*The Republic's Private Navy:
The American Privateering Business
as Practiced by Baltimore during
the War of 1812*

THE AMERICAN MARITIME LIBRARY : VOLUME VIII

The
Republic's Private
Navy

The American
PRIVATEERING BUSINESS
as practiced by Baltimore during
the War of 1812

JEROME R. GARITEE

Published for Mystic Seaport, Inc.
by Wesleyan University Press
Middletown, Connecticut

Library of Congress Cataloging in Publication Data

Garitee, Jerome R   1929–
    The Republic's private navy.

    (The American maritime library; v. 8)
    Bibliography: p.
    Includes index.
    1. Merchant marine—Maryland—Baltimore—History. 2. Baltimore—
Commerce—History. 3. Privateering. 4. United States—History—
War of 1812—Naval operations. I. Title. II. Series.
HE752.M3G37   973.5'25   76-41487
ISBN 0-8195-5004-3
ISBN 0-8195-5005-1 special ed.

Manufactured in the United States of America

FIRST EDITION

To Maria, Meridith, Mary Lynn, and Andrea

Table of Contents

List of Illustrations

Foreword

The privateer brig *Chasseur* of Baltimore, mounting sixteen 12–pounders, heeled with the force of the wind. Under a cloud of canvas on her soaring masts her long, sleek hull seemed almost to fly over the water rather than through it as she raced to overtake the distant sail. On her quarterdeck Captain Thomas Boyle observed with satisfaction the growing outlines of a sturdy merchant brig. Presently within cannon range he fired a gun and unfurled the Stars and Stripes. The merchantman, out of Lisbon for Liverpool, its home port, with wool and fruit, hove to. The *Chasseur* had taken another prize in British waters in this year of 1814.

Boyle was a bold and superbly capable skipper, and his brig, in the words of a fellow American privateersman, "perhaps the most beautiful vessel that ever floated on the ocean. She sat as light and buoyant on the water as a graceful swan." Vessels under Boyle's command captured between thirty and sixty ships during the War of 1812.[1] In this three-months cruise in 1814 through the English Channel and off the coasts of Great Britain and Ireland he took eighteen prizes.

At that time the American coast was under blockade by Admirals Sir John Borlaise Warren and Sir Alexander Cochrane, whose men-of-war were aided in running down American commerce by both British and Canadian privateers. Boyle believed that turnabout was fair play. Anticipating Germany's announcements of World War One with respect to its submarine blockade, Boyle drew up a proclamation which he sent by cartel to London to be posted at Lloyd's Coffee House.

With his tongue in his cheek, he wrote, imitating in part the language of the British blockade announcement, "I do, therefore, by virtue of the power and authority in me vested (possessing sufficient force), declare all the ports, harbors, bays, creeks, rivers, inlets, outlets, islands and sea coast of the United Kingdom of Great Britain and Ireland in a state of strict and rigorous blockade. . . . And I do hereby caution and forbid the ships and vessels of all and every nation in amity and peace with the United States, from entering or attempting

[xi]

to enter, or from coming or attempting to come out of any of the said ports, harbors, bays, creeks, rivers, inlets, outlets, islands or sea coast under any pretence whatsoever"![2]

Such contumacy was not to be tolerated. Ships of the Royal Navy stormed out of port to bring Boyle his come-uppance and let him recover his senses inside Dartmoor Prison, where so many hundreds of American seamen languished. But Boyle was elusive, though on two occasions he was nearly caught. Once a British frigate came close enough to exchange broadsides with him. Another time two frigates and two war brigs had him surrounded, but through adroit maneuvering and fast sailing Boyle slipped out of the trap.

The Baltimore captain ended the war with a fruitful cruise in the West Indies, during which he chased a large schooner off Havana. Thinking her a merchantman, he ranged up alongside her only to have her fire a broadside at him. She was the Royal Navy schooner *St. Lawrence*, fully equal in firepower to the *Chasseur*. In fifteen minutes, however, the contest was over with the schooner striking her colors. The Englishman lost six killed and seventeen wounded; the *Chasseur*, five killed and eight wounded, Boyle among the latter.[3]

Though the *Chasseur*'s record was outstanding, other privateers were notably successful, too. Also in 1814, the *True-Blooded Yankee*, owned by an American in Paris and fitted out and based in French ports, captured twenty-seven ships off the coasts of Ireland and Scotland, destroyed seven ships in a Scottish harbor, and took possession of an Irish island for nearly a week — and all this in a cruise of thirty-seven days. The Baltimore schooner *Rossie* captured nineteen prizes on one cruise. The *Scourge*, of New York, initially rigged as a schooner and then rerigged as a brig, captured or destroyed at least thirty-eight prizes. Most of the privateers, to be sure, enjoyed no such success.

Instances of hard fighting were numerous; the *Chasseur*'s engagement with the *St. Lawrence* was but one. Another was a real epic on October 11, 1814, off Nantucket, involving the privateer *Prince of Neufchatel* and the frigate *Endymion*, which was later to be part of the squadron that captured the U.S.S. *President* in her attempt to escape the British blockading New York. The *Neufchatel* had had many successes during the war, including the present cruise under John Ordronaux, father of the famous lawyer and physician of the same name whose works, during and after the Civil War, on mental disease, particularly its jurisprudential aspects, were of major importance. Because of the number of men drained off as prize crews Ordronaux had remaining on the *Neufchatel* only thirty-three men and officers, with thirty-seven British prisoners confined below decks. He was towing a prize when the frigate was sighted. After first fleeing, he was then becalmed, and had to anchor with his prize close to him to keep from being driven ashore.

The *Endymion* loaded one hundred eleven sailors and marines into five boats and launched an attack about eight-thirty in the evening. Ordronaux opened fire when the boats came within range, but soon found himself sore beset as a boat attacked each bow, each side, and the stern. Cannon, muskets, pistols, pikes, and cutlasses played a deadly role as the desperate Americans repulsed every attempt of the British to find a lodgement on the privateer's deck.

After twenty minutes of the fiercest kind of fighting, what was left of the British withdrew. They subsequently acknowledged a loss of twenty-eight killed and thirty-seven wounded. The Americans also claimed a total of thirty captured. The casualty toll was extraordinary, but the American toll was high too. Ordronaux lost six killed, fifteen badly wounded, and nine slightly wounded, including Ordronaux himself. Only eight men remained intact. Ordronaux, however, had retained his prize, and the next day he carried out a masterful piece of deception when, arming his survivors to the teeth, he persuaded his enlarged total of sixty-seven prisoners whom he transferred ashore to the custody of the U.S. Marshal that he had many more of his crew uninjured and armed lest the prisoners try to capture the ship.[4]

A more portentous, extraordinary, but not more closely fought battle occurred on September 26, 1814, in Fayal in the Azores. The privateer schooner *General Armstrong*, eight long 9–pounders and one 42–pounder (a "Long Tom"), had had a commendable career, even to tangling in 1813 with a frigate off Surinam, a contest from which she was lucky to escape. On September 9, 1814, under the command of Samuel C. Reid, with a crew of ninety, she left Sandy Hook, eluded a frigate and a ship-of-the-line in a long chase, exchanged shots with a war brig on the twelfth, stopped several neutrals on subsequent days but took no prizes, and put into Fayal for water and supplies on the twenty-sixth.

About five o'clock in the afternoon, the British war brig *Carnation* arrived in port, and, learning from the Portuguese pilot boat the nationality of the *Armstrong*, anchored within pistol shot of her. Soon the frigate *Rota* and the ship-of-the-line *Plantagenet* also appeared in the harbor. Alarmed because of the activity aboard these ships and their constant signaling, Reid got out his sweeps and took the *Armstrong* nearer to shore. He anchored, put springs on his cable, and cleared for action.

It was now eight o'clock, bright moonlight, and, aboard the schooner, a tense silence as four heavily armed boats closed in. The *Armstrong* suddenly opened with a heavy fire, which was warmly returned. Soon the boats drew off, the British having suffered severely. Reid had lost one man killed, while his first lieutenant was wounded.

But the British were not done; their main attack was yet to come. The *Carnation* began to tow into the inner harbor a long string of boats crowded with men from the squadron. Then she cut them loose, and the boats, after forming and reforming, approached the *Armstrong* about midnight — all twelve of them in close order.

The privateer opened fire with every gun that could bear, and the boats replied with bow guns, swivels, and small arms fire. When the British were so close that the *Armstrong's* guns were useless, the crew let them have it with muskets and pistols. Then when the British succeeded in getting under the schooner's bow and starboard quarter and tried to board, the *Armstrong's* men went at them, as had the *Neufchatel's* crew, with pikes and cutlasses, as well as small arms.

In the course of the action Reid learned that his second lieutenant had been killed and his third seriously wounded. He himself had just repelled an attack at the stern of the vessel. Sensing that, with his officers out of action, the defense on the forecastle was weakening, he led the whole after division in a wild charge that drove the British into the water and caused them to break off the attack. Several of their boats were adrift, the Americans capturing two of them filled with dead and wounded.

Reid now received a message from the American consul summoning him ashore. The Portuguese governor had sent a note to Captain Lloyd of the *Plantagenet* asking him to desist since Fayal was a neutral port, but Lloyd replied that he was determined to have the privateer at any cost even if the town suffered in the process.

At this point Reid decided to abandon the *Armstrong*. He sent his dead and wounded ashore. Then, as he prepared to leave, the *Carnation* opened fire on him; he drove her off with several well-aimed shots. After that, he scuttled the privateer to prevent the enemy from taking her away. When the British finally boarded her, angered to find her sinking, they completed her destruction by setting her afire. Soon afterward, the privateersmen took to the hills to avoid capture.

The fight had been an epic, particularly the second round which had lasted for a furious forty minutes. Reid lost two killed and seven wounded and, of course, his ship. The British losses were horrendous. The exact tally remains a variable, the number of dead ranging from thirty-four to one hundred twenty, though the latter figure, the American consul's, includes wounded who died after the battle. The number of wounded ranges from eighty-six to one hundred ten. The reported, acknowledged loss when the squadron reached Jamaica was sixty-three killed and one hundred ten wounded, with three lieutenants in each category. Whatever the precise figure, it was a dreadful price to pay for the destruction of one lone American privateer. Two sloops-of-war put into port shortly after the battle, and Lloyd soon sent them off to England, each with twenty-five of the badly wounded aboard. "The attack on the '*General Armstrong*,'" wrote Henry Adams, "was one of the bloodiest defeats suffered by the British Navy in the war."[5]

The squadron under Lloyd was part of the advance element of the expedition bound for the West Indies and the Gulf coast, with New Orleans as the objective. The *Armstrong*'s resistance delayed the British departure for more than a week, time which General Andrew Jackson could and did well use to prepare his defense of the city.[6] Ironically, the battle of New Orleans, in which the British suffered catastrophic losses, was fought two weeks after the peace treaty was signed at Ghent.

But for all the heroics, for all the stalwart evidence of patriotism displayed by privateersmen if the occasion arose, as in the three instances cited, privateering was essentially a business. As Mr. Garitee makes amply evident in his penetrating and exhaustive study of the economics of Baltimore privateering, the lure of profits was irresistible. This was true whether of the syndicate that owned a ship or of the lowliest crewman before the mast. And in its organizational structure, capitalization, method of operation, and distribution of profits, privateering as a business was as soberly directed as any conventional commercial, industrial, or banking enterprise.

Fighting, in fact, received little encouragement. Privateer captains tried to avoid contests at sea, relying on the speed and maneuverability of their ships to slip out of the range of enemy guns. Captain Boyle of the *Chasseur* even felt impelled to explain, almost apologetically, to his owners how it happened that he clashed with the Royal Navy schooner *St. Lawrence*. "I should not willingly, perhaps, have sought a contest with a king's vessel, knowing it was not our object; but my expectations were at first a valuable vessel and a valuable cargo also. When I found myself deceived, the honor of the flag entrusted to my charge, was not to be disgraced by flight." The *St. Lawrence* was so battered that instead of bringing her as a prize to port, he sent her into Havana with the British wounded. As he wrote his owners, "I know you would wish that I should mitigate the sufferings of the unfortunate wounded. I hope you will not be displeased at what I have done, there was no other alternative but to make a cartel of her, or destroy her."[7]

In any business venture there is an element of risk, and in privateering the risks were often high. It was not simply that a privateer might find so few prizes that the venture was a financial failure. Prizes were often recaptured. Privateers themselves were seized, and imprisonment of their crews could last for the duration of the war at Dartmoor or in the hulks. Furthermore, loss of life from gunfire was not uncommon on a privateer, while in prison, especially in the hulks, disease was often rampant and fatal. And, of course, the sea itself offered its own hazards.

The devices resorted to were often daring. Privateers ventured close to enemy harbors to make their captures. Sometimes they actually entered harbors at night to seize or burn shipping. Merchant ships unescorted by men-of-war fell easy prey unless powerfully armed themselves, as many of them were.

The British had recourse to the convoy system as protection against privateers. Often there would be four men-of-war escorting a convoy of mer-

xvi The Republic's Private Navy

chant ships, depending on its size. One warship would be in the van, another to the rear, and one on each flank. Even such protection did not daunt the privateers, who often worked in pairs. While one privateer decoyed the nearest man-of-war, the other would slip in and cut out one or more prizes. Then they would exchange roles, waiting until darkness to cover their approach. They might pursue a convoy for days. One wonders if Admiral Doenitz considered the methods of American privateers before his U-boats launched their wolfpack attacks on Allied convoys in 1942 and early 1943.

By mid–1814, the British blockade of the American coast was so effective that all the principal United States Navy ships were securely locked in except for the *Constitution*, while American merchant traffic had dropped to 11 percent of what it had been in 1811. With such a decline, commercial money and the aggressive commercial spirit often found their principal outlets in privateering. More than five hundred privateers were registered during the war, and of these at least two hundred made one or more cruises. Roaming the waters of the globe, though with special attention to the West Indies and the British Isles, they captured nearly 1350 prizes; had New England entered wholeheartedly into the war, the bag would have been even larger.[8]

Though the German submarine attacks of the two World Wars were immensely more damaging to British shipping, the activity of the American privateers was not inconsequential in its effect. Owing to ship losses and the delays of the convoy system, marine insurance rates, especially evident at Lloyd's, doubled in general what they had been during the struggle with Napoleon, then tripled, while "from England to Ireland they went up from 15 shillings 9 pence per cent to 5 guineas,"[9] an excruciatingly painful blow to the British mercantile pride and purse. Part of the British press became highly critical of the government at the effect of the activities of the privateers. Even more forthright were the merchants of Glasgow, who protested in 1814, after Napoleon had been exiled to Elba and Britain was at peace with all Europe, that it was "distressing and mortifying that our ships cannot traverse with safety our own channels, that insurance cannot be effected but at an excessive premium, and that a horde of American cruisers should be allowed, unheeded, unmolested, unresisted, to take, burn, or sink our own vessels in our own inlets, and almost in sight of our own harbors."[10]

Small wonder that British merchants strongly supported those elements in the government that wanted to bring the American war to a close! One literally could not afford to have many American privateer captains active in British waters like Boyle in the *Chasseur* and Oxnard in the *True-Blooded Yankee*.

Patriotism and profit were so potent as motivation for privateering that it is scarcely surprising that in 1856 Britain worked hard to persuade the great maritime nations to outlaw the practice. A number agreed, signing the Declaration of Paris, but the United States was not one of them. When the Civil War broke out, the South, harking back to the Revolution and the War of 1812, sent a number of privateers to sea. Neither Britain nor France, however, would receive their prizes, and the Union Navy gradually eliminated the raiders. Before 1862 was over, so was Confederate privateering. In fact, the year 1862 virtually marked the disappearance everywhere of the privately owned and armed warship operating under a government license. Thereafter the great threat to a nation's commerce was to come from regularly commissioned Navy warships like the surface raiders C.S.S. *Alabama* and *Shenandoah* of the Civil War and the German cruiser *Emden* of World War One or the submarines of both World Wars.

In its heyday American privateering was always popular and often lucrative. During the Revolution and particularly the War of 1812 privateering interests, frequently in successful competition with the Navy for men and ships, sent swift brigs and schooners to sea under captains who carried the flag over the vast reaches of ocean and boldly harried enemy commerce near and afar: the waters off Halifax, the West Indies, the Irish Channel, the English Channel, the North Sea, the coasts of Africa, the Indian Ocean, and the China Sea — "wherever on the ocean the British merchantmen sailed."[11]

Privateering reached its peak of effectiveness in this country during the War of 1812 and nowhere more completely than in Baltimore. In his admirable study Mr. Garitee clearly reveals why this was so.

WILLARD M. WALLACE

Preface

Any historian investigating the rise of Baltimore in the late eighteenth and early nineteenth centuries, soon realizes that privateering played an important role in that story. Curiosity about the men and circumstances contributing to Baltimore's success overflows into the old institution of privateering. Unfortunately, most studies of American privateering focus almost entirely upon sea exploits. Only scant or secondary attention has been directed toward privateering's entrepreneurial and business aspects, while vital in-port operations preceding and following those well-covered sea exploits have been largely ignored. Such activities, along with the system's impact on its practitioners, their community, and the nation, were integral and significant facets of the full story of privateering and of Baltimore's growth. After discussing the early history of privateering and the rise of Baltimore, this study focuses on Baltimore's privateering activities in the War of 1812 in an effort to analyze every aspect of the privateering business, including limited coverage of sea exploits. Fortunately for the researcher, the merchants and mariners who built Baltimore into a major port in a short period of time were also largely responsible for its activities in the War of 1812. Chronologically, this work begins with a brief account of privateering's origins in Europe at the time of the Crusades and terminates, after concentrating fully on the War of 1812, with a brief discussion of the role of privateering into the twentieth century.

A researcher working on mercantile and maritime sources from the national period discovers obstacles immediately. Business records have disappeared in fires, floods, bankruptcies, family break-ups, or migrations. Scattered and incomplete government records, also devastated by fire, require time and patience, but the locating, sorting, and piecing together of such evidence brings out the detective in the historian. Letters and records in cursive writing are frequently illegible, while name and place spellings are inconsistent. For insights into Baltimore's role, the researcher discovers that the best accounts are stored in other cities where letters from Baltimoreans were received. In an early nineteenth-century port there was little need to write long explanations of local events to neighbors residing within walking distances. In secondary sources, one finds conflicting data and a variety of explanations. As an author's manuscript goes to press, he sometimes discovers new but relevant studies worthy of attention. One such publication is *Tom Boyle: Master Privateer*, by Fred W. Hopkins, Jr. (Cambridge, Md.: Tidewater Publishers, 1976). When pieced together, inexplicably arranged government departmental records, court records, business accounts, and letters and thankfully, the newspapers of the time help to fill in some long-existing gaps. As an analysis of the American privateering system as practiced in Baltimore in the War of 1812, not just its heroics, this study is an addition to the history of privateering, maritime history, the history of the port of Baltimore, and of the national period of American history as well as business and entrepreneurial history, and, finally, the history of the War of 1812.

In the preparation of this manuscript, a number of individuals and institutions have been helpful. Special appreciation is directed toward Professor Roger H. Brown of American University for his vital contributions to the conceptualization, organization, and execution of this entire project. His personal efforts, painstaking analysis, and concern for scrupulosity reflect the best that the historical profession has to offer. Special efforts and significant suggestions were also contributed by Professors Albro Martin and David Brandenburg of American University and Dr. John T. Schlebecker of the Smithsonian Institution. Conversations with that sea-going historian, Dr. Melvin Jackson of the Smithsonian Institution, were also informative. Gary Browne of Wayne State University provided some essential gap-filling leads on manuscript sources and Baltimore merchants while also serving as a sounding board. Appreciation is due Professor Benjamin Labaree of Williams College and the other members of *The American Maritime Library*'s editorial board for their critical analysis of my original manuscript. Conclusions reached in this study are, of course, the responsibility of the author and not of the aforementioned.

Expert and unselfish assistance was furnished by the staffs of the National Archives, the National Record Center at Suitland, the Maryland and Pennsylvania Historical societies, the University of Virginia, and the Maryland Hall of Records. The resourcefulness of friends, Theodore G. Venetoulis and J. Michael Virden, was vital at several points. Without the help of the people mentioned here, this adventure would still be in the stocks.

Baltimore County, Maryland   JEROME R. GARITEE
September 1976

The Republic's Private Navy:
The American Privateering Business
as Practiced by Baltimore during
the War of 1812

ONE

Prologue

Historians have found the exploits of the Baltimore privateer to be an exciting facet of the maritime history of the War of 1812. In heralding the feats of heroic encounters on the high seas, early historians assigned the fascinating story of the preparatory and supportive aspects of the privateering system only secondary importance. The intention in this work is to reverse those priorities by focusing primary attention on the in-port personnel, preparations, and services that necessarily complemented those adventures at sea. Mariners held no monopoly on risk-taking ability, competence, or success in the story of privateering. The investors, shipbuilders, and other shore-bound participants in Baltimore, the preeminent privateering nest in the War of 1812, displayed the same characteristics.

Baltimoreans investing in private armed vessels in the War of 1812 entered an established business with nearly six centuries of history behind it. Before the twelfth century, a merchant who had his seaborne goods pilfered at sea had few retaliatory options. With the sovereign of the day denying any responsibility for private claims, the aggrieved merchant could only wage a private war against his despoilers.[1] Chaos resulted when numerous parties, especially in the Italian city-states, engaged in such private reprisals, and licenses were instituted to give a sovereign a degree of control over those of his subjects seeking redress at sea. The first such reprisal permit was reputedly granted to one Rudolph de Capraja, a resident of Tuscany, in the twelfth century by Emperor Frederic II.[2] It authorized the recipient to use force to compensate himself for an unpaid debt owed to him by the city of Pisa. Similar reprisal permits were issued to merchants victimized by the pirates or corsairs so numerous in the Mediterranean world of the twelfth century.[3] Once such licenses were popularized, any reprisal without a permit became piracy in the eyes of the courts.

Early reprisal license holders were restricted in the amount that they could recover, and their victims were specified on the license. Additionally, all prize goods were sold by the license holder's own government, which then doled out the proper compensation to the license holder while returning any surplus to his

[3]

victims.[4] By the end of the fourteenth century such reprisal licenses were common among mariners operating in the Mediterranean and in other waters. When characterized as "Letters-of-Reprisal" they restricted the holder to raids only in the territorial waters of his own nation. Any raids beyond those waters required a "Letter-of-Marque." But with the undestandable desire of most applicants to operate in home and foreign waters, the two licenses soon became a single "Letter-of-Marque and Reprisal."[5]

While the meaning of "reprisal" is clear, the word "marque" has an uncertain etymological origin. It may have stemmed from a French term for a stamped letter, from the Althochdeutche for "border" or "boundary," or from the old "Letters-of-Mart" given to merchants trading in another's principality.[6] There was no consistency in the title assigned to early reprisal permits issued in England in 1243, 1293, or 1295.[7]

No matter how the reprisal licenses were entitled, they did not provide a safer sea for merchants or their goods. As late as the fourteenth century the Mediterranean area was not only infested with pirates but "the seas were full of privateers — Pisan or Genoese, Catalonian or Greek."[8] Obviously, the licensing of private reprisals, while it saved a sovereign the high costs of a large navy and possibly avoided wars, often invited abuses approximating piracy at sea. The licensed vessels abusing their authority were as dangerous as the open piracy that initially encouraged the development of those very licenses. Nations strove from the twelfth century into the eighteenth century to achieve better controls over their own licensed raiders. Efforts to restrict the issuance of such licenses to particular officers were initiated in England in 1300 and in France in 1400.[9] Also in the 1300s England established an admiralty court to improve its control over marine-related legal cases.[10] An Order-in-Council of 1589 demanded that all prize ships and goods be sent into admiralty courts for adjudication.[11] Even the requirement that licensed raiders provide performance bonds such as those issued John and Martin Frobisher in 1563 and John Hawkins in 1571 failed to curb excesses at sea.

Bond holders pledged that they would observe all government limitations and instructions or forfeit a penal sum. Detailed instructions given to commanders of licensed vessels evolved out of the directions shipowners gave their captains on regular trading voyages. Standardized as "Letters-of-Instruction," they required proof of loss, the posting of a bond, the vital statistics of the vessel as well as descriptions of its crew, provisions, and ordinance. Additionally, the instructions prohibited the commander from opening prize packages at sea and established a system for the distribution of prize money. As a result, port officials could for the first time clearly identify licensed vessels and hopefully deter the selling of prize goods before a court condemnation ensued.[12]

Although impressive on paper, the controls over private armed vessels were ineffective for several reasons. For one, the sea was too large and the public navies too small. The English sovereigns and others were also too dependent upon the private vessels for income and for sea power in emergencies. Queen Elizabeth I actually sent her public vessels out as private armed vessels with Sir Francis Drake and shared in their profits.[13] Such dependence discouraged stringent enforcement of existing controls. The required proof of loss degenerated into a "legal fiction," highly placed officials in the government and admiralty became "silent partners" in private armed vessels, and licenses were openly purchased or simply ignored.[14] At sea expensive licensed vessels took questionable prizes or simply plundered neutral vessels undeterred by a navy too small to patrol the huge stretches of ocean between America and Europe. As Elizabethan England spread to the New World, it became almost totally dependent upon the private initiative and individual enterprise of its privateering establishment. Private armed vessels became the characteristic style of maritime warfare rather than a nuisance factor or a mere supplement to the navy.[15] There was little chance that the Crown could or would discipline the private vessel commander who, frustrated in his search for a Spanish galleon full of silver, simply ravaged a neutral vessel to make expenses or pay a profit to his sponsors.

The European private armed vessel system came to the New World in the ages of exploration and colonization. English vessels engaged in such operations were of necessity armed, and because they functioned on the fringes of the Spanish Empire, it was sensible and convenient for them to acquire a Letter-of-Marque and Reprisal. Such licenses were taken out by Sir Humphrey Gilbert and Sir Martin Frobisher in their search for the Northwest Passage, and Gilbert's North American colonies were valued primarily as privateering bases for raids on Spanish treasure ships.[16]

The combining of raiding with exploratory or colonizing missions served the financial interests of the sponsors, the crew, and the Crown. The colonists benefited from the protection given them by armed vessels and from prize money that offset some of their expenses or found its way into the joint stock companies financing their colony. Sir Walter Raleigh's main purpose in settling Virginia was to set up a raiding base, and until 1590 "nearly all" of the English privateers in the Caribbean were connected with his Virginia enterprise.[17] In fact, it was Captain Simon Fernandez's eagerness to cruise in the West Indies that caused him to divert his Chesapeake-bound colonists to the more southerly but ill-fated site at Roanoke. The combination of licensed raiding against the Spanish and colonization paid well, but the profits from colonies were slow and meagre when compared to the immediate income gained through plunder.[18] The success of Drake, Raleigh, and others in the New World inspired more merchants, captains, seamen, and landlubbers to rush into privateering. Court officers, the upper class, and the nobility furnished new money and provided a protective cover at court for the growing number of outrages and abuses committed at sea.[19] The private armed vessel system transferred from Europe to

America in the Elizabethan era was extensive in size, financially profitable, and largely out of control.

By the seventeenth century a degree of specialization had developed in this system. All commissioned vessels carried the same Letter-of-Marque and Reprisal, but there were functional differences in the roles the vessels performed. In the early days, a shipowner seeking redress at sea simply acquired a reprisal permit and added a few extra guns and men to his cargo-carrying trading vessel. If he captured a prize of opportunity on his voyage to his predetermined market, he was able to reimburse himself. If not, his extra guns were useful for defensive purposes, and his profits resulted, not from prizes, but from the sale of his cargo. His license to raid was secondary in importance.

Sir Leoline Jenkins, an English admiralty court judge, coined the term "privateer" to describe licensed raiders outfitted, not for trading and raiding, but for raiding alone.[20] Such vessels, carrying no commercial cargo, were actually heavily armed private warships or men-of-war. Prizes were their sole objective and their only source of income. Returning from unsuccessful long cruises (not voyages), privateers were more apt than licensed traders to despoil neutrals to meet expenses or to pay their owners a profit. The larger crews on such vessels, unlike the seamen on licensed traders, received no wages except prize money. An observer could differentiate between the two roles by comparing crew sizes, cargo manifests, and armament, or by checking newspaper accounts of privateers clearing for "cruises" and letter-of-marque traders clearing for "voyages." The same commission or Letter-of-Marque and Reprisal authorized both those vessels fitted out for trade and war and those fitted out for war alone in the late seventeenth century.[21] In popular usage, however, the term "privateering" was still used to describe both roles for years.

In the seventeenth and eighteenth centuries private armed vessels thrived as international commerce and colonies grew. National navies, while growing in strength and stature, were unable to meet the demands placed on them, and at the same time, effectively control or replace the private armed vessels. In the single year of 1689, 4,200 English and Dutch prizes were taken by the French, and 4,344 prizes were sold from 1656 to 1783 in Dunkerque alone.[22] In the Caribbean, French *flibustiers* or "Brothers of the Coast" and other private vessels brutally violated the rights of neutrals from 1660 to 1695.[23] The remoteness of the colonies in the New World encouraged abuses, and the transferring of the licensing and adjudication facets of the private system to the colonies was one effort to curb such violations. The governor of the English Puritan colony of Providence Island off Nicaragua, for example, was given a commission as vice admiral and was empowered by the admiralty to issue and supervise Letters-of-Marque and Reprisal and to judge the legality of prizes.[24] In supervising the private vessel system the various colonial governors were ineffectual. An historian of privateering, former privateer commander himself, blamed the "odious entertainment against privateering" on the "piratical age of reckless buccaneers" that existed in the West Indies and the waters of the Spanish Main between 1610 and 1640.[25]

With royal governors in the British North American colonies receiving commissions as vice admirals and with the establishment of admiralty courts in the colonies after 1689, the colonies were ready to expand their privateering role.[26] Shipyards and experienced mariners were on hand, while England provided the wars and the capital and nearby sea lanes offered potential prizes in the form of French, Dutch, and Spanish vessels in the colonial carrying trade. The British North American colonist entering a system developed in Europe over centuries had to acquire a license, post a performance bond, and follow Letters-of-Instruction that were finally formalized in the eighteenth century by Parliament in its General Prize acts.[27]

The English government required that contracts, or "Articles of Agreement," between the vessels' owners and their crews had to be consummated also. The rights and obligations of both parties and a prize distribution scheme were the vital facets of that contract. Once a prize was brought in, the American privateersmen had to file claims (libels), provide written accounts (depositions), and answer a list of questions (standing interrogatory) in an admiralty court. Once a condemnation decree ensued, the prize vessel and its cargo were auctioned and the proceeds were returned to the court for distribution. Any appeals, such as in the case of a decree of restoration, were made before the High Court of Admiralty in England up to 1708 and thereafter to a special commission for prize cause appeals, also in England.[28]

Existing safeguards against abuse on the high seas were no more effective in the colonies than they were in Europe. The lords of the Admiralty complained of American privateering excesses in 1746 and proposed the calling of performance bond sureties to account. Unfortunately, they had given the power for that rare action only to the colonial governors. Threats to revoke licenses and pressure on judges to stiffen condemnation requirements were also unfruitful.[29] The American merchants, governors, and judges were in no mood to restrict private armed vessel operations. During the numerous colonial wars of the eighteenth century any declaration of war led to instant and heavy losses of American and British merchant vessels to French, Dutch, or Spanish private or public vessels. A letter to the *British Newsletter* of May 15, 1704 (during Queen Anne's War) reported that the numerous French privateers out of Martinique alone had taken 130 prizes.[30] Taken off the Chesapeake by a Spanish privateer in 1741, one Maryland vessel was then recaptured by "one of ye Virginia Privateers" within twelve hours.[31] Such perils brought a demand for commissions from the Americans seeking revenge and compensation.

By King George's War (1744–1748), the American colonists were heavily engaged in private armed vessels. They put to sea in 113 commissioned vessels, including 62 from New York.[32] Success brought on a virtual privateering craze that deprived the fishing fleets of Massachusetts of their seamen and placed the hangman's chains around the necks of some captains who failed to end their cruising at the war's termination.[33] In the final colonial war before the American Revolution, the French and Indian or Seven Years' War, the colonists turned to privateering again. New York sent out seventy-five privateers owned by 149 different investors and captured 401 prizes valued at £2,107,700.[34] Massachusetts licensed between three and four hundred private armed vessels in the same war.[35] Incentives to license raiders were increased by the announcement of the British "Rule of 1756." Denying neutral trade to nations not carrying it in peacetime, the rule increased the number of potential good prizes among the neutrals at sea. In 1758 neutral prizes, mostly Dutch, actually outnumbered those taken from belligerent France by English and American privateers.[36]

Another outburst of abuses, neutral protests, and heavy losses to the English insurers of neutral vessels inspired renewed efforts at controlling private vessels in the Seven Years' War. Vessels under 100 tons and those with less than ten nine-pound carriage guns were denied commissions, and the ransoming of prizes was outlawed. The act for "the Encouragement of Seamen and the Prevention of Piracies by Private Ships of War" also led to more vigorous prosecution for raiding without commissions and for other violations of the law.[37] Complaints of the "violent and Piratical Conduct of the English Privateers in the West Indies" and references to "scandalous Disorders" continued, however.[38] King George II finally ordered William Pitt and the colonial governors to halt the abuses by using the "full Authority of the Law" in enforcing the instructions given to commanders in order to "cut up by the Roots, all Excesses and Enormities."[39] Unlike Queen Elizabeth I, the king had a strong navy at a time when the national interest in calming neutrals conflicted with the private interest in profits of owners of licensed vessels.

The larger navies of the Seven Years' War were preoccupied with friendly and enemy privateers in the early years of the war. Because both sides had navies, strategy and prudence dictated the concentration of forces, and unless they sailed into a fleet or squadron, privateersmen found ample unpatrolled areas open for their operations.[40] English naval efforts to contain the numerous French privateers in the western Atlantic and in the Caribbean were largely unsuccessful until the navy in 1761 captured the West Indian bases used by those raiders.[41] That action, combined with a disciplining of English privateers at home and in the colonies, opened the sea lanes to neutral and American shipping.

The stricter English controls over their own and colonial private vessels resulted from a desire to placate angry neutral powers during the war rather than from any intrinsic urge to reform the traditionally undisciplined private force. The result of stronger administrative and court enforcement combined with more policing by an increasingly powerful national navy was, by the end of the Seven Years' War, a better controlled, more standardized, and more professionalized English private armed vessel system.[42] By the time peace was restored, the British North American colonists had clearly demonstrated to their mother country, as well as to the world, their ability to mount a full-blown privateering operation of their own despite tighter regulation.

From the time of the Crusades to the eve of the American Revolution, the private armed vessel system passed through several stages. Originally, a device whereby private individuals used force to gain deserved compensation, it became in the reign of Queen Elizabeth I not only the characteristic and most dynamic maritime power in England, but also a quasi-piratical force. By the end of the Seven Years' War it had been shaped into a better disciplined, readily expandable auxiliary to the newly enlarged national navies. By that time the individual citizen's right to apply force in international affairs was absorbed by strong governments, not solely because of the greater power eighteenth-century monarchies held over individuals or because of the growth of national navies, but largely because private citizens had historically abused the right of private reprisal.[43] In a way, the failure of the privateers to restrain or discipline their own operations actually encouraged the development of large and expensive national navies, especially when their actions threatened to convert neutral powers into belligerents.

Whether it was a nuisance force, a powerful military element, or an auxiliary, some facets of the private system remained constant. Obviously, demands for some kind of license, the need for the adjudication of prizes, and the use of a prize money distribution system, no matter how varied, were basic components of the system from its origin. Also constant was the clash between entrepreneurial desire for profits and governmental interest in regulation. Another vital constant was the willingness of entrepreneurs to invest their capital in the private system. From the French word for "enterprise" meaning "to undertake," the term "entrepreneur" was applied to one who organized and managed a business undertaking while assuming risks for the sake of profits.[44] Entrepreneurs have been characterized not only as "intriguing subjects" for historical study, but also as "elusive characters."[45] Intriguing because of the wide-ranging responsibilities and great financial risks they bore and elusive because of the difficulties historians have had in finding their records and ascertaining their motives and profits, they have been a fascination and a challenge.

When functioning properly, entrepreneurs not only determined the objectives of their business enterprises, but altered those objectives to meet new conditions. To fulfill their objectives, they had to erect and supervise a working commercial organization over a large geographical area, secure financing, and acquire efficient technological equipment. Markets had to be selected for exist-

ing goods and new products found for new demands. In their operations entrepreneurs tried to maintain suitable relations with governments, the international mercantile community, and with society in general. Profits emerged from
constant decision-making, innovations, solid management, and rapid adjustments to changing external conditions.[46] To stand still when conditions
changed was an invitation to disaster because "today's practice" was seldom
adequate for the next day's operations.[47] An ability to fill gaps such as deficiencies in markets, capital and managerial matters, including personnel, while
acting as the prime motivators for their own firm and the ultimate financial risk
takers was another critical side of the entrepreneurs' role.[48] Men fitting this
description in varying degrees invested regularly in vessels and goods in
peacetime, and when the opportunity arose, in private armed vessels in Europe
and America. Attracted to the rising port of Baltimore, such entrepreneurs
provide the connecting link, in this study, between the history of privateering
up to 1763 and the War of 1812.

Entrepreneurial activities inspired the rapid growth of Baltimore before
and during its role as one of the great privateering nests of history in the War of
1812. Baltimore literally absorbed the centuries of entrepreneurial and privateering history preceding its own maturation into an international entrepôt and
raiding base. Any analysis of the private armed vessel system in Baltimore in
the War of 1812 must begin with an account of that port's growth.

TWO

The Rise of a Privateers' Nest

During the colonial period Annapolis preceded Baltimore as Maryland's paramount city and trading center. It retained that status as long as tobacco was the colony's principal crop in value and acreage. Large deep-water anchorages were unnecessary because tobacco planters simply rolled their hogsheads to river landings and transferred them in small boats to sea-going vessels. Annapolis provided the necessary commercial services and functioned as the locus for governmental services as well as a social center for the politically, economically, and socially dominant planter class.

Demands for large deep-water anchorages and warehousing facilities arose only when wheat and flour challenged tobacco in value and acreage planted. Annapolis was unable to capture the bulk of that business because of its limited anchorage, small loading area, and its lack of fresh water feeding into the harbor needed to combat the worms (toredo navalis) weakening the bottoms of wooden vessels.[1] That port, additionally, lacked Baltimore's close proximity to the wheat-growing areas in the central and western counties of Maryland.

Another port bidding for the role of entrepôt for the middle Chesapeake Bay region was Joppa, located slightly north of Baltimore near the mouth of the Gunpowder River. Adjacent to the wheat-growing areas, it flourished temporarily until silting seriously impaired its ability to handle deep-draft vessels. With silting and an erosion of its influence in Annapolis, Joppa's courthouse and jail were transferred to Baltimore in 1768.[2]

Baltimore's initial advantages over its competitors included large protected anchorages and loading areas, gentle tides, and proximity to wheat-growing areas. The silting problem in its inner basin was not significant because Baltimore had an adjacent protected and deep anchorage at Fells Point. Located on the fall line, Baltimore contained many streams for milling operations and for lowering the salinity level of the harbor. It was strategically located on the coastal road between the North and South and was closer to the transmontane trade than Philadelphia. It was several sailing days closer to the West Indies than the more northerly or easterly ports, and farmers in central Pennsylvania,

[11]

New York, and parts of Virginia found the port accessible. Western wheat traveled fewer miles overland to get to Baltimore than to Philadelphia or Norfolk, while return cargoes from the West Indies or Europe were moved to the west through mountain valleys.[3]

Baltimore literally bolted into commercial prominence when its adjacent counties converted from tobacco to wheat. The erection of flour mills in the 1760s on the Patapsco River by Quaker Joseph Ellicott and his brothers encouraged landowners such as the Carrolls to convert to wheat.[4] Soon wheat and flour merchants, following the lead of Dr. John Stevenson in 1750, dispatched their goods to Europe, the West Indies, and the other American colonies. Success and the reluctance of frightened tidewater farmers to move inland after General Edward Braddock's defeat by the French and their Indian allies in 1755 in western Pennsylvania intensified the rate of conversion to wheat into the 1760s. With its convenient location, water power, and deep anchorages, Baltimore staved off competition from Alexandria, Georgetown, and Elkton for the flour and grain trade of the Chesapeake region.[5]

Tobacco did not disappear. Soil exhaustion was not yet serious in many areas, while large investments in slaves trained only for tobacco discouraged wholesale conversions in the lower half of the colony. English markets for tobacco, guaranteed by the Navigation acts, encouraged tobacco planting even when prices were less than ideal. Despite the inroads of wheat, exports of tobacco from the Chesapeake constituted a full third of the 100 million pounds exported from the American colonies in 1775.[6] Less suited to tobacco, northern counties such as Cecil began converting to wheat as early as 1700.[7] A London periodical of 1746 noted that "Maryland planters in great numbers have turned themselves to the raising of grain and livestock, of which, they send great quantities to the West Indies."[8] Conversions in the Baltimore area simply intensified an existing trend at first, but by the Revolution the British army reported that nine-tenths of Maryland's wheat and all of its flour came from its three northern counties closest to Baltimore.[9] Later, the Eastern Shore added its "boat" wheat and flour to a growing stream of "wagon" wheat and flour entering Baltimore from western Maryland, central Pennsylvania, and northern Virginia.

The West Indies became an integral part of a developing trade pattern of Baltimore. Concentrating their production almost totally on sugar to satisfy Europe's sweet tooth, the islands became dependent on outside supplies of wheat. Strategically located for such trade, Maryland raised and Baltimore shipped a variety of wheat resistant to tropical temperatures. Considerable quantities were shipped to the West Indies from 1750 to 1770, while from 1768 to 1770, "810,460 bushels of wheat" were also shipped to new markets in Europe.[10]

Success in wheat and flour transactions attracted new shipping and merchants with capital and commercial experience to Baltimore before the Revolutionary War. Artisans and laborers employable in warehousing, shipbuilding, house construction, and other activities essential to a growing seaport also migrated to the banks of the Patapsco River. Exiled Acadians, congregating in "Frenchtown" in 1756, added their expertise in navigation and oakum production, an essential caulking material for wooden vessels. Two merchants from central Pennsylvania, John Smith and William Buchanan, built two wharves in Baltimore, while merchants William Smith and James Sterett arrived from the same area from 1759 to 1761. They provided a link between their home area and the new port. Jesse Hollingsworth of Elkton came to Baltimore in 1765 and built one wharf and William Spear added another. From Ireland, via Boston, came Cumberland Dugan in 1771 to join new merchants Mark Pringle, James Calhoun, and others. Europeans William Wilson, Barnett Eichelberger, and John McFadon were also attracted by the port's potential. New capital, entrepreneurial skills, and shipping experience were valuable additions to the port.[11]

The letterbooks of a new firm reveal Baltimore's triumphs and troubles in the trying years from 1775 to 1812. John Smith, from central Pennsylvania, established a trading house into which he was able to incorporate his two sons, Samuel and John, Jr. by 1774. The house entitled John Smith and Sons shipped wheat, flour, and other colonial products to Europe in exchange for manufactured goods or shipped the same items to the West Indies for coffee and sugar. West Indian goods were sold locally or sent to Europe, while manufactured goods were consumed locally or reshipped to other colonies. Cargoes to England were consigned to English correspondents or firms that sometimes financed them. Unconsigned cargoes were the responsibility of a captain, or, when his was not a good business head, to a business agent of the firm called a "supercargo" who sailed with the vessel. He or the captain sold the cargo, paid the bills, and selected return loads. Efforts to find a market, good prices, and an appropriate return cargo often required extensive sailing. Advised to try Nice, Marseille, Genoa, or Leghorn in their search for sales, the Baltimore captains and owners had to scramble for profits.[12] The minimal expectation was that any one voyage or adventure would return the costs of the produce, freight, and other attendant charges.

Manufactured goods imported from England demonstrated both the expanding role played by the port as an entrepôt for the entire Chesapeake region as well as colonial dependency on England for such goods. Pins, pots, pewter dishes, shoes, blankets, rugs, glasses, and nails were ordered along with 160 dozen "hatts" including the well-known beaver and, appropriately on the eve of the Revolution, the stylish "Maccaroni" of "Yankee Doodle" fame. Other items shipped to the Smiths were knives, scissors, razors, velvet, thread, broadcloth, combs, buttons, padlocks, hinges, and "chizells." Screws, saws, adzes, augurs, hooks and eyes, files, and other finished products were also ordered for the

Baltimore firm. Orders for feathers, Irish linen, satin shoes, and earrings suggested that some of the wealthy merchants and planters enjoyed a little elegance in their everyday lives.[13]

Despite their location in a tobacco-producing area, the Smiths found it impossible, even upon request from England, to procure tobacco because "in that article we have never done anything." They explained that "the Planters Ship themselves and have their particular friend in London to whom they address, it takes great Interest and trouble to procure their consignments."[14] The Smith firm handled tobacco later, but only after the Revolution altered the existing trade patterns and after a state inspection system provided a rationale for concentrating the previously scattered trade in Baltimore.

The Revolution forced all American merchants to make hard decisions. The Smith firm's correspondence with the English merchants displayed some apprehension, but it also expressed clear confidence in the new cause. Relatively new firms, as were most of those in Baltimore, hoped for new and broader opportunities once the restraints on initiative of the Navigation Acts were removed. The Smiths' interpretation of events led them to assert that Parliament had reacted too severely to the Boston Tea Party, but they were convinced that Parliament's actions (the Coercive acts) would only inspire greater opposition from men "who in our opinion will sell dear their liberties." They anticipated that the London commercial houses engaged in the North American trade would go bankrupt or default on their obligations to American firms. The people of Maryland were determined they wrote and "Seem more willing to lose their Lives than their Liberties."[15]

The Smiths viewed a war with England as "unnatural" but as preferable to the alternative of military occupation, which they characterized as slavery. Accordingly, they suspended their English operations to encourage England to change its policies and informed their correspondents of this. They also told them that the Americans were spirited as well as unanimous and that one thousand men "who will hit the Dollar 200 yards distance" had left the middle colonies for Boston. Fully aware that they would suffer some losses and that failure would invite repression, the Smiths of Baltimore supported the move for independence. On December 6, 1775, the firm saw the options clearly when it wrote that everyone looked "to next Summer as the period which will either fix us Slaves or freemen."[16]

Baltimore shippers supporting the Revolution paid initially through losses to Loyalist privateers in the lower bay. Those privateers were owned by southern and western Marylanders and by non-Marylanders. A handful of Loyalist merchants in Baltimore had their valuable urban property confiscated.[17] At the same time rebel merchants plunged into new economic openings such as feeding the Continental armies, shipping tobacco to markets no longer outlawed by the Navigation acts, and finally, privateering. Both new arrivals in the unblockaded port and more established firms capitalized on the new openings. Grain and flour were shipped to Havana and other non-British West Indian ports for specie or military stores, and when Congress prohibited the shipment of tobacco, the weed went out in flour barrels.[18]

The port served as a depot for Continental army supplies of flour, iron, and salt, and merchants such as Samuel Smith served as purchasing agents for the new government. Baltimore sutlers carried imported supplies to the armies in the field including those at Yorktown. Merchant Stephen Stewart performed as a government purchasing agent, while others such as Jesse Hollingsworth milled flour.[19] An entrepreneur in Baltimore in the Revolutionary War years had little excuse for himself or his capital long remaining idle.

Shipping, the port's main interest, was not neglected. As early as 1775, the Smiths approached the Maryland Council of Safety with a plan to send a ship holding about 2,500 barrels of flour to the West Indies in exchange for sorely needed military stores. Baltimoreans also shared the enormous American commerce with the small Dutch island of St. Eustatius, but even war did not distract them from the basic principles of good shipping. They urged the captain of their brigantine *Speedwell* to be wary of cruisers, and, in words respected by all responsible shippers, reminded him that "the success of all voyages depends on frugality and dispatch."[20] The extent of the port's commerce with St. Eustatius was apparent in one ten day period from January 1 to January 10 in 1780. Of twenty-two vessels clearing Baltimore in that short span, eighteen specified the small Dutch island as their destination.[21] Its capture by the British navy forced the Baltimoreans to utilize other islands for their European trade, but the contacts made at St. Eustatius were useful when the merchants later endeavored to establish a peacetime European trade.

New arrivals in Baltimore during the Revolutionary War included Robert Gilmor from Paisley, Scotland, via Philadelphia, the Netherlands, and the Eastern Shore of Maryland. Gilmor was involved in the tobacco trade; his connections with Robert Morris in Philadelphia and the Baring Brothers banking house in England were, along with his knowledge of shipping and markets, valuable assets.[22] Another experienced merchant with capital settling in Baltimore during the war was William Patterson. Sent from Ireland in 1766 at the age of fourteen, he worked in an uncle's counting house in Philadelphia. In time he invested in vessels and earned a fortune during the Revolution trading with France for powder and arms because, as Patterson recalled, General Washington was so short of such supplies at Boston that he "couldn't fire a salute." After conducting business at St. Eustatius and Martinique, he arrived in Baltimore in 1778 with $100,000 capital. He immediately invested one-half of his money in shipping and privateering (his vessel *Fly* was commissioned in 1778), while placing the other half in real estate because shipping, to Patterson, was "a hazardous and desperate game of chance." Patterson left recklessness to others.[23]

The success of Baltimore merchants and the lack of a blockade attracted other merchants and inspired new activities during the war. William Patterson, as noted, came up from St. Eustatius, and Henry Payson, Michael Diffenderffer, John Schultze, and Christopher Raborg arrived and added their "wealth, credit and enterprize" to the Patapsco port.[24] Displaying a key attribute of good entrepreneurship, Baltimore's merchants found markets for goods pouring into the port. It was reported in 1777 that goods were plentiful and prices were controlled only by a man's conscience.[25] Profits from trade of 100 percent were not uncommon, while demand remained constant. In 1779 new merchant George Salmon reported that while there were 75,000 bushels of salt on hand, there was no sign of a price decline. Tobacco sold for cash in St. Eustatius because its price remained high in France until the last year of the Revolution. The Baltimoreans shipped tobacco and flour to the Danish island of St. Thomas after Britain's Admiral Rodney took St. Eustatius (and 2,000 Americans) in 1781.[26] Hispaniola, Cuba, and other islands were visited by the Baltimoreans in large numbers in 1782 and 1783. William Patterson, Jesse Hollingsworth, Jonathan Hudson, William Taylor, Samuel Smith, William Spear, and Daniel Bowley among others shipped to those markets usually in vessels under one hundred tons.[27]

New Baltimore arrivals in the Revolutionary War were able to move into business without serious opposition from a large entrenched commercial establishment. The newcomers formed new commercial associations and relationships while their profitable experiences in wartime trade and privateering provided the basis for cooperation and growth after the war. The wealth in the city being funneled into young, vigorous houses was invested not only in an expanded commerce, but into banking, insurance, and manufacturing. Unlike wealth in the form of land, profits from privateering and other sea operations were not diminished by taxation and were, consequently, available for reinvestment.[28] Unblockaded, Baltimore and Salem "were able to reap so much profit from their rivals' ills that they flourished for years thereafter," while the British burning of Norfolk set back that promising contender for the Chesapeake's trade.[29] Making full use of its wartime advantages and the vigor of its new merchants Baltimore served both its own entrepreneurial interests and the needs of a revolutionary nation.

Wartime profits from flour, tobacco, salt, iron, and other supplies and trade were injected into new ventures during the war. One of the most appealing, judging from early successes and the numbers involved, was the old institution of privateering. The individual states and Congress assumed the authority to issue letters-of-marque and reprisal. Congress issued an estimated one thousand seven hundred such commissions while another two thousand or so were authorized by the several states, with Massachusetts alone issuing some six hundred.[30] Many shipowners, victimized by Loyalist or British privateers, qualified for commissions under the old "reprisal" approach to privateering, but neither the states nor Congress expected only the aggrieved to apply. Shrewd merchants intensified their investments in raiders as the small American navy declined and the British navy strangled other profit-making ventures. Little inspiration or education was required as the merchants combined "private interests and public duty."[31]

The need for a naval force to supplement the small national navy and the army's incessant pleas for supplies created a national climate favorable to privateering. The merchants' search for profits and an appropriate usage of their many small and swift vessels combined with an existing pool of interested mariners, guaranteed public support for privateering at the local or port level. Congressmen favoring a strong national navy were out-voted by seaport pressure groups as Congress authorized the issuance of letters-of-marque and reprisal in March of 1776.[32] Rhode Island actually anticipated congressional action when it issued commissions in June of 1775.[33] General Washington depended on the newly licensed raiders to provide supplies and to disrupt enemy communications, while owning a share of one privateer himself.[34]

The new American private vessels of war were required to post bond of $5,000 when under 100 tons and $10,000 when larger. Holders of commissions were also required to list a description of the vessel, its officers and crew, as well as its armament and provisions. The new American letter-of-marque was issued by Congress in the name of the "United Colonies." It authorized its holder to attack and seize the vessels of Great Britain and to bring them into American ports for adjudication. Letters-of-instruction were issued to commanders as Congress endeavored to keep raiders' operations within the accepted "usages and Customs of the Nations." While establishing a new nation with new national laws, the Revolution did not alter international maritime customs, and privateering customs were an outgrowth of international rather than national law. An American commission signed by John Hancock, president of the Continental Congress, was issued in 1777 to John Martin, commander of the thirty-ton schooner *Swallow*. Owned by "Hugh Young and others of Baltimore," *Swallow* carried fifteen men and mounted four "Howitzers" as well as "Swivels," a weapon larger than a musket but smaller than a cannon.[35]

In addition to new sources for commissions, the new American privateering system needed its own admiralty courts. Some states contained British admiralty courts when they were colonies, but they now established courts of their own. Maryland, for example, established a Court of Admiralty with a judge, a marshal, and a register in 1776.[36] A Baltimore prizemaster did not have to carry his prize into Baltimore or Maryland, but could have it condemned elsewhere. The privateer *Harlequin* of Baltimore, for example, had a prize condemned in an admiralty court in Williamsburg, but then sold it in Baltimore.[37]

Estimates of the number of privateers fitted out in Baltimore range from one hundred ninety-eight to two hundred forty-eight with the larger figure representing the overall number of commissions, not vessels. The larger figure also included vessels fitted out in Baltimore but owned by outsiders.[38] Even the minimal figure, however, represented a sizeable effort for a relatively new port containing many new merchants. The largest number of private armed vessels sailed in the first four years of the war.

The most popular vessel for Baltimore privateering in the Revolution was the small fore and aft rigged schooner, which with her high wind-catching top sails was both swift and highly maneuverable.[39] Common in the West Indian trade, she managed shallow waters denied to the heavier men-of-war pursuing her and followed even the smallest prizes into coves or inlets. When she was becalmed, her large crew manned her oars while in pursuit or escape. Smallness of hold was a handicap in privateering as it was in the European trade, but a schooner's speed and maneuverability more than compensated for the loss of space. Owners even tailored seemingly appropriate vessels to their own particular privateering tastes. Merchant John Sterett, for example, ordered what was reputedly the first schooner expressly designed for privateering and then handed her over to Captain Jeremiah Yellott, an escaped Englishman of Baltimore.[40] Regardless of the figure one accepts for the Baltimore privateering fleet, about one-half were schooners and three-fourths of the total number of vessels shipped fewer than fifty-one men.[41] Large three-masted, square-rigged ships (used in this work in the specific and not generic sense) were too cumbersome for raiding, while the smaller and less awkward two-masted square-sailed brigs were used on occasion, the fast schooner was most appropriate.

In the early days of the Revolutionary War merchants sent out any small raider to seize unsuspecting enemy merchant vessels still in the sea lanes. This surge of small vessels affected the overall average size for the war and disguised a trend toward larger vessels and larger crews as the war progressed.[42] One of the reasons for that trend was the self-nurturing aspect of raiding as prize money not only inspired but financed new privateering ventures. Profits from supplying government forces and trading were also redirected into privateers when some of the earlier trading outlets were shut off by the British. Additionally, larger prizes were converted into American privateers after the British learned from sad experience and began to sail with more guns and men in an effort to fight off the impudent smaller raiders.

Investors from South Carolina, Philadelphia, France, and other areas joined Baltimoreans in purchasing, outfitting, and commissioning vessels. French investors fitted out one privateer by themselves and Robert Smith, another brother of Samuel, requested commissions for vessels in Havana and Haiti. Family firms such as those of the Smiths, the Buchanans, the McKims, the Pattersons, the Purviances, the Hollingsworths, the Dorseys, and the Van Bibbers were the most active privateer investors in Baltimore during the Revolution.[43] For most it was just one facet of their business activities during the

Revolution, but the experience was valuable as many of the same families as well as individuals such as Jonathan Hudson and William Taylor invested in private vessels again during the War of 1812.

Samuel Smith spent the early years of the war on military duty but then resigned his commission because, as he told General Washington, one-half of his fortune had been expended. Apparently, his privateering profits were not equal to the drain military service made on his pocketbook. The widely held belief that he had made a fortune in raiding stemmed from the last half of the war as his resignation letter and fragments from his father's letters indicated less than smashing success in the early years. His father complained that their privateer *Enterprize* arrived in Martinique "without taking on Prize," while expressing his hope that she "may not run us in debt this Cruize." The nervousness of a privateer owner forced to remain in port while his investment roamed the seas surfaced when the senior Smith expressed his eagerness to dispose of the firm's unproductive privateer, *Beggar*. Privateers without prizes were a drain on any firm's resources, but the Smiths' investments in privateers actually increased significantly as the war progressed so that the potential for great profits or losses existed. The family was financially engaged in at least ten privateers in 1780 alone.[44]

With Revolutionary Baltimore supporting a sizeable fleet on the seas, a shortage of seamen developed despite the payment of bounties and seamen's expenses to vessels' berths in other ports.[45] Service in the privateers was attractive and competition from the navy was negligible. The port's growth from 200 people in 1751 to 5,934 in 1776 may have been a record for urban development, but it could not meet the demands made on it by its own vessels.[46] The importance of privateering was clear to First Lieutenant Campbell of Samuel Smith's militia company. He resigned that position "to be of more Essential Service to his country by distressing the Trade of our Enemies in a Privateer fitted out by a Gentleman of this Town."[47] There were too few Campbells to fill out all the crew lists in Baltimore.

The privateering performance in the Revolution differed from earlier practices in several significant ways. For one, Americans and other Europeans replacing English investors nearly eliminated them.[48] Secondly, licensing, supervision, and adjudication, the roles of English predecessors, were performed by American agencies. Thirdly, the American privateering community's search for profits was accompanied by an unprecedented patriotic concern. Their vessels took risks against English warships, helped each other, and cooperated with the national navy. The old tradition of privateering enjoyed a better public image than it had previously despite minor infractions of the rules.[49] During the Revolution, the Americans depended on their privateers perhaps more than the earlier monarchs of Europe had depended on theirs, but there is little indication that American privateers violated accepted international usage or their own regulations with anything like the impunity of privateers during earlier periods. The professionalism acquired by privateering in the middle of the century was reinforced during the American Revolution.

The flow of merchants with experience and capital, supplemented by Irish and German redemptioners who joined Baltimore's labor pool, continued after the Revolution's end. From Ireland came merchants Robert Oliver, James Wilson, and George Brown, all destined for shipping greatness. Oliver's rise was quite spectacular as he became a millionaire and one of the richest men in America by 1809 after arriving in Baltimore in 1783 with an unspecified amount of capital at the age of twenty-six.[50] From England came John Hollins, a successful Liverpool banker, who went into shipping and insurance. These and other Baltimore entrepreneurs had to meet the acid test of entrepreneurship: that is, to find markets in what was the new commercial world of 1783. Fortunately, the Baltimoreans had tobacco for the Netherlands, Germany, and France, and flour for the West Indies, as well as a maturing American market for European goods.

The new nation's trade suffered from British restraints against foreign shipping in the West Indies. Wheat, for instance, was admitted to the British West Indies only in British bottoms, but colonial produce was exportable to America without restraints. The Americans, however, smuggled produce into the West Indies, or after entering the British islands for repairs, conveniently sold their cargoes to pay for those repairs. Even Horatio Nelson of the British navy was unable to stop the various subterfuges employed in the island trade. Non-British islands provided good markets for grain and flour, with the French islands alone engaging about one hundred thousand tons of American shipping. Baltimore received coffee, cotton, sugar, and indigo from the Dutch West Indies.[51] Between 1783 and 1785 there were over two hundred twenty-five clearances from Baltimore for the West Indies with many vessels returning with colonial products for reshipment to Europe. The majority cleared for the French, Dutch, and Spanish islands, but British islands were also visited. British subjects owned, in name or fact, many of the vessels going to the British islands, but Baltimoreans owned some also.

If, as has been suggested, the postwar tobacco trade to Europe and the flour trade to the West Indies were two bright spots in a relatively depressed national economy after the Revolution, Baltimore was fortunate.[52] Both items were basic to its trade patterns.[53] Tobacco was America's largest single export to France in the 1780s, while Rotterdam, Hamburg, and Bremen also received that item. Flour and tobacco profits kept the Baltimore trading houses active in a trying period and made the port the "boom town of the 1780s."[54] New markets in the East Indies and the Orient were also explored and in 1785 the ship *Pallas* unloaded china, tea, and silk in Baltimore.[55]

There were irritations and some failures in the post-Revolutionary period.

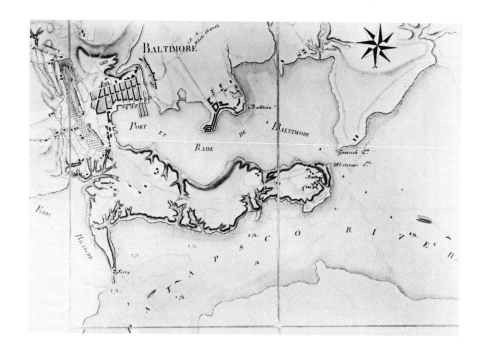

PLATE I

"Ville, port et rade de Baltimore dans le Maryland, 1781,"
original in the Rochambeau Collection, Library of Congress

One new trading house complained of the high cost of locating in and doing business in Baltimore in 1783. Johnson, Johonnot and Company was primarily a New England firm dependent primarily upon commissions for its income. Commissions of 2.5 to 5.0 percent for handling cargoes and related services were supplemented by shipping one's own goods and by charging freight on the firm's own vessels. Johnson, Johonnot and Company found the Baltimore market too limited and, consequently, reshipped imports to New York and Philadelphia for sales. Profits rose and its complaints diminished only when it opened a sugar refinery and purchased a bakery to assist in its sales of sugar and flour.[56] Others were less fortunate and were sorely pressed to meet demands on their resources. Wealthy merchant William Patterson actually threatened to sue his debtors in 1785 in the midst of the postwar economic adjustment.[57]

The firm of John Smith and Sons was dissolved during the Revolution but was reorganized as Samuel and John Smith in 1784 after John Jr.'s return from the West Indies. The new firm's circular to the old firm's correspondents stated that it would handle cargoes at the "usual commission of 5%" and would advance two-thirds on cargoes. The house simply advertised that it had the two key requirements of the entrepreneur, capital and "long knowledge of the commerce of the town, which daily increases with rapidity." The Smith firm offered its correspondents an additional inducement through its ability to ship on its own account, thereby filling space in a foreign shipper's vessel. Such advantages, along with its ownership of vessels, often made the difference between the success and failure of a particular "adventure." Describing the new commercial scene in America and Baltimore in the postwar period, the firm's circular stated:

> A New scene of Commerce has opened with this Country. It now can Import the Commodities of every port of the world. Its wants from its rapid population must Increase every day. Our Tobacco which is One of the Staples of this State, may now freely be exported everywhere. This gives Baltimore a peculiar advantage over Philadelphia and its situation and present great and Established Commerce gives it every advantage over all other ports in the Chesapeake Bay. Here almost all the produce of the Bay must come for Sale for here alone can they receive Cash in payment. From this port Virginia Tobacco is Shipped at a difference of price so trifling as not to equal the Delay generally met with there.[58]

While the firm was trying to attract tobacco orders, it, like most Baltimore trading houses, was not involved in rigid specialization. Conditions and markets were too unstable for such specialization over a long period of time. According to the Smiths, Baltimore not only handled Virginia tobacco with more dispatch than the scattered Virginia planters could ship it from one of that state's ports, but Maryland flour, which was greatly superior to that of Philadelphia. Indeed, they advertised Baltimore as Philadelphia plus tobacco and argued that the Ellicotts, Stumps, and other Marylanders were the "very best millers."[59]

New markets and reentry into British markets were the firm's prime objectives during the period of the Articles of Confederation. To achieve this Samuel and John Smith sought a one-third interest in an East Indian "adventure" with a Lisbon firm and offered tobacco to an Italian merchant. Tobacco was shipped to Hamburg, and in cooperation with a former Liverpool banker, John Hollins, the Smiths sent flour and tobacco to Liverpool. English firms shipped for "the account and risque" of the Smith firm dry goods, gunpowder, wax, hats, lace, lead, dishes, shoes, glass, linens, wire, paper, sheep, copper, needles, screws, and other manufactured items. By 1784 the firm had a "constant trader" to Liverpool, and in 1786 found that it was "absolutely necessary to our English Business" to get into Irish linens. Fast vessels belonging to the Smiths carried European goods as well as American agricultural products to the Caribbean in exchange for sugar and coffee, which was then reexported to Europe.[60]

By the end of the 1780s trade increased so much that the Smiths reported "immense orders for flour from Europe, particularly Liverpool" and revealed that one house there ordered "70,000 Bushels" from Baltimore alone. The new Constitution benefited Baltimore when it gave control of foreign commerce to the federal government, encouraging the Smiths to reflect that formerly the "duty in wine to Maryland was considerably higher than in Pennsylvania." By early 1790 they reported "the demand for produce in Europe" was constant, prices were "enormous," and trade was "brisker than we have ever known it."[61] Both the new Constitution and the French Revolution worked to Maryland's advantage, and Baltimore's growth continued into 1793 when war started in Europe. Describing their port's advantage once more to a correspondent in Spain, the Smiths observed that "Commerce of the port is similar to that of Philadelphia in its Exports and Imports" and added that in wheat "our quantity is equal" while in "Flour and corn we export about two-thirds quantity." In tobacco they boasted, "this Port far exceeds Philadelphia."[62] Indeed, American exports of tobacco attained a level from 1790 to 1792 that would not be duplicated until 1840.[63]

Baltimore trading houses shipped whatever would sell without relying solely on flour or tobacco. When those commodities were too costly or a glut on the market, they shipped pine boards, pig iron, the ever-popular barrel staves, and deerskins to Europe. All Baltimore firms had such locally produced items to fall back on in a pinch, but the early 1790s were good years for most products because France, Spain, and Portugal purchased great quantities. Referring to 1790 as "a Golden Year for America," the Smiths predicted that continuing disruption in Europe "would give a spring to our Commerce." Such entrepreneurial foresight can be seen also in the firm's comment that "Supplies for both fleets and for the islands belonging to both must go from hence" and, more practically, by directions to a schooner captain to proceed immediately to Havana with flour.[64]

The firm had found the key to success in the period from 1790 to 1812. Indeed, the carrying of neutral trade was the next great boost for the port of Baltimore. Always alert, the Smiths also provisioned the American army and, in one case, requested a $40,000 advance from Secretary of Treasury Alexander Hamilton to pay Baltimore contractors. They kept a careful eye on the army and responded to news of an Indian victory and rumors of congressional expansion of the army by asking Hamilton for information so that "Nothing may be wanting on their part."[65] Success resulted from such entrepreneurial alertness and aggressiveness.

The firm changed its name when John Smith declined to participate further in the dry goods importing business because of its high risks. In 1790, Samuel Smith joined with James A. Buchanan, the son of Smith's brother-in-law, William Buchanan, to handle that branch of the business. Their partnership would survive almost three decades and the War of 1812. John Smith, Jr. still participated with Samuel in other aspects of the business. Samuel Smith's involvement in two houses, while also trading under his own name, was not unique as there were often opportunities too risky or too expensive for certain partners to undertake. S. Smith and Buchanan survived 1792, a year in which failures in New York and Philadelphia were described as "very great — the Losses Immense." According to the firm, Baltimore was not "in the smallest Degree affected" by the slump deriving from a lull in European hostilities.[66] It was not wise, of course, to weaken one's reputation by saying otherwise.

Renewed hostilities in Europe enticed the Baltimoreans back into the neutral carrying trade, but the profits of that trade were often matched by its frustrations. S. Smith and Buchanan's captains received several alternatives for landing as ports changed hands or governments changed policies. In 1793 Captain James Porter of the ship *Sidney* was given options including Cork in Ireland, Liverpool, France, and the North of Spain. Captain Anthony Daniels, of the ship *Carlisle* was ordered to Amsterdam, but thereafter he could select Spain or Portugal and return either to the United States or the West Indies. He was also advised of what to do when captured by an English privateer.[67]

The vexations of English and French privateers, starting in the early 1790s, remained with the Baltimore shippers until the signing of the Treaty of Ghent in 1815. One S. Smith and Buchanan captain carried into Jamaica was advised by the firm that his capture was illegal and that "nothing but Ill Temper could have Induced the Privateers to send you into Port," but it then concluded that the high value of the vessel's coffee and sugar was probably the real motivation. Smitten by raiders on numerous occasions, the firm stated on Christmas Eve of 1793 that "The very precarious situation of our Trade with all the Belligerent powers is such that in every case one can see nothing but danger and difficulty."

The firm added that it could not "contrive any precautions sufficient to guard our property from the spoliations of the powers at war."[68] In 1793 the firm was already in a predicament that would help to drive America to war in 1812 as profits earned in entrepreneurial risk-taking ventures were lost in foreign admiralty courts.

Some of those who lost their property in the 1790s had migrated to Baltimore after the Revolution. In the decade after 1783, John Donnell came over from Alexandria and Luke Tiernan from Ireland along with others who would enter the shipping business such as John Carrere, Solomon Betts, and James H. McCulloch. Carrere, Donnell, and Tiernan each lost a number of vessels to privateers. Additional settlers, to the number of 1,000 whites and 500 blacks, arrived in fifty-three vessels from revolution-torn Haiti in 1792. Included was Jérôme Bonaparte whose marriage to merchant William Patterson's daughter was later nullified by his brother the emperor. New arrivals raised the population to 13,503 in 1790 and there was no sign of cessation. In 1790 the port's entrepreneurs owned 102 vessels of which one-third were schooners.[69]

Schooners were the primary carriers of the West Indian trade, which, as S. Smith and Buchanan had predicted, became a flourishing business for the Americans in the 1790s. An estimated 71 percent (or 412) of the 576 vessels entering Baltimore from foreign ports in 1799 were from those islands. Included were 345 Baltimore-owned vessels.[70] Such figures demonstrate the vigorous commerce between Baltimore and the islands in what were privateer- and frigate-infested waters. Baltimoreans, however, had so much confidence in the speed and maneuverability of their schooners on short voyages in known waters that S. Smith and Buchanan told a Philadelphia insurance company, "we seldom insured our West Indian risques."[71] The cost of insurance was certainly a factor in that decision. The 6 percent premiums of 1796 rose to 15 and 25 percent when the French increased their raiding in 1797 and reached 30 to 33 percent in 1798 before the American and British navies drove the French from the seas. By 1800 the rate returned to 10 percent, but even that figure diminished profits significantly.[72]

In contrast to the West Indies trade, tobacco in larger and slower vessels en route to Europe was insured. Full-rigged ships moved coffee or sugar to Europe also when cargo volume and market price justified their use. S. Smith and Buchanan made $50,000 profit from 500,000 pounds of West Indian coffee on the ship *Louis* despite the jettisoning of 60,000 pounds to escape a Bermuda privateer. Impelled to set routes for its captains that would "avoid the Privateers of both Nations," the firm saw its hard-earned profits diverted into the admiralty court accounts of privateersmen.[73] From 1797 to 1800 the French government alone seized 279 American vessels in the West Indies, of which 75 or more were registed in Baltimore.[74] Expectations that claims against those governments for improper seizures insured reimbursements for the aggrieved were abortive. Despite settlements such as those with France in 1800 and 1803, some of the claims were not paid until 1915.[75]

The aggravations of the Baltimoreans can be seen in the depositions made before notary publics for use in the courts. The schooner *Nancy* was seized by the British privateer *Retrieve* in December of 1795, while the French privateer *La Regiscide de la Republique* took a vessel from the same firm, Buchanan and Robb of Baltimore, into Guadeloupe. A mate of the schooner *Experiment* testified that the French privateer *Point à Petrie* captured his vessel in 1795. Impressment, of course, affected seamen more than owners, but owners Oliver and Thompson protested the loss of four men off their ship *Harmony* to a British frigate in 1796. Another captain, in attempting to protect his men, was "knocked down by one of the crew" of the inappropriately named British frigate *Amiable*. Seaman James McDaniel of the Baltimore schooner *Musquitoe* refused to serve on a British frigate when he was assigned to the larboard watch and the "Eighth gun on the main Deck." That refusal nettled him "two dozen lashes and irons for three days," but ultimately he was returned to Baltimore.[76] The sea lanes offered lashes and foreign combat duty to mariners when their luck failed and financial distress or ruin to some Baltimore owners in the same circumstances.

Losses to owners were often critical, injury to individual seamen irreparable, and protests justifiable. When viewed as a percentage of ship registers, certificates of ownership, and registration issued for vessels engaged in foreign trade and replaceable only when the rig, owners, or masters were altered, the losses were not excessive. Of the 3,735 registers issued by the Baltimore collector of customs from October of 1789 to December of 1811, less than 6 percent were noted as condemned in British, French, Spanish or, in rare cases, Danish, or Haitian admiralty courts. From another viewpoint, the 215 condemned vessels amounted to twice the number of vessels owned in Baltimore in 1790. More importantly, certain firms suffered heavy losses. According to government records, S. Smith and Buchanan lost five vessels and their cargoes to France and four to Britain. Michael McBlair of Hollins and McBlair forfeited four vessels to Britain, while Lemuel Taylor lost four to Britain, two to France, and one to Spain. Thomas Tenant yielded three to Britain and two to France.[77] For such owners, and future owners, the condemned vessels represented significant financial losses.

As carriers of neutral trade in wartime, the Baltimoreans suffered at the hands of all belligerents. England captured 92 Baltimore vessels, France took 115, and 2 were taken by both belligerents. The losses to French raiders were numerically greater, but they were usually smaller vessels in the West Indian trade captured before 1800.[78] British condemnations, on the other hand, occurred mostly from 1800 into the War of 1812 and included the larger and more valuable Baltimore vessels engaged in the European trade.[79] By 1812 Baltimore viewed Britain and not France as the primary culprit, although both belligerents taught the Baltimoreans invaluable lessons in blockade running, privateer operations, admiralty law, ship handling, and schooner construction.

The Baltimoreans also gained limited experience in the operation of privateers in 1798 when Congress authorized the issuance of commissions against France's armed vessels. From 1798 to 1800, seventy-four commissions were received by Baltimoreans of which one-half went to schooners.[80] S. Smith and Buchanan, John Hollins, Thomas Tenant, William Patterson, John McFadon, John Carrere, William T. Graham, and William Taylor were among those receiving commissions for their vessels.[81] The American government issued 365 commissions altogether, but the only prizes forthcoming were eighty-five taken by the navy.[82] Vigorous American and British naval operations weakened the French raiders to the point that the 336 American losses of 1797 fell to 153 in 1798.[83] By authorizing "Special Commissions" in "an act further to Protect the Commerce of the United States" of July 9, 1798, Congress allowed the Baltimoreans to defend their trade while employing privateering for retaliatory purposes in peacetime.

The profits of international commerce were such that the Baltimoreans continued to trade despite their losses to the belligerents. The number of registers issued before the War of 1812 offers an insight into the port's growth and risk-taking entrepreneurial efforts in a period when more capital was invested in commerce than in manufacturing. The collector of customs issued only 61 registers in 1791, but signed 159 in 1793 and 254 in 1795. The record number for the prewar period was 196 in 1799 when the neutral carrying trade reached its peak and French raiding was controlled. Peace in 1801, diminishing Europe's need for neutral carriers, encouraged only 149 and 160 requests for registers by Baltimoreans in 1802 and 1803 respectively. The revival of war in Europe in May of 1803 soon renewed Europe's dependence on American bottoms and 311 registers were issued. The Embargo, more painful than even the stodgiest peace years, caused a drop in registers to 68 in 1808, while the years from the Embargo to 1812, during rather inept congressional efforts to restrict or direct trade, saw annual totals ranging from 205 to 256. Grouped in years, the number of registers illustrates the explosive periods of Baltimore's commercial growth. The best years for new ventures were from 1804 through 1807 when 1,038 registers were signed, while second in activity was the period from 1809 through 1812 when 888 registers were issued.[84]

Actual tonnage registered followed the same pattern as impressive gains were made in the period between the ratification of the Constitution and the beginning of the War of 1812. The 34,459 tons in foreign trade in 1794 more than doubled by 1800 and tonnage reached its peak, as did registers, in 1806 and 1807 when it exceeded the 80,000 mark. Tonnage in December of 1812 after six months of war was 69,570 in foreign trade with an aggregate tonnage of 99,135, including smaller vessels either licensed or enrolled in the coasting trade.[85]

Translated into 150-ton vessels that tonnage represented six hundred thirty possible raiders, but some were too old, too small, or too cumbersome for effective raiding.

Any evaluation of Maryland's prosperity must note that the dollar volume of Baltimore's prewar trade included reexported colonial produce. Such reexports did not enrich the farmers of Maryland, Pennsylvania, and Virginia, but they furnished income to shipowners, mariners, shipbuilders, and insurance companies. The rule that such reexports had to be unloaded and reloaded in the United States to qualify for customs duty drawbacks assured stevedores, long-shoremen, and wharfingers some income. The value of all domestic produce shipped out of Baltimore from 1804 through 1807 was almost forty-nine million dollars, while the relative importance of imported and reexported products can be seen in their dollar value of almost thirty-four million. Forty percent of Baltimore's commerce in the peak years was of more benefit to the shipping establishment of Baltimore than it was to the region's farmers or to the federal government customs collectors. Drawbacks on coffee in 1809 and 1810 amounting to three-fourths of the duty collected on that commodity demonstrate Baltimore's penchant for reexporting.[86]

Baltimore's merchants supported the Embargo initially but then grew restive.[87] Raised during Adam Smith's popularity and having recently thrown off British trade restraints, they defined dishonesty to exclude circumvention of what to them were unwarranted government obstructions to commerce. They were reluctant to sit by idly and watch their vessels, capital, and good opportunities waste away under political restraints. Long experience in circumventing the maritime restrictions of foreign governments was utilized to advantage at home. Baltimore vessels violating their own government's laws were reported by American consuls in the years of the Embargo and Non-Intercourse acts to be in Liverpool, Barbados, Cork, Dublin, and other outlawed ports. William Patterson, whose vessels had done so well in all situations from the Revolution to the Embargo, was thought to be the owner of three vessels violating the Non-Intercourse Act in 1809.[88] He had been a supporter of the Embargo at its initiation. Others simply listed coastal ports as their destinations and "blew out to sea" toward a West Indian port or limped into such a port "in distress." The deputy collector at Baltimore reported to the secretary of the treasury in 1807 that several vessels had cleared in ballast for American ports, loaded cargoes somewhere down the bay, and then darted to the West Indies.[89]

Another source of income and experience for the shipbuilders and merchants of Baltimore was the outfitting of foreign privateers. French commissions were issued in America in the 1790s by "Citizen" Edmond Genêt and nearly fifty privateers sailed from Baltimore under French flags.[90] Secretary of Treasury Albert Gallatin, acting on information from the collector at Savannah, asked the collector at Baltimore for the names of owners of a vessel "which it appears has been fitted out in your port for a privateer." A complaint about a French-manned, Baltimore-outfitted privateer came from Savannah.[91] The collector at Baltimore had problems because the sponsors of such operations outfitted what appeared to be perfectly normal merchantmen. But once out of port, those vessels stopped at various inlets, rivers, or towns to load on additional crew and armament or had them floated out to them. The collectors, in general, worked hard at enforcing the laws and the Embargo.[92]

For profits in the period of restricted trade, the shipment of supplies to the British army on the Iberian Peninsula was difficult to surpass. The practice continued with the benefit of British licenses into the War of 1812 itself. The number of American vessels calling at Lisbon almost equaled the British vessels there in 1811 as 802 American vessels stopped at Lisbon, while in 1811 alone Baltimore sent 380,218 barrels of flour to Cadiz and Lisbon.[93] The *Orizimbo* of Baltimore for Lisbon on the exclusive account of the British government secured a profit of 100 percent for its owners from flour costing $9.50 a barrel in Baltimore selling for $20.00 in Lisbon.[94] Such Peninsula trade proved hazardous, though, when the British navy seized licensed vessels after their cargoes were delivered.

By 1812 the body of merchants residing in Baltimore was highly experienced in all aspects of sea-going commerce. Some had participated in every stage of the development of the American economy from colonial times through the periods of Revolutionary War, the Articles of Confederation, and the Napoleonic wars. They traded as belligerents, as normal traders when the world was at peace, and as the carriers of neutral trade when others were at war. The survivors, in the best spirit of the early nineteenth-century entrepreneur, determined objectives, developed organizations, secured financing, acquired suitable equipment (often schooners), while anticipating and meeting consumer demands. Larger merchants such as S. Smith and Buchanan, Didier, Hollins, McBlair, Wilson, Oliver, and others maintained at least reasonably good relations with the public and with society at large while taking risks and making decisions worth, collectively, millions of dollars.[95]

Baltimore's mercantile community had other "essential underlying qualities" of the entrepreneur. The merchants discovered and evaluated new economic opportunities, assumed the sensitive role of ultimate risk bearer, and motivated their own firms. Critical "gap-filling" ability was demonstrated when they compensated for market deficiencies in a period of unstable markets.[96] The absence of a long and stable colonial experience forced the Baltimore firms to scramble for new business almost from their founding. Success and opportunity attracted the better risk-taking and more innovative merchants from other areas in a kind of mercantile selective migration. Success was generally at the expense of other ports and geographical areas rather than at the expense of their own mercantile neighbors in Baltimore. They were a new force "driven by the wind actually blowing," demonstrating an ability to adjust their sails to new conditions better than their competitors.[97]

One success factor was the attention given to shipping details. Extremely wealthy newcomers to trade left such details to others, but while many of the new Baltimoreans started with some capital, few started out as millionaires. The firm of S. Smith & Buchanan advised a supercargo to "lose not a moment" and "every day you hesitate, will probably occasion a fall in price," while telling a new captain to "above all try to be on good terms with your Mates and Crew without which Constant Waste and Injury will arise to your owners." They ordered veteran Captain George Stiles to "fill the Dining room State Rooms with Hats as they come on board" and reprimanded an agent for sending a particular captain to Curaçao because he was "wholly unfit for any Business of the kind." An experienced captain was told to stow his coffee "clear of the Sides under both Decks." In another case a resident agent was directed to improve his knowledge of French so he could function better in the West Indies.[98]

"Sail Duck," a captain was advised, was to be stowed "in the Centre of your Vessel — for if near the Bottom or sides — It will Imbibe the moisture that may be near it." Seven months earlier, while preparing to clear, he was advised to "expend nothing" in England except unavoidable expenses. Speed, proper stowage, and frugality were expected of S. Smith and Buchanan captains, and those who fell short were transferred or released. One captain was transferred from a full-rigged ship after expending an "Enormous Sum" on her operations, to a small brigantine "which will suit his genius much better."[99] The firm's welfare was in the hands of its captains at sea.

The success of the Baltimore merchants was due in a large measure to their initiative and ability as entrepreneurs. It was aided by the existence of an excellent harbor, a supply of staple crops, and a good geographical location for all but the European trade. The city itself blossomed as a market by 1810 when its population with its outlying precincts approximated fifty thousand people.[100] New merchants and workers came from Europe and other states, but the failure of the eastern and southern Maryland counties to grow or even remain constant in population suggests that those areas provided many new Baltimoreans.[101] By 1810 the port was better able to supply the sailmakers, caulkers, iron workers, riggers, shipwrights, and others, skilled and semiskilled, needed by its expanding maritime establishment. Baltimore, particularly Fells Point, was a popular "rendezvous" or recruiting station for naval vessels and merchant vessels of other ports seeking experienced and knowledgeable mariners. One German traveler noted as early as 1800 that the port's captains were highly respected and highly skilled.[102] Each firm had its favorites and some such as S. Smith and Buchanan had whole stables of experienced and proven master mariners by 1812.

Another key factor in the rise of the maritime establishment was the port's shipbuilding capacity. A subsidiary of foreign commerce, American shipbuilding was well established from Maine to Charleston even in colonial times. Entry into what was still a handicraft was easy and substantial profits encouraged competition. Two essentials of the business, timber and labor, were available close to deep water in Baltimore. Worm-resistant white oak was native to the Chesapeake area and live oak, adding longevity to a vessel, along with other woods grew nearby. In time, master carpenters developed or were attracted from other areas and Baltimore, by 1812, had a reservoir of such skilled men. They designed vessels, selected woods, supervised construction, and attended the financial aspects of the business while producing a vessel in six weeks or less upon demand.[103]

Master carpenters of the entire Chesapeake region were experts in the construction of fast-sailing schooners. Such vessels were labeled "sharp-built," "pilot-boat constructed," or "built in privateer fashion." Master carpenters' certificates, required of anyone applying for a ship's register, revealed a variety of Baltimorean schooner builders in the prewar decade. In Baltimore, usually at Fells Point, William Flannigain, William Price, James Cordery, and William Parsons were among the busiest, while Bernard Salnave, Lewis De Rochbrun, John Steele, John Hutton, and Joseph Despeaux, among others, were also productive.[104]

From 1804 to 1812 William Price of Fells Point built schooners in "pilot boat fashion" for merchants later active in private vessels in the War of 1812 such as Lemuel Taylor, Thomas Tenant, and the firm of Hollins and McBlair. William Parsons, also of Fells Point, constructed "sharp built" vessels for William Patterson, George Stiles, Levi Hollingsworth, and others during the same period. The most popular of the Baltimore shipbuilders was the Quaker Thomas Kemp, formerly of St. Michaels on the Eastern Shore. His certificates bore the phrase, "finished privateer fashion," even in prewar years when American private armed vessels were not operative. Even some of Kemp's older vessels, such as the *Rossie* built for Isaac McKim in 1807 and the *Rolla* of 1809, were spectacularly successful in the War of 1812. A brig constructed in 1806 for James Purviance and the firm of Hollins and McBlair was described as suitable for cannon because it was "finished with a flush deck and a privateer waist."[105] Privateer owners during the War of 1812 knew from experience which builders would provide the special equipment needed for war.

Other bay area builders supplied the Baltimore entrepreneurs with vessels in the prewar period. Talbot County builders, William Harrison of James, Noah Richardson, as well as Perry and Richard Spencer were active. Queen Anne's County was the building site for John Denny, and master carpenters in Mathews County, Virginia, provided vessels for Hollins and McBlair, S. Smith and Buchanan, Thomas Tenant, James Bosley, John McKim, Jr., and others.[106] The sharp-built schooner was not solely a Baltimore product or secret.

By 1812 Baltimore had completed five decades of steady growth. Ship-builders, seamen, captains, and most importantly, entrepreneurs such as S. Smith and Buchanan were attracted to the bustling parvenu port by the flour trade, Revolutionary War prosperity, the West Indian trade, and the neutral carrying trade. Wharves, shipyards, manpower, and schooners were all available. Repeatedly challenged to make entrepreneurial adjustments to commercial conditions of someone else's making, the Baltimoreans scrambled and prospered. It was the entrepreneurs' "steady enterprize" that converted a site that thirty years before the Revolution was "occupied by cornfields, cut up ravines, disfigured by high broken hills, or covered by the waters of the basin, swamps and quagmires" into the fourth ranking American port in wealth and commerce. They adjusted to the War of 1812 quickly by converting their port into a full-fledged privateering nest. Before the war was six months old forty-two commissioned vessels dispatched from Baltimore carried 330 guns and 3,000 men into the Atlantic, while the port's yards were outfitting ten more schooners in the 300-ton class.[107] Forced to mature quickly during decades of turmoil, sea-wise Baltimore informed the world that it intended to play a role of leadership in the War of 1812.

THREE

One-Fifth of a City

In the late spring of 1812 many Baltimore-owned vessels were on the high seas heading for the West Indies or Europe. Merchants were anxious to complete profitable transactions, including sales to the British on the Iberian Peninsula, before a prewar embargo or war intervened. By late June, after the declaration of war, emphasis shifted to private armed vessels. In June, a Baltimore newspaper noted that "preparations for privateering are progressing" and anticipated that "several elegant, valuable, and fast sailing schooners will [soon] be ready for sea." It also exhorted owners of the privateers to help a fleet of 150 English vessels sail "into port" or to "lighten their cargoes!" Finally, in July the newspaper reported eight raiders clearing from Baltimore.[1] Other private armed vessels followed soon after as hundreds of Baltimoreans of various backgrounds and means entered into what became Baltimore's most important economic and shipping activity in the War of 1812.

According to surviving documents, Baltimoreans applied for a minimum of one hundred seventy-five commissions of the eleven hundred or more issued by the federal government. Some three-quarters of those were made to the Baltimore Customs Office, the rest to other ports. Allowances for unsubstantiated commissions, especially replacements or renewals required whenever crew size, rig, owners, or commanders were altered, suggest one hundred eighty-five as a reasonable estimate for Baltimore-owned commissions in the War of 1812.[2]

About one-third of the Baltimore commissions for Baltimore-owned vessels were replacements as the investors often followed the old privateering custom of disbanding the informal corporation after one cruise or voyage. Regardless of the number of commissions, the actual vessels involved in the Baltimore fleet was at least one hundred twenty-two.[3] Original or new owners sometimes confounded vessel numbers by renaming previously registered vessels. D'Arcy and Didier's letter-of-marque trader *Maria*, for example, was converted into the privateer *Harpy*, while their licensed trader *Delille* was changed into the privateer *Syren* in New York.[4]

Shareholders in Baltimore's commissioned vessels numbered, when non-

[32]

substantiated possibilities were eliminated, two hundred persons. Allowances for probable but unsubstantiated commissions suggest a range of two hundred to, say, an estimated two hundred twenty persons. About one-half (ninety-eight) of the substantiated owners were one-time investors and may be classified as "marginal" investors even though a number of them were exceptional in that they were the "sole" owners or "dual" part-owners.[5] For this study, the owners were grouped according to their frequency of investment as a measure of their commitment to the private vessel system. Frequency of investment provided a clear picture of which Baltimoreans found private armed vessels to be an appropriate, appealing, or necessary usage for their funds and schooners. The use of the term "marginal," therefore, connotes a one-time investor who lacked either available funds, substitutes for funds in the form of skills or supplies, or full confidence in private armed vessels in the War of 1812.

Fifty-five, or more than one-half of the ninety-eight substantiated marginal investors in Baltimore's private armed vessels, were concentrated in just eight privateers.[6] Such vessels, in contrast to cargo-carrying letters-of-marque traders, required substantial capital for their larger armament, advances to larger crews, and for greater amounts of provisions.

There were no great mercantile houses listed among the twenty-four part-owners of the fifty-five-ton privateer *Wasp*. Captains, marine craftsmen, and small businessmen dominated a syndicate including twenty marginal and four moderate investors. The following list of *Wasp* sponsors is a good example of the tendency of marginal investors to concentrate in one vessel while also serving as an insight into the variegated backgrounds of marginal investors at the time:

Solomon Albers, merchant
John Barkman, double block, tin sheet, and iron manufacturer
John Cooper, blacksmith
John Grosh, sea captain
Leonard Hall, sea captain
John Keys, merchant
John Kipp, oil and paint store proprietor
William Lovell, biscuit baker
George MacKenzie, saddle and harness manufacturer
William McCleary, boot and shoe manufacturer
John O'Connor, doctor (possibly)
Samuel Patrick, merchant
William Porter, dry goods merchant
Thomas Ring, sea captain
Henry Stickney, ship chandler and grocer
John Stickney, distiller and paint and varnish store proprietor
Sebastian Sultzer, biscuit baker

Stephen Turner, occupation not determined
Thomas White, occupation not determined
George Wolpert, ship chandler and grocer
Thomas Kemp, shipbuilder (moderate investor)
Elijah Beam, mariner (moderate investor)
James Curtis, sea captain (moderate investor)
John Snyder, captain, ship chandler and grocer (moderate investor)[7]

Marginal investors sponsoring other commissioned vessels included a ship joiner, a sailmaker, a whitesmith, an auctioneer, a coppersmith and brass founder, a rope store proprietor, a sugar refiner, a keeper of baths, a merchant tailor, and a china store proprietor. Fifty-five marine-oriented craftsmen, small business proprietors, and sea captains dominated the list of single effort investors, while only thirty-two investors were referred to as "merchants." Most, including flour, dry goods, and hardware merchants crippled by the blockade of 1813 to 1814, were seeking substitutes for their usual peacetime incomes. In each vessel one of the part-owners fulfilling the role of agent or "ship's husband" managed that vessel's business affairs for the others. Oil and paint store proprietor John Kipp, a mariner in early life, was ship's husband for the *Wasp*.[8]

A marginal investor could acquire an owner's share without investing a large amount of capital. Chandlers, captains, and shipbuilders were sometimes paid in full or part for their goods and services with shares. Single investor James Cordery, for example, was credited with a one-twentieth share (valued at $1,156.91) in partial payment for constructing the privateer *Amelia*.[9] Captain Thomas Boyle, the most famous of the Baltimore privateer captains, was given "one undivided thirteenth Part" of the *Comet* (valued at $2,307.70) in a last minute registration change on November 10, 1812.[10] The *Comet*'s original owners may have found it advantageous to sweeten the pot to retain Boyle, who had just completed a successful cruise. For captains any income from owners' shares was supplementary to the large blocks of shares assigned to them in the officers' and crew's moiety. Numerous chandlers, grocers, or marine craftsmen in the marginal investor group either chose or were forced by circumstances to accept owners' shares in payment for supplies or services when a vessel's sponsors were low on cash.

Few great merchants were in the marginal investor group. Flour exporters who sold return cargoes of dry goods or hardware invested in private vessels as the only outlet for goods and capital during the British blockade of the Chesapeake from 1812 to 1814. Small general merchants and commission merchants invested limited funds in one private venture also. The few highly reputable shipowning merchants in the group, such as William Patterson, were often sole or dual owners of single vessels.[11] Their wartime investments, while often heavy, were under their own direct supervision. Dual ownership schemes, in seven cases, included one merchant and the vessel's captain. Such arrangements combined counting house and sea expertise while offering a simplified decision-making process and clear-cut areas of responsibility. For maximum profits, efficient decision-making, and effective command, however, it was hard to beat a situation in which the captain was the sole owner. One such captain, a man named Weems, had as his single investment his own *Halcyon*. The heavy loss borne by one man in such cases explains the desperate efforts Weems made to ransom his vessel after its capture.[12] Few of the small businessmen, marine artisans, or captains in the marginal group had significant sums at stake. Most were taking only minimal risks to survive in a wartime economy.

Fifty-two participants in two or three Baltimore-owned commissions constituted a "moderate" investment group. While often renewals, the second or third investment emanated from individual entrepreneurial decisions and, therefore, reflected a commitment to the private vessel system. Some moderate investors simply possessed more capital or vessels than the marginal investors, but others consciously spread their financial risks to avoid the disastrous losses experienced by unfortunate sole, dual, or part-owners whose vessels were captured or lost at sea.

Fewer marine-related craftsmen and artisans were among the moderate investors than among the marginal group. One-third of those making two or three investments were involved in two businesses or a trade and a business. Also noticeable were former captains in business such as James Ramsay, John Snyder, Martin F. Maher, William Price, and Baptiste Mezick. Successfully achieving upward mobility before the war, they became commission merchants, shipyard owners, chandlers, or wharf proprietors.[13] Investing in private vessels was one way of maintaining their achieved status in a mercantile and maritime city in difficult times.

Three prominent shipbuilders made two or three investments in commissions. Shipyard owner Joseph Despeaux from France via Haiti, retained ten shares in the three-masted ship (rare among Baltimore's private armed vessels) *Alexander* after he sold her to a Salem group. He also converted his ship *Father and Son* into a letter-of-marque trader. His owner's "certificate for one share" in the schooner *Caroline* was "on account of repairs, etc. done to said privateer" after half of his bill was paid in cash. The best-known of Baltimore's shipbuilders, Quaker Thomas Kemp from St. Michael's, held shares in the famous privateer *Chasseur*, which his master carpenter's certificate characterized as "finished privateer Built." His certificate for the letter-of-marque schooner *Flight* listed Kemp as one of four owners, while repair work may have led to his share of the privateer *Wasp*.[14] William Price, who had progressed from captain to master carpenter to shipyard owner and wharfinger, also owned shares in two private armed vessels.[15]

In contrast to the marginal group only 10 percent of the moderate investors were sea-going captains. Some, such as J. D. Danels (occasionally spelled Daniels) and Alexander Thompson, were productive privateer commanders. Another highly successful commander in the group was Portuguese-born Joseph Almeda. Unable to write his name, Almeda retained a share of his *Joseph and Mary* after selling her at the war's outset. He was also credited with "one-half share only," valued at $375, in the initial capitalization of the privateer *Caroline*, which he also commanded.[16] For captains and shipbuilders an owner's share accepted in lieu of cash held out the possibility of a bonus in prize money.

Known Baltimore merchants were more obvious among the moderate investors than the marginal group. In addition to the blockade-plagued flour, dry goods, and hardware importers and exporters seen in the marginal group, great shipowning names appeared among the moderates. A Hollins, Buchanan, Didier, Williams, or Patterson name on a letter-of-credit was not challenged in Baltimore. The limited expenditures of those included in the moderate group stemmed from the fact that these investors were the junior partners or relatives of illustrious houses bearing their family name.

Major prewar shipowning merchants among the moderates were sole owners of commissioned vessels who needed no extra capital. A cousin of Samuel Smith, John Donnell, was enticed to Baltimore from Alexandria, Virginia, by his politically and commercially prominent relative. One of his three investments was the wholly owned letter-of-marque trader *Eleanor*.[17] John A. Morton, Baltimore merchant, proprietor of an iron factory and partner in the Bordeaux firm of Russell and Morton, was another sole owner. Sailing to France during the war, Morton serviced Baltimoreans from there as a prize and resident agent.[18] John Carrere, active in the French and West Indian tobacco and coffee trade, kept his solely owned licensed trader *Expedition* racing between France and America throughout the war. Another sole owner in the moderate group was Isaac McKim of the famous postwar clipper-owning family. Sole owner of the reputedly swift and beautiful letter-of-marque traders *Grecian* and *Valona*, he kept them flying to France. Old Revolutionary War shipowner Jonathan Hudson was another moderate but sole owner. The sole ownership of a privateer was rare but moderate investor, sugar refiner, dry goods, and produce merchant Cornelius Specht was listed as the single owner of the privateer *Fox*, a converted prize vessel. Court witnesses, on the other hand, specified one of the *Fox's* officers, Jean-Jacques Bonne, as a dormant owner or "understrapper." Such owners were illegal but Bonne, also referred to as the vessel's captain in contradiction of government documents, was a mysterious figure in Baltimore privateering.[19]

The fifty-two moderate investors were, in conclusion, better known in prewar commerce than the marginal investors. They also invested in larger vessels involving fewer part-owners, while drawing on fewer captains and more merchants (percentage-wise) with shipowning records. The captains, ship-builders, and chandlers among the moderate investors, often engaged in multiple activities, were from the mainstream of the port's commercial and maritime life. With an average of two and one-third commissions per investor, the group's investment rate barely doubled that of the marginal group. With the exception of its sole owners with long shipowning records, the moderate investors appear to be men actually "on the make," endeavoring to achieve the status of great merchants or merchant princes. Unfortunately, the uncertainties of war and private armed vessels could also lower one's status.

The final group of owners and part-owners to be considered is that of the active investors: that is, Baltimoreans who invested in private armed vessels four or more times. Considering only substantiated ownership, those fifty investors must be considered the heart of the Baltimore private armed vessel establishment. Their commitment to private armed vessels was demonstrated clearly by their vigorous participation. The fifty active investors, as owners and part-owners, invested 453 times. This represented an average of about ten (9.96) investments per member, or a rate roughly four and one-half times that of the moderate investors. That average also represented a theoretical investment by each active investor every three months of the war and included only seven who invested in the minimal four commissions. Participating at an extremely active level, twelve investors purchased all or part of fourteen or more commissions, while the maximum number of twenty-three investments was made by only two individuals. There is little doubt that these fifty men were responsible for Baltimore's place in the history of privateering.[20]

How much money was actually needed to buy a share of a private armed vessel? Surviving bills of sale from 1812 and 1813 suggest some beginning costs. Seventeen letter-of-marque traders averaging 195 tons and 3.4 part-owners sold for an average price slightly shy of ten thousand dollars or two thousand nine hundred forty-one dollars per investor. A mixture of old and new vessels, all required additional infusions of capital for alterations, armament, sails, provisions, cargoes, and clearing costs before they could clear for sea. Nine privateers, averaging 192 tons after two fifty-five-ton vessels were excluded, sold in the same period for an average price just shy of fourteen thousand dollars. Increasing the number of part-owners for the more expensive raiders to an average of 11.6 per vessel reduced entry level costs to one thousand two hundred six dollars.[21] Privateers demanded even higher preparatory costs than the traders before clearing and their dividends emanated solely from prizes since they carried extra arms and supplies in lieu of profitable cargoes. Marginal and moderate investors other than sole or dual owners, it can be estimated, came up with somewhere between one and four thousand dollars per share as a working average. For an active investor making the minimal four investments, that estimate ran from four to sixteen thousand dollars, while those making the average ten investments needed forty thousand dollars. For some of the fifty active investors, who often held more than one share in vessels with fewer than average part-owners, forty thousand dollars was minimal.

How significant was the $40,000 minimal investment risked by some of the active investors? First class seamen received $360.00 a year when fully employed in periods of demand, while highly skilled marine carpenters earned $1.87 per day, also in periods of high demand.[22] The secretary of the navy earned $4,500.00 per annum, while the attorney general who maintained no residence or staff in Washington, received only $3,000.00.[23] It would have been difficult for those officials or a craftsman to save enough from their incomes to invest in something like the new 300-ton and sixteen-gun privateer *Tom* said to "cost near 40,000 dollars."[24] For the cost of a share in a first class Baltimore schooner one could have capitalized a business. The 1810 census listed Baltimore coopers, hatters, glovemakers, a breeches maker, shoemakers (one with ten employees), saddleries, farriers, nailmakers, and coachmakers whose capital investments ranged from one to five thousand dollars. An active investor holding multiple shares could have capitalized a Baltimore business requiring, according to the 1810 census report, between eight and twenty-five thousand dollars such as a sugar refinery, a tobacconist firm, a large cooperage firm (employing ten to twenty-one hands), a curriery, or a wagon-making concern.[25]

Because of the higher capital requirements one finds in the active group of Baltimore investors in the War of 1812 even fewer of the marine-related proprietors, artificers, and captains than in the moderate group. No shipbuilders invested in four or more vessels, and while Luke Kiersted, listed as a sailmaker in the 1810 city directory, appeared in the group, he became an active shipowning merchant on the eve of the war. Nicholas Stansbury, a grocer and ship chandler of Bond Street, was interested in seven commissions, more than his prewar shipowning habits would suggest. Most of his investments were privateers for which chandler Stansbury provided the provisions. He may have accepted shares as did shipbuilders Despeaux and Cordery in lieu of cash payments. Among others who invested heavily in private armed vessels was Dennis A. Smith, bank cashier, large Louisiana landowner, stock investor (said to have made a fortune in government bonds during the war), and increasingly an owner of ocean-going vessels. Mill-owning merchants Christian Keller and Francis Foreman (fifteen investments together) and flour merchant Thomas Sheppard (twelve investments) also intensified their shipowning.[26] Once more the particular problems of the flour merchants must be considered as their export product was bottled up in 1813 and 1814 by the blockade.

Forty or more investors of the active group were experienced shipowning merchants in well-established houses, some of whom invested in private armed vessels as far back as the Revolution. They suffered at the hands of privateers and foreign navies in the war-torn decades preceding the War of 1812 when

Baltimore carried neutral trade. Not all active investors were in shipping for twenty years, but there was no merchant of less than five years' experience among the fifty active investors. The experience of the Revolution, when newcomers moved into private armed vessels immediately upon their arrival in Baltimore, was not repeated in the War of 1812. The War of 1812, unlike the Revolution, inspired few new business relationships among the participants in private vessels. A mature mercantile establishment in 1812 provided an adequate base for the port's extensive private armed vessel operations and minimized the need for new merchants and new relationships in Baltimore. Active investors bought shares in vessels whose cooperating part-owners were also established merchants with whom they had previous business relationships. Those sharing vessels in the War of 1812 shared them in the 1790s and 1800s. Ship registers for 1811 alone show Hollins and McBlair, S. Smith and Buchanan, the Williamses, Andrew Clopper, Levi Hollingsworth, Christopher Deshon, Charles F. Kalkman, George J. Brown, George Pitt Stevenson, John Gooding, William T. Graham, D'Arcy and Didier, and Von Kapff and Brune sharing owner's registers. They and other prominent shipowning merchants such as Thomas Tenant, John McKim, Jr., and the Pattersons cooperated with other part-owners in the war, but none was a stranger to the others as a shipowner.[27]

The backbone of Baltimore's private armed vessel establishment (the fifty active investors) consisted of a cluster of merchants built around the firms of Hollins and McBlair and S. Smith and Buchanan. Related by marriage and accustomed to shared ownership of vessels and cargoes, they were intertwined in their social and political lives and in organizations such as the Maryland Insurance Company. The three basic partners of Hollins and McBlair, a firm in the European and Far Eastern trade were former Liverpool banker, John Hollins (five-twelfths), Michael McBlair (five-twelfths), and, after 1810, John's son, John Smith Hollins (two-twelfths).[28] The three partners owned parts of at least seventy commissions for sixteen different vessels and with S. Smith and Buchanan and their partner, Lemuel Taylor, the cluster's interests included ninety commissions for twenty vessels. Relatives of the Hollins-Smith cluster such as Dr. Lyde Goodwin, related to McBlair by marriage, and George Pitt Stevenson, the nephew of Samuel Smith and William S. Hollins, related to John Hollins, owned parts of another thirty-three commissions. Occasional partners of the Samuel Smith and John Hollins firms in peacetime trade, William S. Hollins and George J. Brown, related to banker Alexander Brown (trading as Brown and Hollins), held parts of eleven more commissions. When shares held by Hollins-Smith captains were included, the expanded cluster's total interests ranged from 175 to 200 investments. The cluster had its hand in 40 percent of Baltimore's commissions while investing in 25 percent of its vessels.

Following the shipping and privateering custom of sharing risks, the Hollins-Smith cluster shared its commissions with some from outside its immediate circle. James Williams and Gerrard Wilson, shipowning merchants of great wealth and experience, and S. Smith and Buchanan captain-turned-merchant Christopher Deshon cooperated with the Hollins-Smith cluster. Andrew Clopper of Fulford and Clopper, Charles F. Kalkman, and William T. Graham, bank president, merchant and son-in-law of Alexander Brown, were other established shipowners working with the cluster. The cluster obviously preferred to do its private vessel business with men of experience and means. The new $40,000 privateer *Tom* brought in some lesser merchants, but in all the Hollins-Smith commissions there were only two unidentifiable merchants. Controlling ample capital, the cluster avoided smaller vessels utilizing twenty or more part-owners. It endeavored to spread its risks in larger vessels with a few known and reliable part-owners while sponsoring both letter-of-marque traders and privateers. Privateer profits offset letter-of-marque vessels captured at sea and letter-of-marque trading profits offset privateer losses or augmented their gains. Assuming one share per commission, certainly a rarity among the fifty active investors, the Hollins-Smith group risked at a minimum somewhere between one-quarter and a full million dollars in Baltimore's private armed fleet.

Old mercantile ties and marriage were the glue of another Baltimore cluster of active investors. It centered on Henry Didier, Jr. and John Netherville D'Arcy of the house of D'Arcy and Didier. Formerly based in the West Indies, the firm returned to Baltimore, the home of transplanted Frenchman Henry Didier, Sr., on the eve of war and invested in thirty-eight commissions. German-born trader Bernard Von Kapff, who arrived in Baltimore in 1783, and his partner, former Danish Consul Frederick W. Brune, joined D'Arcy and Didier in ten commissions. Von Kapff and the younger Didier were related by marriage. Dennis A. Smith, bank cashier, successful stock investor, merchant, and owner of large plantations in Maryland and Louisiana, joined the Didier cluster in several vessels. German trader Peter Arnold Karthaus and his son-in-law Ferdinand Hurxthal invested in a privateer with the Didier group. Flour merchants and shipowners Thomas Sheppard and James Williams also cooperated with Didier along with William and James Bosley, large landowners, shipowners, and proprietors of a leather business. In general, the Didier-Von Kapff cluster preferred cargo-carrying letter-of-marque traders to privateers and seemed to be a favorite of the German merchants. Sometimes characterized as "plungers" and "dashers," entrepreneurs D'Arcy and Didier were high in risk-taking ability.[29] They employed first class Baltimore schooners in the war to join scarce products to needy markets. Since part-owners had the legal authority to dispose of his own share without the approval of the syndicate, an anxious investor could withdraw from one owner's syndicate and join another's. A consequence of partnership law was that no one could really control the make-up after the initial shares were sold.[30]

How did one wind up in any one syndicate or in a cluster such as the Hollins-Smith group? Members of the same board of directors of various concerns and bank cashiers as well as old mercantile associates often worked together in private vessels. Six of the nine owners of the privateer *Lawrence*, for example, were directors of the Universal Insurance Company.[31] Successful merchants in the mercantile city of Baltimore continually met and evaluated not only other merchants but directors of banks, insurance companies, and manufacturing concerns. Success in the counting house qualified a merchant for membership on such boards and exposed him to other successful merchants at the numerous board meetings.[32] Social or political status, without counting house success, seldom placed a man in the first rank of Baltimoreans. Twenty mercantile firms and their sometime partners comprised about 80 percent of the active and a significant portion of the moderate investors. Their prominence in trade in the eighteen months preceding America's entry into the war supports mercantile counting house success as the key associational determinant.[33]

Once the rank of major merchant was acquired, associations were sometimes buttressed by other relationships. Baltimore's mercantile society married their own kind and, in time, the established merchant community's foundation rested partly on extended kinship relationships. The Hollins, Smiths, Mc-Blairs, Pattersons, Goodwins, and Stevensons were interrelated as were the Von Kapffs and Didiers, the Hollingsworths, the Partridges, the Williamses, and the Stumps. Few were accepted into such relationships without successful and prior mercantile success.[34]

Shareholders' meetings could have been held among the pews of the city's two Presbyterian churches. The Hollinses, Smiths, Buchanans, Browns, Didiers, and Williamses were active Presbyterians along with investors Thorndike Chase, Joel Vickers, George Stiles, Archibald Kerr, Bernard Von Kapff, and others.[35] Religious activities may have expanded or reinforced relationships, but they had no obvious bearing on investment associations except in the case of Quakers. Nationality, when one scans the names in the city's German Society, was more influential, but the society was founded by well-to-do Germans to assist new arrivals from Germany.[36] Neither marriage, religion, nationality, nor politics, since Republicans and Federalists invested together in the same vessels, were significant associational determinants. In mercantile Baltimore before 1815, status was achieved in the counting houses often after experience as a captain, supercargo, or resident agent abroad.

Five active investors with long experience and unusual resources operated private vessels without any particular associational pattern other than normal business relationships. Peter Arnold Karthaus, John McKim, Jr., and Thomas Tenant owned several whole vessels alone before and during the War of 1812.[37] Relying on well-constructed, swift schooners such as the letter-of-marque schooners *Brutus*, *Spartan*, *Macedonian*, and *Manleus* (*Manelaus?*) owned solely by Thomas Tenant, these independent owners were financially able to move in or out of vessels at will. Richard H. Douglass owned one vessel solely, but his other investments utilized all the different clusters of owners. Former S. Smith and Buchanan captain George Stiles, unique among the active investors, avoided all multiple ownership schemes including those sponsoring privateers. Desiring the first American commission for his solely owned privateer *Nonsuch*, tea and grocery proprietor, merchant, and later mayor of Baltimore Captain Stiles had to settle for a duplicate of that first commission. The port collector's promise of that coveted commission was countermanded by President Madison's own promise to another Baltimorean, Commodore Joshua Barney of Revolutionary War fame.[38] *Siro*, another of Stiles' solely owned fleet, was beefed up after functioning as a letter-of-marque trader so that she could make a privateering cruise in 1813.[39] Stiles did not spread his risks among other part-owners, but the splitting of his money in traders and raiders was a common insurance technique for wartime investors.

Bondsmen were also part of the privateering business. Every commissioned vessel needed two sureties or secondary risk-taking participants for its letter-of-marque bonds. Surety bonds for commissioned vessels were in addition to the usual bonds required of vessels clearing to foreign ports. Signers of letter-of-marque bonds had to be recognized by the collector as merchants whose financial status matched that of the bond. Owners and part-owners traded off this role, but nonshareholders charging a fee were brought into the private vessel establishment in this role. Of 164 substantiated commissions, the names of the letter-of-marque bond sureties survive for three-fourths (77 percent) of them.[40] Among the 109 Baltimore sureties listed, there were sixty owners and part-owners of commissions averaging almost three bonds per signature. The seven most active sureties (all active investors as well) averaged nine bonds each. They bonded vessels for each other in a kind of logrolling, while nonshareowning partners in a firm sometimes signed for their shareowning partner. Relatives acted as sureties for each other, while French and German merchants utilized others of their own national origins in that role. Such practices were logical, of course, because a man's past business associates were familiar with the character of the commission holder and he, in turn, was at least partially informed of their resources. Merchants trading with Germany or France assisted each other in peacetime commerce.

The distribution of the bonds among the commission holders, not surprisingly since they traded off the role, paralleled their activity level in ownership shares. Active investors in commissions signed about the same number of bonds in the sample (127 cases) as the moderate and single investors combined. The most active bond signer, John Smith Hollins, was also the most active commission holder, but his bond signatures amounted to only one-half of his commission holdings. His restraint suggests another risk-spreading technique practiced by the merchants. Two of the most active sureties, George J. Brown and William T. Graham, were related by marriage to the large merchant and banking house of Alexander Brown and Sons for whom bonds were a basic facet of business.

The forty-nine noninvestors who signed surety bonds averaged less than two bonds per member, so the commission owners took care of themselves in seventy-eight cases. Names prominent in Baltimore mercantile history and Revolutionary privateering such as Purviance, Van Wyck, and Sterett, show up as sureties. Whether they lost their need to invest their resources or their nerve is uncertain, but their earlier ownership of commissions demonstrated that they were no opponents of the system. Other prominent mercantile and land-holding names on surety bonds included Henry Thompson, Joshua Dorsey, and Nicholas Ridgely, as well as the Gilmor and Warfield families. The Steretts and the Dorseys (related to Levi Hollingsworth) were the most active bond signers among the nonholders of commissions.[41]

Most numerous in the private vessel establishment and primary risk takers were the officers and crew. The crew's privateer prize tickets provided the only compensation due them at the termination of a cruise. On a letter-of-marque trader a crewman's prize ticket was in addition to his wages and was, in reality, a bonus. Computation of the numbers of such participants was complicated by the in-and-out nature of the schooners and the on-and-off habits of the crews as well as by the tendency of the vessels to pick up crew members in other ports. An estimated four thousand minimum number appears firm, however, since the collector of customs reported, in the first four months of the war, 1,450 officers and crew members on eighteen privateers and 928 men on letter-of-marque traders as clearing from the port.[42] The projection of the collector's partial figures to the entire Baltimore fleet raised the minimum figure to 6,678 men, an enormous number for a city of 50,000 inhabitants.[43] With owners, part-owners, letter-of-marque bond sureties (not to mention other sureties), and crews, the total number of Baltimoreans financially interested in private armed vessels ranged from 4,250 to about 7,500. The engine of this machine was, of course, the 200 entrepreneurs whose capital investments created and sustained the fleet.

Baltimoreans benefitting in wages, goods, or profits from the system without taking personal or financial risks were innumerable. Shipyard and warehouse workers, recruiting agents, lawyers, clerks, owners of piers, wharves and warehouses, as well as auctioneers, draymen, and teamsters swelled the list of those with a vested interest in the system. Their dependence on it increased as normal commerce decreased. Victualers, ammunition and arms merchants, and bidders at prize auctions were also dependent upon the private vessels. Newspaper advertisements aimed at privateering ventures seeking supplies were numerous. Normally, thirty or more firms bought prize goods at auctions in which the names of other prominent Baltimore mercantile families and firms appeared along with those of the auctioneers.[44]

The inclusion of nonrisk-taking participants and their employees suggests that eight or ten thousand Baltimoreans had at least a small financial interest in private armed vessels. For many suppliers and maritime craftsmen it was a modest part of their livelihood, but they earned some income from the system and probably defended it as a legitimate wartime business activity. Without allowances for seamen, farmers selling ship timber or workers who came into Baltimore as temporary help or commuters from the adjacent countryside, approximately one-fifth of Baltimore's 1810 population had more than a casual interest in the tall-masted schooners as they faded from sight past Fort McHenry.

Anyone familiar with the Baltimore mercantile community in the early nineteenth century would notice the absence of well-known commercial names from the roster of private investors. Henry Thompson, whose estate "Clifton" was close to Samuel Smith's but who as a Federalist was politically more distant, did not appear as a shareholder in private armed vessels. He appeared in a secondary role when he successfully bid $16,500 for the prize ship *Henry* taken by the *Comet* in 1812.[45] Other moderate and large merchants purchased sugar, coffee, or dry goods at prize auctions as they endeavored to survive the war.[46] The new firm of Alexander Brown and Sons, not yet heavily engaged in shipping, did not invest in private armed vessels, but two relatives by marriage, William T. Graham and George J. Brown, were active investors. The firm owned large ships appropriate for the large cargoes and long voyages of the European trade but ill-suited for commerce raiding. Alexander Brown and Sons worked closely with some commission owners and shared noncommissioned vessels with D'Arcy and Didier and Dennis A. Smith while shipping tobacco to Liverpool in 1814.[47] The firm advertised newly arrived Irish linens, copper, and hardware for sale on October 29, 1812. The same firm sold coffee, purchased a schooner, and repaired ships, interacting with the private raiders only in the purchase of one prize vessel.[48]

The established firm of Robert Gilmor and Son was a secondary participant in that it had twice signed as sureties for letter-of-marque bonds. The Gilmors owned large three-masted square-rigged ships designed to carry large cargoes in the European trade instead of the smaller and faster schooners that were common in the trade between Baltimore and the West Indies. They bought, stored, and sold tobacco throughout the war along with Charleston rice and cotton while also participating in the Iberian flour trade. The Gilmors shared a ship with Mark Pringle, an old Revolutionary privateer owner who was largely retired from business and completely retired from privateering by 1812.[49]

A final European trading company and owner of bulky ships rather than fast schooners that did not invest in private armed vessels was the house of Robert and John Oliver. Reputedly the wealthiest man in Baltimore, Robert Oliver claimed that he had retired from business in 1810, but that statement conflicted with the actual evidence. Oliver may have meant that he had ceased to expend large sums or full efforts on a constant basis as he had in earlier years. During the war, he traded in nankeens, coffee, tobacco, and copper. The Olivers and Alexander Brown and Sons were the port's "largest purchasers" of tobacco in 1814 as they anticipated peace and increased prices in Europe. They were said, in 1814, to have held several thousand hogsheads of tobacco (over 3 million pounds) each.[50]

The Olivers developed a working relationship with active commission owners D'Arcy and Didier and Von Kapff and Brune before the war and had joined them in the ownership of the 850-ton ship *Hannibal* in 1811. That relationship intensified in the war years as Henry Didier, Jr. reported on December 12, 1814, that "Mr. Oliver and myself are sending out a fast sailing schooner to Havana" and earlier, that "he calls on me daily and is much attached to us." Other merchants also found the great man's influence and knowledge helpful as he assisted a merchant in obtaining a British license to ship supplies to Portugal after the Declaration of War.[51]

The Oliver firm did not completely avoid the private armed vessel business. Indeed, it owned at least two prize vessels, and John Oliver purchased a pistol from the prize cargo of the *Chasseur*.[52] Mr. Oliver had no pressing need for profits, but his avoidance of the private armed vessel business appears unusually determined or his close association with those vigorous investors, D'Arcy and Didier, would have sorely tempted him. Perhaps his Federalism or conservatism restrained him, although one can speculate that another year of war, combined with a blockade, would have forced Oliver and other noninvestors into the business. Their limited participation in the prize and surety aspects of the system and their association with some of the most active investors indicates an absence of moral or ethical objections to the system.

For moral objection to the system one must look to the large Quaker community, long active in Baltimore's growth and trade. The Quakers absolutely rejected military activities of any kind, but their limited wealth prevented them from sitting out the war. One finds shipbuilder Thomas Kemp owning privateers and citing his vessels as "privateer-built" on his master carpenter's certificates. This kind of advertisement was useful because his religion prohibited newspaper advertising. As a shipbuilder and repairer, Kemp's alternatives to wartime activities were few and he may have been inactive in the church while in Baltimore. The Quaker firm of Brown and Wilson found themselves restricted to the coastal and country trade in their effort to survive in wartime. Sales of fresh figs, old Java coffee, and items such as rice, sugar, and salt brought up from Charleston were their alternatives to private armed vessels. They also inaugurated a line of small vessels to run the coast from Boston to Virginia.[53] For them, the war years were entrepreneurially debilitating.

Quakers who joined the Baltimoreans in selling flour to the British army on the Iberian Peninsula were the well-known flour-milling Tyson and Ellicott families. They loaded 2,500 barrels of flour for Cadiz in 1812 and insured it for $30,000, apparently considering such activities nonmilitary. One of the most famous of the Baltimore Quakers, Moses Sheppard, was in the early stages of his mercantile career. From Philadelphia, where his father had been a Loyalist and a partner in the Baltimore firm of Mitchell and Sheppard, he apparently obeyed the Quaker injunction against war activities, including the partaking of the spoils of war in the form of prize goods, but it is difficult to identify individual partners among the many firms purchasing prize goods. Some mercantile families contained one avid Quaker, while the other members of the family rejected that religion. The McKims, investors in private armed vessels, for example, were related to the Baltimore Quaker from Delaware, John McKim, but they did not embrace the religion themselves. Moses Sheppard restricted his trade to the "country trade" in and adjacent to Maryland and survived the war. In fact, the young firm's profits in 1813 were better than those of the two previous years, but $6,000 or so profit of 1813 hardly prepared Sheppard for his immense philanthropic activities in later years.[54]

Exceptions to the general participation in the system of private armed vessels in Baltimore included old conservative aristocrats such as the Carrolls, Quakers, and a few great merchants plus some flour or tobacco exporters. The firm of T. and S. Hollingsworth (Thomas and Samuel) and the house of Hollingsworth and Worthington were flour merchants and nonparticipants in private armed vessels.[55] Owners of large three-masted square-rigged ships built for the European trade and inappropriate for raiding were also nonparticipants. Some nonparticipants preferred a stronger navy or even Jeffersonian gunboats in lieu of the private armed vessel system, but once Congress authorized private armed vessels, the bulk of Baltimore's mercantile and maritime communities plunged into the business in such numbers and with such enthusiasm as to invite retaliation from the British fleet in 1813 and 1814. Bait for the British was prize money, vessels, shipyards, warehouses full of tobacco, cotton, coffee, and flour, and investors who had harassed British commerce and advocated war on Britain. In 1813, the *London Evening Star* suggested its idea of the proper punishment for the numerous Baltimore privateersmen when it wrote that "the turbulent inhabitants of Baltimore must be tamed with the weapons which shook the wooden turrets of Copenhagen."[56] In the dark days of 1813 and 1814, Baltimore's investors holding 15 percent of America's commissions must have had second thoughts about their decision to enter the private armed vessel business.

FOUR

For Purse and Flag

With the long European and American tradition of private armed vessel usage and Baltimore's experience with privateering, its adoption of the system in the War of 1812 was a matter of course. Exhortation was unnecessary. A London newspaper commented matter-of-factly, "From the short period of the declaration of war, the Americans have fitted out two hundred and twenty privateers, which have been very successful in capturing English vessels," and predicted, "Most of their merchants will be converted into this specie of force."[1] Few argued with that conclusion, but the merchants did not all invest for identical reasons. Local circumstances, profit-making, wartime conditions allowing for few entrepreneurial alternatives, and a desire to contribute to the national welfare were possible motives for investing in private vessels. One investor could have been motivated by one, some, or all those reasons.

Shipowning merchants in every American port knew war developed before necessary naval preparations had been completed. They witnessed governmental "bluster and unpreparedness," the construction of Jeffersonian gunboats ill-suited for sea duty, and Madisonian indecision on the eve of war.[2] Those merchants did not expect the small American navy to protect their vessels or to clear the seas for trade despite the navy's reputation for excellence in one-to-one combat. Obviously, merchants themselves had to provide much of any maritime power the republic was to have in the War of 1812. Commissions permitted them to arm their vessels for self-defense as traders or to go on the offensive as privateers. The small American navy, while still operative, drew off the British and forced them to concentrate their vessels for a time. Such concentration left areas of the sea unpatrolled, allowing the merchants' commissioned vessels to trade and raid. The navy's diversion of convoy escorts, called "bulldogs," can be seen in an incident of August of 1812 when British convoy escorts *Shannon*, *Guerrier*, and *Belvedere* left the rich Jamaica fleet of seventy sails to pursue three sails they believed to be an America squadron.[3] The inability of the American navy to meet the British fleet on anything near equal terms motivated American merchants to put their own vessels into action. Another attraction was the presence of English trading vessels operating in the western Atlantic near the American ports, both unaware of the war and unable to defend themselves.

For the Baltimore merchants local motivational factors existed. Many of their vessels were on trading voyages when the war opened, but the port's numerous schooners in the nearby West Indies trade became available quickly. The smallest Baltimore private vessels were adequate in early situations, and the *Wasp* and *Liberty*, both of fifty-five tons, sailed in July of 1812.[4] Three-fourths of Baltimore's 1811 tonnage was for vessels between 70 and 300 tons, and consequently, its fleet was well-suited to private vessel operations.[5] The men who owned and operated that fleet in peacetime, a mixture of Irish, Scottish, German, and French immigrants with little natural affection for Great Britain, had been losing vessels, cargoes, and men to Britain for two decades. The Baltimore merchants, captains, and seamen as well as the port's shipbuilders, sailmakers, ironworkers, and other artificers had prospered from decades of commerce. The war ended their peacetime prosperity and forced them to seek substitutes for it.

One substitute for peacetime commerce was the private armed vessel system. It allowed a merchant to employ both capital and vessels. For craftsmen and mariners, whose resources were less substantial than that of the merchants, service on or for the private armed vessels generated necessary wartime income. Idleness spelled economic disaster for the seamen and smaller merchants and in the case of vessels, a heavy drain on even the large merchants' resources.

For experienced shipowning merchants, entry into the private armed vessel system was a response to what was, historically, another in a series of entrepreneurial challenges. Baltimore's Revolutionary merchant community enlarged a minor business center by launching successful privateering ventures and by their other wartime commercial activities. Strengthened by the addition of new people and new money, they responded to the port's second challenge by finding new markets for the republic's products after the Revolution. The third entrepreneurial challenge was to survive, or, hopefully, to thrive in an Atlantic trading area dominated by warring European powers in the 1790s and early 1800s. For the survivors of the first three challenges the adoption of the private armed vessel system in the War of 1812 was their response to a fourth entrepreneurial challenge.[6] Fortunately for the Baltimoreans, their responses to the first three challenges constituted a valuable apprenticeship for this role in the War of 1812. That apprenticeship included experiences in the operation of private armed vessels, in blockade running, in schooner construction and handling, and in the evasion of enemy warships. Their training over the decades suggested that their performance in private armed vessels in the War of 1812 would be professional and productive.

There was an additional local motivation in the realm of politics. Baltimore, the "rough, disorderly boom-town in the new republic," was "decidedly Republican."[7] Mariners and craftsmen, many of the smaller merchants, and some of the great merchants were Republicans. Political support of the administration was combined with an interest in profits. Hopes that their private armed vessels, "fitted and manned by patriotic citizens" might "add four-fold to their own and their country's welfare" did not eliminate private gain as a motive. The rationalization that the private armed vessels were only recovering from the British "the treasures which they have so clandestinely robbed and pillaged from our citizens" treated profits as fair compensation.[8] Such a view was consistent with the origin of the private reprisal system centuries earlier, but losses no longer had to be proven to get a commission. As a Republican community, Baltimore was pleased that its patriotic support of the administration provided it with an opportunity both to make money and to even a few old scores.

An instinctive drive to generate profits in any or all situations was an integral, if not critical, characteristic of an entrepreneur. His function was to organize and manage a business undertaking while assuming risks for the sake of profits. An investor's individual expertise and degree of risk-taking ability determined how much of his capital would be exposed to what amount of risk in any venture. The addition of wartime conditions was simply another element to be weighed during the decision-making process. For some investors in private armed vessels, the fact that their investments might also serve the national interest was only coincidental and of little or no significance. Profits were the entrepreneur's *raison d'être*, and public service without a profit was self-defeating even though one always kept his relations with the public at an acceptable level. There was no concern for the public interest in Henry Didier, Jr., an active investor in private armed vessels, when he wrote that, "the continuance of war has operated much to our advantage here" after referring to profits of 100 and 200 percent. His admission that, "All that I am afraid of is the war will not last two years more, in that time I expect to make enough for us to retire," exposed little concern for the misery that war meant for others. Much of his success in the war was, however, from letter-of-marque cargo carriers and not from commerce raiders, while his most sanguine hopes were expressed after the British blockade had been terminated. His entrepreneurial instinct for profits after the Treaty of Ghent inspired him to wish for a "war between England and France and some of the Continental powers, that we may make use of our fast sailing schooners."[9] There was little concern for patriotism or public service in his statements, but as the war continued, he expressed pride in American victories.

Profit appears again as the primary motivation in a statement by a partner of Fulford and Clopper, merchants and shipowners. Henry Fulford dispatched two letter-of-marque traders to the West Indies with flour and was interested in another vessel as well. He indicated that, "For a man of my capacity, I shall have a great deal afloat," and, "If nerve lasts, I mean to run the risk, for if two of the three arrive safety I ought to make money." The return loads of coffee and sugar were destined for New York, New England, and France when they could get in. Henry Fulford was satisfied that he had done his own work well, saying his vessels were "well fitted out for their voyage" and in good hands while at sea, but good preparations and officers were not enough and Fulford apprehensively added, "I hope Dame Fortune may protect them." Another Fulford and Clopper commissioned vessel paying a $30,000 profit to Andrew Clopper, principal partner and a very active and successful investor in private armed vessels, prompted Fulford to remark on Clopper's great pleasure. Fulford's concerns in his letter were purely economic, and no interest in public service was expressed, but merchant Fulford cared enough to actually fight at the Battle of Bladensburg.[10]

One motive encouraging an entrepreneur to invest in private armed vessels was a general lack of wartime alternatives. There was, however, a lucrative option available in the war's first seven months. That option was the sale of provisions to the British army in Spain and Portugal. The British were dependent on outside sources of supply before America entered the war, but the trade continued after its entry. American vessels were given special British trading licenses called "Sidmouth's" after an official who rejoined the British government in 1812. Baltimore vessels carrying grain and flour joined those of other ports in the steady traffic to the Iberian Peninsula.[11] There was public opposition to what some branded a traitorous trade, and Fells Point workers and mariners demonstrated vociferously against it while actually damaging some of the vessels loading for the Peninsula, including those of neutrals. Anyone sending "a Barrel of flour to the Enemy" was promised a rope about the neck.[12]

An attack on those selling flour to the British came from another source when Collector of Customs James H. McCulloch, veteran of the Revolution, former merchant, and later a wounded volunteer at North Point, protested. He questioned Secretary of the Treasury Albert Gallatin about the propriety of issuing clearances at Baltimore to American vessels with cargoes of provisions "going to the ports of Lisbon and Cadiz."[13] The secretary's response, perhaps aimed at helping merchants to make money needed in the conduct of the new war, was that the business was legitimate because the United States was not at war with Spain or Portugal. Secretary Gallatin felt that McCulloch was overzealous and reprimanded him by noting that, "The question is not what the law, in your opinion ought to be; but what it is."[14] Gallatin's view of the trade's legitimacy was shared by Baltimore entrepreneurs who shipped eight and ten dollar per barrel flour to the Peninsula for twenty and thirty dollars per barrel. One firm noted that one Lisbon order alone involved 40,000 barrels of flour.[15]

Baltimore's entrepreneurs had almost unlimited access to the wheat and flour of farmers and millers of the entire Chesapeake region, who shared in the

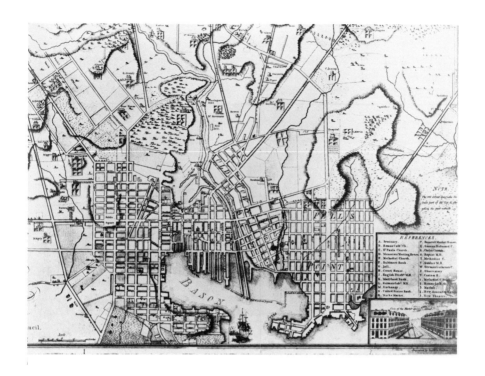

PLATE II

Warner and Hanna's "Plan of the City and Environs of Baltimore, 1801," original in the Maryland Historical Society

profits of the Iberian trade. The port received country or "wagon" supplies at its western end (Howard Street) and Eastern Shore or "boat" supplies at its wharves before the blockade. Other supplies of grain and flour came in about March from the "Rappahannok, Potomack and the mills about the Head of the Bay and the Creeks which empty into the Bay." About the first of April the "Pennsylvania or Susquehanna Flour" made its appearance every year.[16] The British fleet off the American coast respected the Sidmouth licenses in 1812 and for the first few months of 1813, so the demand for flour was high. Alexander Brown and Sons' ship *Armata* reported eight Baltimore vessels anchored in Lisbon in January of 1813.[17] Newspapers and the collector's records reported numerous other Baltimore vessels in the trade.[18] Profits from the trade injected significant amounts of capital into the United States, and to some extent, they financed some private armed vessels in Baltimore.

Merchants in the Peninsula trade profited for a while, but there were obstacles. Officers and supercargoes of traders hid their Sidmouth licenses from some American privateers who delighted in sending them into prize courts for adjudication.[19] Joshua Barney of the privateer *Rossie* believed cargoes on licensed vessels were British property and therefore good prizes. He sent them in even without much hope that they would be condemned.[20] The courts later declared such vessels good prizes.[21] Merchants insured licensed vessels, but some insurance companies charged extra for insurance protecting a vessel "against capture by our own cruisers."[22] The American privateers kept an eye out for the licensed vessels and managed to see British licenses one way or the other. The brig *Hiram* of Baltimore, for instance, showed her license to the commander of a British warship that turned out to be the privateer *Thorn* out of Boston and the *Hiram* was soon on her way to Marblehead for adjudication.[23] The privateersmen delighted in harassing the licensed trade even when they could not get a decree of condemnation.

Risks other than those at sea were insured for those in the Peninsular trade. The Phoenix Insurance Company of Philadelphia insured the *Orizimbo* of Baltimore not only against normal risks but also against "the mob at Baltimore or any loss accruing therefrom."[24] Its Republican owners, disgusted by the clause, remarked that it "has afforded us a hearty laugh and we believe laughing is sometimes conducive to health."[25] The firm ceased laughing when the Baltimore privateer *Sarah Ann* turned its Peninsula-bound *Piscataqua* into Baltimore for adjudication. The firm felt that the Philadelphia privateers were particularly eager to capture Baltimore's licensed flour vessels and that they would get "coats of tar and feathers" if they showed up in Baltimore.[26] Private armed vessels were expected to attack British vessels.

The whole flour trade turned sour abruptly. Baring Brothers, an English banking house serving the American trade, reputedly wrote to Robert Gilmor and Sons that the English government had ceased signing new licenses in September of 1812. The licenses were terminated because the license system was a "measure incompatible with the present state of Warfare," and because Europe's good harvests made the supplies unnecessary. That action in itself did not terminate the business because the British Board of Trade had issued 650 of the permits and their use continued for months. The firm of S. Smith and Buchanan avoided the Peninsula trade, possibly because the Smith's presence in the United States Senate where the trade was much debated. His firm, however, reportedly bought flour for the Peninsula trade after Congress decided not to "meddle" with the business late in 1812. Another Baltimore firm decided that Smith and Buchanan's real object in shipping was simply "to keep their vessels employed."[27] The employment of one's vessels was an important motive for the use of both British licenses and private armed vessels. Those owning full-rigged ships were not apt to commission them, but they used them in the Peninsula trade as long as it was tolerated.

For the Baltimoreans the real end of the Peninsula trade and other commerce, including the coastal trade, occurred in February of 1813. The best alternative to commissioned vessels disappeared when the *Emily* of Baltimore returned to port after clearing for the Peninsula. The British admiral wrote a note on the *Emily*'s register "declaring the Chesapeake in a vigorous state of Blockade." Britain's blockading squadron was actually enforcing its government's earlier decision to end the Peninsula trade, and vessels returning from the Peninsula or anywhere else were turned away from the Chesapeake. British privateers in the West Indies were ordered to "send in every vessel, with or without licenses" and the licensed Baltimore vessels slanting off toward the West Indies after thirty-five dollar per barrel flour prices were out of business.[28]

The cessation of the flour trade to the Iberian Peninsula seriously reduced the entrepreneurial options available to the Baltimoreans. The establishment of the blockade at the same time brought the war home to Baltimore in early 1813. Farmers, importers, and shipowners suddenly became desperate as the "rigor of the Blockade" was increased each day. Flour merchants attempted to get their product to New York or Philadelphia by land as the export business was brought to a standstill. Merchants looking for new alternatives found that only the interior or the West was safe. Sugar and coffee were ordered in "snug small Hogsheads as of easy and safe transportation" because the merchants looked toward "inland speculations."[29] John Hollins noted in February that "perhaps 50,000 barrels" of flour were piled up in Baltimore at the end of February of 1813.[30] At ten dollars per barrel, that was a half million dollars' worth of flour going nowhere.

The port of Baltimore was virtually paralyzed. Hopes that the "Cravings of John Bull's Belly" would end the blockade proved abortive.[31] Products moved only by land and advertisements for wagons increased in local papers. Wagons, referred to as "our wheeled vessels," had their journeys noted in maritime style by days. Wagons reported "no enemy cruisers," as "moving under easy sail," and as having arrived without speaking "any of his British Majesty's cruizers nor an American Privateer."[32] It was unlikely that the frustrated shipowners enjoyed such editorial playfulness. The $10.50 per barrel price of flour in November of 1812 and January of 1813 at Baltimore plummeted to $6.50 by September of 1813 and to a disastrous $5.50 in November of 1813. The $5.50 figure was the lowest average monthly price in the war period and the lowest average monthly price in a decade.[33] Baltimore's merchants needed outlets other than wagons and uses for their expensive and idle vessels. Trade was "as dull as dull can be," one merchant observed.[34]

The blockade strangled Baltimore's sea trade. Chances of clearing port in April of 1813 were so slim that one flour-milling and merchant house used its mill lands for timber cutting "until we have something better to do." Dry goods merchants had empty shelves and could not pay their bills, so they suffered with the flour exporters because "nothing can get in or out of our Bay." Purchases by neutral vessels saved some exporters from starving but, for most, a "most perfect stagnation prevailed in business." Capital not used in vessels or cargoes went into manufacturing, which was reported to be "increasing on every Water fall and by Steam inventions." One active exporting firm contemplated abandoning seaborne commerce altogether if the war were prolonged a few more years.[35] A newspaper reported at the end of 1813 that the city would soon have 20,000 cotton spindles operating compared to none in 1811 and cited advances in wool, copper, brass, nail, and glass production.[36] The port of Baltimore in early 1813 had warehouses full of flour and West Indian produce waiting to be exported, while its hardware and dry goods merchants awaited imports. Private armed vessels were the only option left, so desperate efforts were made to get them to sea. In November of 1813 it was noted that "fifteen or twenty fast sailing schooners have lately got out of our Bay, principally laden with flour."[37] Letter-of-marque schooners, escaping at night or in storms, managed to edge the price of flour up to seven dollars per barrel. John Hollins wrote at the same time that his partner, Michael McBlair, was in New York attending three of the firm's vessels turned away from Baltimore. Successful escapes prompted Hollins to remark that, "The War does not prevent our little fleet vessels from coming and going." Expecting his correspondent to find fifteen or twenty schooners escaping as "extraordinary," he noted that "many more are preparing to depart during the long nights." Recognizing the difficulty of entering at Baltimore, Hollins stated, "they cannot venture back to our Bay — not being able to know where the British vessels may be." In April, John Hollins said only "sharp vessels" were getting out and that he expected the reinforced blockading forces to stop them too. Merchant George Pitt Stevenson also complimented "Baltimore enterprize," but when one of his schooners from France ran "the gauntlet in the Chesapeake with considerable danger and damage," he ordered his vessels to enter at other ports.[38] This was a loss for those whose income was related to servicing such vessels and cargoes, but there were no alternatives as the commissioned sharp-built schooners, with their small cargo area, were the only means of exporting the port's goods.

Flour and dry goods were not the only products in trouble. Maryland's old staple, tobacco, was piling up also. The slightest increase in tobacco's sale price encouraged planters to decrease their wheat cultivation. Despite its low price and attendant soil damage, tobacco was profitable because the planters were able to employ their slaves fully. Only one-fourth or one-fifth of their slaves were needed to cultivate wheat, while maintenance costs continued for the unused labor force. Also, the planters were accustomed to tobacco cultivation and continued to grow it even in a glutted market.[39] All in all, the apprehensions of Revolutionary veterans Thomas and Samuel Hollingsworth expressed at the declaration of war were finally coming true in 1813. They had stated then, "Stocks are falling, Rents reducing and many are already turning their faces towards the Country for returns during the War, resembling the Days of 1776 in Philadelphia."[40] The flour trade to the Peninsula, private armed vessels, and the absence of a blockade had helped Baltimore prosper until 1813, but then a pall settled over the port.

Surprisingly, business failures were not overwhelming in those dismal years. The failure of the Steretts (letter-of-marque sureties) for about ninety thousand dollars was serious, but rich friends helped them. The knowledge that they might drag others down with them and hurt the reputations of other merchants encouraged the merchants to keep such bad news from the public. One Republican firm prayed, in desperation, that "God in his mercy grant us speedily an honorable peace with all the World."[41] Aside from operations in private armed vessels, the merchants experienced difficulties unheard of since 1799 and the years immediately following the Revolution. In those days there was no British blockade and no national war restricting the use of capital or limiting entrepreneurial options.

The leasing of commissioned vessels to the government was one limited option available to some of the shipowners in bad times. The government needed the schooners to return British prisoners, to carry dispatches, and to deliver diplomatic messengers. Leasing allowed an owner to utilize his vessel, but the practice was not widespread enough to aid a sizeable portion of Baltimore's 122 commissioned vessels. The owners were paid operating costs and so much per passenger.[42] This offset maintenance costs and may have allowed some profit. At least two first class Baltimore schooners were actually offered to the government at cost without any thought of profit.[43] Because of the blockade the Baltimore vessels available for leasing were often anchored at other ports. Few of the side benefits needed by wharfingers, stevedores, and other port workers came to Baltimore. The Baltimore schooners were sought by the government because of their speed, small size, and commissions. The government preferred armed vessels for obvious reasons.

Alternatives available to shippers and shipowners at one time or the other were not enough to keep trade moving. The resulting business stagnation and shipping slump affected the entire nation. American imports, after reaching a value of 139 million dollars in 1807, plunged to 77 million dollars in 1812, and to a pitiful 14 million dollars in 1814. Coffee imports, so valuable as a reexport item to the Baltimore entrepreneurs, fell from 59 million pounds in 1807 to 28 million pounds in 1812 and to just 8 million pounds in 1814. Sugar experienced a similar drop. National tobacco exports of 104 million pounds in 1801, dipped to 26 in 1812, to 5 in 1813, and to just 3 million in 1814.[44] Baltimore merchants Robert Oliver and Robert Gilmor together were sitting on three million pounds of warehoused tobacco in 1814.[45] Flour inspections in Baltimore fell from over one-half million barrels each in 1811 and 1812 to about one-quarter million in 1813 and to just one hundred fifty-five thousand barrels in 1814.[46] Undoubtedly, a national and local economic decline existed in 1813 and 1814 and merchants were forced to make adjustments if they wished to survive.

Historically, Baltimore merchants trading on their own accounts and as commission merchants, retreated in bad times into the safe harbor of the commission business. Henry Didier, Jr., trading out of Haiti in 1810, advised a Baltimore firm that he was planning to do nothing but commission business until the market improved. In 1814, anticipating the end of the war, he said his firm preferred to go entirely into the commission business so it could make money "without running any risks."[47] Losses in the commission business fell on the owners of the goods and not on the handlers. Another privateer owner in the war remarked later that his house would be occupying itself "almost exclusively with Commission Business and keeping ourselves Snug for better times."[48] In a war with a naval power such as England, the source of most of Baltimore's commission business along with other European belligerents, that safe harbor was simply not available. Each commercial house had to find its own answer to the question of how to produce profits in a wartime situation.

There were entrepreneurs who invested in private armed vessels early in the war. Incentives for early entry were profits to be made because of the availability of prizes in nearby waters and the easy egress from Baltimore. Early investors had their investments working for them in the dull days of 1813 and 1814 as a kind of insurance against their losses or inactivity in trade. Jeremiah Sullivan of the house of Hollingsworth and Sullivan invested early, and when his firm reported that it knew of "no port to ship to that will pay cost and charges" in 1813, he had his private armed vessels to keep him comfortable.[49] Sullivan's money was in three of Baltimore's best-known privateers, Barney's *Rossie* and the *Comet* and *Chasseur*, both commanded by the incomparable Thomas Boyle.[50] Others waited until the troubled year of 1813 to invest in the private vessels when the armed schooners were the only vessels hazarding clearance in the face of the blockade.[51] All other vessels were wasting away in the harbor.

Late entrants into the private armed vessel system in Baltimore and early entrants who increased their investments in 1813 and 1814 were motivated by a number of factors. Certainly, profit was the primary aim of all the investors no matter when they entered the business. The merchants, however, saw their regular trade and the Iberian flour trade terminated and the blockade instituted all at once. When Congress lowered the duties on prize goods sold at auction in August of 1813, another incentive for investing in private armed vessels occurred.[52] The combination of the end of the flour trade, the establishment of the blockade, and the lowering of the tariff on prize goods, all occurring between February and August of 1813, focused more attention on private armed vessels as a possible profit-making alternative.

Forty-two percent of the 200 Baltimore sponsors of private vessels entered the business after the first six months of war. Viewed in investment groups, almost two-thirds of the marginal or one-time investors were late joiners. Often tradesmen, small merchants, and captains survived as long as some vessels were moving, but the general stagnation in shipping in 1813 forced them to find other sources of income. One-third of the moderate investors (those making two or three investments) entered after the first six months. They were often smaller or moderate merchants who also needed income and vessels capable of getting to sea. The active investors, the 50 men with four or more investments in private armed vessels, were not latecomers. Only one-eighth of them entered the business for the first time after the first six months of the war, although many increased their investments in the later months.[53] The early entry of the active investors suggests that they viewed private vessels as the best profit-making option open to major shipowners in wartime. More of the marginal and moderate investors, on the other hand, waited until other options were gone or until they witnessed the success of the early investors.

There was a price to be paid for late entry that was partially offset by the lowering of the tariff on prized goods. Vessels employed in the private armed vessel system were larger, better armed, and carried larger crews as the war progressed. Late investors had to finance their higher preparatory and outfitting costs. More of the vessels commissioned after the initiation of the blockade in early 1813 were also privateers rather than the less expensive letter-of-marque traders. Only one-third of the commissions issued in the first six months of the war had been for privateers, but then lightly armed traders got to sea without difficulty because there was no blockade. After the blockade the investors resorted to the more expensive, better armed, and larger privateers capable of fighting off the weaker elements of the blockading force. Larger crews on privateers were useful in manning sweeps and in repelling boarders. Two-thirds of the vessels commissioned in the last six months of the war were privateers. Many were commissioned in other ports but, by that time, the British blockade extended to most of the American coast.

The primary motive for investing in private armed vessels was undoubtedly the desire for profits. The profit incentive encouraged some to invest at the war's outset, while the stagnation, blockade, and lowering of the duties on prizes prompted others to invest after 1812. Both groups used the private armed vessel system as a replacement for their peacetime entrepreneurial activities, but the second group tried other options before resorting to private vessels. The existence of a primary motive does not, however, exclude the existence of important secondary motives among the entrepreneurs. They were often men who had participated in the birth and growth of the commercial republic under whose flag they did business. The existence of dual or even multiple objectives or motives did not prevent the investors from remaining loyal to their roles as entrepreneurs.

There is evidence that the Baltimore private armed vessel captains and the owners were not entirely concerned with the profit motive. Private armed vessels, historically, avoided heavily armed opponents and enemy warships, preferring weaker vessels that could be captured relatively undamaged. When private armed vessels were cornered by stronger adversaries, they generally surrendered after attempting to escape by their sailing skills, not their fighting capacity. The private armed vessels of earlier periods avoided serious combat and seldom were concerned with the accomplishment of national objectives such as the weakening of an opponent's general maritime establishment.[54]

Baltimore's fleet fought when cornered and destroyed British shipping when there were no profits involved. The privateer *Mammoth*, owned partly by S. Smith and Buchanan, not only fought a huge troop transport without success, but also burnt and destroyed numerous British vessels having no prize value. The *Mammoth* also scattered the British fishing fleets on the Newfoundland banks. The *York*, a privateer, fought the large troop transport *Lord Somers* at the cost of six men including her commander.[55] Such transports had high sides and massed musketry and were of nominal prize value. The privateer *Grampus* lost her captain and other men in a vicious fight with a British sloop-of-war disguised as a merchantman.[56]

The sailing prowess of the Baltimore schooners was such that they could have broken off some of their engagements with powerful adversaries, including the strong British post office packets, but they did not. The privateers *Rossie* and *Surprise*, in one cruise each, burned or sank nineteen or twenty enemy vessels of little value. The *Surprise* after capturing the valueless brig *James and David* cut off her masts before releasing her.[57] Even two lightly armed letter-of-marque traders, the *Cora* and the *Lottery*, were said to have defended themselves "with great gallantry" when subdued on their way to France in 1813. The privateer *Dolphin* lost thirty men or one-third of her crew before she lowered her flag.[58] The privateer *Hussar*, taken twelve hours out of New York, threw over eight guns, part of her shot, all spars, and lumber on the deck, and her anchors and cables in an effort to escape. The captain, taking a brisk fire, did not lower his flag until requested to do so by his officers to save the lives of his men.[59]

Profits alone were not a satisfactory explanation for such actions by private armed vessels, and "most desperate and bloody action" was not a stranger to them in the War of 1812.[60] It was difficult to produce "a reasonable why or wherefore" for the combat role of the American private armed vessels. The *Rapid*'s efforts to fight off and escape a British frigate inspired the British captain to return the captain's sword of the letter-of-marque trader, "a compliment rarely bestowed on Privateersmen."[61] A Baltimore editor applauded Federalist New England's entry into private armed vessels as a "patriotic effort" to terminate the war as quickly as possible by distressing the enemy.[62] Prizes were profitable but their loss and the burning and sinking of unprizeworthy vessels also hurt Britain.

An example of the fighting spirit of Baltimore's private armed vessels was given by Captain Thomas Boyle's *Chasseur*, the port's pride and joy. Boyle informed the owners' agent George Pitt Stevenson in March of 1815 that he had fought an English warship. His adversary was the British navy schooner *St. Lawrence*, a "large low, pilot-built schooner with yellow sides" showing only three gunports. The *Chasseur*'s approach, however, was greeted by the opening "of a tier of ten ports in a side," soldiers and marines hiding under the bulwark, and a brutal broadside. Boyle reduced the *St. Lawrence*, formerly the privateer *Atlas* out of Philadelphia, to "a perfect wreck, cut to pieces in the hull" with "scarcely a rope left standing" and with all her officers killed or wounded. *Chasseur* had five killed and six wounded.[63]

Captain Thomas Boyle's encounter with a naval vessel was extraordinary enough for a privateer to warrant an explanation from him. Boyle said, "I hope you'll not be displeased with what I have done." He also noted that "I should not willingly, perhaps, have sought a contest with a King's vessel, knowing it was not an object" but having been fooled by her appearance, "the honor of the flag entrusted to my charge was not to be disgraced by flight."[64] There is no doubt that the *Chasseur* could have escaped from her opponent, but Boyle was concerned for something beyond profit. He was part-owner of his former vessel, the *Comet*, and may have been a shareholder in the *Chasseur* as well. He understood that the primary objective of privateering was profit and that a wrecked naval vessel without a cargo was worthless at auction. His adversary was not financially worth the losses and damages suffered by the *Chasseur*. Former privateer captain and historian George Coggeshall described his friend Boyle as a man in whom were "blended the impetuous bravery of a Murat, with the prudence of a Wellington."[65] Prize agent George Pitt Stevenson probably preferred more prudence and less bravery. He kept the *Chasseur*'s accounts with the clerk of the admiralty court and knew Boyle fought the *St. Lawrence* for something other than money. An appraisal of the men on American private armed vessels stating that, in crises, "they were Americans, not privateersmen in quest of plunder, and they would gladly die sooner than hail down the Stars and Stripes," aptly described Boyle and the other Baltimoreans at sea.[66]

Other incidents support the contention that there were motives and concerns other than simple greed. The privateer *Tartar* went aground in a fierce December blizzard while attempting, in company with several other private armed vessels, to glide past the blockading squadron. Six men froze to death but only the "humanity" of her owners, James and William Bosley, prevented greater losses. They supplied heavy winter clothing to the crew at their own expense even though the *Tartar* was not heading for northern waters and winter attire was "not specified in the agreement" signed by the owners and crew.[67] Amos A. Williams, part-owner of fourteen commissions, exhibited a concern for interests other than profit also when he responded to a government request for dispatch vessels by offering two of the fastest "pilot-built schooners" with commissions to the government. He estimated that the *Diamond* cost thirty-five thousand dollars ready for sea, while the *Transit* cost twenty-seven thousand dollars. For their use he asked only costs for himself and the other part-owners because, out of patriotism and with no "mercantile object," they wanted "not one cent of gain."[68] The vessels were to be auctioned off on their return from Europe and, if prices were low, the owners risked a serious loss. Such a use of vessels for cost was better than idleness, but the owners could have either used them in other ways or have gotten some gain from the government.

The Baltimore captains did not dishonor the flag in crises at sea, and the same may be said for the land-based owners when the British attacked Baltimore. The owners were not unpatriotic Shylocks risking only surplus capital. In 1813 and 1814, they sent their families into the country and had the resources and means to flee themselves, but they stayed. Some had suffered at Bladensburg and all knew what had happened to Washington's public buildings in 1814. Their warehouses, counting houses, vessels, and homes, more concentrated than the Washington buildings, would have produced a great conflagration. Henry Didier, Jr., writing to his partner after the British were repulsed at Baltimore in September of 1814 but before anyone knew if they would return, reported that "the British intended to Burn the Town after plundering it," while boasting that Baltimore was now prepared for another round.[69] Baltimoreans realized before the British attack on Fort McHenry that the newly launched frigate *Java* and two navy sloops-of-war in the harbor were "enough to invite the enterprize of the Enemy here."[70] Other vessels in the harbor, warehouses packed with West Indian and prize goods, the port's privateering role, and its Republicanism were immense attractions for British officers seeking prize money and revenge.

The investors in private armed vessels stuck with Baltimore in its hour of need, risking their lives and homes. A survey of military organizations operative during the crises of 1813 and 1814 disclosed, when the captains on sea duty were included, that over 60 percent of the investors, including some great merchants listed as privates, served in militia or volunteer units. Others utilized their skills as quartermasters and clerks.[71]

Sponsors of private armed vessels participated in the defense of Baltimore in various capacities. The Record Book of the Independent Company, a volunteer unit alone listed at least ten investors in its ranks. Attached to the 5th Regiment of the Maryland Militia in 1814, the company went to feel out or harass the British army landing at North Point or Patapsco Neck. Its morning reports listed Levi Hollingsworth (investor in fourteen commissions of private armed vessels), John McFadon (investor in five commissions), and Amos A. Williams (investor in fourteen commissions) as wounded in action.[72] Captain George Stiles, sole owner of a fleet of four private armed vessels, commanded the well-drilled and capable Marine Artillery unit, consisting primarily of ship captains and mates, in 1813 and 1814.[73] Its guns were located in the exposed water battery in front of Fort McHenry during intense bombardment. Merchants- and mariners-turned-land soldiers in the crisis financed "their own guns and carriages," and the businessmen of the city, including private armed vessel investors serving as bank and insurance company directors, collected over one-half million dollars for the defense of their port.[74] Investors in private armed vessels, S. Smith and Buchanan, John Donnell, John Craig, Elie Clagett, and others, provided twenty-four valuable seaworthy vessels to be sunk as obstacles to the British fleet in the harbor.[75] For experienced shipowners proud of their vessels, that was a painful decision. Quaker shipbuilder Thomas Kemp lent his carpenters for three days to Andrew Clopper, an active investor in private armed vessels and an officer in the Sea Fencibles, a volunteer naval unit. Clopper used them to cut apart two ships and a brig for sinking in the harbor. The same carpenters worked on gun carriages and platforms.[76] John A. Morton, an active investor, cast guns for the militia when he could get coal or, in its place, wood from the eastern shore.[77] Active investor Thomas Tenant, the Patterson family, and others utilized their ropewalks and warehouses as billets for the Federal 38th and 14th Regiments of Infantry.[78]

The Baltimoreans, for all intents and purposes, were left to defend themselves, receiving scant assistance from the federal government. Active and multiple investor Jeremiah Sullivan performed as Quartermaster for the 3rd Division Maryland Militia, while Isaac McKim and George Pitt Stevenson functioned as aides to Major General Samuel Smith, the very capable commander of the defense of Baltimore, U.S. Senator and shipowning merchant.[79] Prussian John W. Stump (formerly Stumpf) of the volunteer Baltimore Hussars, set up a series of videttes between Baltimore and Washington following the attack on Baltimore.[80] The two men killed at Fort McHenry's southwest bastion were flour merchants and investors in private armed vessels, John Clemm and Levi Clagett.[81] Active investors Robert Patterson of the William Patterson shipping firm, James Williams, Thomas Sheppard, Dennis A. Smith, Nicholas Stansbury, Gerrard Wilson, Thomas Tenant, Lyde Goodwin, and Lemuel Taylor all held positions in the Maryland Militia. Others such as George Williams and Ferdinand Hurxthal worked with the Sea Fencibles. William Bosley served in the Eagle Artillery. Older men such as John McKim, Jr. and James A. Buchanan sat on the Baltimore Committee of Vigilence and Safety, directing the city's defense. Christopher Deshon belonged to the city's marine and new weapon's committee.[82] These positions and actions were not taken out of naïvete. Levi Hollingsworth and others had been at Bladensburg and witnessed what a fellow-merchant called the "invincible" British columns. The Baltimore investors in private armed vessels were primarily businessmen for whom soldiering was a "miserable employment at best for the Residents of a Commercial city."[83] Their primary aim was to defend home, hearth, and warehouse, but beyond that, they wanted to end the war and get back to trade.

Efforts by the Baltimoreans to terminate the war despite their profits from private armed vessels suggest, along with their military service, that wartime profits were not their sole objective. Senator, militia Major-General and private armed vessel investor Samuel Smith urged the Senate to build a naval force of "thirty fast sailing schooners to depredate on the commerce of your enemy." Baltimore spokesman and editor Hezekiah Niles argued for the same approach to a war against maritime Britain in August of 1812.[84] He continued to plead for a naval raiding force made up of schooners of the Baltimore type throughout the war. Baltimore's congressman Alexander McKim, closely associated with many private vessel owners, made the same plea in November of 1814 in the United States House of Representatives. He argued that the enemy should be attacked where he was "most vulnerable in his commerce." Congressman Robert Wright used the successful cruise of the 376-ton Baltimore privateer *Mammoth* as an example. On that cruise the vessel belonging to S. Smith and Buchanan and John Gooding and James Williams captured or destroyed twenty-one vessels while escaping from many British pursuers.[85] The Baltimoreans showed Congress, through their captures and prizes, how one should fight Great Britain. If their motives in the War of 1812 had been profits alone, the Baltimoreans would not have encouraged their own government to put them out of business. Concern for the nation's survival and a desire for a quick and honorable peace were their reasons for advocating a naval commerce-raiding force.

Baltimoreans knew full well that private armed vessels, by early 1814, were the nation's only effective offensive maritime force. They also realized by the middle of the war that private citizens bore the financial and personal risks of the nation's maritime war. They petitioned Congress, in February of 1814, to pay a bounty for British vessels destroyed by American private vessels. More and more, private vessels were operating in European waters and prizes could not get into blockaded American ports. George Pitt Stevenson, investor and prize agent, presented the petition in which Baltimore's owners stated that they were "sincerely anxious to carry on the war with unabated vigor, by supporting the private armed service, with considerable means and resources." They would "give the best pledge of their sincerity by largely embarking in enterprises against the trade of the enemy," once Congress added the requested financial inducements. The petitioners were "deeply impressed" with the argument that only the destruction of Britain's commerce would bring that nation to its senses. They observed, however, that the nation could not expect "that private adventurers will sacrifice to such an object all prospects of benefit, derived from capture, and expose themselves to the certain loss of an unprofitable cruise."[86] Their motivation for entry into the private system was a combination of a private interest in profits and a public concern for ending the war.

Baltimore's "Merchants and Shipowners" asked for inducements for several reasons. Their main argument was not that the blockade kept out prizes, but that it was discouraging Baltimore's seamen from shipping onto private vessels. Increased remuneration, they believed, would encourage seamen to take greater risks. Then both seamen and owners would be "ready to enter largely into the private armed service and would sanguinely calculate on the increased spirit of our seamen and the enlarged enterprise of our merchants."[87] The destruction of British commerce served both public and private interests. The owners knew they had contributed "three hundred and fifty-four thousand dollars" in duties on prize goods to the treasury in the first six months of the war alone.[88] A reinvestment of some of that and other customs money in private armed vessels would have, in their view, paid even more dividends to the nation.

Circumstantial motives existed for Baltimoreans entering the private armed vessel business, but the primary motivational factor for the participants was still financial profit. That aim was consistent with the objectives of all entrepreneurial activity and with the backgrounds of the Baltimore merchants. The objective here has been to add a very important secondary motivational factor, that of public service. In a crisis at sea, it was not uncommon for that secondary motive to momentarily supplant the primary motive of profit. Profits were sought by the early entrants into the business because the private system was a traditional and appropriate wartime function for investors with commercial and shipowning experience. Later entrants sought profits in the system after other profit-making alternatives faded and conditions in 1813 and 1814 left only private armed vessels as a possibly profitable use of capital and vessels. It was a basic tenet of international maritime and commercial law that ships were "originally invented for use and profit, not for pleasure or delight; to plough the sea, not to be by the walls."[89] "Use and profit" as well as public service were available only through private armed vessels in 1813 and 1814 when investments in those vessels in Baltimore increased dramatically.

Private profit and public service were not necessarily contradictory or mutually exclusive motives. Every British vessel taken was a loss to the enemy and a service to the national interest of the United States. When unprizeworthy vessels were taken, the public interest alone was served, but both private and public interests were satisfied in captures involving prizeworthy vessels. When one accepts the goal of an entrepreneur as something broader than financial profit, the two motives were combined. If profit-making were but one aspect of the entrepreneur's need for achievement, then his actions serving both private and public interests contributed to the attainment of that goal.[90]

The participation of the Baltimore active investors in community service organizations, including volunteer and militia units, supports achievement as an entrepreneurial motivational factor.[91] The struggle between Barney and Stiles for commission number one also buttresses this contention. For some of the small and moderate investors, entrepreneurial survival was the only achievement desired in a wartime situation. Wartime inactivity and losses threatened some with economic extinction or downward mobility. For others, achievement meant ending the war so that they might return to normal commerce. Many merchants had selected Baltimore as an operational base for commerce and war only disrupted commerce. No investor migrated to Baltimore during the war just to invest in private armed vessels.[92]

In conclusion, the case of Baltimore's Samuel Smith should be considered. Symbolic of Baltimore's worth as a commercial city of importance, Samuel Smith played key roles in the military, political, and commercial history of the nation and of Baltimore from the Revolution to 1815. His commercial firm was obviously in business for profits, but his privateering ventures simply compensated Smith for his wartime trade losses and for his private military expenditures in both the Revolution and the War of 1812. To view Samuel Smith as an investor interested only in profits and as a single-minded defender of a profit-oriented private armed vessels system would be an absurdity. A wounded hero of the Revolution, Samuel Smith spoke out in Congress on numerous occasions for a stronger navy as the best instrument for improving America's relations with other nations. A Federalist-turned-merchant-Republican after Jay's Treaty, Smith advocated naval expansion in Congress in 1794, 1797, 1804, 1806, 1808, 1810, and on the eve of the war in 1812.[93] Dependent upon the profits of seaborne commerce, he nevertheless guided Jefferson's Embargo through the Senate and thereafter vigorously fought its repeal. Serving as acting secretary of the navy in the first year of Jefferson's administration, he was one of the few Republicans with any knowledge of naval matters.[94] Smith's support for the private armed vessel system in Congress was actually less vigorous than his support for a stronger navy, and both efforts were tied to a general defense of American commerce.

Samuel Smith's military duty in the Revolution hurt him financially. While in the War of 1812, Smith commanded the militia in Baltimore, organizing the successful defense of the city.[95] There was little comfort or profit in that role. For a man who owned twenty ships as early as 1790 and whose holdings and profits grew steadily up to 1812, his firm's share of five private vessels in the War of 1812 was a minimal effort. Samuel Smith and other active investors in Baltimore were not solely interested in private profit. As merchants in international trade, they would have been pleased with a strong American navy before and during the war. Such a navy would have kept the seas open for their profitable trading vessels. Investments in private armed vessels were but one facet of their total economic, political, military, and social life in the War of 1812. The editor of a Baltimore prowar newspaper needed no convincing of the public service provided by private armed vessels. Baltimore's leadership in commissioning such vessels was, to him, "irrefutable evidence of the practical patriotism" and "patriotic ardor" of the city.[96]

FIVE

A Mercantile and Maritime Elite

The Baltimore investors in private armed vessels had interests and activities other than commissioned vessels. The intention here is to survey the marginal and moderate investors briefly and to analyze the various activities and interests of Baltimore's fifty active investors fully. Their achievements in prewar commerce pushed many of them into the upper levels of what was a mercantile society. Their financial standing, economic activities, and the community organizations to which they belonged were aspects of their community standing. The houses they lived in, their style of life, and their political associations often reflected their status.

Among the marginal and moderate investors in private armed vessels there were many sea captains and tradesmen who serviced the port's vessels.[1] Among them chandlers, shipbuilders, and the successful captains enjoyed good incomes and a relatively high status in the community. A sea captain was at the top of his profession. The sole and dual owners of commissioned vessels were exceptional marginal and moderate investors, and their high standing in the community was based on their prewar commercial activities. Smaller merchants and sea captains among the investors were still climbing and may have viewed their anticipated profits from private vessels as the path to a higher community standing. The absence of the usual peacetime profits and wages from seaborne commerce made profits from private armed vessels one of the few means of keeping an achieved status in a difficult wartime situation. The captains and craftsmen lived in a commercial port heavily engaged in international trade, so their skills were vital to the general welfare of the society and, consequently, worthy of respect.

To have sufficient capital to invest even five hundred dollars in a risk venture set one above the majority of Baltimore's citizens. There were not many opportunities for five hundred dollar investments in private armed vessels; actually, entry sums from one to five thousand dollars were more common.[2] Such sums were not available to many. It has been ascertained that 76 percent of the 1810 property owners of Brooklyn, New York, were worth less than $2,500. Only 1 percent of that city's 5,000 people were worth more than $15,000, and only 8 percent were worth more than $4,000.[3] Baltimore was ten times larger than Brooklyn and had a reputation as a booming commercial city, but when the same criteria were applied to it, only 437 people were worth more than $15,000, and only 3,500 had a value over $4,000. Neither figure would allow frequent or large investments in private armed vessels.

No matter how one views the Baltimore scene, the marginal and moderate investors did not represent the bulk of the population. They were part of a minority that probably included somewhere between one-tenth and one-fourth of the city's population. They have to be viewed as relatively secure in regard to finances or income despite the tendency of the larger merchants to look down upon them. Henry Didier, Jr. referred to some of the lesser capitalists as "the small Beer Gentry," but they were more secure than Baltimore's general population.[4] Certainly, shipyard workers, mechanics, seamen, small farmers, and numerous freed slaves viewed those able to invest any amount in a private armed vessel as fortunate men and as at least borderline members of a mercantile middle class. Such investors enjoyed a better than average (or better than wages) income.

There were marginal investors whose financial standing was greater than their investment record indicated. The standing of a family firm such as that of the Diffenderffers in the china and grocery business, a very diversified business in those days, is difficult to ascertain. Carsten Newhouse, of a sugar importing and refining company of the same name, was in a business requiring substantial capital. Briscoe and Partridge, a flour and dry goods concern, and Charles Appleton, in dry goods also, had to come up with large sums on occasion. Lewis Hart was the proprietor of a public bath, but since he was one of only two owners of the small privateer sloop *Liberty*, he may have had other sources of income.[5] While experiencing financial strain in 1813, John Wallis, Jr. was characterized as a "contemptible little Irishman who keeps a Grog and Bacon Shop — never had $3,000 in his life."[6] Wallis invited the wrath and pejoratives of other merchants worried about public confidence by publicly announcing his momentary insolvency. Not really so "contemptible," Wallis advertised goods for sale in quantity, purchased New Orleans cotton, Dutch canvas, English sail cloth, and molasses while investing (with one other) $13,000 in a privateer in 1812.[7]

Other marginal investors were more impressive. Henry Payson from Roxbury, Massachusetts, was a partner in Payson and Lorman and then Henry Payson and Company where he functioned as a commission merchant and supplier of ships' stores at Bowley's Wharf in the inner harbor. While serving as a director of the Maryland Insurance Company and the Union Bank, Payson was also a proprietor of the Baltimore Manufacturing Company, on the City Council, and on a new court house committee.[8] Described as "the intimate Friend and Correspondent of J. J. Astor," Payson was very active at the Merchants' Exchange.[9] Irish-born merchant Luke Tiernan operated in Hagerstown, Maryland, before moving to Baltimore in 1790. Sending sugar and coffee to Liverpool for hardware and dry goods in his own ships, he lost several vessels to the French in the treacherous 1790s. Tiernan served on a board of relief in 1814 and on the Catholic Cathedral and Washington Monument committees. He also trained Henry Didier, Jr. for his mercantile career and was known for his library and literary taste.[10] Payson and Tiernan were not men of marginal status or influence.

The name of one "merchant prince" also appeared among the marginal investors. William Patterson and one of his sons acquired a commission for the *Torpedo* just as the news of peace arrived in the United States. An old Revolutionary War privateer owner, Patterson migrated to Baltimore with substantial capital in that war. Amassing a fortune in shipping, he nevertheless viewed sea-going commerce as a game of chance. Such a view seemingly precluded private armed vessel investments, but Patterson's alternatives disappeared in 1813 and 1814 while his neighbors raked in their prize money. Their success was both known and infectious and was attested to by an 1814 report stating, "Our Privateersmen speak of their Thousands made as Privateersmen always did."[11] As dual owners the Pattersons had more than minimal investments in the *Torpedo*.

There were merchants of substance as well as strivers among the moderate investors. Baptiste Mezick progressed from captain to sugar and coffee merchant and to part-ownership of a wharf. He fulfilled an ambition held by many literate Baltimore seamen.[12] Another flour firm formerly located in Hagerstown, Elie Clagett and Company (Elie and Levi), imported sugar, coffee, and dry goods, along the lines of Baltimore's popular triangular pattern. Hardware importers, Jesse Eichelberger, formerly of York, Pennsylvania (with John Clemm of Eichelberger and Clemm), became a moderate investor in private armed vessels when his imports ceased.[13] Large flour exporter and mill owner Charles Gwinn, who introduced steam into his mill in 1813, invested in three commissions as his need for profits overcame his disapproval of Mr. Madison's war.[14] Produce merchants James and Thomas Calwell, part-owners of five commissions, opened a chocolate manufacturing concern in 1813. In it they combined their unexportable sugar and chocolate with the candy expertise of George W. Wait from Massachusetts.[15]

There were fewer unknowns or fringe members of Baltimore's mercantile community among the moderate investors. Three-time investor James W. McCulloch (not to be confused with the collector of customs James H. McCulloch) became famous after the war in the case of *McCulloch* v. *Maryland*. An S. Smith and Buchanan clerk before he became a bank cashier, he was not without resources as some have claimed.[16] His three investments were in vessels with only six or eight owners and his investment on the basis of averages of $25,000 per trader and $40,000 per raider was between ten and fifteen thousand dollars.[17] Merchant and captain Thomas Lewis sailed his solely owned *Leo* to France with sugar and coffee in October of 1812. Also a part-owner of the privateer *Kemp*, Lewis sold the *Leo* to that later chronicler of privateering, Captain George Coggeshall.[18] Resident agent in France, iron factory proprietor, overseas prize agent and merchant John A. Morton's wealth was estimated, by his ever-watchful neighbors, to be three hundred fifty thousand dollars in 1806 and seven hundred thousand dollars in 1814.[19] Then moderate investors were struggling as operatives in their field and as entrepreneurs to protect or advance their financial status in wartime.

The focus of this study is not on the status of the marginal or moderate investors but on that of the fifty active investors. Efforts to determine financial worth of the fifty active investors were complicated by a lack of evidence in some cases and by the reluctance of entrepreneurs to admit pecuniary embarrassment. A kind of rough credit rating, often impressionistic, could be ascertained because the merchants of the early nineteenth century extended credit to each other for various periods of time and accepted each other's notes in payment of debts. For such a system to work, an estimate of each other's financial worth was required. The acceptance of another's signature on a note, a draft, or a promise to pay and the collector of customs' respect for one's name on a shipping bond constituted a credit rating. To be sure, a sudden turn in one's affairs such as a loss of an uninsured ship altered things abruptly, but recovery was frequent when one's solvent friends helped out. Robert Oliver, one of Baltimore's richest men, suffered the ups and downs of shipping while experiencing its insatiable appetite for capital.[20] Oliver wrote imploringly in 1785, "I am so distressed for money that I beg you'll make it convenient to let me have one hundred pounds."[21] Shipowning, like slavery, occasionally left one with little cash on hand. William Patterson, as wealthy as Oliver, noted of himself in 1808 that he was "rich in property but without any money."[22] The ratings the merchants had for each other and their own letters provide some insights into their financial status in a period before income tax records.

The wealthiest investors in Baltimore's private armed vessels were the members of the Hollins-Smith cluster. As early as 1799 John Hollins, former English banker, founder and president of the Maryland Insurance Company and closely associated in trade with S. Smith and Buchanan, had an account with one English firm alone balancing out at about four hundred thousand dollars.[23] Years of active shipping through the house of Hollins and McBlair left the two principal partners with reputations that encouraged a neighbor to advise a Philadelphia house in 1814 to "extend them any credit they want" as they prepared to "load two of their sharp vessels lying at New York."[24] In an 1819 trial balance or self-audit, the firm listed creditors to the amount of four hundred thousand dollars.[25] John Quincy Adams spoke of them as doing an "immense business," although Hollins admitted in 1815 that for very large sums he needed help from Samuel Smith and William Patterson.[26] John Smith Hollins owned a share of the Hollins and McBlair firm also.

Samuel Smith's activities, followed in some detail in earlier chapters, were centered in the firm of S. Smith and Buchanan by the War of 1812. Decades of shipping in the European, West Indies, South America, and Far Eastern markets, as well as Revolutionary War privateering activities made Smith one of the wealthiest men in Baltimore. His two-thirds of the proceeds from the disbanded firm of Samuel and John Smith were $237,443.11, while he was still active in other firms and trading in his own name.[27] By 1790 Smith owned twenty ships, a distillery, a retail store in Baltimore, substantial land-holdings in Maryland and Kentucky, warehouses, wharves, several houses, some domestic slaves, and investments in a number of local businesses. During Jefferson's administration, Smith held over $400,000 just in land and stock. He spent over $10,000 in one year's entertaining as a congressman at his new Washington home.[28] Smith's commercial house worked with Robert Oliver and other highly rated Baltimore firms importing specie from Mexico in 1806 and 1807.[29] In 1810 Samuel Smith wrote his daughter, "I believe we cleared last year about $200,000," despite seizures worth $124,000 by the French and British.[30] In 1811 S. Smith and Buchanan's claims against France, Naples, and Holland were valued at more than $200,000.[31] Smith's children were expected to marry into other families of wealth and he periodically advised them of eligible mates worth one or two hundred thousand dollars. One of his own daughters received a dowry of £10,000 sterling.[32] John Quincy Adams stated in 1818 that "Smith and Buchanan have been for many years the greatest commercial house in Baltimore."[33] James A. Buchanan, cousin and partner of Samuel Smith, reported in 1821 that the firm had been extended credit to the amount of $640,000 and that it had over $700,000 in claims against foreign countries.[34] There is little doubt that on the eve of the War of 1812 Samuel Smith and his partners were the great merchants of Baltimore.

Others besides John Hollins, Michael McBlair, Samuel Smith, and James A. Buchanan were in the Hollins-Smith cluster of investors. A silent partner in S. Smith and Buchanan, Lemuel Taylor, engaged in the specie trade with Oliver and others and participated in the commerce and profits of Samuel Smith's firm for years. William Patterson and Sons was another great house, and three of its partners invested in private vessels. William Patterson participated in trade, bought real estate, and was generally considered to have been one of Baltimore's "merchant princes."[35] As early as 1787 the Smiths of Baltimore told English correspondents that the Pattersons "are as safe as it is possible for any men to be."[36] The collector of customs described the Pattersons in 1811 as having "ever been respectable for conduct in business through a long course of years in Baltimore," and "though close in their trade, they are unimpeached as to fairness of character."[37] As a brother-in-law of Samuel Smith, Patterson invested his wealth at least partially with Smith's.

A family enjoying a reputation as great merchants was the Williamses, formerly of Roxbury, Massachusetts. James, Amos A., George, and Cumberland Dugan Williams were active investors in private armed vessels while Dutton Williams was a marginal investor. They were all well established in Baltimore's trade before the War of 1812 and were reputedly "among the leading and wealthiest merchants" of Baltimore.[38] George and Amos also owned a soap and candle factory, while James was heavily engaged in the flour business. Another private armed vessel owner referred to George as "our largest manufacturer of soap, as well as a most wealthy and respectable merchant." A West Indies firm was advised, also in regard to the financial standing of George Williams, "you may deal with him on the most liberal and confidential footing." The same Baltimore correspondent guaranteed George Williams's notes themselves because he was "one of our wealthiest merchants."[39] John Quincy Adams, in 1818, noted that the four Williamses (apparently excluding Dutton) had carried on "an immense business" in foreign trade for years.[40] They belonged in the same category as Hollins, Samuel Smith, and the Pattersons.

Another active investor whose resources were not seriously strained by his investments in numerous private armed vessels was Peter Arnold Karthaus. In the German trade under the name of Peter Arnold Karthaus and Company, he owned numerous vessels in the prewar years. His wartime records show that he did not employ all his capital even though in December of 1813 he listed $472,954.88¾ as owed or paid to him while he owed others but $181,507.39. In December of 1814 Karthaus listed $77,545.28¼ as "captial," suggesting that he did not have it working for him in a wartime situation. In December of 1815 he listed $53,886.56 simply as "cash."[41] His son-in-law, Ferdinand Hurxthal from Harrisburg, Pennsylvania, was also involved in the activities of the Karthaus company. The Karthaus company was able not only to purchase the privateer *Kemp* by itself but to completely outfit it and make unusually high advances of $15,033.83 to its officers and crew.[42] Karthaus's credit with firms in Bremen and Hamburg and in France was extensive as he traded tobacco and West Indian products to them for dry goods.

Another house whose resources and reputation warranted its owners the appelation "great merchants" was that of D'Arcy and Didier. Those two active investors had their ups and downs in trade after starting in Haiti, trading coffee and sugar for European goods. In 1809 Henry Didier, Jr., whose father was a Baltimore merchant, reported that "we now stand A 1" and spoke of keeping $100,000 in capital on hand at all times. A profit of $200,000 from one 1809 transaction alone earned the two partners $60,000 profit. The German dry goods, tobacco, and West Indian produce house of Von Kapff and Brune was related by marriage to Didier and shared vessels and cargoes with D'Arcy and

Didier. Didier was looking for Baltimore vessels to carry the 3 million pounds of coffee the firm owned in Haiti. He apologized to his old Baltimore mercantile mentor Luke Tiernan (a marginal investor in private armed vessels) for his "Dashing way" but explained that he kept his own risks in any one venture at one-fourth. Didier had just sold 300,000 pounds of cotton and explained that his one-fourth interest in ship cargoes was always small enough to be covered by his commission when something went wrong. He also spoke of having two ships at sea with $70,000 specie in each. The D'Arcy and Didier house was in trouble in 1810 when debits of $400,000 were mentioned, but large profits, such as one of $80,000, reduced that debt.[43] By October of 1812 the firm advertised that it had on hand at its new base in Baltimore 1 million pounds of coffee plus goods from Liverpool and London.[44] Another Baltimore firm gave D'Arcy and Didier a credit rating in Philadelphia when they reported, "We should not hesitate to trust D'Arcy and Didier for the sum you mention or a much larger amount — they have dashed, but dashed successfully."[45] In May of 1814 Henry Didier, Jr. offered to send D'Arcy in England £50,000 sterling if D'Arcy needed it for purchases.[46] That offer suggests that Didier was not finding sufficient outlets for his capital in wartime America. John Quincy Adams placed the D'Arcy and Didier house in the same category as S. Smith and Buchanan, Hollins and McBlair, and the Williamses as the major commercial houses of Baltimore in the first two decades of the nineteenth century.[47]

Others of the active investors had ample means. Dennis A. Smith was a bank cashier, investor in Louisiana lands, investor in government bonds, and a sometime shipowner. He was reported by friends to have made $50,000 profit from government bonds in early 1814 and to have purchased in September of 1814, 2 millions of the last loan at $80, "whereby he may clear $200,000."[48] Dennis A. Smith had a reputation as "a keen speculating man" and others watched his moves with more than casual interest.[49] Another extremely active investor in private armed vessels whose credit was vouched for in Philadelphia was Andrew Clopper. One of the most active of Baltimore's prewar shipowners, he was described to the Philadelphia merchants as "a very respectable merchant here."[50] Baltimore's Levi Hollingsworth was a man of means also. Active in commerce and shipowning, he moved flour, tobacco, and dry goods while operating the Gunpowder Copper Works. His copper was used by local shipbuilders and the navy for years and his production of 100 tons a year was second only to the Revere Copper Works.[51] Hollingsworth noted in December of 1812, "I have $70,000 in copper" while engaging in numerous other activities.[52] Another Baltimore entrepreneur, Thomas Tenant, had a long record of shipowning, while he lost vessels to the French and British and to Haiti during that island's upheavals.[53] Tenant also owned a Fells Point wharf and a ropewalk.

Others of the active investors with sizeable prewar shipping records and more than average means were the two Bosleys, John McKim, Jr., George J. Brown, William Hollins, Gerrard Wilson, Harford county landowner John W. Stump, and Jeremiah Sullivan of the house of Hollingsworth and Sullivan. There is little doubt that the resources of such men permitted them to invest in private armed vessels without restraint. All the twenty-five active investors discussed or mentioned so far in this chapter could have absorbed a $20,000 or so loss without injuring their credit rating in the community. Nearly all could drum up from $100,000 to $200,000 in capital, while some made that much profit in one year.

Over one-half of the fifty active investors qualified as men of substantial means and others were close to that category. Another group consisted of relatives and partners of the great merchants who, although they had limited credit of their own, were afforded extra credit because of their marital and commercial ties. On the surface, for example, George Pitt Stevenson, a nephew of Samuel Smith and also related to Hollins and McBlair, appeared to have substantial means since his signature was good for at least $160,000 in customs bonds.[54] A Baltimorean placing his brother in a commercial apprenticeship with Stevenson in 1815 characterized his firm as "one of the most respectable shipping houses in Baltimore."[55] Stevenson, nonetheless, wrote in 1813 to Wilson Cary Nicholas, his uncle in Virginia, on hearing the "awful news" that a powerful British fleet had captured five or six vessels, "God forbid, for I fear, I shall be a serious loser." In May of 1813 he admitted losing $22,000 when an uninsured vessel of his was captured. Stevenson knew the loss, "in times like these, was a serious drawback on mercantile ambition." He admitted in August of 1815, "Engaged as I am in an active business with as you know, a limited capital," he added, "but having a wide field before me and stout heart I look forward with hope." Part of his credit was clearly related to his Baltimore connections as he informed his correspondent that on his own he could accept drafts no larger than $5,000.[56] Stevenson was not of the same financial caliber as a Hollins, Samuel Smith, or Karthaus.

Among the active investors there were some who, on the basis of their positions, had limited resources. Doctor Lyde Goodwin traded through Hollins and McBlair as a sometime minor partner in particular transactions. Related by marriage to Michael McBlair, he served as a resident agent in Calcutta, as a supercargo, and, in time, as the proprietor of his own firm.[57] Working more in commerce than medicine after 1805, he traded in his own name for moderate sums while relying on Hollins and McBlair for larger sums just as George Pitt Stevenson depended on S. Smith and Buchanan. Henry Fulford, a partner of Andrew Clopper, was probably in or close to the same category.[58]

Men who were at sea as captains or supercargoes in the decade prior to the War of 1812 may have had insufficient time to amass any great amount of capital. Charles F. Kalkman and Christopher Deshon were in this category.

The privileges and wages of the captains, the zenith of the marine profession, were abundant. Good wages, bonuses, special fees called "hat money" and "primage," and guaranteed hold space for his own cargo certainly catapulted some captains into merchant status. There was, however, a great difference between a beginning merchant's capital or status and that of a Patterson, Hollins, Smith, Didier, or Karthaus. Supercargoes, often owning parts of the cargoes they supervised while still earning a percentage of the price they brought, were on their way to merchant status also. Of the active investors, Matthew Kelly was still operating as a captain and Henry Holden as a supercargo during the war years.[59] Their resources, and those of sailmaker-merchant Luke Kiersted, chandler Nicholas Stansbury, Captain John Joseph Lane, and some of the flour merchants were significantly less than those of the great merchants. Few of them could say as did Henry Didier, Jr. in May of 1815 that "our note will pass for $100,000."[60]

There were a few active investors whose names were not always accepted on notes or promises to pay. They may have overextended themselves in their private armed vessel investments. John McFadon failed in 1810 but recovered soon thereafter.[61] John Randall was considered a "dasher" or gambler, but unlike D'Arcy and Didier, he was unsuccessful at it. When specie was drained toward New England during the war, some merchants found it difficult to meet all the demands made on them because the banks were not paying their usual discounts.[62] One firm anticipated no "serious consequences" in Baltimore but added, "We may except one instance, John Randall, a dashing, we may say, desperate Trader, who has been embarrassed for a long time; Stopt payment on Tues."[63] Henry Didier, Jr. was concerned about Randall in 1811 when he warned others not to trust Randall, a "good man," for more than $1,000 for six months because he was "too largely in the shipping business" and was not successful. The failure of Randall and a few others in March of 1814 prompted Didier to state that, "We have had several failures here lately but none that can hurt us, mostly among the small Beer Gentry." Randall, whose resources were less than those of some marginal and moderate investors, was an exception among the fifty active investors, but old Revolutionary War private armed vessel owners William Taylor and Jonathan Hudson also had some difficulty remaining solvent.[64]

A collective portrait of the active investors includes facets other than financial ratings or reputations. The active investors, despite their vital interest in ships, cargoes, markets, and commissions, found time to serve the community in other ways. As merchants, the investors in private vessels and others of their class "dominated almost every aspect of urban life."[65] They were active in leadership roles in the city's mercantile, maritime, and military life as well as civic organizations. The fifty investors served on penitentiary committees, medical college lotteries, relief committees, military volunteer committees, fire companies, a new court house committee, and others where salaries or direct profits were absent.[66] There were no investors in private armed vessels, however, among the twenty-four managers of the city's Bible society.[67]

The active investors' business leadership as well as their maritime authority was illustrated by the fact that they held at least twenty bank directorships, bank cashierships, or bank presidencies. Bank connections were vital to entrepreneurs who were outfitting vessels, paying customs bonds, paying seamen, purchasing cargoes and buying vessels. Twenty-seven were officials of insurance companies, usually of the marine type. Their ample resources qualified them for another business role when two-thirds of the fifty active investors signed letter-of-marque bonds as sureties for their shipowning neighbors. Over two-thirds also served as prize agents and ships' husbands, a role reserved for those with considerable shipowning and maritime experience. Some of those not fulfilling such maritime related roles in the port were too busy as proprietors of mills, stores, and factories. Others such as John Netherville D'Arcy were abroad for long periods of time. Captains and supercargoes among the investors were absent at sea for long months.

While the majority of active investors were primarily shipowning merchants, they were also engaged in other entrepreneurial activities. At least thirty-five had interests in nonmaritime enterprises including processing and manufacturing operations in leather, iron, copper, flour, sugar, soap, candles, rope, and textiles as well as turnpikes and canals. The number increased dramatically when banking and insurance companies were added and even more when wharf and warehouse proprietors were included.[68] Obviously, the copper, iron, and rope businesses provided the proprietors with income separate from their vessels whenever raw materials were available. John Hollins observed that his Maryland Insurance Company had "been much benefitted by the war."[69] References to the "Cunning or Knavery or Enterprise of the merchants" were inaccurate in some respects but certainly not in regard to enterprise.[70] Peter Arnold Karthaus and Company, for instance, began the development of a grist and saw mill in 1814 in the town of Karthaus, Pennsylvania, about eighty miles west of Williamsport and sixty miles north of Altoona. Their plans included the mining of coal, clearing of land, and the construction of a special boat to navigate the rapids of the Susquehanna River on the way to the Chesapeake.[71]

In military leadership, always closely related to one's social, economic, and political status in militia and volunteer units, the active investors were also noteworthy. George Pitt Stevenson said that efforts to get commissions ran into interest groups that were "wheels within wheels."[72] Over two-thirds of the active investors and many of the other investors served with military units although a number rejected leadership roles and served as private soldiers. There were seven captains, one major, and, of course, in charge of the defense of Baltimore, Major General Samuel Smith. Four served as aides-de-camp, one as division quartermaster, and one as an assistant division inspector. Others served on committees attending the defense of the city or had younger relatives on the breastworks.[73] Henry Didier, Jr.'s son, Franklin, for example, served as a surgeon at Fort McHenry during its bombardment while still a student at the University of Maryland medical school.[74] Active investors in vessels of war were also active in defending their home port.

Another aspect of the lives of the active Baltimore investors setting them apart from lesser merchants in the community was their ownership of what were known as "country houses" or "country seats." Located in an arc around the city about two to four miles out, they were an effort to imitate the lifestyle of the old landowning aristocrats of America, England, and Ireland as well as an escape from the bustle and yellow fever of a boom city. Few investors had ancestral homes in the area because only one-third of the active investors represented inherited wealth. The rest achieved wealth and status and the "country houses," in addition to being a convenience and a luxury, were status symbols for the merchants.[75] Their "conspicuous outlays on the amenities" testified that they were not inferior to the Carrolls or Ridgelys, their "aristocratic partners in the ruling coalition" of Maryland.[76] Economic achievement in a commercial society rewards achievers with social status almost automatically but the "country houses" were great advertisements of that status.

Active owners with Baltimore country houses were, on the west side, Andrew Clopper, Bernard Von Kapff, and Frederick W. Brune.[77] George Stiles purchased the thirty-one-acre estate Harlem from William Lorman, another 1812 investor in private armed vessels, for $15,000. A brick home with a large piazza in front, lodging rooms for servants, a frame stable and carriage house, a dairy and greenhouse, its grounds also contained a pavilion, an ice vault, a gardener's house, and other buildings. A garden with walks, choice European fruits and all kinds of vegetables as well as a grove or "bosquet" and an orchard were included along with a commanding view of the Patapsco River. Stiles sold the estate in 1815 to Thomas Edmondson for $26,500.[78]

Some merchants lived year round on their estates, riding to their counting houses daily, while others spent only summers on them. One John Gibson, related by marriage to Henry Didier, Jr., described the interrelationships and social ties existent among the "country houses." He wrote his absent wife that he could survive in the country as, "My plan is to sleep at Bolton, breakfast at Rose Hill (where I keep my horse) and dine and drink tea alternately among my country friends."[79] As a Federalist in a Republican city, his circle of friends may have been smaller than that of some of the Republicans.

Dennis A. Smith not only owned Calverton, purchased for $44,000 after the war by the city and county for an elegant almshouse, but also owned a "plantation" on the Gunpowder River and one in Louisiana.[80] John Netherville

D'Arcy built his country house, Netherville, right after the war on the northeast side of Baltimore. Similar to Mount Vernon in appearance, it overlooked the river and was within walking distance of Thomas Tenant's place.[81]

Samuel Smith constructed a large mansion (designed by him) on Washington Square in town in 1796, and several miles out a few years later, built "one of the most outstanding houses of this period" after his own design. Named Montebello after a French victory and resembling Jefferson's original plan for Monticello, it was on the northeast side of the city near Harford Road.[82] In 1810 Smith reported, "Montebello never looked better, our fruit abundant and excellent."[83] Others with country homes worth the expense of at least one schooner and its cargo were the McKims, the Stevensons, the Browns, and the Pattersons as well as the French and West Indian trader John Carrere and moderate investor John Donnell.[84]

John Hollins owned a mansion in the center of town and a country house, Chestnut Hill, while James A. Buchanan constructed a double house in the fashionable center of town.[85] Henry Didier, Jr., whose father had a country house, reported in 1814 that he was "comfortably settled in my handsome two story House at the corner of Light Lane and Church Street" to the north of the city's fashionable center where new residential areas were being developed even during the war.[86] Merchants, lawyers, and doctors moved northerly to higher ground during the war.[87] In town they dined at hotels, attended cotillions and dancing assemblies, or watched the races at Canton. They kept an eye on their counting houses and competitors through evening strolls, luncheons at key places, and in the coffee houses near the waterfront where the shipping news was posted and discussed. A ride to the country for tea, a game of backgammon, a fashionable dinner party, or simply for "strawberries and cream" was not uncommon. At dinner they encountered greater and lesser merchants, political leaders of all factions, military leaders, and great landowning aristocrats as well as sea captains. The captains dined with the upper class in the maritime and mercantile society of the seaport where nearly everyone had been to sea in one capacity or the other and where upward mobility was expected from captains.[88] The top of the mariner's profession often overlapped the beginning of a mercantile career.

The active investors were well-traveled men and they were usually familiar with several languages. They had traveled as resident agents abroad, as supercargoes, and as supervisors of their own trade. Regional travel to other American ports for business reasons was frequent and excursions for rest and recuperation were made to the mineral water and sulphur springs at York, Bedford, Berkeley, and other early resorts.[89] Those in need of serious medical attention visited the celebrated surgeon, Dr. Phillip Syng Physick of Philadelphia.[90] Local land travel was as elegant as the merchants' sea voyages and invited the envy of others. One merchant ordered "a light summer carriage for women and children" such as the one owned by James A. Buchanan. Baltimore's best craftsmen must have been in shipbuilding because the coach makers were reputedly bad and untrustworthy, so a deep green roomy and light carriage lined with green or russet feathers was ordered from Philadelphia.[91] The "colored" people were said to be very impressed by John Netherville D'Arcy's carriage, "raspberry and cream" in color.[92]

Some of the regional travel was a substitute for the restricted social activities of the blockade years. Socially, the city was "very dull" in December of 1813, because parties were rare and cotillion parties were just beginning. Heating was a problem for parties and otherwise, because coal was in short supply. Party clothing was scarce and the "blockading of our ports made every article of clothing" twice the normal price. "Jeans and sattinet" were not to be had and it became fashionable for the "ladies here to make their own boots," but new ladies' "satin boots" were useless because there was "no opportunity of showing them." House guests were numerous and "little sociables" occurred in private homes.[93] The ladies' desire for scarce fashionable fabrics explained the purchases of small pieces of fancy cloth by merchants and captains at prize sales.[94]

The various levels of Baltimore's mercantile and maritime society lived in somewhat segregated areas of the city. Ocean-oriented importers and shipowners, called by one analyst the "body of Importers," resided five or six blocks north or immediately west of the inner basin. "Seafaring men and artificers" lived near the wharves and counting houses on the water's edge and at Fells Point. The merchants were further "divided by" interests, however. The inland traders lived and worked at the western end of a line of buildings that started at the inner basin. Located near the entrances of the "Great Western Roads," they were able to intercept the great wagons from inland, and Howard Street became a major flour milling and sales area matching the mills on the wharves. The great anchorage at Fells Point contained not only the seamen but the maritime artificers, chandlers, and what were primarily the junior partners and agents of the great shipowning firms. The lesser partners and agents met the ships as they came into port.[95]

The fifty active investors as a part of the "body of Importers" had their counting houses and warehouses concentrated in the inner basin area. One could, in a short walk from Bowley's Wharf, Smith's Wharf, or O'Donnell's Wharf, stroll due north for a few blocks to Baltimore Street (commonly called Market Street) and Gay Street near the Customs House, and possibly encounter three-fourths of the active investors. On Bowley's Wharf alone one found the counting houses and warehouses of the Williamses, Von Kapff and Brune, Ferdinand Hurxthal, and Levi Hollingsworth. The proximity of their businesses to one another may have been another associational determinant; convenience should never be underestimated as a factor. Few of the active investors were installed at the western end of the city, although flour merchants Keller and Foreman were at Eutaw Street near Howard close to the western wagon trade. Many of the single and moderate investors were in the west and not, surprisingly, at Fells Point. Of the active investors, Luke Kiersted, the Norwegian sailmaker and merchant, and Nicholas Stansbury, the chandler and grocer, were in Fells Point where their customers were located. One major shipowner, Thomas Tenant, also owned a wharf at Fells Point although the anchorage there was utilized by everyone, and his home was north of the city.[96]

The final facet of the active investors to be discussed, their place in political life, must be considered in relation to a Republican editor's comment that it was "notorious that four-fifths of the population of Baltimore [were] democrats or republicans."[97] Even the British believed Baltimore to be one of the most active proponents of the war and a London newspaper greeted rumors of the city's fall with the observation that, "There is not a spot in the whole United States where an infliction of British vengeance will be more entitled to our applause than in this sink of jacobinical infamy — Baltimore."[98] One could conclude quite erroneously from such statements that the city had no Federalists and no antiwar Republicans.

A Federalist firm noted on the eve of the war that, indeed, there was no organized opposition to the war because, "We are wretchedly divided among the Gallatin, the Smith and the Federal Interests." The Gallatin and Smith Republicans were "greatly opposed to each other if left to themselves, but the least effort of the Federal Interest would serve only to unite the other two."[99] The three-way split in political affiliations complicated the identification of individual investors. They wrote more of business than of politics.

The most easily identified and best-known of the Baltimore political groups was that led by old Jefferson supporter, Senator Samuel Smith. A spokesman for commercial interest in an agrarian party, Samuel Smith advocated strong measures against those nations interfering with America's sea trade. He managed Jefferson's Embargo in the Senate because he believed the needs of the West Indian islands would force the European powers to change their policies.[100] Two years before the United States' entry into the War of 1812 he told his daughter that, "As a Nation we have enriched ourselves greatly altho Individuals may have suffered heavily, but as to our National honor — *C'est un autre chose.*" Smith also wrote, "We are all very angry at the frequent impressments on our Coast." The Maryland senator had been influential in the early Republican years, but his quarrels with Gallatin and Madison reduced that influence by 1812. At the end of 1811 Smith thought President Madison showed "spunk" but felt that it would "evaporate if any man will bring in a bill to authorize letters-of-Marque and Reprisal."[101] He had little hope that Madison would provide the strong leadership needed to protect America's seaborne commerce from the incursions of the French and British. He voted for war but reputedly felt that under existing circumstances, the declaration was the act of "a set of madmen, not to be controaled."[102]

Samuel Smith's political base was the city of Baltimore. A Federalist turned Republican, he had the support of various Baltimore organizations. The Mechanical Society, the Baltimore Republican Society, the Carpenter Society, and the Society of French Patriots backed the spokesman for trade and Revolutionary War hero. As the commander of Baltimore's militia from the time of the Revolution, Smith depended on the votes of the militamen along with those of the seamen of Fells Point. Volunteer fire departments were also useful. Merchants associated with Smith supported his politics. Isaac McKim, James A. Buchanan, William Patterson, John Hollins, and others made Samuel Smith the "most powerful political figure in Baltimore."[103] William Patterson lost faith in the administration as early as 1808, saying "national honor" had been sacrificed.[104] John Hollins, in 1808, thought the actions of the British and French on the sea were shameful.[105] The strength of the Smith faction was estimated by Commodore Joshua Barney to be "at least 2,500" because the "owners, officers and privates of the privateers" were supporting Samuel Smith.[106] A traveler in 1808 heard Smith speak at a barbecue two miles out from the city when a whole oxen and barrels of whiskey and beer were available.[107] In the 1812 presidential election it was reported that Major General Smith would "take the field this ensuing week in favor of Clinton and against Madison — he must have ample means, and is celebrated as a speaker."[108]

Smith's ability as an urban democratic politician and his following did not always give him total command of Baltimore politics. He could not deliver Baltimore to DeWitt Clinton even with the aid of the Federalists.[109] Political rivalry was extremely intense. S. Smith and Buchanan's partner, Lemuel Taylor, fought a duel with that "avowed enemy of the Smiths," Commodore Barney, in 1813.[110] Taylor was wounded. The Smith faction's reservations about the war were not obstacles to their participation in it. Vigorous prosecution of the war was the best way to terminate it on honorable terms.

The group of fifty active investors was predominantly Republican. Twenty-seven were either Smith or Madison Republicans, ten held offices ranging from the City Council to the United States Senate, and others ran as presidential electors.[111] At least eleven were Smith Republicans, while known Madison Republicans among the active investors included Levi Hollingsworth, Jeremiah Sullivan, and the Williamses. They were pictured as being of "the deepest die of Democracy" and "Gallatin men all." They campaigned in nearby counties and collected from twenty to twenty-five thousand dollars for the Madison campaign in Maryland. Several Federalist merchants perceived the fight between the "Clintonians and Madisonians" as a struggle between Democrat and "Jacobin" elements.[112] Thomas and Samuel Hollingsworth, critical of relative Levi Hollingsworth for playing the role of party chieftain, charged that his interest stemmed from his desire for government copper contracts. They observed that while men had been known to sell their country for gold, Baltimore's Levi sold his "for the sake of copper." "Patriotism is now old-fashioned and out of the question," they wrote to their Federalist relative in Philadelphia, also a Levi Hollingsworth. The intensity of political feeling causing the Lemuel Taylor-Joshua Barney duel also encouraged a duel between Baltimore's Levi Hollingsworth and Charles Kilgour. Both were in the Maryland legislature where Kilgour, a victim of anti-Federalist riots in Baltimore verbally attacked Hollingsworth. As a Madison Republican, Levi Hollingsworth supported the declaration of war, but after engaging in several battles, his confidence in the administration's ability to actually fight the war was no greater than that of the Smith Republicans. Levi noted that, "The advantage of discipline, and skill and practice in war is such that I tremble at the idea of a conflict for the preservation of one of our cities."[113]

Baltimore's Madisonians did not support the war out of political loyalty alone. They believed a "real American Interest" was at stake but were anxious to settle the war "Honorably." One merchant wrote, "I thank God that I have lived to see the Dawn of that day, which is to convince England that she is not forever to domineer on the Ocean, that others have rights here as well as She, that they are likewise determined to assert them." The same correspondent believed the war to be among "the most righteous that ever was waged," because the "main object of the War [was] the protection of Native Seamen." Proud of Madison, the Baltimore Republican detested those New Englanders "clamoring for the Dissolution of the Union." When the British threatened Baltimore in 1813, he reported, "If the object for which we are contending can be obtained by a ten years War and a 100 millions of Debt, we shall not have cause to regret that the contest was commenced," and "Few of us are ready to move to Kentucky — if Mr. Clay hoped — he'll be disappointed."[114] The Madisonians applauded the president's efforts "to secure a free and honorable trade" and to protect American seamen when they drank their toasts at a celebration on the new steamboat *Chesapeake* on June 19, 1813. They were celebrating the anniversary of the declaration of war.[115]

The third side of the Baltimore political triangle in the War of 1812 was Federalist. One historian noted that despite its reputation for Republicanism, in "that prosperous commercial city of 50,000 inhabitants" there existed "a sturdy conservative element which had for its organ the *Federal Republican*, edited by Jacob Wagner and Alexander C. Hanson."[116] The supporters of that newspaper and its editors suffered a vicious mob assault in response to its bold criticism of the declaration of war and the administration. It is entirely possible that Federalists in the city were driven underground temporarily as an escape from murder and violent intimidation. One Federalist lady wrote, "We were fearful of muttering our sentiments lest we in turn might be attacked as there is a general denunciation of all Federalists." "The times of Robespierre," she continued, "were not attended with greater fears." Being a member of a Federalist merchant family shipping flour to the British, she complained about their goods

PLATE III

Water color, "View of Baltimore," ca. 1800, artist unknown,
original in the Maryland Historical Society

which escaped the enemy, "and yet fell into those of our own citizens; prizes were taken on all sides by these numerous privateers."[117] "The Feds are quiet at present," reported a Federalist firm in September of 1812.[118]

The Federalists in Baltimore were uncomfortable. Charles Carroll of Carrollton, a signer of the Declaration of Independence, stated after the Baltimore riots, "The occurrences in Baltimore and the temper of this government render a resident insecure in this State, and I may want all the sums I can command to enable me to move out of it."[119] Carroll was not in a leadership role, having been "a mere spectator" after 1800 but he was not the only concerned Federalist.[120] Other Federalists in the Baltimore area, among them the Ridgelys, Steretts, Robert Goodloe Harper, and Henry Thompson, may have found it necessary to leave town or to remain quiet. The active leadership of Federalist Alexander Contee Hanson earned him a visit from the mob, but that action "completely persecuted him into Congress."[121] His public support amounted to small Federalist meetings held north of the city during the war.[122] Merchant Henry Thompson preferred passive resistance. He stayed home on the day set aside by the president for national fasting and ate "as usual" while confiding to his diary that the war was a year old and that "no good has yet resulted."[123] Federalist merchants Thomas and Samuel Hollingsworth kept up a running attack on the Republicans but only in their private letters to Philadelphia. In their view Baltimore was buried beneath a "Torrent of Democracy" and the war was a disaster. The war rendered "life painful as the innocent and the virtuous [were] tormented by the cursed Policy of Madness, folly and Corruption." Republicans, they believed, supported the war as long as they were making money while thinking the war was declared "for the sake of Naturalized Subjects, who care naught for the Country whom we were better without."[124]

There were not many clearly identifiable Federalists among the active investors in private armed vessels, but no political affiliation was found for one-third of the fifty active investors. The party interests of Peter Arnold Karthaus, Von Kapff and Brune, John Gooding, and Andrew Clopper, for example, were not uncovered. Membership in the predominantly Federalist Washington Society, marriages, and other relationships point to Thomas Tenant, the two Bosleys, Dennis A. Smith, and D'Arcy and Didier as probable Federalists.[125] Henry Didier, Jr. married into the Federalist Gibson-Grundy mercantile group. Other Federalists participated in the private armed vessels system as sureties, lawyers, and purchasers of prize goods and vessels. The Steretts, Robert Goodloe Harper, the Olivers, and others, discussed earlier in this study, performed in those roles. Some of the marginal and moderate investors may also have been Federalists. Many of the sea captains had been raised in New England, and one moderate investor, miller-merchant Charles Gwinn, was a Federalist. He had nothing but disdain for "Maddison and his Leatherheaded council."[126]

The attitudes of the Baltimore Federalists changed as the war progressed, and they were proud of the American naval and military victories. One Federalist firm noted, "Federalists in Battle are as conspicuous in these days as they were in the days of '76."[127] The war's prolongation, the British destruction of property, the end of commerce, and the institution of a complete commercial blockade of the American coast, or just national pride, converted them into advocates of resistance. Henry Didier, Jr., proud of Baltimore's defense, was angered by British destruction of property, and by the British 1813 proposals for peace. He said British actions made the war popular in America and observed that a unified United States might even invade Canada in late 1814 or 1815.[128] Staunch Federalists Thomas and Samuel Hollingsworth, severe critics of the war, even came around. By February of 1813 they stated, "A Rigorous War as the safest precursor of early peace is, in our opinion, now most desirable." In November they wrote, "No hopes of peace but in the Conquest of Quebeck and entire possession of the Canadas" was the only way to make "the Lyon humble to the Lambes."[129]

Even Alexander Contee Hanson made a speech in Congress supporting the war effort although his intention was to erode Madison's public support. Concerned because his "letters from Boston convince me a revolution is at hand," Hanson was ready to do military service when his health permitted it.[130] The parties united to defend Baltimore itself in its "hour of danger," while, ironically, Federalist interest in fighting Great Britain increased as Republican interest waned.[131] By the end of the war the Smith Republicans, the Madisonian Republicans, and the Federalists were separated by some issues, but they were united in their belief that only a vigorous prosecution of the war, including use of private armed vessels, could terminate it.

Despite intense political rivalry, some among the three factions cooperated in business functions, including private armed vessels, social affairs, and in the military defense of Baltimore.[132] Such cooperation in the war prepared the way for a period of decreased political tension after the war.

SIX

The Birth of an Adventure

Baltimore's investors in private armed vessels during the War of 1812 were experienced prewar shipowners, shipbuilders, captains, or marine craftsmen. Whether raiding or trading, vessels engaged in letter-of-marque and reprisal operations required the same careful management as peacetime shipping ventures. Because of its commission a private armed vessel needed some extra documents, more men, and, of course, extra equipment. After conceiving, structuring, and capitalizing a private armed vessel enterprise, sponsors focused their attention on the procurement of the required documents and the selection of an in-port manager and a sea captain. The absence of any mandatory documents, sound supervision of preparations, or able leadership at sea endangered the sponsors' intentions, property, and capital.

About three weeks elapsed after the Declaration of War in June of 1812 before any private armed vessels sought clearances from the collector of customs at Baltimore. In the interim, Congress passed letter-of-marque legislation, while the executive branch readied regulations, commissions, and other documentary facets of the system. The actual conceptualization of a private armed vessel venture in the minds of potential sponsors defies tracing. One can only imagine lively conjecture at the Merchant's Coffee House, the Customs House, numerous counting houses, insurance companies, bank offices, and any place, in fact, where shipowning entrepreneurs congregated. With overlapping relationships in marriage, religion, other entrepeneurial and community organizations as well as in their everyday social activities, few potential investors suffered from isolation or remoteness. The business district around the inner basin and Fells Point was geographically compact enough to be covered in an evening's walk. Newspaper reports such as one stating that a "subscription paper was opened at the Merchant's Coffee House for equipping a Letter-of-Marque to the extent of $20,000 in shares of $500 each" were rare.[1] They reflected editorial and public interest, not solicitation. Interest in such opportunities was manifested by those with capital and some knowledge and experience in seaborne commerce. The decision to apply for a commission was sometimes a private matter, especially in

[83]

the cases of sole or dual owners seeking commissions for vessels already owned. When no additional investors were desired, the merchants maintained their usual taciturnity about their shipping or other commercial plans. Any search for new sponsors, a vessel, or a captain exposed one's plans to an ever-widening circle of mercantile and maritime colleagues until those needs were fulfilled.

Efforts to expand ownership of a private armed vessel operation necessitated a movement from a private to a public company. All sponsors publicized their intentions when they applied for official documents, purchased supplies, or, in their most public act, when they opened a rendezvous to enroll a crew. Efforts to limit information, consequently, were successful only in a project's initiatory stages, but some critical aspects such as the owners' instructions to their captains reached only the ears of those with a need to know.

The best-kept secrets existed in cases where an entire private armed scheme was conceived and managed within the walls of a single commercial house. Among dual owners, houses such as W. and J. Bosley, D'Arcy and Didier, Hollins and McBlair, and Fulford and Clopper conceived, owned, and operated private armed vessels solely within their regular peacetime commercial firms. In such an approach they lost the advantages of risk- and cost-sharing but yielded neither profits nor managerial decisions to anyone else. As legal partnerships firms enjoyed advantages over part-ownerships. In partnerships, all aspects of the shipping business were in the hands of proven associates whose partnership contract rested on "mutual respect, confidence, and belief in the entire integrity of each partner, and his sincere devotion to the business and true interests of the partnership." As a permanent part of the firm, a partner was engaging in a project of primary concern and was expected to apply his "skill, industry, diligence or capital" primarily in the firm's interest.[2]

Partners in a particular firm, known as "joint tenants," had full legal powers. Sharing profits and losses, they could legally bind each other as well as the firm, while each could exclude any undesirable new partners. The authority legally to bind other partners of a firm empowered any one partner alone to sell the vessel or even to terminate the venture.[3] The sale and later conversion of two D'Arcy and Didier letter-of-marque traders into privateers in New York was simplified by the fact that each partner had such full powers. With D'Arcy in Europe, partner Didier completed the sale and agreed in the firm's name to the deal that retained a part-owner's role for the sellers.[4] Approval from the absent D'Arcy was unnecessary. Peter Arnold Karthaus and Company, of which Ferdinand Hurxthal was a partner, owned the privateer *Amelia* according to government records. Partner Karthaus, needing no authorization from the other partners, credited four-twentieths of the firm's shares to three merchants in other cities.[5] When such partnership firms owned an entire vessel, they enjoyed maximum managerial flexibility.

Individual investors in the popular part-ownership schemes had no authority over their cosponsors and little flexibility. They were characterized as "tenants in common" and "owners for the season" (a voyage or cruise in this case) in what was considered a temporary relationship. They could not bind one another legally and possibly did not even know the other part-owners. They had the complete right to dispose of their own share or shares only, and they could not exclude other potential part-owners. They were liable "in solido" for the unpaid debts of the operation but retained, in the case of insolvency, a lien on "any property involved." Very common in shipping, such part-owning arrangements were characterized by the courts as "limited" or "special" partnerships restricted to a single operation.[6]

Among part-owners in a "limited partnership" all members were required to pay any additional "contributory shares" necessary for the "preservation" of the enterprise. Such expenditures, however, had to be "indispensible" or authorized by the other part-owners. As a part-owner one's personal preferences for outfitting, staffing, and utilization of the vessel were subordinated to majority opinion on the basis of persons, not interests or shares held. When a minority protested the majority's inactivity or idleness, it anticipated a friendly ear in court because of the common law principle that vessels were "originally invented for use and profit, not for pleasure or delight; to plough the sea, not be by the walls." In a dispute among the various part-owners a court could order a sale of the vessel to "prevent irreparable mischiefs or impending losses."[7] The whole system encouraged consensus among the part-owners while permitting the disenchanted to dispose of their own shares at will. During the War of 1812 the Baltimoreans managed to keep their minority part-owners reasonably contented or at least out of court. Apparently, an adequate consensus existed in a wartime situation when court protests meant only delays and financial disaster.

In arrangements other than sole ownership and closed partnerships shares based on anticipated costs were sold in varying numbers to investors who became "part-owners." If a vessel were already in hand, her seller might retain a number of shares as principal owner but the costs of equipment, provisions and supplies, and advances to the crew as well as other disbursements had to be added to the basic capitalization figure. Suppliers of services and goods, such as Joseph Despeaux who prepared the *Caroline* for a cruise as a privateer, occasionally accepted proprietary shares in lieu of cash.[8] This form of compensation reduced expenditures for the owners while holding out the promise of a bonus for the suppliers and craftsmen.

With over one hundred seventy-five commissions owned in whole or part by Baltimoreans, there was no common formula or pattern to the share arrangements. An example of a common pattern is provided in the case of the new schooner *Tom* as she prepared to sail. The arrangement, as presented in a bill of sale stated:

I, Gerrard Wilson, of the city of Baltimore, merchant, owner and fitter outer of the private Armed Schooner *Tom* of Baltimore, for and in consideration of the sum of $30,000 or whatever may be the cost of said Schooner when her accounts are made up, in money of the United States to me in Hand paid by the Several persons and firms whose respective names are endorsed on the back hereof in the proportion to the number of shares written thereto, do sell, all that said private Armed Schooner *Tom* and appurtenances as she now is and will sail on a cruise from this port, that is to say to each person or from the number of shares or Undivided 30 parts of said Schooner and appurtenances which are written opposite their respective names or firms.

August 1, 1812

James Williams — three Shares or Undivided thirtieth parts
Hollins and McBlair — three Shares or Undivided thirtieth parts
John Gooding — three Shares or Undivided thirtieth parts
William M. Johnson — one Share or Undivided thirtieth parts
Charles Malloy — one Share or Undivided thirtieth parts
Robert Patterson — three Shares or Undivided thirtieth parts
Thomas Wilson — one Share or Undivided thirtieth parts
Christopher Deshon — one Share or Undivided thirtieth parts
William T. Graham — one Share or Undivided thirtieth parts
C. F. Kalkman — one Share or Undivided thirtieth parts
Matthew Kelly — one Share or Undivided thirtieth parts
Luke Kiersted — one Share or Undivided thirtieth parts
J. Lane — one Share or Undivided thirtieth parts
William Whann — one Share or Undivided thirtieth parts
John McKim, Jr. — three Shares or Undivided thirtieth parts
Andrew Clopper — one Share or Undivided thirtieth parts
Gerrard Wilson — four Shares or Undivided thirtieth parts

Thirty Shares or Undivided thirtieth parts[9]

The *Tom*'s initial single share cost of $1,000 bought a new and "superior vessel" ready for sea.[10] Her final cost was impressive even to shipowners accustomed to the heavy demands of seaborne commerce. The *Tom* was relatively large at 286 tons and carried one of the largest crews in the port, requiring provisions and arms for 140 men. Her commander, Thomas Wilson, was a shareholder, but about two-thirds of her shares were owned by major merchants such as Hollins and McBlair, James Williams, John Gooding, Gerrard Wilson, and Andrew Clopper. Gerrard Wilson, former owner of the vessel, was the principal shareholder with four shares. Decisions based on a majority of persons not shares were controlled by experienced shipowners because, with the addition of Christopher Deshon and William T. Graham, such men constituted nine-seventeenths of the syndicate.

Accounts with the clerk of the district court and bills of sale testify that the *Tom*'s arrangement was not unique.[11] Letter-of-marque schooners financed by a number of part-owners required, in general, fewer investors than the more expensive privateers. Thirds, fourths, sixths, and eighths were popular share units in letter-of-marque traders. According to newspaper advertisements of sales and auctions as well as surviving bills of sale, common practice in privateers called for privateer sponsors to reorganize an enterprise after a cruise.[12] Among letter-of-marque traders that practice was less pronounced but still existent. Privateers usually required more part-owners, but there were exceptions. The *Highflyer*, for instance, was financed by just five sponsors on one of its cruises. Ship's husband Thomas Tenant, Robert Patterson, one of William Patterson's sons, and Archibald Kerr each held one-fourth of the shares, while Andrew Clopper and Christopher Deshon owned one-eighth each. Another exception was the privateer *Nonsuch*, owned solely by George Stiles, but the expensive privateers generally employed between ten and twenty part-owners.[13]

Although no owner's certificate or share was located for this study, mercantile correspondence verifies their existence. Shipbuilder Joseph Despeaux was promised by agents in Boston "that a certificate will be given by the agents, that you are a Proprietor of Ten Fiftieth parts of the Ship, as she sailed from Salem."[14] In some cases such certificates or shares were assigned to the vessel itself as the sponsors of letter-of-marque traders considered wear and tear and maintenance costs, since they were apt to retain their vessels for more than one voyage. Sponsors of the *Decatur*, for instance, were listed as Richard H. Douglass (eleven-twenty-fourths), Cumberland Dugan Williams (six-twenty-fourths), and the firm of D'Arcy and Didier (four-twenty-fourths), while the remaining three-twenty-fourths were assigned to "adventure and *Decatur*."[15] The sponsors were removing prize income from the category of dividends and assigning it to operating and maintenance costs. The vessel's share was money from their own pockets but the arrangement saved them an extra assessment or contributory share when the vessel prepared for her next voyage.

When riggers, armorers, and chandlers scrambled over a would-be commissioned vessel, the problem of future assessments was not always a minor matter. The bill of sale of the *Tom* stated a starting share cost but added "or whatever may be the cost of the Said Schooner when her accounts are made up."[16] Such "contributory shares" were authorized in the bill of sale of the letter-of-marque trader *Philaeni* by the phrase "and whatever may be the additional outfits."[17] Richard H. Douglass, ship's husband and prize agent for the new privateer *Lawrence*, informed the other part-owners that, "to enable me to meet Several Cash claims on the new Schooner I find it necessary to call on you for $500 each which you will please pay to the Bearer." That request was repeated for the same sum on February 5, February 25, and March 7, 1814, and was paid within a few days.[18] When Douglass's share of these contributory shares was added along with that of unlisted part-owner William Smith and Company, those assessments brought in $16,000 above the vessel's initial cost. Cost at launching is not known but her builder, James Stoakes of Talbot County, built her for "himself" and probably sold her as a hull or hull and masts only.[19] The vessel brought, outfitted, only $12,000 at a resale soon after the war's end.[20] Investors could not count on the recovery of heavy outfitting and operating costs in a resale at the war's end.

Those shareholders retaining their interest in a vessel after one voyage or cruise anticipated additional requests for funds. Unless they had foreseen both their continued participation and the need for repairs as had the *Decatur*'s owners and set aside prize money, refitting was expensive. When sold or reorganized, a vessel was sold as she arrived from sea even when she was in desperate need of repair. Additional ammunition and provisions as well as advances to a new crew were also financed before the vessel could clear and all before any income accrued from prizes. Joseph Despeaux sold one of his shares in the new Salem privateer ship (three-masted, square-rigged) *Alexander* to chandler and grocer John Snyder. He designated Snyder a debtor for $120 in his account book after he forwarded that sum to the Boston agents of the vessel for "proportionable parts of one share for refitting for the second cruise."[21] With the force of law behind them in peace and war, such periodic demands were one of the financial hazards of shipowning.[22] The cost of entry (the initial share price) was only the beginning of a long drain on a shipowner's funds.

Payment for one's initial shares in a private armed vessel enterprise was often out of profits from decades of prosperity in the neutral carrying trade. Other probable sources were flour and tobacco profits and funds that would have gone into normal trade without the war. Profits of the Iberian flour trade and proceeds of the last few prewar months of the European trade were also available. That money literally poured into the port in the spring and summer of 1812. One firm reported that Baltimore was expecting specie shipments in early July of 1812 of $300,000 to $400,000 as American merchants rushed to get an average of 1.5 million dollars a week in ahead of the British fleet.[23] Return cargoes from Spain or Portugal were nearly always specie with salt as part cargo or ballast. What proportions of the costs of private armed vessels emanated from what particular source is uncertain, but, in time, prize proceeds provided a new source of investment capital.

Manner of payment to the supervising owner or owners was an individual affair. Existing rules of thumb called for no credit for sums under five hundred dollars and credit periods of thirty days to ninety days for larger sums. Longer periods such as six months were allowed in normal commerce involving a foreign or distant correspondent, but a limited partnership's voyage or cruise would have been terminated in that period. Its debts, however, were always collectable in court. The Baltimore owners knew each other's ability to pay and appear to have let individual circumstances influence terms. German dry goods trader Peter Arnold Karthaus sold one-eighth of his letter-of-marque schooner *Bordeaux Packet* to his son-in-law Ferdinand Hurxthal, one-eighth to John Randall, and one-eighth to George Pitt Stevenson. The manner of payment for Hurxthal is unknown, but one can imagine that his son-in-law's assets were familiar to Karthaus and the terms generous. John Randall's credit was questionable, so Karthaus may have been more conservative with him. While not a great merchant in his own name, George Pitt Stevenson was a nephew of Samuel Smith and also related to Hollins and McBlair. His portion of the enterprise was "paid in notes at four months for one-eighth of the vessel and cargo" with interest accruing to Karthaus's account.[24]

With matters of finance and organization at least partially completed, the sponsors were ready to apply for a commission although other items such as preparation of the vessel, her armament, and the acquisition of a crew were still incomplete. Owners had to know enough of their objectives to describe their vessel and her crew on their application. Authorization to issue commissions, shared with the state governments in the Revolution but reserved for the federal government in both the Articles of Confederation and the Constitution, was given specifically to the president in the Declaration of War issued on June 18, 1812. That act stated that the president had the authority:

> to issue to private armed vessels of the United States commissions of marque and reprisal, in such form as he shall think proper, and under the seal of the United States, against the vessels, goods and effects, of the Government of the said United Kingdom of Great Britain and Ireland and the subjects thereof.[25]

Congressional consideration of a system of private armed vessels followed on June 26, 1812, in "An Act Concerning Letters-of-Marque, Prizes and Prize Goods." It instructed applicants to request a commission in writing and to name the vessel while asking for "a suitable description of the tonnage and force of the vessel, and the name and place of residence of each owner concerned therein." The intended size of the crew was required along with the signed application, filed with the secretary of state or any other "officer or person who shall be employed to deliver out such commissions, to be by him transmitted to the Secretary of State."[26]

The main recipient of the hand-carried Baltimore applications was the collector of customs. He was James H. McCulloch, avid supporter of the republic and the administration, former merchant and Revolutionary War maritime veteran and wounded volunteer when the British invaded his bay. His influence was but one of numerous Baltimore contacts with the administration. Baltimoreans also employed Samuel Smith in the Senate and Alexander McKim and

Peter Little in the House of Representatives. Republicans communicated with President Madison and Secretary of State Monroe as well as Treasury and other State Department officials by letter and, being so close, by personal contact. Baltimore's merchants were seldom in ignorance for long about matters involving commissions or commerce in general. Their three-way political split, however, sometimes supplied them with two Republican views and one Federalist account when they listened to party leaders and not to responsible officials.

Baltimore's applications were usually written rather than printed and followed the directions of Congress rather carefully. Figures such as intended crew size, officers' names, and the precise armament were occasionally left blank or incomplete at the time of application. Such data was often unavailable because the vessel's preparation was incomplete at the time of application. Many applications had notations on such matters in the margin, added at a later date. More careless was the failure to list all the owners in some cases where only the ship's husband or managing owner signed the application. Several copies of the application were made with one being forwarded to the State Department.

Applications differed in phraseology. One owner applied for "a letter of Marque Commission" and another for a "commission or license," while others requested a "Letter of Marque" or, most frequently, a "letter-of-marque and reprisal" or simply "a commission." Historically, some differences existed in the meanings of the various phrases, but by 1812, they all granted the authority to take prizes. Applicants may have requested a "letter-of-marque" for a trading vessel or a "commission" for a privateer, but there was no difference in the documents they received.[27]

One applicant, George Williams, husband and prize agent of the letter-of-marque trader *Argo*, did use the ancient phraseology as he requested a "Commission of Letter of Mart and Reprisal."[28] Discussing the phraseology of the private armed vessel papers before the congressional act governing them was passed, a Baltimore editor employed Dutch jurist Cornelius Van Bynkershoek's *Treatise on the Law of War* as his authority. Tracing the topic through the centuries, Bynkershoek (1673–1743) led the editor to conclude that a "Letter of Marque and Reprisal [was] the old technical expression for what we now call Privateer Commissions." He observed that a "Letter-of-Marque [was] a vessel fitted out for war and merchandise, though generally speaking, as trade is more particularly, the object of their destination, the purposing of arming them is rather defense than of offense." The editor's conclusion was that the 1812 variety of a "Commission" authorized the recipient to operate as a letter-of-marque trader, as a privateer cruiser, or if he desired, as both.[29]

Some applications were quite simple. The following was addressed to James H. McCulloch, collector of the port of Baltimore:

Sir:

We request you will grant us a Commission for the Schooner *Rapid* burthen 115 tons, armed with one nine pound cannon, muskets, etc. manned with twenty persons and owned by James Frazier and ourselves.

> Respectfully, We are, Sir;
> Your obedient servant
> HOLLINS AND MCBLAIR [signature]
> Baltimore, October 12, 1813.[30]

Other applicants were more elaborate, describing their Baltimore schooners as a "private armed pilot boat built schooner" or a "private armed pilot boat" and adding in many cases the names of all the officers. Others exposed their intentions in such phrases as "a trading voyage," "to St. Domingo," "for Europe," "intended for Bordeaux with a cargo of Sugars, Coffee and Cotton" or, a "Cargo of flour and lard for Havana." The *Globe*'s application stated that she was "equipt for a cruise as a privateer," while the *Comet*'s stated that she was prepared for an "intended cruise of 120 days." The *Price*'s application stated, in the style of her commission, that she was "to cruise against the shipping and property of the enemies of the United States in the present war." Applications were signed by a "Ship's husband and partowner," by the sole owners' names, a firm's name, or simply by an untitled signature. In very few cases were they signed by a person not listed as an owner, although an agent's signature was acceptable. Time elapsing between the application and the issuance of a commission was frequently less than one day, often two days, and infrequently a week or ten days. The owners of the privateer *Mammoth*, S. Smith and Buchanan, John Gooding and James Williams, waited nine days for Commission No. 969 before receiving it on March 7, 1814.[31]

When a supply of blank commissions was available, the collector's office placed a number corresponding to the actual commission number on the outside of the application. After its filing, a copy and periodic reports were forwarded to the secretary of state. The collector was not likely, however, to turn the commission over to the owners until other requirements of the system had been completed. Owners and the commander (their legal agent and a partner "for the season" at sea) had to "give bond to the United States" with at least two sureties "not interested in the vessel, in the penal sum of $5,000" or, when the crew exceeded 150 in number, $10,000. The bond was assurance that the owners, officers, and men "shall and will observe the treaties and laws of the United States" and the instructions given to them "for the regulation of their conduct." It was an attempt to diminish or control the historical tendency of private vessels of war to lapse into piracy once at sea and to maintain the enterprise's ability to satisfy all later claims for "damages and injuries."[32]

In practice the Baltimore owners avoided the $10,000 bond perhaps because of the smallness of their schooners or simply out of a disinclination to waste money. Privateers out of Baltimore carried as many as 120, 130, or 140 men on numerous occasions, but the closest they came to exceeding the 150 limit on the $5,000 bond was the case of the famous *Chasseur*. Commander Boyle took out 148 men on one cruise and exactly 150 on another. Letter-of-marque traders seldom carried more than 40 men, but the *Chasseur*, when fitted out as a trader, sported a crew of 52 men. The difference between crew sizes on traders and privateers was demonstrated by the *Whig*, which carried 36 men as a trader but 100 as a privateer. The *York* went from 30 men as a commissioned trader to 120 as a cruiser. Crews of the larger traders sometimes actually exceeded those of the smaller privateers. The 356-ton *Chasseur*'s wartime trading crew of 52 men exceeded, for instance, the 55-ton privateer *Wasp*'s fighting crew of 40 men.[33] In peacetime 100- or 200-ton schooners were operated by 8 to 12 men.

The role of surety, as indicated earlier in this study, was often traded off among the owners of private armed vessels. The stipulation that a surety was not to be financially interested in the vessel was interpreted to exclude only actual shareholders. An officer of the privateer *Fox*, Jean-Jacques Bonne, signed as surety for that vessel, but his shares in the crew's prize moiety did not make him an owner with a financial "interest" in the vessel.[34] Common law practice and American court decisions held that such shares were simply a technique for paying wages, and like whaling lays, they bestowed no proprietary or managerial rights on the holders.[35] Another surety, Gaspar Leoni, a brass founder in the employ of shipbuilder Joseph Despeaux, was surety for a Despeaux vessel. Despeaux's failure certainly would have upset Leoni's financial standing, but since he was not directly interested in the vessel, the collector accepted his signature.[36]

The collector's judgment of one's capacity to pay was not entirely impressionistic. He had been judging mercantile solvency for years while he accepted or rejected peacetime Custom House bonds. The fact that several of the sureties failed may have resulted from special wartime conditions or the uncertainty of seaborne commerce. It is unlikely that such collapses represented a failure of the collector to do his duty; surviving records suggest that James H. McCulloch was thoroughgoing. His judgment in most cases was not tested as no sureties were called to account for violations of the law.

Complaints were made, including one privateer accused of making a land raid. A Baltimore editor reported, "It is stated that the privateer *Midas*, of Baltimore, lately from Savannah has made a Cockburn descent on Harbour Island, one of the Bahamas, and burnt or plundered twenty-seven houses, taking from one person 740 doubloons. . . . The destruction of the capital was assigned as a reason for this proceeding."[37] The commission of the *Midas* was revoked on her return by the collector at Wilmington, North Carolina, by authority of the president as passed on by the secretary of state.[38] *Midas* owners James Williams, John Gooding, John W. Stump, and her commander, Alexander Thompson, wanted to return her to sea as a letter-of-marque trader. Ship's husband Williams informed Secretary of State Monroe about a week later that

Captain Thompson's act "was far from being approbated by any of the owners" and that they were loading the *Midas* with flour for a voyage to the West Indies with a new captain who was "a perfect man." He asked that Monroe order the reluctant collector to issue a new commission.[39] Evidence suggests that Monroe agreed with Republican Williams, or that the law had not actually been breached because Commission No. 1057 was issued to the *Midas* under her new captain on January 3, 1815, with Captain Thompson continuing as a part-owner.[40]

The journal of the *Midas* was placed before President Madison and her commission was revoked. The reason was the "wilful deviation of Captain Thompson from the instructions for the private armed vessels of the United States, issued at commencement of the war, which enjoins the strictest regard to the usages of civilized nations." The government and not Captain Thompson was charged, it was pointed out by the secretary of state, with describing the manner and means of retaliation to be made for the burning of Washington.[41] Congress had granted the president such specific authority in 1813.[42] Contrary to later opinions, the *Midas*'s commission was revoked not for waging war on land, although all the documents and laws specified that water was her operating medium and enemy vessels were her objective, but because of the plundering and retaliatory aspects of her actions. The president may have been unusually sensitive to this issue because of the threat of British retaliation. A London news organ reported the case and quoted the American newspaper question, "Is there not too much reason to fear, should not government immediately take up the affair in a proper manner, that the dwelling houses of every seaport on our coast will be burnt to the ground?"[43]

Other complaints, usually involving neutral waters or neutral vessels, were registered. The *America* of Baltimore was said to have robbed some Spanish vessels in the West Indies.[44] The captain of the British brig *26th of October 1812* complained to Secretary of State Monroe that his vessel had been "cut from her moorings" while within Spanish waters and jurisdiction and asked recourse for "so great a breach of the laws of nations." His complaint was against the letter-of-marque schooner *Tuckahoe* of Baltimore owned by Hollins and McBlair, George Pitt Stevenson, Lyde Goodwin, and others. No sureties were called to task, possibly because of the complainant's inability to prove that he was only one mile off the beach.[45] Most Baltimore vessels, however, had no such controversies and were worthy of a New York newspaper's comment: "We observe with such pride and pleasure, that the conduct of our privateersmen is in general so correct and liberal as to command the respect of their enemies, and to afford no room for the clamor of those opposed to the system of privateering."[46] The Baltimore letter-of-marque sureties paid no "penal sums," but the bond itself, as intended, functioned as a strong warning to the owners and captains.

George Stiles was awarded Commission No. 1 for his privateer *Nonsuch*, sharing that honor with Commodore Joshua Barney's *Rossie*. The text of Stiles's bond read as follows:

No. 1

Know all Men by these presents,

THAT WE *George Stiles* Owner of the private armed vessel *of war Nonsuch, one hundred and ten* men and *Twelve twelve-pound carronades, Henry Levely, James Williams and William T. Graham* are held and firmly bound to the United States of America, in the penal sum of *Five thousand and* dollars, money of the United States, to the payment whereof, we bind ourselves jointly and severally, our joint and several heirs, executors and administrators. Witness our hands and seals this *Twenty-ninth* day of *June* in the year of our Lord 1812.

The condition of the above obligation is such, that whereas the President of the United States hath this day commissioned the said private armed vessel as a letter of marque and reprisal; now if the owner, officers and crew of the said armed vessel shall observe the treaties and laws of the United States, and the instructions which shall be given them according to law for the regulation of their conduct, and satisfy all damages and injuries which shall be done or committed contrary to the tenor thereof by such vessel during her commission, and deliver up the same when revoked by the President of the United States, then this obligation shall be void, and other wise remain in full force.

signed, sealed and deliv-   GEORGE STILES [signature and seal]
ered in presence of us, J.   H. E. LEVELY [signature and seal]
BRICE and D. TOTHAM   JAMES WILLIAMS [signature and seal]
[signatures]   WILLIAM T. GRAHAM [signature and seal][47]

After filing an application and a letter-of-marque and reprisal bond, there were other requirements for the captains and owners to meet. Owners had to sign forms for the collector, certifying that they were the owners of the said vessel as well as citizens of the United States. In addition to the captain's oath that he was the master of the vessel and a citizen, he was obliged to list his place of birth or date of naturalization. Both the forms for owners and masters and, in some months, a single form used by both, reflected the government's desire for positive identification by listing the vessel's measurements.[48] Bonds, oaths, and other efforts to minimize the excesses that had become routine features of private armed vessels into the last part of the eighteenth century were managed in an orderly and proper manner by Baltimore's collector. This despite a national dependence after the first year of the War of 1812 on private armed vessels, which approximated that of Elizabethan England, was a feat.

Commissioned vessels were not excused from the normal shipping documentation procedures; consequently, other papers were required. A bill of sale for the vessel, a master carpenter's certificate, and a registry bond were exchanged for a certificate of registry. Without that certificate of registry a vessel could not legally clear for a foreign port. Those vessels making no changes utilized extant certificates of registry, but most old owners, since adding new owners or making other alterations, applied for new certificates. The firm of S. Smith and Buchanan, for example, owned the *Lottery* before the war in conjunction with George J. Brown, William S. Hollins, and John Higenbotham, acquiring Certificate of Registry No. 51 on April 1, 1812, for that vessel.[49] That register was marked as having been surrendered on July 23, 1812, because of "new owners." A new certificate, No. 70, for the same vessel with a commission, was issued to S. Smith and Buchanan and Hollins plus Michael McBlair and, in reference to its earlier certificate, contained the notation, "property partly changed." Portuguese-born captain Joseph Almeda exchanged his 1812 Certificate No. 2 for the *Joseph and Mary* along with a bill of sale when sixteen owners were added for the vessel's role as a raider for new Certificate No. 91.[50]

Change in ownership or rig required a new certificate of registry (and commission). New documents to avoid later embarrassments in admiralty courts were continually sought for private armed vessels because of the habit of reorganizing syndicates after a voyage or cruise. Solely owned vessels used as letter-of-marque traders, such as Isaac McKim's *Grecian*, simply utilized their prewar certificate of registry while adding the necessary documents demanded of commissioned vessels. The *Grecian* without alterations utilized Certificate No. 26 of March 2, 1812, throughout the war.[51]

For letter-of-marque traders carrying cargoes to foreign ports, normal peacetime custom house bonds and papers for their cargo and trading mission were also mandatory. Signatures of the owners, the master, and a surety were required on performance bonds, often involving large sums. One performance bond for $51,000 signed by sole owner John A. Morton, master Joseph Gold, and surety George Williams for the letter-of-marque *Cora*, clearing for Bordeaux, dwarfed her accompanying $5,000 letter-of-marque bond. Surety Levi Hollingsworth signed a performance bond for $34,000 for the *Lynx* on her way to Bordeaux, and John Smith Hollins of Hollins and McBlair did the same for a $44,437 bond on the *Inca* on her way to Nantes, certifying that their vessel would not violate the Non-Intercourse Act. The sum involved was normally twice the value of the vessel and cargo, and, in some cases, such as for the *Flight*, the *Expedition*, or the *Ned*, bound for Bordeaux, approximated seventy-five thousand dollars. Some were for Lisbon- or Cadiz-bound vessels but it must be remembered, as the collector was told, these vessels were not technically trading with belligerent Britain but with neutrals Spain and Portugal. Apparently, value was estimated in terms of the cost of the vessel and cargo in the United

States rather than their value in Europe, the West Indies, or South America.[52]

The collector issued a commission when he was satisfied that all required documents were in order, if he had a blank on hand. Each collector received a block of commissions once Congress and the president authorized and printed such documents. At Baltimore, McCulloch received Commission Nos. 1 through 10 on June 26, 1812, but issued eleven commissions to satisfy the desires of both George Stiles and Joshua Barney for the coveted first commission. One of the explanations for that dilemma was an initial plan specifying issuance of the commissions by the secretary of state before it was decided that the collectors would handle them. Two promises were made by two officials but McCulloch managed to keep both promises. McCulloch got Nos. 324 to 331 on July 13 and similar blocks periodically throughout the war, ending with Nos. 1058 to 1067 in January of 1815. He continually requested new blanks even during the blockade, stating in September of 1813 "but one remains." In November of 1814, as the British abandoned the bay, the Baltimore office asked for at least twenty commissions because many vessels were fitting for sea.[53]

An actual commission, when issued, read as follows:

JAMES MADISON, President of the United States of America.
TO ALL WHO SHALL THESE PRESENTS, GREETING:
BE IT KNOWN, That in pursuance of an Act of Congress passed on the *eighteenth* day of *June* one thousand eight hundred and twelve, I have commissioned, and by these presents do commission, the private armed *Schooner* called the *Patapsco* of the burthen of *159* tons, or thereabouts, owned by Andrew Clopper, Levi Hollingsworth, Amos A. Williams and Henry Fulford of the City of Baltimore _____

_____

_____

_____

mounting *6* carriage guns, and navigated by *40* men, hereby authorizing *James M. Mortimer* Captain, and *William Ross* Lieutenant of the said *schooner Patapsco* and the other officers and crew thereof to subdue, seize and take any armed or unarmed British vessel, public or private, which shall be found within the jurisdictional limits of the United States or elsewhere on the high seas, or within the waters of the British dominions, and such captured vessel, with her apparel, guns and appurtenances, and the goods and effects which shall be found on board the same, together with the British persons and others who shall be acting on board, to bring within some port of the United States; and also to retake any vessel, goods and effects of the people of the United States, which may have been captured by any British armed vessel, in order that proceedings may be had concerning such capture or recapture in due form of law, and as to right and justice shall appertain. The said *James M. Mortimer* is further authorized to detain, seize and take all vessels and effects, to whomsoever belonging, which shall be liable thereto according to the Law of Nations and the rights of the United States as a power at war, and to bring the same within some port of the United States in order that due proceedings may be had thereon. This commission to continue in force during the pleasure of the President of the United States for the time being.

> Given under my hand and seal of the United States of America, at the city of Washington, the *17* day of *September* in the year of our Lord, one thousand eight hundred and *12* and of the Independence of the said states the *Thirty seven*.
>
> By the President JAMES MADISON
> [signature]
> JAMES MONROE Secretary of State[54]
> [signature]

Accompanying the commission, copies of it and the law authorizing the commissions, the sponsors of the private armed vessel were given "suitable instructions for the better governing and directing the conduct of the vessels, so commissioned, their officers and crews." Such instructions were ordered by the law authorizing commissions. Designed along with bonds and other requirements to prevent abuses of the system, they evolved out of the long European struggle to control private armed vessels at sea or to punish them in the courts upon their return. War of 1812 instructions read as follows:

To Captain _____ Commander of the private armed _____ called the _____

INSTRUCTIONS
For the Private Armed Vessels of the United States

1. The tenor of your commission under the act of Congress entitled "An act concerning letters of marque, prizes, and prize goods," a copy of which is hereto annexed, will be kept constantly in your view. The high seas, referred to in your commission, you will understand, generally, to extend to low water mark; but with the exception of the space within one league, or three miles, from the shores of countries at peace both with Great Britain and with the United States. You may nevertheless execute your commission within that distance of the shore of a nation at war with Great Britain, and even on the waters within the jurisdiction of such nation, if permitted to do so.

2. You are to pay the strictest regard to the rights of neutral powers,

and the usages of civilized nations, and in all your proceedings toward neutral vessels, you are to give them as little molestation or interruption as will consist with the right of ascertaining their neutral character, and of detaining and bringing them in for regular adjudication, in the proper case. You are particularly to avoid even the appearance of using force or reduction with a view to deprive such vessels of their crews, or of their passengers other than persons in the military service of the enemy.

3. Towards the enemy vessels and their crews, you are to proceed, in exercising the rights of war with all the justice and humanity which characterizes the nation of which you are members.

4. The master and one or more of the principal persons belonging to captured vessels, are to be sent, as soon after the capture as may be, to the judge or judges of the proper court in the United States, to be examined upon oath, touching the interests or property of the captured vessel and her lading: and at the same time are to be delivered to the judge or judges, all passes, charter parties, bills of lading, invoices, letters and other documents and writings found on board; the said papers to be proved by the affidavit of the commander of the capturing vessel, or some other person present at the capture, to be produced as they were received, without fraud, addition, subduction or embezzlement.

By command of the President of the United States of America.

JAMES MONROE
Secretary of State[55]

The clause in the "Instructions" referring to "the justice and humanity which characterizes the nation of which you are members" may appear quaint to readers in a century characterized by total wars, but in 1812 it reflected the values and self-image of the new republic. Its insertion in a warlike document reflects its general acceptance at the time, while the record of the Baltimoreans at sea suggests that it was taken seriously. Five British masters attested to the good treatment they received on board the Baltimore privateer *Harpy*.[56] The privateer *Kemp* released a British brig "out of humanity to an Italian lady and family" traveling on that brig.[57] The *Sparrow* was praised by a British captain for not touching private items and for purchasing poultry.[58] The *Federal Gazette* received a report on the good treatment of British prisoners on American privateers and commented that this was "as it should be." A New York newspaper applauded the "correct and liberal" conduct of the American privateersmen.[59] Whether the American captains acted as liberally and humanely toward their own crews is another question, but in their dealings with the enemy there is little evidence that they failed to uphold the new republic's standards.

The ancient problem of control at sea encouraged Secretary of State Monroe to send twenty blank commissions to the navy so they might not be duped by forgeries. Monroe stated, "As the flag of the United States, under false commissions of Letter-of-Marque, may, during the prevailing War be prostituted, by unprincipled adventurers, to unlawful purposes, I have deemed it proper to put you in possession of authentic documents for the use of our public armed vessels."[60] The navy needed only twenty examples for its few vessels, while the private armed fleet required over eleven hundred actual commissions.

While all initiatory plans, documents, and financial arrangements were being completed, the vessel was being prepared and a crew was being recruited. Such work was supervised by the ship's husband whose selection or election, in the case of vessels sponsored by a number of part-owners, was a majority decision. The tendency was to select experienced shipowning merchants and, in many cases, those with previous sea experiences were preferred. Those without such experiences may have happily deferred to the likes of former captain and merchant Christopher Deshon, an active ship's husband and later a popular prize agent. Such managing owners (husbands) received a commission identical to the normal commission merchant rate of 2.5 percent on the proceeds. The husband was not required to be a part-owner, but in commissioned vessels nearly all the husbands were shareholders.[61]

As an agent, husband, or superintendent, even in peacetime, the manager was responsible for the vessel's outfitting (with the captain), repairs, the appointment of the master, officers, and mariners, and all the affairs and arrangements "for the due employment of the ship in commerce and navigation." He and the captain signed the crew on and off, selected and purchased stores, and completed contracts of all kinds. He was required to keep regular books and to preserve certificates and documents. To borrow money to pay bills or to ensure a vessel, however, he needed special authorization from the other part-owners. A husband was not permitted to form debts against the proprietary concern but his power to extract "contributory shares" reduced the need for debts. The law permitted an appointment as ship's husband to be in writing or by "parole."[62]

Part-owners of a private vessel of war usually designated the ship's husband, keeper of the vessel's account books, as their prize agent. The prize agent's authority was restricted and defined in the same manner as that of the husband as both were, legally speaking, bound by the law of agency. A prize agent needed written authority, usually in the form of a "letter of attorney," specifying him as prize agent for the owners and, in many cases, the officers and crew. An example of this approach was completed by a group of Baltimore's German traders in May of 1814. Peter Arnold Karthaus, Ferdinand Hurxthal, and Frederick Waesche, owners of the schooner *Pike*, "now on a cruize," appointed the other part-owner, Joel Vickers, as "prize Agent for this cruise" and noted that he was also agent for the officers and crew.[63] The officers and crew, however, had to assign him that role independently of those owners.

Chosen by the ship's husband, the captain was responsible for the "management of the outfit" and the "navigation of the ship." Possession of an owner's share did not guarantee a master mariner a captain's position because that decision was made by the majority with the advice of the husband. When a part-owner, the captain was not protected against removal because the majority of part-owners made that decision.[64] Private armed vessel captains were replaced with regularity, often as a result of changes in ownership or when their privateers were converted to commissioned traders or vice versa. The performance record of a captain, of course, was his best guarantee of continual or new employment, and few were changed while their vessel was employed by one set of owners utilizing the vessel in a single role.

Baltimore's captains were highly respected for their ability and experience, having operated for decades as blockade runners in schooners under an inordinate amount of sail even in rough waters. Commercial houses, such as S. Smith and Buchanan or Hollins and McBlair, and individual shippers, such as the McKims or the Williamses, all had their favorite captains. Captains such as Joshua Barney were more independent, but few had Barney's experience. Beginning his sea career at fourteen years of age, Barney served as a privateer and naval officer in the American Revolution and as a *chef de division* of a French naval squadron in the 1790s. After playing the merchant for a while, Commodore Barney, at the age of fifty, took out Baltimore's *Rossie* during the War of 1812 before returning to public duty as a gunboat flotilla commander.[65] Barney was a naval officer at heart, but he is also an example of the movement of crew members and officers back and forth between the public and private services. His primary objective as a privateersman appears not to have been profits, but injury to the enemy. He reported after the *Rossie* cruise, "I am only sorry my Cruise began so late, or I might have done much more injury to the Enemy — I find small vessels will no longer answer the purpose and have declined proceeding on another Cruise, indeed my Vessel has suffered so much that she is unfit for service being old and worn out."[66]

George Coggeshall, former captain of a privateer and later author of a history of privateering, personally knew Captains Chaytor, Murphy, Barney, Stafford, and Richardson of Baltimore. All were, along with Boyle and Dooley, among the successful commanders of private armed vessels. Coggeshall said that they would "favorably compare with the same class of military men in any army or navy in the world" at a time when even American public commissions were generally reserved for "gentlemen." The 1812 captains he classified with "hardly an exception," as "a dashing brave set of disinterested men, and an honor to their country."[67] American captains, often more literate than their European counterparts, were knowledgeable in mercantile and legal matters as well as navigation and ship management.

A captain was not just another employee. A letter-of-marque captain expected a monthly wage twice that of an experienced seaman (or sixty dollars during the war). The captain also retained the historic prerogatives of masters in the form of percentages, called "hat money" and "primage," for supervising the loading and unloading of cargo and space in the hold for his own merchandise. Furthermore, some captains received a percentage of a voyage's profit. In wartime, captains were allotted the largest number of the crew's prize shares as well as an occasional bonus on dangerous voyages. Amos A. Williams, part-owner and husband of numerous commissioned vessels, stated in 1814, "It is, however, necessary to state that in all our hazardous voyages we have given the commander a complement of 500 dollars to 750 dollars for safe arrival, this we consider money well disposed of."[68] The rewards were ample enough to thrust many captains into the ranks of the merchant class.

About one hundred twenty-five captains commanded Baltimore-owned private armed vessels, with many commanding more than one vessel in the thirty months of war. Seventy surviving masters' oaths listed for captains a place of nativity or simply specified "citizen." Of the seventy oaths in the sample only six listed Baltimore as the captain's birthplace, while fifteen others cited Maryland counties, with the bay counties predominating. The attraction of Baltimore for merchants and master mariners was seaborne commerce, and many were lured to Baltimore during its prewar decades of commercial prosperity. Massachusetts was the birthplace of six captains in the sample, with Nantucket providing three, while Marblehead produced the incomparable Thomas Boyle. Maine was the birthplace of one. Connecticut and Rhode Island were the birthplaces of three each; the bay state of Virginia was listed by six and Delaware by three. New Jersey, Pennsylvania, or North Carolina was each listed by one captain as his place of nativity.[69]

The surprising figure in the masters' oaths sample was the number of "naturalized" citizens. Fifteen captains declared themselves as naturalized citizens, and probably some of those who simply listed "citizen" were in that category. Eleven who listed dates were naturalized from 1798 to 1812, but nine completed that step from 1803 to 1808. With the exception of Portuguese-born Joseph Almeda, who was naturalized in 1805, the names of naturalized citizens were predominantly Anglo-Saxon.[70] This suggests that some of Baltimore's vigorous maritime opposition to Britain was directed by recent English converts to the republic who may well have been English trained. The dangers and government requirements of the years of impressment and the neutral carrying trade encouraged many to acquire their citizenship papers in the decade before the United States' entry into the war. Citizenship was mandatory for private armed vessel commanders.

Captains born outside of Baltimore probably worked their way up through the ranks over a period of years. Those most active in Baltimore private armed vessels during the War of 1812, of whatever origin, were definitely not strangers to the bay or the port of Baltimore. Entrances and clearances, registers, oaths, and other documents for the ten years preceding the war certify that, with a very few exceptions, they served on Baltimore vessels before the war. Fewer than 20 percent of the 125 captains' names were absent from Baltimore's prewar records.[71] Some of those absences were possibly due to promotions during the war or appointments in other ports during the blockade. When it existed, dissatisfaction with a captain was a result of the special stresses of wartime duty and the crowded conditions of oversized and undisciplined crews. Leadership ability was tested fully by the pressures of combat and the difficulties encountered in blockades, but very few captains were removed from command during the life of a single commission. Only eight changes in command were made outside of those following changes in vessel ownership.[72] The developmental process providing the port with captains was effective, while the trying decades preceding the war weeded out those unfit for command in a time of stress. Ship's husbands had a rich pool from which to choose.

The ship's husband and the captain worked on their equipment while they completed the documents and other necessary steps. To be sure, other documents such as a clearance certificate would be needed after the vessel was outfitted, armed, and manned. Such a certificate required another careful description of the vessel. The privateer *Rossie*'s certificate described her as an American-built schooner of 206 tons, carrying eleven guns and 100 men under the command of Joshua Barney. On board were "Ballast and Stores"; her destination was described as "On a cruize," and the certificate was signed by the collector, James H. McCulloch.[73] One of the two No. 1 commissions issued at Baltimore was on her way out to sea. Between the original papers and the clearance, the husband and the captain completed the tasks of vessel procurement, preparation, armament, provisions, and recruitment. Such tasks were more difficult than the routine simplicity suggested by the official language of relevant documents. The fundamental steps, including the completion of papers and other requirements, were carried on in a businesslike fashion by the collector and by the sponsors of private armed vessels. Rules and documents for private armed vessels during the War of 1812 reflected legal principles and governmental practices developed over centuries. Baltimore's owners, husbands, and captains of 1812 dealt with a government fully aware of the dangers inherent in a poorly regulated private armed vessel system.

SEVEN

Readying the Tools of the Trade

Even before the documents discussed in the previous chapter were completed, owners had to obtain and prepare their vessels. Vessels were purchased at auctions through advertisements placed by owners or from custom builders who either built on contract or at their own risk. Although characteristics of the vessels varied, factors such as age, speed, and loading capacity were of vital importance to purchasers. Costs of the popular Baltimore schooners were another vital consideration for those starting a commissioned vessel venture and for builders hoping to make a sale. Prewar owners who simply converted existing vessels to wartime use were spared the search for a vessel but not the preparatory activities required before any vessel cleared for wartime service.

Many of the utilitarian responsibilities of a private armed vessel venture were delegated to a ship's husband or managing owner. The husband, in cooperation with the captain, prepared the vessel for clearance and for sea duty. Often in conjunction with the captain, the husband made decisions regarding sails, armament, provisions, and nautical supplies and was responsible for their procurement. When such items were not available in Baltimore, he sought alternate sources.

Sponsors seeking a vessel after the Declaration of War had several options. One possibility was to place an order with a shipyard to construct a vessel of preferred design. Some owners had already done so in anticipation of the war, but as several months lead time was required by the master carpenter, sponsors ordering vessels in the summer of 1812 were too late to capitalize on the easy prizes of the war's opening months. Another option was to purchase a vessel already constructed from a builder or from a ship's broker. "A New and elegant War-built Schooner" of 230 tons, seventy feet in length and pierced for sixteen guns was advertised for sale in Baltimore on July 10, 1812. The advertisement stated that "good judges" estimated that she would be "a very swift vessel" and was "in every respect well calculated for a first-rate Privateer."[1] Similar advertisements in the early months of the war suggest that the builders had anticipated, in good entrepreneurial fashion, the wartime need for schooners. British and French intrusions upon American trade before the war had encouraged builders to concentrate on schooners for blockade running and for evasion at sea. Alert builders had some in the stocks and others available for conversion when the United States declared war.

Though decreasing in later months, advertisements for new vessels continued in Baltimore throughout the war years. In September of 1813, for example, William Price offered two new schooners of 111 and 195 tons respectively. In October of 1814, Peter A. Guestier, an investor in two commissioned vessels and a ship's broker, offered two vessels for sale. One was a pilot boat schooner of about 150 tons "ready to be launched" and "built with particular care, of the best materials." Another, of 200 tons, was coppered and rigged and "capable on account of her strength, of carrying two long twenty-four pounders."[2] Shipbuilders concentrating solely on vessels designed for wartime use as raiders and cargo runners provided the only vessels capable of eluding the blockade established six months later.

Others in the market for vessels looked to the "country" builders in other towns along the bay. Very active Talbot County builder William Harrison of James, for example, advertised a vessel in November of 1812 before it was launched. He offered her "on the Stocks" but stated that she could be launched within three weeks. According to him, she was "a very handsome copper-fastened Schooner, remarkably sharp built, of the best materials" and about 220 tons on her register.[3] New schooners, then, were available from what were established prewar shipbuilding centers in Baltimore and along the bay, by contract, or at public sale.

Surviving master carpenters' certificates specify, in some cases, the party for whom a vessel was contracted. Thomas Kemp's famous *Chasseur* was built "for William Hollins," and William Price's 330-ton *Maria* (later converted to the privateer *Harpy*) was constructed "for D'Arcy and Didier." Noah Richardson of Dorchester County built his *Macedonian* for Thomas Tenant, a purchaser of numerous Eastern Shore vessels in the prewar years. When a shipbuilder had no contract and built a vessel at his own risk, his certificate specified "for myself." Such entrepreneurial risks were warranted both by the prewar carrying trade and by the war itself, and even popular shipbuilders such as Thomas Kemp built for themselves on occasion.[4] Advertisements offering new vessels for sale suggest that the shipyards had a capacity for production greater than that utilized by their regular shipowning clients. The evidence, however, contains some contradictions. Andrew Descandes publicly offered his shipyard "for any kind of construction" in June of 1812, while in September of the same year shipbuilder Joseph Turner was advertising "immediate employment for five or six men in the ship's carpenter business."[5] Some shipbuilders were busier than others.

Buyers looking for a vessel had the further option of purchasing a proven vessel at auction after she completed a voyage or cruise under other owners. The privateer *Highflyer* was advertised for sale by auction in September of 1812 at the Fells Point wharf of Thomas Tenant, one of her part-owners. Characterized as a "Privateer Schooner," her armament, outfit, and other equipment "as she returned from a cruize" were included in the price. An inventory and terms were available from the auctioneer. Another example of a proven vessel at auction was the *Wasp*, advertised for sale in September of 1813 at Thorndike Chase's Fells Point wharf.[6]

The tiny *Wasp* was auctioned off while the British navy blockaded the bay. That blockade encouraged other owners to advertise their vessels for sale at Baltimore where the vessel was known even though she was moored at another port. In August of 1813 auctioneer and private armed vessel investor William Vance offered the 250-ton schooner *Phaeton* for sale on credit at the Frederick Street dock in the inner basin. She was, he advertised, a first rate sailer, built at Baltimore and being sold after completing one voyage to and from France. The sale included eight four-pound guns, muskets, pistols, cutlasses, and other equipment necessary for cruising. As was customary, the *Phaeton* was to be sold "as she arrived from sea" and an inventory was available. As far as bidders for her were concerned, they considered her condition uncertain as she was deliverable at Wilmington, North Carolina. Another proven vessel, the *Kemp*, with two suits of sails, was offered at auction in 1814 but was also deliverable at Wilmington, North Carolina.[7]

The various sources for vessels, the frequent changes in ownership, and documents outside of Baltimore for some vessels complicated efforts to substantiate the origins and ages of those private armed vessels owned, in whole or part, by Baltimoreans. The utilization of multiple sources, however, led to substantiations for 111 of the 122 different vessels known to have been commissioned by Baltimoreans. Additionally, two D'Arcy and Didier vessels, the *Harpy* and the *Syren*, were previously commissioned vessels whose names were changed in New York. Another vessel, the *Hull*, was a prize vessel converted by Cornelius Specht into the privateer *Fox*. As far as is known, she was the only prize vessel commissioned in Baltimore. Vessels suitable for conversion were too swift to be caught even by the Baltimore schooners.

The number of substantiated vessels increased to 115 with the purchase of one from a French firm. The 290-ton brig *Venus*, formerly *La Venus*, was purchased by active investor John Gooding. He paid the New York agents of the Bordeaux owners $18,000 in two notes in December of 1814 while the vessel was moored at Norfolk, Virginia. Gooding offered to carry government dispatches in his new "first rate sailer" while planning to ballast his vessel "with tobacco to be landed in France" and expecting to take "any British vessels that may fall in her way to France." The captain was "A Gentleman that confidence may be placed in," and because the Norfolk merchants may have been reticent to sign as sureties for a Baltimore-owned vessel, Gooding sent his letter-of-marque bond along to Baltimore. When forwarded to the State Department, it was signed by active Baltimore investors James Williams and Lyde Goodwin. Gooding's action served as an example of a vessel acquired out of Baltimore, of the surety problem in other ports, and of an entrepreneur exploiting every possible opening as he endeavored to combine government service, cargo carrying, and prize taking in his efforts to earn a profit on his investment.[8]

In a period when five years was considered mature for some vessels, an important characteristic of Baltimore private armed vessels was age.[9] The opportunities existing early in the war, when unsuspecting British vessels without naval support were in the sea lanes, encouraged some owners to disregard the age factor. By late 1812, however, when the easy prizes were gone, Baltimore's shipyards were building new schooners. By then, the British navy was omnipresent, and the sponsors of private armed vessels sought newer, larger, and especially designed schooners. The following construction dates of the Baltimore private armed vessels illustrate the pattern:

1805–1	1811– 7
1806–1	1812– 45
1807–4	1813– 28
1809–7	1814– 8
1810–9	1815– 1
	111[10]

Even with the incorporation of vessels of unknown origin and with the assumption that two or three years represented half-life for such vessels, the Baltimoreans employed new or young vessels (built in or after 1811) 72 percent of the time. The bulk of the private service vessels were completed after Congress began deliberations that finally led to the Declaration of War in June of 1812.

Older vessels performed well for the Baltimoreans not only in the early months but throughout the war. Among the stars of the prize lists were the *Rossie* (1807), really old for the period, the *Caroline* (1809), and the *Rolla* (1809). The *Bona* (1809) and the *Comet* (1810) completed the list of older privateers whose prize records were enviable. The oldest Baltimore privateer was the small fifty-five-ton sloop *Liberty*, constructed in 1805 but commissioned September of 1812.[11] Fewer letter-of-marque schooners, so dependent on raw speed, were mature vessels, but Isaac McKim's *Valona* (1806), the *Inca* (1807), and the brig *Female* (1807) made numerous runs through enemy-held waters throughout the war. In other times vessels of their age had already been converted into fishing vessels or, in the language of the collector, "sold to foreigners."[12]

Though known as a Baltimore creation, the sharp-built schooners, constituting at least 90 percent of the Baltimore-owned private armed vessels, were not all constructed along the Patapsco River. Owners utilized "country" ship-builders in Maryland and Virginia bay towns during the war just as they had in the decades preceding the war. Talbot County on the Eastern Shore, particularly St. Michaels, provided one vessel for every two launched at Baltimore. The builder of many of Baltimore's finest vessels was transplanted St. Michael's Quaker, Thomas Kemp. The geographical origins for vessels of all ages were as follows for the 111 substantiated vessels:

Anne Arundel County, Maryland	1
Baltimore, Maryland	60
Dorchester County, Maryland	7
Mathews County, Virginia	4
St. Mary's County, Maryland	1
Somerset County, Maryland	3
Talbot County, Maryland	31
Queen Anne's County, Maryland	4
	111[13]

When vessels of unknown origin are omitted, Baltimore built over one-half of its own private navy.

Baltimore shipbuilders were all experienced master carpenters before the war. They enjoyed a reputation for designing and building "sharp-built" or, as they were sometimes called, "pilot-boat constructed" vessels. John and William Price together built twelve of the seventy-seven Baltimore-built vessels for which certificates were located. All were built during the war, including the successful *Sabine* and the *Revenge*, among the privateers. John Price retained sole ownership of his 330-ton *Eutaw*, commissioned in late January of 1815.[14]

Shipbuilders commonly retained a share in their creations even in peacetime as an investment and as a means of securing new orders and repair contracts. Their share also served as a guarantee of their workmanship.[15] Such a practice reduced the capital needed by a purchaser and gave the shipbuilder a chance, in commissioned vessels, to share in the prize money. Builder James Cordery launched five of the seventy-seven documented new vessels during the war years. One cruised as a privateer and three, including the *Bordeaux Packet*, were active letter-of-marque traders. Another, the *Pike*, performed both roles at different times. William Parsons was responsible for at least seven letter-of-marque traders built during the war years. Parsons built swift, light vessels with larger than usual cargo areas for the Baltimore schooners. Builder Joseph Turner built the *Orb* in 1812 and in 1815 he put over the *Chippewa*. William Flannigain (sometimes spelled Flannigan) built the *Siro* for George Stiles in 1812, and the *Swift* "for himself" in 1814. Andrew Descandes of Federal Hill constructed three vessels, including one rare "xebec" type of three masts with both square and triangular sails. Bernard Salnave built one schooner in the sample of seventy-seven and Joseph Despeaux built two "sharp-built" ships, the *Alexander* and the *Father and Son*, both of which he owned for a time.[16] Few three-masted square-rigged ships were commissioned.

The most famous and most productive of the Baltimore school of shipbuilders was the Quaker Thomas Kemp. He learned the trade at St. Michael's and opened his own yard in Baltimore in 1805, specializing in alterations that added speed to vessels — topsails, topmasts, topgallant yards, and miscellaneous spars.[17] He built vessels for Isaac McKim, Christopher Deshon, Charles F. Kalkman, James Williams, S. Smith and Buchanan, Hollins and McBlair, and other active Baltimore shipowning merchants long before the war. Citing his schooners as "privateer-built" on his master carpenter's certificates, Kemp charged from twenty-three to thirty dollars per carpenter's ton for his vessels as they were launched. That figure held firm even during the war years.[18]

Thomas Kemp's vessels were known for speed and durability although lack of depth in their holds minimized cargo space, making them less suited for trading than for privateering. His 1807 to 1810 creations, the *Rossie, Rolla,* and *Comet,* were great privateering performers under premier commanders during the War of 1812. Of the seventy-seven vessels whose builders were identified, Kemp built nine at his Fells Point yard, including the great *Chasseur,* the *Grampus,* the *Midas,* and the largest of the Baltimore schooners, the *Mammoth.* His weekly Baltimore payroll exceeded one thousand dollars in 1812 and early 1813. The *Whig,* operated almost solely out of New York during the blockade, and the very successful *Surprise* (over forty prizes) were built in St. Michael's where Kemp also maintained a yard with the aid of relatives. Kemp retained part-owner's shares in the *Wasp,* in the letter-of-marque trader *Flight* of 260 tons, which he built in 1812, and in his greatest creation, the *Chasseur.*[19] The use of the phrase "privateer-built" on Kemp's certificates even before the war and the frequent use of his vessels for cruisers testified to the sturdiness and speed of his creations. The extra armament on a privateer required a sturdiness beyond that of a trading vessel, and its more active combat role made sturdy sides and bulwarks desirable.

The Baltimoreans continued to use Eastern Shore shipbuilders during the war years. Shipbuilders' names in the sample of seventy-seven certificates included those of William Harrison (two), Impey Dawson (two), and Perry Spencer (two, including one in 1806), all of Talbot County. In some cases, Eastern Shore shipbuilders sent hulls to Baltimore for completion or outfitting and, consequently, a certificate may have been signed by the builder completing the vessel. In Dorchester County William Harrison, also active in St. Michael's, built the *Delille* (later converted to the privateer *Syren*) and the privateer *Saranac.* Noah Richardson of Dorchester built two commissioned vessels, and Spry Denny of Queen Anne's County built one commissioned vessel. One

Baltimore-owned vessel, the *York*, was built in New York by Forman Chierman for Hollins and McBlair in 1814 when the British controlled Chesapeake Bay.[20]

The American shipbuilding industry had reached a peak in tonnage in 1811 for the entire period from 1789 to 1815. The period from 1812 to 1815, however, was disastrous for many American shipbuilders. Only schooners were in demand, while the tonnage constructed in 1814 amounted to only 20 percent of that launched in 1811. The Baltimore shipbuilders were fortunate in that their skills in the construction of sharp-built schooners gave them a wartime market. The years from 1812 to 1815 were not "boom" years for all the Baltimore shipbuilders since their yards had to produce three to six schooners per year to warrant such a rating.[21] The yards remained operative by building wartime schooners, and surviving records suggest that new construction, alterations, and repair contracts placed the Prices, Cordery, and Parsons near the "boom" category, while Kemp undoubtedly led the pack. Baltimore's orders for hulls and completed vessels were vital in peace and war to the Eastern Shore shipyards.

Unfortunately, costs of new vessels were not quoted in any consistent manner. One could purchase a hull alone, a hull plus masts and spars, or a completely rigged vessel. Rigged, armed, and provisioned vessels or vessels with one or two suits of sails were also available. Kemp's $30 per ton was within a normal range. James Cordery charged Peter Arnold Karthaus $30 per ton for the *Amelia*, but Karthaus had to add at least $19,000 preparing her for sea.[22] The 180-ton *Argo* cost $19 per registered ton, the 276-ton *Tartar* was $21 per ton, and the 33-ton *Arab* sold for eighteen dollars per ton. Their lower costs per ton suggest an incomplete state of readiness when compared to the $108 per ton cost of the privateer *Tom*. Captain Thomas Boyle's *Chasseur* cost her investors, without contributory shares, $78 per ton, ready for sea. The lighter letter-of-marque traders carried fewer guns and less provisions but more sails than the privateers. Their prices, however, were not always lower. The letter-of-marque schooner *Bordeaux Packet*, owned by Peter Arnold Karthaus, cost $89 per ton or 50 percent more than the privateer *Chasseur*.[23] Full preparation doubled or tripled the price of the vessels as they were launched. The dependence on schooners and wartime inflation kept costs up, and a particular owner's preference for quality materials and supplies may have caused him to disregard price. The William Flannigain-constructed letter-of-marque schooner *Siro* was reported to have cost her sole owner George Stiles $40,000 by the time she cleared.[24] That figure represented an unusually high cost of $178 per ton, but the vessel was built of the finest materials. While such costs were more common among privateers, the *Siro* performed as a letter-of-marque trader and as a privateer.

Costs per ton for older vessels also reflected various conditions of preparation and seaworthiness. Older vessels were sold as "they arrived from sea," and buyers anticipated requests for additional or contributory shares from the ship's husband for repairs and further preparations. Prices of older vessels ranged as greatly as those of the new vessels purchased during the war. The small privateer *Sarah Ann* sold for $23 per ton. The small *Wasp* sold for $55 per ton, while the 187-ton *Comet* built in 1810 and ready for sea went for $160 per ton.[25] Such sales seldom represented bare hulls since the vessels had been operative before their resale. Sails, some provisions, partial armament, and other items were included in the price. Their higher state of preparedness as well as demands for vessels early in the war explained the fact that the prices of older vessels were not markedly lower than those of new vessels.

Normal credit for ship purchases was given to the wartime purchasers and was not affected by the buyers' intention of commissioning the vessel. The privateer *America*, for example, was offered at auction in December of 1812, "for approved endorsed notes at four to six months credit."[26] Such a credit period permitted a vessel to complete a cruise before final settlement was demanded, although the note endorsers may not have been enthusiastic about such a risk. Peter Arnold Karthaus paid George Williams $10,000 for the *Kemp* "at five and six months" credit and then invested at least another $18,000 in disbursements and advances to the crew.[27]

The great range in costs per ton among new and old vessels encourages one to look for dollar figures, but the surviving thirty-two bills of sale with dollar figures contain the same wide range as cost per ton. Both figures suggest vessels of varying degrees of preparedness, quality of construction, and size. The amount of demand prevalent at the time of sale also influenced price. The minimum price for a vessel entering the private service was the $1,400 paid for the 1805 built, fifty-five-ton privateer schooner *Wasp*, but this was an exception. Her condition is unknown. The new *Chasseur*'s cost at the shipyard was $27,000, while the *Comet*, built in 1810 but sold in 1812, and the new *Tom* each sold for $30,000.[28] George Stiles's dollar cost for his elegant letter-of-marque *Siro*, ready for sea, was $40,000.[29] The figures indicate that a few smaller vessels, with or without equipment, were available at reasonable prices to smaller investors. Sole owners and wealthy investors, on the other hand, were able to secure large, quality-constructed, and well-equpped vessels for their purposes. George Stiles, for example, demanded quality construction and was willing to pay for it. He had the brig *L'Savage* built for "upwards of $50,000" during the war but did not commission her. Intended for the East Indian trade, the brig used heavy copper, had a large cargo space, and was swift. It was said that never were "such pains taken with any other vessel ever built in this country."[30]

The cost relationship between a hull and a completed vessel cannot be clearly established in each case. The normal relationship, however, was that the cost of the hull represented from 50 to 70 percent of the cost of the completed

Montibello *the* Seat *of* Gen.ˡ S. Smith *Maryland.*

Drawn Engraved & Published by W.Birch Springland near Bristol Pennsylv.ᵃ

PLATE IV

Drawing, "Montibello, the Seat of General S. Smith"
by W. Birch, original in the Maryland Historical Society
(The spelling is usually Montebello.)

vessel.[31] Hollins and McBlair purchased the "Hull, Masts and Spars" of a new, unnamed, and unregistered schooner from shipbuilder Richard Spencer of Talbot County in 1812 for just $5,691.18.[32] That figure represented thirty-six dollars per ton before the armament, outfit (sails), furniture, and provisions were added. The relationship between the basic vessel and her final state of preparation was illustrated by the case of the privateer *Caroline*. Built in 1809, that vessel sold for $17,125 in July of 1812, but the new owners specified in the bill of sale that only $10,000 represented the cost of the vessel. The remainder of the $17,125 was for the further expenses "of outfit and whatever nature and kind till her departure."[33] The vessel was not new, but about 40 percent of her price was designated in the owners' share agreement as preparation costs. Further contributory shares were collected from the *Caroline*'s owners to meet her later expenses. For a privateer, the *Caroline* was a bargain.

The relationship between the cost of a letter-of-marque schooner and her cargo was explained by Henry Didier, Jr. in a clear statement of costs of a first class commissioned trader. In July of 1813 he informed his brother in France that "a first rate Pilot Boat like the *Delille* of 200 Tons would cost here to sea at most $17,000, Cargo to West Indies at most $8,000."[34] A 300-ton schooner, of course, required proportionally higher investment for both the vessel and her cargo. The fifty active investors seldom used anything less than a 200-ton "first rate" schooner, and, consequently, anticipated expenditures of $20,000 to $40,000 per venture. Didier's firm owned the 346-ton *Maria* and, after utilizing it for nine months as a letter-of-marque trader, sold it for $27,500 in New York. The firm retained a twentieth share in the vessel when she was converted to privateering and renamed *Harpy*.[35] Conversion to a privateer necessitated additional expenditures.

An investment of $25,000 covered the cost of a first class, armed, and fully equipped letter-of-marque schooner. Certainly, some, such as the $40,000.00 *Siro*, cost more, but the $25,000 figure is an acceptable average. It included a vessel, sails, armament, cargo, and other preparatory costs or disbursements. But a privateer required even more capital. Construction costs were only a beginning as disbursements for sails, guns, ammunition, small arms, provisions, advances to the crew, and other expenses were seemingly endless. An investment of $40,000.00 was common when one omits the little sloop *Liberty* or the fifty-five-ton *Wasp*. They represent the lowest entry costs for privateers, while $40,000.00 represented privateer creations such as the *Tom*, the *Chasseur*, the *Mammoth*, the *Amelia*, or the *Surprise*. Privateer owners, detailing their costs to Congress in 1813, said the New York privateer schooner *General Armstrong* and her guns cost $28,000.00, while other expenses raised the figure to $42,232.90. The *Governor Tompkins* out of New York but partially owned by Baltimorean Christopher Deshon cost $42,000.00 ready for sea. Both of these schooners were similar to the Baltimore privateers mentioned above. Cost figures for other privateers ranged from $16,000.00 to $54,000.00 with the higher figure representing a full-rigged ship.[36] The $40,000.00 price for armed Baltimore schooner included construction costs and preparations.

Despite wear and tear and occasional combat duty, the Baltimore vessels retained their value. Resale prices represented the basic vessel without all its provisions and ammunition and, in many cases, a vessel in need of refitting and repair. Resale examples are not numerous, but the 285-ton privateer *Revenge* sold for $12,000.00 in September of 1812 and was resold for the same figure in March of 1813 in an unknown condition. The small *Sparrow* of 84 tons exemplifies war-time price increases, selling for $3,250.00 when new in 1811 but bringing $5,666.70 in October of 1812. The addition of partial outfits and armament, however, probably accounted for higher prices along with increased demand.[37]

When a letter-of-marque trader completed a successful voyage or two, any resale income may have been pure profit. Henry Didier, Jr. noted that the *Burrows*, owned by his firm and five other men, sold a $6,000 cargo purchased in New York for $30,000 in the West Indies. Referring to his Baltimore vessels as "the Schooners," Didier noted, "They more than clear themselves in one voyage."[38] Even capture or a loss at sea after several voyages was offset by such profits.

Owners of a vessel did not always sell their vessel after one cruise or voyage. Captain Thomas Boyle brought the privateer *Comet* in after a cruise of eighty-three days, sending in three valuable prize ships and one brig to American ports. He reported "not a man killed during the Cruise" and said the *Comet* had not been chased once. The owners were encouraged to stay with a winning combination and Boyle noted in his log that "the owners of the *Comet* have determined to fit her out again with all possible expedition for a second Cruise."[39] Cornelius Specht, the sole owner of the privateer *Fox*, on the other hand, had good reason to sell his vessel in New Orleans. It was reported that "there was not sufficient property captured on one cruise to reimburse the owners of the said Privateer for more than one-third of the money advanced by them to the crew."[40] Sale of the vessel represented, in such cases, an effort to balance initial costs and disbursements as well as a determination to avoid further losses.

Among the bills of sales listing prices, there were cases of vessels whose value depreciated, causing the owners even heavier losses when they decided to sell. The 228-ton *Kemp*, a privateer, sold for $20,000 in July of 1812 but was down to $14,000 in March of 1813. The *Kemp* had had some trying experiences and vicious fights at sea so her condition was less than ideal. The 176-ton *Orb*, new in December of 1813, cost $13,000 but sold after ten months' service as a letter-of-marque trader, for $10,750.[41] When such resale depreciations were for vessels that had taken prizes or had completed profitable trading ventures, the resale price was not terribly important in the overall profit and loss account. Thirteen or twenty thousand dollars in the *Orb* represented only entry cost, and new owners had to double that investment before they could declare their vessel ready for sea.

In reference to tonnage, the surviving records provided data for the vessels owned by Baltimoreans. The number of vessels in each category was as follows in registered tons:

50–100 tons	8
100–150 tons	26
150–200 tons	22
201–250 tons	27
251–300 tons	24
301–350 tons	11
351–400 tons	3
401–450 tons	0
451–500 tons	1
	122[42]

The largest was a three-masted, square-rigged ship, so the schooners ranged from the 55-ton *Wasp* to the 376-ton *Mammoth*. Ninety-nine of the vessels were in the 100- to 300-ton class, a size combining reasonable cargo- or crew-carrying capacity with speed. Baltimore did not go to extremes in small vessels as did some ports. There were several requests for commissions for rowboats among the applications to other collectors and one for "a light Row Smuggling Boat of about *three fourths* of *one Ton Burthen* and three men" was reported.[43] The State Department on January 21, 1814, prohibited commissions for unsuitable or inferior vessels and for those with less than twenty men because such vessels were often smugglers.[44] Surviving New York quarterly reports for commissions for ninety-two vessels show fourteen of them below 50 tons, while Boston's report on sixty-four commissions listed one-fourth as below 50 tons.[45] Baltimore, with no commissioned vessel below 55 tons, proved the wartime appropriateness of schooners ranging from 100 to 350 tons.

Baltimore investors employed vessels other than schooners from time to time. At least three full-rigged, double-decked, and three-masted commissioned ships sailed during the war. Their slowness handicapped them when the British navy arrived in the Chesapeake, and, consequently, the ships were utilized in other waters. One sloop, the 55-ton *Liberty*, was commissioned and a number of brigs were employed. A brig differed from a schooner only in its sail arrangement, so some vessels were able to change from a schooner to a brig with little difficulty. Shipbuilder William Flannigain demonstrated flexibility of rig when he advertised a 226-ton pilot-boat built vessel for sale that could be "fitted [as] a brig or schooner."[46] With British merchant captains fleeing at the first sight of a schooner-rigged vessel, a brig profile had advantages at sea when one was willing to sacrifice some speed.

The need to allay suspicion was also a factor in the decision to build the 154-ton privateer *Ultor*. Her profile did not remotely resemble the schooner-rigged Baltimore cruisers. She was built by Andrew Descandes in 1813 as a "xebec" or, as her register stated, a "Schebeck."[47] That design originated in the Mediterranean where it was popular among corsairs. A three-masted vessel with square and lateen (triangular) sails, she was easily maneuvered by long oars called sweeps.[48] Over 90 percent of the Baltimore private fleet consisted of the famous two-masted topsail, sharp- or pilot-boat built schooners, while only half of Massachusetts' fleet and two-thirds of New York's consisted of schooners.[49]

The sharp-built Baltimore schooner's hull design originated in England, but similar vessels existed in Bermuda, the Baltic, France, and the Mediterranean. Refinement of the hull design and mastwork was accomplished with small vessels designed to carry pilots out to incoming vessels, largely in the Chesapeake Bay area. In the Chesapeake Bay, such vessels were first known as "Virginia-built." By 1812 they were clearly associated with Baltimore and known as "pilot-boat" or "sharp-built" schooners capable of getting the most out of any available winds and as the principal carriers of the port's West Indian commerce.[50]

Baltimore vessels were easily recognized by their profiles. They were identified by their low profiles and masts raked in the extreme and covered with high but light schooner rigging. The 228-ton *Kemp*, an unusual example of extreme drag, drew five feet three inches of water at her bow and twelve feet four inches aft.[51] Rough waters experienced by other schooners led to losses of men and reports of seas "very near swamping us" and of being "constantly under water." Captains were forced to dump their guns overboard when the seas made it "impossible to open hatches" to store them below in an effort to reduce topheaviness.[52] The high and light spars and yards were in need of frequent repair or replacement and the masts were, because of the strain from the sails, often in need of repair at sea.

William Harrison of James on the Eastern Shore sold his new schooner *Silverheels* to Levin Hall, who resold her to D'Arcy and Didier as the *Delille* in November of 1812 for "value received." Didier later reported the vessel to have cost $17,000 ready for sea, but without cargo.[53] Harrison's certificate described the Baltimore schooner as follows:

> She is sharp-built, has one Deck two Masts and Round Stern and measures Sixty-three feet Six Inches in length, twenty-one feet ten Inches in Breadth and Ten-feet three inches in depth and is One Hundred and Forty-nine and 51/95 ton's Carpenter's Measurement.[54]

As customary, the *Delille*'s measurements in the carpenter's figures were smaller than those cited by customs officials on her register. Harrison's description serves as a good example of the Baltimore schooners used as traders and cruisers because the *Delille* served in both roles. Didier, after using her as a letter-of-marque trader, converted her into the privateer *Syren* in 1814.[55]

The speed of the Baltimore schooners baffled their pursuers and made the vessels objects of nautical curiosity. Schooner logs and newspaper extracts listed numerous chases that left the British far behind. When captured, Baltimore schooners were sometimes brought into the British navy where sailors and captains, inexperienced in the handling of such creations, tried unsuccessfully to sail them. They were seldom over 100.0 feet in length although the two largest, the *Chasseur* of 115.6 feet and the *Mammoth* of 112.0 feet, exceeded the average length.[56] Under some nautical conditions they were difficult to maneuver, but their speed usually permitted them to choose their position so that maneuvering was not always a critical factor. Baltimore seamen had long experience with such vessels, but even they were not anxious to head a schooner around the Horn too often or to remain long in northern latitudes with ice-laden sails on light rigging. The Baltimore creations were effective but dangerous instruments to operate in rough waters and were best suited for the more temperate zones where their unique characteristics were utilized to the greatest advantage.

The effectiveness of the Baltimore schooners encouraged others to copy their design, but such efforts were seldom successful. In 1812 Jefferson encouraged the use of those "swiftest vessels on the ocean" as raiders and noted, "the British cannot counter-work us by building similar ones, because, the fact is, however accountable, that our builders alone understand the construction."[57] The shipbuilders built by eye and kept their ideas regarding design to themselves well into the 1820s.

The swiftness or "fast clip" of the Baltimore schooner encouraged the widespread use of the term "Baltimore Clipper" in the 1830s and 1840s, but that distinctive phrase was also applied to the schooners used during the War of 1812. Two Baltimore merchants noted three days after the Declaration of War that "Six Clippers are fitting out at the Point as Privateers, all of them will be ready for Sea probably in Ten Days" and added, "Our Baltimore Boats are admirably well adapted to the purposes and there seems to be no want of enterprize here."[58] Important to neutrals, speed was absolutely essential to a belligerent America.

The speed of the Baltimore schooners in all kinds of weather was so accepted by those acquainted with nautical matters that the loss of one demanded an explanation. Word that George Stiles's $40,000 letter-of-marque *Siro* had been captured prompted an editor to write, "We presume she must have been laboring under some peculiarly adverse circumstances when taken."[59] Another schooner, the *Racer*, was only three hours out of Baltimore when government dispatches arrived for her. Her agent and part-owner, George Pitt Stevenson, reported that "being a very fleet sailor no means could be taken to put them on board."[60] The same vessel, cornered and captured in the Rappahannock River eight months later, was the object of a ransom effort. It was reported that the British were so impressed with the vessel that the British admiral reportedly laughed at Stevenson, saying, "He would not take a Frigate for her and would not part with her on any account."[61] The captain of the schooner *Sylph* reported in January of 1815, that his 1812 Talbot County-built vessel was so swift that he had no need to fear anything afloat.[62] Another compliment to the speed and handling of the Baltimore schooner was paid by the British when they captured the expensive privateer *Tom*. They told the British public that she was a "remarkably fine vessel" that had "by her superior sailing escaped from eighteen of His Majesty's Cruisers."[63]

Further testimony to the speed of the schooners came from Captain Edward Veazey of the *Lawrence*, a privateer, when he reported to part-owner and agent Richard H. Douglass as he cleared the Chesapeake Bay that "the schooner sails beyond my most sanguine expectation." He later sent word from Europe by a prize master that he had spoken the privateer *Yankee* out of Bristol. With pride he stated, "We tried our sailing with her and beat her in every way," while reporting that he had been chased on the same day by four British war vessels and had "escaped easily."[64] Other examples of relative speed exist, but Captain Joseph Almeda summed up the situation when he told a neutral captain that any thoughts of escape were unrealistic. His *Kemp* was so fast that to try to outsail her, "You may as well try to catch a Bird flying."[65]

Henry Didier, Jr. constantly advised his correspondents to use Baltimore letter-of-marque schooners for his goods because they were hard to catch and, therefore, insurable. "You will ship in no Vessels but Baltimore built Schooners and no matter what part of France they shall sail from, by the schooners *Brutus*, *Ned*, *Inca*, *Engineer*, *Thetis*, or any first-rate Baltimore Schooner," he wrote his brother (and agent) in France. The vessels named were swift letter-of-marque traders that ran regularly between Baltimore and France, but Didier owned a part of the *Expedition* only. He reacted to the capture of one of his cargoes by saying, "had you shipped my goods by a Baltimore Vessel I should have received them, so that for the future you will ship by no other Vessels except first rate Baltimore Schooners." Finally, in October of 1813, he added, "Ship us no goods except in the first rate Baltimore Schooners for those vessels only can be insured."[66]

Premiums even for schooners were high. Insurers asked 50 percent of vessel and cargo value as a premium, forcing owners to seek alternatives to regular insurance. Didier stated that "owing to the impossibility of getting Insurance without paying fifty per cent," he was "determined on dividing my interest" in order to "be my own underwriter."[67] Such a technique was one motivating factor for the owners' habit of buying only a portion of any commissioned vessel, but others simply avoided insurance altogether. George Pitt Stevenson admitted in 1813 that he had made a mistake by not insuring a vessel. He lost $22,000 as a part-owner on the venture and considered it a meaningful loss.[68]

Even though speed was an important factor in avoiding capture, it was not an absolute guarantee of safety for cargo-laden commissioned traders trying repeatedly to slip in and out of ports guarded by the British fleet. The closer they came to a port in Europe or in the United States after the blockade was established, the more difficult it was to avoid the concentrated British warships. To stay at sea without risking entry was obviously financially disastrous. Entry had to be risked eventually, so letter-of-marque traders were lost.

It was essential that the sleek schooners not be overloaded. The Bosleys advertising in New York in 1813 for freight for Bordeaux for their "very superior fast sailing Baltimore Schooner *Ned*, burthen 278 tons, copper fastened and coppered," advised their potential customers of their awareness of load limits. They stated that the *Ned* was "completely armed and equipped" and had an "entire new suit of the best Holland Dutch Sails, and will be loaded to her best known sailing trim only."[69] Few wanted to risk speed by overloading cargo, or in the case of cargo-carrying vessels, to risk capsizing by adding unnecessary guns. The *Ned* carried only six guns and yet, as the Bosleys said, she was completely armed for a letter-of-marque trader. More cargo meant more income but it also increased the chances of being captured.

The speed of the ubiquitous Baltimore schooners served the entire nation by carrying the largest proportion of the nation's trade that got to sea during the war. Editor Hezekiah Niles commented in January of 1814 on that fact as the racers arrived home with regularity and noted, "These wonderfully constructed schooners cannot easily be taken, if not over-loaded, if they have sea room and are uncrippled, and properly managed." He added, "we have lost but four of our privateers — one of them was landlocked and taken in the Chesapeake Bay — one was captured after a severe gale in which she suffered much — one was given up by cowardice, and the other was taken for want of a good look-out." Niles summed up their capabilities by noting, "They go where they please; they chase and come up with everything they see, and run away at pleasure." In April of 1815, when the returning *Chasseur* was saluted at Fort McHenry, Niles observed, in reverence:

> She is, perhaps, the most beautiful vessel that ever floated in the ocean, those who have not seen our schooners have but little idea of her appearance. As you look at her you may easily figure to yourself the idea that she is about to rise out of the water and fly in the air, seeming to set so lightly upon it![70]

Once a vessel, usually a schooner, was acquired, preparations were made by the husband and the captain to ready her for wartime sea duty. If the vessel were used, repairs had to be made; if the vessel were new, sails, armament, and supplies were required. Even a previously owned vessel had to have guns and rigging added, gunports cut, and bulwarks strengthened. Thomas Kemp altered the masts and spars of the *Rolla* for William Hollins and did the same for the letter-of-marque *Express*, both in 1812.[71] Charles F. Kalkman, husband and prize agent of the privateer *Caroline*, built in 1809, put that vessel into Joseph Despeaux's Fells Point shipyard for a month in the fall of 1813 before she went to sea as a privateer. The vessel was not new and had many expensive items on board already, including most of her sails and rope. However, she required tarring and caulking, spikes and other metal work, as well as alterations and replacements in her rig. Six spars ranging from eighteen feet to thirty feet in length and four spars ranging from three and one-half inches to five inches in diameter were installed. The largest spar cost only $6.87 as lumber was available near Baltimore and was cheap. Many feet of timber were also added, perhaps to reinforce the sides and the bulwarks.[72]

The *Caroline* had some food on board, particularly barrels of bread and vegetables such as beans, so Despeaux provided few provisions. He did supply, however, seven barrels of beef at $13.50 each and seven barrels of pork at $18.00 each. It is possible that other items were added later by chandlers and grocers.[73]

The shipyard added some of the mixed armament so common to the Baltimore schooners. One long twelve-pound cannon and two six-pound carronades were put on the *Caroline*, all for $450.00. Ammunition in the form of 984 pounds of twelve-pound shot and 105 pounds of double-headed shot were taken on. About 1,100 pounds of grape cannister and langrage to use against personnel and sails were added by Despeaux and about 1,100 pounds of six-pound shot were included in the bill. Some four-pound shot for guns on the *Caroline* before Despeaux added his, cartridge formers, cartridges, gun screws, rammers, and sponges were also purchased from Despeaux. Powder weighing 121 pounds was included in the final bill of $1,279.00 for what was a partially seaworthy vessel before Despeaux even started his work. The owners, as was customary, paid Despeaux $5.00 for five gallons of rum for the workers and for twenty-one days wharfage at $1.00 per day. Labor costs included thirty-eight and a half days use of carpenters at $1.87½ per day, thirty-seven and one-half days use of caulkers at $1.50 per day and four and one-half days use of "boys" at $1.00 per day. Additionally, supervision, in the form of Despeaux's attendance, cost $2.00 per day for nine days. Despeaux accepted an owner's share in partial payment of his bill, which represented only partial preparation, as the owners had set aside, as noted previously, $7,125.00 for preparatory costs.[74]

In 1812 the Baltimore schooners utilized sails made of American or foreign cotton duck rather than the flaxen sails used before that date and by the navy after that date. Cotton sails held their shape better, were lighter, and required less wetting down to catch a wind than flaxen sails. They were whiter than the flaxen sails and, consequently, helped to identify the American schooners at sea.[75] A "rakish-looking schooner" was identified as American by a captain by the "set of her masts, cut of her sails and color of the canvas."[76] The letter-of-marque *Ned* was advertised as a swift sailer because she had an "entire new suit of the best Holland Dutch Sails."[77] Domestically produced cotton duck, originating in Massachusetts in 1809, was shipped to Baltimore by wagon. Its price reached one dollar per yard during the war, and one Baltimorean handled $20,000 worth in 1812 and 1813 alone.[78] The Union Mills near Ellicott's Mills on the western side of Baltimore manufactured the product also.[79] One of its directors, George Williams, was an active investor in private armed vessels. Investors in private armed vessels such as John Randall, the firms of Von Kapff and Brune, Brown and Hollins, and others offered sail duck for sale during the war years.[80]

The war curtailed the importation of sail duck, but there was enough on hand for one John Goodwin, a relative of active investor Lyde Goodwin, to sell "Sail Duck" worth $17,800 to the navy in 1814.[81] Captains of private armed vessels took advantage of every opportunity to get duck. The crew of the *Kemp*, for example, removed "a new Main Top Gallant Sail" from a prize at sea.[82] The sails and rigging, along with the armament of a commissioned vessel, were of sufficient value to warrant special attention when a vessel went out of service even temporarily. Captain Edward Veazey of the privateer *Lawrence* promised to "deposit the sails, rigging and armament with the agents" at Wilmington, North Carolina, while he proceeded to Baltimore to consult with the owners.[83] A shortage of such a valuable and vital product invited bold entrepreneurial action. Peter Arnold Karthaus dispatched his swift letter-of-marque schooners *Thetis* and *Engineer* for "Dutch Canvas" in 1813. That canvas was later advertised for sale in New York, Philadelphia, and Baltimore.[84]

Sails were not an inexpensive item among the costs of preparation. The privateer *Amelia* had over $1,600 in sheeting, cotton duck, and Russian sheeting listed in her disbursements. The letter-of-marque *Thetis* spent over $800 on eight pieces of "Sail Duck," for her top and lower sails.[85] The sails were replacements for those worn out in the *Thetis*'s first three voyages.

For fire power, the Baltimore private armed vessels depended on a mixed armament. At least one long gun was utilized in most cases as it gave the captain his greatest range. If mounted on a carriage, it moved from gunport to gunport upon demand, and since the schooners seldom carried as many guns as they had gunports, little inconvenience resulted. Such "Long Toms" were the first voice heard by an intended victim. When a long gun's mounting permitted traversing, it was called a "pivot gun." The bulk of the armament was, however, made up of shorter and lighter "carronades." Modeled on those originally designed at

England's Carron Foundry in the eighteenth century, they were very common in the United States by the War of 1812. They threw the same weight shot for a lesser distance than the long guns but were more quickly reloaded and, in privateers, generally replaced long guns of less than twelve pounds. Captain Boyle's *Comet*, as an example, carried two long nine-pounders and ten twelve-pound carronades while letter-of-marque traders were content with four or six carronades as gun weight only lessened their speed and stability.[86]

Not all sea commanders favored carronades. Captain David Porter of the United States frigate *Essex* stated, "Considering as I do that Carronades are merely an experiment in modern warfare and that their character is by no means established I do not conceive it proper to trust the honor of the flag entirely to them."[87] Porter was afraid that a disabled warship armed with carronades would be at the mercy of an opponent's long guns. Commanders of privateers armed with one long gun and carronades did not share his concern because they normally avoided heavily armed warships. Large guns became weight and balance problems on highly rigged schooners, whose favorite tactic was not bombardment but boarding. Damage to an opponent's hull from long guns only reduced the prize master's chances of getting her into a friendly port while lowering the prize's value at auction. The quickly loaded, shorter range carronades in sizes from six to twenty-four pounds suited commissioned vessels.

Baltimoreans acquired guns from local iron foundries, from the navy, and from prize vessels with little difficulty until 1814. Owners of the port's private armed vessels profited from sales of guns to private vessels just as they did from the sale of provisions. Thomas Tenant advertised six twelve-pounders and twenty smaller guns for sale in September of 1813.[88] John Despeaux, shipbuilder and private armed vessel owner, sold four long six-pounders to Andrew Clopper for $65.00 each in 1813.[89] Purchases were also made from the navy as the commander of the Washington Navy Yard was instructed in one of numerous cases to "Please deliver to bearer Mr. George Douglass of Baltimore, one twelve-pound cannon, obligation payable on sight" at $133.33 per ton.[90] John Dorsey's cannon and anchor foundries provided both items to the navy and the private service. Several other foundries such as Hughes at Principio and the Cecil foundry at Havre de Grace, both located northeasterly of Baltimore, and Ridgely's, near the city, also provided long guns, carronades, and shot. Ridgely's furnace advertised cannon balls for sale in the *American* on October 7, 1812.[91] Commodore John Rodgers, in taking command of the *Guerriere* at Philadelphia in 1814, found her armament to be thirty-three long twenty-four-pounders made at the Cecil Furnace and twenty forty-two-pound carronades cast at Dorsey's foundry near Baltimore.[92] The Dorsey works could not keep up with its orders because of a lack of steel for boring the gun tubes despite Dorsey's anguished pleas for steel.[93] With the shortages of guns in 1814, armament became an area where innovation was demanded of the husband, captain, and, of course, the gunners who handled the mixed armament in action. Peter Arnold Karthaus sold six guns to the "concern for the *Pike* and the *Bordeaux Packet*" in 1813 but by 1814 he was compelled to buy shot and guns from five other merchants and the navy for his own privateer *Amelia*.[94]

Prizes coming into Baltimore and other ports provided a source of guns, including a few brass pieces. Thomas Tenant purchased a pair of carronades for $110 and Hollins and McBlair purchased four pair of carronades for $280, all nine-pounders, off the *Tom*'s prize ship *Braganza*. The *Tom* was partially owned by Hollins and McBlair. Tenant, a prize agent, also purchased ten dollars' worth of "Shot and Langrage." Thorndike Chase purchased eighteen-pound carronades for $125 and Joseph Despeaux purchased one long six-pound cannon for $140 from the ship *Hopewell*, prize to Captain Boyle's *Comet*. Chase was a part-owner of the *Comet* and an active prize agent and, like the other owners purchasing prize items, probably realized a profit on their resale even when they sold them to their own private armed vessel. Other examples of investors purchasing prize guns were Isaac McKim and Levi Clagett who purchased guns off the *Comet*'s prize ship *Henry*.[95]

The acquisition of cannon at sea was another source of supply, but a vessel without guns was not in condition to subdue vessels with them. However, there were cases where it was done. Captain James Dooley of the *Rolla* flourished with one gun. Commodore Joshua Barney on the *Rossie* threw six guns over in a severe storm as the "sea struck on board." He had the carpenter construct wooden guns to impress any future victims or would be attackers, but Barney admitted they were a bad substitute. He was determined to get "more guns from the first Englishmen we meet with."[96] Unlike New York, Boston, or Connecticut, where one- or no-gun commissioned vessel clearances were common, Baltimore's fleet all cleared with at least one gun but normally with six or more carriage guns.

Small arms such as pistols, muskets, and cutlasses were also purchased at prize sales after the first months of the war. The navy found such items scarce in Baltimore.[97] Shipbuilder Joseph Despeaux sold Hollins and McBlair twenty-five boarding spikes and other items for the schooner *Hollins*. Despeaux also sold agent Andrew Clopper eighteen pairs of handcuffs for eighteen dollars.[98] Prisoners were an increasing threat to a vessel's security as her crew shrunk after manning prizes, and handcuffs and small arms could also be used on unruly members of hastily assembled crews. Pistols, muskets, and cutlasses were critical in boarding operations.

Small arms were advertised for sale in Baltimore by investors in private armed vessels. Among the numerous advertisers, Frederick C. Graf offered cutlasses at eight dollars per dozen, Von Kapff and Brune advertised French muskets, and Peter Arnold Karthaus offered for sale cutlasses that were "just the right kind for privateers." Another investor, William Hollins, offered 700 muskets at accommodating terms as the owners of the letter-of-marque traders serviced the privateers and each other, importing the needed small arms from France and the West Indies.[99] Captains supplemented their own supplies of small arms from prizes at sea, while owners in port were able to purchase them at prize sales. A prudent captain seldom left large supplies of small arms on a prize when part of her crew was still on board because his prize masters had problems enough without the prospects of prisoner revolts. Finally, in reference to small arms, a captain needed both small arms and cannon. The *Leo* tried to cruise out of France with too few cannon and had to surrender when her small armament proved inadequate against British warships.[100] Peter Arnold Karthaus sold muskets to two vessels in 1813, but in 1814 he had to scramble around for small arms for his *Amelia*. He bought them from fellow-investors George Stiles, William Hollins, Charles Gwinn, and others.[101]

Gunpowder was manufactured in Baltimore but was also available from the DuPont factories in nearby Delaware. Advertisements offered DuPont's "double battle Powder" for large and small guns, Brandywine Gunpowder from the Quaker firm of Mitchell and Sheppard, and Bellona Gunpowder Factory products for sale over the names of private armed vessel owner John Diffenderffer and Gerrard T. Hopkins. One seller offered his gunpowder in assorted types and sizes "so as to be suitable for privateers" whose mixed armament required a variety of powders.[102] Purchases of gunpowder at prize auctions were motivated by low auction prices as well as by scarcity. The privateer *Amelia*'s gunpowder, bought of Nathan Levering, cost $540.[103]

A husband procuring for his vessel also needed water casks, rope, and, as a substitute for the bulkier stones and gravel, pig iron for ballast. For rope, Russian hemp was preferred to American hemp, which rotted more easily. Hemp was still sent to Baltimore from Kentucky, where it was reported the city of Lexington manufactured one-half million dollars' worth in 1814, and was advertised for sale when the blockade kept out foreign supplies.[104] One dealer advertised four- to nine-inch "cables" of "water-rolled hemp from Kentucky and twice as strong as any imported hemp" as well as "Standing and Running Rigging of all sizes."[105] James Piper, owner of a ropewalk and part-owner of the commissioned schooner *Fairy*, promised reduced prices on yarns and cordage "to Owners of Privateers."[106] One "ropemaker's" bill for the *Eutaw* indicates the expense of that item, as he billed owner John Price $1,871.49 for rope work.[107] The port had many ropewalks. When the British attacked Baltimore in 1814, two American regiments of infantry regulars were billeted in eight ropewalks located in just one section of Baltimore.[108]

Three anchors were commonly used on Baltimore schooners, and William H. Dorsey had an anchor factory on Federal Hill in the city. Anchors ran about three or four hundred pounds a piece and were sold for about fifteen cents per pound.[109] Peter Arnold Karthaus paid $11.52 for one anchor and $107.55 for another of 717 pounds for the *Amelia*.[110] The anchor factory had to compete for iron because of the demand for it by cannon and shot makers as well as marine blacksmiths.

As mentioned in the case of the *Caroline*'s preparation, barrels of beef and other provisions were also purchased. Privateer captain and historian George Coggeshall, preparing for a cruise of fifty days, purchased for his crew of 80 to 100 men three tons of bread, thirty barrels of beef, and fifteen barrels of pork as well as other provisions.[111] With its flour supply, mills, and roads leading in from the west, Baltimore was in a position to provide the necessary provisions. Its chandlers and grocers may have accepted owner's shares in payment, accepted terms, or held out for cash, but regardless of the method of compensation, they competed vigorously for the trade. As much as the other tradesmen, they needed substitutes for their great prewar ship supply business. One urged, "Privateersmen Attend!!!" when he offered 3,000 "excellent Salt Petred Venison Hams" for sale.[112] Active investor George Williams offered "New Beef and Hams, suitable for ship Stores," and the firm of Stiles and Williams offered, at the "Sign of the Tea Chest," groceries and "Sea Stores" at the shortest notice.[113] As they had in the case of arms, investors in private armed vessels sold provisions to the private service and realized yet another profit from that system.

Provisions for a privateer's crew were a significant expenditure. The *Amelia* in 1814 purchased pork, hams, corned beef, codfish, coffee, and other items, costing $4,000 from grocers and chandlers. Again, other private investors were often the suppliers. Joel Vickers, George Wolpert, bakers Lovell and Sultzer, Captain John Joseph Lane, James Ramsay, and the Baltimore Water Company were all paid for provisions, water, and water casks loaded on the privateer *Amelia*.[114]

George William Norris, advertising groceries and sea stores when the war opened, informed "those engaged in Privateering, that the most particular attention will be paid having the goods made-up of nice qualities, in good order and on moderate terms."[115] Supplies were less numerous in the last year of the war when the private fleet, the navy, and the army, as well as the general population, drew on existing supplies, while local farmers were reticent to enter a city threatened by the guns of the British fleet. In November of 1814 groceries were actually cheaper in Philadelphia than Baltimore.[116] Colonial products such as sugar and coffee were available in port after the letter-of-marque flyers loaded the warehouses. The privateers' penchant for feeding their men well was illustrated by an attempted mutiny on the *Lawrence*. The cause of the mutinous behavior was not that the food was inadequate, but simply that it and liquor were reduced "to that usually allowed on board of Ships of War of the United States."[117] Court depositions suggest that while food and grog were plentiful on privateers and adequate on national vessels, they were sometimes insufficient on the letter-of-marque traders. Seamen anticipated a daily grog ration but settled for it at least three times a week.[118]

Stores or provisions were replenished in other ports or at sea either from prizes or in the form of purchases from neutrals. The *Wasp* stopped a small vessel of twenty-one tons and "took out some Yams and coffee and let go." The same privateer bought a barrel of sugar for twenty-two dollars from another vessel and when short, served out a pound of pork, a pound of bread, and "plenty of peace" for each man per day. Near the end of the voyage, with provisions dwindling, the men survived on one-half pound of bread per man daily and "as much Turtle Soup as they can devour." The *Kemp's* log noted that two essentials, rum and cordage, were taken out of a prize vessel when needed by the privateer.[119] Captains were permitted to remove items for the use of their vessel, and they usually had a need for food toward the end of a long cruise or voyage.

Clothing was the responsibility of the individual crew members, and the owners accepted no responsibility for providing such items. They did sell clothing on board and owners William and James Bosley provided, at their own cost, winter clothing for the *Tartar's* crew. To outfit himself, a crew member was able to sell part or all of his prize ticket or to spend his small advance from the owners. One court dispute illustrated the cost when a store owner outfitted and loaned money in exchange for a prize ticket. Hezekiah Joel signed onto the *Rolla* in Massachusetts and was sold shirts from $2.00 to $4.00 each, a jacket, a "Superfine Coat ($35.00)," hose, and braces. His shoes cost $2.00, and his two pairs of "Duck Trowsers" were $1.50 a piece. He also purchased, among other items, a mattress, two blankets for $6.00 each, a sea chest for $5.00, and, perhaps for shore use, an umbrella. Joel was outfitted with thirty items for a total of $181.00 according to the store owners.[120] He obviously got what he could for his shares in the *Rolla* while others were content to use their fifteen dollars advance to outfit themselves in a less splendid fashion. Where Joel, perhaps a "greenhand," expected to use a mattress on the crowded *Rolla* is uncertain. Even hammocks were a luxury below decks where space was scarce.

There were other ways to fill the need for clothing. Cotton duck trousers were commonly sewn together from old sails by the seamen. Prize vessels provided clothing also but not always as spoils of war. The *Kemp* sold its own crew $632.75 worth of clothes taken from the prize *Lady Mary Pelham*, but that sum then became part of the *Kemp's* prize account. Seaman John Barnes's account with the agent of the *Kemp* listed $26.00 owed by Barnes for trousers or "slops" purchased on board the vessel.[121]

Charts, compasses, sextants, and other nautical items were available in Baltimore, particularly at Fells Point. James Ramsay, part-owner of the privateers *Sarah Ann*, *Caroline*, and *Fairy*, operated the best-known chandlery and grocery in Fells Point. He advertised charts, compasses, quadrants, sextants, day and night telescopes, lamps, rules, scales, dividers, and other items for sale in October of 1812. Another advertisement placed by John Allen of Thames Street in Fells Point boasted that his was the new and only manufactury in Baltimore of ships' compasses, quadrants, and other instruments and that he also gave navigation lessons.[122]

Navigational instruments were another item taken from prizes at sea. Captain Thomas Boyle of the famous *Comet*, in response to a charge that he had kept prize items for himself and the owners, admitted that nautical instruments were taken from prizes. From the prize ship *John*, Boyle said he also took out among other items signals, canvas, twine, grap shot, and other arms while also distributing liquor and a "few pigs" among the crew. From the *Henry* he took shot, powder, and sailcloth, while the *Hopewell* provided ammunition as well as coffee and sugar, which were "divided among the crew" and a "few Teripins" when the *Comet*'s stores were depleted.[123]

Physical preparations were completed by the addition of navigational instruments. Six weeks were usually required for all preparations but only four were required in some cases. The privateer *Tom* cleared one month after she was launched. Costs, in the case of first rate vessels, went higher than $40,000, but the vessels themselves, according to surviving records, maintained their value reasonably well. Baltimore Congressman Alexander McKim on November 9, 1814, estimated privateer vessel costs at thirty to thirty-five dollars per ton with schooners over 350 tons costing more.[124] The bulk of Baltimore's private armed fleet was new, expensive, and under 350 tons. Investors expected to spend $25,000 for a first class trading schooner and $40,000 or more for a privateer ready for sea. Those seeking a vessel in peak months such as the last months of 1812 and the weeks before the establishment of the British blockade in February of 1813 found few available. "We have not Ships here" one observer noted in December of 1812, but that was a period of high demand when there was a brisk trade to Europe and the West Indies and no blockade of the Chesapeake.[125] When schooners were available, high prices bought speed. The escape of the *Grampus* and the *Patapsco* from the pursuing frigate *La Hague* reportedly motivated the frigate's exasperated captain to rip off his epaulets and throw them on the deck in disgust.[126]

The experience of the Revolution, which saw larger privateers with larger crews as the war progressed, was repeated in the War of 1812. The initial seven privateers out of Baltimore in the summer of 1812 averaged 155 tons and 97 men. Seven privateers reported at sea when the war ended, however, averaged 286 tons each, while the average crew size rose to 116 men.[127] Obviously, the owners sent larger vessels farther away in their search for prizes.

A vessel was ready for clearance, and the husband's job was nearly completed when all the preparations were completed. Christopher Deshon placed a notice in the newspaper as the *Rossie* prepared to clear port, stating that "All persons having bills against the schooner *Rossie*, will please hand them for settlement, in all this week."[128] The payment of these large bills by Deshon and other husbands was essential to the smaller businessmen and craftsmen because the private armed vessel operations served as the major substitute for their normal peacetime maritime business. Those payments also enriched other investors selling items to a private venture. The *Rossie*, of course, had just completed one other important managerial task before she actually weighed anchor. That task involved the recruitment of a crew.

EIGHT

The Shipping of Hands

Completion of the business and documentary aspects of a private armed vessel venture and the procurement and preparation of a vessel left the husband and captain with only one major task. They had to recruit a crew. The husband of a venture had to retain some of the concern's initial capital for recruitment expenses and advances to the crew of the privateer. Previous emphasis on owners, documents, and equipment had now to be diverted toward the hands.

Baltimore's Fells Point anchorage had been a popular rendezvous for public, private, and foreign vessels for decades. Seamen considered service on private armed vessels during the War of 1812 attractive until the British blockaded Baltimore early in 1813. A privateersman of the War of 1812, "for many years Captain in the Merchant Service out of the Port of Baltimore, but now entirely blind," described the scene he had witnessed in Baltimore just fifteen days after the Declaration of War. He recalled that the "most active preparations were in progress to prosecute the war," and, "a number of privateers were fitting out; and everywhere the American flag might be seen flying, denoting the place of rendezvous; in a word, the most intense excitement prevailed throughout the city."[1]

Neither crowded conditions on the private armed vessels nor the risks of combat deterred recruits in the early months of war. The potential or imagined rewards were great for seamen. Even those without nautical experience were attracted to the service because it was an adventuresome and possibly lucrative alternative to the plowing of a Harford County farm or a dull job in town. Such men seldom signed on letter-of-marque traders because those vessels carried fewer men than a privateer and seamen were preferred. Seamen on such vessels earned a wage and prize money and, consequently, the commissioned traders were more appealing than noncommissioned vessels on their way to Spain. Employing three or four times as many hands as a letter-of-marque trader, a privateer needed boys, marines, cooks, clerks, and others without nautical skills. The privateer crews, however, received no pay when there were no prizes. That eventuality was probably ignored by eager recruits.

Many vessels were outfitting in Baltimore in the first six months of the war, but later the guns of the British fleet intimidated seamen hoping to reach salt water. Early in the war a recruit had plenty of choice, but after the blockade he had plenty of risk. Those two conditions explain the absence of competition for positions on the private armed vessels after the initial rush to sea. The fervent move for employment witnessed in Philadelphia and Charleston was not repeated in Baltimore except for Commodore Barney's famous privateer *Rossie*. A Philadelphia commander was obliged to draw lots from numerous applicants before completing his ship's complement "in less than one hour." In Charleston, the *Saucy Jack* opened a rendezvous and signed on 130 "able-bodied seamen" in six hours. An editor responded to that event by commenting, "Probably such a thing is unprecedented even in this country, however remarkable her maritime enterprize."[2] Baltimore's husbands and captains faced more competition in their efforts to acquire full crews.

Service in private armed vessels had its advantages over navy service. The potential for financial gain was greater, there was less desperate combat with warships, and less time was wasted in shipyards. The navy's efforts to man its Jeffersonian gunboats in Baltimore ran afoul of the private service's attractions. Gunboats would not take many prizes. A navy officer reported ten days after the Declaration of War, "I have recruited four or five men notwithstanding the great inducement held out by the owners of Privateers." Three weeks later he wrote that recruiting would take more time because "There are so many Privateers fitting at this Port," and eleven days later, after a squadron of private armed vessels had sailed, he added, "as respects seamen we find it almost impossible to procure *one*, they having nearly all gone in Privateers." In November of 1812, the same officer noted, "in consequence of the impossibility to procure a single man for the Gun Boats on this station" he had "deemed it expedient to close that rendezvous."[3] A report dated September of 1813 from another source repeated identical concern when recruits were sought for a navy sloop being constructed in Baltimore. The desire to open one rendezvous early was motivated by the fact that "the merchants of Baltimore having commenced the equipment of Privateers and Letters of Marque," and an awareness that as soon as those vessels were ready for sea it would be "impossible to procure men."[4] In October of 1812, a Baltimore newspaper advised New England or "Eastern Sailors" that "Seamen are in great demand in Baltimore at thirty dollars per month."[5]

Fells Point was a popular rendezvous during war and a regular stop for navy recruiters. In 1798 Captain Thomas Truxtun directed the *Constellation*'s Lieutenant John Rodgers "to open a Rendezvous at the house of Mr. Cloney, at Fells Point in the City of Baltimore." He wanted 220 men and would pay recruiting agent James Cloney one dollar per recruit.[6] Cloney performed the same service in the War of 1812 on orders, not from the navy, but from the captains and husbands of private armed vessels.

Recruitment was sometimes the sole responsibility of the captain of a private armed vessel. This was justified by the fact that he handled the hastily assembled crew at sea. John Randall, sole owner and husband of the letter-of-marque schooner *Contradiction*, pleaded ignorance when asked by the District Court to verify the service of a particular carpenter on his vessel. With "The shipping of hands being entrusted to the Captain," Randall knew nothing of the ten men on his schooner.[7] In such cases the husband paid the captain a lump sum for his recruiting efforts.

Captains and ship's husbands resorted to recruiting agents whenever they needed more than a handful of men in times of heavy competition. The agents owned boarding houses, groceries, stores, or grog shops on the waterfront where a rendezvous could be established. Joseph Despeaux paid boarding house keeper Daniel James $30.00 for "Shipping Seamen" onto his ship *Alexander* six months before the war started.[8] Despeaux's needs were apparently small but those of the private armed vessels were large. On September 7, 1813, husband Peter Arnold Karthaus paid $400.00 to the same boarding house keeper, Daniel James, for "Shipping Hands" and then paid him $300 more on October 1, 1813. Those men were needed on the letter-of-marque schooner *Thetis*. For a privateer recruitment was often a heavy expense. The privateer *Amelia* cost Karthaus almost $3,000.00 for recruitment without considering the crew's advances. He paid the captain $1,200.00 in four payments "to ship Crew" and paid $1,500.00 to "Ship Sailors" in Philadelphia. Karthaus also paid grocer and boarding house keeper Jacob Myers $107.00 and disbursed another $24.13 to an unspecified person for the same service.[9]

Baltimore had other recruiting agents serving the owners, captains, and seamen. Fells Point grocer and "water man" James Hooper, liquor and grocery store proprietor James Cloney, and boarding house keeper Daniel James engaged in that role along with lawyer William Morrow, tavern and boarding house keeper John Needham, boarding house keeper James Norris, mariner Fitz King, innkeepers Henry Begot and John Degrassier, and others.[10] Recruits received an advance when they signed on and the recruiting agents signed as security for their actual appearance on board at clearance. Two of the *Amelia*'s men, for example, failed to appear so the owners collected $116.32 from their agents or sureties.[11] The same recruiting agents also served as business agents for individual seamen when armed with a power of attorney. The crewmen were often away when prize monies were distributed.[12]

Recruiting agents performed other functions. They were in a position to lend money and to provide clothes, food, drink, and lodging to seamen. In return, they were sometimes given all or part of a seaman's prize ticket. They also purchased large numbers of prize tickets, often at discount prices because seamen were not in a position to drive hard bargains. On occasion, however, seamen sold one ticket twice, perhaps deliberately. One case involving popular recruiting agent and ticket purchaser Fitz King, resulted in a seaman's confession that he sold his ticket twice. The seaman admitted that he did not "know it at the time, being very much intoxicated."[13] Merchant firms such as Agnew and Campbell also served as seamen's agents and purchasers of prize tickets. Active owner, merchant, and prize agent Thomas Tenant held a power of attorney for at least sixty of the *Highflyer*'s crew, while grocer James Cloney signed as security for seventeen men on that privateer.[14] Fees or portions of prize tickets paid to a variety of agents serving seamen disseminated some of the income from the private armed vessel system among a broader segment of Baltimore's population.

Those serving as agents for the seamen were compensated for their services in various ways. One-fourth of a prize ticket was a popular payment, while survivor's rights were sometimes combined with that fractional share. Survivor's rights alone sufficed in some cases, while others charged a simple commission. Lawyer William Morrow agreed to manage the prize funds of seaman John Barry of the *Comet* for a 2.5 percent commission "as a premium."[15] The agents' risks included the chance that a vessel would be unproductive or lost. When he signed as a security for advances to seamen, he incurred some large risks. The *Tom*'s advances in Baltimore before clearance amounted to $2,105. Individual advances were seldom higher than $30, but some owners were more generous than others. The "cabin cook" on the *Fox* was advanced but $8. Daniel James signed (his X) for forty-six men onto the privateer *Pike* and served as security for eleven of them.[16] The *Pike* was only one of many vessels for which James provided men during the war years. He and others had relatively large sums at stake.

Captains and agents for private armed vessels competed not only with the navy but with noncommissioned traders for seamen. Fifteen such noncommissioned vessels cleared from Baltimore in the period from December of 1811 to December of 1812. Their crew lists show a dependence on blacks and youngsters as actual nautical operatives and not merely as supplementary hands. Of the 195 crewmen whose ages were given on noncommissioned traders, 54 percent were twenty-four or younger and about 16 percent were black. Young men and blacks were used in peacetime, but cases such as the noncommissioned schooner *Fox* en route to the West Indies suggest that there were recruitment problems. That vessel sailed with only five men, including two eleven-year-old boys. The brig *Charles* cleared for Oporto with seven men, including five blacks, while the brig *Baltimore* cleared with nine men including a first mate of twenty-one and a second mate of twenty.[17] Noncommissioned full-rigged three-masted ships cleared with only one-third or one-half of the men used on smaller letter-of-marque traders. Even fifteen men were insufficient to man three masts twenty-four hours a day. Noncommissioned vessels were obviously losing men to commissioned vessels but the men they recruited were not available for private armed vessels. Merchant vessels returning from voyages immediately before or during the war provided experienced and eager hands for private armed vessels.

Letter-of-marque trading schooners shipped more men than noncommissioned traders but far fewer than privateers. Surviving crew lists for twenty-five commissioned traders show 90 percent carrying fewer men than proposed in their applications.[18] The *Brutus*, for example, proposed fifty men but cleared with only thirty-seven. Performing as a letter-of-marque trader, the *Rossie* proposed thirty-five men but cleared with twenty-eight. Others cleared with three or four fewer men than proposed. The use of an eight-year-old "apprentice boy of Colour" and a four-feet, three-inch boy with a "light and freckled complexion, blue eyes, and light hair" may have reflected a shortage of men.[19] Boys were commonly used in various roles at sea, however, even in wartime.[20] Of the 537 men whose ages were given, seventeen were under fifteen and ninety-five were under eighteen.[21] That was too many for them all to be cabin boys or powder monkeys.

Baltimore's commissioned traders were handled by young men and a few blacks rather than by "old salts." Of those whose ages were listed 64 percent were twenty-four or younger and 80 percent were under twenty-eight. Only fifteen men, including some mates, were over forty years of age. The blacks listed on the traders numbered thirty-nine, a much smaller portion than used by the noncommissioned vessels. Several vessels, however, carried unusual numbers of blacks. The *Sylph* headed for Bordeaux with twenty-four men among whom ten "men of color" listed Maryland as their birthplace. Other vessels used freemen and slaves belonging to the captain, an owner, or persons not interested in the vessel, but no blacks were listed among the officers. The letter-of-marque *Pilot* employed a twenty-two-year-old first mate and a nineteen-year-old second mate, both white.[22] High rewards for officers on the privateers enticed older, experienced, and available officers away from the traders.

Surviving crew lists for twenty-five letter-of-marque vessels contained the birthplaces of only 246 men. They often listed Baltimore as their residence at their signing, but 19 percent were born in Massachusetts, 13 percent in Louisiana, and 12 percent each in Pennsylvania and New York. Another 10 percent were born abroad, with Germany and Sweden the most popular origins of the foreign born. The sample suggests that over the years the young port of Baltimore collected seamen from the bay area, from other American ports, and from abroad. They were apparently attracted by the same growth in shipping that had drawn many of the merchant owners and captains to the Patapsco River. Letter-of-marque schooners required a high proportion of actual seamen on board, carrying no marines or landsmen and only a few hands who were not required to handle sails. The letter-of-marque *Flight*'s crew was typical. That vessel cleared for Bordeaux with twenty-eight men after proposing thirty. There were three mates, a boatswain, a gunner, a black cook, and twenty-two seamen.[23] The 216-ton letter-of-marque schooner *Engineer* was manned by two mates, a supercargo, a boatswain, a gunner, a carpenter, a cook, a steward, twenty-six seamen, and her captain when she fell prey to the British off Puerto Rico in 1814.[24] Prewar and noncommissioned wartime schooners functioned with a complement about one-half the size of their commissioned counterparts. Two noncommissioned Baltimore schooners, *Coquette* and *Netterville*, for example, utilized only thirteen or fourteen officers and crewmen during the war years.[25] Additional crewmen on letter-of-marque traders handled the guns, boarded and manned prizes, and provided for the vessel's general defense. Recruiting agents sought men with some knowledge of sails and guns for such vessels.

Letter-of-marque traders did not invariably assign one-half of the prize proceeds to the officers and crew. The *Decatur*, ordered to proceed from New York "to Charleston and from thence to France and back to the United States," rejected the routine arrangement. The agreement her owners wrote for the crew specified that profits from her prizes:

> shall not in any case be proportioned in the manner prescribed for the government vessels of the United States but that the same shall be divided and proportioned as follows: that is to say, two thirds of all such prizes or the profits thereof are to belong to the owners, and the other one third to belong to the crew.[26]

Owners sharing two-thirds of the prize money were her agent, Richard H. Douglass (eleven-twenty-fourths), Cumberland Dugan Williams (six-twenty-fourths), and the firm of D'Arcy and Didier (four-twenty-fourths). The final three shares were assigned as an expense account to the "adventure of the *Decatur*."[27]

The officers and crew of the *Decatur* allocated their one-third of the prize proceeds in what was a fairly normal distribution. Captain George Montgomery was assigned sixteen shares and the first lieutenant nine shares, while seven shares were allowed the second mate. The petty officers, including a boatswain, a carpenter, and a gunner were allotted three shares each. Two shares each went to a cook, a steward, and to all the seamen, while the "boys" in the crew settled for one share each. Eight shares were not allocated to positions but were reserved for the "most deserving of the crew." They were to be awarded "as the Captain shall think just and proper."[28] Each crew member was given a prize ticket specifying his particular number of shares. The ticket, his name on the Articles of Agreement, and a certificate of discharge signed by the captain at the termination of the voyage provided proof to the prize agent that he was entitled to a portion of any prize money.

Shares in a letter-of-marque trader were supplementary to monthly wages. The going wartime wage for seamen was $30.00 to $35.00 per month, but a range of $20.00 to $50.00 existed. With few exceptions, the seamen earned more during the war than prior to it. An average of $22.50 per month was paid in 1812 on American vessels before the war.[29] Wages of seamen employed in the short West Indian run near the war's end were not superior. Baltimore seamen signing onto a Philadelphia-owned private armed vessel going to the West Indies in December of 1815 were paid only $20.00 per month. The captain reported later that sum was "the highest wage going in Baltimore" at the time and observed that he "could have had 200 at that rate."[30] Fluctuations in demand raised or lowered wages during the war.

Not all Baltimore letter-of-marque traders followed the distribution scheme employed by the *Decatur*. The *Baltimore* assigned her shares in twentieths with three going to Captain Edward Veazey. One-twentieth each went to the two mates, a boatswain, and a gunner, while twenty-eight seamen shared the remaining thirteen twentieths. The *Patapsco*'s extra petty officers left only eleven twentieths for its twenty-six seamen. One extra petty officer, assigned one-twentieth, was "clerk," supercargo, and active investor, Henry Holden.[31] Most owners who went to sea served as officers and while Holden's shares were allotted to him for his role as clerk, he was probably acting as supercargo or business manager at sea.

When no specific distribution plan existed, the owners and the officers and crew shared the prize proceeds equally according to law. In such cases the officers and crew were assigned individual shares according to a plan authorized by Congress in 1800.[32] There is no evidence that this plan was ever copied exactly by any but navy vessels. The private armed vessels accepted the use of twentieths from the congressional plan but then allocated them according to their own desires.

Privateer crews were recruited in a manner identical to that used by the letter-of-marque traders. Privateers demanded three or four times as many men as the traders, but one-third of them needed no nautical training or experience. Marines (sometimes called landsmen), cooks, stewards, clerks, surgeons, and others without seamen's papers were acceptable. Experienced officers and numerous petty officers were essential, however. Boatswains, armourers, sailmakers, gunners, carpenters, sailing masters, and other skilled petty officers as well as a body of experienced or able-bodied seamen were vital on a private man-of-war. Unable to furnish enough men for every vessel early in the war, Baltimore sent 1,538 men out in privateers alone by October 24, 1812. With the inclusion of crews of letter-of-marque traders, Baltimore recruited 2,800 to 3,000 men by that date.[33] Unsuccessfuly seeking 80 men in December of 1813, the privateer *Rolla* cleared Baltimore with a crew of only 40.[34] Unless the same men went out again and again, the total for the entire war period at least doubled the October, 1812 figure. Apparently men drifted in from neighboring farms or deserted their town jobs, while experienced seamen migrated to Baltimore from smaller bay ports and other American ports because Baltimore, even in the peak trading year of 1806, contained only 1,001 registered seamen.[35]

Arrangements among privateer crewmen for the distribution of prize proceeds were more complicated than those of commissioned traders. The *Highflyer's* Articles of Agreement were typical of privateer staffing and prize distribution schemes. The following plan was utilized:

1 Captain	14 shares
1 1st Lieutenant	9 shares
1 2nd Lieutenant	7 shares
1 Sailing Master	8 shares
1 Surgeon	8 shares
4 Prize Masters	6 shares each
1 Carpenter	4 shares
1 Gunner	4 shares
1 Boatswain	4 shares
1 Clerk	2½ shares
1 Drummer	2½ shares
1 Gunner's Mate	2½ shares
1 Ship's Steward	2½ Shares
1 Boatswain mate	2 shares
1 Carpenter's mate	2 shares
1 Captain's Steward	2½ shares
1 Cook	2 shares
1 Captain of the Forecastle	2 shares
2 Quartermasters	2 shares each
1 Armourer	2 shares
41 First Class seamen	2 shares each
11 Ordinary seamen	1½ shares each
13 Ordinary seamen	1 share each
1 Ordinary seaman	¾ share
1 Boy	1 share [36]

The assignment of 2.5 shares to the drummer suggests that boys did not occupy that position. It required exposure during combat and some drummers, including the one on the privateer *Globe*, were killed in action.[37] Ordinary seamen (eleven of them on *Highflyer*) were normally required to know the common duties of seamen in regard to ropes, sails, and some steering but were not required to be experts. First class or able-bodied seamen were expected to handle all facets of the watch, steering, anchoring, and everything to do with the sails.[38] The *Highflyer* carried forty-one of the all-important first class seamen at two shares each.

The *Highflyer's* articles listed a total of 220 shares for the officers and crew.

Eight and one-quarter "reserved" or "deserving" shares were unassigned in the articles. Two first class seamen names were followed by the notation, "runaway at Baltimore," and one ordinary seaman was marked "returned sick" and then "Discharged." Advances to the crew ranged from ten to thirty dollars except in the case of the surgeon who received seventy-five dollars. Sureties for crew advances were the usual recruiting agents as John Needham signed for sixteen men, James Cloney for seven, and Fitz King for three. Other privateers followed similar but not identical crew positions and distribution patterns.[39]

With the unusual demand for men in peak periods of activity, Baltimore vessels sought men elsewhere. The privateer *Rolla*'s log for November of 1812, only twenty days out of Baltimore, recorded stops at Bristol, Providence, Falmouth, and Boston for men. Her cruise terminated in December of 1812 "for want of officers and men." The privateer *Bona* entered at Norfolk for men, enrolling one black man after he gave proof that "he was not a slave."[40] Commodore Joshua Barney's *Rossie* "touched in at Newport, Rhode Island, for officers and men and proceeded to the West Indies."[41] A Baltimore merchant firm reported that vessels were scarce in December of 1812 and that no men were available when vessels were on hand.[42]

Some shortages resulted from combat losses at sea and from the manning of prizes. The *Syren* cleared with eighty men but in her effort to enter the blockaded Delaware River after a successful cruise, she was handled by only twenty men.[43] The fifty-five-ton *Wasp*, clearing with forty men, found it necessary to ship a boatswain, a seaman, and three Frenchmen at Charleston.[44] Joshua Barney reported the recruitment of six prisoners from prizes to the *Rossie* but carefully noted that they were not British subjects.[45] British subjects were not permitted to serve on American private armed vessels.[46] Apparently, some captains still enrolled them when they were desperate for men.[47] The privateer *Globe*'s journal contained a notation that seven prisoners had "entered" as seamen.[48] Captain Thomas Boyle of the *Chasseur* admitted that he "did accept the Services of some men he took prisoners." Boyle made them sign that they had signed on voluntarily, that they would obey regulations, and that they were to receive one share each.[49] A captain at sea took anyone he could find after his own crew began to shrink. New men might prolong a cruise and increase profits.

Recruiting agents also searched Baltimore for new men to sign onto privateers. Their search provided some recruits, but sometimes those men encountered legal difficulties when it was time to collect their prize money. One father claimed his son had been "lured" onto Captain Joseph Almeda's privateer *Caroline* and argued that the minor's prize money should be paid to him.[50] Runaways were another source of manpower. Numerous newspaper notices offered rewards for their return while cautioning captains about the illegality of hiring them. One notice, in the case of a thirteen-year-old ropemaking apprentice stated that "Masters of vessels and others are forwarned from employing, harbouring, aiding or secreting the said boy at their peril." Another notice predicted the runaway "Will ship on board of a privateer in the city of Baltimore."[51] A ten dollar reward was offered for "sufficient proof" that a "French West Indian Negro, aged twenty-five, had been Shipped on board any vessel." Since the rewards for returning runaways ranged from six cents (for an apprentice in the victualling trade) upward, a captain may have been securing men of marginal ability. Those with experience in ropemaking, carpentry, metal work, food service, including some slaves, on the other hand, brought considerably useful expertise with them. Even a cordwaining apprentice could work on shoes, cartridge cases, and other leather items.[52] Some runaways were worth more than a six cent reward. One slave master offered forty dollars for the return of his sixteen-year-old Negro slave, while promising to prosecute any "masters of privateers" employing him.[53] The appeal of the private armed vessels not only attracted slaves and apprentices but less encumbered types also. "Help Wanted" advertisements in Baltimore were numerous throughout the war, decreasing somewhat only during the blockade.[54]

Some of those who came out of the town or off the farm into private armed vessels lived to regret that move. Individual landsmen, boys, and ordinary seamen, finding life on the crowded private armed vessels less than bearable, deserted. Deserters' shares were remitted to the rest of the crew.[55] On the other hand, advances made to men who later deserted were not always recovered. One Robert Allen deserted two days after signing onto the privateer *Nonsuch* after receiving an unusually high advance on his shares. Allen was last seen on his way to Harford County, "from whence he came," while Captain Henry Levely of the *Nonsuch* offered a ten dollar reward for his return.[56] Others stayed on board but developed regrets later. John Baker, Jr., writing from the infamous Dartmoor prison in England, asked his parents about prize money earned on the privateer *Caroline*. He hoped for a quick peace "so that we shall get out of this place for I long to get Home and I don't think that I shall leave there again in a hurry for if I got as much coming to me as will purchase me a place in the country I mean to get one and stay."[57] Those who served on unproductive vessels or were crippled certainly had cause for regret, while those killed in action paid the ultimate price for their earlier decision to serve on a private armed vessel. At least three hundred men who signed onto Baltimore private armed vessels wound up in British prisoner "Depots" in Halifax, Barbados, and Jamaica, while hundreds more suffered in prisons in England. Postwar government pension records attest to losses of health, limbs, and lives.[58]

There were other sources of manpower. The privateer *Tom* listed a slave, designated the "property of Andrew Crawford" serving as an ordinary seaman.[59] The *Comet* shipped a Negro boy belonging to one B. Ives, "his Master," and Captain William Wade of the *Chasseur* asked for his own prize money and "also my Boy Joseph Kingsbury's proportion."[60] In some cases, the slaveowners authorized payment of a portion of the prize money to the slave. Whether any were able to purchase their freedom from such income is not known. The short-handed privateer *Rolla* stopped at Edgartown, Massachusetts, to recruit several men. The recruits, however, were Chappaquiddick Indians who were not allowed by state law to sign legal contracts without the endorsement of the tribe's official guardians. Additionally, one of the Indians was a "regularly bound apprentice" unable to sell his own services.[61] Slaves were seldom a legal problem, but the case of the Indians suggests that commanders at sea took what they could get, disregarding the later legal entanglements.

The backgrounds of the Baltimore crews of private armed vessels were diverse. Six men from the captured privateer *Sarah Ann* of Baltimore were dispatched to Jamaica to be "tried for their lives" as English deserters. Captain Richard Moore described one as an American navy veteran from Marblehead without parents but with a wife in New York. Another was born in Ireland but had been a resident of Baltimore for some time. A third was a colored seaman from Baltimore holding "free papers," while a fourth was a fifteen-year-old boy from New Jersey who had signed onto the *Sarah Ann* in Savannah.[62] American seamen obviously worked out of all the Atlantic ports, no matter where their residence was officially located. Eighteen of the *Sarah Ann*'s crew and her captain were eventually exchanged, arriving at Charleston in a cartel in November of 1812.[63] Paroles and exchanges for private armed vessel crewmen were allowed only when the commissioned vessel carried fourteen or more guns.[64] This was another incentive encouraging seamen to sign onto privateers rather than letter-of-marque traders carrying from four to eight guns.

The navy veteran on the *Sarah Ann* was not unique. Men terminating a voyage or cruise on a public, commissioned, or noncommissioned vessel tended to sign onto any vessel shipping hands at the moment. Navy personnel wrote to Baltimore frequently asking about prize money earned on earlier private armed vessel tours. Thomas Stevenson, for example, wrote from New London that he could not get home after his tour on the letter-of-marque schooner *Baltimore*. Under those conditions Stevenson said, "I took it in my head to ship on the United States frigate *Commodore Decatur*."[65] Three former members of the *Baltimore*'s crew signed onto the United States frigate *Constitution* at Boston and one entered onto the United States brig *Syren* at Charleston.[66] Some thirty of the petty officers and crew of the United States frigate *President*, on the other hand, signed onto the privateer *David Porter* in Providence.[67] Both the navy and the private service benefited from the exchange of experienced men.

Several key positions on a privateer were difficult to fill. One newspaper carried two advertisements for surgeons on the same day.[68] One was wanted by the *Tom* and the other for an unnamed vessel. The law required a doctor on vessels with large crews and the crew needed the comfort of a surgeon's presence, so the *Tom*'s sailing was delayed until one was found. Another vessel offered "Every encouragement" that the venture could provide to entice a surgeon aboard.[69] One doctor on board a privateer was described as a man who "read physic in a doctor's office, and listened to some half day lectures at a medical college" before he was let off with "a diploma, lancet and pill box to practice upon a credulous public." That particular doctor may have been better or worse than others. His prescription for sick sailors was usually a "pint of salt water" because medicines were too expensive.[70] The large advances given to surgeons on private armed vessels suggest that they paid for their own medicine. Dr. Chidester of the privateer *Dolphin* was thanked publicly for the "very kind and humane treatment" he accorded the captain and crew of the prize ship *Hebe* while they were prisoners.[71]

Another critical role on a privateer was that of the prize master. Experienced captains and officers from Baltimore as well as the entire bay region were available, but privateers needed from four to eight each. Owners offered prize masters three and four times the shares allotted to first class seamen in order to attract good masters.[72] The sponsors of the privateer *Kemp* actually paid their prize masters a separate bounty of seventy dollars for getting prizes into port. Any of the *Kemp*'s regular officers filling in as prize masters after the regular ones were expended also received the bounty at a time when such bonuses were usually restricted to surgeons and captains.[73] Because the role was both vital and hazardous, some grateful owners even added an unassigned prize share to the rewards available to a successful prize master. Before he pocketed any of his rewards, however, a prize master had to manage and navigate his often damaged vessel in enemy infested waters with an undersized crew while simultaneously guarding his prisoners. As the captain of the prize vessel he had to resist any attackers, evade blockading squadrons and cruising frigates, and draw on his commercial expertise in selecting an appropriate foreign port of entry for his particular cargo. Since the other participants in a private armed vessel enterprise were cognizant of the perils of the prize master's role and were dependent upon his success for their own, few begrudged him his extra rewards.

Baltimore and the Chesapeake region were apparently able to provide the numerous petty officer specialists essential to the operation of the privateers, but prize masters, surgeons, experienced seamen, and landsmen were problems. Shortages did not get to the point where extreme measures were taken. There is no record of women enrolling through carelessness such as one British prisoner who, on his arrival at Mill Prison in England, "discovered himself to be a woman." Having survived one shipwreck as a passenger, she then signed onto a privateersman as a "landsman," reportedly earning $200 in prize money.[74] Former privateer lieutenant George Little provided one answer to the question of how desperate American recruiting agents filled their quotas. Contrasting the experienced and disciplined sailors employed on letter-of-marque traders with the "desperadoes and outlaws" dragged from the "lowest dens of wretchedness," Little characterized privateer crewmen as "loafers, highbinders and butcher boys."[75] Meaning "ruffian or gangster" in Little's time, "highbinder" originated as a Chinatown phrase meaning "hired assassin."[76]

Seamen, landsmen, boys, slaves, and others were shaped into a crew by the commander of a privateer. A letter-of-marque trader had less trouble with organization because she had fewer men than the heavily manned privateers. Former navy officer Commodore Joshua Barney organized his privateer crew along the lines of a naval vessel. His "Quarter Bill No. 1" for the *Rossie* illustrates the tight organization used by successful privateer commanders. There were five gun crews consisting of a gun captain, two men, and one boy and one "long gun" crew of a gun captain, four men, and one boy. One officer, a boatswain and four men manned the forecastle, and six men the "Foretop sail," while four men worked the main topsail. The starboard and larboard "Fore Braces" (ropes at ends of yards) were assigned five men each and the "Main Braces," four men. Two men manned the helm and fifteen men, including Barney's marines or landsmen, were positioned in the central or "Waist Fore Sheets" area of the deck. The surgeon, steward, and carpenter waited in the partially protected "Cockpit." The ship's galley held one man, while an "After Guard" at the stern included seven men. Barney utilized his prize masters as part of his chain of command, stationing them in the gun deck, midships, and in the stern. When the commander called for boarders, there were two groups totaling twenty-six men prepared to leap from either side of the privateer. The boarding parties were led by a third lieutenant and six prize masters who fulfilled, in general, roles performed by the more numerous junior and petty officers on naval vessels.[77] Barney's capacity to organize and lead men in battle was a quality all ships' husbands and owners sought in a commander.

The leadership ability of a commander was only one control that officers and owners held over their somewhat motley crews. Crew members signed the Articles of Agreement when they signed on. That document stipulated the rules and regulations for the operation of the private armed vessel and her prizes. Each signature (often an X) was followed by the crewman's position, the shares assigned to him, and any advances made to him. A surety was often, but not always, included for those who took money in advance of the cruise.[78] The original Articles of Agreement remained in the hands of the prize agent who, in most cases, was the ship's husband taking on a new function.

Despite individual variations in phrasing and share allotments, the basic elements of the various Articles of Agreement were constant. The surviving agreement of the privateer *Fox*, signed in September of 1813, was typical. It contained fifteen basic articles covering two major topical categories with the first category defining the managerial rights and obligations of the commander and the owners. Included was the proviso that it was the owners' responsibility, to provide the "necessary provisions, guns, powder, shot, and all other warlike ammunition necessary." Profits, as was customary among privateers, were to be divided into two equal moieties; one for the owners and the other for the officers and crew. The captain was authorized to select his cruising ground unless he received "particular directions from the owners," and to use prize goods for the benefit of his own vessel or crew. The assignment of "deserving" or "reserved" shares was at the sole discretion of the captain.[79]

Other managerial matters were included. The orderly transfer of authority upon the death of the commander was laid out in detail. The tour of duty was specified as "ninety days effective at sea" and in the *Fox's* articles the owners' prize agent was also designated as the crew's agent. (The crew had the right to select a separate prize agent.) The prize agent's responsibility for obtaining all funds accruing in the venture's name at the admiralty court and his authority (a power of attorney) were stated unequivocally. The final article contained a pledge that the signatories would obey the regulations and orders of "the present or any future laws of the United States relative to the conduct and Government of Privateers."[80]

The second category of stipulations in the *Fox's* Articles of Agreement concerned the crew. Unauthorized leaves or absences were prohibited in order to preserve "order and decorum on board." Mutineers, those causing "a disturbance," cowards, and drunkards in a "time of action" were to forfeit their shares. Such persons were to be further punished in court. The Articles of Agreement of the privateer and the foregoing penalties also applied on board any prizes manned for port. A prize master on assignment held the same authority as the commander of the privateer. Anyone hiding or using prize goods for his own use or embezzling the same forfeited his shares. Forfeited shares were returned to the prize account for distribution among the other crew members unless a deserter was actually replaced by a recruit. Any prize money earned by a crew member killed "in action, or in the Ship's service" was assigned to his designated beneficiary after all advances were subtracted.[81]

The articles of the *Fox*, as mentioned earlier, permitted the captain to designate the recipients of the "reserved" or "deserving" shares. The owners, however, designated what particular actions were to earn the extra shares. They selected those actions that were critical in a confrontation at sea. Two merit shares were to be awarded to the first member of a boarding party to actually land on the deck of a prize. Obviously, that man was vulnerable to small arms fire and to swords and knives. The second boarder was to be awarded one "deserving" share, and one-half of a share each went to the third and fourth boarders. Boarding under fire was the most critical action in privateering tactics as well as the most dangerous. The spotting of a sail earned one an extra share, but only if it in fact became a prize. The already well-rewarded prize master

PLATE V

Painting, "Two Baltimore Clippers" by W. J. Huggins, 1815,
original in the Maryland Historical Society

was given further incentive in merit shares. Failure on his part erased any previous success at sea so the owners assigned him one merit share for getting his prize to port. Finally, the *Fox*'s owners assigned $400 to any man who lost a limb in action. That compensation, unfortunately, became a reality only when the prize in the particular action in which the limb was lost proved to be worth the stipulated amount. Extra shares went to those who advanced the interests of the venture or were injured while endeavoring to do so.[82]

Other surviving Articles of Agreement varied in phrasing or share allocation, the length of the tour of duty, or in the number of "reserved" or "deserving" shares. In the case of the *Tom*, the articles were about six feet long after 140 men signed them. The *Highflyer*'s printed articles (others were written) contained one written notation applying them to prizes also and one certifying Thomas Tenant, part-owner, as the venture's prize agent. A tour of duty of 120 days "at sea" was specified in the *Comet*'s articles and because of a problem peculiar to that vessel, a clause asserting, "It is understood that Every man must render Himself on board when called for," was added. The *Pike*'s articles differed from those of the *Fox*, discussed earlier, only in the number of assigned and reserved shares.[83] Such agreements evolved out of hundreds of years of experience in owner-crew relationships and, consequently, they left little to chance. On a commissioned private vessel, violators of her Articles of Agreement were tried by navy Courts Martial boards unless the owners neglected to add the crew's special wartime responsibilities to their normal peacetime agreement. A Courts Martial board dismissed mutiny charges against nineteen crewmen of the letter-of-marque *Chasseur* in 1813 because the crew had signed a normal peacetime agreement.[84] Signed wartime articles were needed to establish naval jurisdiction.

The number of shares assigned to the officers and crew in the articles did not always remain constant. The number not only varied between cruises but also between prizes whenever new recruits or the loss of deserters, forced a new accounting. The *Rossie* listed 285 shares for three prizes, 289 for one, and then 295 for three more, all on one cruise.[85] Additionally, reserved or deserving shares were not always given to individuals. Income from those shares was sometimes simply divided among the whole crew in the proportions listed in the articles.

One's signature on the Articles of Agreement was partial documentary evidence of service. Another part of the evidence was the prize ticket given to the crewman when he signed the articles. One printed prize ticket for the privateer *Lawrence* read as follows:

THIS IS TO CERTIFY, That *Thomas Durham — Seaman* on board the private armed schooner *Lawrence*, Edward Veazey, Esq. Commander, is entitled to *two* shares of any Prizes made by said vessel, provided he complies with the Articles of Agreement signed by him, of which the Captain's Certificate of discharge shall be evidence.

EDWARD VEAZEY [signature]
Commander

Schooner *Lawrence*
Port of Baltimore, March 1st, 1814.[86]

Such tickets immediately became money or at least negotiable paper in Baltimore and, later, in British prisons. The required Certificate of Discharge or evidence the seaman obeyed the articles, had to be signed by the captain before the crewman could receive his share of the prize. Durham's prize ticket was simply a narrow strip of paper containing the written statement that his service in "the Capacity of Seaman" on the *Lawrence* entitled him to "two Shares of all Captures made during her first Cruise." The discharge was signed by Captain Veazey over five months later in Wilmington, North Carolina.[87] It concluded the relationship between seaman Durham and the vessel but not his relations with the system. The seaman still had to deal with the prize agent to get his share of the prize money.

Whatever their reasons, many Americans shipped out on private armed vessels. That their decision was not always an easy one can be seen in the recollections of one experienced mariner who signed onto a privateer in Norfolk in 1812. He recalled that service on such a vessel was an opportunity "of making a fortune; but then it was counterbalanced by the possibility of getting my head knocked off, or a chance of being thrown into prison for two or three years."[88] Such risks were accepted by Baltimoreans in large numbers, perhaps as their only alternative to idleness or undesirable work on shore. As these men on their Baltimore schooners headed down the bay toward sea action one observer noted with justifiable pride, "Our Privateers have been expensively fitted and fully manned generally."[89]

NINE

Seawolves
and Flyers in Action

The clearance of a Baltimore private armed vessel did not conclude the managerial responsibility of those on the vessel or those left in port. The captain, whether he was executing a letter-of-marque voyage or a privateering cruise, operated according to instructions written for him by the vessel's management and, separately, by the government. Through the ship's husband-turned-agent, it was the captain's obligation while at sea to keep the management informed of his progress, prizes, and problems. Once at sea, success was fully in the hands of the captain and his crew as they prowled the Atlantic in search of prey or flew to or from France with valuable cargoes in their holds. Whether a seawolf looking for a prize or a flyer carrying cargo, once a sail was sighted the private armed vessel became a fighting machine, participating in all the dangers and sharing all the hopes inherent in nautical combat. Whether attacking or escaping, the crews of privateers normally anticipated more deadly combat than those on commissioned traders, but the tradition was for them to avoid the kind of bloody battles fought by naval vessels. Cargo-carrying letter-of-marque traders, the second arm of the private service, were primarily interested in profits from the sales of their outgoing and then incoming cargoes. From time to time, however, they also felt the sting of heavy gunfire at sea. Even supreme efforts to prepare a vessel properly on Baltimore's waterfront did not alter the facts that profits from sales came only after the sea lanes had been risked and that prize dividends seldom ensued without the risk of combat.

Even in peacetime it was customary for a ship's husband to provide his captain with written directions from the owners. Wartime conditions and the authorization to take prizes forced the husbands to expand their normal instructions. For letter-of-marque traders the usual commercial advice was still vital in war, needing only supplementary advice on the handling of prizes. For the privateer commander, commercial advice was directed toward prize goods only because such vessels carried no cargoes. The privateer was more interested in cruising grounds and directions for the handling of prizes. One surviving example of instructions to a privateer commander was written early in the War of

1812. Its comments were general except for the specific designation of a cruising ground. British vessels off the American coast at the time were unaware of America's entry into the war, and the British navy was weak in those waters. Consequently, waters off the American coast provided a potentially bountiful and close cruising area from which prizes had only a short distance to travel. Early instructions reflected such factors. Instructions dated July of 1812 read as follows:

Instructions for Joshua Barney, Esquire, of the Schooner *Rossie*

Baltimore, July 11, 1812

Sir,

The Privateer Schooner *Rossie* mounting eleven guns and carrying One Hundred men and upwards which has been by her Owners put under your Command and charge, and being about to proceed to Sea, it has become my duty as Agent for the Owners duly appointed by them to make out your instructions with which I have to request your strict compliance.

In the first place an exact adherance to the Laws of the United States and in particular to the Act of Congress under which the present expedition is made, appears the most indispensible, and a strict attention to the provisions contained in the Sixth and Tenth Sections of the Act is particularly recommended to you.

As it is of the first importance to the success of the Enterprize that the prizes should be brought as speedily as possible within the Jurisdiction of the United States, it is strictly enjoined upon you, that in every case of Capture you dispatch the prize to the nearest and most convenient port in the United States, and that upon no consideration you send a Prize into or attempt to proceed against her in any port or place not within our Jurisdiction, unless she is forced into such port by stress of Weather or by the Enemy, and that in such event, you use all practicable means to dispatch her to the United States unless the risk in your judgement be too great.

It will flow from this part of your Instructions that it would be inadvisable to cruize in the European Seas, as the risk of getting home the prizes would be so great, and in leaving the Cruizing ground to your discretion, this consideration leads me to advise you to confine yourself to the American Coast as much as possible.

On putting a prize Master on board a Prize, you will be careful in instructing him to advise me by the first opportunity which may occur after his arrival in any port of the United States, and by several successive opportunities thereafter of his arrival, of the state of his prize, and of any other matters which he may deem material to communicate, and that he be forbidden to value on any House in such port, but that he wait orders from me, which will prevent the property from falling into unsafe hands. Wishing you Health and happiness and a Successful Cruize.

> I am very respectfully
> your obedt H Servant
> C. DESHON [signature][1]

Joshua Barney was an unusually experienced commander. After commanding public and private vessels in the Revolution and later in the French fleet, he had performed the role of merchant in Baltimore. Deshon's decision to let Barney select his own cruising ground off the American coast, therefore, was justified. As hostilities progressed, other captains gained experience and operated larger vessels, with greater capacities for supplies, prize goods and extra hands for prize crews while the British fleet moved into American waters. It then became necessary to give commanders wider latitude and, in time, to order them into the more distant European waters denied to Barney. Any managing owner or agent restricting a private cruiser to the American coast after 1812 was jeopardizing his vessel and minimizing his chances for success.

Later instructions reflected wartime experience while recognizing new conditions. The instructions given Captain Henry Dashiell of the privateer *Saranac* in January of 1815 reflected experiences gained in two and one-half years of war. Written by Lemuel Taylor, agent for owners Von Kapff and Brune, Henry Didier, Jr., and others, they instructed Dashiell to cruise for ten days east of Bermuda and then to head for Barbados for a twenty-day cruise. If he still had sufficient officers and men to man prizes, he was then to steer for Madeira. After Madeira, off the African coast, the captain was to use his discretion, but he was encouraged to cruise in and off the English and Irish channels. The *Saranac* was to head home only after her prize masters, spare officers, water, and provisions were exhausted. She could enter at any American port east of the Delaware but if there was still space in her hold, she was to cruise in the Grand Banks and off Nova Scotia on the way home. Dry goods (in short supply in the United States) were to be given priority when possible and were to be transferred to the swift *Saranac*'s hold regardless of inconvenience to the crew.[2] The crew, after all, shared in their value. Goods in the hold guaranteed a venture some income even when it was impossible for a prize master to get his vessel into a friendly port.

Operational and commercial advice was an integral part of the *Saranac*'s instructions. The best prize masters were to be used first, and all papers on a prize were to accompany her along with some of the prize's crew. Neither captain, officers, supercargo, nor passengers were to remain on a prize unless humanity demanded it. Advice to select dry goods or other items of high value was a reminder of the business objectives of a private armed vessel. Further commercial advice included information that cargoes of fish were valueless and that French, Spanish, and Portuguese red wines were worth little more than their customs duties. Cotton, flour, and wool were to be directed toward northern ports where better prices prevailed for those items.[3] The entrepreneur at war was still a businessman.

English shipping patterns and other operational insights were also included in the *Saranac*'s instructions. Dashiell was informed that large convoys generally left England in late December and early January for the Mediterranean, the East Indies, Brazil, and the West Indies. Convoys also left the West Indies for England about the tenth of February, the fifth of March, and the first of May. All neutrals were to be examined for British property but were to be treated with respect. Prizes of little value were to be destroyed and no ransom was to be taken in any case. The captain was also instructed to let his nautical position determine what ports his prize masters would utilize. Captain Dashiell was counseled that "rigid discipline" without abuse was his responsibility and that he was to have an "understanding" with his officers. In closing, agent Taylor recognized that the "fortune of War" as well as good intelligence and planning made for an "agreeable and Profitable Cruise."[4] Agent Taylor's 1815 instructions to his captain were far more detailed than those given to Barney in 1812.

Issued through their husband and prize agent, owners' instructions served as a legal protection against unlawful acts at sea. They also assured the owners a measure of control over the captain at sea because his failure to follow his instructions could cost him his large share of the profits. In the case of the privateer *Whig*, the captain was actually denied his sixteen shares of what he claimed was $300,000 worth of prizes. When the captain sued for his shares, agent Lemuel Taylor testified that the officer "did not obey the instructions given him by the owners." According to agent Taylor, the captain failed to execute the role required of a commander and did not faithfully perform his duty "according to his equipment and the nature of her employment."[5] The owners were obviously not satisfied with the *Whig*'s 1814 cruise.

Merchants in peace and war feared unknown or unreliable merchants in other cities. Wanting their prize goods in tested hands, Baltimore owners furnished their captains with the names of reliable commercial firms in other ports. Richard H. Douglass, agent for the letter-of-marque schooner *Decatur*, the privateer *Lawrence*, and other Baltimore private armed vessels, listed firms for the captain of the *Decatur*. Houses known to Douglass were listed for Portland, Boston, New York, Norfolk, Charleston, Savannah, and Wilmington (North Carolina), as well as three other small ports in North Carolina.[6] The captain enjoyed no flexibility. North Carolina and New York were used heavily by Baltimore vessels and their prizes during the blockade because both were physically difficult to blockade.[7] Prewar interfirm relationships between Baltimore and New York, Boston, Charleston, and other ports had taught the Baltimoreans which houses were safe. Some new associations may have been formed during the war, but the impression is that, more often, old associations were strengthened.

A continuous flow of information was another vital need of the entrepreneur. Without it, he could not make necessary adjustments or supervise his investments, so captains and prize masters kept the owners apprised of their activities. Captain George Montgomery of the letter-of-marque *Decatur*, for example, wrote the following letter to agent Richard H. Douglass:

> Dear Sir;
> With pleasure I inform you that I have this day Captured the Brig *Williams* from Senegall loaded with 195,087 lbs. Gum — which I have thought Proper to Send in and hope will meet your approbation. I send my first officer Moses Bears Jr in her as Prize Master with orders to inform you of his arrival immediately — that he should arrive in any port of the United States.
>
> GEO. MONTGOMERY [signature][8]

Another letter of the same day added the news that the crew of the *Decatur* had boarded three other vessels. Unfortunately, all three were already prizes to American private armed vessels. The captain also observed that the *Decatur* performed well "in point of Sailing."[9] Without reports on prizes, owners were unable to advise a cooperating house in another port of the Baltimore concern's intentions. Such a problem did not exist when the prize entered at Baltimore.

Cooperating houses in other ports also fed information to the Baltimore owners. Isaac G. Roberts of Portsmouth, New Hampshire, passed on the unpleasant news that the brig *Hope* and another prize to the privateer *Lawrence* of Baltimore had been recaptured. Another prize was endeavoring to make an American port from the coast of Spain. Roberts reported the happier news that two of the *Lawrence*'s six prizes had entered Portland, while another was directed into a French port for adjudication. Information that the *Lawrence*'s crew was down to fifty men alerted her Baltimore owners that she could not stay out much longer. Roberts also passed on word that the *Lawrence* had sailed in consort with Baltimore's 300-ton *Surprise*. Owned by S. Smith and Buchanan, Hollins and McBlair, and Gerrard Wilson, the *Surprise* was cruising in English and Irish waters but was also low on men and water.[10] S. Smith and Buchanan could expect the *Surprise* to return soon. Additional information on sea activities was available in the daily shipping news section of newspapers and in the logs and journals of returning vessels.

At sea a private armed vessel captain had numerous tactical options, but there were some standard techniques. One popular approach was to cut one prize at a time out of a convoy, working as far away as possible from the escorting warships (called "bulldogs"). A convoy could also be followed ("dogged") until one or more vessels were separated by bad weather or poor sailing. Such tactics were not unlike those used by submarine commerce raiders in later wars. The Baltimore privateer *Sabine* captured the 500-ton East Indiaman, *Countess of Harcourt*, in the English Channel while she carried dry goods, brandy, porter, rum, and gin. Sent into St. Mary's, Georgia, for adjudication, that rich prize was described as "one of the outward bound fleet, separated in a gale of wind."[11] Privateer captain and historian George Coggeshall characterized such tactics as the "taking of sheep without a shepherd." Hopefully, the privateer selected the most valuable of any vulnerable vessels as a target. Coggeshall referred to such selectivity as "capital picking."[12]

A commander of a privateer could simply cruise the great trade routes off the European and American coasts when there was no sign of a convoy. Unescorted vessels were in those sea lanes. Some had become separated from convoys, but not all unescorted vessels were illegal or separated. There was a class of British vessels called "running ships" permitted to sail without escorts. They were usually large, heavily armed, and well-manned vessels carrying expensive cargoes.[13] Only the most powerful and most determined privateers were matches for them.

Whether a private armed vessel dogged a convoy or cruised the sea lanes in search of single vessels, a standard closing technique was employed once a potential victim was sighted. Pursuit was followed by a shot across the bow from the attacker's long-range gun. That shot, combined with the very sight of a low-slung, rakishly masted, and white sailed topsail schooner sometimes encouraged the victim to strike his colors. The captain of a British merchant vessel knew he was confronting a heavily manned, better-armed, and swifter opponent whose crew may well have been more determined than his own. When a British captain elected to run or fight, the private armed vessel closed on his opponent with her long gun and carronades blazing. The intention was not to sink or seriously damage an opponent's valuable hull but to thin out her crew and to damage her rigging and steering. The cannonade also allowed the privateer to get alongside so that massed musketry and boarders, the privateer's best offensive techniques, could be utilized. Victims failing to strike their colors after the long shot, the cannonade, and the musketry, usually did so after boarders hurled themselves onto their deck brandishing swords, knives, pistols, and spikes. The whole operation from long shot to striking seldom took more than one hour. Well-manned and heavily armed British vessels led by determined officers, of course, extended the time and cost of combat. When the victim was a part of a convoy, it was not uncommon for two privateers to work together. One drew off an escorting bulldog, while the other cut out a prize or two.[14]

Most accounts of American privateers in action on the high seas were derived from their own officers, logs, and journals. Another view can be gotten from the victims of the American raiders. The log of the "running ship" *John Hamilton* bound for London from Honduras provides such an account. The captain of that large and well-armed vessel sighted a schooner at two P.M. on November 20, 1812. By six P.M. he identified her as an American privateer under a full press of sail. The next morning when the schooner closed on him with great speed, the British captain fired ten or twelve shots at her and received fire in return as the schooner hoisted an American flag. The Americans then "came across our bow within musket Shot and give us 3 or 4 broadside," which the *John Hamilton* returned. This fire from an unusually strong British vessel forced the American to "sheer off all Night." The next morning the tenacious schooner was "still in sight Doging off us" but soon closed to exchange musketry for about twenty minutes. With three men wounded and with some physical damage to his vessel, the *John Hamilton*'s captain noted in his log "obliged to Strick."[15] He had fought longer than usual before surrendering his 550-ton, sixteen-gun ship to the Baltimore privateer *Dolphin* of just twelve guns. The *John Hamilton*'s cargo included 700 tons of valuable mahogany, used later in the construction of the United States frigate *Java* in Baltimore.[16] Deemed seaworthy, with little damage to her hull, the *John Hamilton* was manned for port.

The ship *John Hamilton* was an exceptionally large and valuable prize, so her capture required more than the usual effort. Smaller victims were taken more abruptly. The little forty-ton schooner *Fame* was such a case. While on her way out of St. Bartholomew's in the West Indies, her captain logged a "calm night" and "wind and weather" the next morning. Without any intervening entries, the captain abruptly scrawled "here this voyage ended" across his log. The *Fame* had become a prize to the Baltimore privateer *Nonsuch*.[17]

Accounts of individual privateer techniques and narratives of particular engagements made for good conversation in the coffee houses. Naturally, shareholders were more interested in black ink on the account books at the completion of an entire cruise. Decisions regarding the next role of the vessel, possible sale of the vessel, changes in captains, and changes in armament were made after full cruises. Profits to the owners were also based on complete cruises.

An American Commission marked No. 4 by the Baltimore collector of customs in July of 1812 was assigned to the privateer *Comet*. Merchants Andrew Clopper, Levi Hollingsworth, Peter Arnold Karthaus, and Jeremiah Sullivan were part of the syndicate sponsoring the *Comet*. They appointed experienced Baltimore schooner master Thomas Boyle commander of the privateer. Boyle of Irish descent, had married a local girl after migrating south at the age of nineteen from his birthplace in Marblehead, Massachusetts. His 187-ton schooner, constructed by Thomas Kemp in 1810, cleared from Baltimore on July 12, 1812, in company with several other Baltimore privateers for a three months' cruise.

Captain Boyle drilled his crew on guns and sails every day as he headed southeasterly from the Chesapeake. On July 26, Boyle "put the Schooner under fighting sail, all hands to quarters" for three hours of pursuit and maneuvering before firing a shot at his prey. It was after twelve minutes of bombardment "when down come the long boasted pride of old England to a Yankee Comet." Boyle had captured the valuable 400-ton ship *Henry* of Hull on her way from St. Croix to London with a mixed cargo that included sugar, fustic, and wine. Transferring the *Henry*'s first and second officers and thirteen seamen to the *Comet*, Boyle placed prize master Seth Long, master's mate Edward Carey, and nine seamen on the prize with orders to bring her, her captain, and four boys into Baltimore.[18]

The *Comet* approached another large ship on August 15, 1812. She hoisted the English flag and fired at the American schooner at three hundred yards. In a warm engagement lasting thirty-five minutes, the *Comet*'s topsails were shot up, while her efforts to board her stubborn opponent were frustrated by the "masterly manner" in which the latter was maneuvered. Backing off, the *Comet* exchanged broadside after broadside with her adversary, while Boyle's marines poured musket fire into the ship. Finally, when "cut all to pieces, scarcely a rope being entire" the heavily armed 346-ton ship *Hopewell*, bound from Surinam in South American to her home port of London, lowered her flag. The *Hopewell* was fully loaded with sugar, molasses, cotton, coffee, and cocoa. Prize master John Hooper and eleven seamen manned the *Hopewell* for Baltimore. On August 26, Boyle captured and sent in the brig *Industry* of and for London also from Surinam, the Dutch colony in South America. The *Comet*'s attack on the brig consisted of musketry alone at pistol range, "without firing a gun."[19]

Many of the vessels Boyle spoke or boarded on his first cruise were neutrals or American vessels engaged in the Cadiz flour trade. In mid-September Boyle pursued another large armed ship. Firing a shot, the Englishman gave the *Comet* three cheers as the privateer closed with him and "commenced firing upon him from the great Guns and musquetry." Within ten minutes, the fourteen-gun, 364-ton ship *John* of Liverpool struck her colors. The *John* and her valuable cargo of sugar, rum, cotton, coffee, copper, and hardwood was entrusted to prize master Purnell Austin and twelve seamen. The *John*'s captain, four passengers, and three boys were sent along with the prize as the *Comet* turned homeward. Boyle completed a successful eighty-three day cruise during which, rather strangely, the *Comet* was not chased once. Boyle was also pleased to report that he had not lost a man. Four large prizes entered at Baltimore and North Carolina, inspiring the *Comet*'s owners to "fit her out again with all possible expedition for a second Cruise" under the same commander.[20]

Refitted, Boyle took his *Comet* (he was now a part-owner) through the British fleet blockading the Chesapeake on a dark stormy night in December of 1812. Off the coast of Brazil, Boyle chose to shoot it out with a large Portuguese man-of-war escorting three heavily armed English vessels. Taking fire from all four vessels at once, the little *Comet*, pouring full broadsides into all of them, forced the Portuguese warship to sheer off while capturing all three English vessels. One English ship was "all cut to pieces and rendered unmanageable," while two brigs were also cut up and disabled with "many shot holes between wind and water and not a rope but what was cut away." Although his badly damaged prizes held perishable cargoes, Boyle got some satisfaction from the fact that the interfering Portuguese had suffered heavily. Privateer captain George Coggeshall, on boarding the Portuguese vessel in London, noted that she carried twenty thirty-two-pound cannons and 165 men and that she was large enough to hoist the *Comet* onto her deck.[21]

The rest of the *Comet*'s second cruise in South American and West Indian waters was a good example of technical and tactical excellence involving frequent escapes from British warships. It was not, however, as financially rewarding as Boyle's first cruise. On January 29, 1813, the *Comet* fired a few guns and then an entire broadside in an effort to slow down a fast sailing "tolerable large ship." After slowing his adversary and sailing "within long musket shot," Boyle unleashed a broadside of "the great Guns and musketry at the same time." After forty minutes of firing the 361-ton ship *Adelphi* out of Liverpool struck her colors. Her eight eighteen-pound cannons had not been enough to protect her from the *Comet*'s punishing fire. Boyle was forced to send a repair crew onto the *Adelphi* before he could man her for port. On February 28, 1813, Boyle was pursued for six hours by the British frigate *Surprise* but "outsailed her with ease." After repairing his damaged foremast at St. Bartholomew's and escaping more British pursuers in the waters surrounding St. Croix, Boyle entered at Baltimore on March 20, 1813.[22] His hold was full of prize goods divested from various victims, but his prize masters were being recaptured in the West Indies or on the increasingly guarded American coast. British prison records at Barbados alone list *Comet* prize masters William Cathell, and William Bartlett, whose prize *Adelphi* foundered at sea, and twenty-four of the *Comet*'s seamen. For Cathell and his crew the records read, "Into the Depot at Barbados for Exchange," but others from the *Comet* were sent to England for what was often a torturous imprisonment.[23]

The owners of the *Comet* and Captain Boyle learned from the experiences of their second cruise. Cruising in the West Indies, Boyle took twenty prizes, but realizing the odds faced by his prize masters, he destroyed most prizes after divesting them of any valuable cargo. In his later cruising on the 187-ton schooner, Boyle again challenged extremely powerful vessels. His unsuccessful effort to take the heavily manned, twenty-two-gun, 800-ton ship *Hibernia* included an eight to nine hour exchange at close range. The cost, three men dead and sixteen wounded on the *Comet*, was inordinately high for a privateer and very unlike Boyle's earlier record.[24] Large high-sided vessels such as transports were physically difficult to board and their large crews could fire down into the low Baltimore schooners. With Baltimore blockaded, Boyle took the battered little *Comet* into Wilmington, North Carolina, in March of 1814. Baltimore and Boyle were finished with the *Comet* after twenty-one months of privateering. In July of 1814 a Baltimore newspaper carried an advertisement for "The well-known, fast sailing schooner *Comet*, Thomas Boyle, late Commander," stating that she would be auctioned off in Baltimore while "lying at Wilmington, N.C. with all her armament and stores, as she arrived from her last cruize."[25] Changing conditions were forcing the Baltimore owners to outfit larger vessels capable of carrying larger guns, more men, and more provisions for more distant cruising over longer periods of time. Larger holds were also needed for goods divested from prize vessels that the capturers felt could not be gotten into a friendly port because of the vessel's condition or value, the distance involved, the blockade, or a combination of those factors. The *Comet* was sold to New Yorkers in December of 1814.

Of the two commissions marked No. 1 by the Baltimore collector of customs, one went to another small and relatively old schooner constructed by Thomas Kemp, the *Rossie*. Owned by eleven Baltimoreans including John McKim, Jr., Thomas Tenant, Robert Patterson, Levi Hollingsworth, Jeremiah Sullivan, and Christopher Deshon, the 206-ton *Rossie* had been launched in 1807. The owners added new sails and rigging, plus her armament and provisions, and convinced Revolutionary War navy and privateering hero Commodore Joshua Barney to command her. The *Rossie*'s commission, her instructions (detailed earlier in this chapter), and her clearance certificate were all dated July 11, 1812, about three weeks after the American Declaration of War.[26] Restricted by his instructions to American waters, Barney headed the *Rossie* with its hand-picked crew toward the Grand Banks of Newfoundland. Outsailing British pursuers without difficulty, Barney cruised off St. John's and along Sable Island and Georges Bank. Barney ran his vessel along navy lines, assigning his men specific combat positions and rehearsing them daily on the *Rossie*'s guns and sails. By the time he turned into Newport, Rhode Island, on August 30, 1812, Barney had taken eighteen vessels. Unfortunately, most were coasting and fishing vessels without great value early in the war when the government was collecting double tariff duties.[27] One of Barney's captures in northern waters was the brig *William* from Bristol bound for St. John's and sent into Boston with a cargo of coal, butter, cheese, pork, hats, shoes, and oakum. A ship, five brigs, and a schooner, all laden with fish and timber, were sunk or burned by Barney because of their low value. A brig and a schooner were sent into Newfoundland with 108 paroled prisoners and a promise to the British admiral there that a larger supply would follow soon. The brig *Brothers* was sent into St. John's with sixty prisoners, while more were kept on board the crowded *Rossie*.[28]

After his entering salute injured a Newport woman on August 30, 1812,

Barney took on some new men, water, and provisions while resting his crew. Barney lodged and dined with Captain George Coggeshall in Newport, leading that gentleman to characterize the commodore as "very agreeable and gentlemanly in conversation."[29] From Newport, the *Rossie* proceeded to the West Indies, passing near Bermuda and then "to the windward of Sombrero Passage, the passage by St. Thomas; Mona Passage, Turks Island passage; the Caycos passage, the Crooked Island passage, then into Gulph, Florida, and home."[30] Entering West Indian waters after his northern swing and after the peak trading period, Barney took just two prizes. One was the well-armed and gallantly defended eight-gun mail packet *Princess Amelia*, taken in a brutal two hour long moonlight fight. On boarding his victim before ordering her manned for Savannah, Barney found that the *Rossie's* fire had left her "in a dreadfull situation, torn to pieces by our shot" with one man killed and seven wounded. While repairing the damaged *Rossie* the next day, Barney noted that British warships "are all out in pursuit of Americans." Perhaps as a result of the British presence, Barney sailed in company with the privateer *Globe* of Baltimore. (Three of her four owners were also part-owners of the *Rossie*.) The two privateers were separated in a gale, which Barney reported "stove in our Larboard waist, from the fore to the main chains, broke off the Stanchions of three ports" and by ripping up the planks supporting his guns, forced him to ditch six of his eleven guns. Rejoining the *Globe*, Barney repaired his damage and shaped wooden guns to fill his empty gunports while resolving to get some real guns from the next English vessel he met.[31]

Commodore Barney was critical of those who broke the law or took advantage of the situation to earn profits. When the *Rossie* and the *Globe*, in consort, stopped a small schooner carrying American Commission No. 12 from Charleston, Barney was suspicious of an armed schooner manned by Frenchmen and Negroes claiming no prizes after a fifty-two day cruise. His log carried the notation that, "my opinion is that they were acting the part of Pirates." After losing a small boy overboard and experiencing high winds and seas in which the *Rossie* averaged ten knots, Barney entered the Gulf Stream on October 18, 1812. As he neared home, he seized the American ship *Merrimac*, carrying dry goods from Liverpool, for violating the Non-Importation Act. After a cruise of ninety days Barney anchored at North Point outside Baltimore on October 22, 1812.[32] The *Rossie* had destroyed or sent in 3,698 tons of British shipping worth an estimated million and a half dollars while capturing 217 prisoners.[33] The damage to Britain was far greater than the proceeds earned in American prize courts. A disenchanted "old and worn out" Barney withdrew from the private service only to reappear in his favorite role as a naval officer when the British invaded Maryland.[34] A newspaper of October 28, 1812, announced the auction of the *Rossie*, characterized by Barney as too old and too small but advertised as "The Elegant Privateer Schooner *Rossie*, as she arrived from the sea, with her armament, Provisions, Water Casks, etc." According to the auctioneer, the *Rossie* was "not excelled in point of beauty or sailing by any vessel belonging to the United States."[35] Purchased by the firm of D'Arcy and Didier in November of 1812, the speedy *Rossie* was converted into a letter-of-marque trader. She was captured near France in January of 1813.

The 117-ton schooner *Rolla* was another older and small Baltimore privateer with an interesting and successful story in the war's early months. Commanded by James Dooley, formerly a lieutenant on the privateer *Dolphin*, the *Rolla* experienced some difficulty in her efforts to recruit seamen. Constructed in 1809, the *Rolla* was too old and too small for some potential recruits but, in any case, there were not many to choose from in October of 1812 after the first rush to sea. Dooley finally cleared, short-handed, in October of 1812 "by beating out of the harbor" only to have his fore-topmast snap. Newport News was utilized for repairs and recruitment before Dooley took the *Rolla* on to Bristol, Providence, Boston, and Falmouth, looking for crewmen. Back at sea, Dooley drilled the crew while stopping mostly American and Portuguese vessels engaged in the Iberian flour trade. Crossing the Atlantic, the *Rolla* captured the fourteen-gun British ship *Mary*, "driven out of Madeira in a gale of wind." Dooley took out provisions for his own men and manned the prize for Baltimore. On the same day, he picked up the ten-gun *Eliza*, also blown out of Madeira in a wind, and manned her for Baltimore. On the following day the wind worked against the *Rolla* when "a sea pooped us on board and very near swamping us." Dooley was unable to open his hatches to store his guns below so, to reduce topheaviness, he threw his guns over. Down to sixty men, the crew asked Dooley to continue the cruise with but one gun. Using grape shot in her one gun and muskets, the *Rolla* captured the sixteen-gun, 400-ton merchantman *Rio Nova* of London, also blown out from Madeira in the storm that had nearly sunk the *Rolla*. Manning the *Rio Nova* for port cost the captain more of his small crew, but Dooley was still able to man the brig *Barroca* on December 17, 1812. That vessel had been separated from the Cork fleet, bound for Jamaica, in a storm. Finally, Dooley drew on his small crew again to man the ship *Apollo*, of and from London for New Providence. After manning her, Dooley was so low on men that he headed for home, reaching Annapolis on January 23, 1813.[36] "One-gun" Dooley had taken seven vessels in a period of twenty-eight days. Four of his prizes got in and from 80 to 100 prisoners were landed at Teneriffe in the Canary Islands and in the Madeira Islands.

The *Rolla* was owned by Hollins and McBlair, two of the Pattersons, William Hollins, and Christopher Deshon. They shared in the profits from the prize auctions of the vessels, hardware, wheat, beef, dry goods, candles, and government supplies, sent in by the *Rolla*. The crewmen reportedly salted away a good six months' wartime wages for the cruise on the *Rolla*. Some went out with Dooley again when he cleared in March of 1813 through the blockade. The ship *David Green*, mistaking the *Rolla* for a British vessel, showed her British license to Dooley. Dooley sent the *David Green* and two brigs in before again throwing over all his guns but one in an escape off Jamaica. The *Rolla* entered at Beaufort, North Carolina, on June 4, 1813, but "One-gun" Dooley would not enjoy his prize income for some time, however. He was captured on a coasting vessel while making his way up to Baltimore and was transferred to England for imprisonment. His vessel was offered at auction while lying at Beaufort, but few were interested in her so the owners sent her out again under George Fellows in December of 1813. She was captured as she came out of a Connecticut port where she had stopped to recruit more men.[37]

The xebec *Ultor* was unique among Baltimore's private armed vessels. With Mediterranean lateen-style sails and three masts, including one raked away from the other two, few British captains suspected that the 154-ton *Ultor* was a Baltimore privateer. Owners Amos A. and George Williams, Andrew Clopper, Peter A. Guestier, the two Gills, and bank cashier James W. McCulloch placed the Andrew Descandes-built xebec in the hands of Captain John Cock. Following Cock's inability to slip through the British blockade, command was transferred to First Lieutenant James Matthews. He made a letter-of-marque run to Havana before clearing the *Ultor* for a cruise in January of 1814. Heading southeasterly, Matthews sent in or sank three vessels carrying fish, oil, or timber. Eight schooners and a sloop were set afire or utilized as prisoner cartels. Chased by a frigate on June 11, Matthews escaped by throwing "a barrel overboard with a fire in it, to decoy the enemy." The *Ultor* outsailed British vessels frequently, eluding a privateer from Antigua and a seventy-four-gun ship of the line. With her small hold bulging with prize goods, the *Ultor* entered Boston in early July of 1814.[38]

The *Ultor*'s second cruise originated from New York in early December of 1814. At midnight on Christmas Eve, the xebec anchored at St. Bartholomew's to repair her sprung foremast. She escaped two English man-of-war brigs and two English privateers by manning her sweeps in a calm. In West Indian waters Matthews avoided a "large two Topsail Schooner, Showing a handsome broadside," supposing her to be an American letter-of-marque trader. Still cruising in March of 1815, unaware of peace, Matthews took and manned the 411-ton, thirteen-gun *Ann* of Liverpool. She surrendered just as the *Ultor*'s boarders were preparing to leap on her decks. The next day the *Ultor* captured the brig *Mohawk* of Jamaica, but her captain went ashore to arrange a payment of 3,000 "Spanish mill Dollars" in ransom to *Ultor* part-owner Peter A. Guestier in Baltimore. Apparently, that effort failed because the *Mohawk* was reported as manned for port. On March 25, 1815, an American schooner informed Matthews of the ratification of the Treaty of Ghent. With the treaty permitting captures in distant waters after the general hostilities ceased, Matthews challenged vessels all the way home. With his hold full of prize goods and prisoners, Matthews entered at Baltimore on April 10, 1815.[39]

The first cruise of the privateer *Lawrence* began while the British navy was very strong in the Chesapeake. The 259-ton schooner, built in Talbot County expressly for war service, was large enough to fight off the smaller vessels of the blockading force. Commander Edward Veazey and his crew of 120 men waited ten days in the Chesapeake before passing the blockading fleet at midnight with the aid of a "stiff breeze from the North and Northwest." After shaking off British pursuers and boarding mostly neutral vessels, Veazey sent in the Swedish ship *Commerce* (captured N 50° 47' and W 10° 41') carrying 280 tons of oats and barley "for the use of English forces in Spain." Questioning Veazey's judgment, an American prize court restored the vessel and charged costs to the *Lawrence* but condemned the cargo. On April 19, 1814, the *Lawrence* sent in the ship *Ontario* with her cargo of brandy, salt, and corkwood and the brig *Pelican*, bound from Bermuda to Liverpool. Far from an American port, Veazey sent the *Pelican* into a French port for adjudication. On April 25, Veazey informed the *Lawrence*'s agent, Richard H. Douglass, that "we at present enjoy good health and the Vessel is in the best possible order."[40] Sent into the United States, the eight-gun brig *Ceres* and her 400 tons of hides, tallow, and horns was mistakenly taken into Nova Scotia by her prize master from the *Lawrence*. A visit ashore inspired him to withdraw quickly. A Baltimore newspaper account of that misadventure also expressed some anxiety about Veazey's habit of sending prizes into the uncertain French ports for condemnation. By 1814 the French were less friendly to the United States and, in fact, would soon close their ports to American prizes.[41]

The *Lawrence* continued to cruise off Ireland, England, and Spain in April and May of 1814, speaking several other American privateers in the area. She diverted cargoes and escaped her pursuers, sending the brig *Hope* with wine and barilla and the brig *Ann* with wine into the United States from waters near the Canary Islands. Heading toward the West Indies in June, Veazey fought several English warships and outsailed others before coming into North Carolina with a hold full of divested prize goods in early August of 1814.[42] After Veazey visited Baltimore, the owners beefed up the *Lawrence*'s armament, acquired a new commission, and retained the resourceful Veazey.[43] Back to sea, the *Lawrence* took at least thirteen prizes, with five of the eight she manned for port actually arriving there. The cargoes consisted primarily of wine, raisins, and other fruit from Malaga and other Mediterranean ports as well as dry goods, hardware, fish, and cork. She captured 3,000 tons of English shipping before terminating her second cruise in Baltimore at the war's end. The *Lawrence* was sold at auction on April 15, 1815.[44]

For skill, courage, determination, and success, it would have been difficult to surpass the record of the 228-ton *Kemp* on her first cruise. After some success as a letter-of-marque trader, including the taking of prizes, she was converted into a privateer in Wilmington, North Carolina, by her new owner, Peter Arnold Karthaus in November of 1814.[45] Karthaus induced the former successful commander of the privateer *Caroline*, Joseph Almeda, to take his vessel to sea. The new owners altered the 100-foot schooner so that she drew five feet, three inches of water forward and twelve feet, four inches aft, an extreme drag, while putting on four nine-pound long guns, four new six-pound carronades, and a new suit of sails. Veteran officers, prize masters, and a crew of 100 men were recruited.[46]

Almeda cleared from Wilmington, North Carolina, on November 29, 1814, right into heavy seas. After experiencing a "dangerous high Sea" and great quantities of water on board, Almeda headed for a fleet of nine sails. Inducing the bulldog, a frigate in this case, to chase him, Almeda lost her in the night and doubled back to the waiting fleet. At a range of three miles, Almeda viewed the entire fleet "formed in line and laid by for combat, a large Ship, the van, three Brigs, two Schooners and a large Ship the rear." The fleet moved upon Almeda "in regular order and commenced firing" as they passed the *Kemp*. After holding his fire until each opponent was within musket range, Almeda opened with his great guns and small arms. With his opponents in confusion, Almeda "fell on board a brig and carried her with one man wounded" while receiving fire from all the other English vessels. An hour later, six men from the *Kemp* under the leadership of First Lieutenant Myers and Sailing Master Fullers "fell on board the Ship" and carried her. A schooner "cried for quarters" as the *Kemp*'s hardened boarders prepared to leap upon her, and a brig struck her colors as Almeda got within pistol range. With so many prizes in hand Almeda could not prevent the schooner from rehoisting her colors, opening fire on her captor, and escaping in company with a brig. Instead of pursuing them, Almeda moved upon the remaining large ship. Her captain, having seen enough, struck her colors immediately. According to Almeda, who now took time to round up his prizes, he had engaged a total of forty-one guns and 143 men while taking 71 prisoners. He lost 1 dead, 3 wounded, and his boarders on the two escaping vessels.[47]

What did Almeda have in hand? The elegant, sixteen-gun, 261-ton ship *Rosabella* with a full cargo of sugar and coffee was sent into Charleston but ran aground. The eight-gun brig *Portsea*, with sugar and coffee, made it into Charleston along with the ship *Princess*, carrying a huge cargo of sugar. A fourth vessel, also carrying sugar and coffee from Havana for London, also got into an American port. Almeda noted proudly in his log that "we can say as the Gallant Perry said, we met the Enemy and they were ours." On December 7 Almeda transferred fifty prisoners from the crowded *Kemp* to a sloop while actually anchoring the prize ship *Princess* personally. In port, the grateful Almeda let sixteen of his men go into town for leave after drawing lots. The few remaining men scraped the *Kemp*'s decks.[48]

Back to sea in company with the privateer *Midas* of Baltimore, Almeda completed a second successful cruise. Among his captures was the new brig

Lady Mary Pelham of ten guns, taken on February 9, 1815. After a "warm contest" of three hours at pistol range, the prudent Almeda removed two brass cannons and most of the brig's small arms before entrusting it to a prize crew. After frequent escapes in the West Indies, Almeda took the large ship *Ottowa* with just one broadside. She contained a valuable cargo of dry goods being carried from Liverpool to Jamaica. The *Kemp* collapsed some of her own water casks to make room for her prize goods. Informed of peace, Almeda "Made all Sail for Baltimore," entering on April 1, 1815. Unable to write, Joseph Almeda placed his mark at the end of his log. Almeda's leadership and the crew's skill on the second cruise earned each seaman $413 per share (most were entitled to two), a neat $9,000 for Almeda, and a small fortune for Peter Arnold Karthaus.[49]

Known as "The Pride of Baltimore" the 356-ton *Chasseur* was as audacious a raider as the *Kemp*. Fast even for a Baltimore schooner, the Thomas Kemp-built vessel outsailed everything she met on the high seas. Frustrated in their efforts to get the schooner to sea as a letter-of-marque trader by the blockade on one occasion and by a mutiny over rations on another, owners Hollins and McBlair sold the beautiful schooner to a Baltimore syndicate.[50] The new owners increased her armament and crew before sending her through the blockade on Christmas Day of 1813 for a privateering cruise under William Wade, formerly Boyle's second officer on the *Comet*. After a productive cruise in European and West Indian waters, Wade brought the big schooner into New York on June 1, 1814. Because of changes in armament and commander, the owners acquired a new commission. While outfitting the vessel and putting on sixteen long twelve-pounders instead of carronades, the owners sent the famous Thomas Boyle to New York to take command. Boyle and a crew of 150 passed Sandy Hook on July 29, 1814, for a cruise.[51]

From Newfoundland waters and on his way to Europe, Boyle sent in the fourteen-gun brig *Eclipse*, the "fine copper fastened brig" *Commerce*, the schooner *Fox*, and the brig *Antelope*, which "struck without firing a gun" while carrying a load of Havana sugar. All British warships pursuing the *Chasseur* were "outsailed with ease." After burning several Scottish vessels, Boyle captured the brig *Marquis of Cornwallis*, valueless after being picked over by several other American privateers in the English Channel. The eight-gun ship *James* and the brig *Atlantic*, sailing in company from South America for London with hides, tallow, bark, and furs, were ordered into American ports in the last week of August of 1814.[52]

Not all of Boyle's messages to the British emanated from the muzzle of a gun. On August 30, while reprovisioning a vessel he had converted into a prisoner cartel earlier, the cocky Irishman informed his British prisoners that he had sent a proclamation of blockade to Lloyd's of London. The impudent suggestion that the *Chasseur* alone could effectively blockade all England, Scotland, and Ireland was Boyle's rejoinder to Britain's declaration that the entire American coast was in a state of blockade. The *Chasseur*'s commander, convinced that the British naval force on the American coast was inadequate for such a task, considered the British effort to be an illegal "paper blockade." His own proclamation read as follows:

PROCLAMATION

Whereas it has become customary with the Admirals of Great Britain, commanding the small forces on the coast of the United States, particularly with Sir John Borlase Warren, and Sir Alexander Cochrane, to declare all the coast of the United States in a state of strict and rigorous blockade, without possessing the power to justify such a declaration, or stationing an adequate force to maintain and blockade —

I do, therefore, by virtue of the power and authority in me vested (possessing sufficient force) declare all the ports, harbours, bays, creeks, rivers, inlets, outlets, islands and sea coast of the United Kingdom of Great Britain and Ireland in a state of strict and rigorous blockade. And I do further declare, that I consider the force under my command adequate to maintain strictly, rigorously and effectually the said blockade. And I do hereby require the respective officers, whether captains, commanders or commanding officers under my command, employed or to be employed on the coast of England, Ireland and Scotland to pay strict attention to the execution of this my Proclamation. And I do hereby caution and forbid the ships and vessels of all and every nation in amity and peace with the United States from entering or attempting to enter, or from coming or attempting to come out of any of the said ports, harbours, bays, creeks, rivers, inlets, outlets, islands or sea coast, under any pretence whatsoever. And that no person may plead ignorant of this my Proclamation, I have ordered the same to be made public in England.

Given under my hand on board the *Chasseur*, day and date as above.

THOMAS BOYLE
By command of the commanding officer,
J. J. Stansbury, Sec.[53]

Undoubtedly, the *Chasseur*'s sailing ability and her sixteen long twelve-pounders assured Boyle that he would never have to explain his concept of blockade to a British court.

The operation of Baltimore schooners such as the *Chasseur* and other American privateers infuriated the British public and the Admiralty. Vigorous efforts were made to catch the American seawolves. In one chase, the *Chasseur* put two broadsides into "a frigate of the second class" but received some punishment in exchange. One twenty-four-pound shot struck Boyle's foremast about twelve feet from the deck and "cut it nearly a third off." Another "struck the gunwale of port No. 5, tore away all the sill and plank shear," dismounted the gun, went through the deck, and wounded three men. Henry Watson was "compelled to have his thigh amputated, and is maimed for life" according to the schooner's journal. After escaping from four men-of-war at once, Boyle perceived a trap set for him by two man-of-war brigs. He "edged down upon one of them, which was of the largest class" but after she fired at him, Boyle "fired a shot to him, displayed the Yanky flag, hauled upon a wind, and outsailed them both with ease." On the very next day, September 6, 1814, Boyle "got among three men-of-war, and narrowly escaped capture" in a calm. On the seventh, Boyle was "chased by 4 men-of-war but outsailed them with ease." Three days later, he outsailed one of five man-of-war brigs sent out especially to nab the *Chasseur*.[54]

Even with the intensified pressure from the British navy, Boyle made more prizes in English waters. Dogging a convoy of thirty-three vessels, Boyle waited until "a perfect gale" separated the ship *Carlbury* of London, bound from Curaçao via Jamaica, before making his move. Leaving bulky items such as cotton, cocoa, tobacco, and hides on the *Carlbury*, Boyle removed the smaller and more valuable goods to the safety of his own hold before ordering the *Carlbury* into an American port. Dogging another convoy in late September, west of Ireland, Boyle jumped the brig *Amicus*, of and for Liverpool from Lisbon. Removing a small quantity of valuable woolens, Boyle sent the brig with her remaining cargo of wool and fruit into port. Down to only sixty men, Boyle brought the *Chasseur* with her hold jammed with prize goods and forty-eight prisoners into New York on October 29, 1814. In three months' cruising in English waters, off Halifax and Bermuda, Boyle had taken eighteen prizes, sending in nine while parolling 150 prisoners. Focusing on the *Chasseur*'s cruise and the productive United States sloop-of-war *Peacock*, a Baltimore editor offered the two cruises as "fresh proof" and "clear indications" that commerce raiding was the best way to defeat Britain. American seamen, the editor boasted, were now "the admiration of Europe and the terror of England."[55]

While Thomas Boyle returned to Baltimore to consult with the owners, *Chasseur*'s foremast and some of her yards were altered to allow her to convert to brig or brigantine rigging at will. Probably because he was planning to cruise in crowded West Indian waters where he would have less elbow room, Boyle replaced ten of his long twelve-pounders with the popular hard-hitting and quickly loaded carronades. Moving from the North River to an anchorage at Staten Island, the brig *Chasseur* broke for the open sea on December 23, 1814. Heavy seas knocked down her "Fore Top Gallant Mast" and cost her one man who was carried "overboard by the Wash of a Sea" and never seen again. After reaching Barbados on January 5, Boyle exchanged shots with a large sloop-of-war, burned a schooner within sight of a British admiral's ship, and escaped a pursuing frigate or seventy-four-gun ship-of-the-line "with ease." On January

15 the sometimes reckless Boyle showed his more prudent side when he refused to take a British ship only a half mile away but "within Neutral limits."[56]

Thomas Boyle was just as resourceful as a situation demanded. With squalls pushing a heavier frigate close upon the fleeing *Chasseur*, the commander threw over ten guns, his spare yards, and started releasing his water to lighten the brig. Finally, as the frigate kept coming, he moved two long twelve-pounders aft. Once he had the *Chasseur*'s rails sawn away to give the guns more play, they drove off his tormentor. On February 3 Boyle beat all hands to quarters, cleared for action, and loaded his remaining guns with round and grape shot. In fifteen minutes the 335-ton ship *Coruna* struck but was unable to follow Boyle's sailing instructions because the crew "was all run below from fear." Boyle replaced his lost guns with those of the *Coruna* and ordered her and her cargo of coal, coarse clothing, cheese, crockery, and hardware into the United States. While dogging a huge convoy of 110 vessels, Boyle's wait for the inevitable laggard paid off when the ship *Adventure*, out of London for Havana, fell behind. Boyle snapped her up, divested some cargo, and sent her into an American port.[57]

Some prizes came easily, but others did not want to come at all. Boyle lost six well-armed ships and two brigs near Puerto Rico after unsuccessfully attempting to separate them. Off Santo Domingo he burned a ketch taken with a volley of musketry while a Jamaica-bound ship struck as soon as the black *Chasseur* pulled alongside and hoisted her flag. It took Boyle two days to divest that vessel's rich cargo. On February 15, 1815, Boyle pursued an innocent-looking schooner showing only three gunports on one side. The *Chasseur*'s commander "hastily made but small preparation for action, expecting no fighting." Much to his chagrin the schooner uncovered a tier of ten gunports and unloosed a broadside when the unsuspecting American was within pistol range. Responding with all his great and small guns, Boyle's closeness, forcing him to try a boarding operation, permitted him to see not only extra men concealed under his opponent's bulwark, but "the blood run Freely from her Scuppers" from the *Chasseur*'s desperate return fire. Boyle's order to board, "quick and cheerfully obeyed," induced the battered adversary, His British Majesty's Schooner *St. Lawrence*, formerly the famous private armed schooner *Atlas* of Philadelphia, to surrender. Carrying fourteen twelve-pound carronades, a long nine-pounder, and seventy-five men plus some marines, the *St. Lawrence* lost at least six men killed and seventeen wounded. She was "a perfect wreck in her hull and had scarcely a Sail or Rope Standing" but the *Chasseur* was hurt in her sails and rigging also. Thomas Boyle, who had lost no men on his first cruise on the *Comet*, had to record five men killed and seven wounded, including four very serious cases. He converted the wrecked *St. Lawrence* into a "flag of Truce" for Havana, carrying the wounded from "motives of humanity" much appreciated by her former captain. Knowing deadly combat with naval vessels was not his object, Boyle wrote an explanation of his actions and his desire to defend his flag to George Pitt Stevenson, the *Chasseur*'s prize agent in Baltimore.[58]

After just missing a water spout on March 1, 1815, the *Chasseur* was informed of peace by an American vessel out of Boston. Coming up the Chesapeake without a pilot, Boyle and the "Pride of Baltimore" were greeted by a rousing salute from the guns of Fort McHenry as they entered their home port on March 20, 1815. Because of a clause permitting captures in different seas for varying periods of time after the peace treaty was ratified, Boyle's prizes were not invalidated by their date of capture. The *Amelia, Kemp, Surprise,* and other Baltimore raiders profited from the same clause. Unlike the national navy, Baltimore's private navy had not been driven from the sea by the British navy in 1814.[59]

Other Baltimore privateers had successful cruises and experienced danger and adventures. Holder of one of the two commissions marked No. 1, the privateer *Nonsuch*, solely owned by George Stiles, fought a bruising three hour and twenty minute battle with two opponents. After exchanging ten full broadsides, Captain Henry Lively had to rely on muskets alone because all twelve of his big guns were knocked loose.[60] While not blockading the Newfoundland banks à la Boyle, S. Smith and Buchanan's 376-ton *Mammoth* under Captain Samuel Franklin did order all British fishing boats off the Grand Banks. The *Mammoth*, Baltimore's largest schooner, was on her way to Europe and a productive cruise.[61] The 161-ton, ten-gun *Dolphin*, another S. Smith and Buchanan privateer, challenged a sixteen-gun ship and a ten-gun brig simultaneously off Spain. Captain William J. Stafford's depleted crew of sixty on the *Dolphin* numbered five less men than his opponent's. A broadside at pistol range and aggressive boarding parties convinced both Englishmen to strike their colors. The determined Stafford also attacked the huge and valuable 550-ton, sixteen-gun ship *John Hamilton* for two days before subduing it.[62]

Hollins and McBlair's 316-ton *York* strove valiantly to capture a stronger opponent. She barely survived a blistering encounter with a huge British army transport in the spring of 1814. Massed musket fire from the soldiers on the high transport killed Captain Enoch Staples, the *York*'s helmsman, a prize master, the wardroom steward, a seaman, the cooper, and one marine on the rolling *York*. With her gun muzzles dipping in and out of the sea, with damage to her hull, her sails torn up, and her masts swaying, the *York* hauled off. The *York*'s boarding operation had been halted at the last minute when troops with fixed bayonets awaited their arrival on the *Lord Somer*'s decks. In addition to her dead, the *York*'s crew suffered one crushed leg, one fractured leg, an amputated arm, two hip wounds, the loss of part of a boy's foot, and six lesser wounds. Such losses would have been severe on a small naval vessel, but the *York*'s council of war decided they would risk a run for port in their damaged schooner rather than surrender. Back into Boston for repairs, the *York* returned to sea in November of 1814. In her successful thirteen week cruise out of Boston, the *York* actually challenged another transport. A Baltimore editor pointed to the *York*'s prizes and jam-packed hold, acquired without the loss of a man, as a lesson to the Navy Department in how to deal Britain the most "essential injury."[63]

The privateer *Globe* suffered unnecessarily during a case of mistaken identity. The *Globe* and other Baltimore privateers often flew Spanish or English flags to enable them to close with an unsuspecting Englishman. For this or other reasons, neither the *Globe* nor her opponent off Portugal in 1813 knew whom she was fighting. After a three-hour fight the 180-ton *Globe* had three feet of water in her hold while her sails and rigging were badly damaged. She had twenty-seven shot holes through her main sail, fifteen through the jib, seven in the flying jib, twelve through the foresail, seventeen in the main sail, two through the main topsail, two in the main boom, and one in the starboard bow. That punishment had been dealt to the *Globe* by a large Algerine sloop-of-war with no real interest in fighting an American privateer.[64] Fortunately for her owners, the *Globe* made several successful cruises. The stubborn 337-ton privateer *Sabine* hooked up with a powerful 500-ton East Indiaman carrying six heavy guns. Both the *Sabine* and her adversary, the *Countess of Harcourt*, pulled away in the English Channel to make repairs in the middle of the battle. The Indiaman, "one of an outward bound fleet, separated in a gale of wind," was finally conquered and sent into Georgia. For the *Sabine*, formerly a letter-of-marque trader, the expensive ship with her great cargo of dry goods, brandy, gin, porter, glassware, and cheese was well worth the trouble. Unfortunately, the *Sabine* was destroyed in September of 1814 when she ran aground.[65]

The 301-ton *Surprise* was another of the large schooners built during the war. Owned by Gerrard Wilson, Lemuel Taylor, and the firm of Hollins and McBlair, her large hold enabled her to make four long cruises in distant waters. After cruising in the English and Irish channels, through the Western Islands, off the Newfoundland banks, and along the coast of Nova Scotia in a 113-day cruise, the *Surprise* entered at Newport on July 12, 1814. Chased sixteen times, she escaped by "superior sailing," while bringing in prize goods and nineteen prisoners under Captain Clement Cathell, one of Boyle's old officers on the *Comet*. In her four cruises under Captains Cathell, James Barnes, formerly of the *Sabine*, and Samuel Barstow, the *Surprise* captured forty-three prizes of which the most valuable, such as the richly laden ships *Kutusoff* and *Star*, made it into American ports. The *Surprise* ran aground and went to pieces with the loss of fifteen lives despite the desperate efforts of her crew and passengers from the navy's *Erie* to save her.[66]

The steady stream of privateers coming out of Baltimore and the tales of combat and prizes that followed their departure have attracted more attention

from historians than the less dramatic operations of the letter-of-marque traders. The traders took some prizes and fought some intense battles, but their
primary objective was to earn profits from trade. Dependent upon their sails
more than their guns, twelve commissioned traders cleared from Baltimore
before November 4, 1812. Seven cleared for Bordeaux, two for Nantes, and one
each for Portugal, Haiti, and Charleston.[67] Some owners loaded their traders
with their own goods, while others carried freight for other merchants. George
Stiles, sole owner of a fleet of commissioned vessels, advertised in October of
1812 that he had five vessels available to carry freight to France, while William
Hollins offered to take 50,000 pounds of coffee or sugar as freight to France in
the *Hussar*. John Carrere called for sugar, coffee, or other colonial produce for
the hold of his *Expedition*.[68] Whether the owners were shy of goods or were
simply reticent of placing all their own eggs in one basket is uncertain. Freight
income helped to defray the operating expenses of the commissioned traders.
Those expenses were estimated to be about one thousand dollars per month at
sea for a 250-ton cargo-carrying schooner.[69]

Letter-of-marque traders were the fastest schooners even though they were
often larger than some privateers. Hold capacity was the vital statistic. Commissioned traders were handled by good officers and seamen, not landsmen or
greenhands. Captain George Little considered the crews on letter-of-marque
traders to be superior in their skill and behavior to those on privateers where
combativeness was often of more value to the venture than sailing skills.[70] The
roughnecks making up boarding parties on privateers were seldom needed on
the traders.

Letter-of-marque traders carried the produce of the middle Atlantic region.
Popular cargoes consisted of flour and tobacco, southern or West Indian cotton
for the European market, or West Indian coffee and sugar. The xebec *Ultor's*
export manifest listed 450 barrels of superfine flour, 400 boxes of soap, and 70
hams when she cleared as a letter-of-marque trader for St. Bartholomew's in the
West Indies.[71] Henry Didier, Jr. loaded flour on the *Harrison* for New Orleans
where he had cotton waiting to go to France. Didier also sent the *Maria* to
Havana with flour before loading her with cotton for France. In 1814 he was
shipping flour to the West Indies before loading the same vessels with tobacco in
North Carolina for France. Didier mentioned the *Midas, Sabine, Sylph, Patapsco,*
and other first rate Baltimore schooners as participating in the Baltimore to the
West Indies to France triangle.[72] By April of 1813 it was reported that "Cotton
is now the only article which promises a sure profit" in France. In November of
1813 sleek Baltimore flyers were a familiar sight in French ports. An American
consular officer reported in November of 1812 that "Fifteen American schooners, chiefly from Baltimore have arrived since the war declaration at the ports of
Nantes, Bordeaux, and La Rochelle, each bringing about one hundred tons of
merchandize."[73] Active investor George Williams offered from twenty-five to

fifty bales of Louisiana cotton "uncommonly hard packed" and averaging four hundred pounds each to "each fast sailing vessel bound to France."[74] Baltimore's entrepreneurs were shipping particular products to a particular market. When markets contracted, they shipped something else or found new markets.

Return cargoes on the commissioned traders varied. Dry goods, wines, and manufactured items, scarce in America by late 1812, sold well, while coffee and sugar could be reexported. The *Pioneer* entered Baltimore with a cargo of brandy, wine, and dry goods in December of 1812, sailing home in company with the Baltimore commissioned trader *Price* after leaving seven other Baltimore schooners in France. The *Tyro* with 70,000 pounds of coffee, the *Philaeni* with coffee, and the *Halcyon* also with coffee, all arrived in Baltimore from Haiti in one short period. The *Midas, Rapid,* and *Eliza* were loading coffee and sugar in Havana in the winter of 1812 to 1813. French wine, almonds, cloth, and wire, offered for sale at the Front Street city auction store, came in on the *Thetis.* The *Patapsco* offered a variety of French goods for sale at Thomas Tenant's Fells Point wharf in April of 1813.[75]

The blockade forced the flyers into other ports. The *Brutus* entered at Portsmouth, New Hampshire, from Nantes in December of 1813, but her agent transferred her cargo of silks, glasses, pencils, ribbons, wax, and other items to the India wharf in Boston for better sales. The *Hollins,* in an eight-day voyage from the West Indies, and the *Express,* with sugar in a fourteen-day run from Cuba, entered at New York.[76] The *Tuckahoe* carried 80 hogsheads, 77 tierces, and 160 barrels of sugar into Philadelphia.[77] Through the house of Hones and Towne, the *Grampus* advertised claret, brandy, oil, champagne, satins, ribbons, silk gloves, boot tops, and other items in New York.[78] The traders were, in good entrepreneurial fashion, trying to fill the home market for dry goods and luxury items. S. Smith and Buchanan's *Lottery* entered at Brazil on her way to Baltimore with dry goods acquired in Calcutta. She and her desirable cargo docked at Baltimore in November of 1812.[79]

The records of captured letter-of-marque traders provide an added insight into cargoes. When taken by two British warships, the *Flight* had on board sixty chests of merchandise, a cask of glasses, gloves, oil, china, wine, and brandy. The *Governor Shelby,* on her way from New York to Amsterdam, was taken by two British warships while carrying 121 hogsheads and 6,000 pounds of tobacco. The *Lynx* was taken by six British warships while her hold contained cotton, coffee, and sugar, a popular mixed export cargo. The *Racer,* cut out of the Rappahannock by Britain's *Victorious* in 1813, carried the same cargo.[80] In these cases the proceeds from prize auctions went to the officers and crews of the eleven British warships that captured the four racers.

Unlike records of prize sales, the records of letter-of-marque sales do not show profits clearly. Henry Didier, Jr., however, reported that his *Philaeni's* cargo of sugar grossed $40,000 and netted $30,000. He noted at another time that the *Philaeni*, the *Argo*, and the *Burrows* were all back after voyages to the West Indies and that they each "made 100% on their Voyages" while the *Harrison* also did well.[81] Those owning all or part of several traders could survive the capture of one when the others returned the kind of profits that Didier mentioned. Even when profits sagged, letter-of-marque traders permitted a merchant to move his goods and to employ his vessels and capital. Nonshipowning merchants also benefited from the system because it was the only way goods could be exported during the blockade. The fact that 114 of Baltimore's 175 or more commissions were for letter-of-marque traders suggests that either they were profitable or that privateers were too expensive and risky for some investors. A few Baltimore schooners such as the *Siro, Sabine,* and *Midas*, alternated as traders and cruisers, but the *Siro* did so under the same commission. Commissioned traders were the quieter arm of the private service, but they were an extremely useful arm for the port. They helped to outfit the privateers while exporting local products, imports, and prize goods and importing scarce items for the nation in general. They also took prizes on occasion.

Once a prize was in hand at sea, the commander of a privateer or the captain of a commissioned trader had decisions to make. For a privateer commander, his judgment at that moment was often critical and the processes he set in motion would determine the financial success or failure of the venture for the privateer's shareholders, his crew, and himself. Privateers survived on prize income alone, while the captain of a letter-of-marque trader knew his prize money was a welcome bonus for all involved. Both wanted to ensure the safe arrival and condemnation of their prizes and the prize goods in their own holds.

TEN

With Prey in Hand

Whether captured after minimal resistance or smashed into submission in desperate combat, a majority of the vessels taken at sea never got to an American prize court. Many were divested and sunk, a number were converted into prisoner cartels, a few were simply let go, and others ran afoul of the weather, went aground, or were recaptured. By lowering his colors, a British captain guaranteed prize money to no one, but he did cause his captor to activate another phase of the private armed vessel system. That phase consisted of the handling and processing of the prize vessel, her crew, and her cargo from the point of capture all the way to the captor's prize agent's collection of the prize auction proceeds from the clerk of the court. When this phase was poorly executed, all that preceded it, including the proper financing, the acquisition of documents, vessel preparation, the recruitment and training of hands, and even the actual capturing of the prize, went for naught in the account books.

After a victim lowered her flag, there was little time for the capturer to lick his wounds or even rejoice. A boat took the officers of the capturing vessel to her victim to inspect her papers, cargo, personnel, and condition. When the captain decided that the vessel was seaworthy, estimated that her cargo was of value, and was satisfied that he could spare a prize master and a prize crew, he had her manned. Most but not all of the officers, some of the crew, any specie or exceedingly valuable and compact cargo such as dry goods were removed to the capturing vessel. Left on the manned prize, some officers and the prize's papers would be needed later in court. The prize master's ability to deliver the prize into an American or friendly port while avoiding recapture, grounding, severe storms, or prisoner insurrections was the key to the entire venture's success.

When the capturing vessel was a letter-of-marque trader carrying no prize masters, an officer was used as prize master. The loss of such officers and even small prize crews, however, was a serious consideration in the decision to man or not to man the prize vessel. Such crew reductions seriously jeopardized a trader's ability to defend herself in future encounters with the British. Of necessity, traders utilized smaller prize crews than privateers and, consequently, their prizes were relatively more vulnerable to recapture or prisoner revolts. Captain George Coggeshall reported that he actually freed a prize taken on his way to France in 1813 simply because he could spare no men at all for her prize crew.[1] Letter-of-marque traders carrying full cargoes were also unable to transfer large prize items or prisoners to their own holds. The privateer *Liberty* had the same problem, not because of a commercial cargo on board, but because of the smallness of the hold of a fifty-five-ton schooner. She divested one prize of her guns and gave her up "for want of room for prisoners."[2] Usually, privateers had more men for prize crews and more space for prisoners and prize cargoes, especially after they had manned prizes.

The captain of the capturing vessel had many things to consider when he had a prize in hand. Once the blockade of the American coast was established, he might divest more cargo and not attempt to run his feebly manned prize through the British blockading squadron. His own vessel was better able to defend prize goods in her hold, and in most cases, she had already demonstrated her ability to outsail her prize. Speed was the critical success factor on the run to a friendly port. When his prize was of little value, the commander might unload some of his prisoners by converting the captured vessel into a prisoner cartel, or he might sink her, set her afire, or simply release her. Ransoming was done but it was not injurious to the enemy because a ransomed vessel remained active. Congress finally outlawed ransom at sea, and a Baltimore editor noted that it was always better to send a vessel "down cellar" than to ransom her.[3] Baltimore's private fleet preferred to sink, burn, or cut off the masts of those British vessels having little monetary value.

In regard to removing prisoners to his own vessel, a captain had to consider the bounty offered by the government. The bounty for each prisoner brought in was $20 in 1812, but it was raised to $25 in 1813 and, finally, to $100 in 1814.[4] A prudent captain worried about insurrection as his prisoners increased and his own crew gradually diminished through casualties and prize crews. Some, however, took the risk. The *Highflyer* came in with sixty prisoners on board in 1812.[5] Probably more typical was the *Amelia*'s eight prisoners for whom the agent noted $800 as "Cash from Washington" in his account book. Prisoners were an additional source of income, but they were a risky and troublesome source. Leaving the prisoners on a manned prize was not an alternative because the small prize crew could not control them. The actual number of British prisoners brought in or paroled at sea is uncertain. Some were captured, exchanged, or paroled and captured again while some cartels never reached port. Others were freed when their captured vessel was retaken by the British. Because surviving but incomplete government prisoner lists named only the capturing vessel and not her home port when vessels out of other ports used the same names as Baltimore vessels, the number of British seamen captured by Baltimore vessels is not clear. After the elimination of questionable vessels the records suggest that Baltimore's private fleet brought in or paroled at sea a minimum of one thousand six hundred British prisoners. The size of any bounties awarded was dependent upon the date and the Congressional act of the moment.[6]

The critical period between capture and condemnation was the voyage home, which was the responsibility of the prize master. Captain George Little characterized prize masters as jolly fellows who rated themselves superior in rank and talent to any on board except the captain "because they'd be commanders before the cruise was over."[7] Some apparently did little while waiting for their command to materialize, but Commodore Joshua Barney used the *Rossie's* prize masters as petty or junior officers and put them in charge of the ever-dangerous boarding operations.[8]

The prize masters' role demanded both navigational and leadership skills. Consequently, former captains were enticed into the role by owners offering them large shares and bonuses. The prize masters on Captain Thomas Boyle's *Comet* serve as an example. Numbered among them were Purnell Austin, a former captain with eighteen years of sea experience, and William Cathell, a master with eight years experience. Also included were Seth Long who had "commanded sundry vessels in his twenty-six years at sea" and former captain James Towers.[9] Unusual among prize masters was one Anthony W. Hayman of the privateer *Dolphin*. Hayman listed himself as a member of the antiwar Quaker sect.[10] There were few alternatives to private armed vessel duty for a mariner in the war years, and the prize masters' role paid well when one was successful.

Prize masters were given special instructions from privateer commanders. A surviving example was given to a prize master of the Philadelphia privateer ship *Young Wasp* who brought his unusually valuable prize into Baltimore for adjudication. He was ordered to "repair on board as soon as possible, and proceed with all possible dispatch to a port in the United States." He was further instructed to inform the privateer's owner, Andrew Curcier of Philadelphia, immediately upon his arrival in an American port. The prize master was authorized to put his crew "on allowance" or short rations, if necessary, and to carry "as much sail as may be proper." In regard to the British, the prize master was advised that "you will no doubt defend the ship as long as you can and not give her up but to a superior force." The privateer's own Articles of Agreement were to be enforced on the prize, and any crew action endangering the prize or her "good management" was to be met with force and irons. The privateer commander assured the prize master, a third lieutenant from the *Young Wasp*, that he would support any use of force that was necessary. The commander promised to "exonerate" the prize master "from any damages whatever," because he was enforcing the "strict laws of the United States for the better government of Privateering."[11] Such concern was justified by the unusual value of the *Clarendon*; the ship and her cargo sold for $278,101.64 in Baltimore.[12]

The prize masters' rewards were great, but so were their risks when less than one-third of all vessels manned by American prize crews ever reached port. One prize master wrote agent George Pitt Stevenson in Baltimore that his prize had lost her foremast and was a complete wreck, while he almost starved before putting into Puerto Rico in distress.[13] Another prize master going into Puerto Rico for provisions lost his vessel to Spanish authorities who restored her to her British owners.[14] That prize vessel and her cargo were a total loss for the privateer *Comet*. Prize master John Clark on the *Ontario*, prize to the *Lawrence*, tried to bring his vessel in with three seamen, five inexperienced youngsters called "green boys," three Swedes from the prize, and three British prisoners. Clark escaped from a British brig-of-war, a letter-of-marque trader, and several other warships. He was boarded by the New York privateer *Scourge* from whom he acquired some coffee and a chart, but his success was short-lived. The prize crew revolted, bound the captain, and took over the *Ontario*. A counterrevolt by two seamen and the green boys proved futile when a British warship recaptured the *Ontario*.[15] After recapturing an estimated seven hundred fifty prizes in the war, Britain sent American prize masters home in prisoner exchanges, including some Baltimoreans who, when stranded in Portland, wrote to Baltimore for money.[16]

The log of one prize vessel illustrates the way prizes were handled in foreign ports. The British brig *Pelican* was captured by the Baltimore privateer *Lawrence* on April 21, 1814 while carrying sugar, cotton, and logwood. Captain Edward Veazey ordered her into France rather than risk the long and dangerous voyage to the American coast.[17] In foreign ports American consuls were charged with the task of hearing prize cases.[18] American merchants in France were appointed agents for the American owners of privateers to supervise their prize cases and the consequent sales. John A. Morton, Baltimore merchant and active investor in private armed vessels, resided in Bordeaux during most of the war. Although he held no shares in the *Lawrence*, Morton was appointed "general agent for the *Lawrence* in all the Ports of France" by letter. Morton, in turn, named the American consuls at Brest and L'Orient as his agents to handle the case of the *Pelican*, the aforementioned prize to Baltimore's *Lawrence*. The whole procedure of condemnation and sale was completed for the *Pelican* just two hours before the publication of a French decree prohibiting the sale of American prizes in France.[19] Changes in the government and the war brought about changes in policy.

The American consul fulfilled the judicial function in foreign ports. That official's role is illustrated by the case of the three-masted, square-rigged ship *Favorite*, prize to the privateer *True Blooded Yankee* of Bristol. The prize master filed a libel with American consul William Bass at Brest, and Bass advised all

PLATE VI

*M. MacPherson's copy of water color in the Peabody Museum
in Salem, Massachusetts, "The Privateer Schooner* SURPRISE
of Baltimore, Maryland, Capturing the British Merchant Ship
STAR, *Armed Indiaman, January 28, 1815," original copy in
the Maryland Historical Society*

those interested to show cause why the case should not be adjudicated. With no protests, the consul then judged the *Favorite*'s register, crew, colors, and cargo to be British and took testimony from the British prisoners present at the time of the capture. Finally, Bass issued a decree declaring the *Favorite* "a good and lawful prize" and authorized a public sale.[20]

France was not the only foreign country utilized by American prize masters. The Philadelphia privateer *Rattlesnake* and New York's *Scourge* together sent twenty-two prizes into Norway. That country was an excellent market for grain and the twenty-two prizes were all coming from Russia with grain.[21] A good captain considered market prizes when he chose particular ports for prize sales. It was reported that the *Rattlesnake* alone sent in over one million dollars worth of prizes into Norway.[22] The *Midas* of Baltimore sent the three-masted, square-rigged ship *Pizzaro* with dry goods, crates, copper, and salt, the ship *Esperanza* with cotton and flour, and the brig *Elsinore* with salt into Havana.[23] Market prices, the conditions of the vessels, and the existence of the blockade were all factors encouraging captains to send prizes into foreign, but supposedly friendly, ports.

The journal of the aforementioned *Pelican*, prize to the *Lawrence*, demonstrates the difficulties faced by prize masters. Placed in the hands of prize master Isiah Lewis and four men, the *Pelican* was ordered into France. Lewis avoided several British warships before he landed in France where "No person could speak English." An American consul visited the vessel, and Lewis wrote to the agent of the *Lawrence*, John A. Morton, in Bordeaux. The prize master went to Brest to sign papers and returned to find "no meat on board and a little moldy Bread." Problems with the crew included a knife attack by a crewman whom Lewis gave a "thrashing," and one black man who nearly died from a stab wound inflicted by another crewman. Lewis had to supervise his crew for eighteen days in port before the cargo was even discharged. A few days later a crewman stole sugar and other items from the *Pelican* while deserting. It was a month or more after landing before condemnation was completed and the cargo sold. Lewis's expenditures for his crew included money for panteloons, shoes, bootmending, and doctor visits. Cash advances to the crew and the cost of mending clothes and shoes were also deducted from the sales proceeds. Agent Morton did not know how to return the remaining sales proceeds to the Baltimore owners of the *Lawrence*.[24]

Not all prize masters were as diligent or as honest as Isiah Lewis. One Hugh Reed, prize master on the *Caroline*, was denied prize money for his six shares in two prize cargoes. It was argued that those cargoes "were embezzled by Reed and smuggled ashore" into Camden, New Jersey, in the dark of the night.[25] Other prize masters ran their vessels aground or lost them in rough weather, prisoner revolts, or to British vessels. The former captain of the English brig *Eagle*, left on board that prize to the *Lawrence* for some reason in

November of 1814, led a revolt against prize master John Hooper. After several of his men were killed, Hooper, with a stab wound, was lashed to the deck for three days and nights without water. Hooper's relief, after his own men regained control, gave way to despair when a British warship recaptured the *Eagle* off New York.[26] The ship *Loyal Sam*, prize to the letter-of-marque *Siro*, was retaken off Portland. Prize master William Furlough, Jr., despite the aid of land guns, was forced to abandon his prize to an English brig and privateer. The *Loyal Sam* ran out of ammunition less than four miles from shore.[27]

British records from Barbados and Halifax list six prizes retaken from Captain Thomas Boyle's *Comet* and one each from the *Globe, Chasseur, Fairy, Amelia,* and *Syren,* all of Baltimore.[28] More recaptured prizes were sent into England and other stations. The prize master of the *Chasseur's* prize schooner *Malpomene,* taken under Captain William Wade, found he had more to fear from his own crew than from the British or the elements. Prize master John Prior found his entire crew of three drunk on deck, unwilling to follow orders. After assaulting Prior and locking him below, the crewmen were compelled to turn the vessel over to her former captain because they could not handle it. Fortunately for Prior, the English captain brought her into Newport where the three mutineers were convicted. "Mulcted" of their prize money from the *Chasseur,* they were also sentenced by the navy court, respectively, to twenty-five, fifty, and seventy-four lashes.[29] Obviously, a prize master operating under less than ideal conditions often earned his shares the hard way.

In cases where a prize was unseaworthy or of little value as a vessel, and in situations where there was no friendly port nearby or no men to man her, a captain sought alternatives. What he usually did was to exercise his business judgment in removing selected goods to his own vessel. Such cargoes slowed his own vessel, but they were often valuable because compact crates, boxes, or trunks contained expensive items. Baltimore investor Levi Hollingsworth suggested the value of such packages when he lost one small trunk containing $7,482.55 worth of black lace.[30] Numerous trunks and cases in the hold often added up to large values. The privateer *Comet* entered Wilmington, North Carolina, with the divested cargoes of twenty prizes in her hold. The *Pike,* run aground while evading a pursuer, had $50,000 worth of prize goods in her hold, including a box of gold coins.[31] The proceeds of the sales of prize goods in the *Kemp's* hold on one cruise amounted to $47,869.18 after costs.[32] Other proceeds from prize cargoes included $33,173.62 for the *Chasseur's* and $50,917.84 for the *Perry's,* which included fifty-five cases and eleven bales of dry goods.[33] The *Whig's* prize cargo brought in $28,152.46, and on another cruise the *Kemp's* prize cargo of dry goods and hardware sold for an unusually high $112,799.19.[34] Such items were scarce in the United States during the war, so prices for them were high. Manufactured goods purchased in the Spanish West Indies for seventeen dollars per unit were sold for eighty dollars in Philadelphia.[35] Additionally, most of the schooners cited here were of the newer model, with larger holds. But, the privateer *Amelia* threw over a cargo of fish on one of her prizes so she could transfer prize goods from her own hold into it.[36]

Whenever possible both prize vessels and privateers carrying valuable prize cargoes in their holds attempted to enter at Baltimore, their port of first choice. An anxious Baltimore owner may have gotten his first hint of success when he saw a prize rowed past Fort McHenry. Others may have informed him at the coffee house or a note may have arrived from his prize agent. The routine, normally, was to raise a flag on the highest point near the harbor, Federal Hill. One observer noted, "A signal is up on the flag staff for an English ship, a prize."[37] Another firm watching its neighbors reap in profits, reported that "Last night a Jamaica Ship with 500 hogsheads Sugar and quantity of Coffee, Cotton and Cocoa came into our River Prize to the *Commet*." The port became accustomed to almost daily arrivals of prizes for a while. The blockade slowed the flow of riches into the Patapsco, but it quickened again once the British departed. In the fall of 1814 there were "numerous arrivals of Prizes to our Privateers."[38] The newspapers kept a running account of prizes entering at Baltimore and other ports.

The prize master entering his vessel at Baltimore did so at the Customs House. His prisoners were handed over to the United States marshal, and papers relevant to his prize were given to the prize agent for the owners. The prize agent was usually the same man who had served as the ship's husband in her preparatory stage. To handle prize accounts one had to be legally designated "prize agent." He held all the vessel's records and accounts as well as her Articles of Agreement, and most importantly, a power of attorney from the owners and often from the crew. The two roles of husband and agent overlapped to the point that Andrew Clopper identified himself as the "prize agent or ship's Husband of the Letter-of-Marque *Patapsco*."[39] As a prize agent Clopper supervised a prize vessel and her cargo, condemnation, sales, and the distribution of the proceeds.

The prize agent assigned his newly arrived prize to the custody of an experienced ship handler. Often the custodians were wharfingers such as private armed vessel investors Thorndike Chase, Baptiste Mezick, or Thomas Tenant.[40] The income they earned from that function was in addition to their owners' shares of prize money. They handled the maintenance, wharfage, supplying, and the transfer of the prize goods to warehouses and vendue houses. In their disbursements for their prize vessels, the custodians frequently paid other private armed vessel investors for goods or services. The prize *Hopewell*, for example, listed empty barrels bought from Peter Arnold Karthaus, empty hogsheads and drayage services from Levi Clagett, locks and whiskey from Fells Point chandler James Ramsay, blacksmith work from Thomas Cockrill, and beef and vegetables from grocer George Wolpert among her disbursements.[41]

All of them were private armed vessel investors and Clagett, Karthaus, and custodian Thorndike Chase were part-owners of the privateer *Comet*, capturer of the *Hopewell*. The sums earned by those investors providing services or goods were not immense, but they were in addition to their shares of the prize money. The impression is that the private investors threw such business to each other and that the care of prize vessels was one more substitute for the port's peacetime marine business.

While the prize vessel was being maintained and serviced, legal proceedings were instituted. These began with the filing of a suit against the prize vessel and her cargo. Such a suit in admiralty law was termed a "libel." The libel or petition was drawn up by admiralty lawyers, called "proctors" in that branch of law when they also argued the case in court for the libelants. Active proctors in Baltimore prize cases were John Purviance, John Meredith, John Aisquith, Nathaniel Williams, William McMechen, William Morrow, Robert Goodloe Harper, Richard Magruder, and James Donaldson.[42] Persons financially interested in a capturing vessel or prize were prohibited from assuming the role of proctor.[43] Consequently, no private armed vessel investors appeared in this particular income-producing role.

A libel in Baltimore was addressed to the United States District Court for Maryland. Federal jurisdiction over admiralty and maritime cases was established in section two of Article III of the United States Constitution and Congress subsequently authorized the new district courts to hear such cases. The act of June 26, 1812, authorizing the issuance of letters-of-marque and reprisal, stated explicitly in reference to prize cases that "the district courts of the United States shall have exclusive original cognizance thereof."[44] The actual filing of a libel was done through the clerk of the District Court.

Certain basic elements were necessary in a libel. The petition had to explain the cause of the action being entered into and list the parties and facts involved. It also had to describe any activity that took place at sea and it closed with a "prayer" for a trial, a decree of condemnation, and a public sale of the prize vessel and her cargo when a vessel was involved. Sometimes called a "Libel as Prize of War," the petition was also required to justify the District Court's jurisdiction in the particular case.[45] Once filed, the petition initiated a process developed over centuries of maritime history. Admiralty law's procedures and principles grew out of international rather than national law and the lawyers had to be knowledgeable in admiralty law to plead a prize case. For their services lawyers or proctors were paid from $50 to $150. John Purviance, an active admiralty lawyer, received fees of $100 and $150.[46] Lawyers drawing up the libels for the owners of the *Kemp* and *Perry* were paid $50.[47] The absence of a vessel in a prize case involving only divested cargoes may have lowered the fee. Admiralty lawyers were replacing their peacetime income while also remaining active in their specialty.

Once the petition was filed, events moved quickly. The judge ordered that interested parties were to be notified (a monition) and that the property in question was to be seized by the marshal (a proclamation of attachment). Such notices were nailed to a prize vessel's main mast or, if the prize were a cargo and not a vessel, they were placed on the doors of the courthouse and sometimes on the doors of neighboring coffee houses. The judge also set a date for the trial, allowing only a few days for all pretrial proceedings to be completed. The libelants, however, were forced to wait until the court was sitting as an admiralty court and not in its more common role of district court. Time was particularly important whenever market prices were high and in cases where spoilage could reduce a prize cargo's market value. In a not unusual sequence of events involving the libel of the privateer *Highflyer* against the prize schooner *Burchall*, the whole process took less than two weeks. John Purviance, proctor, filed his libel on December 21, 1812; the marshal served his papers the next day, including posting "on the Main-Mast"; and the trial was completed on January 6, 1813. The *Burchall* was declared a "good and lawful prize" and a public sale was ordered.[48] Few other than admiralty courts offered such dispatch.

The issuance of a decree of condemnation by the court was dependent upon the libelant's ability to prove British ownership. Documentary evidence, acceptable to the court, emanated from the prize's own papers. Registers, cargo manifests, owners' instructions to the captain, bills of sale of the vessel, bills of lading, and clearance certificates were acceptable evidence. British government permits for guns, convoy assignment papers, or permission for a vessel to sail without escorts also led to condemnation. Witnesses present at the time of capture had to testify that the papers used in evidence were indeed taken off the prize and they had not been altered in any way.

Prisoners brought in with the prize also testified. Officers, petty officers, supercargoes, or passengers taken in the prize answered a list of standard questions called the "standing interrogatory." The number of actual questions was not constant but the topics covered were similar. The questions were aimed at establishing the characteristics, ownership, origin, destination, and cargo of the prize. The residence and citizenship of the captain and crew of the prize were also established.[49] Such documentary and testimonial evidence was the key to condemnation.[50] A prize, in effect, had to condemn herself although the officers of the capturing vessel also swore to the authenticity of the captured papers. Failure to prove British ownership of the vessel or cargo led to the issuance of a decree of restoration for either one or both. Appeals in prize cases in American courts went to the Supreme Court only when the sum at stake exceeded $2,000.[51]

When the judge was satisfied that a vessel was "a good and lawful prize," he issued an informal decree of condemnation and ordered a sale immediately. This was followed by a formal decree of condemnation such as the following:

This cause being submitted by the Proctor for the Libellants and there being no claim interposed for said Ship or Cargo, and the libel and examinations in preparatory as well as the papers and Documents found on board the said Ship *Hopewell* being seen and considered by the Judge, and it appearing that the said Ship *Hopewell* and all the property found on board of her at the time of her Capture were and are good and lawful prize — It is thereupon this nineteenth day of September in the year of Our Lord Eighteen hundred and twelve by James Houston Judge of the United States for Maryland District, and by the Authority of this Court, Ordered, Adjudged and Decreed that the said Ship *Hopewell* and all the property found on board of her at the time of her capture be condemned and confiscated, and that the same be sold by the Marshal of this District; and the proceeds thereof be brought into this Court, to be distributed according to the Law.   JAMES HOUSTON [signature][52]

Next to the actual commission, the decree of condemnation was the most vital document among those employed in the private armed vessel system. It did not tell the owners what their profits would be however. For that information they had to wait for the completion of the court-ordered public sale. Marshal Thomas Rutter advertised prize sales in the Baltimore newspapers. The 400-ton *Braganza*, taken by the *Tom* in a fifty-five minute fight, was condemned on September 2, 1812. The "Marshal's Sale" of 2,111 bags and 30 hogsheads of coffee, some oil, 472,729 pounds of logwood, and the *Braganza* herself was advertised on September 4.[53] The actual sale and completion of the accounts required over two months time and the *Tom*'s agent, Gerrard Wilson, signed for the proceeds on November 12, 1812.[54] That two month period was normal.

The actual vendue process was managed by an auctioneer (vendue master) for the marshal. Prize cargoes were removed to a public vendue hall or to a private vendue house by the custodian of the prize vessel. Samples were displayed and a catalogue was made available to potential buyers. The auctioneers received from 0.50 to 1.0 percent of the proceeds as their commission, or they settled for set fees of $300 to $500.[55] The marshal was compensated with 1.25 percent commission of gross sales receipts and the clerk of the court earned the same percentage. The clerk's percentage, however, was computed after the expenses of the sale were deducted so he received 1.25 percent of the net proceeds. Expenses were the costs of the suit, disbursements for the prize vessel, other custodial costs, and the auctioneer's and marshal's commissions. After the clerk's commission was deducted, another 2 percent was submitted for the government hospital and survivors' fund. In the case of the prize *John Hamilton*, prize to the *Dolphin*, the marshal's commission was $637.55 and the clerk's $597.85, while the hospital fund received $944.60.[56]

The owners of private armed vessels were not satisfied with the pace of the prize sales, the marshal's control of conditions, or the commission rates. To satisfy the owners an act of Congress of January 27, 1813, ordered that sales were to be held within sixty days after the condemnation and that the terms of credit and the ordering of the goods for sale (lots and sequence) were to be determined by the owners of the capturing vessel. The act also limited the period of credit to no more than ninety days. The marshal's and clerk's commissions were lowered to 1 percent and a $250 limit was placed on the commission they could earn on any one prize case. The owners were also permitted to move their prize to another city for the sale when there were no government claims against them.[57] This act was one of many demonstrating the government's support of the private armed vessel system. More importantly for the owners, it increased their income from a heavy investment.

The marshal's sale of prize vessels and goods attracted considerable interest in Baltimore. Private armed vessel owners, including those without shares in the capturing vessel, showed up at the auctions in strength. Of the thirty-two purchasers of prize items from the 400-ton ship *John*, prize to the *Comet*, eighteen were private armed vessel investors. Peter Arnold Karthaus, part-owner of the *Comet*, purchased $7,084.58 worth of coffee and $4,876.09 worth of cotton. Both items were suitable cargoes for entrepreneur Karthaus's swift letter-of-marque traders, such as the *Bordeaux Packet, Thetis, Baltimore,* or *Engineer,* running between Baltimore and France throughout the war. Merchant Elie Clagett paid $4,408.27 and Levi Hollingsworth paid $3,396.12 for cotton. Both were part-owners of the *Comet.* Other *Comet* part-owners purchasing prize items were Andrew Clopper, who paid $10,755 for cotton and $7,435.44 for sugar, and Thomas Sheppard, who purchased $3,659.70 worth of various goods. The flour firm of Keller and Foreman, also part-owners of the *Comet,* paid $14,750 for the prize ship and bought other items as well. Part-owner Thorndike Chase made a number of small purchases including two cannons, some gunpowder, an arms chest, coal, firewood, and some old copper. He may have been outfitting another private vessel or simply looking for good prices for scarce items.[58] The part-owners of the *Comet* knew that they would not have to put up cash for their entire purchase. Their owners' shares of the *Comet* acting as a credit with the clerk of the court would offset the costs of their purchases of prize goods.

Private armed vessel investors not financially interested in the *Comet* herself also purchased prize items at the *John*'s sale. They bought items related to their businesses, weapons suitable for use on private armed vessels, and goods they could export in their letter-of-marque traders. Active investor John Gooding paid $17,244.07 for cotton at the auction of the *John*'s goods.[59] A little over five weeks later, the *Sabine,* a letter-of-marque trader partially owned by Gooding, cleared for Bordeaux with a cargo of cotton.[60] Other private armed vessel investors not involved in the *Comet* purchasing prize goods from the *John* included chandler and grocer Nicholas Stansbury, who purchased rum and sugar,

Solomon G. Albers, who also purchased some rum, and active shipowner George Stiles, who bought jack screws. Chandler James Ramsay bid successfully on provisions, and brass founder Christopher Raborg bought $1,000.00 worth of old copper. Active private armed vessel owner William Hollins paid for a pair of twelve-pound guns and three pairs of six-pound guns appropriate for schooners, and William Bosley bought thirteen muskets for $36.40.[61] Prize sales were obviously filling local wartime needs.

In addition to the part-owners of the capturing vessel, the *Comet*, and the investors in other private armed vessels, other merchants used the prize auctions as a source of low priced or scarce items. Wholesale grocers and dry goods merchants were able to buy goods at vendue that were not available elsewhere. Grocery firms such as those of George William Norris, McDonald and Ridgely, John Okeley, and others bought items at the *John*'s auction.[62] They, too, were looking for substitutes for their peacetime business and the prize sales may have prevented or postponed financial ruin for some of them.

Part-owners, investors in other private armed vessels, and merchants not involved in private armed vessels also purchased goods at the sale of the *Braganza*, prize to the *Tom*. The following is the complete sales account for that auction:

500 Bags Coffee, 71,108 lbs. at 18½, Andrew Clopper	$13,154.98
350 Bags Coffee, 49,638 lbs. at 18¼, Andrew Clopper	9,058.93
7 damaged Bags Coffee, 896 lbs. at 4, Wm. Van Wyck	35.84
350 Bags Coffee, 54,393 lbs. at 17¾, John Gooding & Co.	9,654.75
211 Bags Coffee, 36,681 lbs. at 18½, John Gooding & Co.	6,785.98
180 Bags Coffee, 25,915 lbs. at 18, John Gooding & Co.	4,664.70
30 tierces Coffee, 17,198 lbs. at 19, John Gooding & Co.	3,404.42
336 Bags Coffee, 45,006 lbs. at 18, John McKim Jr.	8,101.08
20 Bags Coffee, 2,792 lbs. at 17¾, Thomas Tenant	495.58
4 Kegs Aril (?) Root, 146 lbs. at 10, Wm. Van Wyck	14.60
1 pr. long 6 pounders, Hollins and McBlair	275.00
1 pr. Carronades, No. 9, Thomas Tenant	110.00
4 prs. Carronades, at 70.00, Hollins and McBlair	280.00
Shot and Langrage Thomas Tenant	10.00
Arms Chest, etc. Faviour	54.00
2 Jack Screws Baptiste Mezick	21.00
4 tierces Beef, 1,300 lbs., John McFadon	52.00
5 bags Bread B. Rynd	3.00
1 tierce and barrel Bread, Wm. Van Wyck	8.00
190 tons Logwood, at 25.25, Christopher Deshon	4,797.50
the Ship *Braganza*, Captain Carr	9,900.00
	$70,881.36[63]

The sale of the *Braganza* and her cargo was dominated by the owners of the

Tom, the capturing vessel. Part-owners of the *Tom*, Andrew Clopper, Hollins and McBlair, John Gooding, John McKim, Jr., and Christopher Deshon, purchased $60,177.44 worth of goods. Another $688.58 was paid by Thomas Tenant, Baptiste Mezick, and John McFadon, all investors in other private vessels. Those who were not investors in private armed vessels bought only $115.44 worth of goods out of the total sale of $70,881.36.[64] Obviously, the investors were using their credit with the clerk whether that credit was in the *Braganza* or other prizes in port at the time. They were also buying goods at prize auction prices to sell later at higher prices. Purchased at seventeen and three-fourths to nineteen cents per pound at the *Braganza*'s September auction, coffee sold for twenty cents per pound in late August in Baltimore and up to twenty-two cents per pound in November.[65] Large sales at a prize auction drove prices down at the auction in particular and in the city in general. The later sale of goods purchased at prize auctions was one more entrepreneurial technique for profiting from the private armed vessel system whether one exported the prize goods on letter-of-marque schooners or sold them locally after waiting for their prices to climb.

Prize sales attracted bidders of different types and from different cities. Philadelphians came to Baltimore looking for sugar, rum, coffee, and other imports. As late as April of 1815 "The Sales of Prize Goods" were "very high and greedily bought at."[66] The auction of the prize goods from the hold of the privateer *Snap-Dragon* in Charleston attracted 300 "from all the towns from Boston to Augusta."[67] That sale brought in nearly four hundred thousand dollars. Merchant John Gibson, related by marriage to active investor Henry Didier, Jr., went to Philadelphia, New York, and Boston in search of prize bargains. His hopes of buying low in the north and selling high in Philadelphia or Baltimore did not materialize. He knew that the "idea is to be there when a public sale is held," but he found the prices to be exorbitant. He even had to wait several days for a seat on the stagecoach back to Baltimore.[68] Many people were looking for bargains and substitutes for their peacetime trade.

The Baltimoreans' desire for goods also encouraged them to bid on prize goods in vessels belonging to owners in other ports. The commissioned ship *Clarendon*, a prize to the *Young Wasp* of Philadelphia, sold for $278,101.64 in Baltimore. Private armed vessel investors William Taylor, Nicholas Stansbury, Martin F. Maher, James Johnson, and Thomas Tenant all bought coffee at her auction. Tenant's purchases of coffee were made after the price per pound was driven from twenty-four cents down to twenty-two and then to twenty-one and one-fourth cents. He purchased a little over $125,000 worth of coffee alone, plus another $500 worth of ivory and beef. Over two-thirds of the proceeds of the *Clarendon* were furnished by Baltimore investors in private armed vessels and the vessel herself was purchased by active investor Gerrard Wilson for $22,000.[69] Baltimore-owned prizes were, of course, being sold in other ports also and those proceeds were sent back to Baltimore.

For anyone shopping for a vessel to purchase prize sales presented an entirely new source. There was no market for the large and slow three-masted, three-decked, full-rigged prize ships in Baltimore during most of the war, but they could be sold to others for a profit. In the early part of the war, such ships with their large holds were useful in the Iberian trade, and firms such as New York's Frances and Gracie kept a watchful eye out for bargains. They had S. Smith and Buchanan, their Baltimore correspondent, evaluate the *John Hamilton*, prize to the *Dolphin*.[70] Only one prize schooner was actually converted into an American commissioned vessel. The prize schooner *Crown Prince*, originally Swedish, was purchased by Cornelius Specht, renamed the *Hull*, and then converted into the Baltimore privateer *Fox*.[71] Henry Didier, Jr. was looking for a "bargain in two or three Prize ships of about 3 or 400 tons each" in 1814 to put into the Liverpool and London trade after the war.[72]

Prize vessels sometimes brought quick profits to an entrepreneur. Archibald Kerr, part-owner of the *Highflyer*, paid $600 for the little thirty-one-ton schooner *Harriet*, prize to the *Highflyer*. He sold her for $750 before the marshal's bill of sale was even signed.[73] Robert Patterson paid $7,300 for the ship *Jamaica*, prize to the *Highflyer*, of which he was part-owner. He resold her on the same day for a neat $4,700 profit to Isaac Iselin, William Bayard, and other New Yorkers. Gerrard Wilson bought the ship *Clarendon*, prize to a Philadelphia privateer, for $22,000 and sold her three weeks later to a Von Kapff and Brune syndicate for $27,135.[74] Among other Baltimore investors in private armed vessels purchasing prize vessels were Peter Arnold Karthaus, Andrew Clopper, Thomas Tenant, and Captain Joseph Almeda.[75]

The Baltimore investors in private armed vessels also purchased prize vessels in other ports. Nicholas Stansbury, George Pitt Stevenson, Peter Arnold Karthaus, Dennis A. Smith, Charles F. Kalkman, John W. Stump, and the two Clagetts each bought prize vessels at the Cape Fear District auctions in North Carolina.[76] S. Smith and Buchanan purchased the 407-ton prize ship *Star* in New York. A prize to their own privateer *Surprise*, she was resold by them to Von Kapff and Brune for $28,000.[77] Active investor Dennis A. Smith bought the brig *Canada* at a North Carolina auction and then sold her to Robert and John Oliver.[78] The Baltimoreans used both prize goods and prize vessels in their entrepreneurial drive for profits.

As bargains, auctions of prize vessels attracted noninvestors in private armed vessels also. The Federalist merchant Henry Thompson bought several prize vessels for use in the Iberian flour trade. His purchase of the *Braganza*, through one of his captains, was for a Richmond merchant, Robert Gamble.[79] George Coggeshall, privateer captain and historian, had his agent pay $25,600 for the 550-ton *John Hamilton*, prize to the *Dolphin*.[80] These and other purchasers were acquiring vessels at prices below construction costs. Only three prizes sold in Baltimore went for less than $800, and only two sold for more than $22,000, while the average prize vessel price was only $6,344.[81] That was a very low average for outfitted sea-going vessels.

Investors in private armed vessels and other Baltimoreans also used the prize sales as a source of scarce luxury goods for personal usage. The *Chasseur* brought in the usual prize cargo of dry and manufactured goods in her hold. From that cargo, Gerrard Wilson purchased a set of bridles, while John Craig bought some knives and forks. Henry Didier, Jr. paid $168 for a twelve volume "Encyclopedia" and Martin F. Maher bought a "Bacgammon board." Captain Thomas Boyle bid successfully on some fine fabrics in small quantities for home use and paid $139 for a "piano forte." Some flutes and fifes were sold from the *Whig*'s prize cargo and small quantities of razors, needles, cheese, glass, and other items were sold from the *Kemp*'s prize cargo. These particular sales possibly resulted from low prices, but prize sales provided the port with luxury and consumer goods unavailable from other sources during the blockade. Thomas Tenant purchased a gig harness, and United States Marshal Thomas Rutter bought twenty-two pounds of cheese. The purchase of 1,700 muskets and carbines from the *Whig*'s cargo by Peter Arnold Karthaus and Company and William T. Graham, though, reflected an interest in the arms market in revolutionary South America and not an interest in hunting.[82]

Prize sales in Baltimore met some particular needs on occasion, but they did not constitute a systematic importation program. Knowledgeable captains sought scarce or valuable goods in prizes, but they were at the mercy of the British shippers who loaded their holds for their own and not American markets. Consequently, the flow of prize goods from privateer prizes was haphazard. Some market gaps were filled, but other facets of the market were flooded or neglected. Coffee and sugar, for example, came into Baltimore in large doses, while the demand for dry goods was never satisfied. For specific market needs, the merchants depended more on the other branch of the private service, the letter-of-marque traders.

The letter-of-marque traders capturing prizes followed the same procedures as those described for privateers. But letter-of-marque traders produced income for their entrepreneurial sponsors even when no prizes ensued. A prize was a bonus for the officers and crew and for the owners. Those investors owning parts of privateers and letter-of-marque traders were able to relate the two types of vessels. Some of the arms, rope, sails, and provisions put onto privateers were brought into Baltimore on commissioned traders, and some of the coffee, sugar, cotton, and other prize goods brought into Baltimore by privateers were exported to France in the traders. The traders, like the privateers, used ports other than Baltimore during the blockade, but some of their goods and most of their profits found their way to Baltimore eventually.

With the prize vessel and cargo in a friendly port and in friendly hands, shareholders knew the moment of truth was near. Court proceedings leading, hopefully and usually, to a condemnation decree and the court-ordered prize auction were executed quickly. Money accruing, in part, to the shareholding owners' and the crew's accounts was deposited by the marshal with the clerk of the court. The final truth would be known only when the prize money was distributed to the concerned parties.

ELEVEN

Distributing the Spoils

The entire proceeds of a prize sale did not reach the hands of the owners and the crew of the capturing vessel. Reduced initially by the expenses of the sale, prize proceeds were subjected to further reductions by the admiralty court before they were distributed to the participants in a private armed vessel venture. For the owners, the distribution of profits was a relatively simple matter. In the case of the officers and crew, however, the distribution system was more complex and contentious. The discussion of the court and prize reductions of the prize sale proceeds and the various distribution schemes in this chapter leads to estimates of earnings for the crews and the owners. The estimates in the case of the owners were based on incomplete data and, consequently, they were constructed through the use of averages and projections. They are intended as "educated guesses" rather than precise audits, but they do provide a rough answer to the question of who made money in private armed vessel ventures.

The proceeds of a prize sale, minus the costs of the auction, were deposited with the clerk of the United States District Court for Maryland. Acting in its corollary role as an admiralty court, that court had condemned the vessel and goods initially and had ordered the marshal to hold a public sale. All further reduction consequent to the clerk's acceptance of the sale proceeds from the marshal required authorization from the court.[1] The largest single item, in what was the second level of reduction, was the customs duty on prize goods. Imported prize goods received no special consideration in 1812, and, as a result, the collector of customs taxed them as routine imports. Routine imports, however, had been subjected to a doubling of the peacetime custom rates in July of 1812.[2] Such double duties, burdensome to the owners and crews of the private vessels, made the federal government a major shareholder in private armed vessel ventures. The federal government was a contributing shareholder because it offered bounties for prisoners, but it also deducted commissions for the court clerk and marshal as well as court costs from the prize sale proceeds.

The impact of duties was apparent in 1812 when prize sale proceeds experienced reductions of 30 or 40 percent because of the double duties. The prize ship *Braganza* and her cargo, for example, sold for $68,925.89, but that figure was then reduced by $29,654.80 in duties. The prize ship *Jamaica* and her cargo brought in $139,675.92, but paid duties of $49,881.39. The sale proceeds of the prize ship *Henry* were $128,641.55, but her account was diminished considerably when she paid $47,154.96 in duties. The cargo of the *Fanny*, prize to the *Dolphin*, was charged five cents per pound for the duty on brown sugar and fifty-six cents per gallon on third proof rum.[3] Prizes often contained such items in thousands and tens of thousands of units, and the Baltimoreans could not absorb all those cargoes unless they could export some of them. The merchants purchasing prize coffee, sugar, or other items were entitled to a drawback (actually a double drawback during wartime) when they exported prize items within a specified period. The drawbacks were an important economic consideration for merchants contemplating bids on prize goods, especially those owning letter-of-marque trading schooners. In such cases high duties were overcome, but not all prize items were of value in foreign markets and not all the sugar and coffee could get out of the port once the blockade was instituted. The customs duties on prize goods, in general, were a heavy expense, and the owners of private armed vessels sought relief from Congress.

Protests to Congress emphasized the large investments required to underwrite private warships. The New York owners of the privateer *General Armstrong* cited $42,232.90 as their investment in the 280-ton schooner, ready for sea. The 270-ton privateer *Governor Tompkins*, owned in Baltimore and New York, was said to have cost her underwriters $42,000. Other petitioners cited costs ranging from $16,000 up to $54,000 for a commissioned full-rigged, three-decked, and three-masted ship.[4] Of the $42,232.90 invested in the *General Armstrong*, $28,000, or two-thirds, was for the vessel and her guns only. Thirty-two Baltimore owners, including Hollins and McBlair and Andrew Clopper, complained to Congresss of high costs and court reductions of prize proceeds.[5] Congress could not deny the need for the services of the private armed vessels as well as the wartime income gained from the prize auctions. It agreed, therefore, to forego some of its income and voted to sustain the private system. In an act signed in August of 1813, Congress authorized a one-third reduction in the duties on prize goods.[6]

One of the supporters of the private armed vessel owners' position in the controversy over duties was Acting Secretary of the Treasury William Jones. As a former merchant, Jones emphasized the "extravagant expenses" of the owners while noting that the double duties sometimes "absorbed the whole proceeds" of a captured vessel. The Treasury Department official was convinced that the hurried prize auctions of large quantitites of some prize items at one time forced the owners to sell at prices 20 to 30 percent below market prices.[7] Prize auction accounts of Baltimore sales corroborated Jones's assertion in the cases of sugar, prize vessels, and other particular items. Coffee, however, sold below the market price but not as far beneath it as Jones suggested.[8] Sellers still preferred quick auctions for perishable cargoes and, if at all manageable, for those commodities commanding a high market price because of serious shortages. Jones blamed the slump in privateering interest in the summer of 1813 on the deficiency of remuneration offered to the owners.[9] It was reported in April of 1813 that the Baltimore "Privateer Owners and sharp-built schooner owners" had "already suffered much," but they may have suffered from the blockade of the Chesapeake as well as from the high duties.[10] William Jones contended that lower tariffs would stimulate merchants to make new investments in private armed vessels and that new vessels would bring in an increased number of prizes. More prizes, according to Jones, would actually increase the government's income from duties even when the actual rates were lower.[11] The enactment of lower duties on prize goods in August of 1813 was followed by an injection of new people and new money into privateering in Baltimore, but once more the blockade was a motivating factor.[12] Only well-armed, heavily-manned, and swift vessels could get to sea. One Baltimore editor recognized the incentive provided by the lower duties on prize goods and characterized that portion of the duties now retained by the owners and crew as a "bounty" of, in some cases, thirty thousand dollars per prize.[13] Increased profits resulting from the lower duties may have motivated the Baltimoreans to challenge the blockading squadron more often.

The court ordered reductions in a prize account other than the customs duties. Any money expended by the custodian of the prize vessel, court costs, wharfage, and fees were also subtracted at this second stage of reduction. The ship *Hopewell* and her cargo were sold for $102,807.29 in October of 1812. Her expenses or disbursements were as follows:

Marshal's commission	$1,285.00
25 days wharfage	37.50
Advertising charge	5.00
Harbour Master's fee	5.00
Cost of the suit	25.75
Captain Thorndike Chase's bill for care of the vessel and her cargo	2,253.77
	$3,612.02[14]

The cost of wharfage (by the day), of advertising, the harbour master's fee, and the costs of the suit for other prize cases were almost identical to those of the *Hopewell*, but the marshal's commission and the custodian's costs were related to sale proceeds and to the type and condition of the goods and vessel involved and were more varied as a result. In addition to the *Hopewell*'s disbursements, the *Comet*'s owner and crew lost $40,373.14 in duties and a commission of 1.25 percent ($735.27) to the clerk of the court and a 2 percent charge ($807.46) for the government hospital fund. At the end of this second, or court-ordered reduction, the *Hopewell's* sale proceeds of $102,807.29 were down to $56,910.42.[15] Even that seriously reduced figure was not ready for division into owners' and crew's shares because the prize agent's expenses and commission had to be deducted.

The diminution of proceeds from the sale of the *Hopewell* and her cargo was not unusual. The *Jamaica* and her cargo grossed $139,675.92 in sales but netted the crew and the owners combined only $83,854.83 before the prize agent's expenses and costs had been deducted.[16] The prize ship *Henry* and her cargo of wine and sugar brought in $128,641.51, but the *Comet's* agent collected only $75,885.08 from the court before deducting his own commission and costs. These and other prize action results supported the contention that the prize proceeds, after the costs of the auction and the court-authorized reductions were deducted and after the final figure was divided into two parts, were not often adequate in relation to the capital invested by the privateer owners. In the case of the unusually valuable *Hopewell*, the owners and the crew were assigned $28,455.21 each, while the federal government received $40,373.74 in duties.[17] The owners and crew were still liable for the agent's expenses and commission, but together they were receiving only 50 or 55 percent of the sale proceeds from the clerk of the court before the duties were lowered. On vessels smaller or less valuable than the *Hopewell* the owners were not doing well. When a captain brought in prize cargoes in his hold instead of sending in a prize vessel where there were no disbursements, and when he divested only those items paying low or no duties, he conceivably stemmed the erosion of sales proceeds. Such options were not always available, but the lowering of the customs duties on prize goods and the setting of limits on commissions paid to the marshal and clerk helped the owners and crew to retain more of the sale proceeds. The prize goods on the *Whig* sold for $28,152.46 in 1815, her expenses were only $784.03, and her duties were only $2,642.38.[18] In a June 20, 1815, case involving a cargo and a vessel, the auction returned $17,038.09 to the court. The court then subtracted only $2,911.96 or 17 percent in duties on a cargo of rum, molasses, and sugar.[19] An erosion of only 17 percent was a substantial improvement over the early losses to duties and expenses. From August of 1813, the crew and owners, in general, were retaining higher proportions of the proceeds from prize sales.[20]

After costs of the auction and court-ordered reductions were subtracted from the sale proceeds, a third reduction occurred. The prize agent drew on the prize proceeds for his expenses and commission. Agents paid the usual merchant's cargo-handling commission of 2.5 percent of the prize proceeds to firms in other ports for handling prize cases for Baltimore-owned vessels. Those firms then managed the prize account with the clerk of their district court for the Baltimore house. Christopher Deshon, popular Baltimore prize agent, paid commissions to other houses for their work on prize cases of the *Rossie*. As a prize agent, Deshon also managed discount and credit terms for the purchasers of prize goods and kept an account of money earned or lost on bills of exchange. Deshon's expenses included the payment of bills presented by the custodian of a prize vessel and traveling expenses of agents he dispatched to Newport, New London, Providence, or Washington to help with prize or private armed vessel business. He also charged the prize account for minor expenses such as printing costs, advertising (probably in newspapers), and for postage.[21]

Not so minor were the legal expenses involving the *Rossie*. Her commander, Joshua Barney, sent in suspicious neutrals, Americans with licensed vessels, or any vessel he suspected of trading with the enemy. As a result, Deshon not only paid the usual $150 lawyers' fees for libels and court presence but also expended $500 to William Pinkney, $500 to Robert Goodloe Harper, and $200 to James Donaldson for "Services at Supreme Court" on appeal cases. William Pinkney, who was United States attorney general until his resignation in 1814, was also paid $100 as a "retainer" by agent Deshon. Finally, Deshon charged the *Rossie*'s prize account a 2.5 percent commission for his own service as prize agent.[22] This third reduction in the prize proceeds ranged from 4 to 7 percent of the proceeds turned over to the agent by the clerk of the court.

Prize agent Christopher Deshon also provided the officers and crew with a summary statement of the *Rossie*'s account. It illustrated the losses suffered in the third reduction stage, but it was not a common arrangement because the commander, Joshua Barney, was assigned 10 percent of the sale proceeds as a bounty. That bounty was in addition to Barney's ten regular shares as the captain and the four reserved or merit shares he awarded to himself.[23] The owners and crew were apparently willing to pay extra to get a captain of Barney's stature. Captain Joseph Almeda of the schooner *Kemp*, also got a 10 percent bonus, but it was taken from the crew's share. Almeda, too, was a distinguished privateer commander by 1814.[24] Agent Deshon's account for the crew of the *Rossie* covered five prizes, and it serves as an example of the third level of reductions in prize proceeds, of the captain's bounty, and of a distribution system for the officers and crew. The significant figures in the crew's account of the *Rossie*'s prizes were as follows:

1st distribution
Amount Net Proceeds of the Brig *William*
and Cargo, the Ship *Jeannie* and Cargo
and Brig *Rebecca*'s goods. $ 36,206.02

Off deductions for the crew's share for
costs, Barney's 10% commission
and Deshon's 2½% commission, leaving $ 31,806.02

the Crew's ½ is $ 15,903.01

which divided by 290¼ Shares
will make each share, $ 55.79 85/1161

2nd distribution
Amount Net Proceeds of the Ship
Euphrates $112,898.68
Off crew's share of costs, Barney's 10%
and Deshon's 2½% commission, leaving $ 96,242.58

the Crew's ½ is $ 48,121.29
which divided by 294¼ Shares
makes each share $ 163.53 1035/1177

3rd distribution
Amount Net Proceeds of the
Princess Amelia, Packet $3284.03
off Deshon's 2½% and
Barney's 10%, leaving $2881.74
The Crew's ½ is $1440.87
which divided by 308¾
makes each share $ 4.66 838/1235[25]

In the *Rossie*'s statement the amount received from the clerk was reduced from 15 to 13 percent before any money was distributed. Without Barney's bounty, the loss would have been from 5 to 3 percent. In typical cases, the proceeds of a sale were lowered by the auction costs, then by the court, and finally, by the prize agent until only one-half of the original sale proceeds remained. As has been noted, the situation improved after the government duties, fees, and commissions were lowered. Prize agent Peter Arnold Karthaus's expenses and records for the privateer *Kemp*'s prize, *Princess*, followed the same pattern as those for the *Rossie* except that he charged the owners only 1 percent for his service as their prize agent. He charged the crew the regular 2.5 percent for the same service.[26]

Once all the reductions were completed, it was time for the actual distributions of proceeds. Part-owners collected their shares from the clerk individually, or they authorized one of their number to collect several shares. With written authorization, it was also possible for the prize agent, on behalf of the owners, to collect the entire owners' moiety. James Williams, John Gooding, and the firm of Hollins and McBlair authorized prize agent Gerrard Wilson to "arrange with the clerk of the Court for our respective Interest" in 1812.[27] The three part-owners held nine-thirteenths of the privateer *Tom*. Wilson also collected the money owed to single shareowners William Johnson and Thomas Wilson from the prize sales of the ship *Braganza*.[28] The clerk's entire account with the owners of the privateer *Tom* in the case of the prize ship *Braganza* was as follows:

to amount of James Williams' proportion	3/30	$ 1915.74
to amount of Hollins and McBlair proportion	3/30	1915.74
to amount of John Gooding's proportion	3/30	1915.74
to amount of John McKim Jr.'s proportion	4/30	2554.32
to amount of Robert Patterson's proportion	3/30	1915.74
to amount of Charles Malloy's proportion	1/30	638.58
to amount of Christopher Deshon's proportion	1/30	638.58
to amount of William T. Graham's proportion	1/30	638.58
to amount of C. F. Kalkman's proportion	1/30	638.58
to amount of Matthew Kelly's proportion	1/30	638.58
to amount of Luke Kiersted's proportion	1/30	638.58
to amount of Andrew Clopper's proportion	1/30	638.58
to amount of William M. Johnson's proportion	1/30	638.58
to amount of Thomas Wilson's proportion	1/30	638.58
to amount of Gerrard Wilson's proportion	4/30	2554.32
to amount of John Lane's proportion	1/30	638.58
		$18,157.40

Amount advanced to 15 sailors and
Disbursements in Newport and deducted
from the owners 1,840.30

$20,997.70[29]

In the case of the *Dolphin*'s proceeds from the sale of the prize ship *John Hamilton*, the receipt for the owners' prize money was signed by Lemuel Taylor, the firm of S. Smith and Buchanan, and the firm of Hollins and McBlair.[30] Different groups collected their prize money in different ways, but there were no court cases involving duplicate payments or claims of underpayment. Obviously, the relationship among the prize agents, other part-owners, and the clerk was well regulated. It had grown out of decades of mercantile experience and mutual trust.

The prize agents maintained separate accounts for each shareholding part-owner in addition to the collective or "adventure" account in the name of the vessel and the account for the officers and crew. Prize agent Christopher Deshon of the *Rossie* provided an account for the flour milling firm of Briscoe and Partridge, holders of one-sixteenth part of that privateer. The *Rossie* earned "per accounts and Vouchers lodged" at Deshon's office "for examination," $4,260.89 for each one-sixteenth share. Deshon deducted $3,021.18 that he had paid to Briscoe and Partridge soon after he received the funds and one-sixteenth of all bills outstanding against the *Rossie*. Since most of the *Rossie*'s preparation bills had been paid when the privateer left Baltimore by Deshon in his role as ship's husband, one-sixteenth of the bills at the end of the cruise amounted to only $14.03. Other small charges were deducted to the point where Briscoe and Partridge retained a credit of $1,213.80 on agent Deshon's books. Apparently, the firm had neglected to draw on its account when the dividend first became available, choosing instead to draw its final amount from Deshon in June of 1814, over twenty months after the *Rossie*'s cruise had terminated. A small part of the final sum was tied up by litigation, but there was no interest cited in the account for any portion of the money.[31] Perhaps the firm had little use for the capital in a wartime situation and felt that the money was safe in Deshon's hands.

The case of the ship *John*, prize to the *Comet*, involved another collection pattern. Each part-owner collected his own share of the proceeds (in twelfths) from the clerk of the court. Some part-owners of the *Comet* were purchasers of prize goods from the *John*, having, in fact, spent their prize money before it was distributed. Andrew Clopper, owner of two-twelfths of the *Comet* and an exceptionally successful investor in private armed vessels, earned $11,746.14 from the *John*. Clopper, however, had purchased $18,190.47 worth of the *John*'s prize goods. On the surface, he owed the clerk over $6,000.00, but he was exporting some of his purchases immediately and, as a result, his account was credited with $6,444.33 in drawbacks on customs duties. Clopper had calculated his account to the very penny, purchasing $18,190.47 in prize goods without drawing on one cent of his own funds. Others among the part-owners of the *Comet* drew the difference between their share earnings and their prize purchases. Thorndike Chase, prize agent for the *Comet*, held two owner's shares, but the clerk subtracted $5,392.34 in prize purchases from the $11,746.14 due Chase. Peter Arnold Karthaus was entitled to $5,873.07 for one share of the *Comet*, but he had made purchases of $8,660.66 from the *John*, so he owed money to the clerk. Thomas Sheppard expended $3,659.70 on prize goods and was entitled to $5,873.07 for his one share before his purchases. Levi Hollingsworth's income from one share was reduced by $3,396.12 for his prize purchases. Levi Clagett spent $2,238.83 of his one share on prize goods, and his partner Elie bought $3,366.25 in goods but held two shares of the *Comet*. The flour-milling firm of Keller and Foreman held one share, but it paid $15,420.05 for the prize ship *John*, so it owed the clerk almost $10,000.00. Jeremiah Sullivan collected his full $5,873.07 for his one share of the *Comet*. Sullivan invested in no letter-of-marque schooners at all, so he may not have been in a position to export prize goods quickly. In summary, three of the nine part-owners of the *Comet* owed money to the clerk, five had spent portions of their prize income before it was distributed, and one broke even. The investors were using their prize income as a credit, buying prize goods and the vessel to profit from their resale.[32] There were numerous profit-making functions in addition to private armed vessel ownership.

The *Comet* had been commissioned on July 10, 1812, and her libel against the prize ship *John* had been filed on October 10, 1812. The court proceedings, condemnation, and prize auction were all completed by December 12, 1812. Levi Hollingsworth, merchant and copper mill proprietor, collected $2,476.55 on January 6, 1813, for the balance of his one share in the *Comet* after his prize purchases had been deducted.[33] International commerce in the early nineteenth century depended on sailing vessels as the quickest means of communication and, consequently, its pace was slow. A voyage to and from Europe, the sales of goods over months, and the bills of exchange and credit arrangements often required a year or more to settle. The period of less than six months involved in the case of the *John* or the *Comet* was, therefore, a quick return on one's investment. In fact, the swiftness of the prize auctions, as discussed earlier, may have cost private armed vessel owners money, but they had no complaint about their prize money being tied up by the process or the court. Once a prize arrived in port, the principal determinant of pace was the traditionally swift admiralty court. Few other courts worked so fast. For the owners, the simplicity of the distribution system also discouraged delay. Obviously, the vessels with eighteen or twenty owners required a little more time, but few agents had to advertise in the newspapers for the owners to congregate in order "to settle their accounts."[34] The one case where this was done involved the *Wasp*, whose agent asked the owners to meet at Pamphillon's Hotel in Fells Point. The *Wasp*, however, was operating as a letter-of-marque trader at the time, and since she could not get through the blockade, her part-owners had to get their cargoes off. No prize accounts were involved. In a prize case, the part-owners were notified by a messenger from the office of the prize agent. It was possibly the same messenger who had knocked at their door months earlier asking for contributory shares for the further preparation of the privateer when she was being readied for sea duty.

The distribution of profits to the owners was but one-half of the distribution system. An entirely separate and different procedure was utilized for the officers and crew. They received one-half of the sale proceeds after the three levels of reductions, including the prize agent's, had been completed. The prize agent then distributed the prize money in accordance with the provisions of the Articles of Agreement signed by the officers and crew before the vessel cleared for sea duty. In the case of the ship *Hopewell*, prize to the *Comet*, the following members of the ship's complement received the shares and amounts listed after their names:

Captain	16 shares	$1,686.24
1st Lieutenant	9 shares	948.51

2nd Lieutenant	7	shares	737.73
Surgeon	11	shares	1,159.29
Sailing Master	6	shares	632.34
Captain of Marines	6	shares	632.34
Carpenter	4	shares	421.54
each able-bodied seaman	2	shares	210.78
each ordinary seaman	1½	shares	158.08½
each greenhand, landsman or marine	1	share	105.39

The *Comet* had 256.75 assigned crew shares at the time the *Hopewell* was captured and 13.25 reserved or merit shares, which were awarded to six deserving individuals.[35] The scheme used by the *Comet* was fairly standard and the income for her able-bodied seamen was equal, in this one prize case alone, to about seven months' pay on a wartime trading vessel.

The officers and crew on a private armed vessel utilized a prize agent also. Usually, he was the same agent employed by the owners and, in some cases, he was designated in the Articles of Agreement. Written authorizations, usually in the form of a collective power of attorney, were also used. The prize agent collected the crew's moiety from the clerk of the court and subtracted his expenses and commission of 2.5 percent. He requested a certificate of discharge, a bill of sale for a prize ticket, or a power of attorney signed by the original owner before he would pay a claimant. Mariners, by the very nature of their trade, were seldom on hand at distribution time, and they frequently gave a power of attorney to a friend, a relative, or a recruiting agent so that their money could be collected. Lawyers, boarding house keepers, tavern owners, and others performed that service for a fee, a portion of the proceeds, or simply for survivors' rights in case of the death of the ticket holder.[36]

Lemuel Taylor was given a power of attorney by eighty members of the crew of the privateer *Dolphin* at one time. Forty-one could not sign their name, and others may have given him such powers at another time. Taylor signed a court receipt for $23,180.77 for the officers' and crew's moiety of the proceeds from the prize ship *John Hamilton*.[37] He then distributed the money to any available shareholders, held the money of absentees, or gave it to another person when that person held a bill of sale, an endorsed prize ticket, certificate of discharge, or a power of attorney. Payment and the name of the recipient, in the event it was someone other than the original ticket holder, were recorded on the Articles of Agreement and by receipt.[38]

The recruiting agents discussed earlier in this work were omnipresent at distribution time in Baltimore. They had purchased parts or all of some prize tickets or were acting as agents for various seamen. Grocer and waterman James Hooper signed many men onto various privateers and he collected the prize money earned by nine of the *Comet*'s crew in the capturing of the *Hopewell*.[39]

Acting as a link between the highly mobile seamen and the more stationary general society, recruiting agents bought and sold prize tickets like lottery tickets. Hooper, for example, bought a ticket worth two and one-half shares for $180 from gunner's mate Edward Venard of the *Comet*. With one prize alone, the *Hopewell*, earning $263.48 for the gunner's mate's ticket, Hooper appeared to be a winner in this transaction. Actually, Hooper sold the ticket to Fells Point grocer and recruiting agent James Cloney for $120, losing sixty dollars in the deal.[40] Third-owner Cloney made over 100 percent profit on the ticket. Purchasers of tickets for unproductive vessels certainly lost money, but buyers such as Hooper, Cloney, Daniel James, James Norris, Fitz King, and others held hundreds of shares so that a few very successful vessels could have offset numerous losses. If the gunner's mate's ticket for two and one-half shares remained valid for both of the *Comet*'s two successful cruises, it may have been worth thousands. The original holder, of course, had settled for his $180 from Hooper plus any advances the owners of the *Comet* gave him. The profits of the private armed vessel system did not always end up in the seamen's small houses in Fells Point.

Other privateers utilized distribution schemes similar to that used by the *Comet*. The *Globe*'s distribution of the proceeds from the schooner *Ann* paid $233.84 for the captain's sixteen shares, $58.36 for the four shares each held by the boatswain, carpenter, sailmaker, and gunner, and $29.18 for the two shares earned by each of her able-bodied seamen. The *Globe* assigned a total of 247.75 shares.[41] The *Highflyer* distributed the profit from the schooner *Harriet* and the three-masted, square-rigged ship *Jamaica*, at one time after it was collected from the clerk by prize agent Thomas Tenant. Captain John Gavet received $2,558.42 (a $20.00 advance was deducted first) for his fourteen shares, and each prize master got $1,076.51, while the able-bodied seamen earned $345.00 each. The total *Highflyer* officer and crew moiety from the two prizes was $46,052.99.[42]

Prizes, of course, varied in value. The surviving records disclose a number of successful full cruises. The following cruises paid the crew the following amounts for single shares:

the *Rossie*'s 1812 cruise	$222.98
the *Lawrence*'s 2nd cruise	$125.11
the *Rolla*'s 1814 cruise	$ 25.10
the *Dolphin*'s 2nd cruise	$158.71
the *Fairy*'s 1814 cruise	$ 42.65
the *Kemp*'s 1st cruise	$169.56
the *Kemp*'s 2nd cruise	$244.56
the *Sabine*'s 1814–1815 cruise	$205.96
the *Caroline*'s 1814 cruise	$152.17[43]

With each able-bodied seaman receiving two shares for a three or four month's cruise, the men on these successful privateers were earning more than wages. The *Kemp*'s second cruise, for instance, was worth $163.00 per month to an able-bodied seaman or five times wartime wages. The average pay-off for the nine cruises in the sample was $149.64 for a single share, but only a minority of the crew was assigned one share. For an able-bodied seaman entitled to two shares, the average pay-off was equal to ten months wages or, for his three month tour, $100.00 per month. In comparison, a skilled sailmaker in the navy was paid $40.00 per month after April of 1814 when his pay was increased, and a corporal in the army received $10.00 per month in December of 1812.[44] For twenty-two individual prize actions, including some with vessels and some without, a single crew share averaged $82.90. The highest was $195.00 per share for the *John Hamilton* and the lowest in the sample was $1.17 per share for various goods taken off a prize vessel.[45] For a seaman entitled to two shares for the *Comet*'s prize sales in Baltimore alone, $773.76 was earned, and only one of every three prizes came into the Patapsco River port. All privateers, however, did not pay off. Men signing onto Baltimore's largest privateer, the *Mammoth*, knew that she had had a fantastic first cruise. The *Mammoth*, however, entered at New York in August of 1815 at the end of her second cruise without a single prize to her credit.[46] The rule was simple: no prize, no pay, except advances.

The officers and crew of letter-of-marque trading vessels also received prize money. Those vessels took prizes of opportunity, but their smaller crews and lighter armament prevented them from capturing the larger, better-manned, and often richer prizes. Crew shares were sometimes higher than some privateer distributions because the letter-of-marque trader carried only one-third or one-fourth as many men as the privateer. Prize money was in addition to monthly wages on the letter-of-marque vessels. The following single share amounts were paid by letter-of-marque prizes:

Point Shares, prize to the *Baltimore*,	$84.48
Maria, prize to the *Patapsco*,	$73.14⅓
Williams, prize to the *Decatur*,	$26.35[47]

The average distribution for a single share in this small sample was $61.36, equivalent to a bonus of two months' wages. Some letter-of-marque vessels, however, paid two shares to their able-bodied seamen.

The letter-of-marque traders sometimes employed distribution schemes unlike those used on privateers. The *Decatur*'s Articles of Agreement, for example, assigned only one-third of all prize proceeds to the crew while retaining two-thirds for the owners. The owners, including Cumberland Dugan Williams, D'Arcy and Didier, and Richard H. Douglass, arranged the owners' shares in twenty-fourths, assigning four of the twenty-fourths to the vessel herself. Those four shares, equalling one-sixth of the venture, were an effort to offset future refitting, maintenance, and operational costs. The crew's one-third of any prize money was divided into ninety-eight shares with sixteen going to the captain. The first officer was entitled to nine shares, the petty officers, three each, and the seamen, two each. In the style of the privateers, seven shares were to be awarded for merit.[48]

Another letter-of-marque trader, the *Patapsco*, assigned one-half of her prize proceeds to her officers and crew but employed the twentieth's distribution system similar to that used by the navy. The captain was assigned three-twentieths while the first officer, second officer, three petty officers, and the clerk were entitled to one-twentieth each. The twenty seamen on the *Patapsco* shared the remaining eleven-twentieths.[49] Other letter-of-marque vessels employed variations of the plans used by the *Decatur*, the *Patapsco*, or other adaptations of the scheme utilized by the privateers.

Like the court and sale phases, the distribution system was relatively quick. It represented, in normal cases, the culmination of the contract initiated by the signing of the Articles of Agreement months earlier. The privateer *Comet*'s distribution to the crew for one prize was completed three months and nineteen days after that vessel cleared from Baltimore. The *Globe* paid off her crew for some prizes in three months, while the *Highflyer* was still paying six months after clearance. Delays were caused primarily by men still at sea or in prisons and by litigation. Appeals concerning the legality of a prize or part of her cargo and challenges to the ownership of prize tickets were the most frequent causes of litigation. In general, however, the private armed vessel distribution system was not lengthy. The sailors from the United States squadron on Lake Erie waited ten months before they were invited to collect their prize money on board the new frigate *Java* in Baltimore.[50]

With the distribution of the prize proceeds to the owners and the crew, the account of a private armed vessel venture was closed. Whether the dreams of riches on the part of the crew or the owners were realized is uncertain. There was some court evidence, however, that individual dissatisfaction existed among the crew members. The prize agents were not able to satisfy all the claimants demanding prize money. They demanded a prize ticket, a certificate of discharge, a bill of sale, or a letter of attorney, but they were still beseiged by what one agent called "a multiplicity of conflicting demands."[51] Some crewmen sold their tickets twice or tried to collect the money themselves after selling them, and the agents were bedeviled with individual claims for years. Michael Pluck and Henry Mayer of the privateer *Sarah Ann* accused their prize agent of withholding their shares. The agent responded that he had paid their money to a Savannah house holding a power of attorney from the two seamen. The Savannah house, however, had gone bankrupt before the two men got their prize money.[52] Peter Myers of the letter-of-marque trader *Baltimore* did not get his money because another man with a prize ticket "represented himself as Peter Myers" and collected the money.[53] Three men sued Captain Thomas Boyle for their shares, but he informed the court that the men "were ignorant of and by no means competent to the duties of ordinary seamen."[54] Boyle refused to sign their certificates of discharge so the agent withheld payment.

Whenever there was a conflict or a question of authenticity, prize agents pressed for a court decree. Their refusal to pay a claimant usually sent him scurrying to a lawyer or to the office of the clerk of the district court. Andrew Clopper, prize agent for the *Patapsco*, pointed out the difficulties faced by the agents. Of eleven claimants for prize money, he noted that one had left the vessel at Havana, four had signed the articles under assumed names, one had been discharged, one had been promoted to prize master, and one was an indentured servant.[55] In regard to assumed names, few of Baltimore's crewmen used names as contrived as "Cuffee Cockroach" or "Jack Jibsheet," names used on the *Yankee*, out of Bristol, although the privateer *Fox* carried a seaman named "Jolly Boy."[56]

The agents' problems varied. Prize agent Christopher Deshon refused to pay several Chappaquidick Indians because they were not allowed to sign contracts (the articles) under Massachusetts law without the endorsement of the tribe's legal guardians.[57] A father trying to collect prize money earned by his minor son was told that two New Yorkers had also claimed the money.[58] Agent George Pitt Stevenson replied to a libel for prize money by noting that the claimants had signed a power of attorney over to two different people. Stevenson asked for a court decree.[59] In some cases the court ordered the agent to pay a claim, while others were compromised or denied. Some were settled out of court, but the district court served the agents and the crewmen well as a simple, quick, and inexpensive instrument for adjudication.

There were crew members who could not claim that they were underpaid. The mother of a landsman (marine) on the *Sabine* was shipwrecked on her way to Baltimore to collect her son's prize money. She wound up in Philadelphia "very low and much bruised" and "dependent upon the humanity" of that city. Unfortunately, Michael McBlair of Hollins and McBlair, agent for the *Sabine*, reported that her landsman son had been advanced $80.75 in Wilmington, North Carolina, New York, Baltimore, and other stops on the cruise, and that $110.00 of the share's value had been paid to others holding a power of attorney. The three-fourths of one share assigned to the marine was worth only $164.75, so he actually owed the agent $25.98.[60] In another case, Christopher Deshon responded to a claim by saying that no funds from the *Rolla*'s cruise remained. Deshon may have overpaid others, but the court ordered him to pay the claimant $627.50 anyhow.[61] Prize master William Cathell was overpaid $116.00 for his shares in the *Hopewell*, prize to the *Comet*.[62] Unless the account was corrected on the next prize case, the agent had to make up the overpayments out of his own commission. With the sales and resales of prize tickets, partial sales, powers of attorney, absent seamen, and the constantly changing crew lists and share arrangements for men added at sea or in other ports, the prize agents had their hands full. The distributions to the owners were far less contentious.

In 1814 a Baltimore shipping firm observed that "Our Privateersmen speak of their Thousands made, as Privateersmen always did — of their wealth we know but little, time will develop that."[63] Because of the fragmented and individualistic nature of the private armed vessel system and because of the wide geographical and international distribution of its records, the century and a half since 1814 has not produced a clear picture of profit and loss. Available records for thirty-five prize actions completed by Baltimore-owned privateers, however, provide the basis for an average prize payment to the owners.[64] The thirty-five prize actions earned the owners alone a total of $498,566.71 before the prize agents' expenses and commission had been deducted in about three-fourths of the cases. That total payment furnished the owners (collectively) of each capturing vessel an average payment of $14,244.76. Allowances for the prize agents' deductions in most of the cases justifies the sum of $13,500 as a reasonable average payment per prize action.[65] The officers and crew received an equal amount so the two interested parties were averaging $27,000 per prize action.

Fewer examples of letter-of-marque prizes have survived. Three cases, however, furnished the following results for the owners of such vessels:

1. the brig *Point Shares*, prize to the *Baltimore* $3,639.21
2. the schooner *Maria*, prize to the *Patapsco* $3,595.58
3. the brig *Williams*, prize to the *Decatur*
   (its owners kept two-thirds of the prize proceeds) $5,185.69[66]

The average payment to the owners of each capturing vessel in this small sample was $4,143.49 for what were smaller prizes. Allowances for the agents' expenses and commissions suggest a figure of $4,000.00 as the owners' average income from a prize to a letter-of-marque trading vessel. The addition of the crew's half raises that figure to $8,000.00. The commissioned traders were not manned or equipped adequately to capture 400- or 500-ton heavily armed and well-manned prizes with huge cargoes so the estimated owners' average prize income of $4,000.00 is reasonable compared to the $13,500.00 average income for the prizes of privateers.

Baltimore's fleet of 122 private armed vessels included thirty vessels performing strictly as privateers. Fifteen others worked as privateers under one or more commissions and as letter-of-marque traders under others. At least two, the *Siro* and the *Midas*, operated as letter-of-marque traders and privateers under a single commission. Twenty-eight vessels or 58 percent of those performing a privateer function at one time or the other were productive enough to be called financially successful.[67] To be termed successful in this study estimated earnings of about $50,000.00 were required to overcome an initial investment of

$40,000.00 plus later operating costs and other regular disbursements. This study classifies privateers for which such an income cannot be estimated as marginal or unsuccessful. The total estimated owners' income for the twenty-eight successful Baltimore-owned privateers was $3,267,437.96. On the basis of an estimated $40,000.00 per vessel, the estimated cost of equipping twenty-eight first class Baltimore privateers was $1,120,000.00. If the owners of the twenty-eight successful privateers collectively held no interests in less successful vessels, they realized a profit of about 200 percent on the basis of a conservative average prize figure. Such an estimate ignores their numerous secondary profit-making activities such as supplying commissioned and prize vessels before a trial. A collective income and profit estimate, however, says little about individual investors.

There were Baltimore owners who invested in none but successful privateers during the War of 1812, but they were a small minority. Of the 200 investors, 102 were financially interested in more than one commission each, and 88 used those commissions for two or more vessels.[68] For most, then, successes and failures were mixed, but those entrepreneurs making only one investment in private armed vessels were either a success or a failure, depending solely upon the productivity of their one vessel. Of the 98 men in the single investment group, the following twenty-three profited from the privateers listed after their names:

Robert Armstrong, *Caroline*
Thomas Boyle, *Comet*
James Briscoe, *Rossie*
John Clemm, *Chasseur*
Thomas Cockrill, *Caroline*
James Cordery, *Amelia*
Philip Dickenson, *Fairy*
Lewis Hart, *Liberty*
William Inloes, *Caroline*
William Johnson, *Tom*
Carsten Newhouse, *Chasseur*
James Partridge, *Rossie*
William Penniman, *Chasseur*
James Piper, *Fairy*
Christopher Raborg, *Chasseur*
Jonathan Rowland, *Sabine*
August Schwartze, *Rossie*
Frederick Schwartze, *Rossie*
Henry Shelton, *Sabine*
William Stewart, *Caroline*

William Vance, *Caroline*
David Wilson, *Liberty*
Thomas Wilson, *Tom*[69]

The successful owners among the one-time investors had a variety of backgrounds. Four were captains of the vessels in which they held an owner's share and, consequently, they also drew the largest number of the crew's shares. An auctioneer, a rope store proprietor, an ironworker, a copper and brass founder, a ship's carpenter, and at least eight merchants were in the group of successful investors. Most of them held shares in vessels with numerous other part-owners so their profits were not immense. Lewis Hart and David Wilson were exceptions because together they owned all of the successful *Liberty*. The *Sabine* had only five owners but the other six privateers owned by the successful single investors attracted from eight to eighteen part-owners. They averaged almost thirteen part-owners per privateer, but no matter how small their investment, they accomplished their objective by making a profit on that investment.

Some profit figures can be estimated for the successful single investors. The firm of Briscoe and Partridge, for example, received $4,260.89 in prize proceeds for their sixteenth share of the *Rossie*.[70] One-sixteenth share of the cost of equipping and operating a first class privateer costing $40,000.00 or more would have been $2,500.00. On that basis, Briscoe and Partridge made an estimated $1,760.89 ($880.00 per partner) or about 70 percent profit. The *Rossie* was not new so the firm may have invested less and made more. William Johnson owned one-thirtieth part of the *Tom*, estimated to have cost at least $40,000.00. According to the estimates used in this study, Johnson at least doubled his small initial investment in the *Tom*.[71] Neither Johnson nor the firm of Briscoe and Partridge profited sufficiently to permit them to use their privateer earnings as a major investment in another shipowning venture. A major or principal part-owner of a vessel needed much larger sums of money.

The other seventy-five one-time investors in Baltimore's private armed vessels were not all losers. Fifty-five of them concentrated their investments in just eight privateers, and of the eight, few were successful. The *Wasp, Joseph and Mary, Revenge, America*, and *Hornet* were either marginal or losing investments. Those unproductive privateers and letter-of-marque schooners, captured before they completed a reasonable tour of duty, accounted for the fact that about fifty of the single effort or marginal investors made no profits. Fifteen of the single investors, including established merchants Henry Payson, William Douglass, and Luke Tiernan as well as Captain George Weems, invested in letter-of-marque traders. Their vessels (one each) were operative, and, therefore, potentially profitable in a period of inflated prices for long periods of time.[72] The fifteen profited from their cargoes but only one out of five of the ninety-eight marginal investors actually profited from the prize-taking authority granted to them in the commissions for private armed vessels. With a total of 39 percent of the single investors clearly profiting from cargo-carrying or prize-taking activities, it is apparent that the private armed vessels were not an adequate substitute for their peacetime business.

The moderate investors (those having two and three commissions) were more successful as a group. With several investments, most of the fifty-two moderate investors had mixed records and their prize proceeds had to be reduced by their losses in other vessels. Again, $40,000 was used as the cost of a privateer and $25,000 for a cargo-laden letter-of-marque trader, and average owners' proceeds of $13,500 for a privateer prize and $4,000 for a letter-of-marque prize were applied. The following twenty-three moderate investors profited from the privateers listed after their name after losses were deducted:

Joseph Almeda, *Caroline*
Thorndike Chase, *Comet*
Elie Clagett, *Comet*
Levi Clagett, *Comet*
Joseph Despeaux, *Caroline*
W. P. Didier, *Harrison*
John Donnell, *Sabine*
Jesse Eichelberger, *Chasseur*
John Franciscus, *Chasseur*
Richard W. Gill, *Ultor*
William L. Gill, *Ultor*
L. G. Griffith, *Harrison*
Peter A. Guestier, *Ultor*
Charles Gwinn, *Lawrence*
Justus Hoppe, *Lawrence*
Thomas Kemp, *Chasseur*
Archibald Kerr, *Highflyer*
James W. McCulloch, *Ultor*
Joseph W. Patterson, *Highflyer* and *Rolla*
William Price, *Revenge*
James Ramsay, *Caroline* and *Fairy*
William Smith, *Lawrence*
Alexander Thompson, *Midas*[73]

Merchants were more prominent in this group of successful entrepreneurs than they were among the successful single effort investors. Fifteen of the twenty-three moderate investors were known merchants, but only two, Joseph W. Patterson through William Patterson and Sons, and John Donnell, had been shipowners on a large scale before the war. Two were captains who received owners' and crew's shares. Well-known shipbuilders Thomas Kemp, William

Price, and Joseph Despeaux were in the group along with the prominent ships' chandler James Ramsay.

Some estimates of profit can be made for successful moderate investors also. The *Comet*'s shares were sold in twelfths on one cruise and in thirteenths on another. Thorndike Chase, captain, wharf owner, and merchant, held two shares of that privateer. He invested an estimated $6,153 for his two shares, without considering contributory assessments, and he earned between $33,000 to $36,000 in prize proceeds. That estimate excludes any income Chase earned from supplying private armed vessels, their prizes, and from the purchase and resale of prize goods. Archibald Kerr, rope store owner and merchant, held one-fourth of the privateer *Highflyer*. If he had $10,000 invested in the privateer and he received an estimated $46,750 of its prize proceeds, he made a 467 percent profit on his investment. The successful moderate investors selected private armed vessels with an average of just eight owners compared to the average of thirteen for the successful marginal investors. Consequently, they received larger shares of the proceeds of productive vessels after making larger initial investments.

There were moderate investors who also shunned privateers. Six, including Jonathan Hudson, Isaac McKim, and Thomas Lewis, put their money into commissioned traders and received lengthy service from them.[74] Twelve others of the fifty-two moderate investors had mixed or unclear income records. The record for the entire group was clearly superior to that of the marginal investors. The percentage of successful moderate investors was twice that of the marginal investors, and only eleven, or one in five, lost heavily on letter-of-marque captures. The sharp decrease in losses may have resulted from the fact that successful vessels sometimes offset the losses of unsuccessful ones, while the single investors, of course, had their total interest in only one risk. Private armed vessels were a reasonably good substitute for the wartime business of over one-half of the moderate investors. Their record, however, was not impressive when it is compared to that of the port's fifty active investors.

On the basis of the averages of $13,500 for a privateer prize and $4,000 for a letter-of-marque prize, the active investors were extremely successful. Forty-four of those investing in four or more commissions profited from their investments in private armed vessels. Nine men shared owners' estimated proceeds with others ranging from $100,000 to $199,000 after their losses were deducted. They were:

George J. Brown	George Stiles
Richard H. Douglass	John W. Stump
Henry Fulford	Joel Vickers
William Hollins	Gerrard Wilson[75]
Matthew Kelly	

With the exception of Kelly, a captain and sometime merchant, all were prewar shipowners. George Stiles, as a sole owner of four vessels, did not share the estimated $119,750 in owner's proceeds earned by his privateer *Nonsuch*. William Hollins of the firm of Hollins and Brown was the sole owner of the privateer *Tomahawk*, but that vessel was captured just two days after clearing from Boston. Hollins, however, also invested in the successful privateers *Chasseur*, *Rolla*, and *Perry*.

Six of the active investors shared in owners' prize proceeds ranging from $200,000 to $299,000. They were:

John Netherville D'Arcy	Ferdinand Hurxthal
Henry Didier, Jr.	Thomas Sheppard
Lyde Goodwin	Thomas Tenant[76]

The firm of D'Arcy and Didier was very active in the European and West Indian trade before the war. Its proportion of privateers was not large. The firm retained only one-twentieth of the letter-of-marque trader *Maria* when she was converted into the privateer *Harpy* in New York. In the successful *Harrison* it held four- and then five-sixteenths, and in the case of the marginally performing *Expedition*, it owned one-sixteenth. The firm was probably happy to have held only one-sixteenth of the unproductive *Saranac*. After its losses were subtracted, the firm shared in $278,655.68 in prize proceeds from its vessels. With the small proportion of owners' shares it held in each vessel, it is unlikely that D'Arcy and Didier earned more than $40,000.00 from prizes. The firm profited more from its ten letter-of-marque traders that raced to and from the West Indies and France throughout the war. Didier spoke of profits of 100 and 200 percent from those wartime trading voyages.[77] The firm used commissions as a supplement rather than a replacement for its entrepreneurial trading ventures.

Others sharing in prize proceeds ranging from $200,000 to $299,000 also invested heavily in letter-of-marque traders while earning money in privateers. In cases where an owner of traders and privateers held a large proportion of his privateers, he may have profited substantially. Thomas Tenant, for example, received an estimated $46,750 for his one-fourth share in the *Highflyer*. His original investment in that privateer was probably less than $10,000. Tenant also owned part of the successful *Rossie* and all or part of four letter-of-marque traders.

A third cluster of active investors shared in estimated owners' proceeds ranging from $300,000 to $399,000. Seven of the eleven entrepreneurs in this category were famous shipping names before the war. The eleven were:

James A. Buchanan	Luke Kiersted	Samuel Smith
Christopher Deshon	Michael McBlair	Lemuel Taylor
John Hollins	John McKim, Jr.	Amos A. Williams[78]
Charles F. Kalkman	Robert Patterson	

Three members of this cluster were involved in one commercial house. Buchanan, Smith, and Taylor were partners in S. Smith and Buchanan, and Smith was related by marriage to the firm of Hollins and McBlair and to the Patterson family. They and the others in this cluster functioned differently from the previous cluster as they relied heavily on privateers and invested in six or fewer vessels. Robert Patterson, of the great house of William Patterson and Sons, owned one-tenth of the successful *Tom*, one-fourth of the successful *Highflyer*, and unknown proportions of the *Rolla* and *Rossie*, both of which were productive. He shared in estimated prize proceeds of $366,874 and, along with a few others, demonstrated that it was not necessary either to buy into ten or fifteen ventures or to diversify into traders to make a handsome profit.

The ample capital of S. Smith and Buchanan (and Lemuel Taylor) permitted them to avoid vessels with more than eight part-owners. They sometimes sponsored whole privateers by themselves. Successful holdings were the privateers *Dolphin*, *Surprise*, and *Mammoth*. They lost a letter-of-marque trader to the British but, in conjunction with Hollins and McBlair, they collected insurance on it.[79] Another trader, the *Pilot*, gave S. Smith and Buchanan a long period of service before she was captured. The firm preferred large shares in large and new privateers, and it shared in estimated earnings of $362,500. If it owned as much as an unusually high one-half of its vessels, it earned $72,500 each year of the war from prizes. If it earned no more from trading, that was a serious decline from its $200,000 per year profit earned in the port's halcyon prewar days.[80]

The firm of Hollins and McBlair shared in owners' prize proceeds of $358,500 after its losses were deducted. It owned parts of fifteen vessels, including eleven privateers. Its junior partner, John Smith Hollins, joined the firm in some successes. The *York*, *Tom*, *Rolla*, *Dolphin*, and *Surprise* all made profitable cruises for part-owners Hollins and McBlair. They lost money on the letter-of-marque traders *Lottery* (insured) and *Rapid* and on the unproductive privateers *Hussar*, *Bona*, and *Sparrow*. The proportions held by Hollins and McBlair, except its one-tenth of the *Tom*, are unknown but even half ownership would not have allowed the firm to replace its annual peacetime business profits.

Three other members of the cluster sharing in estimated prize proceeds ranging from $300,000 to $399,000 were also very active prewar shipowners. John McKim, Jr. of the famous shipping family held four-thirtieths of the profitable *Tom* and unknown proportions of the *Globe* and *Rossie*. He also owned one-sixth of the prize-taking letter-of-marque trader *Diamond*. His share of the *Globe* was large and the *Tom* paid him an estimated ten thousand dollars for his four or five thousand dollar investment in that raider. Active prize agent and former captain Christopher Deshon profited from his holdings in the *Highflyer* (one-eighth), the *Tom* (one-thirtieth), and from his unknown proportions of the *Rolla* and the *Rossie*. Charles F. Kalkman, a familiar name on ships' papers before the war, profited from four successful privateers while losing on the unproductive *Bona* and on the *Revenge* on her losing cruise. Norwegian sailmaker and merchant Luke Kiersted was in on the *Revenge*'s successful cruise and owned parts of the profitable privateers *Fairy*, *Tom* (one-thirtieth), and *Caroline*. He shared in moieties of $300,000 and may have been able to move from sailmaking into a full-time merchant's role with the aid of these profits.

The final cluster of active investors profiting from prize proceeds included nine entrepreneurs who shared in estimated owners' proceeds exceeding $400,000. The nine men, listed in the order of their share earnings after losses were deducted, were:

Peter Arnold Karthaus	$418,054
James Williams	$421,500
Levi Hollingsworth	$481,770
John Smith Hollins	$498,755
Jeremiah Sullivan	$509,174
John Gooding	$521,000
Christian Keller	$534,000
Francis Foreman	$534,000
Andrew Clopper	$799,070[81]

The firm of Foreman and Keller owned parts of the privateers *Comet*, *Chasseur*, and *Harrison*, but those vessels sold in shares ranging from eighths to thirteenths. On the basis of a theoretical twelfth per vessel, the firm's share of the $534,000 earned by its partly-owned vessels was only $44,500 for a thirty month period. The flour-milling merchants also got seventeen months service out of a letter-of-marque trader, but two others, possibly financed by prize proceeds, became operative only in January of 1815. Foreman and Keller's success resulted from its total avoidance of what turned out to be losing vessels.

Another entrepreneur sharing in prize proceeds exceeding $400,000 while investing in what was a relatively few vessels was Jeremiah Sullivan. That partner in the house of Hollingsworth and Sullivan (not Levi Hollingsworth) avoided letter-of-marque traders altogether. Much like Robert Patterson, Sullivan invested only in three successful privateers. They were, however, the famous and well-commanded *Comet*, *Chasseur*, and *Rossie*. Thomas Boyle and Joshua Barney were the most famous commanders in the port, and Sullivan obviously invested in leadership. He apparently placed his winnings from the old *Rossie* and old *Comet* into the new *Chasseur*, also commanded by Boyle. On an estimated investment of ten or fifteen thousand dollars, Sullivan pocketed forty thousand. A partner in two firms, Sullivan may have been accustomed to even more income from shipping in peacetime. For some reason, he made no further investments after the *Chasseur* cleared in December of 1813. All his vessels survived physically, so Jeremiah Sullivan regained some of his original investment when those vessels were sold. Selectivity and restraint were investor Sullivan's strengths.

The remaining six entrepreneurs sharing in owners' proceeds exceeding $400,000 owned parts of more vessels than Sullivan or the firm of Keller and Foreman. They all invested in ten or more vessels, and each one owned at least one share in five or more privateers. Diversification and risk-spreading rather than selectivity and restraint characterized their investment style, and their heavy interest in privateers was their key to success. John Smith Hollins, the junior partner (two-twelfths) of Hollins and McBlair, actually invested in twenty-three commissions for fourteen different vessels. His successes were the privateers *York, Lawrence, Chasseur,* and *Surprise,* and one of his letter-of-marque traders, the *Tuckahoe,* also brought in a prize. He had estimated losses of $195,000 from his numerous holdings, but he still shared in estimated profits of $693,755. The firm of Hollins and McBlair actually entered the private armed vessel business early, possibly because it had vessels on hand, but all three partners made no new investments after the spring of 1814. The firm may have been reacting to persistent rumors of peace or, for unknown reasons, may have become disenchanted with the private armed vessel system. In number of successes, John Smith Hollins actually out-performed his firm's senior partners.

Merchants and mill proprietors Levi Hollingsworth and James Williams were also in the cluster sharing in $400,000 or more in estimated owners' proceeds. Hollingsworth sold flour, coffee, dry goods, and other products while operating a large copper mill. His holdings in eleven private armed vessels included five privateers. His successes were the *Comet* (one-twelfth and then one-thirteenth), the *Rossie,* the *Grampus,* and the *Globe,* while the letter-of-marque trader *Patapsco* brought in two prizes. Levi lost one commissioned trader but got good service from others. He diversified his investments among traders, privateers, tobacco in storage, and copper manufacturing. His relatives' assertion that "He is successful and will be rich" after the *Comet* sent in a prize may have been an accurate appraisal of Levi Hollingsworth's wartime performance.[82] After losses were deducted, Levi shared in estimated owners' proceeds of $481,770. James Williams was a partner in the flour-milling and shipping firm of Stump and Williams, located in Harford County and Baltimore. He was the principal owner of the successful *Sabine,* a one-tenth owner of the *Tom,* and part-owner of the *Midas* and *Mammoth.* He lost money on the unfortunate *Bona,* on two letter-of-marque traders, and on the *Tom* after she converted from privateering to trading. Even with those losses Williams shared in prize proceeds estimated at $421,500. If his proportions ranged from fourths to tenths, he earned from $40,000 to $100,000 personally. The Williamses were among the wealthiest men in Baltimore and may have been accustomed to an even larger income from thirty months of their shipping efforts.[83]

John Gooding shared in estimated proceeds of $521,000 after his losses were subtracted. He owned parts of six privateers and five letter-of-marque schooners. The *Sabine, Midas, Mammoth,* and *Tom* (one-tenth) produced substantial profits for Gooding, but he lost in the *Bona* and *America* (four-twentieths) and on one letter-of-marque trader. The copartnership of Gooding, Hutchins and Company was dissolved by "mutual consent" on June 30, 1812 and Gooding formed John Gooding and Company.[84] One can speculate that inability to agree on what entrepreneurial path to follow during a war may have caused the dissolution of Gooding, Hutchins and Company. With four successful privateers and some successful letter-of-marque operations, Gooding apparently earned a substantial wartime income.

The Baltimore entrepreneur participating in the largest estimated owners' prize proceeds was Andrew Clopper. A partner in the firm of Fulford and Clopper and a bank and insurance company director, Clopper spread his eighteen commissions among thirteen vessels. Eight were privateers and all eight were successful. Clopper owned two-twelfths and then two-thirteenths of the *Comet,* one-eighth of the *Highflyer,* one-third of the *Globe,* and one-thirtieth of the *Tom.* Unspecified proportions of the successful privateers *Rossie, Ultor,* and *Grampus* were also held by Clopper. Two letter-of-marque traders partly owned by Clopper, the *Diamond* and the *Patapsco,* also brought in prizes. He lost the letter-of-marque trader *Arab* to the British navy but his other traders gave him good service throughout the war years. After his losses were deducted, Andrew Clopper shared in estimated prize proceeds of $799,070, and on the basis of his known proportions and a theoretical twelfth for his other vessels, he pocketed between $80,000 and $90,000. He was reportedly "much pleased" by the $30,000 profit he received from one letter-of-marque voyage in 1813, so his wartime income may have been much higher than the prize estimates developed in this study.[85] Even though he was "a very respectable" Baltimore merchant and one of the port's largest prewar shipowners without his prize money, Clopper must have found his wartime income satisfactory.[86] Eight winners out of eight privateer investments was an astounding record.

The final member of the cluster of entrepreneurs sharing in estimated prize proceeds exceeding $400,000.00 was the German trader Peter Arnold Karthaus. Because he held unusually large proportions of several privateers, he may have personally profited more than Andrew Clopper while sharing in a smaller sum than Clopper. The estimated proceeds participated in by Karthaus were $418,054.00. Karthaus owned twelve and three-fourths and then eleven and one-fourth shares of the twenty shares of the successful *Amelia,* held nine-tenths of the lucrative *Kemp,* and was a one-thirteenth part-owner of the *Comet.* According to the records of Peter Arnold Karthaus and Company, he also held five shares of the unsuccessful privateer *Hornet,* but his name appeared on none of that vessel's documents.[87] From the *Kemp* alone Karthaus received $120,532.00 and his total personal share of his vessels' prize proceeds was over $200,000.00.

That figure excludes his commissions as a prize agent, his profits from prize goods resales and from letter-of-marque trading vessels, or his income from supplying privateers and prize vessels. Despite what appears to have been a flurry of entrepreneurial activity during the War of 1812, Karthaus did not employ all his available capital in his ten or eleven vessels. His books showed a profit of $291,447.49¾ from his firm's diverse activities in 1813, $77,545.28¼ available as "capital" at the end of 1814, and $53,886.56 as "cash" on hand at the end of 1815.[88] His reluctance or inability to invest more money in private armed vessels during the war may have been the reason for his instigation of a land, mill, and timber operation in central Pennsylvania in May of 1814.[89] The blockade may have encouraged him to go inland for an entrepreneurial outlet but he remained a very active salt water operative. Karthaus, the Williamses, the Hollinses, Clopper, John McKim, Jr., Gooding, the Pattersons, Levi Hollingsworth, Tenant, and others of the active investors kept their fingers in every profit-making facet of the private armed vessel system from preparation of their vessels to their sale after their service was completed.

Some of Baltimore's fifty active investors were marginal winners in regard to prize proceeds. They shared in amounts so small that their individual proportions were probably unimpressive for a thirty month period of shipping activity. Often large earnings were reduced by heavy losses sustained by the part-owners of several vessels. The following shared in the estimated owners' proceeds below $93,000:

James Bosley	Dennis A. Smith
Frederick W. Brune	Cumberland Dugan Williams
William T. Graham	Bernard Von Kapff[90]
John McFadon	

The small wartime incomes from prizes for a large shipping house such as Von Kapff and Brune or for active shipowners James Bosley and Cumberland Dugan Williams were not satisfactory replacements for their peacetime business. Bank officers William T. Graham and Dennis A. Smith may have been speculating more in government stocks than in vessels. Their prize proceeds were relatively small. John McFadon, as noted earlier in this study, had had financial problems before the war and may have been satisfied with the estimated $86,000 in prize proceeds he shared in during the war.

Finally, there were six apparent losers among the generally successful active investors. In most cases they simply invested in more unproductive vessels than they did in successful ones. Those suffering losses were:

William Bosley — lost on four of his four private vessel investments

John Joseph Lane — lost on two privateers while profiting from a one-thirtieth share of the *Tom*

Charles Malloy — lost on a privateer and a letter-of-marque trader while keeping one trader in service

Nicholas Stansbury — lost on three privateers while holding one share of the profitable *Chasseur*

John Randall — lost two letter-of-marque traders including one owned by him and one other investor, profited from the *Fairy* and one other trader

George Pitt Stevenson — profited from the *Lawrence* and *Patapsco*; may have made expenses on the privateer *Hollins*; lost on two privateers and one vessel acting as privateer and letter-of-marque schooner[91]

William Bosley, junior partner in the firm of J. and W. Bosley, lost an estimated $116,000 on four vessels, and merchant John Randall, financially embarrassed during the war, was unable to use prize proceeds to improve his standing. George Pitt Stevenson, nephew of both Samuel Smith and Wilson Cary Nicholas of Virginia, suffered losses estimated at $212,500 in private armed vessels. It is possible, however, that he owned shares in the *Chasseur* and *Whig* when those vessels operated out of New York while Baltimore was blockaded.[92] With or without any profits from his New York operations, Stevenson failed for a large sum after the war and carried some great entrepreneurial names with him, and while there is no evidence that his private vessel record caused his fall, a better wartime income could have buttressed him against financial strain during the postwar period.

In general, the fifty active investors out-performed the single and moderate investors. Forty-four or 80 percent of them, including two who held shares in only three or four different vessels, profited from their investments. Of the 200 Baltimore investors in private armed vessels during the War of 1812, estimates utilized in this study show 45 percent profited from prize proceeds, 34 percent lost money, while the remaining 21 percent were either unclear cases or operators of successful letter-of-marque traders. When the 21 entrepreneurs who did not invest in privateers were added to the 45 percent who profited from prizes, 55 percent of the 200 investors qualified as being successful. How many improved upon their prewar earnings is uncertain because of the general absence of prewar earnings records. Clopper, Karthaus, Gooding, Hollingsworth, and a few others may have, but firms such as Hollins and McBlair, S. Smith and Buchanan, D'Arcy and Didier, and the Williams and McKim shipping families were accustomed to huge incomes from shipping before the war. The impression is that, in general, the great firms restrained their shipowning during the war and while they earned profits, those funds were substantially smaller than their usual peacetime incomes from seaborne commerce. They did earn additional wartime income, however, from the supplying of prize and private armed vessels, from the resale of prize goods, from their roles as prize agents, and, perhaps most significantly for the moderate and active investors, from their letter-of-marque trading ventures. A general increase in manufacturing in Baltimore, the operation of textile, copper, and other mills, the starting of a land company, and investments in government stocks and stored tobacco suggest that the Baltimore entrepreneurs had substantial capital reserves that were not invested in shipping.

One may conclude, somewhat impressionistically, that shipping attracted a smaller proportion of available capital in wartime than it had in peacetime and that the profits from the private armed vessel system, except for a few cases, were not suitable replacements for peacetime earnings. The private system was not a panacea for the wartime problems of the entrepreneurs. It did, however, provide an outlet for vessels and capital, an opportunity for some profit-making in wartime, and an instrument for hurting England. It was certainly a superior alternative to idleness and stagnation for one's capital and vessels.[1] It was also an outlet for the frustrations of patriotic merchants and mariners who had suffered decades of abuse on the high seas.

TWELVE

The Aftermath

After the distribution of prize proceeds the books of a private armed vessel venture were closed unless the sponsors opted to refit their vessel for another voyage or cruise. After the war and after a particular venture was closed, there was time to analyze losses. At that time also, some consideration could be given to the factors producing either success or failure of the private armed vessel system and to the benefits it afforded to noninvestors. While looking back at the War of 1812, Baltimoreans had to function in the present and keep an eye on the future. Cargoes and markets had to be joined in a peacetime international economy. With a fleet of wartime schooners on their hands, some Baltimoreans looked beyond trade to South American and West Indian operations where their schooners might be used advantageously even without the usual cargoes in their holds. Changes in world shipping and trade patterns presented problems to the port of Baltimore and its entrepreneurs after the signing of the Treaty of Ghent.

At the end of the War of 1812, if not before, Baltimore's shipowning entrepreneurs must have taken at least an informal inventory of the port's wartime fleet. Baltimore had committed at least 122 vessels (two others were simply renamed) to the fray. Entrepreneurs experienced in international commerce were certainly accustomed to occasional losses at sea, and British and French seizures before the war had taught them to expect the worst. The loss of at least fifty-five of their fleet vessels to the British navy or to the sea in the two and one-half years of war was a heavy burden.[1] Nineteen of the losses, including one vessel whose role was uncertain, were well-armed privateers, and eleven of those privateers actually fell prey to British warships. Of eight privateers lost at sea or run aground, at least four were chased so their demise was also attributable to British naval operations. The *Tartar* also went aground in a blizzard while attempting to evade the blockading squadron so, indirectly, the British navy was responsible for her grounding. The nineteen lost privateers represented approximately 40 percent of Baltimore's cruisers and an estimated investment of seven hundred sixty thousand dollars.

Chronologically, the most dangerous year of the war was 1813. Seven privateers were lost or captured in that year, while five disappeared from Baltimore's books in 1814. Those were the years of the greatest British naval strength in American waters, and, of more immediate consequence, that was the period of the blockading and actual invasion of Chesapeake Bay. The blockade was gradually extended from the Chesapeake until all American coastal waters were areas of danger for American vessels. Geographically, thirteen Baltimore privateers were lost in American waters, while only two were taken in the West Indies and one in European waters. Two more privateers were captured after their Baltimore owners sold them to other owners, but the *Fox* and the *Leo* were not included in the calculations used here.

Fifteen Baltimore vessels operated as privateers and as letter-of-marque traders at different times during the war. In this study they were categorized according to the role they were playing at the time of their demise. At least thirty-six Baltimore commissioned traders were lost at sea, run aground, or captured. Depending upon their cargoes, they represented an investment of at least nine hundred thousand dollars. The number of traders varied as some converted to privateering, but about seventy-four functioned consistently as traders. The losses then approached 50 percent of the port's commissioned cargo carriers. Fortunately, many had paid for themselves several times before they were lost, so a vessel loss did not necessarily mean a financial loss on the owner's books.

Chronologically, 1813 was also the most dangerous year for the letter-of-marque traders and for the same reasons. Twenty letter-of-marque traders were lost in 1813, while twelve were put out of action in 1814. Geographically, seventeen of the trader losses occurred in American coastal waters, nine in European waters, four in the West Indies, and six in unknown waters. Unlike the privateers, commissioned traders were forced to come in from the open sea where their speed was such an asset to unload their cargoes. The closer they got to a port, the less flexibility they had in restricted waters crowded with British warships. Five fast traders ran ashore, but only one was actually chased ashore. In a confrontation with even a small British warship, the letter-of-marque traders lacked the extra fire and manpower for defense available on privateers. Larger crews could repel boarders and man sweeps.

The Baltimore schooner losses were serious. Given the extent of the coasts, sea lanes, and open sea to be patrolled by the British navy, the actual capturing of forty-eight or fifty of the swift, well-manned, and ably led Baltimore schooners was an accomplishment. It is true that only a few were captured on the open sea, but the British strategy of concentrating their strength on the coasts and waiting for the schooners' egress or entry was reasonably successful. To have done better at sea would have required the construction of special pursuit vessels such as the destroyers and subchasers used against other commerce raiders in later wars. Near the coasts the British made good use of their superior numbers and fire power. It was common for two, three, or even five major British warships to share in the prize money earned in the capture of one Baltimore privateer or lightly armed letter-of-marque trader.

Even vessels captured or lost at sea often paid dividends to their crews and owners from prizes taken or from trading ventures completed before their loss. All prize actions completed in Baltimore, however, contributed some income to Baltimoreans other than the crews and owners. The warehousemen, shipyard workers, coopers, drayers, and printers benefited from prize-related business. The city's auctioneers also earned commissions and fees from their role in prize sales.[2] The United States marshal's commission on prize sales was lowered during the war, but he still profited from them. Even with the inclusion of seven prize cases where the commission limit of $250 per case applied, former Baltimore shipowning merchant Thomas Rutter earned at least nine thousand nine hundred dollars from his marshal's commission on prize sales.[3] The clerk of the court's commission was computed after the marshal's commission and other costs of the sale were deducted. His income from prize sales was, therefore, only slightly less than that of the marshal.

Anyone looking back upon the private system's operation at the war's end must have envied some of the captains. A number of the successful captains held owners' shares while simultaneously earning 6 or 8 percent of the officers' and crew's moiety. As a result, men such as Barney, Boyle, Almeda, and Dooley entered the postwar period with capital. Joshua Barney, with his bounty of 10 percent written into the *Rossie*'s articles, his ten shares as commander, and the four merit shares that he awarded to himself, received over $32,000.00 for his three month's cruise in the *Rossie*.[4] Thomas Boyle's income with his 16 shares of the *Comet*'s 270 shares, an owner's share (one-thirteenth) in that vessel's second cruise, plus his captain's shares in the *Chasseur* must have earned him over $30,000.00 even without a 10 percent bonus.[5] Joseph Almeda's account with Peter Arnold Karthaus and Company listed his captain's shares and his 10 percent bonus of the *Kemp*'s prizes alone as $16,143.14. Almeda, who also commanded the successful *Caroline*, had a credit of $29,770.37 on the company's books when prizes from other vessels were included.[6]

Even commanders of marginal or losing privateers received their portion of the officers' and crew's moiety when they sent in just one prize or brought in a partial prize cargo in the hold. Unlike the owners, they did not have to overcome or balance an original capital investment in the venture. Letter-of-marque captains received wages, prize money, and even a bonus for safe arrivals as well as their normal peacetime prerogatives such as trading space in the hold and primage. Certainly, captains of successful privateers and of letter-of-marque traders that were operative over long periods of time profited from their role during the war. Others died in action, spent time in prison, or wound up with only their advances to show for their efforts in dangerous times.

Entrepreneurs sponsoring private ventures had other profit-making activities that were related to the private armed vessel system. They furnished supplies to the private armed vessels when they were outfitting for sea and to prize vessels while they awaited a court decree. They bought and resold prize goods and, along with noninvestors, exported prize and other goods in the letter-of-marque schooners. Numerous investors and nearly all of the active investors also performed in the role of ship's husband and prize agent. They received a 2.5 percent commission for that role after the sales and court costs were deducted.

Christopher Deshon's commission on the *Rossie*'s prizes was only slightly less than his dividend from his minimal one-sixteenth owner's share. He earned $3,730.20 commission while his owner's share paid him $4,260.89.[7] Deshon had to subtract his original investment and any later contributory shares from his owner's share but not from his prize agent's commission. He was paid as agent for the successful *Rolla* and several other private armed vessels as well. Andrew Clopper, the entrepreneur sharing in the largest owners' proceeds in Baltimore, received a significant income as the prize agent for the successful privateers *Globe*, *Patapsco*, and *Grampus*. Thomas Sheppard was the prize agent for the lucrative *Chasseur*, and James Williams for the successful privateers *Midas* and *Sabine*. Thomas Tenant served in that role for the *Highflyer*, while Thorndike Chase did the same for the *Comet*.[8]

A prize vessel entering at Baltimore offered profit-making opportunities to many individuals in addition to her sale proceeds. Nearly all levels of Baltimore's population had a chance to earn money from the system. A portion of the wartime income of the port's great and small entrepreneurs, of the proprietors of Fells Point's grog shops and boarding houses, lawyers, seamen, craftsmen, and others came from the private armed vessels. Unless human nature was unique in the War of 1812, some of the system's income also went to the famous prostitutes of Fells Point. The hook of land extending a protective arm around those vessels anchored within it, with its many taverns and seamens' boarding houses, may have given birth to the term "hooker."

Baltimore citizens, including the Quakers, profited from the private armed vessel system indirectly. The federal government's collection of duties on prize goods benefited the entire nation, and city taxes collected from waterfront operations provided Baltimore with income. Wharfage fees alone provided the city with $22,143.52 in the period from 1812 to 1815.[9] That income represented a $10,000.00 drop from the four years preceding the war, but there would have been an even greater loss without the income from private armed vessels. The city also collected $118,500.98 during the war period from a tax on auction receipts. The auction tax receipts of 1812, 1813, and 1815 were the three highest auction tax figures for the entire period from 1807 to 1815. Counting all of 1812 and 1815, the auction tax income was actually twice what the city received from property taxes.[10] Without the waterfront taxes and fees contributed largely by private armed vessels, it may have been necessary to increase the property tax rate.

Any merchant's coffee house or counting house review of the private armed vessel system's operation during the War of 1812 must have eventually asked why some entrepreneurs made money and why some did not. Success and failure factors appropriate to peacetime shipping were also applicable, to a degree, in wartime. Letter-of-marque cargoes and privateer prize cargoes required the same attention to detail so characteristic of the successful Baltimore houses during the prewar years. Henry Didier, Jr., for example, ordered his brother in France to advise his captains "to have all the ropes and patches taken off the Bales of Cotton" and to have the bales "as neatly repaired as possible."[11] Didier knew that French officials charged a tare fee of 8 percent when the ropes and patches were on and only 6 percent when they were off. The proper stowage of a letter-of-marque or prize cargo was as important as proper stowage in peacetime because damaged articles reduced the profitability of a voyage or a cruise. For the merchant shipowners the peacetime concern for prudence, for speculation, regularity in business, and for the placement of one's resources in more than one vessel was not diminished by wartime conditions. The placement of trust in firms with insufficient expertise, capital, or credit also led to bad debts in wartime as it had in peacetime.[12] In letter-of-marque voyages such considerations, and careful attention to the impact of inflation on profits, were more important to an entrepreneur than the possibility of profits from occasional prizes of opportunity.

For letter-of-marque enterprises and privateer adventures, commercial intelligence was another significant success factor. The prices paid for goods in other ports determined whether a commissioned trader with prize or other cargoes or prize vessels with goods in their holds would be sent to certain ports. The Baltimore entrepreneurs had utilized younger brothers, nephews, and junior partners as resident agents in the West Indies and in Europe for decades. Henry Didier, Jr.'s partner John Netherville D'Arcy spent the war in England, while Didier's brother John worked in France. Writing to John Smith in Paris on the eve of the War of 1812, Samuel Smith noted that William Hollins was at Paris.[13] Successful but restrained privateer investor Jeremiah Sullivan received commercial information from his brother in Cadiz during the war.[14] Successful Baltimore investor Levi Hollingsworth spoke of commercial information received from a relative in the West Indies.[15] These and others kept up a flow of intelligence on prices and convoy sailings to the Baltimore trading houses, while foreign business correspondents and returning captains added to the pool of information.

Shipping intelligence was vital to those entrepreneurs preparing instructions for the commanders of their raiders also, and data was acquired from a variety of sources. The brig *Margaretta*, owned by William Patterson and Sons, returned from Portugal in July of 1812. Her captain reported passing a British West Indian fleet of seventy sails and apprising two Norfolk privateers of that fact the next day at sea.[16] A Baltimore newspaper reported in January of 1813 that the British Cork fleet of seventy sails had cleared on November 16, 1812, under the convoy of three British bulldogs. Such advice was often timely enough to permit a swift Baltimore privateer to intercept such slow moving convoys before they reached the West Indies or Canada. Normal seasonal British shipping schedules and patterns were well known but precise sailing dates were always helpful. On March 17, 1813, an editor advised that a fleet of 150 sails had left St. Thomas in the West Indies on February 15, 1813. In November of the same year privateersmen were informed that convoys from India and China, one for China, and the last Baltic convoy of the season were in various locations. In November of 1812 a newspaper reported that the Baltimore privateer *America* had sailed to "intercept the St. Thomas fleet" whose location had been reported earlier. In August of 1813 the whereabouts of the British East India and Brazil convoys were reported along with the strength of their accompanying bulldogs.[17] Another editor advised the cruisers that British vessels carrying specie from Buenos Aires would be found near Newfoundland by the time the newspaper was delivered.[18]

Contacts at sea or in other ports were important and often timely sources of information. Captain Edward Veazey of the privateer *Lawrence* wrote prize agent Richard H. Douglass that he had just captured a new brig from Batavia and that he was informed by her captain that another vessel of twenty-two guns was leaving that port the next morning. Veazey confidently noted that "She is ours."[19] Editor Hezekiah Niles observed that American privateers "have had for a long time secret intelligence with two of the ports on the Irish coast."[20] Perhaps one was the Irish port of Baltimore where Captain Thomas Boyle burned a prize. Dame Fortune played a large role in prize-taking ventures but not everything was left to that lady.

The chances of success were improved by the quality of one's equipment, but the direction given to that equipment by a commander was absolutely vital to success. The "wise selection and management of captains and agents" was a most important factor in business success in peacetime.[21] In wartime a vessel constructed by a first class builder such as Thomas Kemp, the acquisition of a mixed but adequate armament, and the alteration of a vessel's rigging and deadrise in a Baltimore shipyard certainly increased the chances for success. The type of equipment became increasingly significant after the first six months of the war when longer cruises and greater speed were required of cruisers and traders. It was not enough to sail well to take prizes. A crew had to fight and a good performance under fire was a product of able and audacious leadership. Successful captains such as Barney, Boyle, Dooley, and Almeda were stern task masters who carefully organized and drilled their crews while discouraging insubordination. Theirs was no easy assignment with a large, motley, and hastily gathered crew crowded into a small vessel. Boyle kept his men exercising the big guns and small arms, changing sails, and working in various maintenance jobs required on a sailing vessel of war.[22] The Articles of Agreement granted commanders considerable power and their authority to deny a crewman his certificate of discharge at the cruise's termination was a significant controlling factor. There were cases where such controls were either inadequately utilized or irrelevant because a prize was not encountered on the cruise.

Captain Thomas Boyle of the successful privateers *Comet* and *Chasseur* got the maximum response from his men. His second cruise on the *Comet* gave him his choice of men, but his initial crew was somewhat selective also. The importance of full or partial literacy on the part of crew members is uncertain, but, in his first crew, Boyle had a high proportion of men who could at least sign their name. Over three-fourths of his men were able to actually sign the Articles of Agreement.[23] Only one-half of the *Dolphin*'s crew were able to sign and, possibly, to read the articles and other documents. The others placed their "X" on the ship's documents, which were read to them by an officer.

There is little evidence that Thomas Boyle, who ran a tight vessel, had serious difficulties with his crews. He was accused of attacking his captain of marines with a drawn sword when that gentleman fired a musket after a prize had struck her colors.[24] The *Comet*'s drummer testified that Boyle was "very strict and rigid in his Behavior towards the Sailors and Marines, and often damned and abused them, and swore he would knock their Brains out, and such things." Boyle allegedly ordered the drummer "to beat the Drum over the heads" of a prize master and a sailing master when they were asleep.[25] Nevertheless, the boatswain on the *Comet* pointed out that he had served on many vessels and did not "know a better Commander" and that Boyle "was not a Tyrant or a Cruel Man."[26] Obviously, the crew knew who was in command of the *Comet* and *Chasseur*.

Some commanders were accused of being abusive. The mate of the letter-of-marque trader *Pioneer* was charged with attacking a seaman while he was out on a boom in a wind and of threatening to knock him off that boom.[27] The captain of the letter-of-marque trader *Female* allegedly attacked his steward and cook while that person was sick, charging him with "skulking" and beating him "with a rope" and knocking him "senseless with a stick."[28] A seaman on the *Siro* charged that the captain not only beat and flogged him but also forced him to dance for the crew.[29] Numerous other complaints were made in the district court, but the officers sometimes responded that the men had been mutinous, quarrelsome, incompetent, or insolent.

The commanders wanted discipline, but the crews resented abuse. Crew members on privateers that were actually private men-of-war were subject to courts martial, while those on letter-of-marque traders used the navy courts on occasion. Commodore Joshua Barney court martialed one John Marr, a gunner on the *Rossie*, for disobedience of orders. Gunner Marr had improperly filled and prepared cannon cartridges and was charged also with neglect of duty while an enemy vessel was being engaged.[30] Even the entrepreneurs back in Baltimore understood the need for discipline in combat, and Levi Hollingsworth wrote of the advantages "of discipline, skill and practice in war" as the prime determinants of success.[31] But the crew knew abuse when they saw it and could actually instigate a change of command. Henry Didier, Jr. wrote that he had removed Captain James Taylor of the letter-of-marque trader *Delille* because of the crew "refusing to go to sea" with him. Didier observed that Captain Taylor was "a very severe man at sea" but that he was going to assign him to his firm's *Maria* at a later date.[32]

Apparently, the crews accepted severity from their officers when it was combined with the audacity needed for wartime success. They criticized commanders who displayed timidity or uncertainty. The crew of the letter-of-marque trader *Bordeaux Packet* was critical of Captain George Lee after that vessel had fought off and escaped from the British frigate *Nieman* by using sweeps. Unfortunately, the *Nieman* then got between land and the injured schooner when the *Bordeaux Packet*'s condition was such that "our maintop mast was down, yards down, sails unbent and down in the cabin, anchors over the bow and the cables bent, lee guns, square sail boom dragging in the water." The first mate wanted to cut away an anchor to escape, but the captain who "seemed to be thunderstruck and incapable of judging what ought to be done" denied that request.[33] Even the crews of lightly armed (six or eight guns) Baltimore letter-of-marque traders expected their leaders to fight or to escape even when their vessels were distressed.

The inability of a commander to control his crew was an invitation to failure. Captain John Dameron of the privateer *Bona* cleared from Baltimore in July of 1812 with a crew gathered together quickly at a time when many vessels were competing for any available manpower. Dameron worked his "people" on the guns and tried to keep them busy, but cases of disobedience and insubordination cropped up nearly every day. Dameron read the law to the collected crew and lashed one man, but the *Bona*'s failure to meet with the "Phalistean's Fleet" (the British Jamaica fleet) caused great discontent among the "People." The privateer put into Norfolk where two men deserted. Back at sea Dameron stopped the grog allowances of two men for "fighting and Braking my peace." The ship's liquor was raided, illness broke out and the cold weather led to "Salt Warter Boyls" and more discontent. Dameron turned south to milder climate only to find himself assaulted and almost killed below deck. Surviving that, the commander recorded the explosion of cannons and guns in drills and with the combination of injuries and illness, he claimed that he had only "one Seaman amongst the Crew Except the Officers" fit for duty. The *Bona*'s dismal cruise ended on December 20, 1812, when Collector of Customs James H. McCulloch at Baltimore endorsed her log.[34]

Success was also dependent, to some extent, upon the avoidance of serious mistakes. The privateers *Nonsuch* and *Joseph and Mary* fired on each other until three or four men were killed and several others wounded. The firing ceased only when the *Joseph and Mary* struck her colors.[35] Ironically, the government's signalling system for private armed vessels was not put into operation because it was not available before some privateers had cleared.[36] Various Baltimore vessels furnished other Baltimore vessels with their private signals. The signals of the aforementioned *Nonsuch* were given to Joshua Barney of the *Rossie* but not to the captain of the *Joseph and Mary*. The *Nonsuch*'s recognition signals consisted of a sequential exchange of variously colored flags on prescribed masts and one flag with "Nonsuch" printed on it. At night a sequential exchange of fires was utilized. Barney's inventory of flags suggested that close attention was paid to such matters and that American, British, French, and Spanish flags were flown at various times by American privateers. The *Rossie*'s chest also contained seven English ensigns and three English flags of different colors.[37]

A captain needed some luck in locating a prize and some ability and courage in capturing her, but financial success depended on the prize vessels and goods that he and his prize masters were able to get into an appropriate market. Even when he sailed masterfully and fought heroically he could have been an economic failure when his mercantile and commercial expertise was deficient. The quality and condition of prize vessels was probably an easy matter for a master mariner to judge. Prize goods, however, required a trained eye and a knowledge of the market. Items exportable to France such as cotton, sugar, or coffee, at one time or the other, were worth taking. For certain success, a captain would have been wise to have divested or sent in all coffee, sugar, cotton, dry goods, and hardware. For a potential investor the choices of a commander and the prize masters were more important than the newness of the vessel or the quality of her sails, her guns, or her crew.

After the signing of the Treaty of Ghent, the Baltimoreans encountered one more entrepreneurial challenge, while they were still analyzing their performance in the War of 1812. For the first time since the beginning of the French Revolution they were able to engage in an international commerce unaffected by war or revolution in Europe. America's last experience with peacetime trade, during the period of the Articles of Confederation, had been troublesome. Between that period and the signing of the Treaty of Ghent the Baltimore entrepreneurs had learned how to survive and even prosper in wartime circumstances while performing as neutral shippers and as belligerents. Received in Baltimore on February 12, 1815, the news of peace caught some by surprise. Henry Didier, Jr. wrote to his partner that "the peace has come on us quite unexpectedly; we expected that it would take place in the course of this year;

but not before the British Government received the accounts of the defeat of their army at New Orleans."[38]

The problem posed by peace for some Baltimore shipowners was that they still owned small schooners bought for wartime conditions. The firm of D'Arcy and Didier had investments in at least fifteen sleek schooners, both commissioned and noncommissioned, on January 1, 1815. Such a situation prompted Didier to respond to the news of peace by stating, "I am in hopes there will be a war between England, France and some of the continental powers, that we may make use of our fast sailing schooners." Didier was determined not to sell his fast schooners at a loss and hoped that they could be used to carry his Richmond tobacco to the Mediterranean. The prize brig *Canada*, loading cotton in North Carolina for D'Arcy and Didier and the Olivers, was classified as a "fine peace vessel," and Didier thought she would be brought to Baltimore where Richmond tobacco could be added to her cargo. Didier also had fifty hogsheads of tobacco in the ship *William* ready for exportation when the news of peace arrived.[39] Large full-rigged ships and slow brigs were useful in peacetime, but the future of the smaller but faster schooners did not look good in early 1815.

Peace and Andrew Jackson's victory at New Orleans inspired a giant civic celebration in Baltimore. All projects related to the war, including work on a new "Steam Frigate," were suspended and the city looked forward to "a new commencement of life and business." The farmers held their wheat for better prices, while the merchants prepared cargoes for Europe and held their stored tobacco for higher prices. The rents for stores skyrocketed because dry goods importers were preparing stores for large importations. In March, New England vessels began dropping in for the same flour and grain cargoes they had gotten in Baltimore before the war. One trading firm reported that some of its goods had been stolen by "disbanded soldiery prowling our streets."[40] For the first five months of peace outward-bound ships carrying cargoes of cotton and tobacco and incoming ships transporting dry goods passed prizes on their way into Baltimore for adjudication. Reminders of the war did not disappear all at once.

After the war Baltimore's shippers were saved once more by their staple exports, flour and tobacco, and by their reexports. Flour, particularly, experienced a comeback between 1815 and 1819. The following average annual prices per barrel document that product's return to respectability after it reached a monthly low of $5.50 per barrel in November of 1813:

1811	$ 9.38
1812	$ 9.14
1813	$ 7.20
1814	$ 7.37½
1815	$ 9.00

1816	$ 9.75
1817	$11.43
1818	$10.50
1819	$ 5.38
1820	$ 4.33[41]

Flour and the reexport trade provided a postwar boom for a while and aided Baltimore to grow between 1810 and 1820, but the boom expired by late 1818. Baltimore continued to lead the American flour trade until 1827 when New York assumed that role.[42]

With peace, the Europeans began carrying their own West Indian colonial produce while depending on some American food imports because of crop failures.[43] Baltimore and other American merchants also speculated successfully in cotton and tobacco for Europe until 1819.[44] Some products normally shipped by the Baltimoreans fell drastically in price with the news of peace. Sugar in American ports fell from $26.00 to $12.50 per hundred-weight, tea fell from $2.25 to $1.00, both in two days, and coffee and other popular reexport items also declined.[45] Baltimore's warehoused colonial produce lost its value quickly.

After taking off their guns, cutting down their crews, disposing of their commissions, and often converting their schooners into brigs, the Baltimore investors in private armed vessels sought markets and goods. Peter Arnold Karthaus, for example, shipped 200 hogsheads of tobacco to Bremen and Hamburg and sent arms to revolt-torn South America.[46] Henry Didier, Jr. shipped large amounts of muskets and gunpowder to the Spanish Main and to Havana, flour to the Iberian Peninsula, as well as cotton and tobacco to England, France, Holland, and the Mediterranean. In good entrepreneurial fashion, Didier encouraged all his correspondents in Europe and the West Indies to find new markets and new goods. On May 16, 1815, his firm owned parts of one ship on her way to Calcutta, shares in the famous *Chasseur* (converted to a brig) bound for China, portions of four schooners and two brigs headed for South America or the West Indies, part of one brig going to the Madeira Islands, and shares in one schooner sailing for the Mediterranean. Didier had $108,000 invested in those vessels and their cargoes and was counting heavily on the South American arms sales for his profits.[47] Without commissions his fast Baltimore schooners had the best chance to evade the Spanish blockade of the revolutionary South American ports and to evade insurgent privateers when his vessels were carrying cargoes to the Spanish forces.

Others among the entrepreneurs who sponsored Baltimore's private armed vessels during the War of 1812 also sought new outlets and uses for their capital and their vessels in a peacetime world. The neutral carrying trade and commissioned vessels, the sources of profits up to 1815, had to be replaced. Spanish

South America was a customer for arms and a source of hides and other return loads, but the revolutionary privateers in that region also provided the Americans with prize goods. Richard H. and William Douglass of Baltimore authorized their correspondents in Port au Prince, Haiti, to purchase $20,000 worth of prize goods for shipment to Baltimore. There were legal questions involved in such transactions, but the Douglass firm assumed the risk whenever the marks and packaging of the prize goods were altered sufficiently to prevent identification.[48]

The Douglasses reported that business in Baltimore had never been so dull as it was in 1817 despite the search for new markets and new goods. John Donnell's ship, *North Point,* which was coming up the Patapsco, and other Baltimore Indiamen were expected to invigorate business. By 1816 French, German, Russian, and English manufactured and dry goods were a glut on the market, and the Douglass firm as well as other Baltimore trading houses viewed East Indian, Chinese, West Indian, and South American products as "the only goods we want and they bear very good prices, without much fear of a rapid decline."[49]

The entrepreneurs searched for any product that could be shipped for a profit. Prime cotton was purchased for $6,000 in North Carolina for exportation by the Douglasses.[50] Cotton became a very important postwar export, and Baltimore's location permitted its entrepreneurs to enter that trade.[51] The Douglasses, Henry Didier, Jr., John Gooding, John Donnell, and other Baltimore entrepreneurs also investigated the possibility of purchasing Argentina's beef. The Douglass house gathered muskets from merchants in other American ports for Baltimore shippers, particularly D'Arcy and Didier, while reporting to a Bostonian in December of 1816 that "very large shipments have lately been made to Mexico, Buenos Ayres and Chile." Mexico, however, proved to be a problem when the Baltimore vessels were not permitted to land their cargoes of arms. In November of 1817 the Douglass firm reported that the price of Baltimore's flour was holding up "much beyond our expectations and the demand is considerable for the West Indies, Canada, and our Northern Districts." Coffee and sugar, Baltimore's favorite reexport products, brought back as return loads from the West Indies for many decades, recovered somewhat as demand increased.[52] Old reliable export items and new South American and Eastern markets provided the entrepreneurs with a partial solution to their peacetime problems for a few years after the signing of the Treaty of Ghent.

Coffee and sugar were not the only reexports. Linens from Bremen came into Baltimore and were then shipped to Pernambuco, Brazil. Lemuel Taylor and Thomas Sheppard bought muskets imported by Christopher Deshon and reexported them to Havana. Henry Didier, Jr. reshipped European glassware to the West Indies. Von Kapff and Brune imported cloth from Bremen, John Carrere brought silk from France, and Charles F. Kalkman reexported both of those imports to Havana. Dennis A. Smith's China tea came into Philadelphia, but a Baltimore trading house then shipped it to Copenhagen. Didier brought silk stockings from France and reexported them to the West Indies. Calcutta goods brought in by S. Smith and Buchanan were reexported to the West Indies by Martin F. Maher and William Penniman. Other cotton goods from Calcutta were brought in by Peter A. Guestier along with dry goods from Liverpool, and both cargoes were then reshipped to South America. Lemuel Taylor and Michael McBlair bought imported brandy from Robert and John Oliver and then reexported it to Havana.[53] Such reexports helped the entrepreneurs to make profits and to use their vessels, but reexports contributed little to the overall prosperity of Maryland.

The Baltimore entrepreneurs sometimes concentrated on a particular product in their postwar trading. George Williams sent large quantities of soap from his "very large factory" in Baltimore to the West Indies for coffee.[54] Shipbuilder and merchant Joseph Despeaux was advised from France to forego cotton even though he had done well in it and to concentrate on rice.[55] In cooperation with D'Arcy and Didier, Martin F. Maher, grocer and merchant, had cornered all the ginseng (used for medicinal purposes in China) in Baltimore during the war and was attempting to sell 40,000 pounds of it after the war.[56] Tobacco, an item whose price in Europe was not constant, was grown even when its value was low. Maryland tobacco moved better in England and southern Europe. By 1818, the loading of tobacco in the rivers was "almost wholly discontinued," and new warehouses handled the larger quantities coming into the city for exportation.[57] Amos A. and George Williams, William Patterson, and others erected tobacco warehouses in Baltimore after the war. Maryland alone produced 32,234 hogsheads of tobacco in 1818.[58]

Dennis A. Smith, cashier and director of the Mechanic's Bank, was an example of an entrepreneur trying various alternatives after the war. He was reported to have made $250,000 in bank and government stocks in the last year of the war. His total worth in March of 1815 was estimated at $400,000 so he entered the peace years with expendable capital.[59] Smith had shared in estimated owners' prize proceeds of $93,000 in the War of 1812, but his new wealth was largely a result of his stock investments. He owned a plantation in Louisiana and exported large quantities of Louisiana cotton after the war and dispatched vessels to Europe and China with that commodity, flour, and tobacco. One Baltimore merchant characterized Dennis A. Smith in 1815 as "the great head of all speculators here now." The busy banker dispatched John Carrere to France "with some great commercial views" and sent another man to England to prepare for "the Spring Trade." It was said that Dennis A. Smith was "engaged in everything that requires any amount of funds or credit."[60]

Others did not find shipping to be the road to success that it had once been. The Baltimoreans had to compete with New England and European vessels for export and import cargoes after the war. Usually shipowners, the Douglasses invested from \$5,000 to \$15,000 in Mississippi land schemes.[61] In other years that money would have gone into shipping. The turn toward inland trade, to South America, and to the Orient did not provide enough new shipping business for the numerous entrepreneurs who had been attracted to Baltimore from the Revolution to the War of 1812. Merchant prince Robert Oliver characterized American and Baltimore business as being miserable and wretched in 1816. The situation induced that great trading house to withdraw from active trading until things improved. The firm's profits were \$833,618 in 1809, \$38,413 in the middle of the war (1813), and \$22,950 in 1816. In 1817 the firm made only \$162 and in 1819 the Oliver house suffered a loss of \$236. By 1819 the Olivers' resources had been transferred into land, houses, and stocks.[62] The general decline in prices that followed the War of 1812 had discouraged the Olivers and others from reengaging heavily in shipping.

The Douglass commercial house provided a good example of postwar entrepreneurial scrambling. It sought prize business in the West Indies, bought and sold cotton and other commodities, invested in land, and participated in the selling of arms to South America. Somewhat discouraged by June of 1817, it reported frequent failures and a general lack of business confidence in the port of Baltimore. The firm retreated "almost exclusively" into the safe harbor of the commission business aiming to keep itself "Snug for better times." Additionally, it contemplated the Mississippi area as a new mercantile base for the house and for the expanding cotton business.[63] The attraction and potential of Mobile to entrepreneurs in 1817 was similar to that of Baltimore in the period from the Revolution to the War of 1812. The Baltimoreans responded successfully to challenges as long as they employed their shipping, but the postwar period did not always permit the utilization of that shipping to its fullest extent. Finally, in May of 1821, the secretary of treasury ordered reductions in the staff of the collector of customs' office in Baltimore because of "the great reductions of the commerce of this country, since 1817 and 1818."[64] There was simply not enough work for Baltimore's customs staff.

The officers and crew from Baltimore's wartime private fleet had to adjust to peace also. They returned to a simple wage arrangement and found plenty of employment for a while. The port's ability to compete in the early months of peacetime had encouraged a "great importation of masters and mates" from other ports looking for assignments. In late April of 1815, it was reported that at least one hundred fifty mates and masters were on the beach.[65] The prewar decades of shipping success and the wartime demand for mariners apparently overexpanded the supply of such people in Baltimore. Any kind of sea duty was preferable to idleness or shore duty for such men.

In postwar Baltimore there were some who would never forget the battles fought by privateers and letter-of-marque traders. Eleanor Murphy, widow of

Captain John Murphy, slain on the privateer *Grampus*, collected a pension of ten dollars per month, while Margaret Southcomb received twenty dollars per month for the death of Captain John Southcomb, slain on the letter-of-marque *Lottery*. The son of Captain James Stubbs, killed on the privateer *Syren*, was allotted twenty dollars per month after Mrs. Stubbs remarried. Nancy Wilkinson, widow of John Wilkinson, was awarded twelve dollars per month after the death of her husband on the privateer *Nonsuch*. Four dollars per month went to the letter-of-marque trader *Ned*'s Joseph P. Haddock for a "ball still in his right side" in 1819 and to the privateer *Dolphin*'s Peter Matthews for "three fingers of his right hand cut off and his left arm considerably damaged." A quartermaster from the *Dolphin* was also allotted four dollars per month for his left leg "wounded by grape Shot." "Wounded by a musket ball which entered the right side of the backbone" the privateer *Comet*'s disabled master of marines received five dollars per month as did the *Comet*'s William Milford for the loss of a leg. For the loss of two fingers, the *Highflyer*'s Leonard Mattee received three dollars per month along with the *Syren*'s sailmaker, whose arm, fractured by a musket ball "resulted in a caries." For the loss of his thigh, as mentioned in the *Chasseur*'s log, Henry Watson was awarded six dollars per month while Yankey Sheppard received the same amount for the loss of a leg on the same privateer. Ten dollars per month went to prize master Stephen White of an unnamed privateer after grape shot destroyed his left heel and passed through his right foot. The *Hussar*'s Lieutenant John Nantes was entitled to twelve dollars per month after having "the radius of his right arm badly fractured by a musket shot and his left arm so severely wounded as to require amputation" while attempting to escape from the British.[66] These and other pension recipients were still collecting pensions from the Privateer's Fund and nursing memories of the private armed vessel system long after the system became inoperative in Baltimore.

With its schooners, veteran seamen, and experienced entrepreneurs, Baltimore was admirably suited to continue privateering after the signing of the Treaty of Ghent. An opportunity to do just that existed in revolt-torn South America. While Baltimore's "richest and most-favored merchants" supplied both Spanish and rebel forces with arms, the Patapsco port became the "chief center of privateering activities in the United States" for the insurgents.[67] Baltimore was servicing both sides, but its raiding activities became notorious. When Congress was debating a neutrality bill, acerbic John Randolph of Virginia characterized the bill as an effort to make peace between Spain and the port of Baltimore.[68] Blank commissions for insurgent private armed vessels were readily available in Baltimore. Two of the first rebel raiders, the *Orb* and the *Romp*, owned by D'Arcy and Didier during the War of 1812, were outfitted in Baltimore for duty in South America. They were typical 170-ton sharp-built schooners with raked high masts and ten guns. Clearing Baltimore as merchantmen, they added extra men and guns in the bay before a cruise on which their crews reportedly cleared about one thousand five hundred dollars each in prize money. Such service became popular, and an estimated three thousand five hundred American seamen worked on the South American raiders from 1816 to 1821. Capital was provided not only by Baltimore's entrepreneurs but, reportedly, by Judge Theodoric Bland of the District Court, Postmaster John S. Skinner, and the collectors of customs at Baltimore and Savannah.[69] Depositions taken in Baltimore pointed to War of 1812 private armed vessel investors Nicholas Stansbury, Thomas Sheppard, Luke Kiersted, John Snyder, Joseph Karrick, Joseph W. Patterson, John Gooding, James Williams, John Joseph Lane, and Christopher Raborg as probable shareholders, agents, or suppliers of the questionable raiders.[70]

The names of Baltimore's War of 1812 private armed vessel commanders appeared regularly in depositions and court cases involving alleged South American raiding. Captains Almeda (now Don Jose Almeyda), Danels, Stafford (now Captain Estefano), Jenkins, Davey, Chaytor, Taylor, Barnes, Chase, and others commanding the South American raiders were well known by the owners and crewmen of the port's own War of 1812 private armed vessels.[71] Some Baltimoreans were unimpressed by the actions of their mercantile and maritime neighbors, particularly when the South American privateers edged into piracy. Former investor in private armed vessels, Senator Samuel Smith supported a new law curbing American participation in the business. Smith also expressed "great indignation" at what he considered an insult to his commercial house in 1818 when some Buenos Aires commissions were sent to his firm.[72] Public opinion, so favorable to privateering during the war, began to turn against it when protests and complaints about South American adventurers intensified. While the United States was at peace with Spain, the port of Baltimore was seemingly attacking Spanish vessels as well as those of nonbelligerents plying South American waters.

The collector at Baltimore, James H. McCulloch, had struggled with the duties of his office through the years of the Embargo, the Non-Intercourse acts, the licensed flour trade, and the war itself. In the period from 1816 to 1819 his duties were even more difficult to execute. He informed the secretary of the treasury that vessels fitting out in Baltimore to cruise against Spain and Portugal looked too much like "Mercantile projects" for him to detain them. Legitimate cargoes of arms were frequently loaded in Baltimore for South America while extra crewmen were signed at Fells Point or added later and guns, or "gun-nades" as they were called, were simply added after the customs inspection or after the vessel left the port. Cruising with one or more commissions from legitimate or bogus South American republics, the raiders wreaked havoc in West Indian, South American, and Spanish waters. For several years the raiders unloaded disguised prize goods and specie from Spanish, Portuguese, Dutch, and French victims in Baltimore.[73]

Mounting complaints from foreign consuls and agents as well as from

Americans inspired the Baltimore collector to explain the situation in February of 1819. James H. McCulloch reported that "Too many of our people have engaged in the privateering wars of the South American Countries and Baltimore having appeared in name and fact among the naval adventurers has received a larger share of accusations." McCulloch argued that the complaints came from enemies of the revolutionary provinces and from those opposed to American privateering on the basis of principle. Baltimore, he noted, built up a supply of vessels appropriate to cruising during the war and then "sent and sold" them "in all directions" after the war. Those vessels he admitted, were "more numerous in the Spanish royal settlements than anywhere else." Collector McCulloch believed that some of the criticism aimed at himself and Baltimore resulted from circumstances and not from evil intentions. The owners and shipyards of Baltimore outfitted and armed vessels for sale to South Americans after the War of 1812 only to find their officers and crews being persuaded by the insurgents to man those vessels. The Baltimoreans believed they were fighting for the "liberty" of the new nations and that such a worthy cause was popular in the United States. Baltimore attracted the business because it was geographically convenient and technically able to complete the required tasks. Some Baltimore merchants, McCulloch observed, were drawn into the projects only by the insistence of their officers and seamen. Entrepreneurs initially invested in what were seemingly popularly approved ventures but once governmental and public opinion changed, they wanted only to regain their money. Prize-taking privateers under South American colors and papers, once world opinion reacted against their piratical excesses, could find no courts to issue condemnation decrees. Consequently, they entered their spoils into America disguised as regular importations or, failing in that, they simply smuggled them into Baltimore.[74]

Collector James H. McCulloch's apology for Baltimore's privateering satisfied few of his critics. His inability to get great merchants such as Thomas Tenant and William Patterson to testify against their mercantile neighbors prevented him, he claimed, from prosecuting offenders.[75] James Monroe, secretary of state, was so beseiged by Spanish complaints about Baltimore's activities that he ordered the marshal at Baltimore to subpoena the officers of customs who signed the "Ship's Papers, Particularly the Registers and Clearance" of the *Romp*.[76] Monroe informed McCulloch in July of 1816 of Spanish complaints about the outfitting of the *Romp*, *Orb*, and *Comet*, but Monroe was not convinced that those vessels had violated any American statutes. By January of 1817 Monroe informed McCulloch that all testimony in regard to the "South American Cruiser" named the *Mangore* (formerly the letter-of-marque *Swift*) was to be placed in the United States attorney's hands. He also directed the district attorney to assist Spanish victims seeking redress, whenever possible.[77]

Spanish minister Don Luis de Onis, certainly an opponent of insurgent privateering, fired off one protest after another about Baltimore's activities to Secretary of State John Quincy Adams. Onis characterized the former *Sabine* and *Surprise* commander, James Barnes, as one "who has so scandalously violated the laws of nations." Joseph Almeda, formerly of the *Caroline* and *Kemp*, the letter-of-marque *Leonidas*'s old captain, John Chase, and that "well known pirate called Commodore Chaytor" were other recipients of Onis's wrath. Among the Baltimore merchants, Henry Didier, Jr. was accused of both financing a raider and of plundering.[78]

Charges were not convictions. With frequent bills of sales, name changes on the vessels, silent owners, crews charged to secrecy, multiple commissions, and prize goods altered to resemble regular importations, it was difficult to prove the Spanish charges. Finally, in 1818 Elias Glenn, the United States district attorney at Baltimore, reported to the attorney general that popular opinion was turning against those Baltimoreans participating in South American privateering. Glenn actually extracted twenty-five presentments from a Baltimore grand jury against the brig *Fourth of July* for "Piracy" in 1818. Alleged owners included War of 1812 private armed vessel owners Joseph Karrick, John Snyder, and Joseph W. Patterson along with Baltimore postmaster John S. Skinner and one other.[79] The Venezuelan consul at Baltimore, W. R. Swift, after asking the collector to detain the old privateer *Hornet*, now *Alerta*, complained that people indicted for piracy were still walking the streets of Baltimore. The *Alerta* was brought back after a "Pilot Boat" met her in the river with two eighteen-pound cannons, with carriages, rammers, sponges, round and grape shot, and other necessities. Swift said the *Alerta* had changed from one South American flag to another and that her outfit, according to the knowledgeable shipowner Thomas Tenant, was worth $15,000 or $20,000.[80]

A Baltimore attorney characterized Captain J. D. Danels (sometimes spelled Daniels), former commander of Baltimore's *Eagle*, *Rossie*, and *Syren*, as "one of the most distinguished among the piratical privateersmen of this City." After killing forty-two men in taking the brig-of-war *El Nerezda*, Danels brought that powerful prize into Baltimore. Charged with piracy in Baltimore and later at St. Thomas where booty was usually disposed of, Danels was also "publicly outlawed at Buenos Ayres." He returned to Baltimore to prepare a new raider in violation of the American treaty with Spain while reportedly also preparing five vessels to smuggle Portuguese prize goods into the United States without paying duties.[81] Later, others characterized Danels as a captain and hero of the Columbian navy in 1818, saying he outfitted and commanded a naval squadron for that nation without pay. His son was christened Simon Bolivar Danels.[82]

Most of the Baltimore names associated with South American raiding were related to the business only by heresay. J. D. Danels was actually acquitted in his piracy trial at Baltimore, and his case discouraged the government in its efforts to prosecute suspected participants.[83] A case against Almeda's *Orb*, alias

Congreso, for preparing to cruise against Spain when the United States was in amity with that nation (and negotiating for Florida) was finally dismissed in June of 1822.[84] Almeda was also accused of pilfering $5,000 worth of American-owned goods off the Spanish ship *San Iago.* "Don Jose Almeyda" replied to such American charges by proving his vessel was owned by Don Juan Pedro Aguirre of "the United Provinces of Rio de la Plata" and that the *Orb* was bought at a public auction in Buenos Aires. Captain Almeyda informed the court that he was a citizen of the United Provinces and that his vessel entered at Baltimore only in distress after some stormy weather.[85] Entrepreneurs Henry Didier, Jr. and John Gooding were among the three sureties for $16,500 in bonds assuring Almeda's appearance in court. A license listing "Almeyda" as "Capitan de la Golera *Congreso,*" a crew list, and a letter-of-marque, all signed at Buenos Aires on November 18, 1816, were entered in evidence. The crew list contained only two men who actually noted Baltimore as their home, while nine others listed North America.[86] Judge James Houston of the district court was confused by the continually changing names of the raiders and was amused that the Baltimore proctors for "Almeyda," the "Dons Dorsey and Winder," did not even know the names of the various South American republics.

Evidence provided by Almeda, or Almeyda, and others made it impossible to convict them. Theodoric Bland, who replaced James Houston on the bench of the District Court in 1817, was considered friendly toward South American privateering interests. About two-thirds of the cases tried in the United States District Court for Maryland under Houston and Bland were dismissed.[87] Bills of sale and ships' registers actually documented the sales of the *Mammoth, Swift, Orb, Spartan,* and other suspected Baltimore-sponsored raiders such as the *Free Mason* and *Patriot* after the War of 1812. Sometimes other War of 1812 private armed vessel investors purchased them initially, but all those vessels were recorded as having been "sold to foreigners" sooner or later.[88] Silent partners and "wash sales" were, obviously, difficult to expose in court. With appropriate vessels and skilled leaders available, some of the Baltimore entrepreneurs found the quick and nearly certain profits of South American raiding more enticing than the uncertain risks of peacetime commerce. American public opinion turned against such activities, but a decline in the fighting in that area also helped to eliminate the raiding in time.

The slave trade was another shady business utilizing fast Baltimore schooners after the War of 1812. Once more, evidence was hard to find. False or "wash sales," Spanish passengers who became captains when the vessel reached the West Indies, broken voyages, silent partners, and new names for the vessels also appeared in the illegal slave trade. Owners were forbidden by Congress to build or fit a vessel for the slave trade as early as 1794 and the importation of slaves was prohibited in 1808. In 1818 Congress increased the penalties for officers, crews, and owners engaging in the slave trade and, finally, in 1820 the trade was categorized as "piracy, punishable by death."[89] These acts were only as effective as their enforcement, and that was usually negligible.

Baltimore's schooners were ideal slavers no matter what names were on the bills of sale. William Penniman, a War of 1812 investor in Baltimore private armed vessels, fitted out a prize vessel in Baltimore "for a cruise," for a "slave trader," for a "mule carrier," or for any purpose requiring fast sailing in the tropics. The arms and provisions on board, Collector McCulloch charged, were best-suited for slaving. The owner argued that he did not intend to operate the vessel but that it was his right to prepare his vessel anyway he wanted for a sale.[90] In September of 1820 McCulloch reported an American vessel with Spanish papers hidden on board carrying a permanent Spanish passenger designated as the captain on one set of the Spanish ship's papers. Thomas Wilson, another War of 1812 investor in Baltimore's private armed vessels, was charged with the fitting out of a vessel for slave trading or piracy. According to McCulloch, Wilson suffered some shipping losses and thought, since others had done it, that he might recoup some of his losses by selling his vessel after equipping her for slaving.[91] In another instance McCulloch charged former private armed vessel investor Martin F. Maher with "pretendedly" making a sale to a Spaniard and outfitting, in that person's name, a vessel for "a Slaving voyage to Africa with a Spanish captain and supercargo, as usual." McCulloch said Maher's activities were "long notorious." In yet another case the collector reported a vessel's new name "painted on a movable sheet of copper instead of being on the stern."[92] The government prosecuted some Baltimoreans for their slaving activities while directing the attorney general to assist the Maryland district attorney in those cases.[93] The schooner *St. Iago de Cuba* was condemned and sold in Baltimore for violating the laws prohibiting the slave trade.[94]

Baltimore's involvement in the slave trade was encouraged by its ownership of appropriate vessels and by the existence of a market for slaves that lasted for decades after the War of 1812. Slaves were sold in South America and in the West Indies, or smuggled into the United States, sometimes disguised as members of a schooner's crew.[95] The Chesapeake builders continued to construct schooners, demanding only slight alterations for slaving, up to 1855. Between 1836 and 1841 the British captured eighteen slavers originally built on the Chesapeake but "sold to foreigners" later. Schooners such as the *Asp*, the *Lark*, the *Clara*, the *Florida*, and the *Perry Hall* were included.[96] The sharp-built schooner was still useful in the 1840s whenever an owner desired a fast vessel capable of eluding Spanish and British patrols.

Related to both South American privateering and slave trading was the real or pretended sale of Baltimore schooners to foreigners. The immediate postwar period demand for schooners made them "hard to charter or to find" but their prices declined anyway.[97] Schooners costing from $25,000 to $40,000 ready for sea during the war were sold, in varying conditions, for prices from $3,000 to

$20,000 as early as 1815. The *Midas* sold for $14,000, the *Orb* for $6,000, the xebec *Ultor* for $3,000, the *Globe* for $7,900, and the *Amelia* for $8,000 in 1815. The new large schooners, such as the *Mammoth*, *Swift*, and *Chasseur*, usually converted to brigs for peacetime trade, held their value better, selling from $12,750 to $20,000. By 1816 the wartime schooners were selling for only one-half or two-thirds of their already low 1815 prices.[98] The decline in the value of vessels combined with decreases in freight rates and commodity prices encouraged old and new owners to seek better sale prices or a more profitable usage for their vessels. Sales to foreigners in the West Indies provided the best market for schooners. When the sales were authentic, the owners regained some of their investment and cared little about the uses others found for the vessels. On the other hand, when the sale papers represented false or "wash sales," the owners were probably looking for profits from South American privateering or slave trading.

Of the sixty-seven private armed vessels surviving the War of 1812 under American colors, at least twenty-three were "sold to foreigners" from 1815 to 1818.[99] At least four others were lost at sea during the same period, and others were sold to merchants in other American ports. Ultimately, some of these probably wound up in foreign hands also. Most of the foreign sales occurred in the West Indies, particularly Havana. In those sales such famous names as *Comet*, *Chasseur*, *Patapsco*, *York*, *Whig*, *Amelia*, *Kemp*, *Mammoth*, and others disappeared from American records. Fast schooners no longer dominated Baltimore shipping. Schooners constituted two-thirds of all new registers issued in 1814, but with peace, over one-half of the 1815 registers went to two-masted, square-rigged brigs and three-masted, square-rigged ships. Only four ships were registered in 1814, but sixty appeared in the 1815 records, and forty-nine of those were for ships of 300 or more tons.[100] Small, fast schooners were still useful in the West Indian trade, but they were no longer appropriate for the bulk of Baltimore's peacetime business.

Thomas Kemp continued to build sharp schooners at Fells Point and at St. Michaels on the Eastern Shore. For some reason the phrase "privateer-built" remained on his carpenter's certificates. Between 1815 and 1819 he constructed the *Plattsburgh*, *Coquette*, *Patriot*, *Tangent*, *Hippopotamus*, *Montezuma*, a new *Rossie*, and others. Built for wartime private armed vessel investors Isaac McKim, John Gooding, Henry Didier, Jr., Andrew Clopper, James Corner, Henry Payson, and others none of the new Kemp schooners ever saw action as American privateers. Some of the new Baltimore schooners were built for New York owners anxious for a cut of the profits from South American raiding.[101]

From the signing of the Treaty of Ghent to the Panic of 1819, the Baltimore investments in land and manufacturing and a more intensified inland trade provided some outlets for capital and talent. Flour, tobacco, and the reexport business, Baltimore's old reliables, kept some merchants active also. South

American privateering and the slave trading offered entrepreneurial options that lacked the complete approval of the merchant community. Merchants desiring to operate in one port for a period of decades were usually reluctant to irritate those who could damage their reputations, credit, or flow of commercial intelligence. Baltimore's entrepreneurs, in general, appear to have survived the changeover to peace, but there were signs of strain even before the national Panic of 1819.

According to the estimates used in this study, George Pitt Stevenson, nephew of Samuel Smith, had not profited from private armed vessels in the War of 1812. After the war he sold his shares in some private armed vessels but continued to invest in other vessels. He purchased parts of the *Tuckahoe*, the new Kemp-built *General Jackson*, the *Ann*, the *Sarah and Louisa* (with Thomas Boyle), the *Stafford*, and the *Tangent*. Stevenson paid $12,750 for the famous *Chasseur*. While maintaining some of his wartime holdings, Stevenson also bought into older vessels such as the *Exchange*, the *Peter* (sole owner), the *Danae* (sole owner), and the new ship, *General Smith*.[102] By 1816, declining freight rates, decreasing commodity prices, and eroding vessel prices were catching up to Stevenson.

In May of 1816 George Pitt Stevenson complained about the "stagnation of business" and expressed surprise that he had been able to fulfill his financial obligations. Stevenson noted that he had "three large sums" yet to pay and commented, "my hair almost stands on end at the idea and approach of their maturity." He could not sell most of his importations and knew that the few available purchasers were not financially reliable. Foreign markets were not to be had, and his vessels were declining in value. Stevenson contemplated the possibility of retiring from trade, which he characterized as "the chances of traffic and disappointment," and wrote that he was tempted to "turn farmer."[103] In addition to his inability to sell at home or abroad, he lost the old privateer *Hollins* at sea.[104] With unsaleable imported goods in Baltimore furnishing no income, Stevenson struggled to meet the demands of his creditors, the costs of operating his vessels, and requests for payment from the customs collector. Unfortunately, bonds he had posted for customs duties and his credit with other merchants expired before he could sell his goods to earn the money to meet his obligations.

Merchants cosigning or serving as sureties for George Pitt Stevenson's bonds and notes were plunged into a sea of crisis along with him. Michael McBlair's request for an account of Stevenson's unpaid bonds brought a reply from the collector of customs that about $94,000.00 was owed.[105] Stevenson's total debts, including bonds, notes, and other debts, amounted to $254,969.86.[106] McBlair survived the strain placed on him in 1816 by Stevenson, but others did not. Word of "the stoppage of Mr. George P. Stevenson" for "a large amount" and the fear that others would follow was sent to merchants in other cities. A firm in Richmond was apprised that Stevenson had "brought down with him, Mr. Lyde Goodwin" and that others might also be ruined.[107] Goodwin had signed as surety for at least eighteen Stevenson customs bonds and Michael McBlair had signed for fourteen. In Stevenson's private debts, at least fourteen private armed vessel owners in the War of 1812 also suffered losses.[108]

Large firms such as Hollins and McBlair and S. Smith and Buchanan, related by marriage to Stevenson, were damaged by his failure, but their resources allowed them to survive for a time.[109] Stevenson himself went to sea as a supercargo for Isaac McKim in 1817 while applying, in the same year, for a position as a consul at Havana.[110] The former active investor in private armed vessels had fallen from the ranks of the merchants. His failure pointed out the risks of remaining heavily engaged in shipowning and international commerce in the uncertain postwar years without large amounts of capital. The damage done by Stevenson to others exposed the inherent weakness, treated so lighty in earlier years, of having relatives or friends sign numerous and heavy shipping or customs bonds as sureties. A merchant's friends, in such cases, were in more danger than his enemies.

Baltimoreans recovering from Stevenson's failure received an immense shock in 1819 when some of the port's greatest trading houses failed at one time. John Quincy Adams noted on May 24, 1819, that "the houses of Smith and Buchanan, Hollins and McBlair, Didier and D'Arcy, four Williamses, and many others, this day failed."[111] Adams, many Baltimoreans, and merchants around the world were shocked that such firms, particularly S. Smith and Buchanan, a symbol of Baltimore's mercantile greatness, could have collapsed. They knew because of the interrelationships built up over years, that others would follow. One correspondent read the news in the Paris newspapers and wrote a note to Smith's nephew, George Pitt Stevenson, expressing sympathy for the "failure of houses, so respectable as Smith and Buchanan, Lemuel Taylor and Co."[112] Over forty Baltimore firms collapsed with or after the fall of S. Smith and Buchanan.

Reasons for the failure of those merchants who built the port of Baltimore and financed its private navy in the War of 1812 were complex. It was probable that D'Arcy and Didier's confidence in its arms shipments to South America was misplaced. Either belligerent in that part of the world could have seized the arms cargoes, or prices offered in South America may have been inadequate. The trading house of Hollins and McBlair was definitely weakened by its effort to pay George Pitt Stevenson's debts. All the Baltimore trading houses suffered from postwar declines in the value of vessels, freight rates, and commodity prices, while the British carrying of dry goods to America hurt some also. They were all tied too closely together by their habit of acting as bond sureties for each other. Additionally, the Baltimore trading houses suffered from the na-

*Painting, "Baltimore Clipper Privateer Schooner" by Burton
from original in the MacPherson Collection, Salem,
Massachusetts, as reproduced in Howard I. Chapelle's*
THE BALTIMORE CLIPPER

tional Panic of 1819 when the Second Bank of the United States curtailed credit and called in existing loans. Investors in private armed vessels in the War of 1812 were heavily engaged with the Baltimore branch of that bank and the parent bank's orders curtailing credit and loans, caught some Baltimoreans with their credit overextended.

The president of the Baltimore branch of the Second Bank of the United States was James A. Buchanan of the firm of S. Smith and Buchanan. George Williams, merchant and shipowner, served as a director of both the Baltimore branch and the main bank in Philadelphia. Merchant James W. McCulloch, a former S. Smith and Buchanan employee, and an investor in the *Argo*, the *Burrows*, and the xebec *Ultor* during the war, was the cashier of the Baltimore bank. Those three officers and Dennis A. Smith, who profited greatly from his government and bank stock during the war, invested heavily in stock of the Second Bank of the United States.[113] Starting as speculation, their scheme soon involved 3 million dollars in stock, much of which was purchased with borrowed money and without collateral.[114] The inability of the conspirators to produce cash on demand brought ruin to themselves, to the trading houses in which they were partners, and to many of their associates.

George Pitt Stevenson failed because he invested too heavily in the postwar period in vessels and seaborne trade, the old reliables of Baltimore's merchants. Ironically, great crashes occurred in 1819 partly because some of the entrepreneurs strayed from shipping. James A. Buchanan of the famous trading house of S. Smith and Buchanan reported that "the necessity of stopping payment I subscribe entirely to losses in transaction in stock of the Bank of U.S." and observed that the firm's bank stock problems were not anticipated. Samuel Smith was not actively directing the firm when Buchanan engaged in the bank stock speculation with George Williams and James W. McCulloch, but because the law held partners liable for each other's debts, he suffered also. S. Smith and Buchanan's "commercial and shipping business" had been "unquestionably solvent" as late as January of 1818, and only its bank stock speculations brought on failure in May of 1819.[115] Looking back, Samuel Smith said he had not known about $240,000 borrowed by the firm expressly for the purchase of bank stock.

Recovery would have been easier in earlier years. The inability of S. Smith and Buchanan to recover quickly or to help itself or its friends and relatives who had signed its notes and bonds as sureties was partially related to the general conditions of trade and the national Panic of 1819. Smith noted that the firm's vessels had fallen "more than $50,000" in value, that their "Sugar Houses" had cost $50,000 but would sell for less than $10,000, and that a manufacturing plant owned by the firm had been sold for just enough to cover its debts. Real estate and bank stocks had also fallen to ruinous prices. There was no way the firm's assets, in a depressed economy, could have been manipulated or negotiated to settle its obligations to the Second Bank of the United States. Smith wrote, "It is true, too true, Samuel Smith and Buchanan and about thirty or forty other Houses have failed, among the number Hollins and McBlair." He noted in mid-1819 that he was "penniless" and that "never was ruin more complete, I have not a dollar left."[116]

In October of 1819 the unpaid debts of the firm of S. Smith and Buchanan, according to Smith, amounted to $287,519.[117] Sixty years of hard work by Smith and his family in war and peace had led only to disgrace. His partner, James A. Buchanan, and others, perhaps envious of Dennis A. Smith's brilliant and quick success in wartime stocks, had abandoned the combination of entrepreneurial prudence and risk-taking on the sea that had served them so well in previous decades.

The Baltimore mercantile community was in disarray in 1819. Along with S. Smith and Buchanan, Lemuel Taylor, John Hollins, Michael McBlair, John Smith Hollins, D'Arcy and Didier, the four Williamses, and others were prostrate. Federalist Robert Oliver, carefully limiting his own operations after the war, averred in 1819 that "all the Democratic leaders were broke and many of them disgraced." A grand jury presented bills against Dennis A. Smith, James A. Buchanan, James W. McCulloch, George Williams, and others for their operations involving the Second Bank of the United States. They were not found guilty of violating any Maryland law, however.[118]

There were harsh feelings and hard times in Baltimore in 1819. John Gooding, another active investor in private armed vessels during the war also collapsed.[119] Long accustomed to the free use of the credit and standing of the trading house of Hollins and McBlair, Gooding refused to reciprocate when that house needed help in 1819.[120] Privateer and slave vessel operative Martin F. Maher "absconded, being a defaulter at one of the banks" and was not seen again in Baltimore.[121] In 1819 Baltimore suffered merchant and bank failures, followed by some pauperism and actual soup lines as well as yellow fever at Fells Point.[122] Entrepreneurs who had fallen from grace as merchants returned to the sea as masters or supercargoes. Others sought positions as consuls in foreign ports. The names of Baltimore investors in War of 1812 private armed vessels appeared frequently in the government records for not paying duties as Charles F. Kalkman, Andrew Clopper, John W. Stump, Thomas Sheppard, and Nathaniel Stansbury joined other merchants in at least temporary distress.[123]

The broken merchants did not find their new condition and social status very comfortable. Samuel Smith eventually recovered, but in 1819 he was close to insanity or suicide. In time, friends came to his aid, and the Second Bank of the United States finally settled with him.[124] In 1822 John Hollins advised Michael McBlair to restrain his daughter from making an excursion to the seashore. Hollins said "needless unprofitable excursions" ought to be "studiously" avoided because the firm's creditors would complain and heap "censure, if not worse," upon them. The indebted firm, Hollins said, had a "delicate card to play" and since the world was "very ill-natured and ready to catch at any trifle," Hollins believed that any expenditures "should be attended with the greatest circumspection."[125] The small firms that had serviced the great trading houses for decades suffered also. The embattled firm of Hollins and McBlair was asked by King and Johnston to pay a bill of $330 for rigging done to a Hollins and McBlair vessel. In desperation, one partner in that rigging firm wrote in December, "If you ware to see James King's children who are now barefooted and without cloathing, you would have some pity."[126] It was difficult for people to accept the new condition of many of the city's most famous names. From the Baltimore County jail, John Hollins' partner, Michael McBlair, petitioned the commissioners of Insolvent Debtors for relief in October of 1822.[127] Others were forced to do the same, to go back to sea, or to move away. Of the postwar failures, only George Pitt Stevenson's fall was seemingly related to private armed vessel investments during the war, but other investors may have remained solvent or postponed disaster because of earlier prize proceeds.

Not all the War of 1812 investors in private armed vessels failed after the war or in the Panic of 1819. The McKims, Pattersons, and others continued as shipping operatives and business leaders right into the period of clipper ships. They carried on trade with the Orient, South America, and the West Indies in flour, tobacco, coffee, hides, and other products.[128] Investors in private armed vessels during the War of 1812 were instrumental in the establishment of the Baltimore and Ohio Railroad. Entrepreneurs Isaac McKim, Joseph W. Patterson, George J. Brown, and John McKim, Jr. were among the founders of that railroad. Their railroad investments, including prize proceeds from the war, allowed Baltimore to compete with canals linking other ports to large hinterlands. In 1827 former private armed vessel investors Justus Hoppe and Thomas Wilson invested in a railroad to the Susquehanna River.[129] In 1826 Samuel Smith, still active in city and national politics, was released from his bank debt.[130] Smith and others received some assistance from shipping claims settled after Florida was purchased from Spain. Lemuel Taylor, in fact, recovered completely at that time.[131]

Baltimore's population actually grew from 1810 to 1820, rising to 62,738 people in 1820. Among the importers of British dry goods in an 1823 directory was Luke Tiernan and Sons. Among hardware importers, the Hurxthal name survived from the war, and in the flour trade, former investors Charles Gwinn, Keller and Foreman, Stump and David Wilson were still operative. Levi Hollingsworth's copper works were run by John McKim, Jr. after Levi's death. Bankrupt Michael McBlair survived as "agent" for the Warren Cotton Factory, founded in 1816.[132] Former investors in private armed vessels were still engaged in banking and John Donnell, still quite solvent, took command of the trouble-some branch of the Second Bank of the United States. In insurance, John Hollins remained the president of the Maryland Insurance Company despite the failure of Hollins and McBlair. August Schwartze became the president of the Chesapeake Insurance Company, while John McFadon and Samuel Harris directed another insurance firm. The Baltimore Water Company was under the leadership of Isaac McKim, and the president of the Baltimore Exchange Company was William Patterson.[133]

Other War of 1812 investors in private armed vessels were still functioning in business. Some listed in an 1823 directory were the two Bosleys, Thorndike Chase, Christopher Deshon, the Douglasses, Frederick C. Graf, Peter A. Guestier, Justus Hoppe, Archibald Kerr, Charles Malloy, Henry Payson, Thomas Sheppard, Thomas Tenant, Von Kapff and Brune, Frederick Waesche, and others.[134] Numerous great names from the prewar and war days were missing. Those who had been captains, ship's husbands, and prize agents managed to survive, perhaps because their income from their marine services augmented their entrepreneurial income and because they could easily withdraw from trading in tough times.

Many War of 1812 investors in private armed vessels were still engaged in business in 1833. John Franciscus, now president of the Baltimore Shot Tower Company, was still operating a sugar refinery and functioning as a commission merchant. Charles Gwinn was a commission merchant and an agent for twenty vessels running to South Carolina and Virginia. The firm of William Patterson and Sons was designated as "Iron Merchants" as more specialization developed among the merchants. Keller and Foreman sold their flour mill, with an annual capacity of 20,000 barrels, to the city water company for $75,000. The Charitable Marine Society was headed by former sailmaker and private armed vessel investor James Corner, and another seaman's society was led by the aged collector of customs, James H. McCulloch, while Justus Hoppe was president of the German Society. McKim and Son's Copper Works became the new name of Levi Hollingsworth's old copper mill. The Maryland Cotton Factory (formerly the Jericho Factory), operated by Michael McBlair as "principal of the concern," utilized Lyde Goodwin as its Baltimore agent.[135]

Between 1815 and the decade of the 1830s some of the War of 1812 entrepreneurs and captains died. George Stiles died in 1819 after losing his money on a mechanical project involving rotary steam engines, and Joshua Barney, who functioned as the "naval officer" for the port of Baltimore after 1817, died in 1820 at Pittsburgh.[136] In the 1830s and 1840s a long-time resident noted the passing of some of the "old Baltimoreans" who had built the city. In 1835 William Patterson and John Diffenderffer died. In 1836 Collector James H. McCulloch and merchant David Wilson, at the age of eighty-three, were listed as deceased. Death claimed Thorndike Chase in 1838, James A. Buchanan in

1840, and "old Peter Arnold Karthaus" in 1841. John McKim, Jr., "one of our old citizens and merchants," passed away in 1842, and Henry Payson and Thomas Wilson died in 1845. Among the deceased in 1846 was Justus Hoppe, the German trader who "died on a journey westward on a Steamboat on the Ohio River."[137] The passing of the "Old Baltimoreans" was symbolized by the funeral of early merchant, Revolutionary War hero, congressman, senator, mayor, investor in private armed vessels, and defender of Baltimore in the War of 1812, Major General Samuel Smith. Upon Smith's death in 1839 Baltimore newspapers noted "Another Patriot Gone," and, characterizing him as the "founder of commerce in our city," treated him with the honor due the Revolutionary generation. His huge funeral procession, accompanied by the roar of Fort McHenry's cannons, terminated at the cemetery of the First Presbyterian Church.[138]

By the late 1820s and early 1830s, privateering was a thing of the past in Baltimore. Young merchants in the coffee houses and young mariners in the grog shops of Fells Point must have listened in awe to the "Old Baltimoreans'" tales of prize auctions and distributions, of boarding parties, thundering broadsides, and of blockade running. Any ambitions the young ones may have developed while listening would never be fulfilled in private armed vessels. There would be no more Barneys, Didiers, Cloppers, Boyles, or Almedas waiting to collect prize money from the clerk of the District Court or from their prize agents.

THIRTEEN

Conclusions and Epilogue

The British North American colonies and the private armed vessel system grew up together. Baltimore was still a small town when the old European institution of privateering acquired a high degree of professionalism and standardization during the French and Indian War. The young port's participation in the private armed vessel system during the Revolution spurred its growth along with the entrepreneurial accomplishments of mercantile houses such as S. Smith and Buchanan, the Williamses, Hollins and McBlair, and others throughout the second half of the eighteenth century. Baltimore's merchants and mariners gained additional and painful familiarity with privateering during the Napoleonic wars before its own government became a belligerent. With a half century of steady growth and privateering apprenticeship behind it, Baltimore was fully prepared to play a leadership role in the history of privateering, of nautical warfare, and of the American republic when war was declared on Great Britain in June of 1812.

Thousands of Baltimoreans participated in the private armed vessel system during the War of 1812 in one role or the other. Two hundred Baltimore entrepreneurs risked their money or money owed to them for services or goods in at least one hundred seventy-five commissions for 122 vessels. Ninety-eight persons invested, usually in large groups with small individual sums, only one time. These marginal investors were primarily small businessmen engaged in marine-oriented businesses, craftsmen, suppliers, sea captains, or minor merchants. Merchants owning whole vessels were the exception among both the marginal investors and among the fifty-two moderate investors making two or three investments during the war. There were more merchants of substance among the moderate investors, but there were also successful shipbuilders and ships' chandlers. For the greatest involvement in and commitment to the private armed vessel system one has to look at the fifty active investors who made four or more investments during the war. Prominent prewar shipowning entrepreneurs invested large sums in numerous privateers and letter-of-marque traders in the thirty months of war. Representing a mercantile and maritime elite, the fifty active investors had helped to build both the city of Baltimore and the American republic. The growth of the two, from the 1770s to 1819, went hand in hand. The fifty active investors dominated every aspect of urban life in early nineteenth-century Baltimore. Their names were associated with every social, political, entrepreneurial, charitable, and military organization and function. During the War of 1812, they set aside their own interests and very comfortable life styles to respond to the newest challenge to their city and their republic. While risking their money and property in private armed vessels, they risked their lives in the field when the British attacked them at home, probably in response to their support for the war and for their remarkable successes at sea.

There was little doubt in June of 1812 that the Baltimoreans knew how to finance, build, and handle sea-going vessels. They were also experienced with private armed vessels, understanding the system fully. After centuries of refinement, some aspects of the system required few alterations. Facets such as documentation, articles of agreement, prize court procedures, and distribution schemes followed existing models. American governmental controls were neither excessive nor restrictive during the War of 1812. Except for exorbitant customs duties lowered as the war progressed, the government's actions supported the private armed vessel system. Examples of quasi-piratical behavior at sea were rare, while examples of judicious restraint and even humanity were numerous. Baltimore's accomplishments during the War of 1812 were in the realms of vessel design, entrepreneurial and nautical expertise, in-port preparation, and on land and sea, audacious leadership in all endeavors. The port's mariners, builders, and entrepreneurs displayed a remarkably determined capacity for financing, constructing, equipping, staffing, and handling their swift schooners in wartime. Developed over decades in the Chesapeake area, the port's famous schooner design reached perfection, in what was a worldwide competition, just in time for the War of 1812. In a very short time Baltimore schooners inspired British cries of outrage, increases in insurance rates, and pleas for convoy escorts even in home waters, something other European nations using privateers against England had never accomplished. Older and, in some cases, larger American ports, such as New York, Philadelphia, and Salem, failed to match the force mounted by Baltimore private enterprise during the war. At sea Baltimore schooners consistently demonstrated their ability to match or exceed their British adversaries, sail to sail, broadside to broadside and, when necessary, cutlass to cutlass. Audacity and competence at sea were supported by capable management in port where private armed vessel ventures were administered in a businesslike manner by resourceful ship's husbands and prize agents. While risking prewar trading profits, income from the Iberian flour trade, and new prize income in their private fleet, the Baltimore entrepreneurs and mariners displayed a patriotic concern for their republic uncommon in privateering history and contradictory to the entrepreneur's instinctive search for profits. The port's 122 commissioned vessels took over 500 British vessels and over one thousand six hundred prisoners while doing damage in the millions.

Baltimore's wartime efforts, under the leadership of those risk-taking merchants and daring captains who had converted a village into a major seaport, provided mixed results. Profit projections utilized in this study support Henry Adams' assertion that, in general, "privateering was not profitable."[1] The greatest beneficiaries of the system in Baltimore were the prominent prewar shipowners among the active investors such as Hollins and McBlair, Andrew Clopper, John Gooding, the Williamses, Peter Arnold Karthaus, S. Smith and Buchanan, Robert Patterson, John McKim, Jr., Levi Hollingsworth, Thomas Tenant, D'Arcy and Didier, and Jeremiah Sullivan and some of their partners. Only four or five names among the twenty-six investors sharing in estimated owners' prize incomes exceeding $200,000 were not major prewar shipowners. Large incomes from thirty months or more of prize sales, usually reflecting large investments, seldom approached the prewar annual incomes from shipping earned by the active investors who constituted a mercantile and social elite in Baltimore. Even with the nation's largest private fleet, most of the Baltimore investors found private armed vessels to be an inadequate wartime substitute for their prewar earnings. With some large prewar shipowners seriously reducing their investments in vessels during the war while diverting their capital into other channels or simply sitting on it, the private armed vessel system was also an inadequate substitute for Baltimore's prewar capital outlets. Only one-third of Baltimore's 200 investors in private armed vessels actually pocketed substantial profits from prize proceeds. Those making marginal profits on small investments or actually losing out in the prize accounts profited from their participation in the secondary and subsidiary business facets of the system. Income derived from the resale of prize goods, from supplying or outfitting private armed vessels, from supervising prizes in port and from the sale of letter-of-marque cargoes was not listed in the prize accounts. Managerial roles such as those of ship's husbands and prize agents also contributed to an investor's income. Those owning shares of successful vessels during the second half of the war profited more, even from smaller investments, than those paying the higher customs duties early in the war. Many captains and some seamen earned wartime incomes greatly in excess of the wages they could have earned in a peacetime employment period.

There were profits emanating from the private armed vessel system other than those collected by individual participants. There were some indirect dividends paid to the general community of Baltimore. After the first six months of war letter-of-marque flyers carried the only exports getting out of blockaded Baltimore. That provided hard pressed exporters and farmers some relief, while the same flyers and the privateers imported scarce goods for merchants and consumers in the two years of the blockade. Taxes and fees paid to the city as well as wages paid to shipyard and waterfront workers and craftsmen, fees paid to lawyers and clerks, and some of the income earned by boarding house keepers, tavern owners, and those nonshareholding suppliers of private armed vessels were all dependent upon the existence of a private fleet. The system put some bread on a number of tables when alternative sources of income were almost nonexistent.

The greatest beneficiary of Baltimore's private armed vessel success during the War of 1812 was the American republic. Most of its benefits were not monetary, but it did draw a large proportion of the prize proceeds in the form of customs duties, especially in the first year of war, and it continued to collect customs from prize and letter-of-marque imports throughout the war. With Baltimore so active in the prize courts and with its flyers providing the bulk of America's imports at a time when the government had few alternatives, such income was vital to the war effort. The private armed vessel system also damaged the nation's enemy. After the national maritime force was contained, it kept the republic in the war at sea while amost singlehandedly in 1814 upholding the republic's honor. In the second half of the war it constituted virtually the only challenge and the only obstacle to Britain's efforts to strangle America's seaborne commerce. Its carrying of the war home to England's own waters and its successes in 1814 prevented a complete erosion of morale at home while strenghtening the hand of an enfeebled administration at home and abroad.

Baltimore's participation in the War of 1812 was both significant and dramatic. Arming and licensing 122 private vessels, the Patapsco community entered the war in force at an early stage, remained operative in strength even during the blockade, and was still cruising in force months after a peace treaty was concluded. Powerful British forces failed to master Baltimore in their attack on the city in 1814 or in two and one-half years of confrontation at sea. With entrepreneurs willing to invest in the search for profits and in their republic, with shipbuilders ingenious enough to construct an ideal raiding vessel, and with audacious commanders such as Boyle, Almeda, Barney, and Dooley, Baltimore demonstrated to the world how a relatively weak republic could quickly develop an inexpensive but influential second navy. By destroying unprizeworthy British vessels at sea and by attacking stronger opponents, the Baltimore fleet emphasized the point that such a force could perform a valuable public service in addition to its taking of weak but profitable prizes, formerly thought to be its only role. Baltimore also showed a world long-dazzled, if not intimidated, by Britain's naval power how that power's overall maritime dominance and individual blockades could be challenged and even ridiculed. By 1814 America's private armed fleet, with Baltimore in the vanguard, was converted by circumstances into the republic's only maritime force. With national honor

and perhaps survival nailed to their mastheads along with the flag of the republic, those schooners of private enterprise did more than their duty. Succeeding
when the national government had failed, private maritime enterprise in America
refused to be intimidated by the British navy's blockade of the American coast or
by the threat of heavy property, personnel, and financial losses.

Baltimore was the undoubted leader among American ports outfitting private fleets during the War of 1812, but it was also one of the great privateering
centers of maritime history. Without precise studies of ownership, owners'
residences, commission renewals, or commissions for letter-of-marque traders,
statistics from other ports are less than firm. New York is generally credited
with the second largest fleet, but its standing is usually based on privateers alone
and probably includes vessels owned in Baltimore but commissioned in New
York. Salem and Boston were a distant third and fourth respectively.[2] Quarterly reports from the collectors of those ports reveal that the totals from all
three of Baltimore's competing ports included numerous one-gun, one- to
thirty-ton vessels ranging from rowboats to river boats with tiny crews. Every
one of Baltimore's 122 commissioned vessels was a bona fide ocean-going raider,
capable of subduing an armed merchantman. Most of the Baltimore vessels
were about 150 tons and only eight were below 100 tons.

Unfortunately, Baltimore's extraordinary efforts and performance during
the War of 1812 garnered the community few long-term advantages lasting
beyond 1819. Profits from the private armed vessel system were more desirable
than losses from idleness, and they were helpful in the port's efforts to build
railroads and expand manufacturing in the 1820s, but they were inadequate for
the task of maintaining the city's preeminence as a seaport. Privateering turned
out to be Baltimore's single greatest contribution to maritime history. During
the 1820s Baltimore and other Atlantic ports were unable to stem the gravitation
of their trade to the expanding port of New York. Possibly beginning its spurt
of development as early as the Revolution when its occupation by the British
strengthened its commercial ties with Britain, New York attracted more and
more shipping. It benefited from its northern location close to Europe and from
the opening up of vast new hinterlands, first in western New York State and
then in the Middle West, by the construction of the Erie Canal during the
1820s. The implementation of a regularly and frequently scheduled packet
service to Europe in 1818 enticed the Atlantic flour trade, formerly a Baltimore
specialty, southern cotton exports, and immigrant traffic to New York's busy
waterfront.[3]

Baltimore did not yield without a struggle. Applying the same entrepreneurial foresight and nerve, and probably some privateering profits, the city
placed its hopes in the Baltimore and Ohio Railroad during the 1820s. Its goal
was to open up a bigger western market, heretofore limited in scope and population, for Baltimore businessmen and exporters. The port's staples, tobacco to

Europe and flour to the West Indies, were still exported, but those markets were already approaching their maximal limits. Despite its tremendous record of growth and its adaptability in peace and war, Baltimore was losing out by the 1830s. Its great privateering performance during the War of 1812 had only postponed the port's unpleasant adjustment to new peacetime conditions by providing it with wartime income and several years of glory. Baltimore and other Atlantic ports survived the Panic of 1819 and the 1820s in varying degrees, while New York became the major American port on the Atlantic Ocean. The same relative decline was experienced by some European ports on the Atlantic as international commerce was reorganized and concentrated after the Napoleonic wars.[4] In the new Atlantic commercial pattern, Baltimore no longer functioned as an international entrepôt but as a regional entrepôt with a well-defined but geographically limited trade built around the West Indies, South America, the tobacco trade, and an inland market more restricted than New York's hinterland, even with the railroad.

Those entrepreneurs, shipbuilders, and mariners who had converted Baltimore from a village into a major seaport saw many changes after the War of 1812. As the "Old Baltimoreans" retired from their counting houses and decks in the 1820s and 1830s, sail was being replaced or augmented by steam, and the old blue canvassed wagons bringing in western wheat were yielding to the railroad. Banking, railroads, and manufacturing were competing with seaborne commerce for capital and for the title of Baltimore's primary economic activity. For the first time in their lives, Baltimore's entrepreneurs found the private armed vessel system was no longer a significant topic of conversation. In their last days, they would look back with pride at their accomplishments from the beginning of the Revolution to the Panic of 1819. That was a golden age of seaborne commerce for Baltimore, for their schooners, and for American private armed vessels. Even those who lost money in private armed vessels knew they had filled an important gap by providing their young republic with some absolutely essential seaborne muscle in its time of peril.

From the vantage point of the 1820s and 1830s the "Old Baltimoreans" saw that Britain had felt the sting of the American privateers. British losses to American private armed vessels are difficult to ascertain, but *Niles Weekly Register*'s running prize list encouraged its editor to estimate that at least 1,750 vessels, plus 750 that were recaptured, were taken from Britain by American vessels.[5] The total figure, including Newfoundland fishing vessels and small West Indian craft, was probably from 1,300 to 2,500.[6] Of those prizes an estimated 556 were taken by Baltimore's 122 private armed vessels while from 138 to 171, or about 30 percent of the Baltimore prizes, actually arrived in various ports for adjudication.[7] The rest were recaptured, burned, sunk, restored, ransomed, lost at sea, or used as cartels for prisoners. The total figure represented an average of four and one-half prizes per Baltimore commissioned vessel. Even a maritime establishment as large as Britain's in 1815 could not ignore such figures nor enjoy the prospect of greater losses at sea if the war were extended another year or more.

Private armed vessels were the only successful American offensive weapon after 1813 engaged in the War of 1812. According to a Baltimore editor, they "sustained the honor of their country" almost singlehandedly.[8] In doing so, they were one important factor encouraging Britain to terminate the war. British shipowners, colonial merchants, and insurance companies suffered heavy losses, and British vessels paid high insurance rates just to cross the Irish Channel after American privateers began operating in larger numbers in British waters.[9] Losses to British merchants, who bore them as private citizens, were an estimated 40 million dollars.[10] Henry Adams noted that the "American private vessels, the nation's greatest success in 1814, contributed more than the regular navy to bring about a disposition for peace in the British classes most responsible for the war."[11] Alfred T. Mahan, historian and advocate of a strong navy, admitted that private armed vessels "co-operated powerfully with other motives to dispose the enemy to liberal terms of peace."[12] Shipowners and merchants of Glasgow complained in 1814 that the American cruisers were "injurious to our commerce, humbling to our pride and discredible to the directors of the naval power of the British nation." Britain was losing thirty-three vessels per month, or more than one a day, to a nation whose maritime power it had formerly "unpolitically held in contempt." Having set out to weaken Britain's hold on the sea, the Baltimoreans agreed with editor Niles that the war had "Redeemed the Independence of the United States."[13] They fought what privateer Captain George Coggeshall called a "proud, haughty overbearing nation" to a standstill.[14] Private armed vessels, according to Bradford Perkins, had "strengthened Madison's hand as his armies and navies could not."[15] Still operating in strength when the peace treaty was concluded, Baltimore's private navy had given the "Mistress of the Seas" one of its greatest challenges.

The Baltimoreans contributed to peace on land as well as on the sea. Their stubborn defense of their city in 1814 prevented the sacking and burning of a Republican city strongly supporting the war. If Baltimore had burned so soon after the destruction of Washington, the impact could have been devastating to the Republican administration, the war effort at sea, and to the American peace negotiators in Europe. A British success at Baltimore or Plattsburgh would have encouraged the British to ask for stiffer terms in the treaty.[16] Even a feeble American government may have been forced to extend the war by rejecting stronger terms rather than accepting disgrace. In 1814, former Secretary of Treasury Albert Gallatin believed Britain was embarking upon a campaign of "chastisement" and "predatory warfare" upon the United States.[17] If so, the Baltimoreans played a significant role in frustrating that plan on land and, to an even greater extent, at sea. Gallatin observed after the war that the conflict had been "useful" because it raised Europe's opinion of America and designated us, in European eyes, as the one nation able "to check the naval despotism of England."[18] Gallatin was no admirer of private armed vessels, but even he had to admit that a good portion of the new respect accorded the United States abroad had been earned by the sails and guns of the private enterprise system.

Any appraisal of private armed vessels in the War of 1812 should confront some of the criticism of the system. Henry Adams and others argued that the system "injured the navy" by using up available seamen. This may have been true during the first part of the war, but the navy was virtually inoperative if not nonexistent during the last year of the war and could not have employed one-fifth of the nation's able-bodied seamen. The government was short of money for recruitment and pay, Adams admitted, writing that by November of 1814, the Treasury Department "made no further pretence at solvency."[19] Private armed vessels were not a heavy drain on public funds. Furthermore, the army blamed the failure of its recruitment drive not on privateer agents taking lands-men and gunners but on the bounties paid to militiamen and their substitutes.[20] It also admitted that it could not pay its own bounties because of a lack of money.[21] Actually, vessels, timber, and money were probably harder for the navy to acquire than seamen. A frigate required 312 able-bodied and ordinary seamen plus officers and marines, but three or four first class privateers could have been manned by the crew of that one frigate.[22] Whether they would have done more damage to Britain than one frigate is debatable, but the Baltimore schooners were still operative at the war's end and the navy's frigates were not. Certainly, Baltimore's seamen alone could have manned anywhere from twelve to sixteen frigates, but that many American frigates were not available for duty at any time during the war. If the private armed vessels hurt the navy, it was because they drew off the best men, but even this criticism is tempered by the fact that seamen changed from private to public vessels frequently. Fur-thermore, the navy's excellent performance during the early months of the war suggests that it was not getting inferior seamen. Finally, privateers helped the navy by forcing the British to provide bulldogs for its convoys, by encouraging it to use ships in a blockade of the Chesapeake, and by drawing away British warships for patrols and for the defense of various British ports and islands subject to the depredations of the American privateers. The navy's periodic recruitment and other difficulties cannot be blamed solely on the competition from the private armed vessel system.

Another matter worthy of comment was the development of possible alter-natives to the private armed vessel system. With the implementation of the Jeffersonian gunboat policy, an historic American fear of a standing military force and its attendant officer class, a dislike of taxation combined with a dependence on militia, any hope for a moderately strong navy on the eve of the War of 1812 was highly unrealistic. The government's only realistic alternative to the path it actually followed would have been to adopt the concept of a naval commerce raiding force sooner than it did. It is possible that such a national force of schooners or sloops-of-war, unfettered by the need for getting prizes into port, may have produced even better results than the private armed vessels. Such a system, if the government purchased old schooners and ordered the construction of new ones, would have kept the shipowners and builders happy. Whether the use of sloops-of-war as a commerce raiding force, as Henry Adams suggested, would have been feasible is uncertain. Some such raiders were built, but as Adams himself noted, they cost $75,000 each plus operating expenses and wages.[23] They also required twice as many men as the best Baltimore schooners and took longer to build. Even with the sloops-of-war or schooner raiding force, the navy would have been unable to break the British blockade, and, consequently, it would have remained unequal to the most crucial demand made by the war upon the republic's sea power. Guerrilla warfare at sea against merchant vessels was not enough by itself. What was needed was a balanced force of larger war vessels to combat or intimidate a blockading squadron and a commerce raiding force of navy or private armed vessels or, more appropriately for the time, a combination of public and private raiders. If a private raiding force had been implemented and the blockade broken, then commerce would have broken lose. If, however, a naval raiding force had simply replaced the privateers while the blockade continued, commerce would have remained throttled. In that case, the government would have been wise to have authorized not only some private cruisers, but letter-of-marque traders to carry on trade to aid the economy in general and to bolster its own wartime income with customs duties. Another option, that of appointing the government's unemployed naval officers as commanders of privateers, may have been an unacceptable concept to the owners and crews of private armed vessels in 1812 as well as to the naval officers. Shipowners were too accustomed to managing their own investments and selecting their own captains in the early nineteenth century.

There are other conclusions to be drawn about private armed vessels in the War of 1812. Those vessels not only damaged British commerce, but they disrupted its communications and lines of supply while improving American communications. In the Halifax area the British were actually forced to replace dispatch boats with sloops-of-war because of private armed vessel attacks.[24] The American navy was taught that maneuverability was not as essential as speed and weatherliness, The Baltimore schooners proved that "speed in sailing meant survival when the odds were against them" and "victory and the choice of position when the odds were favorable or even." The navy gained a new respect and interest in the Baltimore sharp-built schooners toward the end of the war.[25] In economic matters the Baltimore vessels were forced by the blockade to deal with some new correspondents in other ports, and while they depended primarily upon old friends in port, some new associations were made. Such new associations were useful in the postwar years while a national, as opposed to a regional, economy was developing. Such associations, however, did not support private armed vessel operations after 1820 because of the declining use of the vessels themselves.

For the institution of privateering the War of 1812 and Baltimore's performance represented its historical and professional zenith. The entrepreneurs, builders, and mariners of the Patapsco port developed private armed vessels into what would have been America's characteristic mode of maritime warfare if the republic had gone to war against a major maritime power again in the 1820s or 1830s. But never again would private armed vessels figure so prominently in a major war. Unrestrained operations in South America after the War of 1812 only diminished the favorable reputation acquired by American private armed vessels in the Revolution and War of 1812. Letters-of-marque and reprisal were authorized again in 1815 against Algerian cruisers, but there was no interest in the commissions because the Algerian merchant fleet (the would-be victim) was negligible. Perhaps because of the remoteness of Algeria, Congress increased the minimum letter-of-marque bond to $7,000 (it had been $5,000 during the War of 1812) and for vessels with crews exceeding 150 men, a $14,000 bond was demanded. The regulations and procedures used for private armed vessels during the War of 1812 applied in the Algerian situation.[26] By 1815 the American private armed vessel system had been refined to the point where few adjustments were required for future uses.

Few maritime conflicts in which American private armed vessels could be used advantageously developed after the South American and Algerian wars. The Declaration of War against Mexico in 1846 did not mention letters-of-marque and reprisal. Mexico had little seaborne commerce or navy, and anyone interested in a private armed vessel venture had to consider the higher costs brought about by the adoption of steam power and what were generally larger vessels. Furthermore, the navy in 1846 had more vessels than it could man.[27] The War of 1812 was the private armed vessel system's last major performance.

Europe actually attempted to eliminate private armed vessels in war altogether in 1856. Seven governments, including Austria, France, Great Britain, Prussia, and Russia, signed a declaration abolishing them. Three countries with relatively small navies and long coastlines, the United States, Spain, and Mexico, balked at a move favoring those nations with superior public navies. Before refusing to become a signatory, however, the United States unsuccessfully endeavored to amend the Declaration of Paris by adding a clause outlawing the capture of all private property at sea. Such a clause would have protected vessels and goods at sea whenever the United States carried on trade as a neutral while Europe was at war. Mindful of its War of 1812 experience, the United States was unwilling to eliminate a style of maritime warfare that had served it so well in the first four decades of its existence. In 1857, after the secretary of state had declined to sign the Declaration of Paris, a virtual death notice to privateering, Baltimore's merchants threw a dinner in his honor.[28] As an advocate and former practitioner of the private armed vessel system, the port of Baltimore had excellent credentials as a supporter of privateering and, not knowing the future of privateering, had cause to celebrate.

In the American Civil War, the Union may have regretted its failure to sign the Declaration of Paris. Secretary of State William H. Seward made an unsuccessful effort to add an American signature to that document.[29] His effort was inspired by the Confederacy's issuance of letters-of-marque and reprisal and a desire for some foreign naval assistance in controlling Southern raiders. Six days after the fall of Fort Sumter, President Jefferson Davis invited applications for commissions as the Confederacy adopted a system almost identical to that used during the War of 1812. The hospital fund deducted from prize sales was increased to 5 percent and extra bounties were established.[30] The War of 1812 suggestion of George Pitt Stevenson and other Baltimore owners of private armed vessels was followed when the Confederacy offered a bounty equaling one-fifth of a vessel's value for every prize destroyed at sea.[31] The use of private armed vessels to weaken an opponent's commerce, emphasized by the Baltimoreans during the War of 1812, was being encouraged when a prize was not truly prizeworthy.

The South engaged in the private armed vessel business in a limited manner for a short while. Vessels such as a 30-ton Georgian sailing vessel, a 1,644-ton steamer, and others were commissioned. The steamer's tonnage was equal to four and one-half Baltimore schooners of the *Chasseur* class, but the South may have done better with one real *Chasseur* under Captain Boyle or a *Kemp* under Captain Almeda. The big steamer carried seven guns, twenty-four officers, and 219 men. New Orleans was the South's most active base for private armed vessels.[32] After its initial experiment with private armed vessels, the South depended more on government commerce raiders such as the *Alabama* and captains actually holding commissions in the Confederate navy.[33] Northern newspapers still called the Confederate raiders "privateers" while reporting that Irishmen and Englishmen made up some of the crews.[34] Like the United States during the War of 1812, the South was never able to terminate its opponent's crippling blockade.

The North also flirted with the private armed vessel concept. Private armed vessels were, however, entered into the navy under the command of navy officers under Congressional authority in 1861.[35] The use of private armed vessels was risky because it was apt to irritate the very neutrals President Lincoln and Secretary of State Seward were trying to pacify. The virtual nationalization of the private armed vessels reduced that risk while permitting the government to employ the vessels to its advantage rather than for the profit of their owners. Congress authorized the president to issue regular letters-of-marque in 1863, but execution was contingent upon the South's commissioning of privateers in Europe. When the South did not commission them in Europe, Lincoln's authority was nullified, and no commissions ensued. Secretary of State Seward's plans for a potential private armed vessel system were based on the War of 1812 system and experience while Britain's reticence to engage the Americans in another maritime war emanated also, in part, from its War of 1812 experience.[36]

The Declaration of Paris, according to the United States, invited circumvention and subterfuge when it abolished privateering. That observation was borne out in the Franco-Prussian War of 1870 when Prussia authorized but did not implement the incorporation of private armed vessels into its navy. A 10 percent deposit made to the owner was considered the cost of leasing when a private armed vessel survived the war, while the remaining 90 percent of its value was paid only when the vessel was lost. The government outfitted the vessel, but the owner recruited the crew. That crew was to be sworn into the Prussian navy, issued uniforms, and made eligible for pensions. Bounties were to be awarded the owner and the crew for any prizes taken.[37] The plan provided for a kind of modified or quasi-nationalized privateering force despite the Declaration of Paris to which Prussia was a signatory. As predicted by the United States, the private armed vessel system could not be eradicated so easily, especially when some national navies still depended on supplementary forces.

Between the Civil War and the Spanish-American War the United States became a major naval power and was no longer dependent on private enterprise for its maritime power. Its expensive new steel navy was more than adequate during the Spanish-American War, and no letters-of-marque and reprisal were authorized. Consequently, the United States actually proposed the outlawing of privateering to the first Hague Peace Conference in 1899.[38] The Second Hague International Peace Conference of 1907 finally disposed of private armed vessels when it mandated that all vessels of war, including converted merchant vessels, must be under complete control of the government and that the commanding officer was to be a regular naval officer.[39] The United States and other naval powers agreed because private armed vessels were no longer necessary or appropriate. To be sure, commerce raiding was not eliminated. In the twentieth century it would be carried on effectively by yet another technological innovation, the submarine. Few of its victims, vessels, or crews ever reached a prize court or even a prison. The time was over when, as Jefferson observed in his 1801 inaugural, "every man would meet invasions of the public order as his own personal concern."[40] The entrepreneurs and other private citizens of Baltimore had personally responded to Britain's domination of the sea and its invasion of the Chesapeake in just such a fashion. In its support of the abolishment of private armed vessels, the United States supported a position that would have been inexplicable to the British colonists in North America, to the American

Revolutionaries, and to the entrepreneurs and mariners of early nineteenth-century Baltimore. Their attitudes toward the role of private enterprise in maritime warfare were rooted in an age of relatively small national navies, which was fading in Europe even during the eighteenth century, and in an age of sail whose end began about the time of the War of 1812. The Baltimore entrepreneurs and their bold captains in their swift schooners served Baltimore and their republic superbly for four decades in war, quasi-war, and peace.

Appendixes

Sources for Appendixes A, B, C, and D were the commissions, copies of commissions and applications for commissions in the Baltimore Custom Records (BCR), the War of 1812 Papers (W1812P), and the Navy Privateer Records (NPR) of the National Archives. Other sources used for commissions and for verification and clarification were the Marine Documentation Records (MDR) of the National Archives and the Maryland District Admiralty Cases (MDAC) of the National Record Center of Suitland, Maryland, as well as newspapers and private manuscripts of the Maryland Historical Society (MHS). Sources for the occupations were the *Baltimore Directory* from 1812 through 1815, the various letterbooks and account books used in this study, and newspaper advertisements in the *Federal Gazette* and the *American* in the period from 1812 to 1815.

[A]
SUBSTANTIATED COMMISSIONS FOR PRIVATE ARMED VESSELS OWNED, IN WHOLE OR PART, BY BALTIMOREANS DURING THE WAR OF 1812

Commission Number	Vessel Name	Date of Commission or Application	Place of Origin if Other than Baltimore	Substantiation
1	*Nonsuch*	Jun. 29, 1812		NPR, VI
1	*Rossie*	Jun. 29, 1812		NPR, VI
2	*Dolphin*	Jun. 29, 1812		NPR, VI
3	*Globe*	Jun. 29, 1812		NPR, VI
4	*Comet*	Jun. 29, 1812		NPR, VI
5	*Wasp*	Jul. 6, 1812		NPR, VI
6	*Eagle*	Jul. 8, 1812		NPR, VI
7	*Highflyer*	Jul. 10, 1812		NPR, VI
8	*Hornet*	Jul. 6, 1812		NPR, VI
9	*Bona*	Jul. 14, 1812		NPR, VI
10	*America*	Jul. 14, 1812		NPR, VI
110	*Lawrence*	Sep. 21, 1814	Wilmington (N.C.)	MDAC

Appendix [A] *continued*

Commission Number	Vessel Name	Date of Commission or Application	Place of Origin if Other than Baltimore	Substantiation
58	Sparrow	Aug. 14, 1813	Providence (R.I.)	NPR, VI
127	Atalanta	Aug. 26, 1812	Charleston (S.C.)	NPR, I
191 (?)	Hussar	Jul. 17, 1813	New Bedford (Mass.)	NPR, II
324	Kemp	Jul. 15, 1812		NPR, VI
325	Lynx	Jul. 14, 1812		NPR, VI
326	Cora	Jul. 15, 1812		NPR, VI
327	Contradiction	Jul. 18, 1812		NPR, VI
328	Lottery	Jul. 22, 1812		NPR, VI
329	Sarah Ann	Jul. 22, 1812		NPR, VI
330	Express	Jul. 28, 1812		NPR, VI
331	Experiment	Jul. 6, 1812		NPR, VI
451	Tom	Aug. 1, 1812		NPR, VI
452	Racer	Jul. 31, 1812		NPR, VI
453	Inca	Aug. 13, 1813		NPR, VI
454	Baltimore	Aug. 26, 1812		NPR, VI
455	Tyro	Sep. 1, 1812		NPR, VI
456	Liberty	Sep. 1, 1812		NPR, VI
457	Pilot	Sep. 8, 1812		NPR, VI
458	Valona	Sep. 8, 1812		NPR, VI
459	Joseph and Mary	Sep. 11, 1812		NPR, VI
460	Patapsco	Sep. 15, 1812		NPR, VI
545	Phaeton	Sep. 15, 1812		NPR, VI
546	Thetis	Sep. 18, 1812		NPR, VI
547	Viper	Sep. 8, 1812		NPR, VI
548	Courier	Sep. 22, 1812		NPR, VI
549	Revenge	Sep. 19, 1812		NPR, VI
550	Eleanor	Oct. 1, 1812		NPR, VI
551	Sparrow	Oct. 3, 1812		NPR, VI
552	Highflyer	Oct. 6, 1812		NPR, VI
553	Ned	Oct. 8, 1812		NPR, VI
554	Flight	Oct. 12, 1812		NPR, VI
563	Von Hollen	Dec. 12, 1812		NPR, II
565	Expedition	Oct. 19, 1812		W1812P
566	Rolla	Oct. 20, 1812		NPR, VI
567	Brutus	Oct. 21, 1812		NPR, VI
569	Sylph	Oct. 27, 1812		NPR, VI
570	Hussar	Oct. 30, 1812		NPR, VI
571	Engineer	Oct. 30, 1812		NPR, VI
572	Comet	Nov. 6, 1812		NPR, VI
573	Garonne	Nov. 9, 1812		NPR, VI

Appendix [A] *continued*

Commission Number	Vessel Name	Date of Commission or Application	Place of Origin if Other than Baltimore	Substantiation
574	Climax	Nov. 21, 1812		NPR, VI
580	Leo	Nov. 26, 1812		NPR, VI
581	Rossie	Nov. 26, 1812		W1812P
582	Delille	Dec. 3, 1812		W1812P
583	Siro	Dec. 9, 1812		W1812P
584	Shepherd	Dec. 18, 1812		W1812P
585	Atalanta	Dec. 16, 1812		W1812P
586	Cashier	Dec. 29, 1812		W1812P
587	Halcyon	Dec. 31, 1812		W1812P
588	America	Jan. 1, 1813		W1812P
589	Chesapeake	Jan. 1, 1813		W1812P
599	Tom	Mar. 6, 1813	Charleston (S.C.)	NPR, II
600	Expedition	Jul. 19, 1813	Newport (R.I.)	NPR, VI
641	Price	Feb. 4, 1813	New York (N.Y.)	W1812P
646	Active	Jan. 2, 1813		W1812P
647	Sabine	Jan. 4, 1813		W1812P
648	Bona	Jan. 4, 1813		W1812P
649	Tyro	Jan. 6, 1813		W1812P
650	Globe	Jan. 5, 1813		W1812P
651	Wave	Jan. 8, 1813		W1812P
652	Whig	Feb. 1, 1813		NPR, VI
653	Sidney	Feb. 3, 1813		NPR, VI
654	Grampus	Jan. 27, 1813		NPR, VI
655	Father and Son	Jan. 14, 1813		NPR, VI
659	Chance	Feb. 23, 1814	Norfolk (Va.)	NPR, II
661	Fox	Sep. 8, 1813		NPR, II
662	Female	Feb. 17, 1813		NPR, VI
663	Bordeaux Packet	Feb. 19, 1813		NPR, VI
664	Wasp	Aug. 1, 1813		NPR, VI
665	Chasseur	Feb. 23, 1813		NPR, VI
666	Decatur	Apr. 1, 1813		W1812P
667	Revenge	Mar. 18, 1813		W1812P
668	Arab	Mar. 24, 1813		W1812P
669	Pioneer	Mar. 27, 1813		W1812P
670	Philaeni	Apr. 1, 1813		NPR, VI
698	Thetis	Jun. 16, 1813	Philadelphia (Penna.)	NPR, VI
699	Thetis	Sep. 14, 1813	Philadelphia (Penna.)	NPR, VI

Appendix [A] *continued*

Commission Number	Vessel Name	Date of Commission or Application	Place of Origin if Other than Baltimore	Substantiation
725	Kemp	Apr. 3, 1813		NPR, VI
726	Moro	Apr. 9, 1813		NPR, VI
727	Express	Jun. 10, 1813		NPR, VI
728	Burrows	Sep. 18, 1813		NPR, VI
731	Delille	Jun. 9, 1813	New York (N.Y.)	NPR, II
758	Ned	Jul. 29, 1813	New York (N.Y.)	NPR, II
761	Whig	Aug. 26, 1813	New York (N.Y.)	NPR, II
764	Whig	Aug. 26, 1813	New York (N.Y.)	W1812P
818	Fair American	Dec. 17, 1813	Boston (Mass.)	NPR, I
856	Harrison	Nov. 4, 1814	Savannah (Ga.)	NPR, II
857	James Monroe (?)	Dec. 1, 1814	Savannah (Ga.)	NPR, II
867	York	Jun. 9, 1814	Boston (Mass.)	NPR, I
871	Tuckahoe	Sep. 7, 1814	Boston (Mass.)	NPR, I
894	Fox	Sep. 8, 1813		NPR, VI
895	Ultor	Sep. 22, 1813		NPR, VI
896	Argo	Sep. 24, 1813		NPR, VI
897	Daedalus	Sep. 25, 1813		NPR, VI
898	Rapid	Oct. 12, 1813		W1812P
899	Eliza	Oct. 21, 1813		W1812P
900	Caroline	Oct. 27, 1813		W1812P
901	Pike	Nov. 11, 1813		NPR, I
902	Maria	Nov. 9, 1813		NPR, I
903	Midas	Oct. 16, 1813		W1812P
904	Sylph	Nov. 22, 1813	New Bedford (Mass.)	NPR, I
917	Transit	Mar. 15, 1813		NPR, I
918	Patapsco	Nov. 10, 1813		NPR, I
919	Bordeaux Packet	Nov. 19, 1813		NPR, I
920	Orb	Dec. 4, 1813		NPR, VI
921	Tartar	Dec. 6, 1813		NPR, VI
926	Hussar	Nov. 3, 1813	New York (N.Y.)	NPR, II
927	Governor Tompkins	Nov. 8, 1813	New York (N.Y.)	NPR, II

Appendix [A] *continued*

Commission Number	Vessel Name	Date of Commission or Application	Place of Origin if Other than Baltimore	Substantiation
929	Regent	Nov. 13, 1813	New York (N.Y.)	NPR, II
942	Spartan	Nov. 26, 1813		NPR, I
943	Tuckahoe	Nov. 27, 1813		NPR, VI
944	Grecian	Dec. 6, 1813		NPR, VI
945	Governor Shelby	Dec. 11, 1813		NPR, VI
947	Hollins	Dec. 11, 1813		NPR, VI
948	Diamond	Dec. 11, 1813		NPR, VI
949	Harrison	Dec. 13, 1813		NPR, VI
950	Macedonian	Dec. 15, 1813		NPR, VI
951	Chasseur	Dec. 24, 1813		NPR, VI
955	Active	Jan. 1, 1814	East River (Va.)	NPR, VI
967	Fairy	Feb. 1, 1814		NPR, I
968	Lawrence	Feb. 26, 1814		NPR, I
969	Mammoth	Feb. 26, 1814		W1812P
970	Clara	Feb. 28, 1814		NPR, I
972	Surprise	Mar. 11, 1814		W1812P
973	Amelia	Feb. 16, 1814		W1812P
974	Wasp	May 30, 1814		NPR, VI
975	Orb	Nov. 17, 1814		NPR, VI
976	Croghan	Nov. 25, 1814		NPR, VI
984	York	Feb. 26, 1814	New York (N.Y.)	NPR, II
986	Sabine	Apr. 2, 1814	New York (N.Y.)	NPR, II
1002	Harpy	Apr. 2, 1814	New York (N.Y.)	NPR, VI
1003	Whig	May 3, 1814	New York (N.Y.)	NPR, VI
1004	Hussar	May 17, 1814	New York (N.Y.)	NPR, VI
1005	Patapsco	Jun. 4, 1814	New York (N.Y.)	NPR, VI
1006	Syren	Jun. 4, 1814	New York (N.Y.)	NPR, VI
1007	Daedalus	Jul. 9, 1814	New York (N.Y.)	NPR, VI
1039	Perry	Sep. 3, 1814	New York (N.Y.)	BCR
1057	Midas	Jan. 3, 1815	Wilmington (N.C.)	BCR
1058	York	Nov. 12, 1814	Boston (Mass.)	NPR, I

Appendix]A] *continued*

Commission Number	Vessel Name	Date of Commission or Application	Place of Origin if Other than Baltimore	Substantiation
1067	*Tomahawk*	Jan. 11, 1815	Boston (Mass.)	NPR, I
1110	*Leonidas*	Dec. 12, 1814		NPR, I
1111	*Java*	Dec. 16, 1814		NPR, I
1112	*Manleus*	Dec. 22, 1814		NPR, I
1113	*Vidette*	Jan. 2, 1815		NPR, VI
1114	*Saranac*	Jan. 2, 1815		NPR, VI
1115	*Saturn*	Jan. 7, 1815		NPR, VI
1116	*Charles*	Jan. 5, 1815		NPR, VI
1117	*Swift*	Jan. 23, 1815		NPR, VI
1118	*Chippewa*	Jan. 24, 1815		NPR, VI
1119	*Torpedo*	Jan. 24, 1815		NPR, VI
1120	*Eutaw*	Jan. 15, 1815		NPR, VI
unknown	*Alexander*	Nov. —, 1812		Despeaux Account Book, MHS
unknown	*Ospray*	Dec. 30, 1812		Copy of Commission, MHS
unknown	*Sparrow*	Aug. 14, 1813	Providence (R.I.)	NPR, VI
unknown	*Surprise*	Aug. 14, 1813	Providence (R.I.)	NPR, VI
unknown	*Engineer*	Aug. 1, 1814	New Bedford (Mass.)	NPR, VI
unknown	*Surprise*	Aug. 16, 1814	Newport (R.I.)	NPR, VI
unknown	*Harpy*	Oct. 1, 1814	Portsmouth (N.H.)	NPR, VI
unknown	*Diamond*	Nov. 11, 1814	New York (N.Y.)	noted on register, BCR
unknown	*Kemp*	Nov. 22, 1814	Wilmington (N.C.)	NPR, V
unknown	*Venus*	Dec. 21, 1814	Norfolk (Va.)	NPR, VI
unknown	*Expedition*	late 1814	New Orleans (La.)	NPR, VI
unknown	*Decatur*	1813		Didier Letterbook and Ships' Papers, MHS

[B]
SUBSTANTIATED BALTIMORE ONE-TIME INVESTORS
IN PRIVATE ARMED VESSELS DURING THE
WAR OF 1812 (MARGINAL INVESTORS)

Investor	Occupation	Vessel	Commission Number
Solomon Albers	merchant	Wasp	664
Charles Appleton	wholesale dry goods merchant	Swift	1117
Robert Armstrong		Caroline	900
John Barkman	double block, tin sheet, and iron manufacturer	Wasp	664
Henry Beatty	sea captain	Vidette	1113
James Bett, Jr.	ships' chandler	Sidney	653
John Borie, Jr.	merchant	Phaeton	545
Thomas Boyle	sea captain	Comet	572
James Briscoe	flour merchant	Rossie	1
John G. Brown	merchant	Racer	452
John Clemm	flour and hardware merchant	Chasseur	951
Thomas Cockrill	ironworker	Caroline	900
John Cooper	blacksmith	Wasp	664
James Cordery	shipbuilder	Amelia	973
James Corner	sailmaker	Governor Shelby	945
Hugh Davey	sea captain	Hornet	8
R. Denny	merchant	Governor Shelby	945
Philip Dickenson	sea captain	Fairy	967
Charles Diffenderffer	china and grocery store proprietor	Joseph and Mary	459
John Diffenderffer	grocery and iron store proprietor	Joseph and Mary	459
George Douglass	merchant	Swift	1117
William Douglass	merchant	Decatur	666
William Flannigain	shipbuilder	Joseph and Mary	459
James Frazier	sea captain	Rapid	898
John Gavet	sea captain	Tyro	649
John W. Glenn	printing, oil, and paint supply store proprietor	Joseph and Mary	459
Federick C. Graf	merchant	Charles	1116
John Grosh	sea captain	Wasp	664
James Gwinn		Revenge	549
Leonard Hall	sea captain	Wasp	664
Samuel Hammell		Revenge	549
John Hanna		Daedalus	897
Samuel Harris	merchant	Chesapeake	589

Appendix [B] *continued*

Investor	Occupation	Vessel	Commission Number
Lewis Hart	keeper of baths	*Liberty*	456
Robert Hart	sea captain	*Shepherd*	584
John Hathaway	merchant	*Revenge*	549
William Hays	merchant	*Joseph and Mary*	459
William Inloes	ship joiner	*Caroline*	900
William M. Johnson	sea captain and merchant	*Tom*	451
Joseph Karrick	merchant	*Swift*	1117
John Keys	merchant	*Wasp*	664
John Kipp	oil and paint store proprietor	*Wasp*	664
John Laborde		*Phaeton*	545
William Lorman	merchant	*Fair American*	818
William Lovell	biscuit baker	*Wasp*	664
George MacKenzie	saddle and harness manufacturer	*Wasp*	664
Edward Morgan	accountant (?)	*Tyro*	649
R. D. Mullikan	dry goods merchant	*Swift*	1117
Andrew Myer	brass founder	*Joseph and Mary*	459
William McCleary	boot and shoe manufacturer	*Wasp*	664
James M. McLanahan		*Tyro*	649
Matthew McLaughlin	merchant tailor	*Sidney*	653
Carsten Newhouse	sugar refiner	*Chasseur*	951
John O'Connor	doctor (?)	*Wasp*	664
Kennedy Owen	merchant	*Female*	662
James Partridge	flour merchant	*Rossie*	1
Samuel Patrick	merchant	*Wasp*	664
William Patterson	merchant	*Torpedo*	1119
Henry Payson	merchant and grocer	*Phaeton*	545
William Penniman	merchant	*Chasseur*	951
James Piper	rope store proprietor	*Fairy*	967
William Porter	dry goods merchant	*Wasp*	664
John Price	shipbuilder	*Eutaw*	1120
Christopher Raborg, Jr.	coppersmith and brass founder	*Chasseur*	951
Benjamin Ricaud	merchant	*America*	10
Joseph Richardson	sea captain	*America*	10
Thomas Ring	sea captain	*Wasp*	664
Jonathan Rowland	sea captain	*Sabine*	986
Josiah Rutter	merchant	*Joseph and Mary*	459
August Schwartze	merchant	*Rossie*	1
Frederick Schwartze	merchant	*Rossie*	1

Investor	Occupation	Vessel	Commission Number
Henry Shelton		*Sabine*	986
Daniel Sims	sea captain	*America*	10
Arnold Smith	whitesmith	*Joseph and Mary*	459
Jacob C. Smith	gentleman	*Revenge*	549
Ralph Smith	merchant	*Joseph and Mary*	459
William Spear	sea captain	*Daedalus*	897
Enoch Staples	sea captain	*York*	984
William Stewart	house builder or doctor	*Caroline*	900
Henry Stickney	ship chandler and grocer	*Wasp*	664
John Stickney	distiller and paint and varnish store proprietor	*Wasp*	664
Sebastian Sultzer	biscuit baker	*Wasp*	664
William Taylor	merchant	*Shepherd*	584
Luke Tiernan	merchant	*Female*	662
Stephen D. Turner		*Wasp*	664
William Vance	broker and auctioneer	*Caroline*	900
John Wallis, Jr.	broker, rum and meat store proprietor and merchant	*America*	588
Joseph Watts	sea captain	*Joseph and Mary*	459
George Weems	merchant and sea captain	*Halcyon*	587
William Wescott	sea captain	*Joseph and Mary*	459
William Whann	bank cashier	*Tom*	451
Thomas White		*Wasp*	974
Dutton Williams	merchant	*Sarah Ann*	329
David Wilson	merchant and sea captain	*Liberty*	456
Thomas Wilson	merchant and sea captain	*Tom*	451
William Wilson, Jr.	merchant	*Swift*	1117
George Wolpert	ships' chandler and grocer	*Wasp*	664
Edward Wynn	sea captain	*Saranac*	1114

[C]
SUBSTANTIATED BALTIMORE TWO- AND THREE-TIME INVESTORS IN PRIVATE ARMED VESSELS DURING THE WAR OF 1812 (MODERATE INVESTORS)

Investor	Occupation	Vessel	Commission Number
Joseph Almeda	sea captain	*Joseph and Mary*	459
		Caroline	900
Elijah Beam	mariner	*America*	10
		Wasp	664
William Boyd Buchanan	sea captain and super-cargo	*Whig*	652, 761, 764
James Calwell	merchant and candy manufacturer	*Atalanta*	585
		Ospray	—
Thomas Calwell	merchant and candy manufacturer	*America*	10
		Atalanta	127
		Ospray	—
John Carrere	merchant	*Expedition*	565 and 600
Thorndike Chase	sea captain, merchant, and pier owner	*Comet*	4 and 572
Elie Clagett	flour merchant	*Comet*	4 and 572
Levi Clagett	flour merchant	*Comet*	4 and 572
John Craig	grocer and owner of scows	*Sarah Ann*	329
		Chasseur	951
		Saranac	1114
James Curtis	sea captain	*Wasp*	664
		Argo	896
		Croghan	976
J. D. Danels	sea captain	*Eagle*	6
		Syren	1006
Joseph Despeaux	shipbuilder	*Father and Son*	655
		Caroline	900
		Alexander	—
W. P. Didier	merchant and super-cargo	*Harrison*	856 and 949
John Donnell	merchant	*Eleanor*	550
		Sabine	647 and 986
Jesse Eichelberger	hardware and flour merchant	*Chasseur*	951
		Saranac	1114
John Faulac	gentleman	*Active*	646
		Clara	970
John Franciscus	sugar refiner	*Joseph and Mary*	459
		Chasseur	951

Appendix [C] *continued*

Investor	Occupation	Vessel	Commission Number
Richard W. Gill	merchant	*Ultor*	895
		Argo	896
William L. Gill	merchant	*Ultor*	895
		Argo	896
Jacob Grafflin	sailmaker	*Engineer*	571 and —
L. G. Griffith	merchant	*Harrison*	856 and 949
Peter A. Guestier	ship broker and merchant	*Phaeton*	545
		Ultor	895
Charles Gwinn	flour miller and merchant	*America*	10
		Lawrence	110 and 968
Levin Hall		*Tyro*	455 and 649
		Governor Shelby	945
Benjamin Hardester	sailmaker	*Engineer*	571 and —
Benjamin Hodges	merchant	*America*	10
		Joseph and Mary	459
William S. Hollins	merchant	*Racer*	452
		Sparrow	551
		Wave	651
Justus Hoppe	merchant	*Lawrence*	110 and 968
Jonathan Hudson	merchant	*Sylph*	569 and 904
Thomas Hutchins	merchant	*America*	10
		Chippewa	1118
James Johnson	merchant	*Tyro*	455
		Governor Shelby	945
Thomas Kemp	shipbuilder	*Flight*	554
		Wasp	664
		Chasseur	951
Archibald Kerr	rope store proprietor, pier owner and merchant	*Highflyer*	7
		Orb	920
Russell Kilburn	sea captain	*Whig*	652
		Saranac	1114
William Lansdale	merchant	*America*	10
		Joseph and Mary	459
Thomas Lewis	merchant and sea captain	*Kemp*	324
		Leo	580
Charles C. Maccubbin	merchant	*Tuckahoe*	871 and 943
Martin F. Maher	ships' chandler, grocer and commission merchant	*Revenge*	549
		Fairy	967

Appendix [C] *continued*

Investor	Occupation	Vessel	Commission Number
Baptiste Mezick	sea captain, wharf owner, and merchant	*Tyro*	455
		Governor Shelby	945
John A. Morton	merchant and proprietor of cast iron factory	*Kemp*	324 and 725
		Cora	326
James W. McCulloch	merchant	*Burrows*	728
		Ultor	895
		Argo	896
Isaac McKim	merchant	*Valona*	458
		Grecian	944
Joseph W. Patterson	merchant	*Highflyer*	552
		Rolla	566
		Torpedo	119
William Price	shipbuilder	*Revenge*	549 and 667
		Daedalus	897
James Ramsay	ship chandler and grocer	*Sarah Ann*	329
		Caroline	900
		Fairy	967
William Smith	ropemaker	*Lawrence*	110 and 968
Zedekiah Snow	sea captain	*America*	10
		Atalanta	127
John Snyder	ships' chandler and grocer, and sea captain	*Wasp*	5
		Alexander	—
Cornelius Specht	sugar refiner	*Fox*	661 and 894
Alexander Thompson	sea captain	*Midas*	903 and 1057
Frederick Waesche	merchant	*Garonne*	573
		Pike	901

[D]
SUBSTANTIATED BALTIMORE INVESTORS IN FOUR OR MORE PRIVATE ARMED VESSELS DURING THE WAR OF 1812 (ACTIVE INVESTORS)

James Bosley, *Lawrence*, Nos. 110 and 968; *Joseph and Mary*, No. 459; *Ned*, Nos. 553 and 758; *Wave*, No. 651; *Patapsco*, No. 918; *Tartar*, No. 921; *Regent*, No. 929; *Perry*, No. 1039; *Leonidas*, No. 1110; *Saranac*, No. 1114; *Saturn*, No. 1115; *Swift*, No. 1117.

William Bosley, *Joseph and Mary*, No. 459; *Ned*, Nos. 553 and 750; *Wave*, No. 651; *Tartar*, No. 921.

George J. Brown, *Bona*, No. 9; *America*, No. 10; *Racer*, No. 452; *Sparrow*, No. 551; *Wave*, No. 651; *Chasseur*, No. 951; *Perry*, No. 1039; *Chippewa*, No. 1118.

Frederick W. Brune, *Harrison*, Nos. 856 and 949; *Leonidas*, No. 1110; *Vidette*, No. 1113; *Saranac*, No. 1114.

James A. Buchanan, *Dolphin*, No. 2; *Lottery*, No. 328; *Pilot*, No. 457; *Mammoth*, No. 969; *Surprise*, Nos. 972 and —.

Andrew Clopper, *Rossie*, No. 1; *Globe*, Nos. 3 and 650; *Comet*, Nos. 4 and 572; *Highflyer*, No. 7; *Tom*, 451; *Patapsco*, Nos. 460, 918, and 1005; *Phaeton*, No. 545; *Grampus*, No. 654; *Arab*, No. 668; *Pioneer*, No. 669; *Ultor*, No. 895; *Transit*, No. 917; *Diamond*, Nos. 948 and —.

John Netherville D'Arcy, *Rossie*, No. 581; *Delille*, Nos. 582 and 731; *Female*, No. 662; *Philaeni*, No. 670; *Burrows*, No. 728; *Harrison*, Nos. 856 and 949; *Maria*, No. 902; *Orb*, Nos. 920 and 975; *Regent*, No. 929; *Harpy*, Nos. 1002 and —; *Syren*, No. 1006; *Leonidas*, No. 1110; *Saturn*, No. 1115; *Expedition*, No. —; *Decatur*, No. —.

Christopher Deshon, *Rossie*, No. 1; *Highflyer*, No. 7; *Tom*, No. 451; *Rolla*, No. 566; *Pioneer*, No. 669; *James Monroe*, No. 857; *Governor Tompkins*, No. 927.

Henry Didier, Jr., *Rossie*, No. 581; *Delille*, Nos. 582 and 731; *Female*, No. 662; *Philaeni*, No. 670; *Burrows*, No. 728; *Harrison*, Nos. 856 and 949; *Maria*, No. 902; *Orb*, Nos. 920 and 975; *Regent*, No. 929; *Harpy*, Nos. 1002 and —; *Syren*, No. 1006; *Leonidas*, No. 1115; *Expedition*, No. —; *Decatur*, No. —; *Vidette*, No. 1113; *Saranac*, No. 1114; *Saturn*, No. 1115.

Richard H. Douglass, *Lawrence*, Nos. 110 and 968; *Kemp*, No. 324; *Decatur*, No. 666; *Swift*, Nos. 1117 and —.

Francis Foreman, *Comet*, Nos. 4 and 572; *Phaeton*, No. 545; *Harrison*, Nos. 856 and 949; *Chasseur*, No. 951; *Vidette*, No. 1113; *Charles*, No. 1116.

Henry Fulford, *Patapsco*, Nos. 460, 918, and 1005; *Grampus*, No. 654; *Transit*, No. 917; *Diamond*, Nos. 948 and —.

John Gooding, *Bona*, Nos. 9 and 648; *America*, No. 10; *Tom*, Nos. 451 and 599; *Inca*, No. 453; *Courier*, No. 548; *Price*, No. 641; *Sabine*, Nos. 647 and 986; *Midas*, Nos. 903 and 1057; *Active*, No. 955; *Mammoth*, No. 969; *Venus*, No. —.

Lyde Goodwin, *Chance*, No. 659; *Burrows*, No. 728; *Tuckahoe*, Nos. 871 and 943; *Argo*, No. 896; *Chasseur*, No. 951; *Croghan*, No. 976.

William T. Graham, *Bona*, No. 9; *America*, No. 10; *Lawrence*, Nos. 110 and 968; *Tom*, No. 451; *Inca*, No. 453; *Courier*, No. 548; *Burrows*, No. 728; *Eliza*, No. 899; *Saranac*, No. 1114.

Henry Holden, *Flight*, No. 554; *Patapsco*, Nos. 918 and 1005; *Diamond*, No. —.

Levi Hollingsworth, *Rossie*, No. 1; *Globe*, Nos. 3 and 650; *Comet*, Nos. 4 and 572; *Lynx*, No. 325; *Inca*, No. 453; *Patapsco*, Nos. 460 and 918; *Phaeton*, No. 545; *Price*, No. 641; *Grampus*, No. 654; *Pioneer*, No. 669; *Active*, No. 955.

John Hollins, *Dolphin*, No. 2; *Bona*, No. 9; *Lottery*, No. 328; *Express*, Nos. 330 and 727; *Tom*, No. 451; *Sparrow*, Nos. 551 and —; *Rolla*, No. 566; *Hussar*, Nos. 570, 926, and 1004; *Price*, No. 641; *Chasseur*, No. 665; *York*, Nos. 867, 984, and 1058; *Tuckahoe*, Nos. 871 and 943; *Rapid*, No. 898; *Hollins*, No. 947; *Surprise*, No. 972.

John Smith Hollins, *Dolphin*, No. 2; *Bona*, No. 9; *Sparrow*, Nos. 58 and 551; *Lawrence*, Nos. 110 and 968; *Hussar*, Nos. 191, 570, 926, and 1004; *Lottery*, No. 328; *Price*, No. 641; *Chasseur*, Nos. 867, 984, and 1058; *Tuckahoe*, Nos. 871 and 943; *Rapid*, No. 898; *Hollins*, No. 947; *Surprise*, No. 972.

William Hollins, *Bona*, No. 9; *America*, No. 10; *Sparrow*, No. 551; *Rolla*, No. 566; *Hussar*, No. 570; *Chasseur*, No. 665; *Perry*, No. 1039; *Tomahawk*, No. 1067.

Ferdinand Hurxthal, *Pike*, No. 901; *Bordeaux Packet*, No. 919; *Chasseur*, No. 951; *Amelia*, No. 973; *Saranac*, No. 1114.

Charles F. Kalkman, *Bona*, No. 9; *Express*, No. 330; *Tom*, No. 541; *Revenge*, Nos. 549 and 667; *Von Hollen*, No. 563; *Caroline*, No. 900; *Fairy*, No. 967.

Peter Arnold Karthaus, *Comet*, Nos. 4 and 572; *Baltimore*, No. 454; *Thetis*, Nos. 546, 698, and 699; *Engineer*, Nos. 571 and —; *Bordeaux Packet*, Nos. 663 and 919; *Pike*, No. 901; *Amelia*, No. 973; *Java*, No. 1111; *Saranac*, No. 1114; *Kemp*, No. —.

Christian Keller, *Comet*, Nos. 4 and 572; *Phaeton*, No. 545; *Harrison*, Nos. 856 and 949; *Chasseur*, No. 951; *Vidette*, No. 1113; *Charles*, No. 1116.

Matthew Kelly, *Tom*, No. 451; *Flight*, No. 554; *Patapsco*, Nos. 918 and 1005.

Luke Kiersted, *Tom*, No. 451; *Revenge*, Nos. 549 and 667; *Sidney*, No. 653; *Caroline*, No. 900; *Fairy*, No. 967; *Saranac*, No. 1114.

John Joseph Lane, *Tom*, No. 451; *Revenge*, No. 549; *Wasp*, Nos. 664 and 974.

Charles Malloy, *Sarah Ann*, No. 329; *Tom*, No. 451; *Tyro*, No. 455; *Governor Shelby*, No. 945.

Michael McBlair, *Dolphin*, No. 2; *Bona*, No. 9; *Sparrow*, Nos. 58 and 581; *Lottery*, No. 328; *Express*, Nos. 330 and 727; *Tom*, No. 451; *Rolla*, No. 566; *Hussar*, Nos. 570, 926, and 1004; *Price*, No. 641; *Chasseur*, No. 665; *York*, Nos. 867, 984, and 1058; *Tuckahoe*, Nos. 972 and 943; *Rapid*, No. 898; *Hollins*, No. 947; *Surprise*, Nos. 972 and —.

John McFadon, *America*, Nos. 10 and 588; *Viper*, No. 547; *Atalanta*, No. 585; *Fairy*, No. 967.

John McKim, Jr., *Rossie*, No. 1; *Tom*, No. 451; *Globe*, No. 650; *Diamond*, No. —.

Robert Patterson, *Rossie*, No. 1; *Highflyer*, Nos. 7 and 552; *Tom*, No. 451; *Rolla*, No. 566.

John Randall, *Eagle*, No. 6; *Contradiction*, No. 327; *Bordeaux Packet*, No. 919; *Fairy*, No. 967.

Thomas Sheppard, *Comet*, Nos. 4 and 572; *Hornet*, No. 8; *Experiment*, No. 331; *Shepherd*, No. 584; *Argo*, No. 896; *Caroline*, No. 900; *Orb*, No. 920; *Chasseur*, No. 951; *Croghan*, No. 976; *Hussar*, No. 1004; *Vidette*, No. 1113.

Dennis A. Smith, *Harrison*, Nos. 856 and 949; *Argo*, No. 896; *Orb*, Nos. 920 and 975.

Samuel Smith, *Dolphin*, No. 2; *Lottery*, No. 328; *Pilot*, No. 457; *Mammoth*, No. 969; *Surprise*, No. 972.

Nicholas Stansbury, *Wasp*, No. 5; *Hornet*, No. 8; *Argo*, No. 896; *Governor Shelby*, No. 945; *Chasseur*, No. 951; *Croghan*, No. 976; *Saranac*, No. 1114.

George Pitt Stevenson, *Sparrow*, Nos. 58 and 551; *Lawrence*, Nos. 110 and 968; *Racer*, No. 452; *Cashier*, No. 586; *Wave*, No. 651; *Chance*, No. 659; *Burrows*, No. 728; *Tuckahoe*, Nos. 871 and 943; *Patapsco*, Nos. 918 and 1005; *Bordeaux Packet*, No. 919; *Hollins*, No. 947; *Hussar*, No. 1004; *Daedalus*, No. 1007.

George Stiles, *Nonsuch*, No. 1; *Climax*, No. 574; *Siro*, No. 583; *Moro*, No. 726.

John W. Stump, *Tuckahoe*, Nos. 871 and 943; *Midas*, Nos. 903 and 1057; *Chippewa*, No. 1118.

Jeremiah Sullivan, *Rossie*, No. 1; *Comet*, Nos. 4 and 572; *Chasseur*, No. 951.

Lemuel Taylor, *Dolphin*, No. 2; *Pilot*, No. 457; *Surprise*, Nos. 972, —, and —; *Whig*, Nos. 652, 761, 764, and 1003; *Saranac*, No. 1114.

Thomas Tenant, *Rossie*, No. 1; *Highflyer*, Nos. 7 and 552; *Brutus*, No. 567; *Spartan*, No. 942; *Macedonian*, No. 950; *Manleus*, No. 1112.

Joel Vickers, *Lawrence*, Nos. 110 and 968; *Revenge*, No. 549; *Garonne*, No. 573; *Pike*, No. 901.

Bernard Von Kapff, *Harrison*, Nos. 856 and 949; *Leonidas*, No. 1110; *Vidette*, No. 1113; *Saranac*, No. 1114.

Amos A. Williams, *Globe*, Nos. 3 and 650; *Lynx*, No. 325; *Inca*, No. 453; *Patapsco*, Nos. 460, 918, and 1005; *Phaeton*, No. 545; *Grampus*, No. 654; *Arab*, No. 668; *Ultor*, No. 895; *Transit*, No. 917; *Diamond*, Nos. 948 and —; *Active*, No. 955.

Cumberland Dugan Williams, *Grampus*, No. 654; *Decatur*, Nos. 666 and —; *Arab*, No. 668.

George Williams, *Flight*, No. 554; *Arab*, No. 668; *Burrows*, No. 728; *Ultor*, No. 895; *Argo*, No. 896; *Swift*, No. 1117; *Diamond*, No. —.

James Williams, *Bona*, Nos. 9 and 648; *Lynx*, No. 325; *Express*, Nos. 330 and 727; *Tom*, Nos. 451 and 599; *Inca*, No. 453; *Courier*, No. 548; *Sabine*, Nos. 647 and 986; *Midas*, Nos. 903 and 1057; *Active*, No. 955; *Mammoth*, No. 969; *Orb*, No. 975; *Leonidas*, No. 1110; *Saturn*, No. 1115.

Gerrard Wilson, *Tom*, Nos. 451 and 599; *Revenge*, No. 549; *Sparrow*, No. 551; *Cashier*, No. 586; *Eliza*, No. 899; *Surprise*, No. 972; *Hussar*, No. 1004; *Chippewa*, No. 1118.

[E]
A STATUS INVENTORY FOR THE ACTIVE INVESTORS AROUND THE TIME OF THE WAR OF 1812*

James Bosley — partner in W. and J. Bosley, merchants and shipowners, also curriers; director of the Universal Insurance Company; director of the Farmers and Merchants Bank; manager of Baltimore Hospital Lottery; prize agent and ship's husband; possibly a Federalist.

William Bosley — partner in W. and J. Bosley, merchants and shipowners, also curriers; private in the 1st Baltimore Horse Artillery; letter-of-marque bond surety; possibly a Federalist.

George J. Brown — partner in Brown and Taylor, dry goods merchants; partner in

---

*The sources for this inventory were the *Baltimore Directory*, 1812 through 1815, advertisements and notices in the *American* and *Federal Gazette*, 1812 through 1815, and the letters, records, and account books cited in the body of this study. The works of Griffith, Scharf, Cassell, and Marine were also useful. Papers including records for or references to various individuals are listed in parentheses. The inventory is more suggestive than exhaustive.

Hollins and Brown, merchants and shipowners; director of the Baltimore Insurance Company; director of the Chesapeake Insurance Company; director of the City Bank of Baltimore; proposed superintendent for a new bank; captain in the Eagle Artillerists; prize agent and ship's husband; letter-of-marque bond surety; Republican.

Frederick W. Brune — partner in Von Kapff and Brune, merchants and shipowners; also Brune and Danneman, dry goods merchants; manager of the Linen Manufacturing Company; director of the Universal Insurance Company; director of the Union Insurance Company; manager of the Baltimore and Yorktown Turnpike Road Company; former Danish consul; letter-of-marque bond surety; ship's husband and prize agent.

James A. Buchanan — partner in S. Smith and Buchanan, merchants and shipowners, also sugar refiner; vice president of the China and Calcutta Goods Company; director of the Maryland Insurance Company; proprietor of the Baltimore Water Company; member of the City Council; member of the Penitentiary Committee of Baltimore County; member of the Committee of Vigilance and Safety; member of the City Council Committee for Volunteers; member of the Committee to Draft a Memorial to Congress; secretary of the Coffee House Town Meeting on the Non-Importation Laws; manager of the Washington Monument Lottery; prize agent and ship's husband (as S. Smith and Buchanan); letter-of-marque bond surety; Smith Republican (see Samuel Smith Papers in MHS, University of Virginia, and Library of Congress).

Andrew Clopper — partner in Fulford and Clopper, merchants and shipowners; director of the Commercial and Farmers Bank; director of the Patapsco Insurance Company; second lieutenant in the Baltimore Fencibles; prize agent and ship's husband; letter-of-marque surety (see Hollingsworth MSS in HSP).

John Netherville D'Arcy — partner in D'Arcy and Didier, merchants and shipowners, also D'Arcy Dodge and Company (Haiti); prize agent and ship's husband; was abroad during most of the war; Federalist (see Didier Letterbook in MHS).

Christopher Deshon — captain, merchant, and shipowner; director of the Chesapeake Insurance Company; member of the Committee to Examine a New Mode of Harbor Defense; member of the City Marine Committee; agent and ship's husband; letter-of-marque bond surety; Republican.

Henry Didier, Jr. — partner in D'Arcy and Didier, merchants and shipowners, also D'Arcy Dodge and Company (Haiti); director of the City Bank of Baltimore; proposed superintendent of a new bank; offered directorship of the Mechanic's Bank; prize agent and ship's husband; letter-of-marque bond surety; Federalist (see Didier Letterbook and Gibson-Grundy Papers in MHS).

Richard H. Douglass — partner in R. and W. Douglass, merchants and shipowners; director of the Universal Insurance Company; prize agent and ship's husband (see Douglass and Ships' Papers in MHS).

Francis Foreman — partner in Keller and Foreman, flour millers, merchants, and shipowners; proprietor of a mill on Jones Falls; private in the 51st Regiment of the Maryland Militia.

Henry Fulford — partner in Fulford and Clopper, merchants and shipowners; also Lorman and Fulford, merchants and shipowners; private in the Independent Company.

John Gooding — partner in Gooding, Hutchins and Company, merchants and shipowners, also John Gooding and Company; prize agent and ship's husband; letter-of-marque bond surety.

Lyde Goodwin — doctor, merchant, and shipowner; former supercargo and resident agent in Calcutta; sometime partner of Hollins and McBlair, merchants and shipowners; officer of the Savage Manufacturing Company; director of the Universal Insurance Company; first lieutenant 6th Cavalry District of the Maryland Militia; prize agent and ship's husband; letter-of-marque bond surety; Republican (see McBlair Papers in MHS).

William T. Graham — merchant and shipowner; former ship's surgeon; president of the Farmers and Merchants Bank; director of the Universal Insurance Company; letter-of-marque bond surety.

Henry Holden — supercargo, merchant, and shipowner.

Levi Hollingsworth — merchant and shipowner; proprietor of the Gunpowder Copper Works; director of the Chesapeake Insurance Company; manager of the Washington Monument Committee and Washington Monument Lottery; member of the State Senate; member of the Relief Committee for Easton (Talbot County); member of the Penitentiary Committee; member of the Fourth of July Committee; private in the Independent Company; letter-of-marque bond surety; Madison Republican (see Levi Hollingsworth Papers in MHS and Hollingsworth MSS in HSP).

John Hollins — partner in Hollins and McBlair, merchants and shipowners; founder and president of the Maryland Insurance Company; member of City Council; member of the City Council Committee of Supplies; member of the Committee of Vigilance and Safety; proprietor of the Baltimore Water Company; proprietor of the Savage Manufacturing Company; prize agent and ship's husband; private in the 51st Regiment of the Maryland Militia; Smith Republican (see McBlair Papers in MHS and Wilson Cary Nicholas Papers and Samuel Smith Papers, University of Virginia).

John Smith Hollins — partner in Hollins and McBlair, merchants and shipowners; director of the Universal Insurance Company; manager of the Susquehanna Canal Lottery; member of the City Council; first lieutenant in the Independent Company; prize agent and ship's husband; letter-of-marque bond surety; Smith Republican (see McBlair Papers in MHS).

William Hollins — partner in Brown and Hollins, merchants and shipowners; also sometime partner of Hollins and McBlair; private in the Independent Company; prize agent and ship's husband; letter-of-marque bond surety; Smith Republican.

Ferdinand Hurxthal — partner in Hurxthal and Hasenclaver, merchants and shipowners, also F. Hurxthal and Company, and sometime partner of Peter Arnold Karthaus, merchant and shipowner; private in the Baltimore Fencibles; prize agent and ship's husband; letter-of-marque bond surety (see Karthaus Records in MHR).

Charles F. Kalkman — merchant and shipowner; former supercargo; director of the Patapsco Insurance Company; prize agent and ship's husband; letter-of-marque bond surety.

Peter Arnold Karthaus — principal partner in Peter Arnold Karthaus and Company, merchants and shipowners; director of the City Bank of Baltimore; director of the Patapsco Insurance Company; proposed superintendent of a new bank; prize agent and ship's husband; letter-of-marque bond surety; proprietor of a new land development, flour and saw mill, coal mining and boat building (for Susquehanna rapids) project in Karthaus, Pennsylvania (see Karthaus Records in MHR).

Christian Keller — partner in Keller and Foreman, flour millers, merchants, and shipowners; proprietor of a mill on Jones Falls; director of the Patapsco Insurance Company; member of the Inspection Committee of the Committee of Relief.

Matthew Kelly — captain, merchant, and shipowner; private in the Marine Artillery.

Luke Kiersted — sailmaker and merchant and shipowner; officer of the Columbian Fire Company; captain of the 6th Regiment Maryland Militia; prize agent and ship's husband; Smith Republican.

John Joseph Lane — captain, merchant, and shipowner.

Charles Malloy — merchant and shipowner; prize agent and ship's husband; letter-of-marque bond surety.

Michael McBlair — partner in Hollins and McBlair, merchants and shipowners; former supercargo; director of the Maryland Insurance Company; proprietor of the Savage Manufacturing Company; prize agent and ship's husband; letter-of-marque bond surety; Smith Republican (see McBlair Papers in MHS).

John McFadon — captain, ship chandler, and grocer; proprietor of a linen factory; prize agent and ship's husband; letter-of-marque bond surety.

John McKim, Jr. — merchant and shipowner; director of the City Bank of Baltimore; director of the Union Manufacturing Company; proprietor of the Baltimore Manufacturing Company; commissioner for the New Court House; proposed superintendent for a new bank; member of the Committee to Draft a Memorial to Congress on the Non-Importation Laws; member of the Committee of Vigilance and Safety; aide-de-camp of the 3rd Division of the Maryland Militia; letter-of-marque bond surety; Madison Republican.

Robert Patterson — partner in William Patterson and Sons, merchants and shipowners; director of the Baltimore Insurance Company; director of the Chesapeake Insurance Company; director of the City Bank of Baltimore; proposed superintendent of a new bank; assistant division inspector of the 3rd Division of the Maryland Militia; letter-of-marque bond surety; Smith Republican (see William Patterson Papers in MHS and Wilson Cary Nicholas Papers in University of Virginia).

John Randall — merchant and shipowner; captain of the Rifle Company of the 36th Regiment of the Maryland Militia; prize agent; letter-of-marque bond surety (in Hollingsworth MSS, HSP).

Thomas Sheppard — flour miller, merchant, and shipowner; director of the Mechanic's Bank; manager of the Baltimore-Havre de Grace Turnpike Road Company; proprietor of the Athenian Society (insurance); president of the Columbian Fire Company; member of the Committee to Examine a New Mode of Harbor Defense; member of the Committee of Relief for Easton (Talbot County); member of the Committee to Uniform Volunteers; candidate for Presidential elector; captain of the 6th Regiment of the Maryland Militia; prize agent and ship's husband; letter-of-marque bond surety; Smith Republican.

Dennis A. Smith — merchant and shipowner; also partner in J. Creighton and Company, merchants and shipowners; cashier and director of the Mechanic's Bank; manager of the Medical College Lottery; sponsor of the Merchant's Exchange; commissioner of Bedford (Pennsylvania) Bath Company; treasurer of the Baltimore and York-town Turnpike Road Company; private in the 36th Regiment of the Maryland Militia; possibly a Federalist (see McBlair and Didier Papers in MHS).

Samuel Smith — partner in S. Smith and Buchanan, merchants and shipowners; wharf owner; distillery owner; director of Bank of Baltimore and Bank of Maryland; director of the Maryland Insurance Company; manager of the Susquehanna Canal Lottery; proprietor of the Baltimore Water Company; member of the Washington Monument Committee, major-general of the 3rd Division of the Maryland Militia and commanding officer at the defense of Baltimore in 1814; prize agent and ship's husband (as S. Smith and Buchanan); Smith Republican (see Samuel Smith Papers in MHS, University of Virginia, and Library of Congress).

Nicholas Stansbury — ship chandler and grocer; merchant and shipowner; director of the Marine Bank (Fells Point); director of the Columbian Fire Company; private in the 6th Regiment of the Maryland Militia; candidate for presidential elector; letter-of-marque bond surety; Smith Republican.

George Pitt Stevenson — merchant and shipowner; sometime partner of Hollins and McBlair; also partner in Stevenson and Goodwin (New York), commission merchants; director of the Universal Insurance Company; captain, adjutant, and aide-de-camp of the 3rd Brigade of the Maryland Militia; prize agent and ship's husband; letter-of-marque bond surety; Smith Republican (see Wilson Cary Nicholas Papers, University of Virginia and Samuel Smith Papers, MHS, University of Virginia, and Library of Congress).

George Stiles — captain, merchant, and shipowner; also partner in Stiles and Williams, tea and grocery dealer; member of the City Council and mayor in 1816; director of the Chesapeake Insurance Company; member of the City Rules Committee for Volunteers; member of the Relief Committee for Easton (Talbot County); member of the City Marine Committee; captain of the 1st Marine Artillery of the Union; prize agent; letter-of-marque bond surety; Republican (see Samuel Smith Papers in MHS, University of Virginia, and Library of Congress).

John W. Stump — partner in Stump and Williams, flour millers, merchants, and shipowners; also in John and Samuel Stump; proprietor of a flour mill; director of the Bank of Baltimore; Cornet, second lieutenant and quartermaster in the 1st Baltimore Hussars; Republican.

Jeremiah Sullivan — captain and partner in Hollingsworth and Sullivan, merchants and shipowners, also J. and J. Sullivan; director of the Commercial and Farmers Bank; manager of the Medical College Lottery; manager of the Liberty Engine House Lottery; division quartermaster of the 3rd Division of the Maryland Militia; letter-of-marque bond surety; Madison Republican.

Lemuel Taylor — partner in S. Smith and Buchanan, merchants and shipowners, also Lemuel Taylor and Company; member of the City Council; director of the Maryland Insurance Company; manager of the Washington Monument Committee and the Washington Monument Lottery; proprietor of the Baltimore Water Company; member of the Committee to Investigate the Baltimore Riots; member of the City Rules Committee for Volunteers; member of the Relief Committee for Easton (Talbot County); captain and adjutant of the 5th Cavalry District of the Maryland Militia; prize agent and ship's husband; letter-of-marque bond surety; candidate for position as presidential elector; Smith Republican (see Samuel Smith Papers, MHS, University of Virginia, and Library of Congress).

Thomas Tenant — merchant and shipowner; wharf owner; ropewalk owner; director of the Bank of Baltimore; director of the Baltimore Insurance Company; vice president of the Charitable Marine Society of Baltimore; sponsor of the Merchant's Exchange; member of the Fourth of July Committee; member of the Relief Committee for Easton (Talbot County); major in the 6th Regiment of the Maryland Militia; prize agent and ship's husband; letter-of-marque bond surety; Federalist (see Didier Letterbook in MHS).

Joel Vickers — captain, merchant, and shipowner; also partner in Vickers and Bishop, grocers; director of the Marine Bank (Fells Point); director of the Universal Insurance Company; member of the City Council; member of the City Rules Committee for Volunteers; member of the Relief Committee for Easton (Talbot County); corporal in the 1st Marine Artillery of the Union; prize agent and ship's husband; letter-of-marque bond surety; Republican.

Bernard Von Kapff — partner in Von Kapff and Brune, merchants and shipowners; director of the Patapsco Insurance Company; ship's husband and prize agent.

Amos A. Williams — merchant and shipowner; sometime partner of George Williams; proprietor of a soap and candle factory; director of the Union Insurance Company;

director of the Farmers and Merchants Bank; licensed to erect a tobacco inspection warehouse (1816); private in the Independent Company; prize agent and ship's husband; letter-of-marque bond surety; Madison Republican (see Douglass Papers, MHS).

Cumberland Dugan Williams — merchant; ship's husband and prize agent; private in the Sea Fencibles; Madison Republican.

George Williams — partner in B. and G. Williams, merchants and shipowners; sometime partner of Amos A. Williams; proprietor of a soap and candle factory; director of the Union Bank; director of the Union Cotton Works; licensed to erect a tobacco inspection warehouse (1816); private in the Baltimore Fencibles; prize agent and ship's husband; letter-of-marque bond surety; Madison Republican (see Williams and Douglass Papers, MHS).

James Williams — partner in Stump and Williams, flour millers and merchants; proprietor of a flour mill; director of the Maryland Insurance Company; manager of the Washington Monument Lottery and Washington Monument Committee; captain in the 3rd Cavalry District of the Maryland Militia; prize agent and ship's husband; letter-of-marque bond surety; Madison Republican (see Douglass Papers in MHS).

Gerrard Wilson — merchant and shipowner; sometime partner of Stump and Williams; captain in the 6th Regiment of the Maryland Militia; prize agent and ship's husband; letter-of-marque bond surety; Republican.

[F]

BALTIMORE OWNERS' PROCEEDS FROM THIRTY-FIVE
PRIVATEER PRIZE ACTIONS
1812–1815*

1.	Schooner *Francis* and her cargo, prize to the *Dolphin*	$ 445.84
2.	Ship *Braganza* and her cargo, prize to the *Tom*	$18,892.20
3.	Ship *John* and her cargo, prize to the *Comet*	$34,218.68
4.	Ship *Hopewell* and her cargo, prize to the *Comet*	$28,455.21
5.	Ship *Jamaica* and her cargo, prize to the *Highflyer*	$41,927.42
6.	Schooner *Harriet* and her cargo, prize to the *Highflyer*	$ 4,125.58
7.	Prize goods in the *Hollins*	$ 2,718.73
8.	Prize goods in the *Chasseur*	$14,894.81
9.	Prize goods in the *Perry*	$23,026.08
10.	Prize goods in the *Whig*	$13,684.22
11.	Brig *William* and her cargo, prize to the *Lawrence*	$14,851.64
12.	Ship *Henry* and her cargo, prize to the *Comet*	$37,942.54
13.	Schooner *Fanny* and her cargo, prize to the *Dolphin*	$ 3,077.37

---

*Various Accounts and Distributions to the Owners of Private Armed Vessels, 1812–1815, NRC-S and Admiralty Cases; Prize Dockets 1812–1815; NA (Suitland), RG 118, Records of United States Attorneys and Marshals; and for the *Rossie*, Prize Agent Christopher Deshon's Statement of the Cruize of the Private Armed Schooner *Rossie*, May 31, 1814, MHS, Partridge Papers.

14. Ship *John Hamilton* and her cargo, prize to the *Dolphin* $23,180.77
15. Schooner *Ann* and her cargo, prize to the *Dolphin* $ 3,589.71
16. Schooner *James* and her cargo, prize to the *Dolphin* $ 234.30
17. A box of gold from the brig *Orion*, prize to the *Pike* $ 2,898.10
18. Prize goods in the *Ultor* $ 500.58
19.–21. Brig *William* and her cargo, the brig *Rebecca* and
    her cargo, and the ship *Jeannie* and her cargo, prizes
    to the *Rossie* $15,903.01
22. Ship *Euphrates* and her cargo, prize to the *Rossie* $48,121.29
23. Brig *Portsea* and her cargo, prize to the *Kemp* $23,221.43
24. Brig *SB* and her cargo, prize to the *Kemp* $12,309.42
25. Ship *Princess* and her cargo, prize to the *Kemp* $32,772.62
26. Bounties for prisoners on the *Kemp* $ 2,718.86
27. Prize goods in the *Kemp* $49,096.59
28. Packet *Princess Amelia*, prize to the *Rossie* $ 1,440.87
29. Schooner *Resolution* and her cargo, prize to the *Kemp* $ 6,444.88
30. Schooner *Maiden Lass* and her cargo, prize to the *Kemp* $ 6,297.35
31. Brig *Lady Mary Pelham*, her cargo and clothing sold
    to the privateer crew, prize to the *Kemp* (consolidated
    for this study) $ 4,488.22
32. Brig *Porgy* and her cargo, prize to the *Highflyer* $ 6,615.45
33. Schooner *Burchall*, prize to the *Highflyer* $ 975.82
34. Ship *Ann* and her cargo, prize to the *Ultor* $12,743.88
35. Prize goods in the *Lawrence* $ 6,755.33

[G]
ESTIMATED OWNERS' PROCEEDS FROM TWENTY-EIGHT SUCCESSFUL BALTIMORE PRIVATEERS IN THE WAR OF 1812*

Vessel	*Prizes*	*Owners' Proceeds*
Nonsuch	7 prizes into port and prize cargo in hold	$ 94,500 (estimated)
Dolphin	4 prize sales in records netted $26,718; one other prize into port and prize cargo in hold	$ 54,000 (estimated)

*Niles Weekly Register's running account of over 1,600 prizes maintained throughout the war was the basic source for these estimates. Only vessels "satisfactorily accounted for" were included by Niles but licensed or "traitor" vessels were omitted (notes in prize lists of October 31, 1812, February 19, 1814, March 26, 1814, and January 7, 1815). Other sources utilized were the Maryland District Admiralty Cases 1812–1815 and the marine news sections of the *American* and *Federal Gazette*, 1812–1815. Additional sources were

Appendix [G] *continued*

Vessel	Prizes	Owners' Procceds
Globe	1 prize sale in records netted $3,589.71; 7 others into port, $4,000 in specie divested, and 2 prize cargoes in hold	$130,000 (estimated)
Comet	3 prize sales in records netted $100,616.43; 6 others into port, 4 ransomed (estimated at $2,500 each for the owners because of the number of times $5,000 was the cost of ransom), and 2 prize cargoes in the hold	$220,000 (estimated)
Highflyer	4 prize sales in records netted $53,644.27, 1 other estimated at $50,000 by observers; 4 others into port and 2 prize cargoes in the hold	$187,000 (estimated)
Tom	1 prize sale in records netted $18,892.20, 2 others into port, estimated $2,500 in ransom and 2 prize cargoes in hold	$ 75,500 (estimated)
Liberty	3 prizes into port, estimated $2,500 in ransom and prize cargo in hold (This privateer was of only 55 tons burthen so $7,000 instead of the average prize action was used for the value of its cargo.)	$ 50,250 (estimated)
Rolla	7 prizes into port and prize cargo in hold	$118,000 (estimated)
Grampus	5 prizes into port and prize cargo in hold	$ 81,000 (estimated)
Revenge	4 prizes into port, $3,500 in specie	$ 57,500 (estimated)
Ultor	1 prize sale in records netted $12,743.88; 4 others into port, $2,500 ransom and 1 prize cargo in hold in records netted $500.58	$ 70,000 (estimated)
Midas	7 prizes into port, and prize cargo in hold	$108,000 (estimated)

---

the Partridge Papers, the Didier Letterbook, Ships' Logs and Papers, and other manuscript sources of the MHS. The compilations of Coggeshall (*op. cit.*, pp. 415–421) and Crane and Cranwell (*op. cit.*, pp. 373–400), based largely on Niles, were also consulted. Each capturing vessel's estimated owners' income was computed by assigning the averages erected in Chapter XI of this work, by using actual court records or the reports of newspapers, or other observers when known. The results should be considered educated guesses in most cases.

Appendix [G] *continued*

Vessel	Prizes	Owners' Proceeds
Harrison	2 prizes into port, $2,500 in ransom, 1 divested of unspecified amount of specie, 1 prize cargo in hold estimated at $45,000, and 1 other prize cargo in hold	$ 93,000 (estimated)
Chasseur	14 prizes into port, 1 divested of unspecified amount of specie, 1 cargo in hold in records netted $14,894.81, and 1 other prize cargo in hold	$221,000 (estimated)
Patapsco	3 prizes into port and prize cargo in hold	$ 54,000 (estimated)
Perry	5 prizes into port and one prize cargo in hold in records netted $23,026.81	$ 90,500 (estimated)
Harpy	12 prizes into port, $3,000 in prisoner bounties, $7,500 in specie divested, $1,000 in ransom, and 2 prize cargoes in hold	$201,500 (estimated)
Fairy	4 prizes into port and prize cargo in hold	$ 67,500 (estimated)
Lawrence	9 prizes into port, 1 prize cargo sale in records netted $6,755.33, and 1 other prize cargo in hold	$141,755 (estimated)
Surprise	9 prizes into port, 2 prize cargoes in hold, and estimated $30,000 in specie divested	$178,500 (estimated)
Mammoth	7 prizes into port and prize cargo in hold reportedly worth $50,000 to owners	$144,500 (estimated)
Amelia	8 prizes into port, $4,000 in prisoner bounties, and prize cargo in hold	$125,500 (estimated)
York	5 prizes into port and 2 prize cargoes in hold	$ 94,500 (estimated)
Sabine	1 prize worth an estimated $50,000 to the owners; 1 prize (East Indiaman) reportedly netted $75,000 to owners, and 2 cargoes in hold	$193,500 (estimated)
Whig	1 prize sale in records netted $13,684.22, 1 other prize cargo netted a reported $35,000; $1,150 in prisoner bounties	$ 49,834.22 (estimated)
Caroline	10 prizes into port, estimated $2,500 in ransom, and 2 prize cargoes in hold	$164,500 (estimated)

Appendix [G] *continued*

Vessel	Prizes	Owners' Proceeds
Rossie	5 prizes netted $68,174.30 per court statement of agent Christopher Deshon before final settlement was determined	$ 68,174.30
Kemp	6 prize sales in records netted $83,404.37; prisoner bounties netted $2,650.89, prize cargoes in hold netted $47,869.18, all per agent and sole owner Peter Arnold Karthaus's court statement	$133,924.44

[H]
COMMENTARY ON INDIVIDUAL COMMISSIONED VESSELS OWNED BY BALTIMOREANS IN THE WAR OF 1812*

1. *Active*, Commission No. 646, letter-of-marque trader; cleared for La Guayra from Baltimore, January, 1813; entered Baltimore from Havana, June, 1813; Commission No. 955, letter-of-marque trader.
2. *Alexander*, Commission No. —, privateer, largely owned in Salem, paid dividends; brought coffee into Norfolk from the West Indies in 1813; captured, April, 1813, and sent into Halifax.
3. *Amelia*, Commission No. 973, successful privateer, see Appendix G; entered Baltimore from Havana, September 19, 1813; sold to foreigners at Havana in 1816.
4. *America*, Commission No. 10, unsuccessful privateer, did not make expenses; Commission No. 588, letter-of-marque trader, cleared for Havana from Baltimore, January, 1813, prize; *America* cast away in Chesapeake, March, 1813, operative two months.
5. *Arab*, Commission No. 668, letter-of-marque trader; captured in Rappahannock River two weeks after clearing while carrying flour and sent into Halifax.
6. *Argo*, Commission No. 896, letter-of-marque trader; entered at Philadelphia from Havana with molasses, August, 1814; vessel sold in Philadelphia, summer of 1814.

---

*The sources used for this commentary were the same as those utilized for Appendix G. Additional information secured from Baltimore certificates of registry, letter-of-marque bonds, entrance and clearance records, and bills of sale for vessels in the War of 1812 Papers, Marine Documentation Records, Navy Privateer Records, and the Baltimore Customs Records in the National Archives. Ships' records in the Maryland Historical Society, Dow's Halifax records (*op. cit.*, XLV to XLVII), and the *Gentleman's Magazine* (London), 1812–1815, were also helpful. This commentary indicates the operational scope of the Baltimore vessels and is not intended to be a complete account.

7. *Atalanta*, Commission No. 127, letter-of-marque trader; entered from St. Bartholomew's, November, 1812; cleared for St. Domingo, December, 1812; Commission No. 585, letter-of-marque trader, entered Baltimore from Aux Cayes, February, 1813; cleared for St. Domingo, February, 1813; entered Baltimore from St. Bartholomew's, November, 1813; captured off the American coast, December, 1813.
8. *Baltimore*, Commission No. 454, letter-of-marque trader; cleared for Bordeaux August, 1812; one prize into port; captured off Spain, October, 1812; operative for six weeks.
9. *Bona*, Commission No. 9, privateer, unsuccessful; Commission No. 648, letter-of-marque trader, cleared for Havana with flour and lard, January, 1813; captured in Chesapeake Bay, March, 1813; operative for three months.
10. *Bordeaux Packet*, Commission No. 663, letter-of-marque trader; cleared for Bordeaux, February, 1813; Commission No. 919, letter-of-marque trader; captured off the American coast; operative one year.
11. *Brutus*, Commission No. 567, letter-of-marque trader, cleared for Cuba, August, 1812; cleared for Bordeaux, October, 1812 from Baltimore; one prize ransomed in France, February, 1813; cleared from Boston for Bordeaux, June, 1813; into Bordeaux, July, 1813; entered Portsmouth from Nantes, December, 1813 with wine, pencils, wax, and dry goods; sold in Boston, September, 1814 and operated as a privateer from that port.
12. *Burrows*, Commission No. 728, letter-of-marque trader; cleared from Baltimore, September, 1813; sold in New York in 1813 and commissioned there; sold to foreigners in 1816.
13. *Caroline*, Commission No. 900, successful privateer in Appendix G; lost at sea in late 1815.
14. *Cashier*, Commission No. 586, letter-of-marque trader; cleared for Bordeaux from Baltimore, December, 1812; captured, February, 1813; operative for two months.
15. *Chance*, Commission No. 659, cleared from Norfolk, February, 1813.
16. *Charles*, Commission No. 1116, letter-of-marque trader; cleared for Havana, January, 1815; had cleared for Portugal, October, 1812, and for West Indies, March, 1813, apparently without a commission; entered Baltimore from Cuba, March, 1815.
17. *Chasseur*, Commission No. 665, letter-of-marque trader; loaded but could not clear for France because of crew problems and blockade; was converted in Commission No. 951 to successful privateer, see Appendix G; sold to foreigners in 1816.
18. *Chesapeake*, Commission No. 589, letter-of-marque trader; cleared for Bordeaux, December, 1812; at Nantes, April, 1813; captured off France, October, 1813; operative for eleven months.
19. *Chippewa*, Commission No. 1118, letter-of-marque trader; cleared from Baltimore, January, 1815; sold to foreigners at Havana in 1816.
20. *Clara*, Commission No. 970, letter-of-marque trader; cleared from Baltimore, February, 1814; captured off American coast, May, 1814; operative for three months.
21. *Climax*, Commission No. 574, letter-of-marque trader; cleared for Cuba from Baltimore, November, 1812; entered Baltimore from Havana, February, 1813; captured off Cuba, April, 1814; operative for sixteen months; recaptured by Baltimore privateer *Amelia*.

22. *Comet*, Commission No. 4 and No. 572, successful privateer, see Appendix G; leased to navy for short while; sold to New Yorkers at Charleston, December, 1814; sold to foreigners at Havana in 1816.

23. *Contradiction*, Commission No. 327, letter-of-marque trader; cleared from Baltimore for Coro (?), July, 1812.

24. *Cora*, Commission No. 326, letter-of-marque trader; cleared from Baltimore for Bordeaux, July, 1812; in Bordeaux port, December, 1812; one prize restored; captured in Chesapeake Bay, February, 1813 while carrying brandy, wine, and silks from Bordeaux; operative for six or seven months.

25. *Courier*, Commission No. 548, letter-of-marque trader; cleared from Baltimore for Nantes, September, 1812; in French port, December, 1812; captured off France, March, 1813; operative for five and one-half months.

26. *Croghan*, Commission No. 976, letter-of-marque trader; entered Baltimore from Havana, April, 1813; sold to foreigners in late 1815, nearly 1816.

27. *Daedalus*, Commission No. 897, letter-of-marque trader; at Cuba, December, 1813; Commission No. 1007, letter-of-marque trader and maybe privateer, no prizes; captured off American coast, September, 1814; operative for four months on last commission.

28. *Decatur*, Commission No. 666 and Commission No. —, letter-of-marque trader; cleared from Charleston for France, August, 1814; one prize into port; sold to foreigners at Havana in 1816.

29. *Delille*, Commission No. 582, letter-of-marque trader; cleared for Bordeaux, December, 1812; entered New York, May, 1813 by using sweeps; Commission No. 731, letter-of-marque trader; into New Orleans, September, 1813, from Haiti; some prizes divested; sold in part in New York and converted to the privateer *Syren*.

30. *Diamond*, Commission No. 948 and Commission No. —, letter-of-marque trader; one prize with 240,000 pounds of coffee; sold to foreigners after the war.

31. *Dolphin*, Commission No. 2, successful privateer, see Appendix G; captured in Rappahannock River, April, 1813.

32. *Eagle*, Commission No. 6, letter-of-marque trader; cleared from Baltimore for Haiti, July, 1812; entered at Baltimore from Puerto Rico, September, 1812; cleared for St. Bartholomew's, November, 1812; captured by British, November, 1812; operative for four months.

33. *Eleanor*, Commission No. 550, letter-of-marque trader; at Havana, December, 1813; one prize into port; captured off Europe (?), October, 1813.

34. *Eliza*, Commission No. 899, letter-of-marque trader; at Havana, December, 1813; one prize into port; captured.

35. *Engineer*, Commission No. 571 and No. —, letter-of-marque trader; cleared for Bordeaux, November, 1812; arrived Bordeaux, December, 1812; entered New Bedford, December, 1813, from Bordeaux with silks, hardware, wine, and brandy for sales at Boston; into Baltimore from France, April, 1813, with brandy, wine, and dry goods; arrived in Bordeaux from New York, September, 1813; captured off Puerto Rico, September, 1814.

36. *Eutaw*, Commission No. 1120, letter-of-marque trader; cleared from Baltimore, January, 1815; sold to foreigners in Cuba in 1816.

37. *Expedition*, Commission No. 565, letter-of-marque trader; cleared for France with coffee and sugar, September, 1812; one prize into Boston and out for New Orleans, October 13, 1813; entered New Orleans, November, 1813; four small prizes, one of which sold for $4,000, may have made expenses; sold in part in New Orleans in August, 1814; lost at sea in 1816.

38. *Experiment*, Commission No. 331, letter-of-marque trader; cleared from Baltimore, July, 1812; captured off Spain, October, 1812; operative for three months.
39. *Express*, Commission No. 330, letter-of-marque trader; cleared from Baltimore for Nantes, July, 1812; in France, December, 1812; into Baltimore, January, 1813; Commission No. 727, cleared for Bordeaux, June, 1813; into New York with sugar in fall of 1813; aground in blizzard, December, 1813, sails and rigging off; into New York, December, 1813 with sugar from Cuba; into Philadelphia from Cuba, August, 1814; lost at sea in 1814.
40. *Fair American*, Commission No. 818, letter-of-marque trader; gave up cargo and $150,000 ransom to French vessel in 1813; lost at sea in 1817.
41. *Fairy*, Commission No. 967, successful privateer in Appendix G.
42. *Father and Son*, Commission No. 655, letter-of-marque trader (ship); could not get past blockading force and turned back in January, 1813.
43. *Female*, Commission No. 662, letter-of-marque trader; cleared from New York for Bordeaux, December, 1813; entered Cuba in distress December, 1813; an expensive brig, she was sold to foreigners at Cuba, February, 1814.
44. *Flight*, Commission No. 554, letter-of-marque trader; cleared for Bordeaux, October, 1812; captured in Chesapeake Bay, April, 1813, while carrying French manufactured goods, brandy, wine, and oil; sent into Halifax; operative for five months.
45. *Fox*, Commission No. 661, privateer; did not make expenses; Commission No. 894, privateer; may have made expenses; sold at New Orleans in 1814 and then captured.
46. *Garonne*, Commission No. 573, letter-of-marque trader; cleared for Bordeaux from Baltimore, November, 1812.
47. *Globe*, Commission No. 3 and No. 650, successful privateer, see Appendix G.
48. *Governor Shelby*, Commission No. 945, letter-of-marque trader; cleared from Baltimore, December, 1813; captured off American coast, July, 1814, while carrying tobacco; sent into Halifax; operative for eight months.
49. *Governor Tompkins*, Commission No. 927, owned largely in New York; reported to be successful; captured in eastern Atlantic.
50. *Grampus*, Commission No. 654, letter-of-marque trader; cleared for Bordeaux, January 20, 1813; entered Bordeaux, April, 1813; in France, July, 1813; into New York from Bayonne, September, 1813, with silks, cloth, and brandy; Commission No. —, successful privateer, see Appendix G; sold to navy in late 1814; became the *Spitfire*.
51. *Grecian*, Commission No. 944, letter-of-marque trader; into Baltimore from La Teste, January, 1813; cleared for Cuba, October, 1813; captured in Chesapeake Bay, May, 1814; operative for five months.
52. *Halcyon*, Commission No. 587, letter-of-marque trader; entered Baltimore from Port au Prince, March, 1813, with coffee; captured in Chesapeake Bay, September, 1813; ransomed; cleared with flour October, 1813.
53. *Harpy*, Commission No. 1002 and No. —, successful privateer, see Appendix G; was formerly the letter-of-marque trader *Maria*.
54. *Harrison*, Commission No. 856, letter-of-marque trader; one prize ransomed; Commission No. 949, letter-of-marque trader; possible commission in late 1814, or cruised under No. 949; successful privateer, see Appendix G.
55. *Highflyer*, Commission No. 7 and No. 552, successful privateer, see Appendix G; captured off American coast, December, 1812; used by British; recaptured by United States Frigate *President* and sold at prize auction for $11,000.
56. *Hollins*, Commission No. 947, letter-of-marque trader; entered at New York with

sugar from Havana, August, 1814; may have had another commission in late 1814 or cruised under No. 947; one prize into port and prize cargo in hold; made expenses; lost at sea in 1816.

57. *Hornet*, Commission No. 8, unsuccessful privateer; chased ashore on American coast and bilged, September, 1812.

58. *Hussar*, Commission No. 197 (?), letter-of-marque trader; cleared for Nantes, October, 1812; Commission No. 570, in French port, February, 1813; No. 926, into New Orleans from New Bedford, October, 1813; No. 1004, unsuccessful privateer; captured twelve hours out of New York, July, 1814.

59. *Inca*, Commission No. 453, letter-of-marque trader; cleared from Baltimore for Nantes, August, 1813; in French port, December 1813; into Beaufort, North Carolina, in distress; from Nantes, May, 1813, with brandy, wine, and silks; at La Teste, July, 1813; into Charleston, November, 1812; wrecked after chase October, 1813; operative for fourteen months.

60. *Jamess Monroe*, Commission No. 857, letter-of-marque trader; cleared from Savannah, December, 1814.

61. *Java*, Commission No. 1111, letter-of-marque trader; cleared from Baltimore, December, 1814.

62. *Joseph and Mary*, Commission No. 459, unsuccessful privateer; one small prize sent into Haiti, earned estimated owners' proceeds of $9,000; captured off St. Domingo, November, 1812; operative for two months; sent into Jamaica.

63. *Kemp*, Commission No. 324 and No. 725, letter-of-marque trader; cleared from Baltimore for Bordeaux, July, 1812; into Baltimore with brandy and claret, October, 1812; at Nantes, December, 1812; into Baltimore from Nantes, February, 1813; cleared for Bordeaux, April, 1813; was blockaded in Chesapeake Bay for eight and one-half months; Commission No. —, successful privateer in Appendix G; sold to foreigners at Havana in 1816.

64. *Lawrence*, Commission No. 110 and No. 968, successful privateer, see Appendix G.

65. *Leo*, Commission No. 580, letter-of-marque trader; cleared for Bordeaux, November, 1812, with coffee and sugar; sold in France and operative as a privateer under Captain George Coggeshall; captured, December, 1814.

66. *Leonidas*, Commission No. 1110, letter-of-marque trader; cleared from Baltimore, December, 1814; sold to foreigners at Martinique in 1816.

67. *Liberty*, Commission No. 456, successful privateer, see Appendix G.

68. *Lottery*, Commission No. 328, letter-of-marque trader; entered Baltimore from Havana, May 12, 1812; cleared from Baltimore for Pernambuco, Brazil, November 5, 1812; captured off American coast, February, 1813; operative for six months.

69. *Lynx*, Commission No. 325, letter-of-marque trader; cleared from Baltimore for Bordeaux, July, 1812; entered Baltimore from Nantes, January, 1813, with stockings, gloves, tin, files, perfume, champagne, etc.; cleared for Bordeaux, March, 1813; captured in Rappahannock River, April, 1813, while carrying cotton, coffee, and sugar; sent into Halifax; operative for eight months.

70. *Macedonian*, Commission No. 950, letter-of-marque trader; one prize ransomed; sold in October, 1814, and operated out of Salem as a privateer.

71. *Mammoth*, Commission No. 969, successful privateer, see Appendix G; may have had second commission; second cruise was unsuccessful; sold to foreigners in 1816.

72. *Manleus*, Commission No. 1112, letter-of-marque trader; cleared from Baltimore, December, 1814; sold to foreigners at Havana in 1819.

73. *Maria*, Commission No. 902, letter-of-marque trader; cleared from Baltimore for

Havana, July, 1812; entered Baltimore from St. Bartholomew's, December, 1812; partly sold in New York in 1814 and converted into the privateer *Harpy*.

74. *Midas*, Commission No. 903, letter-of-marque trader; at Havana, December, 1813; made successful privateering cruise in 1814, see Appendix G; had her commission revoked for plundering; Commission No. 1057, letter-of-marque trader.

75. *Moro*, Commission No. 726, letter-of-marque trader; entered Havana with flour, July, 1814.

76. *Ned*, Commission No. 553, letter-of-marque trader; cleared for Bordeaux, October, 1812; in French port, December, 1813; prize into North Carolina; Commission No. 758, letter-of-marque trader; cleared from New York for Bordeaux, June 1813; captured off Spain, September, 1813.

77. *Nonsuch*, Commission No. 1, successful privateer, see Appendix G; sold to navy and sailed from Charleston in January, 1813 as United States Schooner *Nonsuch*.

78. *Orb*, Commission No. 920, letter-of-marque trader; Commission No. 975, letter-of-marque trader; sold to foreigners at Havana in 1816.

79. *Ospray*, Commission No. —, letter-of-marque trader; entered Norfolk, March, 1813, from Jacqmel with coffee; cleared for Cuba with flour December, 1813.

80. *Patapsco*, Commission No. 460, letter-of-marque trader; cleared for Nantes, September, 1812; entered from La Rochelle and chased into Severn River, March, 1813; cleared for Havana, November, 1813; Commission No. 918, letter-of-marque trader; into Baltimore from La Rochelle, March, 1813, with brandy, wine, dry goods, steel, oil, etc.; one prize into port; Commission No. 1005, successful privateer, see Appendix G; leased to government in 1813 as United States Schooner *Patapsco*; sold to foreigners in 1816.

81. *Perry*, Commission No. 1039, successful privateer, see Appendix G.

82. *Phaeton*, Commission No. 545, letter-of-marque trader; cleared for La Rochelle, November, 1812; entered Baltimore, August, 1813; in French port, December and January, 1813; aground and bilged in Bahamas, February, 1814.

83. *Philaeni*, Commission No. 670, letter-of-marque trader; entered Baltimore through ice from Port au Prince, January, 1813, with coffee; cleared for St. Domingo, April, 1813; into Philadelphia, August, 1814, from Puerto Rico with sugar, crates, and tin plate.

84. *Pike*, Commission No. 901, letter-of-marque trader; may have had another commission as privateer in 1814; one prize into port, cargo in hold, and $10,000 divested; chased ashore off Savannah, February, 1814; made expenses at least.

85. *Pilot*, Commission No. 457, letter-of-marque trader; cleared from Baltimore for New York, September, 1813, with wine and dry goods from Bordeaux; into Savannah, December, 1813; one prize into port; one prize ransomed; captured in European waters, January, 1814.

86. *Pioneer*, Commission No. 669, letter-of-marque trader; entered Baltimore from France, April, 1813, with brandy, wine, and dry goods; ashore and bilged on New Jersey coast, January, 1814; operative for nine months.

87. *Price*, Commission No. 641, letter-of-marque trader (?); captured, April, 1813, leaving New York; operative for two months.

88. *Racer*, Commission No. 452, letter-of-marque trader; cleared for Bordeaux from Baltimore, August, 1812; into Baltimore from Bordeaux, January, 1813, with brandy, dry goods, etc.; cleared for Bordeaux, March, 1813; captured in Rappahannock River, April, 1813, while carrying coffee, cotton, and sugar; sent into Halifax.

89. *Rapid*, Commission No. 898, letter-of-marque trader; at Havana, December, 1813; captured off Havana, December, 1813; operative for two months.

90. *Regent*, Commission No. 929, letter-of-marque trader; cleared from New York, November, 1813.

91. *Revenge*, Commission No. 549, unsuccessful privateer; Commission No. 667, successful privateer, see Appendix G; leased by navy temporarily in war.

92. *Rolla*, Commission No. 566, successful privateer, see Appendix G; Commission No. —, December, 1813; captured eighteen hours out in December, 1813; sent into Halifax.

93. *Rossie*, Commission No. 1, successful privateer, see Appendix G; Commission No. 581, letter-of-marque trader; cleared for Bordeaux from Baltimore, December, 1812; captured in European waters, January, 1813; operative for three months.

94. *Sabine*, Commission No. 647, letter-of-marque trader; cleared from Baltimore for Bordeaux with sugar, coffee, and cotton, January, 1813; entered at Nantes from Baltimore, July, 1813; into Boston, September, 1813, from Nantes; Commission No. 986, successful privateer, see Appendix G; ashore in North Carolina, September, 1814; cargo salvaged.

95. *Sarah Ann*, Commission No. 329, unsuccessful privateer; may have made some expenses; captured in West Indies, September, 1812; operative less than two months.

96. *Saranac*, Commission No. 1114, unsuccessful privateer; no prizes into port; sold to foreigners in 1816.

97. *Saturn*, Commission No. 1115, letter-of-marque trader; cleared from Baltimore, January, 1815.

98. *Shepherd*, Commission No. 584, letter-of-marque trader; cleared from Baltimore for New Orleans, December, 1812; captured off American coast, December, 1813; operative for one year.

99. *Sidney*, Commission No. 653, letter-of-marque trader; cleared from Baltimore, February, 1813; captured off American coast, March, 1813; operative for one month.

100. *Siro*, Commission No. 583, letter-of-marque trader; cleared for Bordeaux from Baltimore, December, 1812; divested $23,000 in specie; cleared for France, October, 1812; into Portland from Bordeaux, June, 1813; made sixty day cruise as privateer with seventy-five men out of Portland; into Savannah, September, 1813, with brandy, soap, candles, and fish; captured in European waters, January, 1814; recaptured by United States navy's *Wasp*.

101. *Sparrow*, Commission No. 58, unsuccessful privateer; divested two schooners; Commission No. 551, unsuccessful privateer; two prizes divested and one small prize into port; made some expenses; Commission No. —, letter-of-marque trader; chased ashore and captured in New Jersey, November, 1813, while carrying sugar and pig lead; recaptured by United States navy flotilla.

102. *Spartan*, Commission No. 942, letter-of-marque trader; cleared from Baltimore, November, 1813.

103. *Surprise*, Commission Nos. 972, —, and —, successful privateer, see Appendix G; aground in storm en route to Baltimore from New York, April, 1815.

104. *Swift*, Commission No. 1117, letter-of-marque trader; cleared from Baltimore for Europe, January, 1815.

105. *Sylph*, Commission No. 569, letter-of-marque trader; cleared for Bordeaux from Baltimore, October, 1812; at Bordeaux, March, 1813; into Boston from Bordeaux via New Bedford, June, 1813; Commission No. 904, letter-of-marque trader; entered at St. Bartholomew's, July, 1814.

106. *Syren*, Commission No. 1006, unsuccessful privateer; formerly the letter-of-marque

trader *Delille*; may have made expenses from prize cargo in hold; aground and burnt on Cape Cod, November, 1814.

107. *Tartar*, Commission No. 921, unsuccessful privateer; aground in blizzard, December, 1813, two weeks after clearing from Baltimore.

108. *Thetis*, Commission No. 546, letter-of-marque trader; cleared from Baltimore for Bordeaux, September, 1812; sold French cloth, wine, wire, etc. in Baltimore, March, 1813; into Philadelphia, May, 1813, with Dutch sail duck; Commission No. 698, June 16, 1813, letter-of-marque trader at Philadelphia; Commission No. 699, letter-of-marque trader at Philadelphia; at Bordeaux, November, 1813; into Philadelphia via Egg Harbor, New Jersey, with dry goods from St. Bartholomew's, July, 1814.

109. *Tom*, Commission No. 451, successful privateer, see Appendix G; Commission No. 599, letter-of-marque trader; captured on way to Bordeaux, April, 1813; sent into England; operative for six weeks.

110. *Tomahawk*, Commission No. 1067, unsuccessful privateer; captured two days out of Boston, January, 1815; sent into Halifax.

111. *Torpedo*, Commission No. 1119, letter-of-marque trader; cleared from Baltimore, January, 1815; sold to foreigners in Rio de Janiero in 1819.

112. *Transit*, Commission No. 917, letter-of-marque trader; cleared from Baltimore, March, 1813; chartered to government as dispatch vessel in 1814.

113. *Tuckahoe*, Commission No. 871, letter-of-marque trader; Commission No. 943, letter-of-marque trader; one prize into port; into Philadelphia, November, 1814 with 80 hogsheads, 77 tierces, and 160 barrels of sugar; sold to foreigners in 1817.

114. *Tyro*, Commission No. 455, letter-of-marque trader; cleared for St. Bartholomew's from Baltimore, September, 1812; entered Baltimore with sugar and coffee from St. Bartholomew's, October, 1812; cleared for Haiti, November, 1812; entered Baltimore with 70,000 pounds of coffee from Haiti, December, 1812; Commission No. 649, letter-of-marque trader; captured off Chesapeake Bay, February, 1813; operative for one month.

115. *Ultor*, Commission No. 895, successful privateer, see Appendix G; was unable to elude blockade as letter-of-marque trader.

116. *Valona*, Commission No. 458, letter-of-marque trader; cleared from Baltimore for Bordeaux, September, 1812.

117. *Venus*, Commission No. —, letter-of-marque trader; cleared from Norfolk for France with cotton, December, 1814.

118. *Vidette*, Commission No. 1113, letter-of-marque trader; cleared with flour from Baltimore for West Indies; may have been captured illegally in West Indies after Treaty of Ghent was ratified.

119. *Viper*, Commission No. 547, letter-of-marque trader; cleared from Baltimore for Nantes, September, 1812; in French ports, December, 1812, and April, 1813.

120. *Von Hollen*, Commission No. 563, letter-of-marque trader; cleared from Baltimore for France, December, 1812; reported wrecked February, 1813, but apparently survived; sold to foreigners in 1817.

121. *Wasp*, Commission No. 5, unsuccessful privateer; two prizes into port; $300 as ransom; made some expenses; Commission No. 664, unsuccessful privateer; could not elude blockade; Commission No. 974, letter-of-marque trader; cleared for Cuba, May, 1814; entered Baltimore from Haiti, July, 1814; leased to navy temporarily during war.

122. *Wave*, Commission No. 651, letter-of-marque trader; cleared for Havana from

Baltimore, January, 1813; captured in Chesapeake Bay, early 1813; operative for three or four months.

123. *Whig*, Commission No. 652, letter-of-marque trader; entered New York from Bordeaux, July, 1813 with silk; Commission No. 764, letter-of-marque trader; arrived in France from New York, November, 1813; Commission No. 1003, successful privateer, see Appendix G; sold to foreigners at Martinique in 1815.

124. *York*, Commission Nos. 867, 984, and 1058, successful privateer, see Appendix G; sold to foreigners in 1816.

Notes

Foreword

1. "More than thirty. . . ." Harry L. Coles, *The War of 1812* (Chicago, 1965); "60 captures." E. B. Potter and Chester W. Nimitz (eds.), *Sea Power* (Englewood Cliffs, N.J., 1960), p. 214.
2. George Coggeshall, *History of the American Privateers and Letters-of-Marque During . . . 1812, '13 and '14* (New York, 1856), p. 367; *Niles Weekly Register,* 75 vols. (Baltimore, 1811–1849), Vol. VII, p. 128.
3. Coggeshall, pp. 362–365; *Niles Register,* Vol. VIII, pp. 61–62; A. T. Mahan, *Sea Power in Its Relations to the War of 1812* (2 vols., Boston, 1905), Vol. II, pp. 237–240; Henry Adams, *History of the United States. . . .* (8 vols., New York, 1889–1891), Vol. VIII, pp. 196–197.
4. Coggeshall, pp. 241–244, 466–472; Adams, Vol. VIII, pp. 207–209.
5. Adams, Vol. VIII, p. 207.
6. For the *Armstrong's* resistance, see *ibid.*, pp. 207–209; Coggeshall, pp. 370–383; *Niles Register,* Vol. VIII, pp. 253–255, Supplement, pp. 167–172; Carroll Storrs Alden and Allan Westcott, *The United States Navy* (Philadelphia, 1943), p. 91; John K. Mahon, *The War of 1812* (Gainesville, 1972), pp. 255–256.
7. Coggeshall, p. 365.
8. Alden and Westcott, pp. 90–91; Potter and Nimitz, pp. 213–214.
9. Alden and Westcott, p. 92; G. J. Marcus, *The Age of Nelson: The Royal Navy, 1793–1815* (New York, 1971), p. 473.
10. Quoted in Alden and Westcott, p. 92; see also Adams, Vol. VIII, pp. 197–201.
11. Theodore Roosevelt, *The Naval Operations of the War Between Great Britain and the United States, 1812–1815* (New York, 1910), pp. 247–248.

Chapter One

1. Albert E. Hindmarsh, *Force in Peace: Force Short of War in International Relations* (Cambridge, Mass.: Harvard University Press, 1933), p. 11.
2. Frederick Rockwell Sanborn, *Origins of Early English Maritime and Commercial Law* (New York: The Century Company, 1930), p. 227.
3. Hindmarsh, *op. cit.*, p. 44.
4. *Ibid.*, pp. 49–50.
5. *Ibid.*, p. 51.
6. Francis R. Stark, *The Abolition of Privateering and the Declaration of Paris,* Vol. III, No. 3 of the Columbia University Studies in History, Economics and Public Law (New York: Columbia University Press, 1897), pp. 272–73; Sanborn, *op. cit.*, p. 225 and for the last explanation, Melvin Jackson, Curator of Marine Transportation, Smithsonian Institution, in an address delivered at the Maryland Historical Society on February 11, 1974.

7. Charles Wye Kendall, *Private Men-of-War* (London: Philip Adler and Company, 1931), pp. 3–5; Stark, *op. cit.*, p. 271, and Reginald Geofrey Marsden, *Documents Relating to the Law and Customs of the Sea*, 2 vols. (London: Publications of the Navy Records Society, 1915), I, p. 19.
8. Iris Orego, *The Merchant of Prato: Francesco di Marco Dantini* (New York: Alfred A. Knopf, 1957), p. 59.
9. John Gallisan, "Privateering," *The North American Review*, XI (July, 1820), p. 174, and Stark, *op. cit.*, p. 275.
10. C. John Colombos, *A Treatise on the Law of Prize* (London: Longman Green and Company, 1949), No. 5 of the Grotius Society Publications, p. 15.
11. Marsden, *op. cit.*, I, p. 252.
12. *Ibid.*, I, pp. 173, 190, and 236.
13. M. Oppenheim, *A History of the Administration of the Royal Navy and of Merchant Shipping in Relation to the Navy* (London: John Lane, 1896), p. 140, and Kenneth R. Andrews, *Elizabethan Privateering: English Privateering During the Spanish War, 1585–1603* (Cambridge, Eng.: University Press, 1964), pp. 94 and 157.
14. Andrews, *op. cit.*, pp. 3–4.
15. Kenneth R. Andrews, *Drake's Voyages: A Re-Assessment of Their Place in Elizabethan Maritime Expansion* (London: Weidenfeld and Nicholson, 1967), pp. 94, 157, and Kendall, *op. cit.*, p. 3.
16. Andrews, *Elizabethan Privateering*, pp. 16–18.
17. *Ibid.*, pp. 163 and 191.
18. David Beers Quinn, *England and the Discovery of America, 1481–1620* (New York: Alfred A. Knopf, 1974), pp. 196–300.
19. Andrews, *Elizabethan Privateering*, p. 26.
20. Stark, *op. cit.*, p. 272, and Kendall, *op. cit.*, p. 3.
21. See a discourse on Dutch jurist Cornelius Van Bynkershoek's *Treatise on the Law of War* in *The American and Commercial Daily Advertiser* [Baltimore] (hereinafter referred to as *American*), June 25, 1812, on this topic. For "voyages" and "cruises," see the maritime news section of American port newspapers, 1812–1815, and for example of classification, see British Registers of United States Prisoners in Halifax, Barbados, and Jamaica, November, 1805, to March, 1815, 3 volumes wherein captured vessels were designated as "privateers," "merchant," or "letter-of-marque." National Archives, Record Group 45, Naval Records Collections of the Office of Naval Records and Library; also George Coggeshall, *History of the American Privateers and Letters-of-Marque During Our War With England in the Years 1812, 1813 and 1814* (New York: Published by and for the author, 1856).
22. Kendall, *op. cit.*, pp. 72–73.
23. Stark, *op. cit.*, pp. 96–100.
24. Commission from Providence Island Company to Governor Nathanial Butler as Vice Admiral, April 23, 1638, in *Privateering and Piracy in the Colonial Period: Illustrative Documents*, ed. John Franklin Jameson (New York: MacMillan Company, 1923), pp. 1–3; also an extract of the patent granting admiralty powers to the Providence Island Company in Marsden, *op. cit.*, I, p. 470.
25. Coggeshall, *op. cit.*, xliv–xv.
26. Jameson, *op. cit.*, x–xii.
27. Marsden, *op. cit.*, II, vii–ix.
28. Jameson, *op. cit.*, xii–xiii.
29. Marsden, *op. cit.*, p. 327.
30. In Jameson, *op. cit.*, p. 276.
31. Letter, Stephen Bordley, Annapolis, to Matt Harris, October 1, 1741, Maryland Historical Society (hereinafter referred to as MHS), Bordley Letterbook.
32. James G. Lydon, *Pirates, Privateers and Profits* (Upper Saddle River, N.J.: The Gregg Press, 1970), p. 152.
33. Samuel Eliot Morison, *The Maritime History of Massachusetts, 1783–1860* (Boston: Houghton Mifflin Company, 1921), p. 20.
34. Lydon, *op. cit.*, pp. 159 and 275–80.
35. Allen Westcott, et al., eds., *American Seapower Since 1775*, rev. ed. (Philadelphia: J. B. Lippincott Company, 1952), p. 4.

36. Stark, *op. cit.*, p. 294.
37. *Ibid.*, p. 295.
38. Letters, Governor B. Wentworth, Portsmouth, New Hampshire, to William Pitt, February 3, 1758, in *Correspondence of William Pitt When Secretary of State With the Colonial Governors and Military and Naval Commissioners in America*, 2 vols., ed. Gertrude Selwyn Kimball (New York: The MacMillan Company, 1906), I, p. 179, and William Pitt, Whitehall, to the Governors in North America, September 16, 1757, *ibid.*, p. 105.
39. *Ibid.*
40. Julian S. Corbett, *England in the Seven Years' War: A Study in Combined Strategy*, 2 vols. (London: Longman, Green and Company, 1907), I, p. 392.
41. *Ibid.*, II, pp. 392 and 178.
42. Lydon, *op. cit.*, pp. 83–100.
43. Evelyn Speyer Colbert, *Retaliation in International Law* (New York: Columbia University Press, 1948), p. 58.
44. *Webster's New World Dictionary of the American Language.*
45. William J. Baumol, "Entrepreneurship in Economic Theory," *American Economic Review* (May, 1968), p. 64.
46. Arthur H. Cole, "An Approach to the Study of Entrepreneurship: A Tribute to Edwin F. Gay," *The Journal of Economic History*, Supplement VI (1946), pp. 6–7.
47. Baumol, *op. cit.*, p. 65; and G. H. Evans, "Business Entrepreneurs: Their Major Functions and Related Tenets," *The Journal of Economic History* XIX (June, 1959), p. 256.
48. Harvey Leibenstein, "Entrepreneurship and Development," *American Economic Review*, LVIII (May, 1968), p. 74.

CHAPTER TWO

1. Ralph H. Brown, *Mirror for Americans: Likenesses of the Eastern Seaboard, 1810* (New York: American Geographic Society, 1943), p. 229; Ronald Hoffman, "Economics, Politics and the Revolution in Maryland," Ph.D. diss., University of Wisconsin, 1969); William Thomas Calman, "Toredo," *Encyclopaedia Britannica* XXI (1954), pp. 946–47; and Clarence P. Gould, "The Economic Causes of the Rise of Baltimore," in *Essays in Colonial History Presented to Charles McLean Andrews by his Students* (New Haven: Yale University Press, 1931), pp. 238–39.
2. Thomas W. Griffith, *Annals of Baltimore* (Baltimore: William Woody, printer, 1824), p. 44.
3. Constance McLaughlin Green, *American Cities in the Growth of the Nation* (New York: Harper and Row, 1957), p. 13.
4. Charles Byron Kuhlmann, *The Development of the Flourmilling Industry in the United States* (Boston: Houghton Mifflin Company, 1929), p. 28.
5. Thomas Courtenay Jenkins Whedbee, *The Port of Baltimore in the Making* (Baltimore: F. Bowie Smith and Son, 1953), p. 4; also *The Maryland Journal* (Annapolis), March 25, 1785, and the *News-Post* (Baltimore), January 28, 1798.
6. Jacob M. Price, "The Economic Growth of the Chesapeake and the European Market, 1697–1775," *The Journal of Economic History*, XXIV, No. 4 (December, 1964), pp. 497–99.
7. Gould, *op. cit.*, p. 225.
8. *The Farmers Register*, V, p. 83 in Lewis Cecil Gray, *History of Agriculture in the Southern United States to 1860*, 2 vols. (Washington, D.C.: Commercial Institute, 1933), I, p. 167.
9. Gould, *op. cit.*, p. 226.
10. Avery O. Craven, *Soil Exhaustion as a Factor in the Agricultural History of Virginia and Maryland 1606–1860*. Vol. XIII of University of Illinois Studies in the Social Sciences (Urbana: University of Illinois Press, 1926), p. 67.
11. Griffith, *op. cit.*, pp. 36–65.
12. Letters, John Smith and Sons to G. and J. Wombwell Sons and Company, September 21, 1774; to Joseph Jones and Son, Bristol, November 21, 1774; and Sailing Instructions to Captain Thomas Drysdale of the Ship *Sidney*, December 15, 1774, MHS, Smith Letterbooks, I.

13. List of Goods to be Shipped, March 23, 1775, *ibid.*
14. Letter, John Smith and Sons to Murrell and Moore, June 16, 1775, *ibid.*
15. Letters, John Smith and Sons to Dattera and Ryan, April 23, 1775; to John Roberts and Son, April 24, 1775; and to P. Bulkeley and Company, May 14, 1775, *ibid.*
16. Letters, John Smith and Sons to G. and J. Wombwell, Sons and Company, June 24, 1775; to William Rathbone, August 7, 1775; to George C. Fox, August 12, 1775; and to others; to Ford, Curtays and Company, July 17, 1775; to Gregory and Guill, July 17, 1775; and to Joseph Jones and Son, December 6, 1775, *ibid.*
17. Richard A. Overfield, "The Loyalists of Maryland During the American Revolution" (Ph.D. diss., University of Maryland, 1968), pp. 257, 357–82.
18. Robert A. East, *Business Enterprise in the Revolutionary Era*, Columbia University Studies in the Social Sciences (New York: AMS Press, 1969, originally published by Columbia University Press, 1938), p. 151.
19. *Ibid.*, pp. 164, 171–72.
20. Letter, John Smith and Sons to Maryland Council of Safety, December 4, 1775, and Sailing Directions for the *Speedwell*, January 17, 1777, MHS, Smith Letterbooks, I.
21. Baltimore Clearances for 1780–1786, National Archives, Records of the Bureau of Customs, Record Group 36, Records of the Collector of Customs at Baltimore (hereinafter referred to as NA, Balto. Customs Records).
22. William Gilmor, Family Memoranda, and extract from the family Bible of Robert Gilmor, MHS, Robert Gilmor, Jr. Papers; also Ralph W. Hidy, *The House of Baring in the American Trade and Finance: English Merchant Bankers at Work, 1763–1801*, XIV of Harvard Studies in Business History, ed. N. S. B. Gras and Henrietta M. Larson (Cambridge, Mass.: Harvard University Press, 1949), p. 22.
23. William Patterson, "Preliminary Introduction to My Will," MHS, Patterson Account Books; and Hamilton Owens, *Baltimore on the Chesapeake* (New York: Doubleday, Doran and Company, 1941), p. 113.
24. Griffith, *op. cit.*, p. 80.
25. Robert Greenhalgh Albion and Jennie Barnes Pope, *Sea Lanes in Wartime: The American Experience*, 2nd ed. (New York: Archon Books, 1968), p. 64.
26. East, *op. cit.*, pp. 147, 166, 168, 177.
27. Baltimore Entrances for 1782 and 1783, NA, Balto. Customs Records.
28. East, *op. cit.*, pp. 172, 179, 214; Scharf, *The Chronicles of Baltimore* (Baltimore: Turnball Brothers, 1874), pp. 212–88; Griffith, *op. cit.*, pp. 104–40.
29. Albion and Pope, *op. cit.*, pp. 60–63.
30. Henry Steete Commager and Richard B. Morris, eds. *The Spirit of Seventy-Six: The Story of the American Revolution as Told by Its Participants*, 2 vols. (Indianapolis: The Bobbs-Merrill Company, 1958), II, p. 964. The total of 3,700 translates into voyages or cruises, not vessels. New commissions were required when there was a change of master, rig, owner, or armament. Westcott, et al., *op. cit.*, p. 7, states that Congress issued 1,697 commissions and that another 2,000 or so were issued by the states. Edgar Stanton Maclay, *A History of American Privateers* (New York: D. Appleton & Company, 1899), ix, says there were 712 American privateer vessels in the Revolution.
31. Commager and Morris, *op. cit.*, p. 965.
32. Owens, *op. cit.*, pp. 100–01.
33. Stark, *op. cit.*, p. 337.
34. James Thomas Flexner, *George Washington in the American Revolution, 1775–1783* (Boston: Little, Brown and Company, 1967), p. 193.
35. Commission of the *Swallow*, July 23, 1777, MHS, Vertical File.
36. Griffith, *op. cit.*, p. 73.
37. Letter, James Calhoun to Major General Nathaniel Greene, no date, MHS, Vertical File.
38. Bernard C. Steiner, "Maryland Privateers in the American Revolution," *Maryland Historical Magazine*, III, No. 2 (June, 1908), p. 99, lists 224 commissions issued by the federal government but that figure includes new commissions for vessels changing rigs, owners, commanders, armament, and the like. Rear Admiral Elliot Snow of the Navy Department, Bureau of Construction and Repair, in his "Lists of Public and Private Armed Vessels of the North

American Colonies Fitted Out in the United States During the Revolutionary War, 1776–1783, Accredited to Maryland," March 12, 1926, MHS, Vertical File, lists 198 national and private armed vessels. Snow in a letter to W. Grace Carroll, October 23, 1927, MHS, Vertical File, mentions 220 Maryland privateers. Owens, *op. cit.*, uses the 248 figure.

39. Howard I. Chapelle, *The History of American Sailing Ships* (New York: Bonanza Books, 1935), p. 133.
40. Griffith, *op. cit.*, p. 78.
41. Snow, *op. cit.*
42. William H. Browne, et al., eds., *Archives of Maryland: Journal and Correspondence of the State Council of Maryland*, sub-series vols. I through VIII, Documents Relating to the Revolutionary War (Baltimore: published by authority of the state under the direction of the Maryland Historical Society, 1892–1931), vols. I–VIII, passim.
43. *Ibid.*, V, pp. 264, 284; VIII, pp. 103, 125, 198, 322, 357, and East, *op. cit.*, p. 172.
44. Letters, Samuel Smith to George Washington, May 18, 1779, and to Samuel Smith, August 12, 1777, MHS, Samuel Smith Papers. There is, on the back of this letter, a list of eight captains and their expenses, indicating the extent of the firm's shipping involvement even early in the war. How many of the eight vessels involved were raiders is uncertain. Also William H. Browne, et al., *op. cit.*, XVII, 35, p. 267.
45. Letter, John Smith to Samuel Smith, August 16, 1777, MHS, Samuel Smith Papers.
46. Carl Bridenbaugh, *Cities in Revolt: Urban Life in America, 1743–1776* (New York: A. Knopf and Company, 1955), p. 267.
47. Letter, Samuel Smith, Baltimore-Town, to the Maryland Council of Safety, May 1, 1776, copy in MHS, Vertical File (original in the Maryland Hall of Records, Annapolis).
48. Miriam Beard, *History of the Business Man* (New York: MacMillan Company, 1938), points out that some British capital managed to find its way into American privateers during the Revolution, p. 514.
49. Coggeshall, *op. cit.*, xliv.
50. Stuart Weems Bruchey, *Robert Oliver, Merchant of Baltimore*, Series LXXIV, No. 1, The Johns Hopkins University Studies in Historical and Political Science (Baltimore: The Johns Hopkins Press, 1956), p. 19; and for John Hollins, Griffith, *op. cit.*, p. 104.
51. Merrill Jensen, *The New Nation: A History of the United States During the Confederation, 1781–1789* (New York: Alfred A. Knopf, 1950), pp. 162–63, 199–206.
52. East, *op. cit.*, p. 248.
53. Samuel and John Smith Circular, April 15, 1784, MHS, Smith Letterbooks, I; and Green, *op. cit.*, pp. 13–14.
54. Jensen, *op. cit.*, pp. 192, 204–06; and Baltimore Entrances and Clearances for 1780 to 1790, NA, Balto. Customs Records.
55. Baltimore Entrances and Clearances for 1783 to 1785, NA, Balto. Customs Records.
56. Rhoda M. Dorsey, "The Conduct of Business in Baltimore, 1783–1785," *Maryland Historical Magazine*, Vol. 55, No. 3 (September, 1960), pp. 230–40.
57. East, *op. cit.*, p. 259.
58. Letter, Samuel and John Smith to William Rathbone, September 30, 1783, and "circular" of April 15, 1784, MHS, Smith Letterbooks, I.
59. Letter, Samuel and John Smith to Paul Seiman, Hamburg, June 25, 1789, advising him of Captain George Stiles's cargo en route to Europe, *ibid.*, II.
60. Letters, Samuel and John Smith to Daniel Bowden and Sons, Lisbon, April 24, 1784; to Burn and Son, Lisbon, April 26, 1784; to William Orr, Leghorn, April 26, 1784; to Opley and Hancock, Hamburg, May 12, 1784; to Vander Smisson and Son, Hamburg, May 12, 1784; with John Hollins to James Astley and Company, Liverpool, June 7, 1784; Invoice of Sundry Goods to be Shipped by Messrs. Forrest and Stoddert, London, August 24, 1784; Invoice from John Noble, Bristol, August 24, 1784, *ibid.*, I; letters, Samuel and John Smith to Lecky and Willson, Dublin, December 13, 1786; to Peel, Yates and Company, October 5, 1789; Instructions to Captain John Stran of the Schooner *Ardent*, January, 1789, and Instructions to Captain George Stiles of the Brigantine *Louis*, April 15, 1789, *ibid.*, II.
61. Letters, Samuel and John Smith to Rathbone and Benson, London, November 28, 1789; to D. Bowden and Sons, Barcelona, December 21, 1789, and Instructions to Captain John Fitzsi-

mons of the sloop *Lambert*, February 17, 1790, as she cleared for Haiti with flour, *ibid.*, II.

62. Letter, S. Smith and Buchanan (the firm's 1790 name) to Pedro Lessea, Barcelona, April 12, 1790, *ibid.*, II.

63. Gordon C. Bjork, "The Weaning of the American Economy: Independence, Market Changes and Economic Development," *Journal of Economic History*, XXIV (December, 1969), p. 544.

64. Letters, S. Smith and Buchanan to Atherton and Astley, Liverpool, May 29, 1790; to William Gibbon and Company, Bristol, June 28, 1790; to M. and T. Gregory and Company, June 28, 1790, and Instructions to Captain Daniel Jones of the Schooner *Peggy*, July 9, 1790, MHS, Smith Letterbooks, II.

65. Letters, S. Smith and Buchanan to Alexander Hamilton, August 17, 1790, November 20, 1791, and December 11, 1791, *ibid.*

66. Circular of January 13, 1790, to fourteen European correspondents. Samuel Smith also had an interest in the house of Lindenberger, Buchanan and Company. Letter, S. Smith and Buchanan to M. and J. Willink, Amsterdam, May 8, 1792, and letter to W. Gibbons and Company, Bristol, May 12, 1792, *ibid.*

67. Instructions to Captain James Porter, November 18, 1792, and to Captain Anthony Daniels, August 27, 1793, *ibid.*

68. Letters, S. Smith and Buchanan to Captain Thomas O'Brien, Jamaica, September 4, 1793; to Taylor, Ballantine and Fairley, Kingston, Jamaica, September 4, and September 19, 1793; and to Rathbone and Benson, Liverpool, December 24, 1793, *ibid.*

69. Griffith, *op. cit.*, pp. 131, 132, 140, 141.

70. Rhoda Dorsey, "Comments" in *The Growth of the Seaport Cities, 1790–1825*, ed. David T. Gilchrist, Proceedings of a Conference sponsored by the Eleutherian Mills-Hagley Foundation, March 17–19, 1966 (Charlottesville: University Press of Virginia, 1967), pp. 65–66. The percentage is for "bottoms" and not tonnage or dollar value of cargo. These vessels were generally smaller than those in the European trade. Also, the 412 is not the number of vessels but the number of voyages. Some of the vessels may have stopped at the West Indies on the way home from Europe.

71. Letter, S. Smith and Buchanan to Cunningham and Company, Philadelphia, August 12, 1794, MHS, Smith Letterbooks, III.

72. Albion and Pope, *op. cit.*, p. 83.

73. Letters, S. Smith and Buchanan to Johann Abrams and Retberg and Sons, Bremen, March 5, 1795; to Rathbone and Benson, Liverpool, March 5, 1795; and Instructions to Captain Josiah Reiter of the Schooner *Peggy*, April 20, 1795, MHS, Smith Letterbooks, III.

74. Ulane Bonnel, *La France, Les États-Unis et la Guerre de Course, 1797–1815* (Paris: Nouvelle Editions Latine, 1961), pp. 319–403.

75. Albion and Pope, *op. cit.*, p. 84.

76. Depositions of Buchanan and Robb, December 6, 1794 and December —, 1794; of Pierre Lelande, Mate, September 2, 1795; of the Captain of the Ship *Harmony*, May 7, 1796; of Captain John Smith of the Ship *Ardent*, September 14, 1796, and of James McDaniel, Mariner on the Schooner *Musquitoe*, September —, 1796, MHS, Donaldson Protest Book: Copies of Depositions taken before Thomas Donaldson, Notary Public of Baltimore-Town 1793–1796, Consisting chiefly of depositions by Master of Vessels and others relating to captured, damaged vessels and cargoes.

77. Abstracts of Registers of Vessels, Baltimore, October, 1789, to December, 1811, NA, Balto. Customs Records. While the 3,753 registered vessels represented any number of vessels, the 215 losses consisted of one vessel each.

78. Bonnel, *op. cit.*, pp. 319–66.

79. Abstracts of Registers of Vessels, Baltimore, October, 1789 to December, 1811, NA, Balto. Customs Records.

80. Letter, L. A. Coob, Assistant Secretary, Treasury Department, to Richard D. Fisher, Baltimore, November 19, 1908, MHS, Vertical File. According to Coob, some of these records were destroyed in an 1858 Baltimore Customs House fire before the balance was transferred to the Treasury Department in 1887 for use in the French Spoliation Claims cases.

81. *Ibid.* Also letter-of-Marque Commissions Authorized by the Act of July 9, 1798 in Dudley W. Knox, comp., *Naval Documents Related to the Quasi-War Between the United States and France*, 7 vols. (Washington, D.C.: GPO, 1935–38), II, pp. 151–95, and VII, pp. 405–36.

82. Evelyn Speyer Colbert, *Retaliation in International Law* (New York: Columbia University Press, 1948), p. 116.
83. Bonnel, *op. cit.*, p. 367. The French took 1,434 American vessels in the period from 1797 to 1815, pp. 309–10.
84. Abstracts of Registers of Vessels, Baltimore, October, 1789, to December, 1812, NA, Balto. Customs Records.
85. "Abstracts of Tonnage of the Several Districts of the U.S.," *American State Papers, Commerce and Navigation*, I, pp. 331, 495, 701–02, 828, 998–99.
86. Timothy Pitkin, *A Statistical View of the Commerce of the United States of America* (New York: James Eastburn Company, 1817), pp. 52–55; and "Treasury Department Register's Office Report on Drawbacks in 1809, 1810, and 1811," November 19, 1812, in *Niles Weekly Register*, January 2, 1813.
87. Louis Martin Sears, *Jefferson and the Embargo* (New York: Octagon Books, 1966, originally published in 1929 by Duke University Press), pp. 221–26; and Letters, William Patterson to Wilson Cary Nicholas, May 11, 1808, and December 1, 1808, University of Virginia, Wilson Cary Nicholas Papers. Patterson supported the Embargo in May but was concerned about the problems it caused in December.
88. Letters, Albert Gallatin to James H. McCulloch, Collector of Customs at Baltimore, May 9, 1809, July 12, 1810, November 14, 1809, and December 3, 1810, NA, General Records of the Department of Treasury, RG 56, Letters Sent by the Secretary of Treasury to the Collectors of Customs at all Ports, 1789–1847.
89. Letter, Deputy Collector at Baltimore J. Brice to Albert Gallatin, December 28, 1807, NA, General Records of the Department of State, RG 56, Correspondence of the Secretary of Treasury, 1789–1833.
90. *Maryland Gazette* (Annapolis), April 10, 1795; and for Genêt's activities in Charleston, see Melvin H. Jackson, *Privateers in Charleston, 1793–1796*, No. 1, Smithsonian Studies in History and Technology (Washington, D.C.: Smithsonian Institution Press, 1969).
91. Letters, Albert Gallatin to James H. McCulloch, February 7, 1810; Richard Wall, Collector at Savannah, to Albert Gallatin, January 26, 1810, NA, General Records of the Department of Treasury, RG 56, Letters Sent by the Secretary of Treasury to the Collectors of Customs at all Ports, 1789–1847.
92. Leonard D. White, *The Jeffersonians: A Study in Administrative History, 1801–1829* (New York: MacMillan Company, 1951), pp. 453–54.
93. *Niles Weekly Register*, April 18, 1812 and March 21, 1812, and *American State Papers, Commerce and Navigation*, I, p. 956.
94. Anna C. Clauder, *American Commerce as Affected by the Wars of the French Revolution and Napoleon, 1793–1812* (Philadelphia: University of Pennsylvania Press, 1932), p. 228; and Albion and Pope, *op. cit.*, p. 109. A bond for $72,075 was taken out on the *Orizimbo* on October 14, 1812, by sole owner David Easterbrook as she left for Cadiz, Spain, NA, Bond No. 59, Bonds for Letters-of-Marque and Reprisal 1812, Balto. Customs Records. Despite the collection's label, some non-letter-of-marque bonds are included in the group.
95. Criteria from Cole, *op. cit.*, p. 6.
96. Harvey Leibenstein, "Entrepreneurship and Development," *American Economic Review*, Vol. 58 (May, 1968), pp. 74–75.
97. Henri Pirenne, "The Stages in the Social History of Capitalism," *The American Historical Review*, Vol. CIX, No. 3 (April, 1914), pp. 494–515.
98. Instructions to Supercargo James Purviance, September 29, 1793; to Captain Boyd Buchanan, February 25, 1793; to George Stiles, May 20, 1793; letter, S. Smith and Buchanan to James Donnell, Port au Prince, March 15, 1792; to Captain William Furlong, June 11, 1791; and letter, S. Smith and Buchanan to James Donnell, January 31, 1791, MHS, Smith Letterbooks, II.
99. Sailing Directions to Captain Henry Travers, November 29, 1790, and May 29, 1790, *ibid.*, II; letter, S. Smith and Buchanan to William Wallace, October 11, 1784, *ibid.*, I.
100. *Niles Weekly Register*, December 21, 1811.
101. J. R. Pole, "Constitutional Reform and Election Statistics in Maryland," *Maryland Historical Magazine*, Vol. 55, No. 4 (December, 1960), pp. 285–92.
102. Anonymous, "Reise von Hamburg nach Philadelphia," in *This Was America: As Recorded by*

European Travelers in the 18th, 19th and 20th Centuries, ed. Oscar Handlin (New York: Harper and Row, Publishers, 1949), p. 105.

103. John G. B. Hutchins, *The American Maritime Industries and Public Policy, 1789–1914: An Economic History*, Vol. LXXI of Harvard Economic Studies (Cambridge, Mass.: Harvard University Press, 1941), pp. 73–89; 100–20.

104. Master carpenter Certificates, 1790–1819, NA, Records of the Bureau of Marine Inspection and Navigation, Record Group 41 (hereinafter referred to as NA, Marine Documentation Records).

105. *Ibid.* A single name on a certificate may have been the agent or "ship's husband."

106. *Ibid.*

107. *Niles Weekly Register*, May 1, 1813, and October 24, 1812.

CHAPTER THREE

1. *American*, June 24, July 4, 11, 13, 1812.

2. See Appendix A (Substantiated Commissions for Private Armed Vessels Owned, in Whole or Part, by Baltimoreans During the War of 1812). An example of omissions is the application for the *Whig*'s Commission No. 1003, May 3, 1814, in New York in which the writer's name, part-owner Lemuel Taylor, appears without the names of the other part-owners. National Archives, Navy Records Collection of the Office of Naval Records, Record Group 45, Letters from the Collectors of Customs to the Secretary of State Relative to Commissions of Privateers, 1812–1815, VI (hereinafter referred to as NA, Navy Privateer Records).

3. Applications for Commissions, 1812–1815, NA, Navy Privateer Records, VI.

4. Letter, Henry Didier, Jr. to John N. D'Arcy in England, June 7, 1814, MHS, Didier Letter-book. Such changes were not clearly indicated in the government records.

5. See Appendix B (Substantiated Baltimore One-Time Investors in Private Armed Vessels During the War of 1812).

6. Applications for Commission Nos. 1, 10, 451, 459, 549, 664, and 951, NA, Navy Privateer Records, VI, and No. 900, National Archives, General Records of the Department of State, War of 1812 Papers, Record Group 59, Letters Received Concerning Letters-of-Marque 1812–1814 (hereinafter referred to as NA, War of 1812 Papers).

7. Application for Commission No. 664, August 1, 1813, NA, Navy Privateer Records, VI; Griffith, *op. cit.*, William Fry, *Baltimore Directory 1810, 1812, 1814* (Baltimore: G. Dobbin and Murphy Printers, 1810, 1812, 1814) (hereinafter referred to as *B D*); J. Thomas Scharf, *History of Baltimore City and County* (Philadelphia: L. E. Evarts, 1881); and *Chronicles;* and advertisements in *American*, 1812–1815, and *Federal Gazette and Baltimore Daily Advertiser*, 1812–1815 (hereinafter referred to as *Federal Gazette*).

8. Nontitled collector's resumé of Baltimore Commission, 1812–1815, NA, Navy Privateer Records, II.

9. Entry of April 25, 1814, Maryland Hall of Records, Peter Arnold Karthaus and Company Shipping Accounts (hereinafter Maryland Hall of Records referred to as MHR).

10. Baltimore Bills of Sale, November 10, 1812, and Baltimore Certificates of Registry Nos. 141 and 142, November 10, 1812, NA, Marine Documentation Records. Boyle reputedly was a part-owner of the *Chasseur* also, but no substantiation was located.

11. Master Carpenter's Certificate for the *Eutaw*, January 25, 1815, NA, Marine Documentation Records.

12. Application for Commission No. 1119, January 24, 1815, NA, Navy Privateer Records VI; also William Patterson, "Preliminary Introductions to My Will," Maryland Historical Society, Patterson Account Books.

13. See Appendix C (Substantiated Baltimore Two- and Three-Time Investors in Private Armed Vessel Commissions During the War of 1812).

14. Entry of November 10, 1812, Maryland Historical Society, Despeaux Account Book. His ten shares in the *Alexander* were valued, initially, at $8,500, but he sold one to Captain John Snyder soon after (December 1, 1812). Refitting costs were, in addition to the initial $8,500, at

least $120 per share. An entry of November 12, 1813, valued Despeaux's *Caroline* share at $750. Also Master Carpenter's Certificate for the *Flight*, October 12, 1812, "finished privateer fashion" and Master Carpenter's Certificate, January 8, 1813, for the *Chasseur*, NA, Marine Documentation Records; also Florence M. Bourne, "Thomas Kemp, Shipbuilder and his Home, Wades Point," *Maryland Historical Magazine*, LXIX N. 4 (December, 1954), pp. 271–89, based on Kemp's account books which were not located for this study.

15. Applications for Commissions Nos. 549, September 19, 1812, and 897, September 25, 1813, NA, Navy Privateer Records, VI.

16. Bill of Sale of *Joseph and Mary*, September 11, 1812, and Bill of Sale of the *Caroline*, October —, 1813, NA, Marine Documentation Records.

17. Letter, S. Smith and Buchanan to Fenwick and Mason, Liverpool, December 12, 1791, MHS, Smith Letterbooks, II.

18. Notice in *Federal Gazette*, March 17, 1813.

19. Depositions of Prize Master John J. Mitchell of the *Fox* (Case of *George Dumenill v. Cornelius Specht*), January 31, 1816, National Record Center, Suitland, Maryland, Maryland District Court Records, Admiralty Cases, Record Group 21 (hereinafter referred to as NRC-S, Md. District Admiralty Cases).

20. See Appendix D (Substantiated Baltimore Investors in Four or More Private Armed Vessels During the War of 1812).

21. Bills of Sale of Vessels, 1812, and January and February, 1813, NA, Marine Documentation Records; and untitled Collector's resumé of Baltimore commissions for 1812 and 1813, NA, Navy Privateer Records, II.

22. Account for Carpenter's Wages, November 5, 1812, and May 6, 1813, MHS, Despeaux (shipyard) Account Book.

23. Henry Adams, *History of the United States of America*, 9 vols. (New York: Charles Scribner's Sons, 1891), VII, p. 398.

24. Letter, T. and S. Hollingsworth to Levi Hollingsworth and Son, Philadelphia, Historical Society of Pennsylvania, Hollingsworth Manuscripts, Correspondence (hereinafter referred to as HSP, Hollingsworth MSS, Correspondence).

25. Baltimore City Census, NA, Third United States Census (1810).

26. Abstracts of Registers of Vessels, October 1789 to December 1811, NA, Balto. Customs Records; also *B D*, 1812, 1814, and advertisements in *Federal Gazette* and *American*, 1812–1815.

27. Abstracts of Registers of Vessels, October, 1789, to December, 1811, NA, Balto. Customs Records; and MHS, Customs Papers; also Entrances and Clearances at Baltimore, 1780 to December 1811, NA, Balto. Customs Records.

28. Letter, R. L. Gatt to Michael McBlair, undated but after 1820, MHS, McBlair Paper.

29. Letter, Hollingsworth and Worthington to Levi Hollingsworth and Son, Phila., May 9, and March 10, 1814, HSP, Hollingsworth MSS, Correspondence.

30. Joseph Story, *Commentary on the Law of Partnership as a Branch of Commercial and Maritime Jurisprudence* (Boston: Charles C. Little and James Brown, 1841), p. 630. This work covers the topic from Roman law to English and American law.

31. Application for Commission No. 968, February 26, 1814, NA, Navy Privateer Records, I.

32. Entries of December 26, 1812 and February 7, 1814 of bank directors at Henry Thompson's house for dinner, MHS, Henry Thompson Diary, Vols. III and IV; and newspaper notices of board meetings, *Federal Gazette* and *American*. See, for example, *Federal Gazette*, February 2, June 10, June 29, June 25, October 12, and December 2, 1812; October 12, December 2, and 7, and December 13, 1813; and October 4, and 14, and September 2, 1814.

33. Certificates of Registry, 1811, and January to June, 1812, NA, Marine Documentation Records.

34. *Genealogy and Biography of Leading Families of the City of Baltimore and Baltimore County* (New York and Chicago: Chapman Publishing Company, 1897), passim; *Biographical Encyclopedia of Representative Men of Maryland and the District of Columbia* (Baltimore: National Biographical Publications Company, 1879), pp. 10, 159–60, 248–49, 393, 547; also MHS, Partridge Papers, McBlair Papers, Samuel Smith Papers, Didier Letterbook, William Patterson Papers, and HSP, Hollingsworth MSS. Correspondence.

35. James E. P. Bouldin, *Presbyterians of Baltimore; Their Churches and Historic Graveyards* (Baltimore:

William K. Boyle and Son, 1875), passim; and John C. Backus, *Historical Discourse on Taking Leave of the Old Church Edifice of the First Presbyterian Congregation in Baltimore* (Baltimore: John Woods, Printer, 1860), appendix, pp. 95–97. This work is useful for marriages also.

36. Louis P. Henninghausen, comp., *History of the German Society of Maryland* (Baltimore: The German Society, 1909), pp. 171–73. Von Kapff, the Schwartzes, Hoppe, Eichelberger, Waesche, Brune, Diffenderffer, Karthaus, Keller, Graf, Albers, Hurxthal, Vickers, and, for some reason, Jeremiah Sullivan were members.

37. Abstracts of Registers of Vessels, October, 1789, to December, 1811, NA, Balto. Customs Records.

38. Letter, Secretary of State James Monroe to the Collector at Baltimore, NA, Navy Privateer Records, III; Barney Commission in the Revolution and Commission No. 1 for the *Rossie*, HSP, Joshua Barney Papers, I.

39. Untitled Collector's resumé of Baltimore commissions for 1812–1813, NA, Navy Privateer Records, II; and *Federal Gazette*, August 11, and August 28, 1813. No new commission was located for this change and it is, therefore, an example of possible but unsubstantiated Baltimore commissions and of the capacity of the vessels to change their character.

40. Bonds for Letters-of-Marque and Reprisal of 1812 (fifty-four bonds). NA, Balto. Customs Records; War of 1812 Papers; and Navy Privateer Records, I through VI (seventy-three more surities listed).

41. *Ibid.*

42. Untitled collectors' resumé of commissions, 1812–1813, NA, Navy Privateer Records, II.

43. Baltimore Collector's Return of November 1, 1814, NA, War of 1812 Papers. The collector's figure for eighteen privateers averaged out to 80 officers and men per vessel, and thirty other Baltimore armed vessels cleared as privateers so 3,850 men is a basic estimate of the crews in those vessels. Some were not manned in Baltimore but most after the first four months carried more than 80 men, and many went out on two or more cruises changing only part of their crew each time. The collector's figure for letter-of-marque traders averages 38 men (including officers) per vessel for the first twenty-four vessels. If the fifty other Baltimore-owned commissioned traders are added, they raise the crew figure for letter-of-marque traders to 2,828. The total number of crew openings, not counting reenlistments, was then an estimated 6,678.

44. Libels, Prize Vessel Disbursement and Expense Accounts, Prize Sales Accounts and other 1812–1815 records, NRC-S, Md. District Admiralty Cases; MHS, Despeaux (shipyard) Account Books; and advertisements in *Federal Gazette* and *American*, 1812–1815.

45. Marshal's Sale of the Ship *Henry*, August 28, 1812, NRC-S, Md. District Admiralty Cases; Owner and Citizenship Oaths for the *Eagle*, August 12, 1812, NA, Marine Documentation Records.

46. See various Sales at Prize Auctions, 1812–1815, NRC-S, Md. District Admiralty Cases.

47. Letter, Henry Didier, Jr. to John N. D'Arcy in England, December 14, 1814, MHS, Didier Letterbook; and Scharf, *Chronicles*, p. 468.

48. *Federal Gazette*, October 29, and October 8, 1812; Master Carpenter's Certificate (Thomas Kemp), October 21, 1814 for schooner (125 tons) *Romp*, NA, Marine Documentation Records; entry of December 27, 1815, MHS, Despeaux Account Books.

49. Letter, H. Didier, Jr. to John N. D'Arcy in England, June 4, 1814, MHS, Didier Letterbook; advertisements in *Federal Gazette*, September 8, 1812, December 17, 1813, April 14, 1814; and letter, Hollingsworth and Worthington to Levi Hollingsworth and Son, Phila., October 1, 1812, HSP, Hollingsworth MSS, Correspondence.

50. Owner's Oath, October 28, 1812 for the Ship *Stapleton*, and Bill of Sale of the Ship *London Packet*, March 16, 1814, NA, Marine Documentation Records; letter, H. Didier, Jr. to John N. D'Arcy in England, June 4, 1814 and December 6, 1814, MHS, Didier Letterbook; Bruchey, *op. cit.*, pp. 357–58, and advertisements in *Federal Gazette*, April 2, November 20, 1813.

51. Certificate of Registry No. 186, November 20, 1811, NA, Marine Documentation Records; letters, Henry Didier, Jr. to John N. D'Arcy, November 19, 1814, MHS, Didier Letterbook; and Hollingsworth and Worthington to Levi Hollingsworth and Sons, Phila., October 28, 1812, HSP, Hollingsworth MSS, Correspondence.

52. Owner's Oath for the Brig *Canada*, July 10, 1815, NA, Marine Documentation Records; Sales of the Cargo of the *Chasseur*, NRC-S, Md. District Admiralty Cases.
53. Master Carpenters' Certificates, 1790–1819, NA, Marine Documentation Records; advertisements in *Federal Gazette*, August 1, 18; 1812, May 3, 1813, and October 25, 1814; and James G. Wilson and John Fiske, eds., *Appleton's Cyclopaedia of American Biography*, 6 vols. (New York: D. Appleton and Company, 1900), I, p. 557.
54. Letter, Hollingsworth and Worthington to Levi Hollingsworth and Son, Phila., September 19, and October 8, 1812, HSP, Hollingsworth MSS, Correspondence; Bill of Sale of the Ship *Stapleton*, October 12, 1812, NA, Marine Documentation Records; *Appleton's Cyclopaedia, op. cit.*, V, p. 496; and Bliss Forbush, *Moses Sheppard: Quaker Philanthropist of Baltimore* (Philadelphia: J. B. Lippincott Company, 1968), p. 36.
55. Letters, T. and S. Hollingsworth and Hollingsworth and Worthington to Levi Hollingsworth and Son, Phila., 1812–1815, HSP, Hollingsworth MSS, Correspondence. Which Hollingsworth is a partner in Hollingsworth and Worthington is uncertain. It seems to be Stephen but may be Francis. T. and S. were the brothers Thomas and Samuel, who came to Baltimore from Elkton, Maryland, after the Revolutionary War. There were nine other brothers.
56. Quoted in *Niles Weekly Register*, April 3, 1813.

CHAPTER FOUR

1. *The Gentleman's Magazine* (London), LXXXII, Part 2, September, 1812.
2. Alfred T. Mahan, *Sea Power in Its Relation to the War of 1812*, 2 vols. (Boston: Little Brown and Company, 1905), I, p. 394.
3. *Niles Weekly Register*, September 5, 1812.
4. Clearances for 1812, NA, Balto. Customs Records.
5. Certificates of Registry for 1811, NA, Marine Documentation Records.
6. The adjustments to be made after the signing of the Treaty of Ghent represented a fifth challenge, and perhaps the response to the Panic of 1819 was a sixth.
7. David Hackett Fischer, *The Revolution of American Conservatism: The Federalist Party in the Era of Jeffersonian Democracy* (New York: Harper and Row, Publishers, 1965), p. 217.
8. Toasts at a Fourth of July celebration at the Pamphilion Hotel, Fells Point, reported in *American*, July 8, 1812. Several investors in private armed vessels were officials at that fête.
9. Letters, Henry Didier, Jr. to John N. D'Arcy in England, October 23, 1814, December 6, 1814, and February 27, 1815, MHS, Didier Letterbook.
10. Letter, Henry Fulford to ———, November 21, 1813, in William Bowner Crane and John Cranwell, *Men of Marque: A History of Private Armed Vessels Out of Baltimore During the War of 1812* (New York: W. W. Norton and Company, 1940), p. 345; also in William M. Marine, *The British Invasion of Maryland, 1812–1815* (Hatboro, Pa.: Tradition Press, 1965, originally published in 1913), pp. 19–21.
11. Baltimore Clearances for 1812 and 1813, NA, Balto. Customs Records. Henry Addington, as 1st Lord Sidmouth, issued the licenses as a member of the cabinet. He served in that body three times between 1805 and 1812.
12. Letters, Hollingsworth and Worthington to Levi Hollingsworth and Son, Phila., July 9, 1812, and June 27, 1812, HSP, Hollingsworth MSS, Correspondence. The firm writing the letter was a Republican flour-exporting house. Its partners pretended to be part of the mob attacking a vessel in order to minimize the damage, but they continued shipping flour to the Peninsula, saying, "if the Rope comes it must be borne."
13. Letter, James H. McCulloch to Albert Gallatin, July 2, 1812, NA, General Records of the Department of Treasury, RG 56, Correspondence of the Secretary of the Treasury with the Collectors of Customs, 1789–1833.
14. Letter, Gallatin to McCulloch, July 15, 1812, *ibid.*; also, letter, William Jones, Acting Secretary of Navy to Henry Dearborn, Collector of Customs at Boston, Massachusetts, September 22, 1813, noting the absence of any United States statute against British licenses, *ibid.*

15. Letters, Hollingsworth and Worthington to Levi Hollingsworth and Son, Phila., January 23, 26, and 29, 1813, HSP, Hollingsworth MSS, Correspondence.
16. Letter, Hollingsworth and Worthington to Levi Hollingsworth and Son, Phila., February 15, 1813, *ibid.*
17. *Federal Gazette*, March 6, 1813.
18. Marine news sections of *Federal Gazette* and *American* June 1812 through February 1813 and clearances from Baltimore for the same period. NA, Balto. Customs Records.
19. Letter, Hollingsworth and Worthington to Levi Hollingsworth and Son, Phila., October 1, 1812, HSP, Hollingsworth MSS, Correspondence.
20. Joshua Barney's Report of the *Rossie's* Cruise, December, 1812, HSP, Joshua Barney Papers, II.
21. *Niles Weekly Register*, March 26, 1814. Editor Niles noted that such prizes were not counted in his prize accounts list and that such prizes would add millions to the total value of prizes taken by American vessels.
22. Letter, Hollingsworth and Worthington to Levi Hollingsworth and Son, Phila., October 1, 1812, HSP, Hollingsworth MSS, Correspondence.
23. *Federal Gazette*, November 9, 1812.
24. *Ibid.*, November 25, 1812.
25. Letters, Hollingsworth and Worthington to the Phoenix Insurance Company of Philadelphia, October 19, and 21, 1812, HSP, Hollingsworth MSS, Correspondence.
26. Letters, Hollingsworth and Worthington to Levi Hollingsworth and Son, Phila., November 12, and August 24, 1812, *ibid.*
27. Letters, T. and S. Hollingsworth to Levi Hollingsworth and Son, Phila., November 12, 1812; Morewood and Forsyth, London, to Levi Hollingsworth and Son, Phila., October 7, 1812; Hollingsworth and Worthington to Levi Hollingsworth and Son, Phila., December 29, 1812; and Owings and Cheston to Levi Hollingsworth and Son, Phila., February 11, 1813, *ibid.*
28. *Federal Gazette*, February 16, 1813 and April 6, 1813.
29. Letters, Hollingsworth and Worthington to Levi Hollingsworth and Son, Phila., March 17, 1813, March 9, and 17, 1813; and T. and S. Hollingsworth to Levi Hollingsworth and Son, Phila., February 14, 1813, HSP, Hollingsworth MSS, Correspondence.
30. Letter, John Hollins to ———, February 28, 1813, University of Virginia, Wilson Cary Nicholas Papers.
31. Letter, Hollingsworth and Worthington to Levi Hollingsworth and Son, Phila., February 17, 1813, HSP, Hollingsworth MSS, Correspondence.
32. *Federal Gazette*, September 3, 13, 14, 1813.
33. Price of Flour at Baltimore from July 1, 1802 to January 1, 1822, *American State Papers, Commerce and Navigation*, II, p. 657.
34. Letter, George P. Stevenson to Wilson Cary Nicholas, July 10, 1813, University of Virginia, Wilson Cary Nicholas Papers.
35. Letters, Hollingsworth and Worthington to Levi Hollingsworth and Son, Phila., April 22, 1813, and May 19, 1813; T. and S. Hollingsworth to Levi Hollingsworth and Son, Phila., October 26, 1813; T. and S. Hollingsworth to Levi Hollingsworth and Son, Phila., May 26, 1814, and March 22, 1814. HSP, Hollingsworth MSS, Correspondence.
36. *Niles Weekly Register*, November 20, 1813.
37. Letters, Hollingsworth and Worthington, November 8, 1813, and Charles Gwinn and Company, November 9, 1813, to Levi Hollingsworth and Son, Phila., HSP, Hollingsworth MSS, Correspondence.
38. Letters, John Hollins to Wilson Cary Nicholas, November 6, 1813 and April 8, 1814; and George P. Stevenson to Wilson Cary Nicholas (his uncle), February 26, 1813, University of Virginia, Wilson Cary Nicholas Papers.
39. Letter, Hollingsworth and Worthington to Levi Hollingsworth and Son, Phila., March 20, 1813, HSP, Hollingsworth MSS, Correspondence.
40. Letter, T. and S. Hollingsworth to Levi Hollingsworth and Son, Phila., June 21, 1812, *ibid.*
41. Letter, Hollingsworth and Worthington to Levi Hollingsworth and Son, Phila., June 1, 1814, *ibid.*
42. For cartel usage, see Anthony G. Dietz, "The Use of Cartel Vessels During the War of 1812," *The American Neptune*, XXVIII, No. 3 (July, 1968), pp. 165–94.

43. Letter, Amos A. Williams to Naval Agent James A. Beatty, and Beatty's Memorandum to Secretary of Navy William Jones, July 29, 1814, NA, General Records of the Department of State, RG 59, Misc. Letters of the Department of State, 1789–1906.
44. United States Department of Commerce, *The Statistical History of the United States from Colonial Times to the Present* (Stamford, Connecticut: Fairfield Publishers, 1965), pp. 538 and 549.
45. Letter, Henry Didier, Jr. to John N. D'Arcy in England, June 4, and December 6, 1814, MHS, Didier Letterbook.
46. "Baltimore," *Hunt's Merchants Magazine*, XXIII, No. 1 (July, 1850), p. 51.
47. Letters, Henry Didier, Jr. to Luke Tiernan, April 20, 1810, and to John N. D'Arcy in England, June 7, 1814, MHS, Didier Letterbook.
48. Letter, Richard H. Douglass to Sanforth and Blunt, London, June 14, 1817, MHS, Douglass Letterbook.
49. Letter, Hollingsworth and Sullivan to Levi Hollingsworth and Son, Phila., January 4, 1813, HSP, Hollingsworth MSS, Correspondence.
50. See Appendix D for Sullivan's holdings.
51. See Appendix D for latecomers, especially Von Kapff and Brune, Lyde Goodwin, Frederick Hurxthal, John W. Stump, and Dennis A. Smith.
52. Richard Peters, ed., *The Public Statutes at Large of the United States of America*, 17 vols. (Boston: Charles C. Little and James Brown, 1848–1873), III, p. 75.
53. See Appendixes A, B, C, and D.
54. Albion and Pope, *op. cit.*, p. 23.
55. *Niles Weekly Register*, October 6, 1814, and May 21, 1814.
56. Coggeshall, *op. cit.*, p. 157.
57. *Niles Weekly Register*, September 17, 1812; October 6, 1814 and July 30, 1814.
58. Letters, Hollingsworth and Worthington to Levi Hollingsworth and Son, Phila., February 17, 1813; T. and S. Hollingsworth, April 8, 1813, and Charles Gwinn and Company, April 9, 1813 to Levi Hollingsworth and Son, Phila., HSP, Hollingsworth MSS, Correspondence; and "Extract of Captain Stafford's Journal on the *Dolphin*" printed in *Federal Gazette*, April 24, 1813.
59. *Federal Gazette*, July 9, 1814.
60. Letter, George P. Stevenson to ——, Richmond, April 8, 1813, University of Virginia, Wilson Cary Nicholas Papers.
61. *Federal Gazette*, December 5, 1812.
62. *Niles Weekly Register*, July 25, 1812.
63. Letter, Captain Thomas Boyle, at Sea, to George P. Stevenson, March 2, 1815, printed in *Niles Weekly Register*, March 25, 1815.
64. *Ibid.*
65. Coggeshall, *op. cit.*, p. 368.
66. Ralph D. Paine, *The Old Merchant Marine: A Chronicle of American Ships and Sailors*, vol. XVII of The Chronicle of America Series, ed., Allen Johnson (New Haven: Yale University Press, 1919), p. 126.
67. *American*, July 29, 1813.
68. Letter, Amos A. Williams to Naval Agent James A. Beatty, and Beatty's Memorandum to Secretary of Navy William Jones, July 29, 1814, NA, General Records of the Department of State, RG 59, Misc. Letters of the Department of State, 1789–1906.
69. Letter, Henry Didier, Jr. to John N. D'Arcy in England, September 23, 1814, MHS, Didier Letterbook.
70. Letter, T. and S. Hollingsworth to Levi Hollingsworth and Son, Phila., August 1, 1814, HSP, Hollingsworth MSS, Correspondence.
71. Marine, *op. cit.* (with an appendix of 11,000 Maryland participants in the War of 1812 completed by Louis H. Dielmand added to the original 1913 edition for the 1965 publication), pp. 195–98.
72. Reports from August 19, to September 13, 1814, MHS, Baltimore Independent Company Record Book.
73. *Niles Weekly Register*, June 5, 1813.
74. Letter, Samuel Smith to Secretary of War John C. Calhoun, February 7, 1818, University of Virginia, Samuel Smith Letterbook; and Frank A. Cassell, *Merchant Congressman in the Young*

Republic: Samuel Smith of Maryland, 1752–1839 (Madison: University of Wisconsin Press, 1971), pp. 188–89.

75. Letter, Samuel Smith to Joseph Anderson, Treasury Department, October 18, 1822, University of Virginia, Smith Letterbook; and Walter Lord, *The Dawn's Early Light* (New York: Norton Company, 1972), p. 272. The owners of those "block vessels" sought compensation from Congress after the war.
76. Bourne, *op. cit.*, p. 281.
77. Letter, Isaac McKim, Aide de Camp to Major General Samuel Smith, to J. P. Pleasants, May 1, 1813, Library of Congress, Samuel Smith Papers.
78. Billeting List, September —, 1814, *ibid.*
79. Letters of September and October, 1814, *ibid.*
80. Letter, John W. Stump to Major General Samuel Smith, October 27, 1814, *ibid.*; and Cassell, *op. cit.*, pp. 181–209.
81. Marine, *op. cit.*, pp. 245–47; and letter, G. T. Warfield to Levi Hollingsworth and Son, Phila., September 14, 1814, HSP, Hollingsworth MSS, Correspondence.
82. Marine, *op. cit.*, pp. 195–98; and military notices in the *Federal Gazette* and *American* 1813 and 1814. For identification of the active investors' military positions, see Appendix E.
83. Letters, Samuel Hollingsworth to Levi Hollingsworth and Son, Phila., August 26, 1814, and August 10, 1814, HSP, Hollingsworth MSS, Correspondence.
84. *Niles Weekly Register*, February 5, 1814; August 15, 1812, November 6, 1813, and other dates.
85. Thomas Hart Benton, *Abridgements of the Debates of Congress*, 16 vols. (New York: Appleton and Company, 1860), V, pp. 358–59.
86. George P. Stevenson *et al.*, "Memorial of the Merchants and Shipowners of Baltimore," February 4, 1814, in *American State Papers, Naval Affairs*, I, p. 300.
87. *Ibid.*
88. Benton, *op. cit.*, IV, p. 704.
89. Story, *op. cit.* p. 587.
90. D. C. McClelland, *The Achieving Society* (Princeton: Princeton University Press, 1961),pp. 233–37.
91. See Appendix E for the activities of the active investors.
92. Charleston had attracted a privateering interest group in the 1790s. See Jackson, *op. cit.*, pp. 23–24.
93. Cassell, *op. cit.*, pp. 56, 49, 75, 117, 127, 142, 154, and 189; and Dorothy Marie Brown, "Party Battles and Beginnings in Maryland, 1786–1812" (Ph.D. diss., Georgetown University, 1961), pp. 111 and 140.
94. Cassell, *op. cit.*, pp. 139, 141 and 106.
95. *Ibid.*, pp. 177–209.
96. *American*, August 18, 1812.

CHAPTER FIVE

1. See Appendix B and C for the occupations of the marginal and moderate investors.
2. Estimate based on a $40,000 privateer with anywhere from four to forty shares and a $25,000 letter-of-marque trader with anywhere from five to twenty-five shares. One scheme using shares of $500 was advertised in *American*, June 25, 1812.
3. Edward Pessen, "The Egalitarian Myth and the American Social Reality; Wealth, Mobility and Equality in the Era of the Common Man," *American Historical Review*, LXXVI, No. 4 (October, 1971), pp. 1024–25, and pp. 1034–35.
4. Letter, Henry Didier, Jr. to John N. D'Arcy in England, June 7, 1814, MHS, Didier Letterbook.
5. Application for Commission No. 456, September 1, 1812, NA, Navy Privateer Records, and *Federal Gazette*, July 2, 1812.
6. Letter, Hollingsworth and Sullivan to Levi Hollingsworth and Son of Phila., May 13, 1813,

HSP, Hollingsworth MSS, Correspondence. The Hollingsworths of Elkton, Philadelphia, and Baltimore were all in the flour business to varying degrees and were all related.

7. Advertisement in *Federal Gazette*, November 3, July 7, 1812, and Bill of Sale of *America*, December 23, 1812, NA, Balto. Customs Records.

8. *Federal Gazette*, October 10, 1812, and October 7, 1814, and Griffith, *op. cit.*, p. 180.

9. Letter, Hollingsworth and Worthington, April 13, 1813, to Levi Hollingsworth and Son, Phila., HSP, Hollingsworth MSS, Correspondence.

10. Charles B. Tiernan, *The Tiernans and Other Families* (Baltimore: William J. Gallery and Company, 1901), pp. 56–58. The fact that a number of Baltimore dry goods merchants initially settled in Hagerstown, Maryland, suggests that they thought they could handle the western trade at that place. Their movement to Baltimore indicates that one did better at the entrepôt itself. Tobacco and flour people moving to Baltimore from neighboring towns may have found proximity to shipping advantageous for outgoing and return cargoes. *Representative Men of Maryland and District of Columbia*, pp. 497–98; and advertisements in *Federal Gazette*, July 8, and October 17, 27, 31, 1812; April 3, June 11, 22, and July 1, 1813.

11. Application for Commission No. 1119, January 24, 1815, NA, Navy Privateer Records VI; also William Patterson, "Preliminary Introductions to My Will," MHS, Patterson Account Books; and letter, T. and S. Hollingsworth to Levi Hollingsworth and Son, Phila., February 17, 1814, HSP, Hollingsworth MSS, Correspondence.

12. *B D*, 1812, and 1814; and Expenses for the Prize Ship *Braganaza* (wharfage bill), October 10, 1812, NRC-S, Md. District Admiralty Cases.

13. Advertisement in *Federal Gazette*, October 10, 1812.

14. Letters, Charles Gwinn to Levi Hollingsworth and Son, Phila., 1812–1815, HSP, Hollingsworth MSS, Correspondence.

15. Notice in *Federal Gazette*, March 17, 1813.

16. Bray Hammond, *Banks and Politics in America: From the Revolution to the Civil War* (Princeton: Princeton University Press, 1957), pp. 251–285; and Fritz Redlick, "William Jones' Resignation from the Presidency of the Second Bank of the U.S.," *Pennsylvania Magazine of History and Biography*, LXXI (July, 1947), pp. 203–47.

17. Letter, David Baillee Warden, acting consul-general at Paris, July 19, 1813, to the Duke of Bassano, MHS, Warden Letterbook, Book A; and Log of the Brig *Pelican*, Prize to the Privateer *Lawrence* of Baltimore, April 21, 1814 to June 3, 1814, MHS, Ships' Logs and Papers.

18. Advertisements in *Federal Gazette*, October 16, 1812, July 14, 1814.

19. Didier Notebook, 1815–1817, MHS.

20. Bruchey, *op. cit.*, p. 19.

21. Letter, Robert Oliver to Samuel and Robert Purviance, January 25, 1785, University of Virginia, Samuel Smith Papers.

22. Letter, William Patterson to Wilson Cary Nicholas, June 3, 1808, University of Virginia, Wilson Cary Nicholas Papers.

23. J. MacKenzie and A. Glennie in Account Current with John Hollins, December 16, 1814, MHS, McBlair Papers.

24. Letter, Charles Gwinn and Company to Levi Hollingsworth and Son, Phila., May 16, 1814, HSP, Hollingsworth MSS, Correspondence.

25. Self-audit of April 1, 1822 for 1819, MHS, McBlair Papers.

26. Entry of April 6, 1820 in Allan Nevins, ed., *The Diary of John Quincy Adams, 1794–1845: American Political, Social and Intellectual Life from Washington to Polk* (New York: Longman Green and Company, 1928), p. 238; and letter, John Hollins to ———, November 6, 1815, University of Virginia, Wilson Cary Nicholas Papers.

27. Letter, Samuel Smith to Eliza Thompson, March 25, 1815, University of Virginia, Smith Letterbook and MHS, Smith Letterbooks, I, II, and III.

28. Cassell, *op. cit.*, pp. 42, 103, and 102.

29. Bruchey, *op. cit.*, p. 298; and for the specie trade, see Vincent Nolte, *Fifty Years in Both Hemispheres or Reminiscences of the Life of a Former Merchant* (New York: Redfield, 1854), pp. 95–97.

30. Letter, Samuel Smith to Mary B. Mansfield, London, June 8, 1810, University of Virginia, Samuel Smith Papers.

31. Letter, S. Smith and Buchanan "In Senate" to the Secretary of State, February 23, 1815, NA, General Records of the Department of State, RG 59, Misc. Letters of the Department of State, 1789–1906.

32. Letters, Samuel Smith to Mary B. Mansfield, London, October 25, 1811, and Samuel Smith to J. MacKenzie and A. Glennie, London, November 2, 1802, University of Virginia, Samuel Smith Papers.

33. Nevins, ed., *op. cit.*, p. 197.

34. James A. Buchanan's answer to Interrogations by the Creditors of S. Smith and Buchanan, June 1, 1821, University of Virginia, Samuel Smith Papers.

35. William Patterson, Introduction to My Will, MHS, Patterson Papers; and Bruchey, *op. cit.*, p. 298.

36. Letter, John and Samuel Smith to Joseph Yates, Manchester, June 5, 1787, MHS, Smith Letterbooks, II.

37. Letter, James H. McCulloch to Albert Gallatin, December 24, 1811, NA, General Records of the Department of Treasury, RG 56, Correspondence of the Treasury with the Collectors of Customs, 1789–1833.

38. *Representative Men of Maryland and District of Columbia*, p. 248.

39. Letters, Richard H. Douglass to Hannibal Price, September 20, and December 23, 1817, MHS, Douglass Letterbook.

40. Nevins, ed., *op. cit.*, p. 238.

41. Entries of December 1813, 1814, and 1815 in Peter Arnold Karthaus and Company Journal, MHR, Karthaus Accounts.

42. Statement of Advances Retained from the Crew of the Schooner *Kemp* to the Credit of the Owners of Said Vessel, undated, MHR, Peter Arnold Karthaus and Company Shipping Accounts.

43. Letters, Henry Didier, Jr. in London to D'Arcy, Dodge and Company, Haiti, May 15, 1809; to Bernard Von Kapff, Baltimore, May 29, 1809; to Luke Tiernan and Company, May 31, 1809; in Haiti to Greaves, Sharp and Fisher, London, June 6, 1810; to John N. D'Arcy in England, July 28, 1810; and to D'Arcy, Dodge and Company, Haiti, December 1, 1811, MHS, Didier Letterbook.

44. *Federal Gazette*, October 26, 1812. At a low price of twenty cents per pound, the coffee alone was worth $200,000.

45. Letter, Hollingsworth and Worthington to Levi Hollingsworth and Son, Phila., May 9, 1814, HSP, Hollingsworth MSS, Correspondence.

46. Letter, Henry Didier, Jr. to John N. D'Arcy in England, June 7, 1814, MHS, Didier Letterbook.

47. Nevins, ed., *op. cit.*, p. 197.

48. Letters, Henry Didier, Jr. to John N. D'Arcy in England, February 9, and September 23, 1814, MHS, Didier Letterbook.

49. Letter, Hollingsworth and Worthington to Levi Hollingsworth and Son, Phila., April 13, 1813, HSP, Hollingsworth MSS, Correspondence.

50. Letter, Levi Hollingsworth, Baltimore, to Levi Hollingsworth and Son, Phila., May 17, 1813, *ibid.*

51. Petition of Levi Hollingsworth (of Baltimore) to the House Committee of Commerce and Manufacturing, February 6, 1813, *American State Papers, Finance*, II, p. 602.

52. Letter, Levi Hollingsworth, Baltimore, to Levi Hollingsworth and Son, Phila., December 22, 1812, HSP, Hollingsworth MSS, Correspondence.

53. Letter, Henry Didier, Jr. to D'Arcy, Dodge and Company, Haiti, May 13, 1811, MHS, Didier Letterbook.

54. Stevenson Accounts, undated, MHS, McBlair Papers.

55. Letter, John C. Pawson to William Pawson, October 26, 1815, MHS, Pawson Papers.

56. Letters, George P. Stevenson to Wilson Cary Nicholas, Richmond, April 8, March 9, May 16, 1813, and August 29, and March 9, 1815, University of Virginia, Wilson Cary Nicholas

Papers. Hemp shipments from Nicholas's Ohio River plantation were shipped via Pittsburgh to Baltimore where they were sold by Stevenson. Both men counted on the blockade driving up the price because the preferred Russian hemp was not available to the numerous Baltimore ropemakers.

57. Various letters, MHS, McBlair Papers.
58. Crane and Cranwell, *op. cit.*, p. 346. Fulford thought he had "a great deal afloat" considering his resources.
59. *B D*, 1812–1815.
60. Letter, Henry Didier, Jr. to John N. D'Arcy in England, May 18, 1815, MHS, Didier Letterbook.
61. Letter, Henry Didier, Jr. to D'Arcy, Dodge and Company, Haiti, December 29, 1810, *ibid.*
62. Letter, Hollingsworth and Worthington to Levi Hollingsworth and Son, Phila., March 10, 1814, HSP, Hollingsworth MSS, Correspondence; Douglass C. North, *The Economic Growth of the United States, 1790–1860* (New York: W. W. Norton, 1966), pp. 57–58; and Walter B. Smith and Arthur H. Cole, *Fluctuations in American Business, 1790–1860* (Cambridge, Mass.: Harvard University Press, 1935), p. 28.
63. Letter, Hollingsworth and Worthington to Levi Hollingsworth and Son, Phila., March 10, 1814, HSP, Hollingsworth MSS, Correspondence.
64. Letters, Henry Didier, Jr. to D'Arcy, Dodge and Company, Haiti, November 7, 1811; to John N. D'Arcy in England, June 7, and December 14, 1814; and to D'Arcy, Dodge and Company, Haiti, December 29, 1810, MHS, Didier Letterbook.
65. Cassell, *op. cit.*, p. 42.
66. See Appendix E (A Status Inventory for the Active Investors Around the Time of the War of 1812).
67. *Federal Gazette*, September 28, 1813.
68. See Appendix E.
69. Letter, John Hollins to Wilson Cary Nicholas, November 6, 1813, University of Virginia, Wilson Cary Nicholas Papers.
70. Letter, Hollingsworth and Worthington to Levi Hollingsworth and Son, Phila., November 23, 1812, HSP, Hollingsworth MSS, Correspondence.
71. *American*, May 5, 1814. Karthaus was advertising for labor. The enterprise must have had a degree of success as the town can still be located on a map of Pennsylvania (in Clearfield County).
72. Letter, George P. Stevenson to Wilson Cary Nicholas, May 16, 1813, University of Virginia, Wilson Cary Nicholas Papers.
73. See Appendix E.
74. Bouldin, *op. cit.*, p. 107.
75. Russell Blaine Nye, *The Cultural Life of the New Nation, 1776–1830* (New York: Harper and Row, 1960), p. 106.
76. Yale Brozen, "Determinants of Entrepreneurial Ability," *Social Research*, XXI (October, 1954), p. 349.
77. *Federal Gazette*, September 1, 1812, and April 9, 1813.
78. Edith Rossiter Bevans, "Harlem," typewritten paper in the Maryland Room, Enoch Pratt Free Library, Baltimore, Maryland.
79. Letter, John Gibson to Eliza Gibson, Frederick, Maryland, June 27, 1814, MHS, Grundy-Gibson Papers.
80. Scharf, *Chronicles*, p. 74–75.
81. Amy D'Arcy Wetmore, "Some Old Country Houses of Old-Time Baltimoreans," *The Sun* (Baltimore), November 11, 1906; and Eugene Lemoine Didier, "The Social Athens of America," *Harpers Magazine*, LXV (June, 1882), pp. 30–31.
82. Mayer Brantz, *Baltimore, Past and Present* (Baltimore: Richardson and Bennett, 1871), p. 465; and Robert L. Raley, "The Baltimore Country House 1785–1815" (Masters' thesis, The University of Delaware, 1959), pp. 62–68, 147–48.
83. Letter, Samuel Smith to Mary B. Mansfield, London, September 12, 1810, University of Virginia, Samuel Smith Papers.

84. Warner and Hanna's Map of Baltimore, 1801, republished in facsimile by the Peabody Institute Library, Baltimore, 1947. About fifty such country houses were illustrated on this map. See also Richard H. Howland and Eleanor P. Spencer, *Architecture of Baltimore* (Baltimore: The Johns Hopkins Press, 1953), passim.

85. William Stump, "Sketch of John Hollins," *The Sun* (Baltimore), September 25, 1949; and William Boyd Buchanan, "1852 Recollections," *The Baltimore News*, January 25, 1902.

86. Letter, Henry Didier, Jr. to John N. D'Arcy in England, December 6, 1814, MHS, Didier Letterbook.

87. *American* and *Federal Gazette*, announcements, 1813–1814.

88. Entries for 1812–1815, MHS, Henry Thompson's Diary, III and IV.

89. Letters for 1812–1815, MHS, Didier Letterbook; and HSP, Hollingsworth MSS, Correspondence.

90. Letters, Mary Grundy to George Carr Grundy in London, December 8, 1813, MHS, Grundy-Gibson Papers; and from Henry Didier, Jr. to D'Arcy, Dodge and Company, September 11, 1811, MHS, Didier Letterbook.

91. Letter, Samuel Hollingsworth to Levi Hollingsworth and Son, Phila., June 27, 1814, HSP, Hollingsworth MSS, Correspondence.

92. Wetmore, *op. cit.*

93. Letters, Mary Grundy to George Carr Grundy in Liverpool, December 8, and 9, 1813, and January 7, 1814, MHS, Grundy-Gibson Papers.

94. Prize Auction Accounts, 1812–1815, NRC-S, Md. District Admiralty Cases.

95. Letter, James H. McCulloch, Collector of Customs, to William H. Crawford, Secretary of the Treasury, February 8, 1817, NA, General Records of the Department of Treasury, RG 56, Correspondence of the Secretary of the Treasury to the Collectors of Customs, 1789–1833. This description of the city was related to a search for a new Customs House site.

96. *B D*, 1810, 1812, 1814; and advertisements in *Federal Gazette* and *American*, 1812 to 1815. See Plate II for locations.

97. *Niles Weekly Register*, July 11, 1812.

98. Quotation in *Niles Weekly Register*, December 24, 1814.

99. Letter, T. and S. Hollingsworth to Levi Hollingsworth and Son, Phila., June 7, 1812, HSP, Hollingsworth MSS, Correspondence.

100. Cassell, *op. cit.*, pp. 57, 139.

101. Letters, Samuel Smith to Mary B. Mansfield in London, July 19, 1810, May 22, 1811, and November 6, 1811, University of Virginia, Samuel Smith Papers.

102. Letter, T. and S. Hollingsworth to Levi Hollingsworth and Son, Phila., July 4, 1812, HSP, Hollingsworth MSS, Correspondence. For Smith's policies at a national level see Cassell, *op. cit.*; Norman J. Risjord, *The Old Republicans: Southern Conservatism in the Age of Jefferson* (New York: Columbia University Press, 1965), p. 116; Frank A. Cassell, "Samuel Smith: Merchant Politician 1792–1812" (Ph.D. diss., Northwestern University, 1968); and John S. Pancake, "The Invisibles: A Chapter in the Opposition to President Madison," *Journal of Southern History*, XXI (February, 1955), pp. 17–35.

103. Cassell, *Merchant Congressman in the Young Republic*, p. 71.

104. Letter, William Patterson to Wilson Cary Nicholas, December 1, 1808, Library of Congress, Wilson Cary Nicholas Papers.

105. Letter, John Hollins to Wilson Cary Nicholas, April 5, 1808, *ibid.*

106. Quoted in Irving Brant, *James Madison, Commander-in-Chief, 1812–1836* (Indianapolis: Bobbs-Merrill Company, 1961), p. 105. For another Barney criticism of Samuel Smith, see letter, Joshua Barney to James Monroe, October 30, 1812, NA, General Records of the Department of State, RG 59, Misc. Letters of the Department of State, 1789–1906.

107. Henry Marie Breckenridge, "Memoirs" in *Baltimore As Seen by Visitors 1783–1860*, ed. Raphael Semmes, Studies in Maryland History, No. 2 (Baltimore: Maryland Historical Society, 1953), p. 43.

108. Letter, T. and S. Hollingsworth to Levi Hollingsworth and Son, Phila., October 11, 1812, HSP, Hollingsworth MSS, Correspondence.

109. Benton, *op. cit.*, IV, p. 711.

110. Letter, Hollingsworth and Worthington to Levi Hollingsworth and Son, Phila., September 6,

1813, HSP, Hollingsworth MSS, Correspondence; and *Federal Gazette*, September 4, 1813.

111. See Appendix F for political offices and loyalties; and Scharf, *Chronicles*, p. 305–06.

112. Letters, T. and S. Hollingsworth (Federalists) to Levi Hollingsworth and Son, Phila., September 23, 1813, and January 3, 1814; September 28, and 23, 1812; HSP, Hollingsworth MSS, Correspondence.

113. Letters, T. and S. Hollingsworth to Levi Hollingsworth and Son, Phila., June 7, 1812, and January 12, 1813; and Levi Hollingsworth of Baltimore to Levi Hollingsworth and Son, Phila., September 21, 1814, *ibid.*

114. Letters, Hollingsworth and Worthington to Levi Hollingsworth and Son, Phila., October 1, 1813, February 20, 1815, April 3, 1813 and May 6, 1813, *ibid.*

115. *Federal Gazette*, June 19, 1813.

116. Kendric Charles Babcock, *The Rise of American Nationality, 1811–1819*, Vol. XIII of The American Nation: A History, ed. Albert Bushnell Hart (New York: Harper and Brothers, 1906), p. 71.

117. Letter, Mary Grundy to George Carr Grundy, England, August 28 and September 8, 1812, MHS, Grundy-Gibson Papers.

118. Letter, T. and S. Hollingsworth to Levi Hollingsworth and Son, Phila., September 8, 1812, HSP, Hollingsworth MSS, Correspondence.

119. Letter, Charles Carroll of Carrollton to Charles Carroll, Jr., August —, 1812, in Kate Mason Rowland, *The Life of Charles Carroll of Carrollton, 1737–1832, With His Correspondence and Public Papers*, 2 vols. (New York: G. P. Putnam and Sons, 1898), II, p. 291.

120. Fischer, *op. cit.*, p. 357.

121. Letter, T. and S. Hollingsworth to Levi Hollingsworth and Son, Phila., October 7, 1812, HSP, Hollingsworth MSS, Correspondence.

122. Fischer, *op. cit.*, p. 368.

123. Entry of June 18, 1813, MHS, Henry Thompson's Diary, IV.

124. Letters, T. and S. Hollingsworth to Levi Hollingsworth and Son, Phila., October 14, 1814, June 30, 1813, April 14, 1814, February 14, 1813, and December 22, 1812, HSP, Hollingsworth MSS, Correspondence.

125. MHS, Didier Letterbook, 1812–1815; MHS, Thompson Diary, July 28, 1812, October 10, and 24, November 14, 20, and 25, 1812, III; and April 26, June 26, February 3, 1815, IV.

126. Letter, Charles Gwinn to Levi Hollingsworth and Son, Phila., December 1, 1814, HSP, Hollingsworth MSS, Correspondence.

127. Letter, T. and S. Hollingsworth to Levi Hollingsworth and Son, Phila., December 8, 1812, *ibid.*

128. Letter, Henry Didier, Jr. to John N. D'Arcy in England, October 23, 1814, MHS, Didier Letterbook.

129. Letters, T. and S. Hollingsworth to Levi Hollingsworth and Son, Phila., February 14, 1814, and November 22, 1813, HSP, Hollingsworth MSS, Correspondence.

130. Letters, Alexander C. Hanson to Robert Goodloe Harper, October 11, November 2, and 7, 1814, MHS, Harper-Pennington Papers.

131. *Federal Gazette*, May 5, 1813; and Libero Marx Renzulli, "Maryland Federalism: 1787–1819" (Ph.D. diss., University of Virginia, 1962), p. 378.

132. Dinner parties, 1812–1815, MHS, Henry Thompson's Diary, March 25, October 5, November 4, 1812, January 16, and March 20, 1813, III; May 23, November 14, and 17, 1813, and April 5, May 5, and 11, December 2, 1814, January 27, and February 9, 1815, IV. Samuel Smith, the Williamses, Hollinses, Pattersons, Levi Hollingsworth, the Steretts, Didier, and others came to dinner with the Federalists in groups.

CHAPTER SIX

1. *American*, June 25, 1812.

2. Story, *op. cit.*, pp. 261, 272.

3. *Ibid.*, p. 124.

4. Letter, Henry Didier, Jr. to John N. D'Arcy in England, June 7, 1814, and October 23, 1814, MHS, Didier Letterbook.
5. Entry of April 7, 1814, MHR, Peter Karthaus and Company Shipping Accounts.
6. Story, *op. cit.*, pp. 6, 67, 620–35, and 107. Within one firm, share partnerships were difficult to calculate as it was an accepted practice in England and America for individuals to use their firm's name even though their partners were not investors in a particular venture. In commissioned vessels the owners' oath sometimes straightened out such matters. Depositions of clerks and merchants in the *United States* v. *the Ship* Severn, December 12, 1807, NA-S, Records of the United States Attorneys and Marshals, RG 118, Decrees in Admiralty 1806–1808.
7. Story, *op. cit.*, pp. 587–630.
8. Entry of October 28, 1813, MHS, Despeaux Account Book.
9. Bill of Sale of the *Tom*, August 1, 1812, NA, Marine Documentation Records, RG 41. The *Tom* was constructed by John Price at Baltimore in May, June, and July of 1812 for Gerrard Wilson, Master Carpenter Certificate, July 30, 1812, *ibid.*
10. *Federal Gazette*, July 1, 1812.
11. Bills of Sales of Vessels, 1812–1815, NA, Marine Documentation Records.
12. *Ibid.*, and *Federal Gazette* and *American*, 1812–1815.
13. The Owners of the Privateeer Schooner *Highflyer* in Account Current with Philip Moore, clerk of the District Court, December 7, 1812, NRC-S, Md. District Admiralty Cases, and for the *Nonsuch*, applications for Commission No. 1, June 29, 1812, NA, Navy Privateer Records, VI.
14. Letter, T. K. Jones and Company, Boston, to Joseph Despeaux, September 22, 1812, MHS, Joseph Despeaux Papers. The ship involved was the *Alexander*, built and formerly owned by Despeaux.
15. Proceeds of the Brig *William* and Cargo, May 22, 1815, MHS, Ships' Papers, *Decatur*.
16. Bill of Sale of the *Tom*, August 1, 1812, NA, Marine Documentation Records.
17. Bill of Sale of the *Philaeni*, April 1, 1813, *ibid.*
18. Letters, Richard H. Douglass to Joel Vickers, John S. Hollins, George P. Stevenson, James Bosley, William T. Graham, and Charles Gwinn, one undated, but marked as "paid" in January and February of 1814, February 5, 25, and March 7, 1814, MHS, Ships' Logs and Papers.
19. Master Carpenter's Certificate for the *Lawrence*, November 27, 1813, NA, Marine Documentation Records.
20. Bill of Sale of the *Lawrence*, April 17, 1815, *ibid.*
21. Undated entry in the Despeaux Account Book, MHS.
22. Story, *op. cit.*, p. 594.
23. Letters, Hollingsworth and Worthington to Levi Hollingsworth and Son, Phila., July 7, 1812, HSP, Hollingsworth MSS, Correspondence; also, Secretary of Treasury Albert Gallatin to President Madison, June —, 1812, in Henry Adams, ed., *The Writings of Albert Gallatin*, 3 vols. (Philadelphia: J. B. Lippincott and Company, 1879), I, p. 521. The frigate *Constitution* stopped the Baltimore ship *Diana* on July 19, 1812 while she was carrying $80,000 in specie from Lisbon for Baltimore. Amos A. Evans, USN, *Journal Kept on Board the Frigate Constitution, 1812* (Lincoln, Mass.: Reprinted for William D. Sawtell from *The Pennsylvania Magazine of History and Biography*, 1967), p. 157.
24. Notes on the Bills of Sale of the *Bordeaux Packet*, February 25, 1813, NA, Marine Documentation Records, RG 41.
25. *Annals of Congress*, 12th Congress, 1st Session (Washington: Gales and Seaton, 1853), pp. 2322–23.
26. *Ibid.*, p. 2327.
27. Applications for Letters-of-Marque and Reprisal, 1812–1815, NA, Balto. Customs Records; War of 1812 Papers; and Navy Privateer Records.
28. Application for Commission No. 896, September 24, 1813, NA, Navy Privateer Records, VI.
29. *American*, June 25, 1812.
30. Application for a commission for the *Rapid*, October 12, 1813, NA, Navy Privateer Records, VI.
31. Applications for Letters-of-Marque and Reprisal, 1812–1815, NA, Balto. Customs Records;

War of 1812 Papers; Navy Privateer Records; and application for No. 969, February 26, 1814, War of 1812 Papers.

32. *Annals of Congress*, 12th Congress, 1st Session, pp. 2327–28.
33. Applications for Letters-of-Marque and Reprisal, 1812–1815, NA, Balto. Customs Records, War of 1812 Papers, and Navy Privateer Records.
34. Bonds for Letters-of-Marque and Reprisal, 1812 (six months), NA, Balto. Customs Records.
35. Story, *op. cit.*, p. 62.
36. Bonds for Letters-of-Marque and Reprisal, 1812 (six months), NA, Balto. Customs Records.
37. *Niles Weekly Register*, November 5, 1814.
38. Letter, Robert Cochran, Collector at Wilmington, North Carolina, to James Monroe, December 8, 1814, NA, Navy Privateer Records, V.
39. Letter, James Williams to James Monroe, December 16, 1814, NA, General Records of the Department of State, RG 59, Misc. Letters of the Department of State, 1789–1906.
40. Returned Commission No. 1057, Suspended April 11, 1815, NA, Balto. Customs Records, RG 36.
41. Letter, Secretary of State James Monroe to Robert Cochran, Collector at Wilmington, North Carolina, November 25, 1814, in *Niles Weekly Register*, December 24, 1814.
42. An Act Vesting in the President of the United States the Power of Retaliation, March 3, 1813, in Peters, ed., *op. cit.*, I, p. 829.
43. Extracts from *The Evening Post* (New York), and *Courier* (Charleston), reprinted in *The Gentleman's Magazine* (London), LXXIV, II, December, 1814.
44. *Federal Gazette*, March 8, 1813.
45. Letter, Captain J. A. Brush, Kingston, Jamaica, to James Monroe, May 19, 1814, NA, General Records of the Department of State, RG 59, Misc. Letters of the Department of State, 1789–1906.
46. Extract from a New York newspaper of August 20, 1812, quoted in Coggeshall, *op. cit.*, p. 60.
47. Bond No. 1 for the *Nonsuch*, June 29, 1812, NA, Balto. Customs Records, Bonds for Letters-of-Marque and Reprisal, 1812.
48. Owners and Master Oaths of Ownership and Citizenship, 1812–1815, NA, Marine Documentation Records. These forms were sometimes for owners alone or masters alone but most were for both as the collector used whatever forms he had available. The citizenship oath requirement was established in "An Act to Amend an Act Entitled, 'An Act Concerning the Registering and Recording of Ships and Vessels,'" March 27, 1804, in Peters, ed., *op. cit.*, II, pp. 296–97.
49. Certificate of Registry No. 51, April 1, 1812, NA, Marine Documentation Records.
50. Certificate of Registry No. 70, July 23, 1812, and Certificate of Registry No. 2, January 1, 1812, and No. 91, September 12, 1812, *ibid.*
51. Certificate of Registry No. 26, March 2, 1812, *ibid.* All surviving registers were called in for replacement by "An act authorizing the Secretary of the Treasury to provide new Certificates of Registry" of March 3, 1813, as new and free certificates were to be provided after December of 1814, Peters, ed., *op. cit.*, II, p. 818. Other normal shipping requirements included a registry bond of $1,200.00 for vessels from 100 to 200 tons, $1,600.00 for those from 200 to 300 tons, and $2,000.00 for those over 300 tons demanded in "An act concerning the registering and recording of ships or vessels," December 31, 1792, Peters, ed., *op. cit.*, I, pp. 287–99.
52. Bonds for Letters-of-Marque and Reprisal, 1812, NA, Balto. Customs Records. Despite the collection's title, these non-letter-of-marque bonds are included.
53. Periodic Lists of Commissions for Private Armed Vessels Sent from the Department of State, NA, Navy Privateer Records, V; and for requests for additional blank commissions, III.
54. Returned Commission No. 460, NA, Balto. Customs Records.
55. Copies in NA, War of 1812 Papers and in *Annals of Congress*, 12th Congress, 1st Session, pp. 2329.
56. *Niles Weekly Register*, April 15, 1815.
57. *Federal Gazette*, August 18, 1814.
58. Coggeshall, *op. cit.*, p. 116.
59. *Federal Gazette*, August 13, 1812, and extract from a New York newspaper in Coggeshall, *op. cit.*, p. 60.

60. Letter, James Monroe to Secretary of Navy Paul Hamilton, July 18, 1812, NA, Navy Privateer Records, V.
61. Prize Accounts, 1812–1815, NRC-S, Md. District Admiralty Cases; and undated resumé of Baltimore commissions, NA, Navy Privateer Records, II.
62. Story, *op. cit.*, pp. 588–94.
63. Letter-of-Attorney by the Owners of the *Pike*, May 28, 1814, NRC-S, Md. District Court Admiralty Cases.
64. Story, *op. cit.*, pp. 601–07.
65. For documents on Barney's Revolutionary, French, and *Rossie* experience, see HSP, Joshua Barney Papers, 1782–1818, 2 vols. For a sketch of his career, see James Fenimore Cooper, *The History of the Navy of the United States of America*, 2 vols. (London: Richard Bentley, 1839), II, pp. 358–60.
66. Report of Cruise to Secretary of State, undated, HSP, Joshua Barney Papers, II.
67. Coggeshall, *op. cit.*, xlvii.
68. Letter, Amos A. Williams to Naval Agent James Beatty, July 29, 1814, NA, General Records of the Department of State, RG 59, Misc. Letters of the Department of State, 1789–1906.
69. Owners and Masters Citizenship Oaths (mixed forms), 1810–1818, NA, Marine Documentation Records.
70. *Ibid.*
71. *Ibid.*, and Abstracts of Registers of Vessels, 1789–1812, NA, Marine Documentation Records; and Entrances and Clearances, 1782–1824, NA, Balto. Customs Records.
72. Baltimore Endorsements of Changes of Masters, 1800–1815, NA, Marine Documentation Records.
73. Clearance Certificate, July 11, 1812, HSP, Joshua Barney Papers, II.

CHAPTER SEVEN

1. *American*, July 10, 1812.
2. *Federal Gazette*, September 15, 1813, and October 26, 1814.
3. *Federal Gazette*, November 11, 1812.
4. Master Carpenters' Certificates, 1790–1819, NA, Marine Documentation Records.
5. *American*, June 16, 1812, and September 9, 1812.
6. *Federal Gazette*, September 8, 1812, and September 28, 1813.
7. *Ibid.*, August 25, 1813, and October 3, 1814. The *Governor Shelby*, 186 tons or 1,000 barrels, was advertised as for sale in New York, *American*, May 27, 1814.
8. Bill of Sale of *La Venus*, December 13, 1814; Application for a commission for the *Venus*, December 21, 1814; Letter-of-Marque Bond for the *Venus*, December 21, 1814; and letter, John Gooding, Baltimore, to Stephen Pleasanton, Department of State, December 21, 1814, all in NA, Navy Privateer Records, VI.
9. Hutchins, *op. cit.*, p. 78.
10. Baltimore Certificates of Registry, 1811–1815, and Master Carpenters' Certificates, 1790–1819, NA, Marine Documentation Records.
11. Prize Lists, *Niles Weekly Register*, 1812–1815, and Master Carpenters' Certificates, 1790–1819, NA, Marine Documentation Records.
12. Baltimore Certificates of Registry, 1800–1820, NA, Marine Documentation Records.
13. *Ibid.*, and Master Carpenters' Certificates, 1790–1819, NA, Marine Documentation Records.
14. Master Carpenters' Certificates, 1790–1819, NA, Marine Documentation Records.
15. Hutchins, *op. cit.*, p. 128.
16. *Ibid.* Salnave's *Expedition* of 320 carpenter's tons was said to be a "complete model and the largest of her rig in the United States" at the time, *American*, August 19, 1812. The *Chasseur*, *Mammoth*, and others exceeded her size later.
17. Bourne, *op. cit.*, pp. 274–75. This work was based on Kemp's account books, which were not located for use in this study.
18. Master Carpenters' Certificates, 1790–1819, NA, Marine Documentation Records.

19. Bourne, *op. cit.*, p. 279. The Chesapeake Maritime Museum at St. Michael's, Md. has a model of the *Surprise*.
20. Master Carpenters' Certificates, 1790–1819, and Certificates of Registry, 1810–1815, NA, Marine Documentation Records.
21. Hutchins, *op. cit.*, pp. 185–86 and 127.
22. Distribution Defrayed on the Schooner *Amelia*, November, 1813 to April 1, 1814, MHR, Peter Arnold Karthaus and Company Shipping Accounts.
23. Bills of Sale of Vessels, 1812–1815, NA, Marine Documentation Records.
24. *Niles Weekly Register*, April 30, 1814.
25. Bills of Sale of Vessels, 1812–1815, NA, Marine Documentation Records.
26. *Federal Gazette*, December 1, 1812.
27. Distribution for the Privateer *Kemp*, October and November, 1814, and Statement for the Officers and Crew of the Private Armed Schooner *Kemp*, undated, MHR, Peter Arnold Karthaus and Company Shipping Accounts.
28. Bills of Sale of Vessels, 1812–1815, NA, Marine Documentation Records.
29. *Niles Weekly Register*, April 30, 1814.
30. Letter, Henry Didier, Jr. to John N. D'Arcy, March 27, 1815, MHS, Didier Letterbook. Didier purchased the vessel from Stiles for $18,000 after the war.
31. Hutchins, *op. cit.*, p. 126.
32. Bills of Sale, NA, Marine Documentation Records.
33. Bill of Sale of the *Caroline*, July —, 1812, *ibid.*
34. Letter, Henry Didier, Jr. to John Didier, July 24, 1813, MHS, Didier Letterbook. Didier's letter-of-marque schooner was more expensive than any of the fifteen Salem privateers captured by the British by November of 1813. None of the three most expensive, a schooner, a brig, and a ship, was valued at more than $24,000. This suggests that the Baltimore vessels were larger or better equipped. The Salem figures are in *Niles Weekly Register*, November 20, 1813.
35. Letter, Henry Didier, Jr. to John N. D'Arcy, June 7, 1814, MHS, Didier Letterbook.
36. *Niles Weekly Register*, January 2, 1813.
37. Bills of Sale of Vessels, 1812–1815, NA, Marine Documentation Records.
38. Letter, Henry Didier, Jr. to John N. D'Arcy, December 6, 1814, MHS, Didier Letterbook.
39. Entry for October 6, 1812, in the *Comet*'s Log, MHS, Ships' Logs and Papers.
40. Deposition of Simon Dupuis, Prize Master of the *Fox*, December 18, 1815, NRC-S, Md. District Admiralty Cases.
41. Bill of Sale of *Kemp*, July 14, 1812, March 15, 1813, and Bill of Sale of *Orb*, December 6, 1813, NA, Marine Documentation Records.
42. Certificates of Registry, 1812–1815, NA, Marine Documentation Records
43. Letters from the Collectors at New London, September 18, 1813, and Lake Champlain, November 30, 1813, NA, Navy Privateer Records, IV. New York's collector reported at least seven commissioned "boats" ranging from three to twelve tons.
44. Circular from Secretary of State James Monroe to the Collectors of Customs, January 21, 1814, NA, Attorney General Papers, RG 60, Letters Received from the Department of State, 1813–1831.
45. Collectors Quarterly Reports, 1812–1815, NA, Navy Privateer Records, I, II.
46. *American*, June 19, 1812.
47. Certificate of Registry No. 56 for the *Ultor*, September 23, 1813, NA, Balto. Customs Records. Though said to be unique, other xebecs existed. One was advertised for sale in *American*, October 26, 1814, and at least one more, the *Shark*, was commissioned on March 1, 1814, in New York. See Copy of Commission, NA, War of 1812 Papers.
48. Howard I. Chapelle, *The Search for Speed Under Sail, 1700–1855* (New York: Bonanza Books, 1967), pp. 131–32.
49. Collectors Quarterly Reports, 1812–1815, NA, Navy Privateer Records, I, II.
50. Chapelle, *History of American Sailing Ships*, pp. 236–37; *The Baltimore Clipper: Its Origin and Development* (Hatboro, Penna.: Tradition Press, 1965, originally published in 1930 by the Marine Research Society), Foreword. Although it was commonly used in the early 1800s, there is little agreement today as to whether "sharp-built" referred to a sharpness of the bow

for an ocean-going vessel of its time, a tapering of width from the bow area to the stern, or some other physical characteristic.

51. Entry in *Kemp*'s Log, November 29, 1814, MHS, Ships' Logs and Papers.
52. Entries in *Rolla*'s Log, December 13, 1812, and *Wasp*'s Log, November 14, 1812; in *Chasseur*'s Log, January 30, 1815; also logs of *Lawrence*, *Bona*, and *Comet*, *ibid*.
53. Bill of Sale, October 19, 1812, NA, Marine Documentation Records and letter, Henry Didier, Jr. to John Didier, July 24, 1813, MHS, Didier Letterbook.
54. Bill of Sale, October 19, 1812, NA, Marine Documentation Records.
55. Letter, Henry Didier, Jr. to John N. D'Arcy, June 7, 1814, MHS, Didier Letterbook.
56. Certificates of Registry, 1812–1815, NA, Marine Documentation Records.
57. For letter, Thomas Jefferson to President James Madison, June 29, 1812, see H. A. Washington, ed., *The Writings of Thomas Jefferson*, 9 vols. (Washington, D.C.: Taylor and Maury, 1853 and 1854), Vol. VI, pp. 70–71.
58. Letter, T. and S. Hollingsworth to Levi Hollingsworth and Son, Phila., June 21, 1812, HSP, Hollingsworth MSS, Correspondence.
59. *Niles Weekly Register*, April 30, 1814.
60. Letter, George P. Stevenson to James Monroe, August 12, 1812, NA, General Records of the Department of State, RG 59, Misc. Letters of the Department of State, 1789–1906.
61. Letter, T. and S. Hollingsworth to Levi Hollingsworth and Son, Phila., April 13, 1813, HSP, Hollingsworth MSS, Correspondence.
62. *American*, January 10, 1815.
63. *The Gentleman's Magazine* (London), Supplement, LXXXIII, Part I, January to June, 1813, p. 653.
64. Letter, Captain Edward Veazey to Richard H. Douglass, March 4, and May 18, 1814, MHS, Ships' Logs and Papers.
65. Entry in *Kemp*'s Log, February 11, 1815, *ibid*.
66. Letters, Henry Didier, Jr. to John Didier, July 24, and October 10, 1813, MHS, Didier Letterbook.
67. *Ibid*., September 22, 1813. The 50 percent premium was national in 1813, Mahan, *op. cit*., II, p. 182.
68. Letter, George P. Stevenson to Wilson Cary Nicholas, Richmond, May 16, 1813, University of Virginia, Wilson Cary Nicholas Papers.
69. *Federal Gazette*, June 17, 1813.
70. *Niles Weekly Register*, January 8, 1814, and April 15, 1815.
71. Bourne, *op. cit*., p. 279.
72. Account for Repairs Done to the Privateer Schooner *Caroline*, Captain Almeda, entry of October 28, 1813, MHS, Despeaux Account Book.
73. *Ibid*.
74. *Ibid*. Wages were higher during the war than during normal times but not as high as those of some of the prewar boom years when carpenters had gotten as much as $2.50 a day. *Niles Weekly Register*, December 19, 1812. Labor, timber, and copper were high cost items in shipbuilding. See Hutchins, *op. cit*., pp. 74 and 123.
75. Chapelle, *Search for Speed Under Sail*, pp. 210–11; Hutchins, *op. cit*., p. 124; and Basil Lubbock, "Ships of the Period and Development in Rig," in *Trade Winds: A Study of British Overseas Trade During the French Wars, 1793–1815*, ed. Cyril N. Parkinson (London: George Allen and Anwin, 1948), p. 92.
76. George Little, *Life on the Ocean, or Twenty Years at Sea: Being the Personal Adventures of the Author* (Boston: Waite, Peirce and Company, 1846), p. 216.
77. *Federal Gazette*, June 17, 1813.
78. Chapelle, *Search for Speed Under Sail*, p. 211.
79. Richard H. Townsend, "The Diary of H. Townsend 1683–1789," 3 vols., typed copy of original WPA MSS at the Enoch Pratt Free Library, Baltimore, Maryland, I, p. 119.
80. See for example *Federal Gazette*, July 15, 1812, February 3, and 9, and May 20, 1813; August 8, and October 22, 1814; and *American*, June 19, and July 14, 1812; and January 25, 1813.
81. Secretary of the Navy William Jones to James Beatty, Naval Agent at Baltimore, April 1, 1814, NA, Naval Records Collection of the Office of Naval Records and Library, RG 45,

Letters Sent by the Secretary of the Navy to Commanders and Naval Agents, 1808–1865.

82. Entry in *Kemp*'s Log, December 9, 1814, MHS, Ships' Logs and Papers.

83. Letter, Captain Edward Veazey to Agent Richard H. Douglass, July 30, 1814, MHS, Ships' Logs and Papers.

84. *Federal Gazette*, May 20, 1813.

85. Disbursements Defrayed on the Schooner *Amelia*, April 23, 1814 and Disbursements for the Schooner *Thetis* at New York, February 26, 1814, MHR, Peter Arnold Karthaus and Company Shipping Accounts.

86. Howard I. Chapelle, *The History of the American Sailing Navy* (New York: W. W. Norton and Company, 1949), pp. 133 and 238. The xebec *Ultor*, an exception to the mixed armament, went out with only two twelve-pound long guns. See *Niles Weekly Register*, January 6, 1816. Captain Boyle's *Chasseur* was another vessel not utilizing the usual mixed armament. He used sixteen long twelve-pounders on one cruise. See Coggeshall, *op. cit.*, p. 358.

87. Letter, Captain David Porter to Secretary of the Navy Paul Hamilton, October 12, 1811, NA, Navy Records Collection of the Office of Naval Records and Library, RG 45, Letters of the Secretary of the Navy to Commanders and Naval Agents, 1808–1865.

88. *Federal Gazette*, September 15, 1813. Private vessel owner Thorndike Chase advertised four- and six-pound cannon with carriages for sale also, *American*, April 1, 1813.

89. Entry of November 25, 1813, MHS, Despeaux Account Book.

90. Letter, William Jones, Secretary of the Navy, to Commodore T. Tingey, January 31, 1814, NA, Navy Records Collection of the Office of Naval Records and Library, RG 45, Letter of the Secretary of Navy to Commanders and Naval Agents, 1808–1865. John Gooding reputedly sold his share in the *Sabine* when the government would not sell him ten eighteen pound carronades in September of 1814, Crane and Cranwell, *op. cit.*, p. 284.

91. *American*, October 7, 1812.

92. Charles Oscar Paullin, *Commodore John Rodger: Captain, Commodore and Senior Officer of the American Navy, 1772–1838* (Annapolis: U.S. Naval Institute, 1967, originally published by Arthur H. Clark Company, Cleveland, 1910), p. 281.

93. Letter, Hollingsworth and Worthington to Levi Hollingsworth and Son, Phila., March 22, 1814, HSP, Hollingsworth MSS, Correspondence.

94. Entry of August 30, 1813, and April 23, 1814, MHR, Peter Arnold Karthaus and Company Shipping Accounts.

95. Sales at Auction on Account of the Owners of the *Tom* of the Prize Ship *Braganza* and Cargo, September 9, 1812; of the Owners of the *Comet* of the Prize Ship *Hopewell* and Cargo, August 28, 1812, and of the Owners of the *Comet* of the Prize Ship *Henry* and Cargo, August 28, 1812, NRC-S, Md. District Admiralty Cases.

96. *Federal Gazette*, January 29, 1813, for the *Rolla*; and entries of September 28, 29, and October 4, 1812, HSP, Dreer Collection, Vol. 1, *Rossie*'s Log.

97. Letter, Captain C. G. Ridgely to William Jones, Secretary of the Navy, August 13, 1813, NA, Navy Records Collection of the Office of Naval Records, RG 45, Letters Received by the Secretary of Navy from Commanders, 1804–1886.

98. Entry of November 26, and 29, 1813, MHS, Despeaux Account Book.

99. See for example, *American*, July 7, 18, and 21, 1812; and *Federal Gazette*, August 4, 12, 17, and 21, 1812; and January 25, February 9, November 20, 1813; and April 6, 1814. A privateer such as the *Caroline* carried forty muskets. See Application for Commission No. 900, October 1813, NA, War of 1812 Papers.

100. Coggeshall, *op. cit.*, p. 255. A captain was also well advised to check his small arms and ammunition carefully. Captain Edward Veazey of the *Lawrence* reported to his agent that a partial count of a box of 3,000 musket cartridges showed 355 cartridges missing and that he thought he found fewer than 2,000 in the box. Letter, Captain Edward Veazey to Richard H. Douglass, March 2, 1814, MHS, Ships' Logs and Papers.

101. Entries of November 6, 1813, and April 23, 1814, MHR, Peter Arnold Karthaus and Company Shipping Accounts.

102. See for example, *Federal Gazette*, November 18, 1812; March 4, July 6, and 24, September 15, and 30, November 13, and December 16, 1813; also July 5, 19, and 27, August 16, and 19, and October 12, 1814.

103. Entry of April 23, 1814, MHR, Peter Arnold Karthaus and Company Shipping Accounts.
104. *Niles Weekly Register*, June 11, 1814.
105. *Federal Gazette*, December 3, 1813.
106. *American*, December 28, 1813.
107. *Samuel H. Hodskis* v. *the Agent of the Schooner* Eutaw, February 26, 1815, NRC-S, Md. District Admiralty Cases.
108. Letter, 3rd Divison Quartermaster Jeremiah Sullivan to Major General Samuel Smith, October 9, 1814, Library of Congress, Samuel Smith Papers.
109. Libel of *William H. Dorsey* v. *Schooner* Divers *and Her Owners*, January 3, 1813, *ibid.*; and *Federal Gazette*, July 2, 1813.
110. Entry of April 23, 1814, MHR, Peter Arnold Karthaus and Company Shipping Accounts.
111. Coggeshall, *op. cit.*, pp. 254–55.
112. *American*, July 21, 1812.
113. *Federal Gazette*, November 3, and 7, 1812.
114. Disbursements Defrayed on the Schooner *Amelia*, April 23, 1814, MHR, Peter Arnold Karthaus and Company Shipping Accounts.
115. *American*, July 14, 1812.
116. Letter, John Stump and Company to Levi Hollingsworth and Son, Phila., November 3, 1814, HSP, Hollingsworth MSS, Correspondence.
117. Answer of Captain Edward Veazey to the Libel of William Johnson for His Shares, November, 1815, NRC-S, Md. District Admiralty Cases. Johnson's four shares were forfeited because of his mutinous conduct.
118. Depositions in Mutiny trial of Nineteen Crewmen of the Private Armed Schooner *Chasseur* (functioning as a letter-of-marque trader), November 18, 1813, NA, Records of the Office of the Judge Advocate General (Navy); RG 125, Records of General Courts Martial and Courts of Inquiry of the Navy Department, 1799–1867, November 11, 1812–February 19, 1814.
119. Entry in *Wasp's* Log, August 27, 1812; entry in *Kemp's* Log, February 20, 1815; entries in *Wasp's* Log, September 7, October 12, and November 1, 1812; and entry in *Kemp's* Log, February 20, 1815, MHS, Ships' Logs and Papers.
120. *Thomas Millwater* v. *Agent Christopher Deshon*, June 30, 1813, and Hezekiah Joel's account with Thomas Millwater, February 22, 1813, NRC-S, Md. District Admiralty Cases.
121. Entry in *Kemp's* Log, February 16, 1815, MHS, Ships' Logs and Papers, and Account of John Barnes in *Barnes* v. *Peter Arnold Karthaus*, December 4, 1816, NRC-S, Md. District Admiralty Cases.
122. *Federal Gazette*, October 17, 1812, and January 20, 1813.
123. Thomas Boyle's Answer to a Libel, November 4, 1812, NRC-S, Md. District Court Cases.
124. Benton, *op. cit.*, V, p. 358. The costs of Salem privateers lost in the first half of the war averaged less than $25,000. See *Niles Weekly Register*, November 20, 1813.
125. Letter, T. and S. Hollingsworth to Levi Hollingsworth and Son, Phila., December 22, 1812, HSP, Hollingsworth MSS, Correspondence.
126. *Federal Gazette*, August 3, 1814.
127. *Niles Weekly Register*, October 24, 1812, and January 6, 1816.
128. *American*, July 14, 1812.

CHAPTER EIGHT

1. Little, *op. cit.*, pp. 194–95.
2. *Federal Gazette*, July 1 and July 28, 1814.
3. Letters, Captain Charles Gordon to Paul Hamilton, Secretary of the Navy, June 28, July 17, and 28, and November 16, 1812, NA, Navy Records and Library, RG 45, Letters Received by the Secretary of the Navy from Commanders, 1804–1886.
4. Letter, Robert Spence to Secretary of Navy William Jones, September 4, 1813, *ibid.*
5. *Federal Gazette*, October 21, 1812.
6. Letter, Captain Thomas Truxtun to Lieutenant John Rodgers, April —, 1798, Knox, *op. cit.*, I, p. 49.

7. Answer of John Randall to the Libel of Master Carpenter John Berwick, February 10, 1813, NRC-S, Md. District Admiralty Cases.

8. Entry of January 1, 1812, MHS, Despeaux Account Book.

9. Entries of September 7, and October 1, 1813, and Disbursements Defrayed on the Schooner *Amelia*, April 23, 1814, MHR, Peter Arnold Karthaus and Company Shipping Account.

10. Court Records, 1812–1815, NRC-S, Md. District Admiralty Cases; and *B D*, 1810 through 1815.

11. Disbursements of the Privateer *Amelia*, Second Cruise, December 23, to April 7, 1815, MHR, Peter Arnold Karthaus and Company Shipping Accounts.

12. Articles of Agreement, Prize Distribution Accounts, Bills of Sale of Prize Tickets, Letters of Attorney, NRC-S, Md. District Admiralty Cases.

13. Depositions of *John Norton and Fitz King* v. *Christopher Deshon*, March 3, 1813, *ibid.*

14. Articles of Agreement, 1812–1815, and Articles of Agreement of the Privateer *Highflyer*, September 22, 1812, *ibid.*

15. Bills of Sale of Prize Tickets and Letters of Attorney, 1812–1815, and Bill of Sale of Prize Ticket from John Barry to William Morrow, October 10, 1812, *ibid.*

16. Articles of Agreement of the Privateer *Tom*, October 23, 1812, of the Privateer *Fox*, September —, 1813, and of the Privateer *Pike*, March 23, 1814, and Daniel James's affidavit, May 14, 1814, *ibid.*

17. Crew Lists, 1812–1815; Crew Lists of the *Fox*, October 13, 1812; of the *Charles*, October 15, 1812, and the *Baltimore*, December 23, 1812, NA, Balto. Customs Records.

18. Crew Lists, 1812–1815, *ibid.*

19. Crew Lists of the *Brutus*, October 21, 1812; of the *Rossie*, December 3, 1812; of the *Courier*, September 29, 1812, and the *Inca*, August 13, 1812, *ibid.*

20. The English ship *John Hamilton*, prize to Baltimore's *Dolphin* had apprentices aged eleven, thirteen, fourteen, and two aged sixteen on board. London Customs House Certification of Indentures, June 30, 1812, *ibid.*

21. Crew Lists, 1812–1815, *ibid.* All the surviving crew lists were for the period from August 13, 1812, to February 4, 1813, and they included some vessels that cleared twice.

22. *Ibid*, and Crew Lists of the *Sylph*, October 27, 1812, and of the *Pilot*, September 8, 1812, *ibid.*

23. Crew Lists, 1812–1815, and Crew List of the *Flight*, October 15, 1812, *ibid.*

24. Entry of September 21, 1814 in Registers of United States Prisoners in Halifax, Barbados, and Jamaica, November, 1805, to March, 1815, NA, Navy Records Collection of the Office of Naval Records and Library, RG 45, Barbados vol. The 261-ton letter-of-marque *Vidette* operated with thirty-one men including a supercargo and a pilot when she was captured on February 14, 1815, *ibid.*

25. Entries of November 29, 1813, and December —, 1814, *ibid.*

26. Agreement of the Crew of the Letter-of-Marque Schooner *Decatur*, New York, July 1, 1814, MHS, Ships' Papers.

27. Prize Shares of the Schooner *Decatur* in the Brig *Williams* and Cargo, *ibid.* The total proceeds in this case amounted to $7,778.53 of which the owners got $5,185.69.

28. Agreement of the Crew of the Letter-of-Marque Schooner *Decatur*, New York, July 1, 1814, MHS, Ships' Papers.

29. Samuel Eliot Morison, *The Maritime History of Massachusetts, 1783–1860* (Boston: Houghton Mifflin Company, 1921), p. 111; and the *Federal Gazette*, October 21, 1812.

30. Deposition of Captain Matthews in *Samuel Smith and Others* v. *Peter A. Guestier, Agent of the Adeline*, September 2, 1816, NRC-S, Md. District Admiralty Cases.

31. Crew List and Stations of the Letter-of-Marque Schooner *Baltimore*, August 26, 1812, and Distribution of Prize Money to the Officers and Crew of the Schooner *Patapsco* from the Sales of the Schooner *Maria*, June 18, 1814, *ibid.*

32. Section 4 of "An Act Concerning Letters-of-Marque Prizes and Prize Goods," June 26, 1812, *Annals of Congress*, 12th Congress, 1st Session, p. 2328.

33. *Niles Weekly Register*, October 24, 1812. Baltimore's large schooners required more men than the smaller vessels of ports such as Salem, where the first seven privateers clearing averaged only forty-five men and two and one-half guns each, *Federal Gazette*, July 15, 1812. Estimates based on the 2,800 figure suggest, as described in Chapter IV, that Baltimore vessels carried from 4,000 to 6,678 men altogether.

34. Crane and Cranwell, *op. cit.*, p. 175.
35. Brown, *op. cit.*, p. 285. Boston had the largest number of registered seamen with 1,043.
36. Articles of Agreement of the Privateer *Highflyer*, September 22, 1812, NRC-S, Md. District Admiralty Cases.
37. *American*, August 29, 1812.
38. Depositions of First Lieutenant Thomas Ring, Prize Master James Towers and others in *Caldwell, Ferguson and Dougherty* v. *Thomas Boyle of the* Comet, November 4, 1812, NRC-S, Md. District Admiralty Cases.
39. Articles of Agreement of the Privateer *Highflyer*, September 22, 1812; of the Privateer *Tom*, October 23, 1812; of the *Globe*, July 11, 1812; and others, *ibid.* Most of the variations in crew stations involved petty officers and the number of first class and ordinary seamen as well as marines or landsmen. Ten or fifteen marines were the rule.
40. Entries of November 10 to November 16, 1812, in the *Rolla*'s Log, and of October 13, 1812, in the *Bona*'s Log, MHS, Ships' Logs and Papers.
41. *Federal Gazette*, October 24, 1812.
42. Letter, T. and S. Hollingsworth to Levi Hollingsworth and Son, Phila., December 22, 1812, HSP, Hollingsworth MSS, Correspondence.
43. *Niles Weekly Register*, January 7, 1815.
44. Entries of August 11, and 12, 1812 in *Wasp*'s Log, MHS, Ships' Logs and Papers.
45. Letter, Joshua Barney to Secretary of State James Monroe, October 30, 1813, NA, General Records of the Department of State, RG 59, Misc. Letters of the Department of State, 1789–1906.
46. A law of March 3, 1813 specified that only citizens of the United States or persons of color, natives of the United States could sign onto private armed vessels. See *Federal Gazette*, March 15, 1813.
47. Maclay, *op. cit.*, p. 228.
48. Extract of the Journal of the Privateer Schooner *Globe* in *Niles Weekly Register*, September 5, 1812.
49. Thomas Boyle's Answer to the Libel of Manuel Santo and Manuel Morriss, March 7, 1816, and Exhibit "A" in *Santo and Morriss* v. *Thomas Boyle*, September 11, 1814, NRC-S, Md. District Admiralty Cases.
50. Libel of *John Davis* v. *Charles F. Kalkman*, prize agent of the privateer *Caroline*, May 2, 1816, *ibid.*
51. *Federal Gazette*, August 17, 1814, and February 22, 1813.
52. *American*, July 18, and July 14, 1812.
53. *Federal Gazette*, December 30, 1813.
54. See for example, *American*, September 9, 1812; and *Federal Gazette*, November 18, 1812; March 3, 15, and 27, April 1, May 29, and November 26, 1813.
55. For example, the prize agent for the *Amelia* entered $264.38 to the credit of her prize account for "Prize Money" forfeited by deserters. Disbursements of the Privateer *Amelia*, December 23, to April 7, 1815, MHR, Peter Arnold Karthaus and Company Shipping Accounts.
56. *American*, July 14, 1812.
57. Letter, John Baker, Jr., Dartmoor Prison, to John Baker, June 16, 1814, MHS, Joseph Despeaux Papers. Despeaux was a part-owner of the *Caroline*.
58. Registers of United States Prisoners in Halifax, Barbados and Jamaica, November, 1805, to March, 1815, NA, Navy Records Collection of the Office of Naval Records and Library, 3 vols., RG 45, and Navy Pension Payment Records, Baltimore, Maryland, 1816–1849, NA, Records of United States General Accounting Office, RG 217, 6 boxes.
59. Distribution of the *Braganza*'s Prize Money Among the Crew of the *Tom*, October 23, 1812, NRC-S, Md. District Admiralty Cases.
60. Account of the Distribution of the Officers and Seamen of the Privateer *Comet* in the Case of the Ship *John* and her Cargo, December —, 1812; and letter, Captain William Wade to Philip Moore, Clerk of the Court, January 10, 1814, *ibid.*
61. Prize Agent Christopher Deshon's Answer to the Libel of Benjamin White, June 19, 1814; and a Letter of Attorney from Hezekiah Joel to Thomas Cooke of Edgartown, Massachusetts, undated, *ibid.*

62. Captain Richard Moore's description of his crewmen in *Niles Weekly Register*, November 14, 1812. His account was originally written in Nassau, October 18, 1812.
63. *Federal Gazette*, November 6, and 10, 1812. A total of 112 prisoners including other Baltimore captains of private armed vessels were returned on the cartel *Ann*.
64. Maclay, *op. cit.*, p. 365.
65. Letter, Thomas Stevenson to "Dear Mom," August 4, 1813, NRC-S, Md. District Admiralty Cases.
66. Letters of Attorney, November 22, and 5, 1813, *ibid*.
67. Maclay, *op. cit.*, p. 336.
68. *American*, July 16, 1812.
69. *Federal Gazette*, February 26, 1813.
70. Little, *op. cit.*, p. 219.
71. *Federal Gazette*, February 16, 1813. A Thomas Chidester was commissioned as a surgeon in the United States Navy on July 24, 1813 according to Naval Register for 1815.
72. Various articles of agreement, 1812–1815, NRC-S, Md. District Admiralty Cases.
73. Disbursements for the Privateer Schooner *Kemp*, November 28, 1814, MHR, Peter Arnold Karthaus and Company Shipping Accounts.
74. Report from Plymouth, England of May 12, 1813, in *Federal Gazette*, July 14, 1813.
75. Little, *op. cit.*, pp. 197–220.
76. *Webster's New World Dictionary of the American Language*.
77. Quarter Bill No. 1 for the Privateer *Rossie*, undated, HSP, Joshua Barney Papers, II.
78. Various articles of agreement, 1812–1815, NRC-S, Md. District Admiralty Cases.
79. Articles of Agreement of the Privateer *Fox*, September —, 1813, *ibid*.
80. *Ibid*.
81. *Ibid*.
82. *Ibid*. Congress also provided benefits for those killed or wounded in private armed vessels, assessing the private vessel 2 percent of her prize money for that fund. Section 17 of "An Act Concerning Letter-of-Marque Prizes and Prize Goods," June 26, 1812, *Annals of Congress*, 12th Congress, 1st Session, p. 2332.
83. Articles of Agreement of the Privateer *Tom*, August 1, 1812; of the Privateer *Highflyer*, September 22, 1812; of the Privateer *Comet*, June —, 1812, and of the Privateer *Pike*, March 23, 1814, NRC-S, Md. District Admiralty Cases.
84. Courts Martial Record of John Lord and Eighteen Others of the Crew of the Private Armed Schooner *Chasseur*, November 15, to November 20, 1813, NA, Records of the General Courts Martial and Courts of Inquiry of the Navy, 1799–1867, November 20, 1813 to February 19, 1814, RG 125, Records of the Office of the Judge Advocate General (Navy).
85. Prize List of the Schooner *Rossie*, September and October, 1812, HSP, Joshua Barney Papers, II.
86. Prize Ticket No. 80, MHS, Ships' Logs and Papers.
87. Thomas Durham's Certificate of Discharge, August 13, 1814, *ibid*.
88. Little, *op. cit.*, p. 196. Little went on board a Norfolk privateer in July of 1812 as a first lieutenant, carrying only a small trunk and a clothes bag.
89. Letter, T. and S. Hollingsworth to Levi Hollingsworth and Son, Phila., August 21, 1812, HSP, Hollingsworth MSS, Correspondence.

CHAPTER NINE

1. Instructions for the Schooner *Rossie*, July 11, 1812, HSP, Joshua Barney Papers, II. Section 6 of the congressional act prohibited the breaking of bulk (the opening of prize packaging) and specified the district courts of the United States as the proper court for prize cases. Section 10 required the commander to maintain a journal. *Annals of Congress*, 12th Congress, 1st Session, pp. 2327–32.
2. Crane and Cranwell, *op. cit.*, pp. 357–59. The original instructions were in the hands of a descendant of Captain Dashiell in 1940.

3. *Ibid.*
4. *Ibid.*
5. Libel of *Captain Joseph Skinner, Jr.* v. *Lemuel Taylor*, July 15, 1816; and Lemuel Taylor's Answer to Skinner's Libel, December 6, 1816. Taylor's case was apparently less than watertight. He compromised with Skinner. Letter, Joseph Skinner, Jr. in New York to William A. Winder (his attorney in Baltimore), April 26, 1817, NRC-S, Md. District Admiralty Cases.
6. Letter, Richard H. Douglass to Captain George Montgomery, June 26, 1814, MHS, Ships' Papers.
7. Shipping reports in *Federal Gazette* and *American*, 1813–1815; and Albion and Pope, *op. cit.*, p. 120.
8. Letter, George Montgomery, at sea, to Richard H. Douglass, August 31, 1814 (received November 20, 1814), MHS, Ships' Papers.
9. Letter, Samuel Dorsey, at sea, to William Douglass, August 31, 1814, forwarded from Elizabeth City, North Carolina, *ibid.*
10. Letter, Isaac G. Roberts, Portsmouth, New Hampshire, to Richard H. Douglass, July 1, 1814, *ibid.*
11. *Federal Gazette*, August 16, and 17, 1814.
12. Coggeshall, *op. cit.*, pp. 111–12.
13. *Ibid.*, p. 113; and Maclay, *op. cit.*, p. 20.
14. Logs and journals of the *Wasp, Lawrence, Kemp, Bona, Ultor, Rolla, Chasseur, Decatur,* and *Comet*, 1812–1815, MHS, Ships' Logs and Papers; log of the *Rossie*, HSP, Dreer Collection II; Albion and Pope, *op. cit.*, p. 29; Maclay, *op. cit.*, p. 19; Coggeshall, *op. cit.*, passim; and various journal and log extracts in the *Federal Gazette, American,* and *Niles Weekly Register*, 1812–1815. See, for example, *Federal Gazette*, September 1, and November 21, 1812; January 25, April 24, June 15, and 17, 1813; July 11, August 18, October 28, and November 11, 1814.
15. Log of the Ship *John Hamilton*, July 1, to November 21, 1812, NRC-S, Md. District Admiralty Cases.
16. *Niles Weekly Register*, December 19, 1812.
17. Log of the Schooner *Fame*, March 27, 1812, NRC-S, Md. District Admiralty Cases.
18. Journal of *Comet*'s First Cruise, July 12, 1812 to October 6, 1812, MHS.
19. *Ibid.*
20. *Ibid.*
21. Journal of the *Comet*'s Second Cruise, MHS; and Coggeshall, *op. cit.*, p. 136.
22. Journal of the *Comet*'s Second Cruise, MHS; *Niles Weekly Register*, March 27, 1813; and *Federal Gazette*, March 20, 1813.
23. *Niles Weekly Register*, March 27, 1813; *Federal Gazette*, March 20, 1813, and Register of United States Prisoners in Halifax, Barbados, and Jamaica, November, 1805, to March, 1815, NA, Navy Records Collection of the Office of Naval Records and Library, Barbados vol., RG 45.
24. Coggeshall, *op. cit.*, pp. 165–66; Crane and Cranwell, *op. cit.*, pp. 129–44; Mahan, *op. cit.*, II, pp. 234–35; and *Niles Weekly Register*, April 2, 1814.
25. *Federal Gazette*, July 18, 1814.
26. Clearance Certificate for the Private Armed Schooner *Rossie*, July 11, 1812, HSP, Joshua Barney Papers, II.
27. Log of the *Rossie*, HSP, Dreer Collection, II; *Rossie* Journal Extracts in Coggeshall, *op. cit.*, pp. 84–87; and *Federal Gazette*, October 24, 1812.
28. Log of the *Rossie*, HSP, Dreer Collection, II; *Federal Gazette*, August 27, 1812; *Niles Weekly Register*, September 5, and 17, 1812; and Quarter Bill No. 1, for the Private Armed Schooner *Rossie*, HSP, Joshua Barney Papers, II.
29. Coggeshall, *op. cit.*, p. 61.
30. *Federal Gazette*, October 24, 1812.
31. Log of the *Rossie*, HSP, Dreer Collection, II; and *Niles Weekly Register*, October 17, 1812.
32. *Niles Weekly Register*, November 7, 1812.
33. *Federal Gazette*, October 24, 1812.
34. Report, Joshua Barney to Secretary of State James Monroe, October —, 1812, HSP, Joshua Barney Papers, II.

35. *Federal Gazette*, October 28, 1812.
36. Log of *Rolla*, MHS; and *Federal Gazette*, January 25, and 30, 1813.
37. *Federal Gazette*, May 20, 21, June 12, and July 8, 1813; Crane and Cranwell, *op. cit.*, pp. 172–75; and Clifford Lindsey Alderman, *The Privateersmen* (New York: Chilton Books, 1965), p. 82.
38. Extracts from the Log of the *Ultor* in *Federal Gazette*, July 11, 1814; *Niles Weekly Register*, May 28, and July 30, 1814; and Crane and Cranwell, *op. cit.*, pp. 200–03.
39. Journal of the xebec *Ultor* on her Second Cruise from New York, MHS; *Niles Weekly Register*, May 28, July 30, 1814, and April 15, 1815; and Crane and Cranwell, *op. cit.*, pp. 205–08.
40. Journal of the *Lawrence*, MHS; Crane and Cranwell, *op. cit.*, pp. 275–78; *Federal Gazette*, August 8, 1814; and letter, Captain Edward Veazey on board the Schooner *Lawrence* to Richard H. Douglass, Baltimore, April 25, 1814, MHS, Ships' Logs and Papers.
41. *Niles Weekly Register*, June 25, 1814.
42. Journal of the *Lawrence*, MHS; and *Federal Gazette*, August 8, 1814.
43. Letter, Captain Edward Veazey, Fort Johnson, North Carolina, to Richard H. Douglass, Baltimore, July 30, 1814, MHS, Ships' Logs and Papers.
44. *Federal Gazette*, October 22, 1814; *Niles Weekly Register*, April 15, 1815; and Crane and Cranwell, *op. cit.*, pp. 278–81.
45. *Federal Gazette*, February 13, March 5, and June 14, 1813; July 30, and August 18, 1814.
46. Log of the *Kemp*, MHS; Coggeshall, *op. cit.*, pp. 312–13; Alderman, *op. cit.*, pp. 149–51; and Crane and Cranwell, *op. cit.*, pp. 214–17.
47. Log of the *Kemp*, MHS; *Niles Weekly Register*, January 7, 1815. Niles says that Almeda actually faced forty-six guns and 134 men.
48. Log of the *Kemp*, MHS; and *Niles Weekly Register*, January 7, 1815.
49. Log of the *Kemp*, MHS; and Crane and Cranwell, *op. cit.*, p. 225.
50. *American*, December 15, 1812; *Federal Gazette*, December 17, September 25, and November 4, 1813.
51. Crane and Cranwell, *op. cit.*, pp. 228–35; and "Extract from the Journal of the *Chasseur*'s Cruize" in *American*, November 2, 1814; and *Federal Gazette*, November 1, 1814.
52. "Extract from the Journal of the *Chasseur*'s Cruize" in *American*, November 2, 1814.
53. "Proclamation of Blockade," *ibid.*
54. "Extract from the Journal of the *Chasseur*'s Cruize" in *American*, November 2, 1814; for English complaints, see *Niles Weekly Register*, October 21, November 12, and 26, 1814.
55. "Extract from the Journal of the *Chasseur*'s Cruize," *American*, November 2, 1814; and *Federal Gazette*, October 30, 1814.
56. Journal of the Private Armed Brig *Chasseur*, Thomas Boyle, Commander, from New York on a Cruise, MHS.
57. *Ibid.*; and *Niles Weekly Register*, April 15, 1815.
58. "Extract from the Journal of the *Chasseur*'s Cruize," *American*, November 2, 1814; and letter, Captain Thomas Boyle to George P. Stevenson, printed in *Niles Weekly Register*, March 25, 1815.
59. "Extract from the Journal of the *Chasseur*'s Cruize," in *American*, November 2, 1814; *Niles Weekly Register*, April 15, 1815; Adams, *op. cit.*, VIII, pp. 196–98; Crane and Cranwell, *op. cit.*, pp. 236–59, Mahan, *op. cit.*, II, pp. 237 and 358–68, and Owens, *op. cit.*, pp. 177–85.
60. *Federal Gazette*, November 10, and 21, 1812; and Coggeshall, *op. cit.*, pp. 87–88.
61. *Niles Weekly Register*, October 6, 1814; *American*, May 24, 1814; Adams, *op. cit.*, VIII, p. 196; and Crane and Cranwell, *op. cit.*, pp. 285–87.
62. *Niles Weekly Register*, February 20, 1813; *Federal Gazette*, December 11, 1812; April 9, 24, and 28, 1813; and January 19, and 27, 1813; Log of the Ship *John Hamilton*, NRC-S, Md. District Admiralty Cases; Coggeshall, *op. cit.*, pp. 128–30; and Crane and Cranwell, *op. cit.*, pp. 100–13.
63. *American*, April 18, 1814; Crane and Cranwell, *op. cit.*, pp. 261–69; *Niles Weekly Register*, October 29, 1814; and *Federal Gazette*, July 19, August 9, and October 26, 1814.
64. "Extract from the Log of the *Globe*," in *Federal Gazette*, June 15, 18, and 26, 1813; *Niles Weekly Register*, May 15, 1813; Coggeshall, *op. cit.*, pp. 55–56, 103–04, and 160–63; Crane and Cranwell, *op. cit.*, pp. 85, 94–100; Mahan, *op. cit.*, II, pp. 226–28; *American*, August 29, 1812; and *Niles Weekly Register*, August 24, September 5, 1812; and May 1, 1813.

65. *Federal Gazette*, June 1, July 16, September 8, and September 10, 1813; August 16, 17, and 19, 1814; *Niles Weekly Register*, August 20, 1814; Adams, *op. cit.*, VIII, p. 198; Crane and Cranwell, *op. cit.*, pp. 283–85.

66. *Federal Gazette*, July 14, 1814, "Extracts from the Log of the *Surprise*," July 19, 1814; *Niles Weekly Register*, October 6, 1814, and April 15, 1815; Crane and Cranwell, *op. cit.*, pp. 287–92.

67. *Federal Gazette*, July to November 4, 1812.

68. *American*, October 7, and September 28, 1812.

69. Letter, Deputy Collector John Brice to John Graham, State Department Clerk, December 22, 1814, NA, General Records of the Department of State, RG 59, Misc. Letters of the Department of State, 1789–1906.

70. Little, *op. cit.*, pp. 197–220.

71. Export Manifest of the *Ultor*, November —, 1813, found with Bills of Sale for November, 1813, NA, Marine Documentation Records.

72. Letters, Henry Didier, Jr. to John Didier in France, December 4, and September 27, 1813; November 19, 1814, and December 14, 1813, MHS, Didier Letterbook.

73. Letters, David Baillee Warden to James Monroe, April 5, 1813; to John Graham, State Department Clerk, November 12, 1812, MHS, Warden Letterbooks, A.

74. *Federal Gazette*, September 28, 1812.

75. *Ibid.*, December 31, and 28, 1812; March 1, December 20, March 5, and April 6, 1813.

76. *Ibid.*, December 7, 23, 1813; August 26, 1814, and December 31, 1813.

77. Cargo Manifest of the Schooner *Tuckahoe*, November 25, 1814, MHS, McBlair Papers.

78. *Federal Gazette*, October 4, 1812.

79. *American*, November 4, 1812.

80. George F. Dow, "Records of the Vice-Admiralty Court at Halifax, Nova Scotia: The Condemnation of Prizes and Re-captures of the Revolution and the War of 1812," *Historical Collections of the Essex Institute*, XLVI, pp. 259, 264, and 321; XLVII, p. 193.

81. Letters, Henry Didier, Jr. to John N. D'Arcy in England, November 19, and September 23, 1814, MHS, Didier Letterbook.

CHAPTER TEN

1. Coggeshall, *op. cit.*, p. 181.

2. *Niles Weekly Register*, June 12, 1813.

3. *Ibid.*, January 29, 1814, and October 9, 1813. The bill passed the House of Representatives by a vote of eighty to fifty-seven, suggesting that Congress wanted the private armed vessels to damage British commerce and not to enrich American citizens. The British had outlawed ransoming also.

4. Act of June 26, 1812, *Annals of Congress*, 12th Congress, 1st Session, p. 2329; of August 3, 1813, *ibid.*, 13th Congress, 1st Session, p. 2773; of March 19, 1814, *ibid.*, p. 2803.

5. *American*, September 2, 1812.

6. Undated entry, Peter Arnold Karthaus and Company Shipping Accounts, MHR; Register of British Prisoners of War in the United States, July 1812–March 1815, NA, Navy Records Collection of the Office of Naval Records and Library, 2 vols., RG 45.

7. Little, *op. cit.*, p. 219.

8. Quarter Bill No. 1 of the *Rossie*, undated, HSP, Joshua Barney Papers, II; Crane and Cranwell, *op. cit.*, p. 21, stated that prize master had no duties before a prize was actually captured.

9. Depositions of Austin, Cathell, Long, and Towers in *Caldwell, Ferguson and Dougherty v. Thomas Boyle*, November 4, 1812, NRC-S, Md. District Admiralty Cases.

10. Deposition of Anthony W. Hayman, December 22, 1812, NRC-S, *ibid.* As a prisoner, Hayman retook a prize from the British and sued for salvage money.

11. Captain's Instructions to Prize Master Lieutenant Thomas Audenae, Ship *Young Wasp* at Sea, January 23, 1815, *ibid.* The prize in this case, the ship *Clarendon*, held a British letter-of-marque and reprisal against the United States.

12. Sales at Auction of the Prize Ship *Clarendon* and her Cargo, June 1, 1815, *ibid.*

13. Letter, Prize Master John Paul to George P. Stevenson, March 5, 1815, *ibid.* The 104,060 pounds of good cocoa and 5,963 pounds of damaged cocoa were gotten ashore before the prize broke up.
14. *Niles Weekly Register*, March 19, 1814.
15. Letter, Prize Master John Clark, Halifax, to Agent Richard H. Douglass, May 31, 1814, MHS, Ships' Logs and Papers.
16. *Niles Weekly Register*, August 13, 1815, and January 6, 1815; letter, James Cunningham, Portland, to Richard H. Douglass, July 30, 1814, *ibid.*
17. The Convention of 1800 between the United States and France authorized American private armed vessels to send their prizes into French ports. Jackson, *op. cit.*, p. 106; and *American State Papers, Foreign Relations*, I, p. 296.
18. Circular from David Baillee Warden to Consuls and Vice Consuls of the United States of America in Ports of France, Paris, August 1, 1812, MHS, Warden Letterbooks, A.
19. Letter, John A. Morton, Bordeaux, to Richard H. Douglass, July 16, 1814, MHS, Ships' Logs and Papers.
20. Decree of Condemnation for the Ship *Favorite*, January 26, 1814, NA, Marine Documentation Records. This document was found loose with the bound 1815 Certificates of Registry.
21. *Niles Weekly Register*, November 6, 1813.
22. Maclay, *op. cit.*, p. 262.
23. *Niles Weekly Register*, September 10, 1814.
24. Journal of Isiah Lewis, Prize Master on board the Brig *Pelican*, taken by the Privateer *Lawrence* of Baltimore, Edward Veazey, Commander, on the 21st of April, 1814; and letter, John A. Morton, Bordeaux, to Richard H. Douglass, July 16, 1814, MHS, Ships' Logs and Papers.
25. Agent Charles F. Kalkman's Answer to the Libel of Hugh Reed for his Six Prize Shares, March 18, 1815, NRC-S, Md. District Admiralty Cases.
26. *Niles Weekly Register*, March 15, 1813.
27. *Federal Gazette*, June 28, 1813.
28. Registers of United States Prisoners in Halifax, Barbados, and Jamaica, November, 1805 to March, 1815, NA, Navy Records Collection of the Office of Naval Records and Library, 3 vols., RG 45, Barbados and Halifax Stations.
29. Crane and Cranwell, *op. cit.*, pp. 233–34.
30. Letter, Levi Hollingsworth (Baltimore) to Levi Hollingsworth and Son, Phila., November 29, 1814, HSP, Hollingsworth MSS, Correspondence. As an entrepreneur matching goods to markets, Levi Hollingsworth of Baltimore was shipping his trunk to the Spanish West Indies where black lace was fashionable.
31. *Niles Weekly Register*, April 2, and October 6, 1814.
32. Statement for the Officers and Crew of the Private Armed Schooner *Kemp*, ———, 1815, NRC-S, Md. District Admiralty Cases.
33. Account of Sales of the Cargo of the *Chasseur*, June 21, 1815; Account of Sales of the Cargo of the *Perry*, undated, *ibid.* The *Perry*'s goods were landed at Philadelphia but were shipped to Baltimore for sale.
34. Account of Sales of the Cargo of the *Whig*, May 24, 1815; Account of Sales of the Cargo of the *Kemp*, June 12, 1815, *ibid.*
35. Letter, Henry Didier, Jr. to John N. D'Arcy in England, October 23, 1814, MHS, Didier Letterbook.
36. *Niles Weekly Register*, April 15, 1815.
37. Letter, Hollingsworth and Worthington to Levi Hollingsworth and Son, Phila., August 21, 1812, HSP, Hollingsworth MSS, Correspondence.
38. Letter, T. and S. Hollingsworth to Levi Hollingsworth and Son, Phila., September 6, 1812, and April 18, 1815, *ibid.*
39. Andrew Clopper's Answer to the Libel of Frederick Travers, November 8, 1815, NRC-S, Md. District Admiralty Cases.
40. Captain Thorndike Chase's Bill for the Disbursements of the Prize Ship *Hopewell* ($2253.77), October 24, 1812; Baptiste Mezick's Bill for the Expenses of the Prize Ship *Braganza*, December 10, 1812, and for Tenant, Sales Goods in the *William*, April 21, 1815, *ibid.*
41. Disbursements of the Ship *Hopewell*, Prize to the *Comet*, October —, 1812, *ibid.*

42. Admiralty Dockets for the Maryland District Court, 1812–1815, NA (at Suitland), Records of the United States Attorneys and Marshals, RG 118.
43. Arthur Browne, *A Compendious View of the Civil Law and the Law of Admiralty*, 2 vols. (London: J. Butterworth and John Cooke, 1802), II, p. 230. This particular volume was owned by proctor Theodorick Bland. He succeeded James Houston as judge of the United States District Court for Maryland after the war.
44. *Annals of Congress*, 12th Congress, 1st Session, p. 2328.
45. Erastus C. Benedict, *The American Admiralty, Its Jurisdiction and Practice with Practical Forms and Directions*, 3rd ed., revised by Robert D. Benedict (New York: Banks and Brothers, Law Publishers, 1894), pp. 212–16; and numerous examples of War of 1812 libels in NRC-S, Md. District Admiralty Cases.
46. Expenses of the Ship *Braganza*, Prize to the *Tom*, October 10, 1812; Disbursements of the Ship *Henry*, Prize to the *Comet*, September 22, 1812, NRC-S, Md. District Admiralty Cases.
47. Disbursements of the Schooner *Resolution*, Prize to the *Kemp*, May 20, 1815, and Account of Sales of the Goods in the *Perry*, April —, 1815, *ibid*.
48. Libel, Order to the Marshal, and Condemnation Decree in the Case of *Captain Jeremiah Grant and Others* v. *the Schooner* Burchall, *ibid*.
49. See for examples: Answers to Interrogation by the Late Master of the *Jamaica*, prize to the *Highflyer* (twenty-one questions), October 8, 1812; Interrogation of Captain John Mason of the *Hornet*, Prize to the *Highflyer* (twenty-nine questions), September 2, 1812; Interrogation of Captain Simes of the *Braganza*, Prize to the *Tom* (thirty-one questions), October —, 1812; and others, *ibid*.
50. Benedict, *op. cit.*, p. 288. Benedict says "this peculiarity is the very essence of the administration of prize law."
51. *Ibid.*, pp. 291 and 359. Appeals relating to admiralty matters other than prize cases went to the United States Circuit Court.
52. Certified Copy of the Decree of Condemnation and Sale in the Case of *Thomas Boyle and Others* v. *the Ship* Hopewell *and Cargo*, September 19, 1812, found with the Marshal's Bill of Sale of the Prize Ship *Hopewell*, NA, Marine Documentation Records. For other decrees of condemnation see NRC-S, Md. District Admiralty Cases.
53. *American*, September 4, 1812.
54. Gerrard Wilson's Receipt for the *Braganza*'s Prize Money, November 12, 1812, NRC-S, Md. District Admiralty Cases.
55. Various Accounts of Sales of Prize Vessels and Goods by Auction, 1812–1815, *ibid*.
56. Costs of the Prize Ship *John Hamilton*, Prize to the *Dolphin*, December —, 1812, *ibid*.
57. An Act in Addition to an Act Concerning Letter-of-Marque Prizes and Prize Goods, January 27, 1813, *Annals of Congress*, 12th Congress, 2nd Session, pp. 1319–21.
58. Sales of Auction on Account of the Owners of the Prize Ship *John* and her Cargo by Caspar Otto Muller [vendue master], November 24, 1812, NRC-S, Md. District Admiralty Cases.
59. *Ibid.*
60. Application for Commission No. 647 for the *Sabine*, January 4, 1813, NA, War of 1812 Papers.
61. Sales at Auction of the Prize Ship *John* and Cargo, November 24, 1812, Md. District Admiralty Cases.
62. *Ibid.*
63. Sales at Auction on Account of the Owners of the Prize Ship *Braganza* and Cargo, September 9, 1812, *ibid*.
64. *Ibid.*
65. Price Currents in the *Federal Gazette*, August 25, and November 3, 1812. Coffee from the prize ship *John* sold as low as eighteen and one-half cents per pound on November 24, 1812 when it was quoted at twenty to twenty-two cents per pound in the *Federal Gazette*, November 18, 1812. Sugar was quoted at seventeen dollars per hundredweight in the *Federal Gazette* on August 25, 1812 but that in the sales of the prize ship *Henry* sold from $14.80 to $11.40 per hundredweight on August 28, 1812, NRC-S, Md. District Admiralty Cases.
66. Letters, T. and S. Hollingsworth to Levi Hollingsworth and Son, Phila., October 7, 1812, and April 27, 1815, HSP, Hollingsworth MSS, Correspondence.

67. *Federal Gazette*, October 27, 1813.
68. Letter, John Gibson in Philadelphia to Elizabeth Gibson, October 21, 23, and 25, 1814, MHS, Grundy-Gibson Papers.
69. Letter-of-Marque and Reprisal for the *Clarendon*, issued by George III on March 4, 1814, and Sales at Auction on Account of the Owners of the Ship *Clarendon*, May 13 and 14, 1815, NRC-S, Md. District Admiralty Cases. Employed by Philadelphians as their Baltimore agent on previous occasions, Tenant may have been purchasing prize coffee for Philadelphia buyers. See Power of Attorney from Andrew Curcier and others to Thomas Tenant, October 14, 1812, *ibid.*
70. Letter, Hollingsworth and Worthington to Levi Hollingsworth and Son, Phila., February 2, 1813, HSP, Hollingsworth MSS, Correspondence.
71. Letter, James Monroe to Collector James H. McCulloch, June 7, 1813, NA, Navy Privateer Records, II.
72. Letter, Henry Didier, Jr. to John N. D'Arcy in England, June 7, 1814, MHS, Didier Letter-book.
73. Marshal's Bill of Sale of the Prize *Harriet*, November 4, 1812, and Bill of Sale of the *Harriet*, October 2, 1812, NA, Marine Documentation Records.
74. Marshal's Bill of Sale of the Prize *Jamaica*, February 6, 1813, and Bill of Sale of the *Jamaica*, February 6, 1813; Marshal's Bill of Sale of the Prize *Clarendon*, June 22, 1815, and Bill of Sale of the *Clarendon*, July 3, 1815, *Ibid.*
75. Marshal's Bills of Sale of Prize Vessels, 1812–1815, *ibid.*
76. *Ibid.*
77. Bill of Sale of the *Star*, May 15, 1815, *ibid.*
78. Bill of Sale of the *Canada*, June 30, 1815, *ibid.*
79. Marshal's Bill of Sale of the Prize Ship *Henry*, September 29, 1812; of the Ship *Ann*, September 19, 1815; of the *Braganza*, September 29, 1812 (through Captain Carr), *ibid.*
80. Marshal's Bill of Sale of the Prize *John Hamilton*, February 6, 1813, *ibid.*
81. Marshal's Bills of Sale for Prize Vessels, 1812–1815, *ibid.*
82. Sales of the Cargo of the *Chasseur*, April 17, 1815; of the *Whig*, May 17, 1815, and of the *Kemp*, May —, 1815, NRC-S, Md. District Admiralty Cases.

CHAPTER ELEVEN

1. Benedict, *op. cit.*, p. 347.
2. An Act of July 1, 1812 Doubling Duties on Goods Imported from any Foreign Port or Place. See Peters, ed., *op. cit.*, II, p. 768; also *American*, July 14, 1812.
3. Accounts of the Sales of the Prize Ship *Braganza* and her Cargo, September 2, 1812; of the Prize Ship *Jamaica* and her Cargo, October —, 1812; of the Prize Ship *Henry* and her Cargo, September 15, 1812; and Statement of the Duty on the Cargo of the *Fanny*, July —, 1812, NRC-S, Md. District Admiralty Cases.
4. Costs of the Private Armed Vessels *General Armstrong*, *Governor Tompkins*, and others, November 12, 1812, *American State Papers, Finance*, II, p. 592; and *Niles Weekly Register*, January 2, 1813.
5. "Memorial of the Merchants and Owners of the Private Armed Commissioned Vessels of the War of the City of Baltimore, November 23, 1812" (Washington, D.C.: Printed by Roger C. Weightman by order of the United States Senate, 1812), pp. 3–4.
6. An Act Reducing the Duties Payable in Prize Goods Captured by Private Armed Vessels of the United States, August 22, 1813, *Annals of Congress*, 13th Congress, 1st and 2nd Sessions, p. 2766.
7. Letter, William Jones, Treasury Department, to the Honorable Hugh Nelson, Chairman of the Naval Committee of the House of Representatives, July 21, 1813, in *Niles Weekly Register*, August 7, 1813.
8. Various Prize Sale Accounts, 1812–1815, NRC-S, Md. District Admiralty Cases; and price currents in *American* and *Federal Gazette*, July, 1812 to August, 1813.

9. Letter in *Niles Weekly Register*, August 7, 1813.

10. Letter, T. and S. Hollingsworth to Levi Hollingsworth and Son, Phila., April 13, 1813, HSP, Hollingsworth MSS, Correspondence.

11. Letter, *Niles Weekly Register*, August 7, 1813.

12. See Appendix A for the dates of new commissions.

13. *Niles Weekly Register*, April 30, 1814.

14. Disbursements of the Ship *Hopewell*, Prize to the *Comet*, October —, 1812, NRC-S, Md. District Admiralty Cases.

15. Costs of the Prize Ship *Hopewell*, October 24, 1812, *ibid.*

16. Account of the Clerk of the Court with Thomas Tenant, Agent for the *Highflyer*, October —, 1812; Distribution of the Prize Money of the *Jamaica* to the Officers and Crew of the *Highflyer*, December 5, 1812, *ibid.*

17. Costs of the Prize Ship *Hopewell*, October 24, 1812, *ibid.*

18. Account of the Sale of the Cargo of the Schooner *Whig*, May 24, 1815, *ibid.*

19. Sales at Auction of the Schooner *Resolution*, Prize to the *Kemp*, June 20, 1815, *ibid.*

20. The June, 1815, date for a prize sale resulted from the provisions of the Treaty of Ghent. Article 2 of that treaty permitted the capturing of prizes in the Atlantic, twelve to thirty days after the treaty's ratification, depending on the location of the prize. Prizes could be taken in the North Sea, Baltic, and Mediterranean for forty days, south of the equator to the Cape of Good Hope for sixty days, for ninety days for the rest of the sea below the equator, and for 120 days in all other parts of the world "without exception," *Niles Weekly Register*, February 18, 1815.

21. Statement of the Cruize of the Schooner *Rossie*, Privateer, filed December 6, 1815, NRC-S, Md. District Admiralty Cases.

22. *Ibid.*

23. Prize List of the Schooner *Rossie*, undated, HSP, Joshua Barney Papers, II.

24. The Owners of the Private Armed Schooner *Kemp* in Account with Agent Peter Arnold Karthaus, April —, 1814, MHR, Peter Arnold Karthaus and Company Shipping Accounts.

25. Statement of the Dividends of Prize Money from the Cruize of the Private Armed Schooner *Rossie*, filed December 6, 1815, NRC-S, Md. District Admiralty Cases. The net proceeds for the third distribution or the reductions are incorrect because a reduction of 12.5 percent should have left $2,873.53.

26. Account of the Sales of the Ship *Princess*, Prize to the *Kemp*, undated; and Disbursements of the Schooner *Kemp*, May 20, 1815, MHR, Peter Arnold Karthaus and Company Shipping Accounts.

27. Authorization Notice by the Owners of the *Tom*, November 10, 1812, NRC-S, Md. District Admiralty Cases.

28. Gerrard Wilson's Account with Philip Moore, Clerk of the District Court, endorsed by Wilson, undated, *ibid.*

29. Owners of the Privateer Schooner *Tom* in Account Current with Philip Moore, Clerk, District Court, October 30, 1812, *ibid.*

30. Receipt of the Owners of the Private Armed Schooner *Dolphin* for the Prize Money from the *John Hamilton*, March 30, 1813, *ibid.*

31. Briscoe and Partridge in Account with Christopher Deshon — Concerning the Schooner *Rossie*, June, 1813, to June, 1814, MHS, Partridge Papers.

32. Sales of the Prize Ship *John* and her Cargo, November 24, 1812; and the Owners of the Privateer Schooner *Comet* in Account Current with Philip Moore, Clerk, District Court, December 12, 1812, NRC-S, Md. District Admiralty Cases.

33. Levi Hollingsworth's Receipt for his Share of the Prize Ship *John* and her Cargo, January 6, 1813, *ibid.*

34. *American*, August 4, 1814.

35. Distribution of the Prize Money to the Officers and Crew of the *Comet* in the Case of the Ship *Hopewell* and her Cargo, October 29, 1812, NRC-S, Md. District Admiralty Cases.

36. Various Letters of Attorney, Bills of Sale of Prize Tickets, 1812–1815, *ibid.*

37. Power of Attorney to Lemuel Taylor from the Crew of the Privateer *Dolphin*, October 31, 1812; and Lemuel Taylor's Receipt for the Prize Money of the *John Hamilton*, March 30, 1813, *ibid.*

38. Various Receipts for Prize Money, and Articles of Agreement, 1812–1815, *ibid.*
39. James Hooper's Receipt, November 9, 1812, *ibid.*
40. Bill of Sale of a Prize Ticket, October 22, 1812, *ibid.* A written endorsement on the ticket transferred it to Cloney.
41. Distribution to the Officers and Crew of the Privateer *Globe* of ½ Net Proceeds of the Prize Schooner *Ann* and its Cargo, September —, 1812, *ibid.*
42. Distribution of the Proceeds of the Prize Ship *Jamaica* and her Cargo and the Schooner *Harriet* and her Cargo to the Officers and Crew of the Privateer *Highflyer*, endorsed by Tenant on December 5, 1812, *ibid.*
43. Distributions to the Officers and Crew 1812–1815, *ibid.*; for the *Sabine*, Distribution, ————, 1815, MHS, McBlair Papers.
44. Peters, ed., *op. cit.*, III, p. 136, and II, p. 788. The competition for men from the private armed vessels may have been a factor encouraging Congress to increase the pay in the army and navy.
45. Distributions of Prize Money and Answers to Libels, 1812–1815, NRC-S, Md. District Admiralty Cases.
46. *Niles Weekly Register*, August 12, 1815.
47. Distribution of the Prize Money to the Officers and Crew of the Schooner *Baltimore* from the Sales of the *Point Shares*, signed at various times between 1813 and 1818, and to the Officers and Crew of the Schooner *Patapsco* from the Sales of the Schooner *Maria*, June 18, 1814, NRC-S, Md. District Admiralty Cases; also Proceeds of the Brig *Williams* and her Cargo, Prize to the Schooner *Decatur*, undated, MHS, Ships' Papers.
48. Proceeds of the Brig *William* and her Cargo, Prize to the Schooner *Decatur*, undated, MHS, Ships' Papers.
49. Distribution of the Prize Money to the Officers and Crew of the Schooner *Patapsco* from the Sales of the Schooner *Maria*, June 18, 1814, NRC-S, Md. District Admiralty Cases.
50. *Niles Weekly Register*, August 27, 1814.
51. Peter A. Guestier's Answer to the Libel of Edward McCue and Seven Others to the Xebec *Ultor*, March 8, 1819, NRC-S, Md. District Admiralty Cases.
52. Answer of James Ramsay Prize Agent of the *Sarah Ann*, to the Libel of Michael Pluck and Henry Mayer, June 15, 1814, *ibid.*
53. Letter, Captain Edward Veazey of the *Baltimore* to United States Marshal Thomas Rutter, April 4, 1816, *ibid.*
54. Captain Thomas Boyle's Answer to the Libel of James Caldwell and Two Others, November 23, 1812, *ibid.*
55. Andrew Clopper's Answer to the Petition of John Young, Master of the Schooner *Patapsco*, June 18, 1814, *ibid.*
56. Wilfred Harold Munro, "The Most Successful American Privateer: An Episode of the War of 1812," *Proceedings of the American Antiquarian Society*, XXIII (1913), p. 17; and an entry of December 26, 1814 in Registers of United States Prisoners in Halifax, Barbados and Jamaica, November, 1805 to March, 1815, NA, Naval Records Collections of the Office of Naval Records and Library, RG 45, Barbados vol.
57. Christopher Deshon's Answer to the Libel of Benjamin White for David York's Share, June 19, 1814, NRC-S, Md. District Admiralty Cases.
58. Answer of Andrew Clopper to the Libel of Frederick Travers, the Elder, November 8, 1815, *ibid.*
59. Answer of George P. Stevenson to the Libel of Dixon, Lockwood, Hartnett and Fewery, October —, 1815, *ibid.*
60. Letter, J. W. F. ———— [indiscernible], Philadelphia, to Michael McBlair, March 23, 1815, MHS, McBlair Papers.
61. Christopher Deshon's Answer to the Libel of John Leeds, Carpenter on the *Rolla*, February 8, 1814, NRC-S, Md. District Admiralty Cases.
62. Notation in Account of the Distribution of the Privateer *Comet* in the Case of the Ship *John* and her Cargo, December to March, 1813, *ibid.*
63. Letter, T. and S. Hollingsworth to Levi Hollingsworth and Son, Phila., February 17, 1814, HSP, Hollingsworth MSS, Correspondence.
64. See Appendix F (Baltimore Owners' Proceeds from Thirty-five Privateer Prize Actions,

1812–1815). This sample consists of prize vessels and cargoes of all types and sizes and some prize cargoes in the holds of privateers. It includes prize cases both before and after the fees and duties were lowered and some cases from other ports. Only Baltimore-owned and -directed capturing vessels are included. Some prisoner bounties are included but not for all cases because they were not part of the court record.

65. *Ibid.* Duties were sometimes added to the owners' proceeds by the clerk of the court as a bookkeeping technique. Such cases were corrected for this study. Drawbacks on duties were not always listed by the purchaser's name so they have been omitted entirely in this sample.

66. Peter Arnold Karthaus, Owner of the Private Armed Schooner *Baltimore* in Account with Philip Moore, Clerk, District Court, November 11, 1812, and Distribution of the Prize Money to the Officers and Crew of the Schooner *Patapsco* from the Sales of the Schooner *Maria*, June 18, 1814, NRC-S, Md. District Admiralty Cases; Proceeds of the Brig *Williams* and her Cargo, Prize to the *Decatur*, undated, MHS, Ships' Papers.

67. See Appendix G (Estimated Owners' Income from Twenty-eight Successful Baltimore-owned Privateers in the War of 1812).

68. See Appendixes C and D for substantiated owners of two or more commissioned vessels.

69. See Appendix B for ownership substantiation, Appendix G for a list of successful privateers, and Appendix H for individual vessel performance.

70. Agent Christopher Deshon's Statement of the Cruise of the Private Armed Schooner *Rossie*, May 31, 1814, MHS, Partridge Papers.

71. See Appendix G for the estimated income of the privateer *Tom*.

72. See Appendix H for comments on individual private armed vessels. Six months is used as an adequate period for a letter-of-marque trader to earn her costs of about $25,000. The period is long for West Indian voyages, but the blockade kept vessels in port for inordinate periods of time and the West Indian vessels often went to Europe also.

73. See Appendix C for ownership substantiation, Appendix G for a list of successful privateers, and Appendix H for the performances of individual vessels.

74. See Appendix C for substantiated ownership and Appendix H for individual vessel performances.

75. See Appendix D for substantiated ownership, Appendix G for successful privateers, and Appendix H for individual vessel performances.

76. See Appendix D for substantiated ownership, Appendix G for successful privateers, and Appendix H for individual vessel performances.

77. Letters, 1812–1815, MHS, Didier Letterbook.

78. See Appendix D for substantiated ownership, Appendix G for successful privateers, and Appendix H for individual vessel performances.

79. Letter, John Hollins to ———, February 28, 1813, University of Virginia, Wilson Cary Nicholas Papers. John Hollins was president of an insurance company.

80. Letter, Samuel Smith to Mary B. Mansfield, London, June 8, 1810, University of Virginia, Samuel Smith Papers.

81. See Appendix D for substantiated ownership, Appendix G for successful privateers, and Appendix H for individual vessel performances.

82. Letter, T. and S. Hollingsworth to Levi Hollingsworth and Son, Phila., September 6, 1812, HSP, Hollingsworth MSS, Correspondence.

83. Letters, Richard H. Douglass to Hannibal Price, September 20, and December 23, 1817, MHS, Douglass Letterbook; John Quincy Adams, *op. cit.*, p. 238.

84. Notice in *American*, July 27, 1812.

85. Crane and Cranwell, *op. cit.*, p. 345.

86. Letter, Levi Hollingsworth to Levi Hollingsworth and Son, Phila., May 17, 1813, HSP, Hollingsworth MSS, Correspondence; Bourne, *op. cit.*, p. 281.

87. Entry for December, 1813, MHR, Peter Arnold Karthaus Company Journal.

88. Entries for December, 1813, 1814, and 1815, *ibid.*

89. *American*, May 5, 1814.

90. See Appendix D for substantiated ownership, Appendix G for successful privateers, and Appendix H for individual vessel performances.

91. See Appendix D for substantiated ownership, Appendix G for successful privateers, and Appendix H for individual vessel performances.

92. Crane and Cranwell, *op. cit.*, pp. 376 and 399, credit Stevenson with owners' shares in those vessels but his name does not appear on their documents.

CHAPTER TWELVE

1. See Appendix H for vessels captured or lost at sea.
2. Prize Dockets, 1812–1815, NA (at Suitland), Records of United States Attorneys and Marshals, RG 118.
3. Even with prize business about one-half of the city's vendue houses folded during the war. Letter, Hollingsworth and Worthington to Levi Hollingsworth and Son, Phila., May 12, 1813, HSP, Hollingsworth MSS, Correspondence.
4. Statements of the Dividends of Prize Money from the Cruize of the Private Armed Schooner *Rossie*, filed with the Clerk, December 6, 1815, NRC-S, Md. District Admiralty Cases; May 31, 1814, MHS, Partridge Papers; Prize List of the Schooner *Rossie*, undated, HSP, Joshua Barney Papers, II.
5. Distribution of the Prize Money of the Officers and Crew of the *Comet* in the Case of the Ship *Hopewell* and Cargo, October 19, 1812, NRC-S, Md. District Admiralty Cases.
6. Captain Joseph Almeda's Account with Peter Arnold Karthaus and Company, June 1, 1815; and Joseph Almeda's Account Credit on Peter Arnold Karthaus' Books, undated, MHR, Peter Arnold Karthaus and Company Shipping Accounts.
7. Statement of the Cruize of the Private Armed Schooner *Rossie*, May 31, 1814, MHS, Partridge Papers.
8. Resumé of Baltimore Commissions, July 10, 1812 to December 24, 1813, NA, Navy Privateer Records.
9. J. H. Hollander, *The Financial History of Baltimore*, extra volume XX of the Johns Hopkins University Studies in History and Political Science, ed. Herbert B. Adams (Baltimore: Johns Hopkins Press, 1899), pp. 378–81.
10. Reports of the Baltimore city collector, p. 382; *ibid.*
11. Letter, Henry Didier, Jr. to John Didier in France, September 27, 1813, MHS, Didier Letterbook.
12. Stuart Weems Bruchey, "Success and Failure Factors: American Merchants in Foreign Trade in the Eighteenth and Early Nineteenth Centuries," *The Business History Review*, XXXII, No. 3 (Autumn, 1958), p. 274.
13. Letter, Samuel Smith to John Smith in Paris, May 25, 1812, Library of Congress, Samuel Smith Papers.
14. Letter, Hollingsworth and Worthington to Levi Hollingsworth and Son, Phila., November 10, 1812, HSP, Hollingsworth MSS, Correspondence.
15. Letter, Levi Hollingsworth (Baltimore) to Levi Hollingsworth and Son, Phila., September 21, 1814, *ibid.*
16. *American*, July 28, 1812.
17. *Federal Gazette*, January 19, and March 17, 1813; November 7, and August 13, 1813.
18. *American*, July 20, 1812.
19. Letter, Captain Edward Veazey, at Sea, to Richard H. Douglass, May 18, 1814, MHS, Ships' Logs and Papers.
20. *Niles Weekly Register*, January 16, 1814.
21. Stuart Weems Bruchey, *The Roots of American Economic Growth, 1607–1861: An Essay in Social Causation* (New York: Harper and Row, Publishers, 1968), pp. 150–51.
22. Logs of the *Comet* (two cruises) and *Chasseur*, MHS, Ships' Logs and Papers.
23. Articles of Agreement of the *Comet*, July 7, 1812; of the *Tom*, August 1, 1812; of the *Pike*, May 8, 1814; and Power of Attorney to Lemuel Taylor from the Crew of the *Dolphin*, October 31, 1812, NRC-S, Md. District Admiralty Cases.
24. Deposition of Samuel Dougherty, First Sergeant of Marines on the *Comet*, March 15, 1813, *ibid.*
25. Deposition of George Riggs, Drummer on the *Comet*, March 15, 1813, *ibid.*
26. Deposition of John E. Smith, Boatswain on the *Comet*, March 15, 1813, *ibid.*

27. Libel of *John Hutchins* v. *William Hoffer*, Mate of the *Pioneer* for Assault and Battery, December 7, 1812, *ibid.* Hoffer, according to a notation dated February 23, 1813, agreed to pay Hutchins.
28. Libel of *Jeremiah Mead* v. *Samuel Childs and the Brig* Female, May 28, 1813, *ibid.*
29. Libel of *John Will* v. *David Gray* of the *Siro*, August 16, 1815, *ibid.*
30. Copy of the Charges and Specifications Preferred Against John Marr, Late Gunner of the Private Armed Schooner *Rossie* of Baltimore at a Naval Court Martial held at the Navy Yard, Baltimore, undated, HSP, Joshua Barney Papers, II.
31. Letter, Levi Hollingsworth (Baltimore) to Levi Hollingsworth and Son, Phila., September 21, 1814, HSP, Hollingsworth MSS, Correspondence.
32. Letter, Henry Didier, Jr. to John N. D'Arcy in England, June 23, 1813, MHS, Didier Letterbook.
33. Depositions of John Powers, Chief Mate and of the Second Mate, Boatswain and Gunner of the *Bordeaux Packet*, November 29, 1815, NRC-S, Md. District Admiralty Cases.
34. Log of the *Bona*, MHS, Ships' Logs and Papers.
35. *Niles Weekly Register*, November 28, 1812.
36. Circular from the Secretary of State to the Commanders of Private Armed Vessels, July —, 1812, NA, War of 1812 Papers. The circulars arrived in Baltimore after some vessels had cleared so the signals were not used, but the *Rossie* had a copy of the circular.
37. Private Signals of the Schooner *Nonsuch*, undated; and Number of Colours on Board the *Rossie*, undated, HSP, Joshua Barney Papers, II.
38. Letter, Henry Didier, Jr. to John N. D'Arcy in England, February 27, 1815, MHS, Didier Letterbook.
39. *Ibid.*
40. Letters, T. and S. Hollingsworth to Levi Hollingsworth and Son, Phila., February 20, 1815; Hollingsworth and Worthington to Levi Hollingsworth and Son, Phila., February 27, 1815; T. and S. Hollingsworth to Levi Hollingsworth and Son, Phila., March 16, 1815; Hollingsworth and Worthington to Levi Hollingsworth and Son, Phila., March 19, 1815; and T. and S. Hollingsworth to Levi Hollingsworth and Son, Phila., April 4, 1815, HSP, Hollingsworth MSS, Correspondence.
41. Price of Flour at Baltimore from July 1, 1802 to January 1, 1822, *American State Papers, Commerce and Navigation*, II, p. 657.
42. North, *op. cit.*, p. 62 and pp. 178–79; and Robert Greenhalgh Albion, *The Rise of New York Port, 1815–1860* (Hamden, Conn.: Archon Books, 1961), p. 92.
43. Bruchey, *Robert Oliver*, p. 340.
44. Smith and Cole, *op. cit.*, p. 20.
45. Mahan, *op. cit.*, II, p. 206.
46. Entries of June 28, September 23, and other 1815 dates, MHR, Peter Arnold Karthaus and Company Shipping Accounts.
47. Letters, Henry Didier, Jr. to John N. D'Arcy in England, March 27, April 7, May 5, May 16, 1815, MHS, Didier Letterbook.
48. Letters, Richard H. and William Douglass to William S. Cooper, Port au Prince, November 23, 1816; to William Taylor, Port au Prince, November 14, and 23, 1816; to David Corry and Company, Port au Prince, January 4, 1817, MHS, Douglass Letterbook.
49. Letters, Richard H. and William Douglass to J. J. Hoogerwerff, Boston, April 5, 1817; and to Stanforth and Blunt, London, November 1, 1816, *ibid.*
50. Letter, Richard H. and William Douglass to James Townes and Company, Fayettevill, North Carolina, December 24, 1816, *ibid.*
51. North, *op. cit.*, p. 67.
52. Letters, Richard H. and William Douglass to Stevens and Mactier, New York, November 20, and 21, 1817; to William Tucker, Boston, December 20, 1816; to William Tucker, Boston, December 21, 1816; and to Miller and McLeod, Kingston, Jamaica, November 2, 1817, MHS, Douglass Letterbook.
53. Export Bond Book, 1815–1818, NA, Balto. Customs Records.
54. Letter, Richard H. and William Douglass to Hannibal Price, Jacmel, December 23, 1817, MHS, Douglass Letterbook.

55. Letter, Russel and La Farge, Havre, October 17, 1816, to Joseph Despeaux, October 17, 1816, MHS, Joseph Despeaux Papers.
56. Letter, Martin F. Maher to Levi Hollingsworth and Son, Phila., March 22, 1815, HSP, Hollingsworth MSS, Correspondence.
57. Scharf, *Chronicles*, p. 394.
58. Griffith, *op. cit.*, p. 226.
59. Letters, Henry Didier, Jr. to John N. D'Arcy in England, March 27, 1815; and to John Didier in the West Indies, March 5, 1815, MHS, Didier Letterbook.
60. Letter, Hall Harrison to Hugh Thompson in Ireland, September 27, 1815, MHS, Hugh Thompson Papers.
61. Letters, Richard H. and William Douglass to William Tucker, October 28, and November 18, 1816, MHS, Douglass Letterbook.
62. Bruchey, *Robert Oliver*, pp. 359–61.
63. Letter, Richard H. and William Douglass to Sanforth and Blunt, London, June 14, 1817, MHS, Douglass Letterbook.
64. Letter, William Crawford to James H. McCulloch, May 5, 1821, NA, General Records of the Department of Treasury, RG 56, Letters Sent by the Secretary of Treasury to Collectors of Customs at all Ports, 1789–1847.
65. *Niles Weekly Register*, April 29, 1815.
66. Payment to Privateer Pensioners, 1816–1829, NA, Records of the United States General Accounting Office, RG 217, Statements of the Account of the President of the Branch Bank of the United States at Baltimore, Payments to Privateer Pensioners, in Navy Pension Payment Records, Baltimore, 1816–1849, 6 boxes, 1 and 2. Joshua Barney, former navy captain and commodore, commanding the flotilla service in the Chesapeake Bay was receiving a navy pension of fifty dollars per month.
67. Arthur P. Whitaker, *The United States and the Independence of Latin America, 1800–1830* (New York: W. W. Norton and Company, 1964, originally published by The Johns Hopkins Press in 1941), pp. 139 and 219.
68. *Ibid.*, p. 219; *Annals of Congress*, 14th Congress, 2nd Session, p. 732.
69. Charles Carroll Griffin, *The United States and the Disruption of the Spanish Empire, 1810–1822: A Study of the Relations of the United States with Spain and the Rebel Spanish Colonies*, No. 429 of the Columbia University Studies in History, Economics and Public Law (New York: Columbia University Press, 1937), pp. 100–01 and pp. 104–26. There may have been some confusion of the two McCullochs here.
70. Various Depositions, 1818–1819, NA, General Records of the Department of State, RG 59, Miscellaneous Piracies — Depositions in re Privateers Fitted Out in Baltimore and their Depredations in South American Waters, 1818–1819.
71. *Ibid.*; Griffin, *op. cit.*, p. 105.
72. *Annals of Congress*, 14th Congress, 2nd Session, p. 732; and Charles F. Adams, ed., *Memoirs of John Q. Adams*, 12 vols. (Philadelphia: J. B. Lippincott and Company, 1875), IV, pp. 44–45.
73. Letter, James H. McCulloch to Secretary of Treasury A. J. Dallas, June 24, and September 2, 1816, NA, General Records of the Department of Treasury, RG 56, Correspondence of the Secretary of Treasury with the Collectors of Customs, 1789–1833; Various Depositions, 1818–1819, NA, General Records of the Department of State, RG 59, Misc. Piracies — Depositions in re Privateers Fitted Out in Baltimore and their Depredations in South American Waters, 1818–1819.
74. Letter, James H. McCulloch to Secretary of Treasury William H. Crawford, February 2, 1819, NA, General Records of the Department of Treasury, RG 56, Correspondence of the Secretary of Treasury with the Collectors of Customs, 1789–1833.
75. Letter, James H. McCulloch to Secretary of Treasury William H. Crawford, February 3, 1821, *ibid.*; public complaints in *Niles Weekly Register*, January 8, 1820.
76. Letter, James Monroe to the Marshal of Baltimore, December 7, 1816, NA, General Records of the Department of State, RG 59, Domestic Letters, 1784–1906.
77. Letters, James Monroe to James H. McCulloch, July 19, 1816, January 3, and February 15, 1817, *ibid.*
78. Letters, Don Luis de Onis to John Q. Adams, February 12, and 22, March 11, and 26, and

June 2, 1817, also one undated, in Thomas B. Wait, comp., *State Papers and Publick Documents of the United States*, 12 vols. (Boston: T. B. Wait, 1819), XII, pp. 139 and 149–53.

79. Letters, Elias Glenn to William Wirt, October 9, and December 17, 1818, NA, Attorney General Papers, RG 60, Maryland Correspondence, 1812–1862.
80. Letters, W. R. Swift to William Wirt, December 17, 19, 1818, *ibid.*
81. Letter, David Hoffman to William Wirt, June 28, 1818, *ibid.*
82. *Appleton's Cyclopaedia*, II, p. 72.
83. Letter, Secretary of the Treasury William Crawford to Samuel Smith, April 3, 1819, Library of Congress, Samuel Smith Papers.
84. The *United States* v. *Schooner Orb alias* Congresso, March 25, 1817, and June 5, 1822, NRC-S, Md. District Admiralty Cases.
85. Libel of *Jonathan Manro and Others* v. *Captain Almeda*, May 17, 1817, *ibid.*
86. Letter, James Houston, Chestertown, Maryland, to Philip Moore, Clerk of the Maryland District Court, March 29, 1817, *ibid.*
87. Various Cases 1817 to 1822, NA (Suitland), Records of United States Attorneys and Marshals, RG 118, Admiralty Dockets, 1814–1822.
88. Bills of Sale and Certificates of Registry 1815 to 1818, NA, Marine Documentation Records.
89. Chapelle, *Search for Speed Under Sail*, p. 299.
90. Letter, James H. McCulloch to Secretary of the Treasury William H. Crawford, June 9, 1819, NA, General Records of the Treasury Department, RG 56, Correspondence of the Secretary of Treasury with the Collectors of Customs, 1789–1833.
91. Letter, James H. McCulloch to Samuel D. Ingham, May 11, 1829, *ibid.*
92. Letter, James H. McCulloch to Attorney General William Wirt, January, 1824, NA, Attorney General Papers, RG 60, Maryland Correspondence, 1812–1862.
93. Letters, Secretary of State Henry Clay to William Wirt, May 16, 1826 and January 2, 1827, NA, Attorney General Papers, RG 60, Letters from the State Department, 1813–1831.
94. Libel of the *United States* v. *the Schooner* St. Iago de Cuba, NA, Letters Received by the Treasury Solicitor from United States Attorneys, Clerks and Marshals, RG 206, United States Attorney's Statement of Cases for the Maryland District Court, September, 1820.
95. Owens, *op. cit.*, p. 213.
96. Chapelle, *Search for Speed Under Sail*, pp. 301–03.
97. Letter, Richard H. and William Douglass to Mumford Beverly, May 12, 1817, MHS, Douglass Letterbook.
98. Bills of Sale, 1815 and 1816, NA, Marine Documentation Records.
99. Bills of Sale and Certificates of Registry, 1815–1819, *ibid.*
100. Certificates of Registry, 1814–1815, *ibid.*
101. Master Carpenters' Certificates, 1790–1819, NA, Marine Documentation Records; and Albion, *op. cit.*, p. 168.
102. Bills of Sale of Vessels, 1815 and 1816; and Certificates of Registry for 1815 and 1816, NA, Marine Documentation Records.
103. Letter, George P. Stevenson to Wilson Cary Nicholas, May 5, 1816, University of Virginia, Wilson Cary Nicholas Papers.
104. Register No. 154, May 20, 1815, NA, Marine Documentation Records.
105. Letter, Michael McBlair to James H. McCulloch, October 29, 1818, MHS, McBlair Papers; entries for 1815 to 1819 in Abstract of Bonds in Suit, December 31, 1819, and Index to Bonds in Suit, 1818–1836, NA, Balto. Customs Records.
106. Stevenson's Accounts, undated, MHS, McBlair Papers.
107. Letters, Richard H. and William Douglass to Stevens and Mactier, New York, October 4, 1816, to Kirkpatrick, Grevignee and Company, Malaga, Spain, November 2, 1816; to D. W. and C. Warwick, Richmond, October 4, 1816, and to D. W. and C. Warwick, Richmond, October 4, 1816, MHS, Douglass Letterbook.
108. Stevenson's Accounts, undated, MHS, McBlair Papers.
109. Customs House Bonds Account, October 3, 1818 or 1819, *ibid.*
110. Letters, Richard H. and William Douglass to Stevens and Mactier, April 10, 1817, MHS, Douglass Letterbook, and George P. Stevenson to ———, October 25, 1817, University of Virginia, Wilson Cary Nicholas Papers.
111. Allan Nevins, ed., *op. cit.*, p. 197.

eorge. *Life on the Ocean or Twenty Years at Sea: Being the Personal Adventures of the*
or. 12th ed, Boston: Waite, Peirce and Company, 1846.

, Reginald Geofrey. *Documents Relating to the Law and Customs of the Sea.* Vols. I
II. London: Publications of the Navy Records Society, 1915.

Allan, ed. *The Diary of John Quincy Adams, 1794–1845: American Political, Social and*
ectual Life from Washington to Polk. New York: Longman Green and Company,
.

incent. *Fifty Years in Both Hemispheres or Reminiscences of the Life of a Former*
hant. New York: Redfield, 1854.

ichard, ed. *The Public Statutes-at-Large of the United States of America.* Vols. I, II,
III. Boston: Charles C. Little and James Brown, 1848–1873.

, Kate Mason. *The Life of Charles Carroll of Carrollton, 1737–1832, With His Corre-*
ence and Public Papers. Vols. I and II. New York: G. P. Putnam and Sons, 1898.

Raphael, ed. *Baltimore as Seen by Visitors, 1783–1860.* Studies in Maryland His-
No. 2. Baltimore: Maryland Historical Society, 1953.

omas B., comp. *State Papers and Publick Documents of the United States.* Vol. XII.
on: T. B. Wait, 1819.

on, H. A., ed. *The Writings of Thomas Jefferson.* Vol. VI. Washington, D.C.:
or and Maury, 1853 and 1854.

nent Documents and Correspondence

tes Archives. Suitland, Maryland.
rds of United States Attorneys and Marshals. Record Group 118.
dmiralty Dockets for the Maryland District Court, 1812–1817, 2 vols.
strict Court Decrees in Admiralty, 1806–1808, 1 vol.
aryland District Court Prize Dockets, 1812–1815, 1 vol.

tes National Archives. Washington, D.C.
rney General Papers. Record Group 60.
tters Received from the Department of State, 1813–1831, 1 box.
aryland Correspondence, 1812–1862, 1 box.
ral Records of the Department of State. Record Group 59.
mestic Letters of the Department of State, 1784–1906. Microcopy No. M-40.
Roll No. 14.
scellaneous Letters of the Department of State, 1789–1906. Microcopy No.
M-179. Rolls Nos. 25, 26, 27, 28, 29, 30, 31, and 32.
ar of 1812 Papers of the Department of State, 1789–1815. Letters Received
Concerning Letters-of-Marque, 1812–1814. Microcopy No. M-588. Rolls Nos.
, 3, and 5.
scellaneous Piracies — Depositions in re Privateers Fitted out in Baltimore and
Their Depredations in South American Waters, 1818–1819, 1 box.
ral Records of the Department of Treasury. Record Group No. 56.
rrespondence of the Secretary of Treasury with the Collectors of Customs,
789–1833. Microcopy No. M-178. Rolls Nos. 2, 3, and 8.
tters Sent by the Secretary of Treasury to Collectors of Customs at all Ports,
789–1847. Microcopy No. M-175. Rolls Nos. 1 and 2.
Records Collections of the Office of Naval Records and Library. Record
p 45.

112. Letter, Antonio de Arias to George P. Stevenson, July 7, 1819, MHS, McBlair Papers.
113. Hammond, *op. cit.*, pp. 260–61; Ralph C. H. Catterall, *The Second Bank of the United States* (Chicago: University of Chicago Press, 1902), p. 39.
114. Hammond, *op. cit.*, pp. 260–61; Cassell, *op. cit.*, p. 223.
115. Answers of James A. Buchanan to the Interrogations of the Creditors of S. Smith and Buchanan, June 18, 1821, University of Virginia, Samuel Smith Papers.
116. Letters, Samuel Smith to Nicholas Biddle, June 20, 1823, and to Colonel James Morrison, Kentucky, July 8, 1819, University of Virginia, Samuel Smith Letterbook.
117. Letter, Samuel Smith to Langdon Cheves, October 4, 1819, *ibid.*
118. Letter, Robert Oliver to General Robert Goodloe Harper, July 4, and 26, 1819, MHS, Harper Letters; Hammond, *op. cit.*, pp. 268–72.
119. Letter, John Glenn to Attorney General William Wirt, December 13, 1822, NA, Attorney General's Papers, RG 60, Maryland Correspondence, 1812–1862.
120. Letter, Michael McBlair to John Gooding, May 23, 1819, MHS, McBlair Papers.
121. Letter, James H. McCulloch to William Wirt, January —, 1824, NA, Attorney General's Papers, RG 60, Maryland Correspondence, 1812–1862.
122. Griffith, *op. cit.*, p. 231; for four soup kitchens plus street carts, see *American*, September 18, 1819; and for yellow fever, Scharf, *Chronicles*, p. 394.
123. Index to Bonds in Suit, 1818–1836, NA, Balto. Customs Records. Joseph Karrick was declared insolvent once in Baltimore and then again in England, *Niles Weekly Register*, February 10, 1821.
124. Cassell, *op. cit.*, pp. 224–31.
125. Letter, John Hollins to Michael McBlair, July 7, 1822, MHS, McBlair Papers.
126. Letter, Mathias Johnston for King and Johnston to Hollins and McBlair, December 16, 1822, *ibid.*; *Niles Weekly Register*, October 23, 1819, doubted that the formerly wealthy merchants were as poor as they pretended when they declared themselves insolvent.
127. Petition of Michael McBlair to the Commissioners of Insolvent Debtors for the City and County of Baltimore, October —, 1822, MHS, McBlair Papers. Sixty insolvent debtors were listed on one day in the *Federal Gazette*, October 18, 1819. Seven had been private vessel investors.
128. Scharf, *Chronicles*, p. 407; and Baltimore Entrances and Clearances, 1782–1824, NA, Balto. Customs Records.
129. Griffith, *op. cit.*, pp. 258 and 266.
130. Cassell, *op. cit.*, pp. 225–26.
131. Letters, Samuel Smith to Secretary of the Treasury Joseph Anderson, June 10, 1822, and June 21, 1824, University of Virginia, Samuel Smith Letterbook.
132. J. C. Kayser, *Baltimore Commercial Directory* (Philadelphia: J. C. Kayser and Company, 1823), pp. 66 and 73–77. As "agents" the bankrupt merchants performed as employees and not proprietors. Their creditors could not get the courts to confiscate the mill property.
133. *Ibid.*, pp. 69–72.
134. *Ibid.*, pp. 69–72.
135. Charles Varle, *Complete View of Baltimore with a Statistical Sketch* (Baltimore: Samuel Young, 1833), pp. 40–45, 86–98, 102, 132, 143, and 206.
136. Griffith, *op. cit.*, pp. 232 and 234; and Appointment, December 16, 1817, HSP, Joshua Barney Papers, II. For Stiles's rotary steam engine, used to bore cannons during the War of 1812 and on the steamboat *Surprise* in 1817, see *Niles Weekly Register*, October 16, 1819.
137. Townsend, *op. cit.*, pp. 188, 197, 213, 230, 265, 269, 322, 344, and 359.
138. *Niles Weekly Register*, April 27, 1839; *The Sun* (Baltimore), April 25, 1839, *American*, April 23, and 26, 1839, all cited in Cassell, *Merchant Congressman in the Young Republic*, pp. 263–64.

CHAPTER THIRTEEN

1. Adams, *op. cit.*, VII, p. 335.
2. Maclay, *op. cit.*, p. 2.
3. Albion, *op. cit.*, pp. 156–57, and *Square Riggers on Schedule* (Princeton: Princeton University Press, 1939), pp. 49–50.

4. François Crouzet, "Wars, Blockade and Economic Change in Europe, 1792–1815," *Journal of Economic History*, XXIV, No. 4 (December, 1964), pp. 569–72.
5. *Niles Weekly Register*, August 13, 1815, and January 6, 1816.
6. Maclay, *op. cit.*, VIII. According to Maclay, 517 American "privateers" captured 1,300 prizes.
7. Crane and Cranwell, *op. cit.*, p. 401; Owens, *op. cit.*, p. 185; and, for the higher figure, Appendix G (Estimated Owners' Proceeds from Twenty-eight Successful Baltimore Privateers).
8. *Niles Weekly Register*, March 4, 1815.
9. Adams, *op. cit.*, VIII, pp. 198–99; *Niles Weekly Register*, November 26, 1814.
10. Paine, *op. cit.*, p. 118.
11. Adams, *op. cit.*, VII, p. 331.
12. Mahan, *op. cit.*, I, p. 288.
13. *Niles Weekly Register*, November 26, 1814.
14. Coggeshall, *op. cit.*, xlix.
15. Bradford Perkins, *Castlereagh and Adams: England and the United States 1812–1823* (Berkeley: University of California Press, 1964), p. 37.
16. *Ibid.*, p. 98; Matthew Page Andrews, *History of Maryland: Province and State* (New York: Doubleday, Doran and Company, 1929), p. 443. Andrews suggests that the Madison administration would have been unable to relocate at Washington, D.C., if the British had taken Baltimore and used it as a naval base.
17. Letter, Albert Gallatin in London to James Monroe, June 13, 1814, in Henry Adams, ed., *op. cit.*, I, pp. 628–29.
18. Letter, Albert Gallatin in New York to Thomas Jefferson, September 6, 1815, *ibid.*, pp. 651–52.
19. Adams, *op. cit.*, VII, pp. 337–38, and VIII, p. 245.
20. Letter, James Monroe to William Branch Giles, October 26, 1814, *American State Papers, Military Affairs*, I, p. 518.
21. Report of the Paymaster, October 26, 1814, *ibid.*, p. 519.
22. *Niles Weekly Register*, December 26, 1812.
23. Adams, *op. cit.*, VII, p. 338, and VIII, p. 181.
24. Perkins, *op. cit.*, p. 18.
25. Chapelle, *History of the American Sailing Navy*, p. 292.
26. An Act for the Protection of the Commerce of the United States Against the Algerine Cruisers, March 3, 1815, in Peters, ed., *op. cit.*, II, p. 230; *Niles Weekly Register*, March 11, 1815.
27. K. Jack Bauer, *The Mexican War, 1846–1848*, in The Macmillan Wars of the United States series, ed. Louis Morton (New York: Macmillan Publishing Company, 1974), pp. 69–70.
28. Stark, *op. cit.*, pp. 135–48 and 151.
29. *Ibid.*, p. 155.
30. William M. Robinson, *The Confederate Privateers* (New Haven: Yale University Press, 1928), pp. 1, 18–23, and Stuart L. Bernath, *Squall Across the Atlantic: American Civil War Prize Cases and Diplomacy* (Berkeley: University of California Press, 1970), p. 2.
31. Robinson, *op. cit.*, pp. 22–23.
32. *Ibid.*, pp. 30 and 243.
33. Stark, *op. cit.*, p. 156.
34. *New York Herald*, February 1, 3, and 20, 1862.
35. Robinson, *op. cit.*, p. 315.
36. Julius W. Pratt, *A History of United States Foreign Policy*, 3rd ed. (Englewood Cliffs, N.J.: Prentice-Hall, 1972), p. 157, and Charles S. Campbell, *From Revolution to Rapprochement: The United States and Great Britain, 1783–1900* (New York: John Wiley and Sons, 1974), p. 97.
37. Stark, *op. cit.*, p. 157.
38. Maclay, *op. cit.*, XXIII.
39. Crane and Cranwell, *op. cit.*, p. 17.
40. Mahan, *op. cit.*, II, p. 213.

Selected Bibliograp

A. PRIMARY SOURCES

1. Published Documents, Narratives, Letters, and Memoirs

Adams, Charles F., ed. *Memoirs of John Q. Adams.* Vol. IV. Pl and Company, 1875.

Adams, Henry, ed. *The Writings of Albert Gallatin.* Vol. I. Pl and Company, 1879.

American State Papers. Commerce and Navigation. Vols. I and Relations. Vols. I and II. *Military.* Vol. I. *Naval Affairs.* and Seaton, 1832–1861.

Annals of Congress. 3rd, 12th, 13th, and 14th Congresses. W Seaton, 1853.

Benton, Thomas Hart. *Abridgements of the Debates of Congress.* Appleton and Company, 1860.

Browne, William H.; Hall, C. H.; Pleasants, J. H.; Sen Richard C. *Archives of Maryland: Journal and Corresp Maryland.* Vol. XVII and sub-series Documents Relati Vols. I through VIII. Baltimore: published by autho land Historical Society, 1892–1947.

Commager, Henry Steele, and Morris, Richard B., eds. Story of the American Revolution as Told by Its Participar Bobbs-Merrill Company, 1958.

Evans, Amos A. *Journal Kept on Board the Frigate Const* Reprinted for William D. Sawtell from the *Pennsy Biography*, 1967.

Handlin, Oscar, ed. *This Was America: As Recorded by Eu and 20th Centuries.* New York: Harper and Row, Pu

Jameson, John Franklin, ed. *Privateering and Piracy in Documents.* New York: The Macmillan Company, 1

Kimball, Gertrude Selwyn, ed. *Correspondence of William* the Colonial Governors and Military and Naval Commiss New York: The Macmillan Company, 1906.

Knox, Dudley W. *Naval Documents Related to the Quasi-V France.* Vols. II and VII. Washington, D.C.: Gov 38.

Letters from the Collectors of Customs to the Secretary of State Relative to Commissions of Privateers, 1812–1815, 6 vols.
Letters Received by the Secretary of the Navy from Commanders, 1804–1886. Microcopy No. M-147. Rolls Nos. M-4, 5, and 6.
Letters Sent by the Secretary of Navy to Commandants and Naval Agents, 1808–1865. Microcopy No. M-441. Rolls Nos. 1 and 2.
Register of British Prisoners of War in the United States, July, 1812–March, 1815, 2 vols.
Registers of United States Prisoners in Halifax, Barbados and Jamaica, November, 1805 to March, 1815, 3 vols.
Records of the Bureau of Customs. Record Group 36. Records of the Collector of Customs at Baltimore.
Abstracts of Bonds in Suit on December 31, 1819, 1 vol.
Abstracts of Registers of Vessels. October, 1789 to December, 1811, 1 vol.
Bonds for Letters-of-Marque and Reprisal, 1812, 3 bundles.
Bond Receipt Book, 1815–1823, 5 vols.
Crew Lists, 1812–1813, 3 boxes.
Export Bond Book, 1815–1818, 1 vol.
Entrances and Clearances, 1782–1824. Microcopy No. T-257, 1 reel.
Index to Bonds in Suit, 1818–1836, 1 vol.
Returned Privateer Commissions, 11 commissions.
Records of the Bureau of Marine Inspection and Navigation. Record Group 41.
Baltimore Bills of Sales of Vessels, 1812–1818, 11 boxes.
Baltimore Certificates of Registry, 1810–1818, 8 vols.
Baltimore Endorsements of Changes of Masters, 1800–1815, 1 vol.
Baltimore Master Carpenter Certificates, 1790–1819, 2 boxes.
Baltimore Owners' and Masters' Oaths of Ownership and Citizenship, 1812–1815, 6 vols.
Baltimore Registry Bond Books, 1811–1814, 3 vols.
Records of the Office of the Judge Advocate General (Navy). Record Group 125.
Records of General Courts Marshal and Courts of Inquiry of the Navy Department 1799–1867. Microcopy No. 273. Roll No. 6.
Records of the General Accounting Office. Record Group 217.
Navy Pension Records, Baltimore, Maryland, 1816–1849, Payment to Privateer Pensioners, 6 boxes.
Records of the Third United States Census.

United States Records Center. Suitland, Maryland.
Maryland District Court Records. Admiralty Cases. Record Group 21.
Maryland District Admiralty Cases, 1812–1815, 3 boxes.

3. Manuscript Collections

Historical Society of Pennsylvania. Philadelphia, Pennsylvania.
Dreer Collection, 1492–1917. Vol. I: American Navy.
Hollingsworth Manuscripts. Correspondence, 1761–1887. 1812–1815 Correspondence, 14 boxes.
Joshua Barney Papers, 1782–1818. Vols. I and II.

Library of Congress
>Samuel Smith Papers, 1762–1911. Boxes 5 through 8 (or University of Virginia microfilm copy. Rolls, 2, 3, and 4).
>Wilson Cary Nicholas Papers, 1765–1831, 7 vols. (or University of Virginia microfilm copy. Roll 2).

Maryland Hall of Records. Annapolis, Maryland.
>Peter Arnold Karthaus and Company Journal, 1813 to 1818, 1 vol.
>Peter Arnold Karthaus and Company Shipping Accounts, 1812–1817, 1 vol.

Maryland Historical Society. Baltimore, Maryland.
>Baltimore Custom House Papers, 1796–1798, 1 box.
>Baltimore Independent Company Record Book, 1814, 1 vol.
>Bordley Letterbook, 1727–1759, 5 vols.
>Commission of the *Ospray*. Vertical File.
>Commission of the *Swallow*. Vertical File.
>Despeaux Account Book, 1807–1820, 1 vol.
>Didier Letterbook, 1807–1820, 1 vol.
>Didier Notebook, 1815–1817, 1 vol.
>Donaldson Protest Book, 1793–1796, 1 vol.
>Douglass Letterbook, 1816–1818, 1 vol.
>Gilmor Family Memoranda, 1813, 1 vol.
>Grundy-Gibson Papers, 1783–1840, 1 box.
>Harper Letters, 1817–1912, 1 box.
>Harper-Pennington Papers, 1701–1899. Boxes 3, 4, 5, and 9.
>Henry Thompson Diary, 1802–1836. Vols. III, IV, and V.
>Hollingsworth Papers, 1732–1891, 1 box.
>Hugh Thompson Papers, 1813–1824, 2 boxes.
>Joseph Despeaux Papers, 1778–1884, 2 boxes.
>Letter. James Calhoun to Major General Nathaniel Greene. Vertical File.
>Letter. Samuel Smith to Maryland Council of Safety. Vertical File.
>Logs of the *Chasseur*, 1814–1815 and *Rolla*, 1812–1813, 2 vols.
>McBlair Papers, 1797–1855. Boxes II and X.
>Partridge Papers, 1713–1906, 3 boxes.
>Patterson Account Books, 1770–1906, 3 boxes.
>Pawson Papers, 1814–1820, 1 box.
>Samuel Smith Papers, 1776–1836, 1 box.
>Ships' Logs and Papers, 1812–1815, 4 vols. and 1 package.
>Ships' Papers. *Ultor* and *Decatur*, 1814–1815, 8 items.
>Smith Letterbooks, 1774–1821, 3 vols.
>Warden Letterbooks, 1804–1845. Vol. A.

University of Virginia, Alderman Library. Charlottesville, Virginia.
>Letterbook of General Samuel Smith, 1811–1829, 1 vol.
>Samuel Smith Papers, 1726–1924, 2,800 items.
>Wilson Cary Nicholas Papers, 1779–1824. Boxes 9, 10, 11, and 12.

4. Newspapers and Periodicals

The American and Commercial Daily Advertiser (Baltimore), 1812–1815, 1819.

The Baltimore News, 1902.
Federal Gazette and Baltimore Daily Advertiser, 1812–1815, 1819.
The Gentleman's Magazine (London), 1812–1815. Vols. LXXXII through LXXXV.
Maryland Gazette (Annapolis), 1795.
Maryland Journal (Annapolis), March 25, 1785.
Niles Weekly Register (Baltimore), 1812–1821.
News-Post (Baltimore), 1798.
New York Herald, 1862.
The Sun (Baltimore), 1839, 1906, and 1949.

5. Miscellaneous

"Memorial of the Merchants and Owners of the Private Armed Commissioned Vessels of War of the City of Baltimore." November 23, 1812. Washington: Printed by Roger C. Weightman by order of the United States Senate, 1812.
Townsend, Richard H. "The Diary of Richard H. Townsend; Containing Historical, Biographical and Genealogical Information for 1683–1879." Vol. I. WPA, completed 1851–1879. Copy of original manuscript. Baltimore. Enoch Pratt Free Library, 1937. (Typewritten.)
Warner and Hanna's Map of Baltimore — 1801. Republished in facsimile. Baltimore: Peabody Institute. Library, 1947.

B. SECONDARY SOURCES

1. Books

Adams, Henry. *History of the United States of America.* Vols. VII and VIII. New York: Charles Scribner's Sons, 1891.
Albion, Robert Greenhalgh. *Square Riggers on Schedule.* Princeton: Princeton University Press, 1939.
————. *The Rise of New York Port, 1815–1860.* Hamden, Conn.: Archon Press, 1961.
———— and Pope, Jennie Barnes. *Sea Lanes in Wartime: The American Experience.* 2nd ed. New York: Archon Books, 1968.
Alderman, Clifford Lindsey. *The Privateersmen.* New York: Chilton Books, 1965.
Andrews, Kenneth R. *Elizabethan Privateering: English Privateering During the Spanish War, 1585–1603.* Cambridge, Eng.: University Press, 1964.
————. *Drake's Voyages: A Re-Assessment of Their Place in Elizabethan Maritime Expansion.* London: Weidenfeld and Nicholson, 1967.
Andrews, Matthew Page. *History of Maryland: Province and State.* New York: Doubleday, Doran and Company, 1929.
Babcock, Kendric Charles. *The Rise of American Nationality, 1811–1819.* Vol. XIII: The American Nation: A History. Edited by Albert Bushnell Hart. New York: Harper and Brothers, 1906.
Backus, John C. *Historical Discourse on Taking Leave of the Old Church Edifice of the First Presbyterian Congregation in Baltimore.* Baltimore: John Woods, Printer, 1860.
Bauer, K. Jack. *The Mexican War 1846–1848.* In The Macmillan Wars of the United States series. Edited by Louis Morton. New York: Macmillan Publishing Company, 1974.

Beard, Miriam. *History of the Business Man.* New York: Macmillan Company, 1938.

Bendict, Erastus C. *The American Admiralty, Its Jurisdiction and Practice with Practical Forms and Directions.* 3rd ed. Revised by Robert D. Benedict. New York: Banks and Brothers, Law Publishers, 1894.

Bernath, Stuart L. *Squall Across the Atlantic: American Civil War Prize Cases and Diplomacy.* Berkeley: University of California Press, 1970.

Biographical Cyclopaedia of Representative Men of Maryland and District of Columbia. Baltimore: National Biographical Publications Company, 1879.

Bonnel, Ulane. *La France Les États-Unis et la Guerre de Course, 1797–1815.* Paris: Nouvelle Editions Latine, 1961.

Bouldin, James E. P. *Presbyterians of Baltimore: Their Churches and Historical Graveyards.* Baltimore: William K. Boyle and Son, 1875.

Brant, Irving. *James Madison, Commander-in-Chief, 1812–1836.* Indianapolis: The Bobbs-Merrill Company, 1961.

Brantz, Mayer. *Baltimore, Past and Present.* Baltimore: Richardson and Bennet, 1871.

Bridenbaugh, Carl. *Cities in Revolt: Urban Life in America, 1743–1776.* New York: A. Knopf and Company, 1955.

Brown, Ralph H. *Mirror for Americans: Likenesses of the Eastern Seaboard, 1810.* New York: American Geographic Society, 1943.

Browne, Arthur. *A Compendious View of the Civil Law and the Law of Admiralty.* Vols. I and II. London: J. Butterworth and John Cooke, 1802.

Bruchey, Stuart Weems. *Robert Oliver, Merchant of Baltimore.* Series LXXIV, No. 1: The Johns Hopkins University Studies in Historical and Political Science. Baltimore: The Johns Hopkins Press, 1956.

———. *The Roots of American Economic Growth, 1607–1861: An Essay in Social Causation.* New York: Harper and Row, Publishers, 1968.

Campbell, Charles S. *From Revolution to Rapprochement: The United States and Great Britain, 1783–1900.* New York: John Wiley and Sons, 1974.

Carse, Robert. *Ports of Call.* New York: Charles Scribner's Sons, 1967.

Cassell, Frank A. *Merchant Congressman in the Young Republic: Samuel Smith of Maryland, 1752–1839.* Madison: University of Wisconsin Press, 1971.

Catterall, Ralph C. H. *The Second Bank of the United States.* Chicago: University of Chicago Press, 1902.

Chapelle, Howard I. *The History of American Sailing Ships.* New York: Bonanza Books, 1935.

———. *The History of the American Sailing Navy.* New York: W. W. Norton and Company, 1949.

———. *The Baltimore Clipper: Its Origin and Development.* Hatboro, Penna.: Tradition Press, 1965. Originally published in 1930.

———. *The Search of Speed Under Sail, 1700–1855.* New York: Bonanza Books, 1967.

Clauder, Anna C. *American Commerce as Affected by the Wars of the French Revolution and Napoleon, 1793–1812.* Philadelphia: University of Pennsylvania Press, 1932.

Coggeshall, George. *History of the American Privateers and Letter-of-Marque During Our War with England in the Years 1812, 1813 and 1814.* New York: Published by and for the author, 1856.

Colbert, Evelyn Speyer. *Retaliation in International Law.* New York: Columbia University Press, 1948.

Cole, Arthur H., and Smith, Walter B. *Fluctuations in American Business, 1790–1860.* Cambridge, Mass.: Harvard University Press, 1935.

Colombos, C. John. *A Treatise on the Law of Prize.* No. 5, Grotious Society Publications. London: Longman, Green and Company, 1949.

Cooper, James Fenimore. *The History of the Navy of the United States of America.* Vol. II. London: Richard Bentley, 1839.

Corbett, Julian S. *England in the Seven Years' War: A Study in Combined Strategy.* Vols. I and II. London: Longman, Green and Company, 1907.

Crane, William Bowner and Cranwell, John. *Men of Marque: A History of Private Armed Vessels Out of Baltimore During the War of 1812.* New York: W. W. Norton and Company, 1940.

Craven, Avery O. *Soil Exhaustion as a Factor in the Agricultural History of Virginia and Maryland, 1606–1860.* Vol. XIII: University of Illinois Studies in Social Sciences. Urbana: University of Illinois Press, 1926.

Cunz, Dieter. *The Maryland Germans: A History.* Princeton: Princeton University Press, 1948.

East, Robert A. *Business Enterprise in the Revolutionary Era.* Columbia University Studies in the Social Sciences. New York: AMS Press, 1969. Originally published in 1938.

Essays in Colonial History Presented to Charles McLean Andrews by his Students. New Haven: Yale University Press, 1931.

Fischer, David Hackett. *The Revolution of American Conservatism: The Federalist Party in the Era of Jeffersonian Democracy.* New York: Harper and Row, Publishers, 1965.

Flexner, James Thomas. *George Washington in the American Revolution, 1775–1783.* Boston: Little, Brown and Company, 1967.

Forbush, Bliss. *Moses Sheppard: Quaker Philanthropist of Baltimore.* Philadelphia: J. B. Lippincott Company, 1968.

Fry, William. *Baltimore Directory 1810.* Baltimore: G. Dobbin and Murphy Printers, 1810.

———. *Baltimore Directory, 1812–1814.* Baltimore: G. Dobbin and Murphy Printers, 1814.

Genealogy and Biography of Leading Families of the City of Baltimore and Baltimore County. New York and Chicago: Chapman Publishing Company, 1897.

Gilchrist, David T., ed., *The Growth of the Seaport Cities: 1790–1825.* Charlottesville: published for the Eleutherian Mills-Hagley Foundation by the University Press of Virginia, 1967.

Gray, Lewis Cecil. *History of Agriculture in the Southern United States to 1860.* 2 vols. Washington, D.C.: Commercial Institute, 1933.

Green, Constance McLaughlin. *American Cities in the Growth of the Nation.* New York: Harper and Row, 1957.

Griffin, Charles Carroll. *The United States and the Disruption of the Spanish Empire, 1810–1822: A Study of the Relations of the United States with Spain and the Rebel Spanish Colonies.* No. 429: Columbia University Studies in History, Economics and Public Law. New York: Columbia University Press, 1937.

Griffith, Thomas W. *Annals of Baltimore.* Baltimore: William Woody, printer, 1824.

Hammond, Bray. *Banks and Politics in America: From the Revolution to the Civil War.* Princeton: Princeton University Press, 1957.

Harman, Joyce Elizabeth. *Trade and Privateering in Spanish Florida, 1732–1763.* St. Augustine, Fla.: St. Augustine Historical Society, 1969.

Henninghausen, Louis P., comp. *History of the German Society of Maryland.* Baltimore: The German Society, 1909.

Hidy, Ralph W. *The House of Baring in the American Trade and Finance: English Merchant*

Bankers at Work, 1763–1801. XIV: Harvard Studies in Business History, ed. N. S. B. Gras and Henrietta M. Larson. Cambridge, Mass.: Harvard University Press, 1949.

————. *The Formative Era of American Enterprise*. Boston: D. C. Heath and Company, 1967.

Hindmarsh, Albert E. *Force in Peace: Force Short of War in International Relations*. Cambridge, Mass.: Harvard University Press, 1933.

Hollander, J. H. *The Financial History of Baltimore*. Extra Vol. XX: Johns Hopkins University Studies in History and Political Science. Edited by Herbert B. Adams. Baltimore: Johns Hopkins Press, 1899.

Howland, Richard H. and Spencer, Eleanor P. *Architecture of Baltimore*. Baltimore: The Johns Hopkins Press, 1953.

Hutchins, John G. B. *The American Maritime Industries and Public Policy, 1789–1914: An Economic History*. Vol. LXXI: Harvard Economic Studies. Cambridge, Mass.: Harvard University Press, 1941.

Jackson, Melvin H. *Privateers in Charleston, 1793–1796*. No. 1: Smithsonian Studies in History and Technology. Washington, D.C.: Smithsonian Institution Press, 1969.

Jane, Fred T. *The British Battle Fleet: Its Inception and Growth Throughout the Centuries to the Present Day*. Vol. 1. Boston: David D. Neckerson and Company, 1912.

Jensen, Merrill. *The New Nation: A History of the United States During the Confederation, 1781–1789*. New York: Alfred A. Knopf, 1950.

Kayser, J. C. *Baltimore Commercial Directory*. Philadelphia: J. C. Kayser and Company, 1823.

Kendall, Charles Wye. *Private Men-of-War*. London: Philip Adler and Company, 1931.

Kuhlmann, Charles Byron. *The Development of the Flourmilling Industry in the United States*. Boston: Houghton Mifflin Company, 1929.

Lord, Walter. *The Dawn's Early Light*. New York: Norton Company, 1972.

Lydon, James G. *Pirates, Privateers and Profits*. Upper Saddle River, N.J.: The Gregg Press, 1970.

Maclay, Edgar Stanton. *A History of American Privateers*. New York: D. Appleton and Company, 1899.

Mahan, Alfred T. *Sea Power in Its Relation to the War of 1812*. Vols. I and II. Boston: Little, Brown and Company, 1905.

Marine, William M. *The British Invasion of Maryland, 1812–1815*. Hatboro, Penna.: Tradition Press, 1965. Originally published in 1913.

McClelland, D. C. *The Achieving Society*. Princeton: Princeton University Press, 1961.

Morison, Samuel Eliot. *The Maritime History of Massachusetts, 1783–1860*. Boston: Houghton Mifflin Company, 1921.

North, Douglass C. *The Economic Growth of the United States, 1790–1860*. New York: W. W. Norton, 1966.

Nye, Russell Blaine. *The Cultural Life of the New Nation, 1776–1830*. New York: Harper and Row, 1960.

Oppenheim, M. *A History of the Administration of the Royal Navy and of Merchant Shipping in Relation to the Navy*. London: John Lane, 1896.

Orego, Iris. *The Merchant of Prato: Francesco de Marco Dantini*. New York: Alfred A. Knopf, 1957.

Owens, Hamilton. *Baltimore on the Chesapeake*. New York: Doubleday, Doran and Company, 1941.

Paine, Ralph D. *The Old Merchant Marine: A Chronicle of American Ships and Sailors*. Vol. XVII: The Chronicle of America Series. Edited by Allen Johnson. New Haven: Yale University Press, 1919.

Parkinson, Cyril N., ed. *Trade Winds: A Study of British Overseas Trade During the French Wars, 1793–1815.* London: George Allen and Anwin, 1948.

Paullin, Charles Oscar. *Commodore John Rodgers: Captain, Commodore and Senior Officer of the American Navy, 1772–1838.* Annapolis: United States Naval Institute, 1967. Originally published in 1910.

Perkins, Bradford. *Castlereagh and Adams: England and the United States, 1812–1823.* Berkeley: University of California Press, 1964.

Pitkin, Timothy. *A Statistical View of the Commerce of the United States of America.* New York: James Eastburn Company, 1817.

Pratt, Julius W. *A History of United States Foreign Policy.* 3rd ed. Englewood Cliffs, N.J.: Prentice-Hall, 1972.

Quinn, David Beers. *England and the Discovery of America, 1481–1620.* New York: Alfred A. Knopf, 1974.

Risjord, Norman J. *The Old Republicans: Southern Conservatism in the Age of Jefferson.* New York: Columbia University Press, 1965.

Robinson, William M. *The Confederate Privateers.* New Haven: Yale University Press, 1928.

Sanborn, Frederic Rockwell. *Origins of Early English Maritime and Commercial Law.* New York: The Century Company, 1930.

Scharf, J. Thomas. *The Chronicles of Baltimore.* Baltimore: Turnbull Brothers, 1874.

————. *History of Baltimore City and County.* Philadelphia: L. E. Evarts, 1881.

Sears, Louis Martin. *Jefferson and the Embargo.* New York: Octagon Books, 1966. Originally published in 1929 by Duke University Press.

Smith, Walter B. and Cole, Arthur H. *Fluctuations in American Business, 1790–1860.* Cambridge, Mass.: Harvard University Press, 1935.

Stark, Francis R. *The Abolition of Privateering and the Declaration of Paris.* Vol. III, No. 3: Columbia University Studies in History, Economics and Public Law. New York: Columbia University Press, 1897.

Story, Joseph. *Commentary on the Law of Partnership as a Branch of Commercial and Maritime Jurisprudence.* Boston: Charles C. Little and James Brown, 1841.

Tiernan, Charles B. *The Tiernans and Other Families.* Baltimore: William J. Gallery and Company, 1901.

United States Department of Commerce. *The Statistical History of the United States from Colonial Times to the Present.* Stamford, Conn.: Fairfield Publishers, 1965.

Varle, Charles. *Complete View of Baltimore with a Statistical Sketch.* Baltimore: Samuel Young, 1833.

Wernham, R. B. *Before the Armada: The Emergence of the English Nation 1485–1588.* New York: Harcourt Brace and World, 1966.

Westcott, Allen F., ed.; and Fredland, J. Roger; Jeffries, William W.; Kirk, Neville T.; and McManus, Thomas F. *American Seapower Since 1775.* Revised edition. Philadelphia: J. B. Lippincott Company, 1952.

Whedbee, Thomas Courtenay Jenkins. *The Port of Baltimore in the Making.* Baltimore: F. Bowie Smith and Son, 1953.

Whitaker, Arthur P. *The United States and the Independence of Latin America, 1800–1830.* New York: W. W. Norton and Company, 1964. Originally published in 1941 by The Johns Hopkins Press.

White, Leonard D. *The Jeffersonians: A Study in Administrative History, 1801–1829.* New York: Macmillan Company, 1951.

Wilson, James Grant and Fiske, John, eds. *Appleton's Cyclopaedia of American Biography.* Vols. I, II, III, IV, V. New York: D. Appleton and Company, 1900.

2. Essays and Articles

"Baltimore." *Hunt's Merchants Magazine*, XXIII, No. 1 (July, 1850): 34–52.

Baumol, William J. "Entrepreneurship in Economic Theory." *American Economic Review* (May, 1968): 58–71.

Bjork, Gordon C. "The Weaning of the American Economy: Independence, Market Changes and Economic Development." *Journal of Economic History*, XXIV (December, 1969): 541–60.

Bourne, Florence M. "Thomas Kemp, Shipbuilder, and his Home, Wades Point." *Maryland Historical Magazine*, LXIX, No. 4 (December, 1954): 271–89.

Brozen, Yale. "Determinants of Entrepreneurial Ability." *Social Research*, XXI (October, 1954): 339–64.

Bruchey, Stuart Weems. "Success and Failure Factors: American Merchants in Foreign Trade in the Eighteenth and Early Nineteenth Centuries." *The Business History Review*, XXXII, No. 3 (Autumn, 1958): 272–92.

Buchanan, William Boyd. "1852 Recollections." *The Baltimore News*, January 25, 1902.

Calman, William Thomas. "Toredo." *Encyclopaedia Britannica* XXI (1954).

Cochran, Thomas C. "Economic History, Old and New." *American Historical Review*, LXXIV, No. 5 (June, 1969): 1561–72.

Cole, Arthur H. "An Approach to the Study of Entrepreneurship: A Tribute to Edwin F. Gay." *The Journal of Economic History*, Supplement, VI (1946): 1–15.

Crouzet, François. "Wars, Blockade and Economic Change in Europe, 1792–1815." *Journal of Economic History*, XXIV, No. 4 (December, 1964): 567–88.

Didier, Eugene Lemoine. "The Social Athens of America." *Harpers Magazine*, LXV (June, 1882): 30–31.

Dietz, Anthony G. "The Use of Cartel Vessels During the War of 1812." *The American Neptune*, XXVIII, No. 3 (July, 1968): 165–94.

Dorsey, Rhoda M. "The Conduct of Business in Baltimore, 1783–1785." *Maryland Historical Magazine*, Vol. 55, No. 3 (September, 1960): 230–40.

Dow, George F. "Records of the Vice-Admiralty Court at Halifax, Nova Scotia: The Condemnation of Prizes and Re-captures of the Revolution and the War of 1812." *Historical Collections of the Essex Institute*, 1911, XLV: 69–71; 150–60; 161–84; 221–24; 309–32. XLVI: 69–71; 150–60; 157–72; 317–24. XLVII: 20–24; 189–96; 236–49.

Evans, G. H. "Business Entrepreneurs: Their Major Functions and Related Tenets." *The Journal of Economic History*, XIX (June, 1959): 250–70.

Gallisan, John. "Privateering." *The North American Review*, XI (July, 1820): 166–96.

Leibenstein, Harvey. "Entrepreneurship and Development." *American Economic Review*, LVIII (May, 1968): 72–85.

Munro, Wilfred Harold. "The Most Successful American Privateer; An Episode of the War of 1812." *Proceedings of the American Antiquarian Society*, XXIII (1913): 12–62.

Pancake, John S. "The Invisibles: A Chapter in the Opposition to President Madison." *Journal of Southern History*, XXI (February, 1955): 17–35.

Pessen, Edward. "The Egalitarian Myth and the American Social Reality; Wealth, Mobility and Equality in the Era of the Common Man." *American Historical Review*, LXXVI, No. 4 (October, 1971): 989–1034.

Pirenne, Henri. "The Stages in the Social History of Capitalism." *The American Historical Review*, Vol. CIX, No. 3 (April, 1914): 494–515.

Pole, J. R. "Constitutional Reform and Election Statistics in Maryland." *Maryland Historical Magazine*, Vol. 55, No. 4 (December, 1960): 275–92.

Price, Jacob M. "The Economic Growth of the Chesapeake and the European Market,

1697–1775." *The Journal of Economic History*, XXIV, No. 4 (December, 1964): 496–511.

Redlick, Fritz. "William Jones' Resignation from the Presidency of the Second Bank of the U.S." *Pennsylvania Magazine of History and Biography*, LXXI (July, 1947): 203–47.

Steiner, Bernard C. "Maryland Privateers in the American Revolution." *Maryland Historical Magazine*, III, No. 2 (June, 1908): 99–103.

"The Stevensons." *The Baltimore News*, January 28, 1898.

Stump, William. "Sketch of John Hollins." *The Baltimore Sun*, September 25, 1949.

Wetmore, Amy D'Arcy. "Some Old Country Houses of Old-Time Baltimoreans." *The Baltimore Sun*, November 11, 1906.

3. Unpublished Materials

Bevans, Edith Rossiter. "Harlem." Vertical File, Maryland Room, Enoch Pratt Free Library, Baltimore. (Typewritten.)

Brown, Dorothy Marie. "Party Battles and Beginnings in Maryland, 1786–1812." Ph.D. dissertation, Georgetown University, 1961.

Cassell, Frank A. "Samuel Smith: Merchant Politician 1772–1812." Ph.D. dissertation, Northwestern University, 1968.

Hoffman, Ronald. "Economics, Politics and the Revolution in Maryland." Ph.D. dissertation, University of Wisconsin, 1969.

Overfield, Richard A. "The Loyalists of Maryland During the American Revolution." Ph.D. dissertation, University of Maryland, 1968.

Raley, Robert L. "The Baltimore Country House 1785–1815." M.A. thesis, University of Delaware, 1959.

Renzulli, Libero Marx. "Maryland Federalism: 1787–1819." Ph.D. dissertation, University of Virginia, 1962.

Snow, Elliot. "Lists of Public and Private Armed Vessels of the North American Colonies Fitted Out in the United States During the Revolutionary War, 1776–1783, Accredited to Maryland." March 12, 1926, Vertical File, Maryland Historical Society, Baltimore.

Index